NEWLY REVISED AND EXPANDED FIFTH EDITION

CORROBORATING EVIDENCE V

Cleveland Torso Murders

The Case Against William Heirens

Murder of the Black Dahlia

Phantom Killer of Texarkana

Zodiac Killer

Comparisons between the Zodiac Killer and the Eyeball Killer

Mysterious Murder of Valerie Percy

Murder of Richard Robison and His Family

Freeway Phantom

Santa Rosa Hitchhiker Murders

Connecticut River Valley Killer

Colonial Parkway Murders

Bedford Highway Killer

and

The Murder of JonBenet Ramsey

NEWLY REVISED AND EXPANDED FIFTH EDITION

CORROBORATING EVIDENCE V

A True Crime Story

Cleveland Torso Murders
The Case Against William Heirens
Murder of the Black Dahlia
Phantom Killer of Texarkana
Zodiac Killer
Comparisons between the Zodiac Killer and the Eyeball Killer
Mysterious Murder of Valerie Percy
Murder of Richard Robison and His Family
Freeway Phantom
Santa Rosa Hitchhiker Murders
Connecticut River Valley Killer
Colonial Parkway Murders
Bedford Highway Killer
and
The Murder of JonBenet Ramsey

William T. Rasmussen

Interior design by Booknook.biz

Library of Congress Cataloging-in-Publication Data:
William T. Rasmussen., 1948-

Corroborating Evidence V: A true crime story/by
William T. Rasmussen-Newly rev. and expanded 5th ed.
Includes bibliographical references and index

ISBN 979-8-9904804-2-1 (Paperback)
979-8-9904804-0-7 (Hardcover)
979-8-9904804-3-8 (eBook)

"No one knows what will be the fate of the child he begets. This weary world goes on begetting . . . and all of it is blind from the beginning to end. I don't know what it was that made these boys do this mad act, but I know there is no reason for it. I know they did not beget themselves . . . . We are all helpless . . . . But when you are pitying the father and mother of poor Bobby Franks, what about the fathers and mothers of all the boys and girls who thread a dangerous maze in darkness from birth to death? . . . I am sorry for all the fathers and mothers. The mother who looks into the blue eyes of her little baby cannot help musing of the end of the child--whether it will be crowned with the greatest promises that mind can imagine--or whether he will meet death upon the scaffold. All she can do is to rear him with love and with care, to watch over him tenderly, and to meet life with hope and trust and confidence, and leave the rest to fate."

"Everybody is a potential murderer."
—Clarence Darrow, from the trial of
Loeb and Leopold, 1924

SOLUTION TO THE CLEVELAND TORSO MURDERS AND THE BLACK DAHLIA MURDER

In 1937, Cleveland Detective Peter Merylo investigated a 17-year-old suspect in the Cleveland Torso Murders whose last name was "Wilson." This "Wilson" was born in 1920, and was employed at the Great Lakes Exposition in Cleveland in 1936. The Cleveland Torso Murders took place from 1934-1938. His birth certificate indicates that his father was Walter F. Wilson and his mother was Helen Wilson. Cleveland Detective Orley May reported on a tip regarding the Torso Murders in 1937, as follows:

> Detective Musil and I received information from a person who does not want her identity revealed and who stated that while she was in the workhouse, a woman by the name of Helen O'Leary, who was the former wife of a man who was shot and killed several years ago-since got married to Gas House O'Malley, a stage hand, told her that she knew the man that killed Florence Polillio. She asked him who it was and she said "You know, his name is Jack Wilson." We learned from the informer that Jack Wilson was a former butcher and worked for Sam who operated a grocery store and meat market on St. Clair Avenue, and that he was known to carry a large butcher knife. Informant also stated that this Wilson was a sodomist, and that he committed sodomy on a number of persons known by the informant and

> is committing these decapitated (sic) murders in Kingsbury Run and may be killing them for the purpose of committing Sodomy on the victims, and would be a good suspect in the above murder.

All of the original Cleveland police reports, on the Cleveland Torso Murders, have been either destroyed, lost or misplaced. Luckily, Detective Merylo had made copies of the reports for his personal use. When Merylo died in 1958, his files were transferred to his daughter, Marjorie Merylo Dentz, in Rockville, Maryland. In 2004, I traveled to Rockville and was given permission from Mrs. Dentz to review all of Detective Merylo's files of the Cleveland Torso police reports. I found the two entries mentioned above in Detective Merylo's copies.

Max Allan Collins wrote in his book, *Angel of Death*, on pages 269-270:

> "You had a suspect...some fag butcher..." "A young homosexual, yes, who worked on St. Clair Avenue. Like Waterson, he liked to prowl the skid row sections of town, preying on society's dregs. And his name, as you've guessed, was Arnold Wilson.". . . "Yes, but the description of the St. Clair Avenue butcher shop boy was not common: he was a very pockmarked kid, very thin, very tall, Merylo said . . . perhaps as much as six four."

In the late 1960's, Los Angeles author, John Gilmore, was contacted by Arnold Smith, regarding the murder of Elizabeth Short (The Black Dahlia). Gilmore tape recorded Arnold Smith's third party (Al Morrison) confession of the Black Dahlia Murder. See complete "Confession" on pages 83-92. In the early 1980's Gilmore contacted Los Angeles detective John St. John regarding Arnold

Smith. After listening to the taped recording, Detective St. John determined that Al Morrison was a made up name, that Arnold Smith was an alias of Jack Anderson Wilson and that he knew more about the Black Dahlia Murder than the police did. Jack Anderson Wilson became a prime suspect in the Black Dahlia Murder. The suspects in the Cleveland Torso Murders and the Black Dahlia Murder shared the same characteristics:

1. They were 17-years-old in 1937.
2. They were born in 1920. Detective St. John's suspect in the Black Dahlia Murder was originally from Canton, Ohio.
3. Their last name was "Wilson" and they were further identified as "Jack Wilson."
4. Detective Merylo's suspect was a sodomist. Detective St. John's suspect was a convicted sodomist.
5. They were suspects in the Cleveland Torso Murders and the Black Dahlia Murder.
6. Their height was 6' 4".
7. They were thin and may have walked with a limp. (To verify, see Jack Anderson Wilson's police rap sheets at the Los Angeles County and Oakland County, California Police Departments). Georgette Bauerdorf Murder: See page 71. The sheriff's record states: "Jack Anderson Wilson is a possible, plausible suspect for the Bauerdorf murder and the murder victim Short (the Black Dahlia)." "A possible suspect was identified as a 6' 4" soldier who walked with a limp, whom the victim was said to have expressed she was afraid of him (see page 201, *Severed* by John Gilmore).
8. They were suspects in a series of murders whereby the victims were killed in one area and their blood was drained from their bodies. They were dismembered in the Cleveland cases and bisected in the Black Dahlia Murder, then their body

parts were transferred to different locations where they were dumped.

9. In both cases victims were dismembered or bisected by someone with "skill of a surgeon."
10. Some of the Cleveland Torso victim's genitalia were severed from their bodies (See pages 23-26).The Black Dahlia's autopsy indicated that "Within the vagina and higher up there is lying loose a piece of skin with fat and subcutaneous tissue attached. On this piece of loose skin there are several crisscrossing lacerations." The genitalia had been mutilated.
11. Some of the victims Cleveland Torso victims had been tortured. The Black Dahlia was tortured.
12. Victim's bodies in both cases had been cleaned following their murder (See page 2).
13. In the Cleveland Torso Murders there were signs of possible necrophilia anal sex (See photo of victim No. 5, Edward Andrassy, on page 3.)The autopsy of the Black Dahlia indicated that "The anal opening is markedly dilated and the opening measures 1 1/4" in diameter . . . There are lacerations, including the dilation of the anal opening that were done after the woman's death" (possible signs of necrophilia anal sex.)
14. The Cleveland Torso Murders and the Black Dahlia Murder were not ordinary murders. They were quite rare and unique.
15. Merylo's suspect "Wilson" worked at the Great Lakes Exposition in Cleveland in 1936. While incarcerated at the Oakland City Jail in 1958, Detective St. John's suspect, Jack Anderson Wilson, told an inmate that he had seen a queer's head in a glass box, Johnny Weissmuller and Sally Rand at the Great Lakes Exposition in Cleveland, in 1936.

Detective Merylo "thinks it possible that (the Cleveland Torso Killer) perpetrated the Black Dahlia Murder" (see page 94, *Butcher's Dozen and Other Murders*, 1952, by John Bartlow Martin). By the time Detective St. John began to focus on Jack Anderson Wilson, Peter Merylo had died and all of the original Cleveland police reports on the Torso Murders had disappeared. Detective St. John might not have realized that Merylo's copies of the police reports were housed in a closet at Mrs. Dentz's home in Rockville, Maryland. If Detective St. John had discovered that Detective Merylo's suspect in the Cleveland Torso Murders, matched the description of his suspect, Jack Anderson Wilson, in the Black Dahlia Murder, then Detective John St. John would have connected the corroborating evidence and these cases would have been solved a long time ago.

* To completely verify that Jack Anderson Wilson was responsible for both sets of murders, compare the DNA (if available and not completely degraded) in both cases. A rape kit should have been used and samples collected in the Black Dahlia case. In the event no DNA samples exist in the Cleveland Torso Murders, Jack Anderson Wilson's mother is buried in the Newland Cemetery, Newland, Avery County, North Carolina, d/o/d 5/18/1973. Her mitochondrial DNA might suffice.

(See pages 1-33; 69-141; 383-405 and 463-540)

CONTENTS

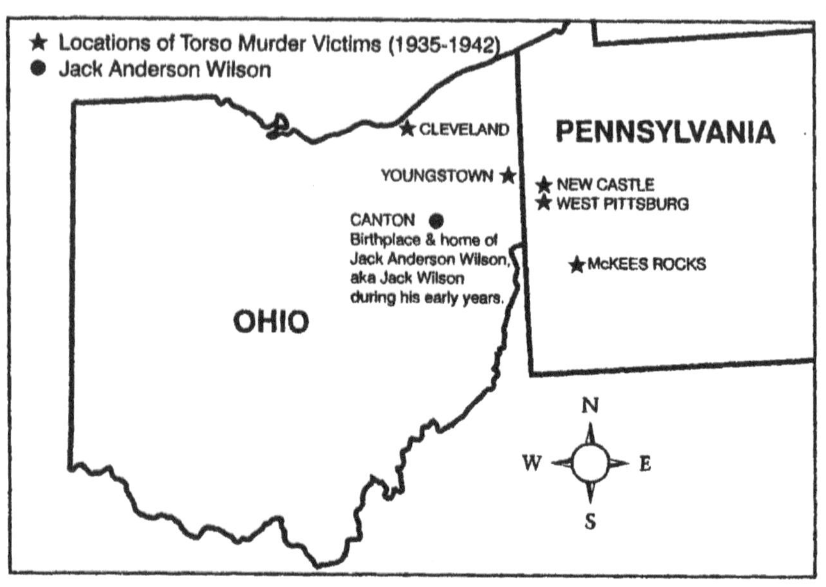

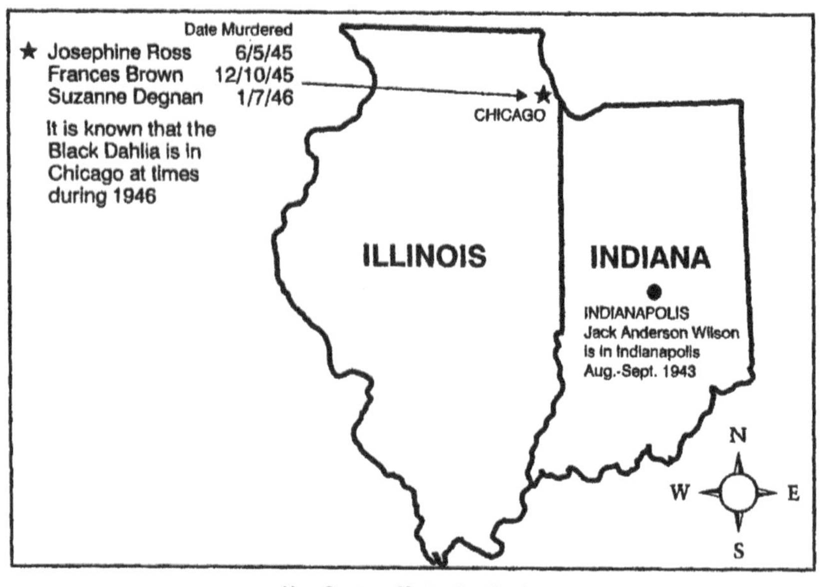

Maps Courtesy of Forton Graphics, Inc.

INTRODUCTION

The Torso Murders

Someone was killing, decapitating and dismembering other human beings for some unknown reason. A sadistic serial killer was on the loose but no one at the time realized it. The Great Depression had thrown millions of Americans into poverty and despair. Feeding a family, staying alive and healthy during these lean times were no easy tasks. Jobs, especially good-paying ones, were few and often out of reach for the average person. Thousands of men, down on their luck, put the responsibilities of the world behind them, became hobos and "rode the line." Some of these hobos, along with other unfortunates that fit a similar profile, became targets of one of the most horrific serial killers in the history of the United States.

From September, 1934, to August, 1938, a total of thirteen Torso Murders were committed in Cleveland, Ohio, by a psychopathic killer who became known as "The Mad Butcher of Kingsbury Run." In 1938, the Torso Murders in Cleveland "officially" ended. The Torso killings were bad for business in Cleveland, so even though the killer was never apprehended, the authorities publicly announced that the Torso killings had ended. That's one way to end a crime spree, just declare that it is over. It's obvious that a killer such as this would pay little attention to such a public utterance. On December 23, 1938, someone in Los Angeles mailed a letter addressed to

Cleveland's Chief of Police George J. Matowitz, claiming, among other things, to be the Butcher.

Between 1939-1942, New Castle, Pennsylvania, experienced at least five Torso Murders similar to the murders committed earlier in Cleveland. Was the same person or persons killing and dismembering individuals in Pennsylvania and Ohio? Was he traveling by train to and from the various locations in Pennsylvania and Ohio? Was he killing and dismembering his victims in railroad boxcars? Cleveland's detective Peter Merylo was convinced that there was one killer operating in both states and that he was doing just that. Killing several victims, then dismembering their bodies with surgical skill, including decapitation, and then draining the blood from their corpses would take a very rare, unique person, according to one detective. The odds of there being another killer with the same skill, intelligence, capability, stomach and sleuth as the Mad Butcher, operating in a different (but adjacent) state-- at times that didn't overlap or conflict--are very slim. A copycat killer might get away with a single killing duplicating the methods of the Mad Butcher, but not a series of nearly identical murders. Not every person, hell-bent on killing someone, has the fortitude to decapitate and dismember a human body and then completely drain the blood from the corpse and remove the remains to a different location, where they were deposited. This takes a rare type of psychotic killer with sadistic tendencies. One that, thank goodness, doesn't come along every day. If the other detectives who didn't accept Merylo's theory were correct in their assumptions, then there would have been at least three different persons who were committing the murders in New Castle and Cleveland, all in the same manner as the Mad Butcher of Kingsbury Run. I submit that detective Merylo was probably correct in his evaluation that there was only one person, possibly with a subservient assistant, who was committing all of the Torso Murders in Pennsylvania and Ohio. There weren't two Jack the Rippers, two Zodiac Killers, two Ted Bundys or two Green

River Killers, and there probably weren't two different Torso Killers. If the police agencies in each jurisdiction and the Federal Bureau of Investigation had fully cooperated in a concerted effort with a full exchange of information, the odds of apprehending the culprit would have been much greater.

Now here is where the plot thickens. What happened to the Mad Butcher of Kingsbury Run after 1942? I have a couple of theories and some clues that may shed some light on the identity of the elusive Butcher. I may or may not be correct, but if nothing else the story is interesting and may lead to additional clues and evidence that could solve this mystery. One thing is for sure, if the Butcher was alive and not in prison or in a mental institution in the decade that followed the Torso Killings, he was still killing and dismembering someone somewhere. The questions are, Who and where?

The Case Against William Heirens

On June 5, 1945, a woman by the name of Josephine A. Ross was savagely murdered in Chicago. The Red Line, a passenger railway, was located near her apartment, where she was murdered. On December 10, 1945, Frances Brown was also murdered in her apartment close to where Ross lived. Her killer left a message written in red lipstick on her living room wall. The message read: "For heavens sake catch me before I kill more I cannot control myself." Less than one month later, on January 6, 1946, 6-year-old Suzanne Degnan was kidnapped from the first-floor bedroom of her parents' apartment on North Kenmore Avenue, strangled to death, and dismembered, then her body parts were discarded in the Chicago storm sewer system. A few months later a 17-year-old boy by the name of William Heirens was arrested for burglary in a nearby Chicago neighborhood. He was brutally interrogated by the police for his possible involvement in the Ross, Brown and Degnan murders. After being held in "protective custody" for over a month, he eventually signed a purported confession and pled guilty to the crimes. Heirens was sentenced to three consecutive life sentences for the murders of Ross, Brown and Degnan and one year to life for burglaries and assaults. There has been speculation over the years that certain evidence may have been planted at the scene of the killings, including a "rolled fingerprint" that may have been lifted from Heirens' fingerprint card at the police station. William Heirens was incarcerated in Illinois from 1946, until he died in a prison hospital on March 5, 2012. There is something about this file that just doesn't seem to add up. The autopsy report and the police files on these cases have disappeared from the records department at the Chicago Police Department. Did William Heirens commit the crimes that he pled guilty to, or was someone else, someone more sinister, prowling the streets of Chicago at that time? The dismemberment of Suzanne Degnan took place four years after the last known Torso Murder in Pennsylvania and almost one year before the Black Dahlia was murdered and professionally bisected in Los Angeles.

Georgette Bauerdorf, the Black Dahlia, Jeanne Axford French and other Los Angeles Victims

On October 12, 1944, a young, pretty socialite by the name of Georgette Bauerdorf was found murdered in her apartment on West Fountain in Hollywood, California. Her killer left her body lying face down in her bathtub. She had been strangled and raped.

On January 15, 1947, the severed corpse of Elizabeth Short was discovered near the corner of 39th and Norton Avenue in Los Angeles. Elizabeth Short was known by her friends and others in her social group as the Black Dahlia. On February 10, 1947, the body of Jeanne Axford French was found near Grand View Avenue and National Boulevard in Los Angeles. Some of the detectives thought that whoever killed the Black Dahlia also killed Georgette Bauerdorf and Jeanne French, but who?

These murders, and other associated murders in Los Angeles between 1947-1949, have never been solved. Had the Mad Butcher of Kingsbury Run traveled to Los Angeles in the late 1930's, traveled back to Pennsylvania and then reappeared again in Los Angeles in 1942? Did he travel to Chicago in 1945-1946 and then relocate in Los Angeles between 1947-1949? The timing is right: a letter sent by someone in Los Angeles in 1938 to the Cleveland Chief of Police indicated that he might have. Several other clues and documented evidence seem to be pointing in the direction of the Mad Butcher of Kingsbury Run as being the killer of the Black Dahlia and other females in Los Angeles and Chicago. Was the person who killed the Black Dahlia, Josephine Ross, Frances Brown and Suzanne Degnan somehow connected to the Cleveland Torso Killer? The clues and evidence indicate that he may have been.

The Phantom Killer of Texarkana

On February 22, 1946, Jimmy Hollis and Mary Jeanne Larey were parked in a secluded area on Richmond Road near Texarkana, Arkansas, when a hooded stranger wielding a pistol approached them in the dark. The stranger forced Hollis and Larey from their vehicle and assaulted the couple. Both survived, but they were the lucky ones. On March 24, 1946, Richard Griffin and Polly Ann Moore were murdered near Texarkana under similar circumstances. One month later James Paul Martin and Betty Jo Booker were murdered in Spring Lake Park in Texarkana.

The local newspapers dubbed the killer the "Phantom Killer of Texarkana." On May 3, 1946, the Phantom Killer struck again, this time by firing a 22 semi-automatic through a window of a farm house near Texarkana into the head of a farmer by the name of

Virgil Starks. A serial killer was at work in Texarkana. The Phantom Killer of Texarkana has never been identified. After the murder of Virgil Starks, was this the Phantom's last murder, or was it just the beginning of a long history of murders that he committed and that went unsolved, to be stored in cold case files?

The Zodiac Killer

In June, 1963, seventeen years after the last known murder by the Phantom Killer of Texarkana, Robert Domingos and Linda Edwards were killed on a secluded beach near Santa Barbara, California. On October 30, 1966, 21-year-old Cheri Jo Bates was killed in Riverside, California. She was stabbed one time in each breast. Six months later her father received a letter that read, "Bates had to die there will be more." A letter following the Phantom Murders included the words, "there will be more." On December 20, 1968, Betty Lou Jensen and David Faraday were shot and killed at night on an isolated road a few miles east of Vallejo, California. On July 5, 1969, Michael Mageau and Darlene Ferrin were shot by the same assailant at night on a lover's lane four miles from Vallejo near Blue Rock Springs Golf Course. Ferrin died from her wounds and Mageau survived the attack.

The killer mailed taunting letters with ciphers and codes to the police and newspapers.. In one of the letters, received on August 7, 1969, the killer identified himself as the "Zodiac." On September 27, 1969, Bryan Hartnell and Cecelia Shepard were assaulted near Berryessa Lake north of Napa, California. Cecelia was stabbed twenty four times including one time in each breast. She died from her wounds, but Hartnell survived the attack. Zodiac wore a hood over his head with slits for the eyes and mouth but not the nose. The taunting letters continued. On October 11, 1969, a taxi driver by the name of Paul Stine was murdered in his taxi by the Zodiac. Two days later the *San Francisco Chronicle* received a letter from the

Zodiac with a scrap of Stine's bloody shirt enclosed. Several more letters were mailed by the Zodiac.

In 1972, Santa Barbara Sheriff John Carpenter issued a press release suggesting that Zodiac may have been responsible for the murders of Domingos and Edwards in 1963.

The Zodiac has never been identified and the Zodiac Murders have never been solved. Rasmussen compares the interests, background, skills and personality traits of the Zodiac Killer and a known serial killer by the name of Charles F. Albright a/k/a The Eyeball Killer.

The Mysterious Murder of Valerie Percy

On September 18, 1966, 21-year-old Valerie Percy, daughter of Illinois Senator Charles H. Percy, was brutally murdered in the Percy home near the shores of Lake Michigan in Kenilworth, Illinois. Someone entered the occupied building in the early morning hours and silently crept up the stairs and into the bedroom where Valerie lay sleeping. The intruder viciously struck her four times in the head with a heavy object similar to a ball peen hammer or fireplace poker. He then proceeded to stab her six times around the nose and left eye. She was stabbed one time in each breast and twice in the abdomen. Investigators speculated that a bayonet fished from off shore a short distance from the Percy property may have been the murder weapon.

Valerie died from her wounds. Her killer escaped and has never been identified.

The Murders of Richard Robison and his Family

The State of Michigan's most famous mass slaying of an entire family has never been solved. On June 25, 1968, Richard Robison and his entire family were shot and killed in their secluded cottage off Lake Michigan near Good Hart in Emmet County. Someone approached the cottage at around 8:30 pm and fired a 22 semi-automatic through a window pane on the north side of the building. Mr. Robison was shot as he sat in his easy chair in the living room. Then Mrs. Robison was shot and killed. A bullet grazed the head of 7-year-old Suzie Robison and she fell bleeding to the floor. The killer then entered the cottage and shot and killed all three of the Robison sons. He used a carpenter's hammer to smash the heads of Mr. Robison and little Suzie. The killer then dragged Mr. Robison down a hallway and placed his body on a floor furnace. Then he dragged one of the Robison sons down the hallway and placed his body on top of Mr. Robison's dead body. The lifeless body of Suzie Robison was placed next to her brother. The killer then went into the living room, pulled down Mrs. Robison's undergarments and stabbed her seven times with a sharp instrument in her Kotex. He then covered Mrs. Robison with a red plaid blanket, pulled all of the shades in the cottage, turned the heat up, placed a note on the outside north door, put a piece of cardboard over the bullet holes in the window, and left the cottage through the rear entrance after securing the lock.

Investigators have long suspected that Robison's business associate, Joseph Scolaro, committed the murders. Circumstantial evidence and failed polygraph tests certainly point in Scolaro's direction as being the killer. But was Scolaro the killer? Based on witness reports, Scolaro didn't have time to commit the murders and return to his home near Detroit during the rain storm on the night of the murders. If Scolaro didn't actually pull the trigger, then investigators speculated that he must have hired a hit man to commit the crimes. If Mr. Robison was the intended target, why was the entire family murdered? It seems that a hit man would have singled out Mr. Robison. Would a hit man have gone through all of the steps that were taken by the killer after the family was murdered?

In August, 1968, following the Robison Murders, the *Detroit News* Secret Witness Program received a tip from someone who wrote that he had information, but in order to get it law enforcement officials had to place a specific ad in the News personals section.

Could this have been a letter from the Zodiac Killer? Was there a hidden message in the tip?

The Robison Murders have never been solved and new clues point to someone other than Joseph Scolaro or a hit man hired by Scolaro as the perpetrator.

The Freeway Phantom, Santa Rosa Hitchhiker Murders, Connecticut River Valley Killer, Colonial Parkway Murders and the Bedford Highway Killer

The Zodiac Killer abducted Kathleen Johns and her young daughter on March 17, 1970, near Modesto, California. Letters thought to have been written by the Zodiac were received by newspapers and the authorities in 1974 and 1978. The question is: Did the Zodiac continue killing after 1970 and if so, where did he start again and whom did he kill?

There were a series of murders in Santa Rosa, California between February, 1972 and December 22, 1973, that may have been committed by the Zodiac. There were also a series of murders committed in Washington D.C. and in the states of New Hampshire, Virginia and Massachusetts from 1971-1989, that remain unsolved. Could the Zodiac Killer have changed "the way the collecting of slaves," as he wrote in his November 9, 1969, letter to the *Chronicle,* and moved his base of operation to the eastern side of the United States, far from the state of California, and into new jurisdictions, thinking that the authorities might not be as apt to crosscheck specific facts and circumstances that could connect the murders?

Several clues presented in Chapter Nine may justify focusing on the Zodiac Killer as the person responsible for several of these unsolved murders.

The Murder of JonBenet Ramsey

Six-year-old JonBenet Ramsey was brutally murdered in the Ramsey's family home in Boulder, Colorado, sometime in the night of December 25-26, 1996. Her killer has never been identified. Detectives from the Boulder Police Department investigated several suspects and researched several theories but primarily focused on members of the Ramsey family.

Rasmussen suggests, that if the authorities haven't already done so, they should examine the families and associates of other pageant and dance contestants who competed in those contests the Ramsey girl had competed in, including families and associates of girls who were planning to compete in contests scheduled for dates following her death. The list should include those associated with contestants likely to compete, even if not already registered to do so, based on previous participation in contests JonBenet had won.

NOTE TO THE READER

References enclosed in parenthesis in the footnotes after chapters refer to the notes at the back of this book; page numbers after each such reference indicate the page in the publication that is referenced.

Chapter 1

THE TORSO MURDERS

New Castle, Pennsylvania; Youngstown and Cleveland, Ohio

In 1934, dismembered torsos and body parts of murdered victims began appearing in Cleveland, on a fairly regular basis. Many of the headless victims were never identified. The killer became known by a variety of names, including the "The Cleveland Torso Murderer," "The Head Hunter of Kingsbury Run," "The Mad Butcher of Kingsbury Run," and "The Mad Butcher." In each murder the killer used a sharp instrument similar to what a butcher would use when slaughtering an animal. The lower half of the first Cleveland victim, a female, showed up on September 5, 1934, found partially buried in the sand near 156th Street in Cleveland close to the water's edge of Lake Erie. It was determined that the torso had been in the water for approximately three months before it was discovered. Two weeks earlier the upper portion of her torso had been found on a beach thirty miles east in North Perry. Her killer had applied a preservative to the corpse "that turned the skin reddish, tough and leathery." Medical authorities later determined that the preservative applied to the body was either calcium hypochloride or chloride of lime. The woman has never been identified and to this day is known as "The Lady of the Lakes." Her limbs were skillfully removed except for the right arm. The butcher had missed this joint and completed the separation with a saw. In an apparent attempt to eliminate members of the medical profession as the killer, Cuyahoga County Coroner Arthur J. Pearce indicated, "No surgeon ever would have used a saw; he would have known how to manipulate a knife around the joint."

In an effort to locate and identify the Mad Butcher of Kingsbury Run, the City of Cleveland hired famed "Untouchable," Elliot Ness, as director of Public Safety in 1935. Prior to this time Ness had successfully battled organized mobsters, including Al Capone in Chicago. As it turned out the Mad Butcher was much more of a challenge to Ness than all the Chicago hoodlums combined.

The headless corpse of Edward Andrassy, a white male, described as Victim No. 1, was found on September 23, 1935, at the foot of Jackass Hill in Cleveland. His body was found stripped, except for his stockings, completely drained of blood, emasculated and cleaned. A substance had been found on the body which "turned the skin reddish, tough and leathery." The authorities thought the killer may have tried to burn the body. "The head was found buried in the ground about twenty feet from the body; just enough hair showed above the surface of the loose earth to ensure the police would find it" (Note 1, p. 31).

Was the killer experimenting on the dead bodies with some sort of preservative?

Thirty feet away from Andrassy's body the police found Victim No. 2. He also had been emasculated. The severed genitals of both men lay in a pile next to the corpses. Found near the bodies were several pieces of rope, a railroad torch and a two-gallon water bucket containing crankcase oil. Dr Samuel R. Gerber, who succeeded A. J. Pearce as Coroner of Cuyahoga County, declared, "Appearances, together with certain findings, seem to indicate that the body, after death, was saturated with oil and fire applied. The burning, however, was only sufficient to scorch, hence the peculiar condition of the skin" (Note 1, p. 36). Each victim had been decapitated after his hands were tied, then stripped of clothing, and further mutilated. The presence of rope burns on one of the victim's wrists indicated he may have been conscious when he was decapitated.

Decapitated body of Victim No. 5, found July 22, 1936, on Cleveland's west side. (photo courtesy of the Cleveland Police Historical Society)

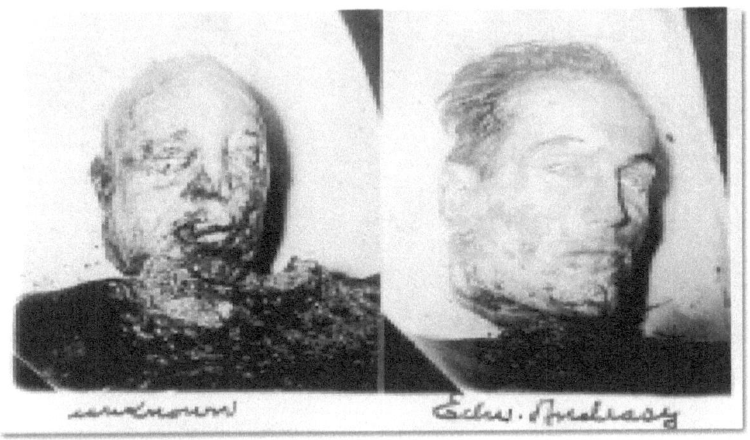

Decapitated heads of Victim No. 2 and Edward Andrassy found at the foot of Jackass Hill in Cleveland, September 23, 1935 (photo courtesy of the Cleveland Police Historical Society)

On January 26, 1936, body parts, some of which were located neatly wrapped in half-bushel baskets, were discovered behind Hart Manufacturing Plant in Cleveland. The murdered woman was later identified as Florence (Flo) Polillo, "a part-time waitress, part-time barmaid, part-time prostitute" (Note 1, p. 51). She became known as torso Victim No. 3. It is curious to note that embedded in her skin were cinders and coal dust. An indention of a lump of coal was found in the lower portion of her torso. Had she been butchered in a coal bin?

Police photograph of Flo Polillo, Victim No. 3, taken approximately 1934 (photo courtesy of the Cleveland Police Historical Society)

Remains of Flo Polillo found behind Hart Manufacturing Plant in Cleveland, January 26, 1936 (photo courtesy of the Cleveland Police Historical Society)

On June 5, 1936, Victim No. 4 was discovered in Kingsbury Run. His head had been wrapped up in his pants and placed in a burlap bag. Drawn on parts of Victim No. 4's body were six tattoos: A butterfly on the left shoulder; the comic strip character, Diggs, on the surface of the left calf; crossed flags with the letters WCG on the left forearm; a heart and anchor also on the left forearm; a cupid and anchor on the outer surface of the right calf; and the names Helen and Paul on the right forearm. Investigators believed the dead man may have been a sailor.

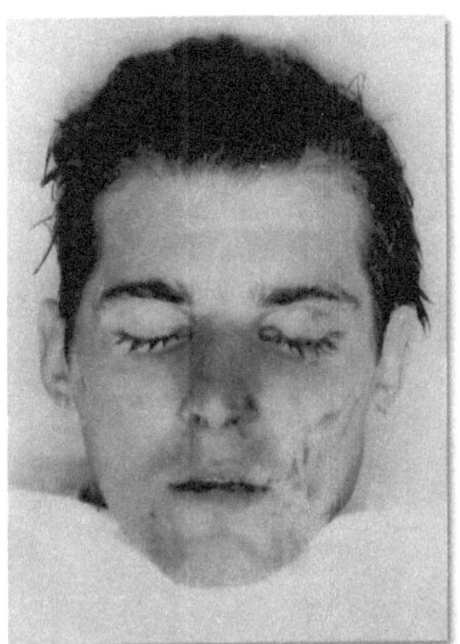

The head of the "Tattooed Man," Victim No. 4, located in Kingsbury Run, June 5, 1936 (Cleveland Press Collection, courtesy of Cleveland State University Library)

Remains of the "Tattooed Man," Victim No. 4, found in Kingsbury Run, June 5, 1936 (photo courtesy of the Cleveland Historical Society)

In June, 1936, in an area near New Castle, Pennsylvania, a couple of Pittsburgh and Lake Erie Railroad inspectors found the naked, headless body of a white male. Located near the body were pages from newspapers including a Cleveland newspaper dated August 30, 1933.

Victim No. 5 was found on Cleveland's west side, just south of Clinton Road, July 22, 1936, decapitated and lying about a hundred yards from the tracks of the B & O Railroad. The head and clothes were found approximately ten feet from the victim's body. Coroner Pearce indicated that, "The killer would have to possess the skill and anatomical knowledge of a surgeon to sever the head and body so cleanly" (Note 1, p. 71).

Sheriff O'Donnell, Detective Harry Brown, jailer Mike Kilbane & (stooped)
Dr. E. F. Ecker inspecting a tub used in a dismemberment
by the Cleveland Torso Killer
(Cleveland Press Collection courtesy of Cleveland State University Library)
Also see chapters 2 and 3.
Sinks and tubs were used in the murders and dismemberment of victims.

Sometime in October, 1936, a decapitated body of a white male was discovered along the train tracks near Haverstraw, New York. The killer had used a saw to sever the head from the torso. Curiously, the New York Central runs past Haverstraw.

Victim No. 6 was discovered September 10, 1936. The head had been severed between the third and fourth cervical vertebrae. The killer had severed the torso about two inches above the navel between the third and fourth lumbar vertebrae. The stomach and both kidneys were cut in the process. Based on the method of amputations, it was determined that the killer had gained knowledge of anatomy as a medical student or as a butcher.

Cleveland detectives searching for body parts of Victim No. 6, September 11, 1936, in a stagnant pool near Kingsbury Run (Cleveland Press Collection courtesy of Cleveland State University Library)

Storm drain at the end of Superior Avenue in Cleveland where a piece of Victim No. 6's leg was recovered (photo courtesy of Marjorie Merylo Dentz)

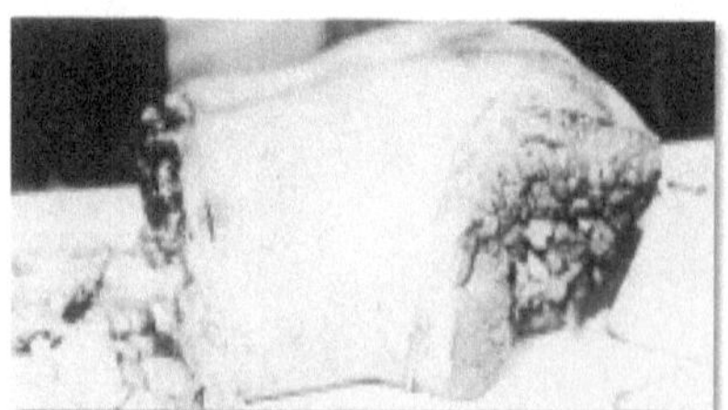

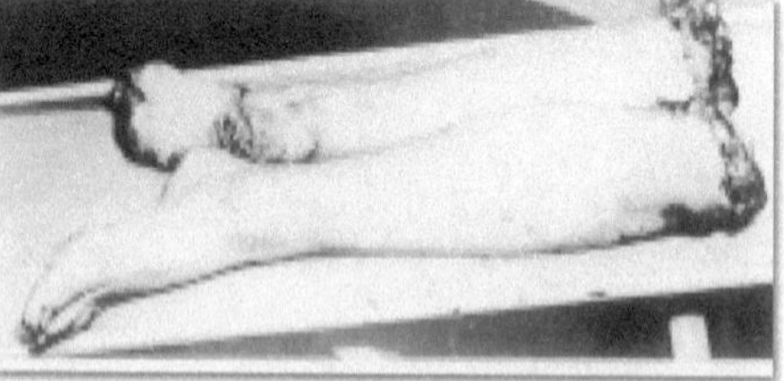

Body parts of Victim No. 6 found September 10, 1936, in Kingsbury Run near 37th Street (photo courtesy of the Cleveland Police Historical Society)

Throughout my study of the torso murders, Cleveland's Detective Peter Merylo seems to have offered the most probable analysis based on the known facts at that time. He determined that the Cleveland, New Castle and additional torso killings in Youngstown, Ohio, were committed by the same person or persons. Detective Merylo thought that similar murders during this time period in Pennsylvania and in Cleveland were committed by the same individual. He also determined that the killer traveled from one location to another by rail and may have used a boxcar as his laboratory to butcher his victims. Merylo also toyed with the idea that more than one person acting together were committing these crimes. Based on the known evidence, I concur with his conclusion. Elliot Ness also studied the idea that the New Castle and Cleveland torso murders might somehow be connected. He sent his assistant, John R. Flynn, to New Castle to investigate a possible link between the two locations.

Detective Peter Merylo
(photo courtesy of his daughter,
Marjorie Merylo Dentz)

Detective Peter Merylo searching for clues (and body parts?) in a Cleveland storm sewer. Notice the shovel and pick (by the boot of the standing detective) that were used to open the heavy sewer cover. This search for body parts in a sewer compares to the search for body parts in chapter 2.
(photo courtesy of Marjorie Merylo Dentz)

Picture of New York Central freight cars near Kingsbury Run
(photo courtesy of Marjorie Merylo Dentz)

Detective Peter Merylo with Lieutenant Moffitt; Cleveland's Director of Public Safety and former head of the Chicago "Untouchables," Elliot Ness; Sergeant Massey; and Lieutenant Schanadam, October 19, 1938
(photo courtesy of Marjorie Merylo Dentz)

On May 5, 1937, the upper torso of Victim No. 7 was found located in the cold waters of Lake Erie just off East 30th Street in Cleveland. The killer had inserted a pants pocket inside the woman's rectum. The rectum had been stretched to accommodate the foreign object.

The skull of Victim No. 8 was located on June 6, 1937, under the Lorain-Carnegie Bridge in Cleveland. The head of this victim had been separated from the body and the torso had been placed in a burlap bag. The victim was later identified as a black woman named Rose Wallace. On the day she disappeared, according to witnesses, she left a laundry with a dark-skinned, white man named "Bob."

Cleveland police searching under Sidaway Bridge in Kingsbury Run (Cleveland Press Collection courtesy of Cleveland State University Library)

On July 6, 1937, Cleveland police and the Ohio National Guard began searching the banks of the Cuyahoga River for body parts of Victim No. 9.

On July 9, 1937, the lower half of a man's torso was discovered floating in the Cuyahoga River. For the first time, drugs were detected in the body. Was the killer introducing drugs into the victims before killing and dismembering them? The drug was determined to be morphine. He left deep gashes in the thighs of Victim No. 10.

Cuyahoga County Coroner Samuel R. Gerber had speculated that the killer could be a doctor. If drugs were introduced, then this could explain why the torso victims were dismembered without showing signs of putting up much defense. The *Cleveland News* included an editorial in a September 12, 1936, edition:

> That this creature, sly, crafty inhumanly skilled in butchery is a menace to every man, woman and child who walks the streets of Cleveland does not have to be emphasized. Why these dead? Why the darkest of all Cleveland murder mysteries? He kills for the thrill of killing. He kills to satisfy a bestial, sadistic lust for blood. He kills to prove himself strong. He kills to feed his sex-perverted brain, the sight of a beheaded human. He must kill for decapitation is his drug, to be taken in closer-spaced doses. Yes he will kill again. He is of course insane.

In March, 1937, Coroner Gerber reviewed the known facts covering the first seven torso murders in Cleveland:

> It is particularly the peculiar dissection of the bodies which groups these seven cases together. All cases show that the heads were severed from the bodies through the intervertebral discs . . . by means of a sharp knife. Cases No. 3, 6, and 7 showed further that the bodies were cleanly dismembered at the shoulder and hip joints apparently by a series of cuts around the flexure of the joints and then by a strong twist wrenching the head out of the joint cavity and cutting the capsule. The torsos were further sectioned through the abdomen, the knife being carried in cases No. 3 and 6 through the intervertebral discs . . . . Case No. 3 (Flo Polillo) was further mutilated by disarticulating the knee joints roughly, fracturing the mid-portion of the bones of the lower legs and slashing the abdomen down through the pubic bones . . . All the skin edges, muscles, blood vessels and cartilages were cut squarely and cleanly, apparently by a long sharp knife such as a butcher or heavy bread knife. There is relatively little hacking of the tissues and relatively few hesitation marks . . . .

> the direction of these marks indicate . . . a right handed individual . . . . (knife marks) indicate they were cut through anteriorly down to the vertebral spines and then the section completed from behind in all cases. The procedure followed in these cases suggests to us that the dissection was done either by a lay person, or persons, highly intelligent in recognizing the anatomical landmarks as they were approached, or else, as is more likely, by a person, or persons, with some knowledge of anatomy, such as a doctor, a medical student, a (male) nurse, orderly, prosector butcher, hunter or veterinary surgeon. (. . . the bodies may have been sectioned as they were, to facilitate transportation and disposition.)

On the afternoon of August 16, 1938, in a dumpsite near the southwest corner of Lake Shore Drive and East 9th Street in Cleveland, the torso of Victim No.11 was found. Shortly thereafter other body parts were discovered in the same area wrapped in heavy brown paper like the kind used by butchers. At 5:30 that afternoon a fellow by the name of Tom Bartholomew spotted the bones of Victim No.12 at the Cleveland dump site. The murders in Cleveland "officially ended" in 1938.

On December 29, 1938, a letter addressed to Cleveland's Chief of Police George Matowitz, dated December 23, 1938, was found in the dead letter office at the Cleveland Post Office. The letter reads:

> Chief of Police Matowitz
>
> You can rest easy now, as I have come out to sunny California for the winter. I felt bad operating on those people, but science must advance. I shall astond the medical profession, a man with only a D.C. What did their lives mean in comparison to hundreds of sick and disease twisted bodies? Just laboratory guinea pigs found on any public street. No

> one missed them when I failed. My last case was successful. I know now the feeling of Pasteur, Thoreau and other pioneers.
>
> Right now I have a volunteer who will absolutely prove my theory. They call me mad and a butcher, but the truth will out.
>
> I have failed but once here. The body has never been found and never will be, but the head, minus the features is buried on Century Boulevard, between Western and Crenshaw. I feel it my duty to dispose of the bodies as I do. It is God's will not to let them suffer.
>
> (signed) X

Whoever wrote the 1938 letter seemed to know that the killings in Cleveland were ending, at least for the time being.

On August 7, 1939, Detective Finnis W. Brown wrote Detective Merylo from Inglewood, California. Brown's letter is as follows:

> He needed to direct attention away from Cleveland for a short time, so he evidently sent a letter, to be re-mailed from there. Then while all attention was focused on Los Angeles, he disposed of his dangerous evidence. I fully expected to hear of the discovery of another torso murder victim soon thereafter and sure enough, a short time later, part of a woman's body was found. Well, he is on his guard right now, but as time passes without discovery, he will gradually gain confidence in his ability to outsmart the police—and he'll try his luck again. For he must have heads for his experiment, and get them he most likely will. Best wishes.
>
> F.W. Brown #719 West Kelso St., Inglewood, Calif.

In 1942, Los Angeles detectives had tentatively identified the author of the 1938 letter as one Charles August DiVere, a quack doctor. No positive link was ever established between DiVere and the Cleveland Torso Murders. Whoever wrote the December 23, 1938, letter may have had access to information printed in Cleveland newspapers, but one has to wonder if someone in Los Angeles in 1938 would have read that the heads of the Cleveland and New Castle torso victims had been buried.

The Cleveland Police Department has been unable to locate the files on the Cleveland Torso Murders. Fortunately, Detective Merylo was a very dedicated police officer. While in office he accumulated duplicate copies of thousands of notes and letters associated with the Torso Murders, which he studied at home after completing his shift at the department. I personally reviewed all of the known copies that were in Detective Merylo's care. In one of the letters, dated July 20, 1937, Merylo wrote a letter to Lieutenant Harvey Weitzel:

Copy of envelope mailed from Los Angeles to Cleveland Chief of Police Matowitz postmarked December 22, 1938 (photo courtesy of Marjorie Merylo Dentz)

Dec. 21,1938

Chief of Police Matowitz,

You can rest easy now as I have came out to sunny California for the winter. I felt bad operating on those people but science must advance. I shall soon astonde the medical profession-- a man with only a D.C.

What did their lives mean in comparasion to hundreds of sick x and disease twisted bodies. Just laboratory guinea pigs found on any public street. No one missed them when I failed. My last case was sucessful. I know now the feeling of Pasteur;Thoreau and other pioneers.

Right now I have a volunteer who will absolutely prove my theory. They called me mad and a butcherer but the"truth will out".

I have failed but once here. The body has not been found and never will be but the head minus features is buried in a gully on Century Blvd. between Western and Century Crenshaw. I feel it is my duty to dispose of the bodies I do .It is God's will not to let them suffer.

Copy of December 21, 1938, letter mailed from Los Angeles to Cleveland Chief of Police Matowitz (photo courtesy of Marjorie Merylo Dentz)

Sir

Reported for duty 8:30 a.m. and with Detective Zalewski, assigned to further investigate Torso Murders.

In reference to letter received by the department from North Hollywood, California, pertaining to the Torso murders, in which one suspect being mentioned, who is now employed at the Great Lakes Exposition, we checked up on this suspect from various sources unbeknown to him and will continue to do so until every angle has been thoroughly checked and a report will follow when the investigation is completed. We also located a woman with whom he made a date, but after a confidential inquiry, she could not tell us anything that would substantiate the information received in the letter from North Hollywood, California.

I further wish to state that we detailed ourselves at the exposition ground watching the movements of the suspect mentioned in the above letter, but up to this time have learned nothing that would warrant the arrest and detention of the suspect. Reported off duty at 6:00 p. m. Respectfully Peter Merylo, Det.

Detective Merylo wrote another letter July 20, 1937, to Lieutenant Weitzel:

Report on letter received from North Hollywood, California

Sir;

On July 10, 1937 a letter was received by this department in reference to the Torso Murders. The writer of the letter gave a detail of the suspect that is suppose to have been connected with the Great Lakes Exposition. It was considered at that time and still is until a thorough investigation proves otherwise that her information was very important. The writer refuses to sign her name but requested that we communicate with her through a personal column of the Los Angeles, Calif. newspapers. The Los Angeles Herald and Express. With the permission of Inspector Sweeny and Chief Matowitz the ad was inserted in said newspaper and the same ran for a period of one week. This transaction was accomplished through the Los Angeles Police Dept., and we were successful in receiving a reply through said ad which gave us the name of the person and additional information. On this date we received a bill from Chief of police, Los Angeles, Calif. In which he stated that he had paid the bill as instructed by our Chief's office which amounts to $9.24 and the same is attached. Respectfully, Peter Merylo, Det.

Detective Merylo determined that the suspect mentioned in the 1937 letter from North Hollywood was a 17-year-old boy, who's last name was "Wilson." Wilson was employed at the Great Lakes Exposition in 1936. Merylo also learned that the suspect's mother's name was Helen Wilson and his father was Walter F. Wilson. Merylo related this information to Lieutenant Weitzel. The 17-year-old boy was ultimately dismissed as a possible suspect.

On August 16, 1938, the severed head of Victim No.12 was found in a Cleveland dump site in a tin can, separate from the body. One of the New Castle torso victims' heads was found buried in the ground near the unburied body.

In the spring of 1950, a man approximately fifty years old was seen sunbathing for about twenty minutes each day close to East 22nd Street and Lakeshore in Cleveland. One day the man disappeared and did not return to his sunbathing activity. On July 22 of that year near the location where the man sunbathed a dismembered torso of a white male was found. The sunbather was thought to be the killer of the person later identified as Robert Robertson, a forty-year-old alcoholic from Boynton, Pennsylvania. Robertson had not been seen since June 12. Was the sunbather someone who soaked up the sun during the winters in "sunny California"? At the scene of this murder investigators found something new: two pages from a telephone book covering the letter "K" (See pages 522–523).

Similarities Between the Cleveland Torso Murders and the Pennsylvania Torso Murders

1. None of the timings of the murders overlap.
2. There was decapitation of victims in both states.
3. There was dismemberment of victims in both states.

4. All of the murders occurred in close proximity to railroad tracks.
5. The New York Central Railroad traveled to and from Cleveland and Youngstown, Ohio; New Castle and West Pittsburgh, Pennsylvania; Haverstraw, New York, and Chicago. The New York Central passes by Kingsbury Run.
6. In all cases there are similarities in the victim profiles.
7. In Cleveland, Edward Andrassy's severed head was found buried in the ground near his unburied body. One of the Pennsylvania torso victims' heads was located buried in the ground near the unburied body.
8. The Mad Butcher of Kingsbury Run used a saw to finish separating the shoulder of the Lady of the Lakes. A murder in New Castle in late 1939 mirrored the Cleveland torso murders. In the New Castle murder the killer used a saw or a knife with serrated teeth to remove the head from the victim's body. The killer of the victim in Haverstraw, New York, used a saw to sever his head from the body.
9. Bloodstained underwear was found near the victims.
10. Decapitation was "clean and expert" in each state.
11. Several of the victims' decapitated heads were never found.
12. Several of the murdered victims were never identified.
13. Several victims in both states were located in remote areas.

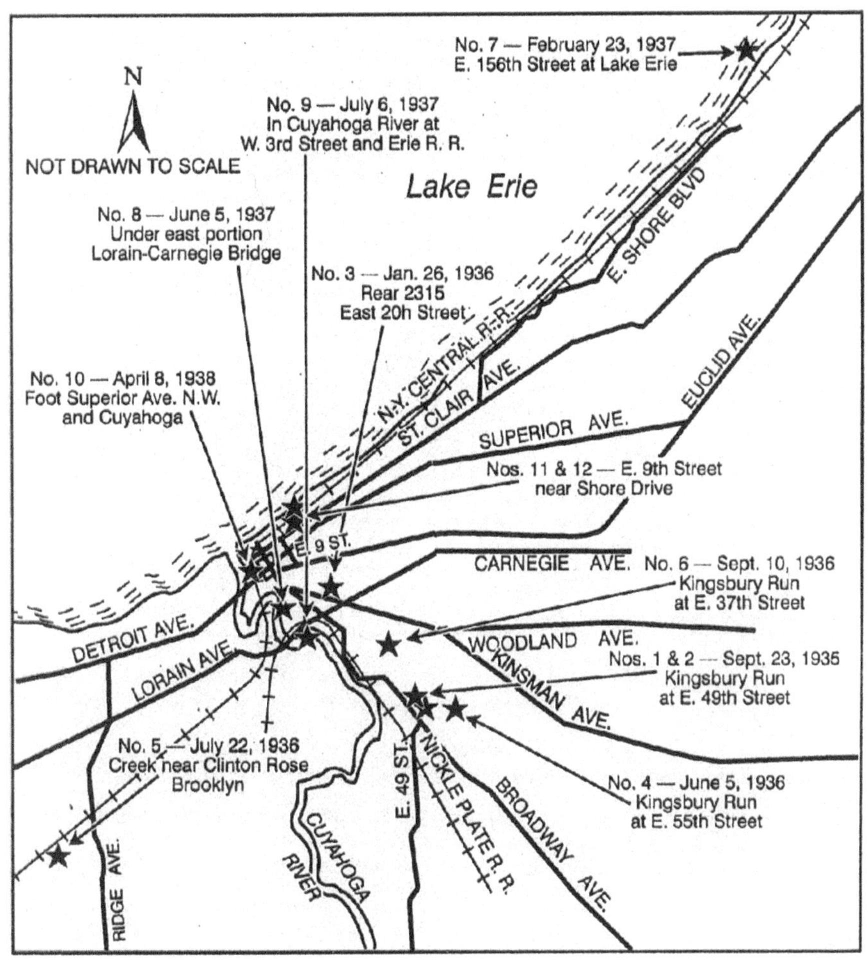

Cleveland Map 1: Location of Torso victims.

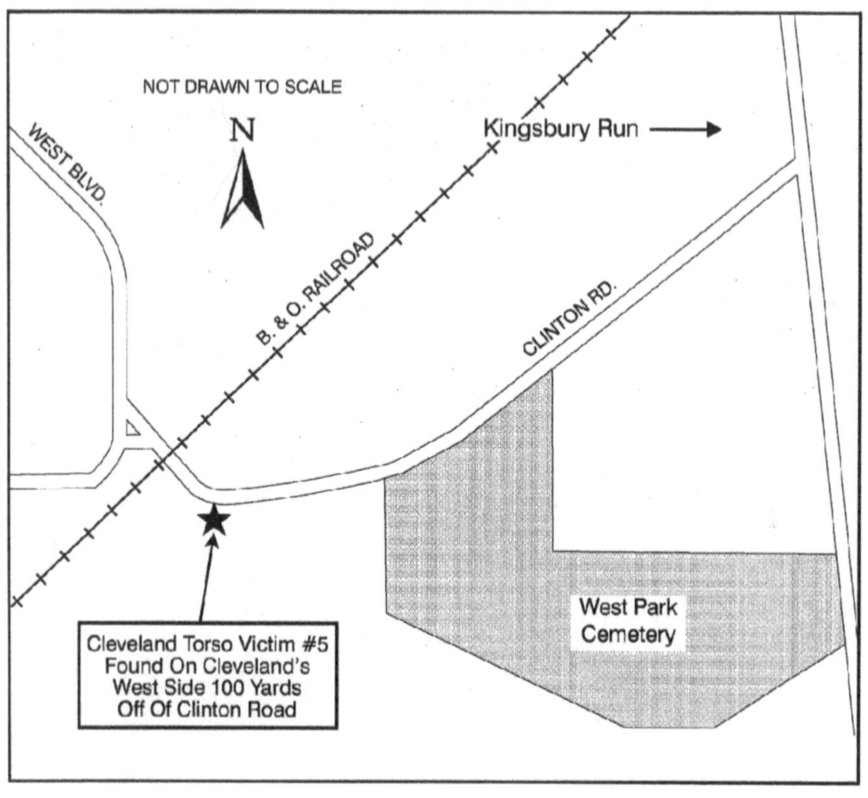

Cleveland Map 2: Location where Torso Victim No. 5 was found on Cleveland's West side.

Detective Peter Merylo kept a separate ledger on ten of the torso murders. His notes, courtesy of his daughter, Marjorie Merylo Dentz, include the following:

Torso Victim:

Case No. 1

Name	Unknown		
Address	Unknown		
Sex:	Male	*Color:*	White
Date Found	July 23, 1935	*Duration of Death*	7-8 days

Approximate date of death	July 15, 1935		
Estimated age	40 to 45	Height 5 ft.6 in. Weight 160	
Location found	Kingsbury Run at East 40th Street		
Parts Recovered	Head, body		
Parts Missing	Left testicle		
Neck	Disarticulated mid-portion.		
Body			
Extremities	Intact		
Cut surfaces, soft tissues,	Sharply cut, muscles retracted		
Genitalia	Left testicle excised (?)		
Blood in Body ?			
Contents of stomach			
Identification marks	two scars middle third right thigh one inch and two in diameter.		
Cause of Death	Decapitation		

Torso: Victim:

Case number 2			
Name	Andrew W. Andrassy		
Address			
Sex	male	*Color*	white
Date found	July 23rd, 1935	*Duration of death*	2-3 days
Approximate date of death	July 20th, 1935		
Estimated Age	28 years	*Height* 5 ft. 11 in. *Weight* 150	
Location found	Kingsbury Run at east 40th Street		
Parts recovered	Head, body, genitalia		
Parts Missing			
Neck	Disarticulated mid-portion		
Body			
Extremities	Intact (Rope burns on wrist)		
Cut Surfaces, soft tissue	Sharply cut, muscles retracted		
Genitalia	Scrotum and penis amputated		

Blood in Body — Heart and large vessels empty

Contents of stomach — Recently ingested vegetable meal

Identifying marks — Appendectomy scar, small scar forehead, Gold-capped left upper lateral incisor tooth

Cause of Death — Decapitation

Torso Victim:

Case number 3.

Name — Florence Polillo alias Martin

Address

Sex — Female Color white

Date found — January 26, 1936

Approximate date of death — January 23, 1936

Estimated age — 42 *Height* 5 ft 5 in. *Weight* 160

Location found — 2315-2325 East 20th Street

Parts Recovered — upper and lower half of torso, four extremities

Parts missing — head

Neck — Disarticulated C4-5

Body — Disarticulated L 3-5. Also longitudinal section

Extremities — All extremities disarticulated also at the knee joints Cut surfaces, soft tissues all surfaces sharply cut, no retraction of muscles. Few hesitation marks

Genitalia — none veneris and symphysis incised

Blood in body — Heart and large vessels empty

Contents of stomach

Identifying marks — vaccination mark right thigh. Mid-line lower abdominal laparotomy wound

Cause of death — Decapitation

Torso Victim:

Case number 4

Name — Unknown

Address — Unknown

Sex — Male *Color* white

Date found	June 5, 1936 June 6, 1936	*Duration of death*	2-3 days
Approximate date of death	June 2nd, 1936		
Estimated age	25	*Height* 5 ft. 11 in. *Weight* 150	
Location found	Kingsbury Run, East 55th Street		
Parts Recovered	Head, body		
Parts Missing			
Neck	Disarticulated C 1-2		
Body			
Extremities	Intact		
Cut Surfaces, soft tissues	Sharply cut. Few hesitation marks *Genitalia* Intact		
Blood in body	Heart and large vessels empty		
Contents of stomach	Small amounts of undigested food (Baked beans) in stomach		
Identification marks	Tattoo marks 1. butterfly; 2. Picture of Jiggs. 3. Hearty and Arrow. 4. Flag with "W.C.G." 5. Cupid and anchor. 6 Dove with "Helen and Paul."		
Cause of death	Decapitation		

Torso Victim:

Case number 5

Name	Unknown		
Address	Unknown		
Sex	Male	*Color*	white
Date found	July 22nd, 1936	*Duration of death*	1-2 months
Approximate date of death	May 22nd, 1936		
Estimated age	35-40		
Location found	Big Creek, Clinton Road, Brooklyn Village, Ohio, near Rayon Silk		
Mills. *Parts recovered*	Head, body		
Parts missing			
Neck	Disarticulated C 3-4		

Body			
Extremities	Intact		
Cut surfaces, soft tissues?			
Genitalia?			
Blood in body?			
Contents of stomach			
Identifying marks?			
Cause of death	Decapitation (?)		

Torso Victim:			
Case number 6			
Name	Unknown		
Address	Unknown		
Sex	Male	*Color*	white
Date found	September 10, 1936	*Duration of Death*	1-2 days
Approximate date of death	September 8, 1936		
Estimated age	25-30	*Height* 5 ft. 10 in.	*Weight* 145
Location found	Kingsbury Run at East 37th Street		
Parts recovered	Upper half torso, lower half torso, thighs and legs.		
Parts missing	Head, both upper extremities, Genitalia		
Neck	Disarticulated C 3-4		
Body	Disarticulated L 3-4		
Extremities	All extremities disarticulated, also at knee joints		
Cut surfaces, soft tissues	Sharply cut, few "Hesitation" marks on neck. No retraction of muscles		
Genitalia:	genitalia amputated		
Blood in Body	Heart and large vessels empty		
Contents of stomach	Kernels of corn in stomach		
Identifying marks	None		
Cause of death ?			

Torso Victim:
Case number 7
Name Unknown
Address Unknown
Sex Female *Color* white
Date found February 23, 1937 *Duration of death* 3-5 days
Approximate date of death February 17th, 1937
Estimated age 25-35 *Height* ? *Weight* 100-120
Location found Lakeshore Boulevard at East 156th Street
Parts recovered Upper half torso
Parts missing Head, lower half torso, all four extremities
Neck Disarticulated C-7-T 1
Body Disarticulated L 1 (through body)
Extremities All extremities disarticulated
Cut surfaces. Soft tissues Sharply cut. Numerous hesitation marks on neck
Genitalia?
Blood in body blood clots in heart and large vessel
Contents of stomach
Identifying marks None except extremely flat breasts
Cause of death ?

Torso Victim:
Case number 8
Name Unknown
Address Unknown
Sex female *Color* Colored
Date found June 6th, 1937 *Duration of death* 1 year
Approximate date of death June, 1936
Estimated age 30-40 *Height* 5 ft. 0 in. *Weight* 100-110
Location found Cuyahoga River Basin, region of West 3rd Street Bridge

Parts recovered	Skull, entire vertebral column, ribs and pelvis
Parts missing	Bones of all four extremities
Neck	Disarticulated C 4 C 5
Body ?	
Extremities	Apparently disarticulated at the shoulders and hip
Cut surfaces, soft tissues ?	
Genitalia ?	
Blood in body ?	
Contents of stomach ?	
Identifying marks	Gold bridge upper left side cuspid 1st, 2nd bicuspid
Cause of death ??	Decapitation

Torso Victim:

Case number 9

Name	Unknown		
Address	Unknown		
Sex	Male	*Color*	White
Date found	July 6th, 1937	*Duration of death 2* days	
	July 10th, 1937		
Approximate date of death	July 4, 1937		
Location found	Cuyahoga River region of West 3rd Street bridge		
Parts Recovered	Upper and lower halves torso, both arms, both legs, both thighs, both forearms.		
Parts Missing	Head, neck		
Neck	Disarticulated C 6 C 7		
Body	Body disarticulated L1 L2		
Extremities	Disarticulated at shoulders, hips, elbows and knees		
Cut surfaces, soft tissues	Sharply cut, hesitation marks on skin of out surfaces. Retraction muscles of neck. Body eviscerated.		
Genitalia	Intact		
Blood in Body	Blood vessels empty, heart excised		

Contents of stomach ?	Eviscerated		
Identifying marks	Blue pigmented cross on left leg. Two linear scars dorsum right thumb		
Cause of death ??	Decapitation		

Torso Victim:

*Case number 10**

Name	Unknown		
Address	Unknown		
Sex	Female	*Color*	White
Date found	8th, 1936	*Duration of death*	3-7 da.
	May 2nd, 1936 27-34 da.		
Approximate date of death	January 5th, 1936		
Location found	Cuyahoga River, region upper West 3rd Street bridge		
Parts recovered	Left leg, thorax, abdomen, both thighs, left foot.		
Parts missing	Upper portion 2nd and 3rd cervical		
Neck	Disarticulated 12 T 1 L		
Body	Disarticulated L 1 through body		
Extremities	All extremities disarticulated		
Cut surfaces, soft tissues	Sharply cut, hesitation marks on skin of cut surfaces. Some retraction of muscles		
Genitalia	Intact		
Blood in Body	Heart and blood vessels empty		
Contents of stomach	Empty		
Identifying Marks	Old scar 4 inches long horizontally in right lower quadrant abdomen. Midline scar lower mid abdomen 5 inches long.		
Cause of death ??	Decapitation		

* A letter from Detective Merylo to Lieutenant Tozzel indicated that the torso victim found May 2, 1938, was a female and "her privates were cleanly shaved."

DEPARTMENT OF POLICE: CLEVELAND. O.
Bureau of Criminal Identification.

September 4th, 1938

The following is the List of Murders - (TORSO) committed in Cleveland, Ohio, evidently by a Homicidal Maniac.

- -

NO.- 0 - Torso of an UNKNOWN white woman found at the foot of East 156th, st, evidently washed ashore (buttock & thighs only) on Sept. 5th, 1934

NO.- 1) - On September 23rd, 1935 the nude bodies of two white men were
NO.- 2) found on the side of a hill in Kingsbury Run, Cleveland, Ohio they had been dead probably about four days when found.
The heads, penis, and testicals had been severed from the bodies none of their clothing had ever been found. they were not killed at the spot where the bodies were found, but no doubt were brought there.
One of the men was identified by his finger prints but the other was never identified (Identified as Edw. Andrasy of 5708 Storer Ave, Cleveland, Ohio.
There were no marks on either of the bodies, only at the neck where the head had been severed and this was very neatly done.

NO.- 3 - On Sunday January 26th, 1936 the Pelvis, Thighs and Right Arm of a white woman was found in an alley back of 2315 East 20th, st, Cleveland, Ohio.
The head of this woman had been hacked away from the body and was never found, also the legs and arms had been clumsily hacked from the body.
This woman was identified by the prints of her right hand as Florence Martin alias Clara Dunn alias Florence Polillo alias Florence G. Sawdey she was married to an Andrew Polillo with whom she lived in Buffalo, N.Y. for some time.
The remains were turned over to her relatives January 30, 1936 and taken to North Girard, Pa, for burial.
This woman was a prostitute and a hard drinker.

NO.- 4 - On June 5th, 1936 the headless body of a white man was found in a place known as Kingsbury Run in Cleveland, Ohio, this place is a ravine or gully close to the Nickle Plate Ry. The water being about three feet to fifteen feet in depth.
This mans head was found about 200 feet from the body under a tree wrapped in this victims clothing. He was never identified and there were no marks on the body only at the neck where the head was severed.

NO.- 5 - On July 22nd, 1936 the dead body of a white man was found near Clifton Rd, & Big Creek in Brooklyn Township a Suburb of Cleveland, Ohio. The head had been very expertly severed from the body, there were no marks of violence on the body only at the neck. The head was found a short distance from the body wrapped in the victims clothing and was under a low growing bush, the place where this crime was committed is very isolated and close to a railway tracks as have all of the others.
This man was never identified and all the bodies which have been found have been stripped of the clothing after death.

September 4, 1938, list of first five Torso Murders in Cleveland prepared by the Cleveland Police Department (photo courtesy of the Cleveland Police Historical Society)

On April 15, 1939, Detective Merylo made a request to Lieutenant Harvey Weitzel of the Cleveland Detective Bureau that the following letter be sent to the Baltimore, Maryland, Police Department:

> Sir;
>
> I respectfully request that a letter be sent to the Baltimore, Maryland Police Department asking them to furnish us with details of the human body found there dissected recently. What we particularly would like to know is, was the body dissected at the joints, did it appear that any other instrument than a knife was used to dissect the body. What was the condition of the parts found as to blood, was there any blood left in the veins? We understand the body was wrapped in the comic section of the newspaper. Will you kindly advise what newspaper and the date of same. Were the hands found, and if so can you send us fingerprints of same. In what section of the city was the body found? Since 1935, we have had in the city a series of so called "torso" murders, that is where the body has been found dissected and in most instances decapitated and the heads have never been found. Respectifully, Peter Merylo, Detective

Another letter of interest was received by the Cleveland Police Department in the late 1930s that was among the letters in the Peter Merylo file. This typed letter provided the following:

Chief of Police
Homicide Bureau
Cleveland, Ohio

Dear Sir;

Being particularly interested in discovering the identity of the Cleveland Torso Slayer for a long time. I thought I would write you my impressions on seeing the photo of Edward Andrassy. What he is sitting on appears like a bench used by a Professional Photographer. The back ground doesn't seem to be clear and may be disguised. What about doing a quiet investigation of places of this sort within a radius of a mile from the Run. Its likely that this fellow may be one who hasn't a first class place. Just a small neighborhood affair. Hence the few pictures in the rear which may at first appear to be a private residence. Again, he may be and likely is a man of foreign extraction. Also, a former butcher or orderly who does work either on a full or parttime. In this manner he may get acquainted with the history of his intended victims. He also may do the strip tease stuff on the side. Would suggest getting a youthful plain clothes man or men do a round of these places by getting a few negatives developed. And in this way size up the owner there. There's an outside chance that it may be a woman with previous nurse experience. Again this party is likely to have a car. Also, a large developing lab situated in a spot of this kind could be a good blind. Persons in this line too get a large part of the News. Would advise to take your time as this person is crazy but no fool. Sincerely, Lewis Wilson Appleton, Jr.

Could this letter have been written by the Cleveland Torso Killer? He signed his name as Lewis Wilson Appleton, Jr. Perhaps he was sending a clue to the police: Lewis (Clue is) Wilson? The writer advised the police to "take your time." This may be of importance when compared to a note, referred to in Chapter 3, sent by the Black Dahlia Avenger, in which the writer wrote: "Go Slow Man Killer Says." Also note that this letter refers to a "former butcher" (See tip reported to Detective Orley May on page 100 in which the informant refers to Jack Wilson as a "former butcher").

Chapter 2

THE CASE AGAINST WILLIAM HEIRENS

Forty-three-year-old Josephine Ross lived in an apartment building at 4108 North Kenmore Avenue in Chicago's Edgewood District. An elevated passenger railway, known as the, "Red Line," is located within one block of her apartment. The train makes scheduled stops at Thorndale Avenue near her apartment. At 9:00 a.m. on June 5, 1945, after Josephine's daughter, Jacqueline, had gone to work, Josephine went to bed. When her daughter came home for lunch she discovered her mother's blood-soaked body lying on the bed. Sometime between 9:00 a.m. and 1:00 p. m. Josephine Ross was savagely murdered. Her throat had been stabbed several times. The killer had wrapped her head in a dress. The custodian of the apartment building and another tenant reported to detectives that they had seen an "unfamiliar, swarthy, dark-haired male in white sweater and dark trousers, seemingly without purpose, wandering through the building." Janitor Elmer Nelson estimated the stranger to weigh in at about 190 pounds; lodger Bernice Folkman called him slender.

Six months later, on December 10, 1945, the body of Frances Brown was found in room 611 at the Pinecrest Apartments, 3941 Pine Grove, in Chicago near the apartment rented by Josephine Ross and the near the Red Line. A large knife was found lodged in her throat, and there was a bullet hole in her skull. Her head was

4108 North Kenmore Avenue, Chicago, Illinois

wrapped in her pajamas. Written in red lipstick on her living room wall were the words, "For Heavens sake catch me before I kill more. I cannot control myself." "The words had been written a full six feet from the floor and the hand that wrote them seemed to be heavy." The red lipstick message may have been written by a tall man.

3941 Pine Grove, Chicago, Illinois

Less than one month later, on January 7, 1946, six-year-old Suzanne Degnan was kidnapped from her parents' home at 5943 North Kenmore Avenue in Chicago and murdered. The Degnan family lived on the first floor, and the Flynn family occupied an apartment on the second floor. Suzanne's abductor may have placed a ladder against the side of the building and gained access through a first-floor window. The killer or killers left a ransom note behind in the girl's bedroom. The note read, "Get $20,000 reddy & waite for word. Do not notify FBI or police. Bills in $5's and $10's." On the back of the ransom note was a warning: "Burn this for her safty." Cecelia Flynn later recalled hearing two men talking in the street the evening of the abduction. She thought one of the men said, "This is the best-looking building around." Suzanne's body could not be found until an anonymous telephone call, by someone who was never identified, was received by the police. The caller directed the authorities to neighborhood storm sewers. The police immediately began searching and located the dismembered body parts of Suzanne Degnan discarded where the caller indicated they would be found. It was later determined that a basement washtub in an apartment located at 5901-03 Winthrop was the place where she was dismembered (Note 14).

On the night of the abduction a witness saw a woman carrying a large bundle in both arms in the vicinity of the Degnan home. "She got into what seemed to be an awaiting automobile where a balding man sat behind the wheel." Another witness recalled seeing a large dark man carrying a shopping bag near the Degnan house at the time of her disappearance. None of these individuals has ever been identified.

A 17-year-old University of Chicago college student and part-time petty burglar by the name of William Heirens was at the wrong place at the wrong time searching for something to steal when he was arrested and eventually charged with the murders of Josephine

William Heirens at Vienna Correctional Center, Illinois Correctional Facility in 2004 (photo courtest of Dolores Kennedy)

Ross, Frances Brown and Suzanne Degnan. While in the custody of the Chicago police he was interrogated relentlessly for days, often brutally. He was physically beaten, kept awake, interrogated by several detectives, paraded past the electric chair on a daily basis and threatened with its efficiency. He was given sodium pentathol, had ether applied to his scrotum and was given a painful spinal tap. The five Chicago daily newspapers headlined the Heirens story 157 times over a ten-week period (Note 14).

He faced up to fifty years in prison for the burglaries alone. His attorneys strongly advised him to plead guilty, and his chances for a fair trial in Chicago had all but evaporated. Public sentiment towards his condemnation and political pressure were taking their toll on Mr. Heriens. He finally agreed to plead guilty, in his words, "so I could live." As an example of the interrogation methods that might have been used on William Heirens, consider the case of another earlier suspect in the Degnan murder, Hector Verburgh, the janitor at the Winthrop Apartments where Suzanne was dismembered. Mr. Verburgh was arrested under suspicion of murder. After his ordeal, Mr. Verburgh told reporters:

> Oh, they hanged me up, they blindfolded me. I can't put up my arms, they are sore. They had handcuffs on me for hours and hours. They threw me in a cell and blindfolded me. They handcuffed my hands behind my back and pulled me up on bars until only my toes touched the floor. I no sleep, I no eat, I go to the hospital. Oh I am sick. Any more and I would have confessed anything (Note 17, p. 52).

Following Mr. Verburgh's release from custody he was hospitalized for ten days with a separated shoulder. "Immediately following his recuperation, he filed a $125,000.00 lawsuit against the department. After the investigation the Verburghs were awarded $20,000" (Note 13). Author John Bartlow Martin wrote an applicable segment in *Butcher's Dozen and Other Murders:*

> Several policemen whom I originally met professionally have become my personal friends; my wife and I visit their homes. A few weeks ago one of them startled my neighbors as he drove away by turning on a siren. The next I heard of him was a few days ago: an ex-convict had run amok in downtown Chicago and after being pursued by a couple of hundred cops had been trapped in a washroom in a railroad station, and my friend happened to be the man who killed him with a sub-machine gun. This was the first man he ever killed. He often told me he hoped he'd never have to kill anybody, and I called him up to see how he felt about it. He said he didn't know. 'It was just one of those things. He was in the washroom and couldn't get out any other way.' Some policemen like to kill criminals.
>
> All policemen hate sex criminals and criminals who harm children. Many good cops hate all criminals, and in a truly personal way. I have sat in the little back rooms in police

stations where prisoners are questioned and have watched a squad bring in a man, and their hatred and contempt is clear even in the way they close the door behind him. They seem bitter, affronted, outraged by his crimes. Frank Pape, a detective who figures in 'Cops and Robbers,' once told me how he had killed a murderer in a dark tenement the night before, and, shaking his head, Pape said seriously, 'He was a bad man, John, a bad man.' It was reproach. Another time Pape told me how he and other detectives had found parts of the body of the child, Suzanne Degnan. Pape has a couple of kids of his own. Though he, and the other policemen too, had worked on many cases, they were as horrified by what happened to Suzanne Degnan as any of the thousands of Chicago parents who woke up nights and looked in at their own sleeping children during the time that the murderer was at large. I remember Knifey Sawicki, a foolish kid who had spent his youth in reform schools and who one weekend killed a policeman and three other people: detectives pleaded to have fifteen minutes alone with him; the captain said correctly, "He's too hot—if you lay a hand on him you'll throw the case away." Sawicki had killed a cop who had a wife and two children and who was just minding his own business; Sawicki had killed him just because he didn't like cops. One can hardly blame the detectives who wanted to beat him up.

Police brutality is not as common as most people think but it is common enough. One team of detectives I know beat a confession out of a man and as soon as he was safe in the county jail he repudiated it and got a lawyer, who turned up a second man who also confessed to the murder; the first man was released and the second acquitted. The detectives had thrown the case away. I remember spending an evening

> listening to a detective (now dead) try to justify beating a prisoner. "Hanging her over a door," as he and the other cops call it—the practice of tying a prisoner's wrists behind his back, hoisting him off the floor so that his body hangs by the armpits from a door with his arms on the back of the door and the rest of the body on the front, then beating him across the stomach with a baseball bat. The woman they had just done this to had a previous criminal record and was the leader of a gang of stickup men who made a practice of going into a crowded tavern and pistol whipping or shooting the customers before emptying the cash register. They finally killed a good policeman who, on his way home, chanced to drop into a tavern they were holding up. My detective friend explained that through he was positive the woman was guilty he might have had a hard time proving it in court without a confession, that he had beaten her rather than take a chance on letting her go free to commit more crimes, that there was tremendous pressure on the case from the public and from higher police officials, that policemen in self defense can't afford to let a criminal get away with killing another policeman (the one alarm on the police radio that will bring every squad running is "Policeman needs help"), and that policemen never beat respectable people or ones of whose guilt they are in doubt. (This is almost true—you or I wouldn't get beaten up by the cops—but it isn't quite true, as has been shown. Cops are fallible.) (Note 18, p. 218-119).

Policeman have a sworn duty to "serve and protect," not to punish. In our system of justice it is the court's duty to hand out punishments to those who break the law. Pursuant to the United States Constitution, all men are presumed innocent until proven guilty. There is nothing contained in the Constitution that allows the police to inflict punishment on anyone suspected of a crime, no matter how outrageous the crime might be. To condone police activity that allows them the right to inflict punishment on those suspected of a crime undermines the foundation of our legal system.

William Heirens was in "protective custody" for over one month before he finally pled guilty to the Chicago murders in June, 1946. After he confessed, one of the five Chicago daily newspapers ran an article that read, "The Werewolf was in Chains." He received three consecutive life sentences and one year to life for burglaries and assault. He was spared the death penalty.

Following the murder of Suzanne Degnan, Chicago's Mayor Kelly received the following note: "This is to tell you how sorry I am I couldn't get ole Degnan instead of his girl. Roosevelt and OPA made their own laws. Why shouldn't I and a lot more?" (OPA stood for Office of Price Administration.) Keep in mind that during this time there was a nation-wide meat packer's strike in progress. Representative Jenkins, Republican from Ohio and chairman of the Republican Congressional Food Study Committee, was quoted in 1946, as follows: "The OPA is to blame for this strike which no one in the industry really wanted." Jenkins told the House, 'The single point at issue is an adjustment of meat prices so that the industry can afford to pay its employees higher wages." Senator Eastland (D. Miss) told the Senate a continuance of the meat strike would eventually make rationing of milk and dairy products necessary (Note 9). Could someone associated with the meat-packing industry or a butcher have something to do with the murder of Suzanne Degnan? The *Chicago Daily Tribune* reported on January 14, 1946, that "Police last night posted a guard at the home of Marion Isbell, wealthy restaurant owner and former top executive of the OPA, after receipt of two mysterious telephone calls at the home inquiring if there were any children there." The OPA agents did enter another murder in Chicago at about the same time as the Suzanne Degnan investigation because there were reports that the murder might have been the result of black market operations in meat. The head of the person killed was nearly severed.

In the investigation of the Degnan murder, certain members of the Chicago police department homicide division "believed that the kidnapper-killer must have driven a car the few blocks to the dismemberment; that carrying a 74-pound child through the streets would have drawn too much notice" (Note 14). Keep in mind that somehow the Mad Butcher of Kingsbury Run managed to dismember the bodies, often large bodies, in one location, transport and deposit the pieces in another location without being detected.

Several other women had been killed in Chicago during the previous six months immediately preceding the Degnan murder. In each case the body had been meticulously cleaned. In each instance the killer demonstrated a form of psychopathic cleanliness. I have already mentioned that the Heirens'case doesn't add up, and there may be a good reason for this. I would render a guess that whoever killed Josephine Ross, Frances Brown and Suzanne Degnan would have to be classified as an "organized killer."

Suzanne Degnan was kidnapped, a ransom note was left at the scene, and she was dismembered at a location other than where she was kidnapped. The killer used a basement tub and drain to complete the dismemberment. She was expertly dismembered. Her remains were discarded in nearby sewers. After the murder the Chicago Police Department, the FBI and every vigilante within fifty miles of Chicago had entered the race to find the killer. In other words, the heat was on, big time. So what was William Heirens doing at this time? Was he following the performance of an organized killer? Did he fit the part? I don't think so. William Heirens was a petty thief. He robbed houses, apartments and stores. He accumulated furs, men's suits, radios, utensils and guns. He got a thrill out of stealing things. On June 26, 1946, according to author

Dolores Kennedy, Heirens was in the process of stealing a wallet from a third floor apartment of the Wayne Manor apartments on Wayne Avenue in Chicago. A neighbor in an adjacent apartment witnessed the theft of the wallet and yelled at Heirens. Heirens fled the building. Another tenant spotted Heirens and called the police. The police arrived, a scuffle ensued, and Heirens was hit on the head with a flower pot. He was arrested, and the rest is history. Now you have to ask yourself, does this sound like an organized serial killer or a 17-year-old kid who was on a mission to commit another robbery? Had William Heirens been an organized killer he would not have risked apprehension by stealing a wallet from an occupied apartment building at a time when all of Chicago's police force was looking for the murderer of a six-year-old child that had been brutally killed and professionally dismembered. With this in mind, remember how meticulously the killer of Suzanne Degnan acted to complete the kidnapping, murder, ransom note, dismemberment and disposal of her body. I will say it again: The case against William Heirens just doesn't add up.

The kidnapping, murder and dismemberment of Suzanne Degnan may have been patterned somewhat after the famous kidnapping case of Colonel Charles A. Lindbergh's 20-month-old son on March 1, 1932 and if it was then it is possible that the killer knew it would cause a sensational response from law enforcement and the media, which it obviously did. If this was a motive then again William Heirens does not fit the profile. Someone like the Cleveland Torso Killer would relish the publicity.

In comparison to the Lindbergh case consider the following: Suzanne Degnan's kidnapper may have used a ladder to gain access to an occupied residence. In the Degnan case the person responsible kidnapped a small child, left a ransom note demanding $20,000, requested the bills be in $5's and $10's, and killed the child in a manner that would shock the nation. The kidnapper in the Lindbergh case used a ladder to gain access to an occupied home, kidnapped a small child, left a ransom note in the child's nursery demanding "50,000$, $25,000$ in $20 bills 15,000$ in 10$ and 10,000$ in 5$." On March 12, 1932, the kidnapper increased his ransom demand by 20,000$.

1. The Cleveland Torso Killer may have killed a man in October, 1936, in Haverstraw, New York, along a railroad track. Coincidentally, Haverstraw is located within 60 miles of Hopewell, New Jersey, where the Charles Lindbergh mansion was located and the Lindbergh kidnapping took place.
2. The Reading Railroad tracks pass by Hopewell, New Jersey, not far from where the New York Central Railroad line ends in New York.
3. A ladder was used in the Lindbergh case to gain access to an occupied house.
4. A ladder may have been used in the Degnan case to gain access to an occupied house.
5. The ransom note in the Lindbergh case read in part, "Have 50,000$ Redy . . ."
6. The ransom note in the Degnan kidnapping read "Get $20,000 Reddy . . ." (The word "reddy" has been written "ready" in the book *William Heirens: His Day In Court.* Arthur C. Becker, noted musician scholar indicated in 1946, that the spelling was "Reddy." I am not exactly sure how the killer spelled this word.)
7. The Lindbergh ransom note demanded in part 5$ bills and 10$ bills.
8. The Degnan ransom note demanded bills in 5's & 10's.
9. In the Lindbergh kidnapping case a small child was kidnapped and killed. The murder shocked the nation.

10. The ransom note in the Lindbergh case also read: "We warn you for making anyding (sic) public or for notify the polise the child is in gute care."
11. A note written in the Black Dahlia case read, "We're going to Mexico City-catch us if you can. (signed) 2k's" (See chapter 3).
12. In the Lindbergh case the ransom note was found on the window sill of the nursery.
13. In the Degnan kidnapping case the detectives speculated that the wind blew the ransom note onto the floor from her bed. The ransom note was found in her bedroom.

The events in the life of William Heirens can be found in Dolores Kennedy's book *William Heirens: His Day In Court.* I would recommend her book as a background to the following summary of the Heirens' confession and for a review of the disputed trace evidence used against William Heirens. The entire text of Mr. Heirens' confession can be found at the end of this book. I would like to summarize the text of Mr. Heirens' confession and then show that what he confessed to doing was nearly physically impossible. In the "confession" he admitted:

1. Murdering and kidnapping Suzanne Degnan early Monday morning January 7, 1946
2. Cutting up her body and depositing it in different storm sewers in the neighborhood
3. Cutting her up with his knife
4. Depositing the knife on elevated train tracks
5. Walking North and boarding the Jackson Park Express at Grandville "L" Station after the murder and dismemberment
6. Arriving at school (University of Chicago located at 57th and Ellis) at 6:00 a.m.

7. Not going to bed and staying up and studying
8. Having previously been in the vicinity of the murder scene in an apartment of a man named Gold located just to the north of the Degnan home
9. Not having observed the Degnan home while at the Gold apartment
10. First observing the Degnan home at 2:45 a.m. on the morning of January 7, 1946, never having observed the house before
11. Finding a ladder but not yet knowing where he was going to "burglarize"
12. Feeling "dizzy"
13. Entering the Degnan home through a window
14. Having a flashlight with him
15. Shining the flashlight in the direction of the person in bed
16. Strangling the person in bed
17. Carrying the 78 pounds of dead weight down the ladder, and out with no idea where he was taking this dead person (Suzanne's weight was reported as 78 pounds in the Coroner's Report)
18. Proceeding to the alley and turning north, and from there not knowing what happened
19. Taking the child to a basement of an apartment building on Winthrop Avenue
20. In the basement of the apartment house, writing the ransom note after discarding all of the body parts down separate neighborhood sewers
21. Not remembering cutting up the body
22. Claiming that the knife he used was carried in his "regular coat pocket"
23. Washing the tubs after dismembering the body
24. Then washing the knife

25. Not remembering he got into the basement of the apartment where the body was cut up
26. Having no light in the basement apartment
27. Carrying the body 150 feet from the Degnan home
28. Not remembering cutting the head off
29. Not remembering cutting the torso, the body, the arms and legs off
30. Not remembering where the head, left leg, torso or buttocks and right leg were found
31. Noticing the open window at 2:45 a.m.
32. Coming down the alley a block and a half or two blocks from where the knife was thrown next to the "L" station and burning his coat
33. Remembering that the reason he burned the coat was that there was blood on a sleeve
34. Remembering that he had a gun on him and that it was a .32 caliber
35. Remembering that he had a wire in his coat pocket that he always carried with him
36. Remembering that after depositing the body parts he went back to the apartment where he had dismembered the body of Suzanne Degnan, washed the tubs and his knife, and wrote the ransom note
37. Going back to the Degnan home and leaving the ransom note in her bedroom (The police thought it was on the bed and it was blown by the wind. This would mean that Heirens must have reentered the bedroom to leave the ransom note on the bed. Could the ransom note have been left on the window sill and been blown onto the floor?
39. Taking the ladder away from the window and leaving it in the alley

40. Going south across the lawn at the Degnan house to Kenmore, north on Kenmore until he reached Glenlake and to the alley beside the elevated where he disposed of the knife and sheath

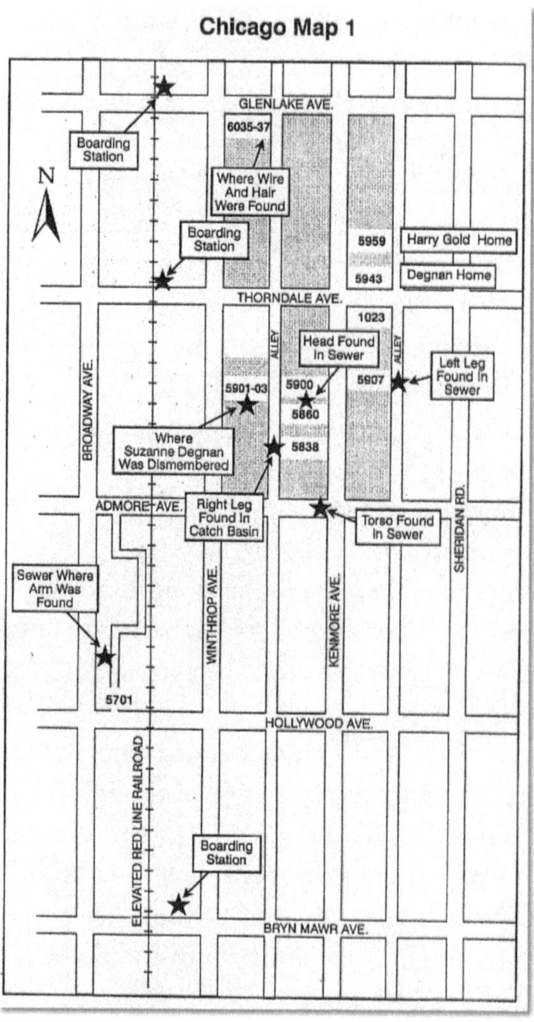

Map with the locations of Suzanne Degnan's murder, dismemberment and disposal of her body parts

According to the William Heirens' "confession," he was "dizzy." Later in his "confession" Heirens acknowledges that he had consumed six shots of alcohol earlier that evening. He entered the Degnan house, a house he had never seen before this night, at 2:45 a.m. When he carried Degnan's dead body out of the Degnan home, he had no idea where he was taking her. Miraculously, within a block of the Degnan home, he found an occupied apartment building with a basement that he could access without being noticed, that had tubs and running water in working condition that could be used when he dismembered Suzanne's body. Then, with the aid of a single flashlight and a knife he carried in his jacket pocket, he performed an anatomical feat by expertly dismembering a human body, cutting off a head, legs, arms and buttocks. During this entire process he only managed to get blood on the wrists of his jacket. Then he took separate body parts, in the middle of the night, to separate storm sewers in the neighborhood. He opened the extremely heavy, iron sewer covers with his bare hands and deposited the body parts, each time moving farther away from the place of dismemberment.

Photograph of heavy iron storm sewer cover where one of Suzanne Degnan's legs was found January 8, 1946

The arms were the last parts to be deposited in a sewer near Hollywood and Broadway Streets, near the elevated train. Close to this point is a boarding station. At this sewer the "confession" indicated that Heirens dropped a heavy sewer cover and injured a finger on his right hand. According to the "confession," Heirens then returned to the place where the body was dismembered, and with his injured finger on his right hand he washed the tubs, cleaned his knife, wrote a ransom note, put oil on the ransom note to obliterate any clues, and then returned to the Degnan home and left the ransom note in the bedroom because "he didn't want her parents to worry." Once he left the Degnan residence, he made his way back to a boarding station further west of where he had originally gotten off the train. To top this off he stopped on the way back to the University of Chicago, after performing what must have been one of the goriest dismemberments of a human body in Chicago's history, and had donuts and coffee. When he arrived at his dorm room, he began studying. According to Heirens' "confession," he went from a bumbling thief to bumbling kidnapper to a calculating murderer all in the same evening.

The body parts were located, after an anonymous telephone call tipped off the police, in separate sewers throughout the Kenmore/Thorndale neighborhood. The Heirens "confession" indicates that William Heirens used his fingers to open the sewer covers. In another part of his "confession" Heirens indicated that he used the butt of his pistol to pry open a sewer cover. Chicago street sewer covers are very heavy. They are intentionally constructed that way so that people cannot lift them off the sewer hole and create a hazard in the middle of a street. Lifting a heavy, cold, iron sewer cover without the necessary and proper tools, would be literally impossible for most people. It may be possible for an extremely strong person to lift a sewer cover, but if one is dropped or mishandled, someone in this populated neighborhood would probably have heard something.

Once the sewer covers are removed, the dirt and grime embedded near the rim of the sewer cover become separated. When the covers were replaced, there would have been obvious indications that someone had removed the covers. "Detectives Lee O'Rourke and Harry Benoit had noticed that the ground surrounding the sewer in the alley behind a building on Winthrop had been disturbed. They lifted the sewer cover, and peering into the blackness, saw a blond head on top of the sewer muck" (Note 17, p. 44). It may have taken both of the detectives to lift and replace the heavy sewer cover. I spoke with three members of the Sanitation Department for the City of Chicago, and they all indicated that it would be very difficult if not impossible for someone to physically lift the sewer covers without the aid of a proper tool. It is extremely difficult to see anything down one of these sewers, let alone some object submersed in sewer muck. A concerned citizen in the neighborhood might have noticed the disturbed ground near a sewer cover and, not wanting to get involved, for good reason, made an anonymous telephone call reporting that the girl might be found in the sewers. If he reported that "body parts" could be found in the sewers, or that the police should look in "sewers" instead of a "sewer," I would suspect that the caller knew a little more about the murder than an ordinary concerned citizen. It is interesting to note that the direction of the catch basin and sewers from the basement where the dismemberment took place appears to be from Winthrop to Admore to Hollywood, close to the elevated train track. Just down an alley, beyond the location of the storm sewer where the arms were found, is a boarding station for the Red Line at Bryn Mawr. The logical direction the killer took after the dismemberment is away from the basement apartment and away from the Degnan residence. That is not the route Heirens indicated he traveled.

The Heirens "confession" does not make much sense for a number of reasons:

- **a.** In order to successfully carry out this type of crime it would seem logical that the perpetrator would have had to preplan his movements and have access to secure locations in advance. It would also seem that the killer would have intended to kidnap, murder, possibly sexually assault her body after she was dead, dismember her body, and dispose of the body parts in separate sewers, long before the kidnapping took place.
- **b.** The kidnapper would have had to know where the room was that he could use to dismember the body before she was kidnapped.
- **c.** The kidnapper would have had to have the necessary expertise and tools to complete the dismemberment. It is a major undertaking to expertly dismember a human body. "It's a hell of a job to remove a human head anyway," according to an unidentified homicide detective present at the autopsy of Edward Andrassy in 1936. Had a dismemberment been performed with the sole aid of a "flashlight" and a knife that he "carried in his jacket pocket," there would have been blood located on more than the sleeves of his jacket. Blood would have been all over everything.
- **d.** The kidnapper would have had to known ahead of time where all of the sewers were located, and he would have had to have the necessary tools to remove the sewer lids in order to deposit the body parts.
- **e.** Suzanne Degnan was kidnapped from 5943 Kenmore Avenue. Five wisps of yellow hair matching Suzanne's were found on a rough stairway board at the rear of 6035-37 Winthrop Avenue near the same spot the wire and handkerchief were located. She was dismembered at 5901-03 Winthrop Avenue.
- **f.** The person was probably an organized killer who carefully planned every detail of his crime.

g. The killer must have had past experience in dissecting humans or animals.

h. By all accounts William Heirens was not an organized killer and he lacked the skills necessary to expertly dissect a human body.

The most logical explanation for the murder of Suzanne Degnan is as follows:

> The killer was an "organized killer." He had cased the area ahead of time. If he used the ladder, he knew where the ladder would be well before the early hours of January 7, 1946. He knew that a basement apartment was located nearby the Degnan residence. He knew ahead of time that the little girl would be in her room because he had seen her through the first floor window before this night. He knew ahead of time that he would have access to the basement apartment where the dismemberment took place. He knew ahead of time that the basement apartment contained tubs with running water and working drains that could be used to wash away the blood from a dismembered body. He would know prior to the dismemberment where the individual sewers were located in the dark, cold streets and alleys. He would have been a person who brought with him or had stored in the basement of the apartment the tools necessary to complete a dismemberment of a human body. He would have brought the necessary tools to open the extremely heavy iron storm sewer covers. He would have known that the blood would have to be drained from the corpse in the tubs before the body parts were transported to another location for disposal.
>
> Whoever kidnapped, killed and dismembered Suzanne had experience in this type of crime. The killer, or killers, com-

mitted this crime for the thrill of it and to create fear and attention on a national level. Whoever killed her succeeded just as the person or persons who committed the Cleveland Torso Murders had. The murder and dismemberment of this little girl went off like clockwork. Whoever committed this crime was very clever, very diabolical. He managed to kidnap a small child from an occupied residence, take her to an occupied apartment building and dismember her body in a laundry room that just happened to have frosted windows so no one could see in, discard the body parts in several different sewers and catch basins throughout the neighborhood, all without being detected. (There is some evidence that the killer may have taken her to a third apartment building where she was strangled with a wire wrapped with a handkerchief.) This was no ordinary killer. The person, or persons, who killed Suzanne had expert skills. The killer(s) were experts at dismembering a human body. "Dr. William D. McNally, toxicologist, reported to Coroner Brodie that a sharp knife had been used to dissect Suzanne and that the expertise could only have come from a butcher or a hunter accustomed to the dissection of animals." Coroner Brodie concurred, telling the press that: "It was a very clean job with absolutely no signs of hacking as would be evident if a dull tool was used. The bones were all intact, carefully wrenched from their sockets." Dr. Jerry Kearns, the coroner's expert, declared that "the killer had to be an expert in cutting meats because the body was separated at the joints. Not even the average doctor could be so skillful. It had to be a meat cutter." Chief Storms told reporters that the girl's murderer "was either a physician, a medical student, a very good butcher, an embalmer or perhaps a livestock handler" (Note 17, p. 49). Dr. Kearns reported that the killer was "a person with a knowledge of

> anatomy, either a man whose profession required the study of anatomy or one with a background in dissection."
>
> How in the world seventeen-year-old William Heirens, with no known expertise in any of these fields, could manage, on his first attempt, to skillfully dismember a small child with this amount of precision using a knife he carried in his jacket pocket and with the aid of a flashlight is beyond me. In my opinion, the possibility of William Heirens completing this crime, according to the statements contained in his "confession," and based on the actual facts in this case, on a scale of 1 to 100, is about a 2, and that is being generous. The coroner reported that the death of Suzanne occurred between 12:30 a.m. and 1:00 a.m. The Heirens "confession" reflects that the murder was committed after 2:45 a.m., another "minor" inconsistency.

Consider this: If the body parts were never discovered the killer's grandiose scheme would not be complete. An anonymous tip to authorities suggested that they search the storm sewers. Low and behold, there they find the body parts. Now, you not only have a small, innocent six-year-old-girl kidnapped and butchered, but also her killer dumping her body parts in a sewer. What else in this tragedy could possibly summons more fear, anger and notoriety in the general public? The killer (possibly killers) accomplished exactly what he had set out to accomplish. In addition, he received the satisfaction that the police arrested and the courts sentenced someone else for these crimes.

Ask yourself these questions:

1. Why didn't the killer strangle the victim in her bedroom and leave her there?
2. Why didn't the killer dispose of her body in any number of waste receptacles that were located in the nearby back alleys?

3. Some evidence suggested that the kidnapper did not strangle Suzanne in her bedroom, but, instead, carried her to an apartment house at 6035-37 Winthrop Avenue, where he strangled her with a handkerchief and a wire. If this was the case, then why did the killer have to enter an occupied building at 6035-37 Winthrop to kill Suzanne Degnan? Why didn't he kill her outside the building? Why risk being caught entering an occupied building with a six-year-old girl in the early hours of the morning?
4. If she was strangled to death at 6035-37 Winthrop, why didn't her killer leave her body there and flee the murder scene?
5. After dismembering the body, why didn't her killer hide the body in the basement laundry room or in the coal room?
6. Why didn't the killer dispose of all of the body parts in one sewer? There certainly was enough room, and it had to be very difficult to locate and open four separate sewer covers on that dark, cold evening.

I think that whoever killed Suzanne intended to kidnap, kill, sexually assault, dismember and dispose of her body parts in the sewers long before he exited the Red Line at the Thorndale Station and arrived at the Degnan residence at 5943 North Kenmore Avenue.

Recall the death of Frances Brown. Her killer left a large knife stuck in her throat. By doing this, whoever killed her was sending a message, but no one paid attention. In my estimation there is a very high probability that in the mid-1940's, the Mad Butcher of Kingsbury Run was visiting Chicago, the former home of his old nemesis, Elliot Ness. There certainly seems to be a substantial number of similarities.

Famous mystery writer/researcher Craig Rice pored over the records, interviewed the principals (including State's Attorney Touhy and Heirens himself), and then to the chagrin of the newspaper that hired Rice responded: "Let's think about Billy Heirens. I've seen him. I've talked to him (and) I believe him innocent" (Note 13).

Coroner's Time of Death:

On the bases on undigested food found in Suzanne Degnan's stomach, the experts at the coroner's office fixed the time of death at 12:30 or 1:00 a.m. Monday January 7, 1946 (Note 10). A report to Coroner Brodie by Dr. William D. McNally, Toxicologist, disclosed that the killer had attempted to rape the child. Coroner Brodie indicated, "It appears that a hatchet, ax or *meat cleaver* was used to decapitate the girl" (Emphasis added) (Note 8).

Witness Statements:

12:50 a.m. Miss Ethel Hargrove, a maid in the Flynn apartment, came home from visiting friends. Shortly after she got to bed, she said, she heard the dogs barking and loud voices, men's voices, downstairs (Note 13).

1:00 a.m. "George Subgrunski, a serviceman enjoying furlough on January 6, 1946, had gone to the police shortly after the Degnan murder to report that he had seen a man walking toward the Degnan home at about 1:00 a.m. on the night of the crime, carrying a shopping bag. Subgrunski said he had taken his girlfriend to her apartment at Glenlake and Kenmore Avenues, and had returned to his car when he saw the man walking west on Glenlake Avenue. The man turned south onto Kenmore Avenue, then crossed the street towards the Degnan home. Subgrunski described the man 'as about five feet nine inches tall, weighing 170 pounds, about thirty-five-years-old, and dressed in a light-colored fedora and a dark overcoat with the belt drawn tight'" (Note 17, p. 95-96). Subgrunski's report may have been dismissed by some because of its inconsistency.

1:30 a.m. Cab driver Robert Reisner saw a man and a woman parked in an automobile in Thorndale Avenue just east of the alley behind the Degnans' home. Albert Johnson reported seeing a woman carry a bundle in both arms and that the man opened the door for her. "This woman is described as about 130 pounds, five feet six inches tall, wearing a gray coat with a dark fur collar and a small hat. A man was observed in the front seat of this car. He was bareheaded and had gray hair" (Chief Walter G. Storms).

1:45 a.m. Another witness reported that the dogs in the Flynn apartment above the Degnans' home were barking.

2:30 a.m. A Miss Crawford of 5900 Kenmore Avenue reported that at about 2:30 a.m. that morning she was sitting in a car with a friend on the west side of Kenmore Avenue, just south of Thorndale, when she noticed a gray-colored sedan containing a man and a woman driving up and down the street several times (Note 17, p. 47).

3:00 a.m. "A second witness, Mrs. Marian Klein of 6033 Winthrop Avenue, also saw a stranger in the areaway which separates the building in which she lives from the building at 6035-37 Winthrop. Yesterday Mrs. Klein was questioned by Capt. John L. Sullivan of Summerdale Station. She said that she and a friend, Jake DeRosa, of 742 North Springfield Avenue, were sitting at a window of her apartment about 3 a.m. January 7, when she saw a strange man fumbling at the areaway gate. He seemed in a hurry; he may have been carrying something, she added. Mrs. Klein described him as 35-40, stocky, and wearing a gray hat and tan coat. Detective Storm said the man tried to get into the laundry room but was frightened away." Heirens was 17 years old (Note 10).

3:40 a.m. Mrs. Frieda Meyer, who lived in the first-floor apartment just above the basement laundry room in which the little girl's body was dismembered, said she heard footsteps in the areaway beneath her window. "The man, she said, walked to the laundry room from the alley, and remained there no longer than 10 to 15 minutes. She then said he returned to the alley, stayed there about 10-15 minutes, and returned to the basement. He stayed in the basement only a minute or two, she said, and returned again to the alley, where he stayed for 10 to 15 minutes. He made a third trip to the basement and stayed only a moment. Mrs. Meyer said she heard footsteps of only one person. She said she did not hear the noise of an automobile stopping or starting, although her bedroom window was open about six inches and overlooks the areaway to the alley."

5:20 p.m. January 7, 1946, police found the child's head in a catch basin 16 hours after the kidnapping.

Suzanne's torso was discovered wrapped in a 50-pound *sugar bag* (Note 4). One of the clues in the Cleveland Torso murders was a sugar sack.

The *Cleveland Press* reported on August 17, 1938, "A ragged blue coat, a patchwork quilt, a cracker box, a frozen fish container, and a *sugar sack* apparently stained with blood—These were the clues on which the detectives based their hopes of sifting out the identity of the Cleveland Torso Killer, following the finding today of additional bones of his 12th victim near the scene of yesterday's recovery of the 13th victim."

Pathological Report—Suzanne Degnan

An autopsy was performed on Suzanne Degnan on January 8, 1946. "The head was removed at the level of the 4th cervical vertebra. The trunk was divided at the level of the umbilicus anteriorly and the 2nd lumbar vertebra posteriorly. The left lower extremity has been removed at the level of the hip joint in a direction slightly oblique to the transverse direction medically at the level of the perineum from left to right; the joint cavity contains some black powder and granular material. The upper extremities have been removed at the level of the shoulder joints in a vertical direction; and are absent. The skin and subcutaneous tissues and muscles at the site of the amputation show no tissue retraction." The coroner's opinion as the cause of death was: asphyxiation by strangulation.

Following the murder of Suzanne Degnan, Chicago Chief of Detectives Walter G. Storms received a letter that could have been sent by her killer. It is interesting to note that in the Cleveland Torso Murder case a letter was addressed to Cleveland Chief of Police

Matowitz, dated December 23, 1938, from someone who could have been the Mad Butcher of Kingsbury Run. In the case of the Black Dahlia a pasted note, possibly from her killer, was addressed to Los Angeles Police Captain Donahoe (See chapter 3, page 120, #23). In all three cases, following a murder in which the victim was dismembered, someone, possibly the murderer, wrote a letter to the chief investigator in the city where the murders took place. Could the same person have written all three letters?

Similarities Between the Cleveland Torso Murders and the Murder of Suzanne Degnan (and other possibly related Chicago killings)

Cleveland Torso Murders	Suzanne Degnan and Eunice Rawlings Murders
1. The killer carried body parts in a burlap produce bag.	**1.** Witnesses saw a woman (or someone dressed as a woman) in the vicinity of the Degnan home carrying a large bundle in both arms at approximately the time when she was murdered. Another witness saw a large, dark man carrying a shopping bag near the Degnan home when she was murdered. Earlier a woman wearing a man's overcoat and a shawl over her head was reported by housewives near the Degnan home to have chased children on the streets. She offered them candy and, one mother said, she scratched her little boy's face with her long bright red fingernails (Note 3).

2. The Cleveland Torso Killer murdered and dismembered several individuals possibly as early as 1935, definitely from 1935-1938, and possibly again from 1938-1942.	**2.** Suzanne Degnan was murdered and dismembered in Chicago in 1946. The Cleveland Torso Killer may very well have been alive and actively pursuing his trade in Chicago at this time.
3. The Torso Killer may have placed dismembered body parts of victims in Cleveland sewers. On September 10, 1936, Victim No. 6 was found. The lower portion of the trunk, its legs amputated at the hips, was discovered nearby. Both halves had apparently emerged from a sewer near the bridge (Note 19, p. 76-77).	**3.** Suzanne Degnan's killer discarded her body parts in Chicago storm sewers.
4. The Torso Killer killed in Cleveland from 1934-1938, where Elliot Ness was Director of Public Safety. The killer taunted Ness.	**4.** Suzanne Degnan was killed and dismembered in Chicago in 1946. Chicago was the former home of the Untouchable Elliot Ness.
5. The Torso Killer could, among other things, have been a "prosector butcher" (Note 18, p. 79).	**5.** The killer of Suzanne Degnan had "the skill of a butcher." In fact the police arrested a local butcher named George Carraboni, who they suspected might be the Cleveland Torso Killer, but eventually released him. In 1946, the Chicago detectives must have considered the possibility that the Mad Butcher of Kingsbury Run might have been responsible for the murder and dismemberment of Suzanne Degnan. Chicago police even referred to the killer as "the Mad Butcher of Kenmore Ave" (Note 11).

6. The Torso Killer applied oil to the body of a victim.	**6.** An oily substance was found on the Suzanne Degnan ransom note.
7. Detective Merylo considered the possibility that one or more persons acting together committed all of the Torso murders. If so, then the Torso Killer murdered victims in more than one state.	**7.** On the night of Suzanne Degnan's abduction a neighbor, Cecelia Flynn, thought she heard voices of the two men on the street. One of the men was heard to say, "This is the best-looking building around."
8. The Torso Killer murdered victims in one location and transported them to another site, where they were dismembered. Some of the victims were then discarded in a third location.	**8.** Suzanne Degnan was kidnapped from one location and moved to another location, where she was dismembered. She was then discarded in a third location.
9. The description of Victim No. 3, Flo Polillo, included the following: "Cinders of coal dust were embedded in the skin, and the lower portion of the torso bore the indentations of lump coal (Note 2, p. 51).	**9.** There were four laundry tubs in the basement of the building on Winthrop Avenue, just one block south of the Degnan home and in the drain of one of them clung bits of human flesh and matted blond hair. **Further investigation located blood stains in the coal bin underneath a new shipment of coal. They had found the place of the dismemberment** (Note 17, p. 45). The Degnan Pathological Report contains the following: "the joint cavity contains some black powder and granular material." The *Chicago Daily Tribune* reported on January 20, 1946: "An examination of the windpipe showed no coal dust, indicating that Suzanne was dead when her body was taken to the basement at 5901 Winthrop Avenue."

10. The Torso Killer murdered Flo Polillo, dismembered her corpse in one location, wrapped pieces of her body in newspapers in January, 1936 (winter in Cleveland); deposited some of the body parts at one location (behind Hart Manufacturing Plant) and dumped the additional body parts in another location (in a vacant lot on Orange Avenue.) Referring to Victim No. 6, Lieutenant Harvey Weitzel stated, "It is my opinion that the missing parts were **not** thrown into the creek when the torso was thrown in" (Emphasis added) (Note 2, p. 82). When Victim No. 7 was found a few feet offshore in Lake Erie, they noted that "a couple of storm sewers emptied into the lake nearby but blockage from snow and ice prevented immediate search" (Note 4, p. 126). I believe Merylo thought that some of the body parts had been deposited by the Mad Butcher of Kingsbury Run into the city sewers and eventually drained into Lake Erie. A piece of Victim No 10's leg was found at an opening to a storm drain at the foot of Superior Avenue.	**10.** The killer of Suzanne Degnan dismembered her corpse in one location, wrapped pieces of her body with rags, placed the body parts in bags, and deposited the body parts in four separate sewers and a catch basin.

11. The Torso Killer murdered and dismembered several individuals near railroad tracks and Lake Erie in Cleveland. Then he killed an individual in West Cleveland.	**11.** Suzanne's killer committed the murder and dismemberment near railroad tracks and Lake Michigan. This murder took place after and west of the Ross and Brown murders. The pattern of murders is similar to the Cleveland Torso murders (from east to west along the lake).
12. Detectives in the Torso murders could not determine how the killer moved the heavy bodies without being detected. There was speculation that he used a pushcart. Chicken feathers found in one of the bags containing body parts became a clue.	**12.** Detectives located a metal cart in a boiler room at 5860 Kenmore with blood on it. The blood was later determined to be chicken blood.
13. "The killer was large and strong. The bodies of the first two victims—and probably that of the Tattooed Man as well—had been carried, not dragged, some distance by the murderer. It was obvious, Director Ness remarked, that the Torso Murderer was 'a big man with the strength of an ox.' Coroner Pearce agreed that all the knife wounds had been executed by an 'exceptionally strong individual.' Since at least three of the victims had been conscious or at least alive when they were beheaded, the suggestion that the killer overpowered his victims reinforced the belief that he was a physically powerful man."	**13.** Her killer may have carried the body from her bedroom, down a ladder, and 150 feet to the place where she was dismembered. The killer also managed to lift four extremely heavy iron storm sewer covers and replace them without being detected.

14. Parts of Flo Polillo's body were found in a burlap bags, bloodstained with chicken feathers adhering to them (Note 2, p. 51). Pieces of victim No. 10 were found in a burlap sack pulled out of the Cuyahoga River May 2, 1938 (Note 2, p. 131). August 16, 1938, the bodies and heads of two victims of the Torso Killer were found in a Cleveland dumpsite at East 9th and Lake Shore. **A piece of striped pillowcase was found with the bodies. A bloodstained sugar sack was discovered nearby** (Note 19, p. 140).	**14.** Her right leg was found in a manhole inside a paper shopping bag. **Her torso was discovered wrapped in a 50-pound sugar bag. Also found was a white striped pillow cloth** (Note 5).
15. The torso of the Lady of the Lakes was found on a Lake Erie beach at the foot of 156th Street.	**15.** "The disappearance of a North-side girl (18-year-old Eunice Rawlings) last January 14 was investigated today in connection with the headless, armless body on the beach near Scott" (Note 4). It is interesting to note that Eunice Rawlings lived in an apartment close to where Josephine Ross and Frances Brown lived. Her death was ruled a suicide.
16. The head of Victim No. 4, the "Tattooed Man," was found wrapped in his pants in Kingsbury Run **June 5, 1936** (Note 2, p. 60-61).	**16.** The killer of Josephine Ross stabbed her in her throat several times and then wrapped her head in a dress on **June 5, 1945.**

17. The upper torso of Victim No. 9 had been wrapped in three-week old newspapers and packed in a burlap bag. The bag also contained one of the most perplexing clues the police would deal with in the entire series—a cheap woman's silk stocking, in good condition save for a single runner which contained a lone black and white dog hair and several short blond human hairs (Note 19, p. 110 & Note 4, p. 118).	**17.** The head of Josephine Ross was found wrapped in a dress secured by a tightly bound silk stocking (Note 17, p. 35).
18. "Suddenly, Orley May's words from the previous February took on a prophetic, haunting echo: 'He (the Mad Butcher of Kingsbury Run) gives us one every five months."	**18.** On June 5, 1945, Josephine Ross was murdered in Chicago. Just over six months later, on December 10, 1945, Frances Brown was murdered in Chicago. Less than one month later on January 7, 1946, Suzanne Degnan was murdered.
19. When dismembering the body of Flo Polillo, the Mad Butcher of Kingsbury Run "cut the skin around the arms and legs and then '**wrenched them from the sockets**'" (Note 2, p. 57-58).	**19.** Coroner Brodie told the press, "it was a very clean job with absolutely no signs of hacking as would be evident if a dull tool was used. The bones were intact, **carefully wrenched from their sockets"** (Note 17, p. 49).

20. A letter dated December 23, 1938, possibly mailed by the Mad Butcher of Kingsbury Run, was received in Cleveland. The letter was addressed to Cleveland Chief of Police Matowitz. (Both killers may have mailed letters to the Chief of Police in the respective jurisdictions following a murder) William Heirens died March 5, 2012, at the University of Illinois Medical Center, Chicago, Ilinois. He was still a prisoner at the Dixon Correctional Center Minimum Security Prison in Dixon, Illinois at the time of his death.	**20.** Following the dismemberment of Suzanne Degnan in 1946, Los Angeles Chief of Police Storm received a communication, possibly sent by her killer.

The detectives in the Cleveland Torso murders were never able to determine where the killer dismembered the bodies and drained the blood from his victims. The coal dust and indentions of lump coal on the torso of Flo Polillo may indicate that she was placed in a basement furnace/laundry room where coal was stored, just like Suzanne Degnan years later. If this is in fact the case, then it would suggest that the Mad Butcher of Kingsbury Run may have paid a visit to the Windy City in the mid 1940s. Cleveland is not that far from Chicago. The New York Central runs from Cleveland to Chicago.

Chapter 3

GEORGETTE BAUERDORF, ELIZABETH SHORT (THE BLACK DAHLIA), JEANNE AXFORD FRENCH (THE RED LIPSTICK MURDER) AND OTHER LOS ANGELES VICTIMS

Georgette Bauerdorf

A young socialite by the name of Georgette Bauerdorf was found murdered, lying face down in the bathtub in her Los Angeles apartment October 12, 1944. Her killer had removed the lower portion of her pajamas. Dr. Frank R. Webb surmised that she had been strangled with a square of toweling that was thrust deep into her throat. She was then raped, as she lay dying or already dead. Detective A.L. Hutchinson said, "The automatic light over the outside entrance to her apartment had been unscrewed two turns so that the switch wouldn't turn on. Prints lifted off the light bulb . . . and whoever turned the globe must have stood on a chair or used some other physical assistance to reach the electrical outlet which was nearly eight feet from the floor." "Or someone fairly tall," said Sheriff's Captain Gordan Bowers (Note 27, p. 42).

It is interesting to note that in the William Heirens "confession" to the Suzanne Degnan murder, the following dialog took place between the interrogator, Mr. Crowley, and William Heirens: (See pages 415–416)

Mr. Crowley

Q: Did you do anything to that light?
A. No, then I went east, north, I went west then, and I turned that corner in sort of "Z" corner, I went in and looked for a window that was least lighted, I found it and I entered.
Q. Did you use a ladder?
A. Yes.
Q. Before you entered the room did you do anything to the electric light that was lighted outside?
A. No.
Q. Did you hit the bulb with your hand in order to break it?
A. No.
Q. You went into the room with the electric light on?
A. Yes.
Q. Was it pretty well lit up back there?
A. Yes.

I suspect, based on this line of questioning, that the outside yard light at the Degnan home may have been tampered with by her assailant on the night of the kidnapping just as the outdoor light bulb at Georgette Bauerdorf's apartment had been unscrewed prior to her murder. According to June Zeiger, a friend of Georgette, "Georgie dated a very tall soldier." He said he was a first lieutenant in the Air Force. According to Sgt. Gordon R. Aadland, Georgette seemed nervous and excited about a trip the next day to El Paso, Texas. She told him she was rushing home so she wouldn't miss a call from her boyfriend Jerry (private Jerome M. Brown, stationed at Fort Bliss), a soldier she had met six months before at the Hollywood Canteen (Note 32, p. 168). She planned to celebrate his military graduation in Texas and had purchased an airline ticket during the first week in October. "Detective Al Hutchinson responded to the dead body call at Georgette Bauerdorf's apartment. His personal view based on what 'floated' around included the idea of a possible suspect a soldier, about 6'4, who walked with a limp that the victim dated until she thought he was a bad egg. Georgette expressed that she was afraid of him." Sheriff's files identified the soldier as Jack A. Wilson "DOB 8/5/20 other 8/5/24". Hutchinson said, "The guy would've been tall enough to easily unscrew the bulb in the victim's foyer without a ladder or stool, which nobody found." She was murdered before she could use her ticket to Texas. Following her death, Georgette's car was stolen and then abandoned on East 25th Street near San Pedro. Agness Underwood, a top crime reporter for Hearst's *Herald-Express*, received a tip that a tall, thin man with a limp, dressed as a soldier, was seen near her abandoned vehicle.

It is interesting to note that in the December 10, 1945, murder of Frances Brown in Chicago, to which William Heirens pled guilty, her killer removed the bottom portion of her pajamas and draped her over a bathtub. It is also interesting to note that in the Suzanne Degnan case the weather the morning of the kidnapping was above freezing, the ground was moist and soft. Yet no dirt, no mud, no marks were found on the window sill or in the room. Nor was any mark left by the kidnap ladder against the window sill of the child's bedroom, if in fact a ladder was used by the kidnapper. However, Sgt. James Penny of the Sunnydale station said it was possible for the kidnapper to have avoided making mud tracks. A concrete walk extends from the street around the Degnan home to a point under Suzanne's bedroom. But generally the area was soil. (Note 21) Another explanation may have been that a very tall man gained access through her first floor window without the aid of a ladder, possibly the same tall man who killed Georgette Bauerdorf and the victims of the Cleveland Torso murders.

Elizabeth Short (The Black Dahlia)

Elizabeth Short was born July 29, 1924, in Hyde Park, Massachusetts. She lived with her mother, Phoebe Short, in Medford, Massachusetts, until age 16, when she moved to Miami. Eventually Elizabeth ended up in Los Angeles seeking fame and fortune. Her hair was black, and the clothing she wore was black. She, like thousands of other young pretty girls, may have migrated to Los Angeles with hopes of becoming a famous, rich movie star. Servicemen began calling her the "Black Dahlia" because a movie showing at the time was entitled the "Blue Dahlia," starring Alan Ladd and Veronica Lake.

Elizabeth Short (the Black Dahlia) in 1946, age 22, 5' 6", 118 lbs, green eyes, very attractive (photo courtesy of the Delmar Watson Archives, Hollywood, California)

Elizabeth left California in September, 1943, and did not return until April, 1946 (Note 32, p. 95).

It has been verified that Elizabeth traveled by train from Los Angeles to Chicago in 1945 (Note 27, p. 45–47). True crime writer John Gilmore wrote in *Severed* on page 173, "The Dahlia's path was traced back from Massachusetts to Chicago, to St. Louis and Indianapolis, and to Miami through Hollywood and the movie crowd, then to Long Beach again, and San Francisco, Texas, New Orleans, Santa Barbara, and back to Boston—an almost impenetrable, ever-eddying pool of mystery." In 1951, Detective Finnis Brown received a news tip about the Black Dahlia: "It came from Chicago, about a doctor in [Hammond] Indiana who'd examined the girl last spring before her murder." (That would have been in the spring of 1946, shortly after Suzanne Degnan was murdered in Chicago.) Records indicated a woman, who might have been Elizabeth Short, was referred by a Chicago doctor to an Indiana urologist in 1946. All medical records of women with gynecological problems were routinely checked by the Chicago authorities as possible abortions. The handwritten medical report listed the woman as B. Fickle from Lexington, Massachusetts, Age 21, Blood Type: AB. The notations by the Chicago doctor seem to have been:

AB/ND.CO;
F/21/W/AB
HERED.GEN.
Referred to David Stine URO

The name B. Fickle, as written by the doctor, could have been a hastily scrawled B. Fickling. Bette's age, 21, was the same as the patient's. Bette had the same uncommon blood type, AB. The note seemed to indicate that the patient had an inherited problem (HERED) that was either genital (GEN.) or genetic" (Note 32, p. 109-110).

"By the spring of 1946, Bette had re-kindled her war-time romance with Lt. Gordon Flicking. She was on her way to meet Fickling in Long Beach, California, where he was to be mustered out of the service. En route, Bette would have to change trains in Chicago. Extending her layover in order to consult with a specialist was well within the realm of possibilities" (Note 31, p. 110). Detective Finnis Brown indicated that the Hammond, Indiana, doctor, "identified Short as the girl who had visited him at one time." Joseph Gordon Fickling was interviewed by detectives in North Carolina about a letter dated January 8, 1947, six days before Elizabeth Short was murdered in Los Angeles. "Fickling told Charlotte detectives he had received a final letter from Elizabeth dated January 8, 1947, in which she told him not to write to her anymore at her address in San Diego because her plan was to relocate to Chicago." It has been suggested that Elizabeth Short was also in Chicago in early 1946, posing as a newspaper reporter covering the death of Suzanne Degnan. (I do not have verification of this report, but it should be further investigated.) In 1947, a woman by the name of Dorothy French told the *Examiner*, "that Beth's trunk had been shipped from Chicago and held by Railway Express for nonpayment of storage charges. The *Examiner* tracked it to the warehouse in L.A. but called detective Donahoe at the same time to alert the police that they were not interfering or tampering with evidence" (Note 27, p. 137-138). The week after Christmas, 1946, Elizabeth Short wrote a letter to "Duffy" in Chicago (Note 27, p. 110).

Did Elizabeth Short come in contact with her killer on the Chicago to Los Angeles train, or could he have been stalking her as she traveled from California to Massachusetts? There isn't much doubt that the Mad Butcher of Kingsbury Run traveled by train. Is the fact that Elizabeth Short was in Chicago at times during 1945 and 1946 somehow connected to the murders of Josephine Ross, Frances Brown and the murder/dismemberment of Suzanne Degnan?

On January 15, 1947, Elizabeth Short was found murdered and bisected at the corner of 39th and Norton Avenue in Los Angeles. Her nude body had been mutilated and cut in half at the waist. Her arms were positioned above her head. Portions of her skin were missing from her torso. Her mouth had been cut, causing a grotesque smile on her face. There was an unsubstantiated report that her breasts had been burned with what appeared to be cigarettes. Both halves of her body had been drained of blood and washed clean. Grass had been forced into her vaginal cavity. There were rope marks on her ankles, wrist and neck. One of the investigating officers, Detective Lieutenant Jess Haskins, said, "Looks like strangulation, but seems that she was trussed up by ropes or maybe wire from some of the marks, maybe spread eagle or bound upside down the way you would hang a carcass—that nut's probably lining up another one right now." It was determined that she may have been forced to eat feces before being murdered. There were multiple criss-cross lacerations in the suprapubic area which extended through the skin to the soft tissues. At least three of the criss-cross marks in this area appeared to be in the shape of the letter "X." Detective Herman Willis indicated that, "the killer had cut out parts of some basic female organs." (There is some speculation that the organs were not developed and were not there to start with.)

Detective Lieutenant Haskins described the body as, "someone's idea of a dirty postcard that suddenly materialized into real life." It was determined by the authorities that the victim had been killed and mutilated in one location and afterwards transported to the corner of 39th and Norton Avenue.

Elizabeth Short's severed body found on January 15, 1947, near the corner of 39th and Norton Avenues in Los Angeles. Onlookers include Will Fowler (in straw hat), reporter for the *Los Angeles Examiner.* Mr. Fowler closed Elizabeth's eyes at the crime scene. He died at age 81 in 2004 (photo courtesy of the Delmar Watson Archives, Hollywood, California)

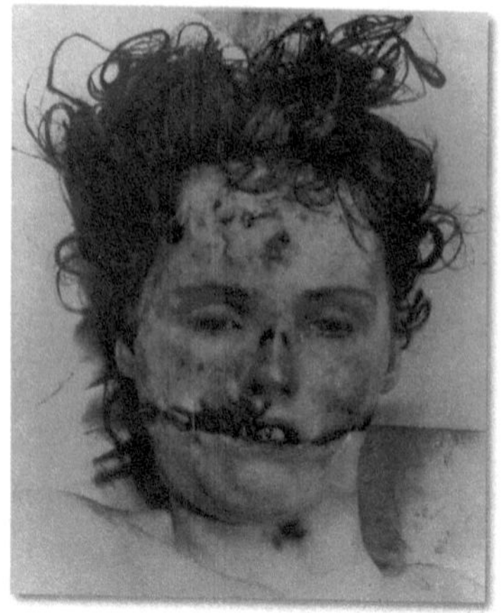

Elizabeth Short (the Black Dahlia) in the Los Angeles Morgue, January 15, 1947, after being tortured, murdered and bisected most likely by Jack Anderson Wilson (photo courtesy of the Delmar Watson Archives, Hollywood, California)

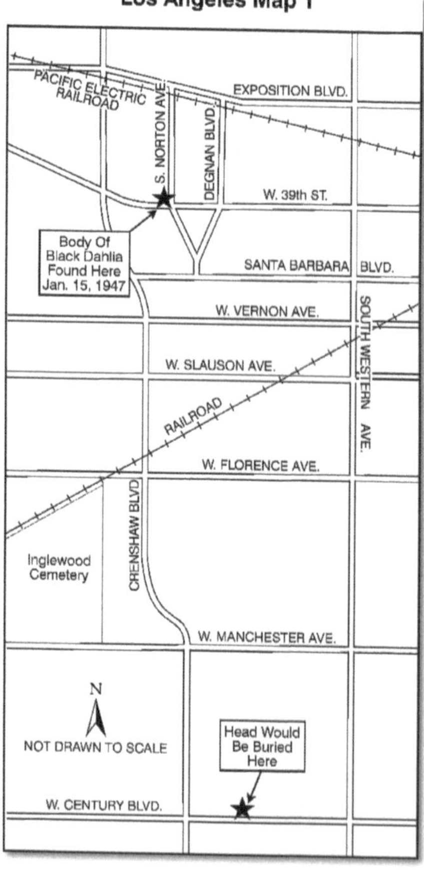

Los Angeles map showing the corner of 39th and Norton Avenues, where the severed body of Elizabeth Short was found January 15, 1947. Also, approximate location where the writer of the December 21, 1938, letter mailed from Los Angeles indicated a severed head would be found on Century Boulevard between Western and Crenshaw Boulevard

Following the murder of the Black Dahlia, her killer began writing and mailing postcards and notes to Los Angeles newspapers. On January 23, 1946, James Richardson, city editor of the *Los Angeles Examiner*, received a telephone call from a man who identified himself as the killer of the Black Dahlia. Richardson described the call in his autobiography, *For the Life of Me: Memoirs of a City Editor*. Richardson described the conversation as follows:

> The story dwindled to a few paragraphs and was about to fade out altogether when one day I answered the phone and the voice I'll never forget. "Is this the city editor?" it asked. "Yes." "What is your name, please?" "Richardson." "Well, Mr. Richardson, I must congratulate you on what the *Examiner* has done in the Black Dahlia case." "Thank you," I said, and there was a slight pause before the voice spoke again. "You seem to have run out of material," it said. "That's right." A soft laugh sounded in the earpiece. "Maybe I can be of some assistance," the voice said. There was something in the way he said it that sent a shiver up my spine. "We need it," I said and there was that soft laugh again. "I'll tell you what I'll do," the voice said. "I'll send you some of the things she had with her when she, shall we say, disappeared?" It was difficult for me to control my voice. I began scribbling on a sheet of paper the words: "Trace this call." "What kind of things?" I asked as I tossed the paper to my assistant on the desk. I could see him read and start jiggling the receiver arm on his phone to get the attention of the switchboard girl. "Oh say, her address book and her birth certificate and a few other things she had in her handbag." "When will I get them?" I asked, and I could hear my assistant telling Mae Northern the switchboard girl to trace my call. "Oh within the next day or so. See how far you can get with them. And

> now I must say goodbye. You may be trying to trace this call." "Wait a minute," I said but I heard the click and the phone was dead (Note 28, p. 163-164).

A package *wrapped in brown* paper and addressed "To the *Los Angeles Examiner* and Other Papers" was located in a mailbox at the Biltmore Hotel. Elizabeth Short's purse was in the package. The purse contained an address book, business cards, Elizabeth Short's birth certificate and Social Security card, several photographs of her with different servicemen, and claim checks or stubs for suitcases she'd checked at the Greyhound depot. According to Detective Herman Willis, "Everything had been soaked in gasoline to remove any trace of latent prints" (Note 27, p. 147-148). Detective Brown stated that the package was the killer's genuine work because, "It was the same kind of psychopathic cleanliness he'd used in handling the corpse."

Another note received by a Los Angeles newspaper read, "A certain girl is going to get the same as E.S. got if she squeals on us. We're going to Mexico City catch us if you can. (signed) 2 k's." This note indicates that two individuals may have been involved, one way or another, in the death of Elizabeth Short.

Elizabeth Short did become famous as a result of the terrible death she suffered at the hands of a mad butcher. If the person who killed Elizabeth Short was also responsible for the Cleveland Torso Murders and if Elizabeth Short was in Chicago at different times during 1945-1946, when Josephine Ross, Frances Brown and Suzanne Degnan were murdered, then there is a possibility that the same person who killed Elizabeth Short may be responsible for all of the murders of Ross, Brown and Degnan in Chicago. The clues and evidence seem to indicate that the same person might have committed the murders in Cleveland, Chicago and Los Angeles.

Cleveland Detective Peter Merylo, "suggested that the Black Dahlia murder and some other similar Los Angeles homicides that followed might have been the work of the Torso murderer. His theory was not taken seriously by the California authorities or by anyone else" (Note 31, p. 190). Had his theory been vigorously pursued by the Los Angeles detectives at that time, the case against William Heirens might have had a completely different outcome.

Hundreds of investigators tried to solve the Black Dahlia murder. Included among them was Los Angeles Detective John St. John, a/k/a "Jigsaw John." It is interesting to note that Detective St. John's assessment of the December 23, 1938, letter mentioned in Chapter 1 is as follows: "There was no connection," St. John said. "That had been checked out thoroughly. The Cleveland killer had a particular signature. All the Cleveland victims were killed quickly and decapitated. Those were two elements which never deviated"(Note 32, p. 133). St. John explained: "Signature is different from MO," he said. "Signature is the extra things a predator does, the obsessive things he needs to do that aren't necessary if his objective is to kill someone. Killing quickly was the Cleveland killer's MO; the decapitation was his signature. Torture and posing the body was not involved, like in the Elizabeth Short murder" (Note 32, p. 133). In her book *Childhood Shadows: The Hidden Story of the Black Dahlia Murder,* author Mary Pacios wrote about her interview with Detective St. John: "St. John said the murder of Elizabeth Short was unique. 'There was never one like it before, and there hasn't been one like it since. The perpetrator combined a number of elements that have never been seen together—a unique signature.' St. John was adamant. He believed the killer struck only once. St. John said that Finnis Brown and Harry Hansen were the only two people who watched the autopsy being performed—no reporters or other policemen were present. St. John hedged when I asked him if the killer had any medical training or had used medical equipment. 'I can't go into that,' he said and then laughed. 'Our job is to get information, not give it . . . The perpetrator may have had some knowledge of anatomy, but he wasn't necessarily in the medical profession'" (Note 32, p. 132-133). John St. John was in my opinion an excellent detective, but he made a mistake here, the same mistake detectives continue to make when searching for highly intelligent serial killers: they fail to accept the fact that the killers intentionally change locations to cross jurisdictional lines and alter their methods of killing, intending to throw their pursuers off course.

Several years after the murder of Elizabeth Short the Los Angeles Police Department received a tip that a certain individual had information regarding her murder. The individual was being paid by an informant to supply information to the police department about someone who might have had information about the murder of the Black Dahlia. The whole affair was orchestrated so that the entire conversation amounted to hearsay and was not admissible against anyone named. The individual brought a tape recording and other information to Los Angeles Detective Marvin Enquist. "Enquist, in turn, called upon St. John and his partner, Kirk Mellecker to hear the informant repeat his story." The informant related facts on tape to Detective Enquist, including how the body was severed, that the body had been severed on 31st Street near San Pedro and that the person, "who had told the informant these facts was using the name Arnold Smith." The informant described Smith as, "very tall, over 6', very thin, with one leg shorter than the other. Smith blamed the murder and bisection of the Black Dahlia on a female impersonator he called "Al Morrison." St. John determined that there was no Al Morrison and that Al Morrison was a made-up person who was in reality a 6'4" sodomist by the name of Arnold Smith (Jack Anderson Wilson). "What Smith is doing," St. John said," is airing what he possibly knows of the murder first hand, while putting the words in someone else's mouth, an as-told-to story, if you get my drift" (Note 29, p. 95).

According to the information given, the informant had met "Smith" quite a few years earlier at an apartment in the Silver Lake area occupied by a man named "Eddie" and a girl. According to the informant, "Smith said that wasn't where the cops had been looking, Eddie told us that Smith had known the Black Dahlia and he'd seen a photograph of them together . . . I asked him about it, but mostly Smith talked to me about some other guy, a female impersonator from Indianapolis" (Note 27, p. 180-181).

"Eddie" was a fence for burglarized electronics. He was suspected by the F.B.I. of being involved in an earlier kidnapping" (Note 27, p. 227).

"Of the time the informant met with Smith, he said the man never referred to Elizabeth Short by name, He did not call her Elizabeth, or the Short girl, or Beth. He would say 'her, who we're talking about,' if I didn't follow what he was saying and asked me what I meant" (Note 27, p. 181).

Keep in mind the Cleveland Torso victim No. 2, Edward Andrassy, had a friend by the name of "Eddie" (Note 30, p. 60). Author John Bartlow Martin wrote on pages 59-60 in his article about the Torso Murders in the book *Butcher's Dozen*:

> Now, the murderer had emasculated the bodies of both Andrassy and the unidentified man (the genitalia were found near the bodies). The police believed this indicated that the murderer was a sexual pervert and they wondered if Andrassy was one himself. The evidence was contradictory. During the summer Andrassy visited a nightclub several times, each time with a different woman, including a Chinese. On the other hand, a woman recalled that her son said Andrassy had picked up another boy in a park and had taken him to a speakeasy. A married couple told the queerest story of all. The man, who had known Andrassy most of his life, said that early in the

summer Andrassy had remarked "how bad" the man's wife looked. "She had female trouble," the police reported, and then Andrassy spoke up and told them that he was a "female" doctor and that he would like to examine her. In doing so Andrassy committed sodomy upon her (it isn't clear whether her husband did not protest because he didn't understand or because Andrassy was bigger than he). "He then told Mr. and Mrs.____ that if he would go home and get his instruments he could fix her within a month, so that she could have children." But they "told Andrassy not to bother." Searching Andrassy's room later, detectives reported finding "two doctor books and five physical magazines." A while later the couple moved, and one night the man found Andrassy and a stranger standing in the dark outside the door of his new home. Andrassy said they were considering sleeping in the adjoining apartment, which was empty. Andrassy introduced his friend as "Eddie," a chauffer for a wealthy woman in suburban Lakewood whom Andrassy "was doctoring . . . for the same trouble," The host invited them in for coffee, but "Eddie" seemed very nervous and they left in a large new touring car, a Lincoln or a Buick. "Eddie" was described as "28-30, 5-6, 150 good looking very good set of teeth, appeared to have had a broken nose and wore a dark trousers blue shirt, checkered gray cap, and dark brown hair." The detectives never could find "Eddie." The couple said he was not the unidentified man found dead a month later with Andrassy. But oddly, they said a cap found near the bodies was his.

A person by the name of Eddie was also described in the Cleveland Torso murder of Flo Polillo: "About six weeks after the death of Edward Andrassy, Flo Polillo returned to her hotel, this time with 'an unknown Italian,' described as twenty-seven-years old, five feet eight or nine, 135 pounds, dark complexioned, wearing a dark suit and dark cap, a description that nearly matched the description of Andrassy's friend, 'Eddie'" (Note 30, p. 65).

A transcript at the Los Angeles County Sheriff's files includes the following statement from Arnold Smith (Jack Anderson Wilson): Smith is talking about his fictitious character "Al Morrison." The transcript was developed from the tape recordings of Smith provided by the informant to Los Angeles Sheriff's Detective Marvin Enquist:

> She'd told Morrison she slept on the couch downstairs in Hassau's after he spotted her walking to the corner of Hollywood across the street from the Roosevelt Hotel. So he says, "Hey, what the hell are you doing?" She got in the car and sat with him for awhile, and then she got out and was walking away from the car.
>
> She gets sad and gets back into the car, and he heads south on La Brea. She wanted to know where he was going and he headed down to Washington and then east as far as Flower. Then he drove down that way, going south from there to San Pedro Street. They drove further south, to another hotel near 29th Street, also called the Roosevelt Hotel, but not connected to Hollywood's Roosevelt Hotel.
>
> He got the key there, that guy that knew the blond—this is the one that shacks up with the Chinaman, and she had the key. Then he drove her to the Chinaman's house on 31st, but he couldn't get into the place.
>
> There was something wrong with the key, as I remember the situation, as it had been described to me. Morrison had to drive to a small factory on the corner, around on 33rd Street and Trinity, to straighten out the problem with the key. She was complaining about having to get back because of Henry's wife. Later on, I asked him, "You think she was

trying to get back to see me?" He turned red when I said that. You see, the first thing is you couldn't fuck her at all. He said he'd screwed her and I said he was a liar. See, she made my dick hard every time I looked at her mouth. But I swear to God, I never put it in her, and I knew he was a lying sonofabitch.

There was a red bottle, had a glass stopper you use for putting fancy perfume in. And he could've taken her eyes out with that. But you understand, that's what he said. Because his mind has gone. You know, half those hoods had their mind eaten away because of syphilis. I know his mind has gone to have done what he did to her, and knowing he did it all along, but knowing it was just that he had to do it, you see what I am saying, so there was an excuse in part of this.

I remember being told something about pulling the car into the dirt driveway and to the back by the incinerator. The car was parked there so that it was close to the building. There was just so much room, so you get out and go around front to the building, since the back door's locked.

This is the Chinaman's house in the 200 block on East 31st Street by San Pedro Street and Trinity . . . . This is an older two-story brown wood-framed building that rented rooms and units.

You go up to the place by these steps right in front that're wood and you go in the hall. Right there is the stairs going up. So what we're talking about, he goes up behind her to the second floor. This place smells so bad like it's been closed up for a long time. Right away he opened the beer and sat on the couch, but he didn't pull that goddamn drape back. That's the problem, there, because she says she can't breathe because it is so dusty, but he doesn't say anything—he is just waiting there.

He has to tell her to be quiet, again. But she says she has to make a call and when she starts to use the phone there he says, "You can't." He put it back down. She said something like she is a prisoner and he says, "That's right. You're a prisoner." She says she is going to make a call from the market . . . She means the market where they just were. She gets her handbag up, and he says, "No, you're not going." But she was starting out, just starts out of the room. He came out of the hall up there and goes to the head of the stairs where she is standing, and he says, "You better come back inside of here. You better not go outside now."

She didn't say anything and he said okay. And he went to her and grabbed her arm like this, and started to pull her back and she hauled off and let him have it with the purse. Just swing it out and caught him across the side of the face. He slugged her once and her knees got weak. He pulls her back into the room, and he leans her against the door while he locks the door with the key. She just stayed there as though she was unsure exactly what would follow or admit it. He said he then grabbed her and pushed her and she fell down like it was against or on the couch. Then off that and is on the floor with her dress on her body. He said he stood over her and said something about he was going to screw her ass.

She started to yell so he bent down and slugged her again. He said he put his hand on her neck and holds her head still for a couple of times. She didn't move. Now he didn't know what he was going to do, except he went out of the room, through the door he had locked and went downstairs to the rear of the first floor to the kitchen . . . . He knew what was going to happen.

When he got outside he heard the funniest sounds he'd

heard. He couldn't tell whether it was the people making noises inside the joint or whether hearing people over the fences in those crummy houses. He wasn't sure. He could almost hear voices like they were talking, you understand? Anyway, he checked the gas in the car and checked under the seat in the car. He had to get north. He went back upstairs and through the back door, through the back part, there was this concrete. They were cementing a walk for the back part there, and he had to step over it or sink his shoe in the dirt, the mud there. He remembered a hose that was going. It was leaking and the water was running down the back, just leaking and going back by the incinerator.

It was on his mind all the time. Everything that was going to happen. He said he didn't have to think about anything, because it was laid out in front of him.

He got a small knife or he got the knife on the back of the porch, like a paring knife, and on the back of the porch was a rope, this clothesline hunk of a rope. This is what he had in mind for the waitress. Then he said there was a larger knife, like a long butcher knife that was two inches, the width of the blade near the handle. He said he thought that such a knife could be used to dismember the body. He said he didn't know what he was going to do with the knife, except to scare her or keep her back up in the room. He went upstairs but she hadn't gotten up off the floor, but up on an elbow or an arm and was looking around.

She was on the edge of the couch, I think maybe he had her arm—up here at this part of the arm—and had brought her to the couch, but this wasn't a couch like you think; it was a studio bed on a metal frame, only it was littler than a regular bed you'd consider for that, and he said, "You had enough trouble?" She said she had so he opened this bottle . . . .

This is what he said, oh, and had this opened from the sink place downstairs, the washtub just before you went to the back door. She kept saying, "What are you going to do?"

Drinking that, and she said her mouth hurt. She was scared of the knife and got up and was moving but he ran to her and hit her again, but it didn't put her out and didn't seem to stop her. So it was necessary at this point to indicate that he was going to hurt her with the knife.

He tore at the clothes, not tearing but cutting at the clothing. I don't know what . . . , I didn't know he said something and I can remember him scared or his face was white and his eyes didn't even look anywhere near like it was real eyes. Like they were glass and they were shining and he was cold but he was sweating and he turned the light away . . . . This light, like a desk light, and it was bright as this is. It was like when you see flashes of light when you get hit in the head. But he put a rag in her mouth. He used her underpants and he knocked her out a few times. She was all tied up to that couch and she'd been stripped of all the clothes and cut up bad.

I couldn't tell you how bad it was. I mean, this is the information I have that I know about. I knew it had to be some other Chinese. They'd cut her mouth across it and there was blood on the couch. He knew he'd stuck her with it and had to get rid of it.

She was naked, only he'd tied her hands and these were up over her head like this, and he stabbed her with a knife a lot, not deep, not enough that would kill you, but jabbing and sticking her a lot and slitting around one tit, and then he cut her face across it. Across the mouth. After that she was dead.

Her legs weren't tied at this particular point, but it was plain that they had been tied by the rope—this hunk that had been tied was cut, but it was still anchored at the frame, and there was the piece of it that was still there.

The knife was on the floor next to where the rope pieces were, a small knife, a paring knife that had been used to stick her with. I think it was seeing the rope down in the back, and the wire stuff, like a gauge heavier. I don't mean the wire part of the hanger but like you got on the other kind of hanger, that's the hook on the top part of it, going over the clothes pole, but it wasn't like that, it was soft and around the frame part. That's what stands out in one's mind.

There was the matter of getting rid of her, and what probably was the first thing was the incinerator out back. Burn the clothes and things and the knife. He got the knife idea from the situation that someone had put the rope around her neck, and held her down on the couch. Now these underpants or these ladies pants, they were all clotted with her blood, like a wad of some blood that was hard to see right off since the material was black, but blood does show on black, and there were these other particles of material that probably didn't belong to her and the problem that these had to be burned as well. So, it is easier to try to think what he told me about all this situation, though you look at a movie, you see what I am saying?

There is a larger knife that can be used, but he had to go back and outside and get these boards they were using for forms. Maybe there were three of these boards, or maybe there were four of them back upstairs, and went through the room she was in and into the bathroom which was off this one room, but there was a short hall. It's not a hall in that sort of sense except with—well, this window and you can see the roof of the car and the trunk of the car if you look out. And on the other side is the alcove, not a closet because there is no door, but it is arranged with a clothes pole going across, and some curtain material that is a bathtub shower curtain, there is one of these in front of where the clothes pole is across. But in the bathroom these boards are put across the tub, straight across it—set out that way. She was brought into the bathroom first, if I recall exactly what the information is. So, partly brought into the bathroom. I think dragged the rest of the way, and looking down at her, is the way I understand it. He had fooled around with her stomach, too, using the knife on her, the decorations in that manner. He had done a few other things to the body, figured she'd still been alive, and seeing how she could take it.

As much as possible, you understand, well . . . . There was a purpose to this in such a way though a person undergoes so much and it's possible that this person has to be, what you would call—anesthesia. It's a word in a crossword puzzle . . . .

There was this other muscle portion or the part of the jaw, during the time she was dying. But this had been taken care of, and she had to be laid across the tub, on top of the boards. Then he tied the arms and tied the hands to the faucet handles and the shower, the pipe. And then put a leg, the one that was nearest hanging over the side of the tub. Her leg was put on the tub, on the boards, the board that was arranged for that part of the leg, she was laying across one board just underneath the back part, and the other was underneath the hips here, under the ass—see, a rope around each leg and pulled them downwards, pulling them so that you then tied these ropes around the bottom of the can—the toilet bowl, but there is the pipe. There is not the wall section of the water storage, the tank. It is the vacuum housing part there and the water pipe, so he had her drawn and fixed down, because there wasn't a particular way of getting into the tub with that kind of knife. That particular knife.

The idea was first cutting off the legs at the top of her thighs but then this would have to be done twice, so the decision to separate, to cut this in half, that way to move the two parts easily, and get her there was the way to transport . . . .

Burning of the body in the incinerator was not the actual plan, but that the body could be separated for disposal purposes so there was this commencing with a different approach. The body was on the planks over the bathtub. Her middle was over the tub and the boards were width-wise so she was open, at the waist and back, and so the cut was across the middle, pulled tight like she was, as it could go clean through and have her body opened.

The knife was a larger knife. I would say it was approximately ten inches long, the length of the blade and there were two inches at the handle part, not the handle of it but just at the end of the blade. It went in further than figured with this knife and went all the way across and down through her body. The drain was into the tub below. But blood did not come out and onto the boards and some even jumped out of her, came out and upwards in such a way, but it was clean through, and then there was some trouble with going through her backbone of the bone's part there. The important thing is that the starting of it has to be finished. If one would intend to make the separation as to what we're talking about.

When the board was removed from underneath the rear part, that low section went down into the tub, but hanging on an angle, and drained in this manner. The same with the top half which hung down into the tub and there were marks that were made on the body's back, the upper part. Both sections of the body drained in this way, leaning, you could say laying down at an incline into the bathtub, but the bottom half, the hips and these parts of the leg was leaning against the slope of that part of the tub, but the upper part was straight down, not straight as the back of a chair, but straight more down than the lower section. She stayed in the tub and the boards were taken down and out back. The boards and stuff went into the incinerator.

The broom was where the mop was and the mop and the rags were used, and then these things went down and were put in the incinerator and lighted on fire.

The covers and the mattress padding—it wasn't a padding, but it was like thick as felt, like a heavy material. It was covered with shit. It was messed so bad, and these were bundled, put into a bundle. They were not put on top of her, but the water was in the tub. It had run before, the tub had been filled with the water. So it was put up around where the hands were, up around where the faucets were and this way not in the tub. The blood was thinned out by the water. It was on the chain, a stopper, down in the drain, but it was plugged-in first and then the water made the body rise, and it came up as the water filled the tub.

There was some worry about the rope areas, and these were then cut. He said he was sitting on the toilet and he cut the rope, the part that went around the base of the bowl and these then were taken off of the places of the body where they were tied around. It was in the water but was drained and it was filled again and the body was in the water at this time. The body tended to stay higher with the surface as it came up. There was movement in the bathtub with the body when the tub was filled with water. And whatever skin contact there was, this was removed when there was the draining. And it was removed by cleaning it off. There was this idea that she was not dead because her eyes were open and they had a look in them that she was not dead. This, I think, what it was, that he was scared and getting more scared and knowing that they had to be gotten rid of. I think it was that the water drained and ran in and around the open parts of the body . . . . It was not excitement or that sort of feeling, but because of the jaw that I said earlier, it made it so it was necessary to take care of the rest of it.

The skin contact had been taken care of, and then back downstairs was the oilskin tablecloth off the kitchen table. But this wasn't enough, so there were these curtains and shower curtain from the hall there by the pipe. She was wrapped over in the curtains, both parts in the two curtains, and what was it . . . . It was used to pull on the tablecloth or I think it was the shower curtain to take the sections downstairs. The bag was on the floor of the truck. This was the cement bag from the rear of the house.

She was put into the trunk of the car, and then drove until the place was reached that he could put the body—put her out of the car. The top section was carried by the arms held up and put down on the ground and the bottom section was on the bag and put down that way. The body was put down in the manner that the bottom was put down and moved this way. Moved by one leg this way, more away from the sidewalk, and then the top part was picked up again and put in order.

The cement sack was left where it was when he took hold of the ankle and put away from the sidewalk. The shower curtain and the tablecloth were in the trunk of the car. There was nothing of the clothes that was not cut, except the shoes and purse. The pocketbook was on the floorboard. It was put into a storm drain. All of this was put into a storm drain (Note 27, p. 185-193).

Los Angeles County Sheriff's Detective Joel Lesnick determined that Smith, as Grover Loving, Jr., first appeared in Los Angeles in the late 1930's, then did not reappear there until 1942, as Jack Anderson Wilson. The Cleveland Torso murders "officially" ended in 1938, at or about the same time Cleveland Chief of Police George Matowitz received the letter from someone purporting to be the Mad Butcher of Kingsbury Run. Additional Torso murders were reported in Pennsylvania from 1938-1942. Most of Wilson's early years were spent growing up in Ohio (Note 27, p. 199). Lesnick was able to obtain documentation that Wilson (a/k/a Smith) while incarcerated during the fall of 1958, in Oakland City Prison, California, told an inmate a story about a queer's head he'd seen in a glass box in Cleveland. He'd said this was at the time he saw Johnny Weissmuller as Tarzan. "It would seem to me to tie in," Lesnick says, "with Wilson saying Elliot Ness had been outsmarted by a Cleveland killer that was never caught" (Note 27, p. 199). Forensic Psychologist Paul Cassenelli pointed out what Wilson had said about Sally Rand, the striptease artist, that he had "jacked off" in his pants while watching her dance in Cleveland. Sally Rand was featured at the 1936 Great Lakes Expo held in Cleveland. Ester Williams appeared in the aquacade with Johnny Weissmuller, and the city of Cleveland had a police exhibit dealing with the Cleveland Butcher, which included a replica of one of the victim's heads contained in a glass box. Although Wilson talked about the decapitated head as that of a homosexual, and spoke derogatorily about homosexuals in general, his rap sheet showed arrests for crimes against nature—sodomy and he seemed to prefer the skid row homosexual bars and juke joints. (Recall the 1937 letter referred to in Chapter 1 sent to the Cleveland Police Department from someone in North Hollywood. In that letter a suspect in the Cleveland Torso Murders was identified as a person with the last name "Wilson." This suspect was identified as being 17 years old in 1937. Jack Anderson Wilson's birth certificate shows that he was born in 1920. He would have been 17 years old in 1937. Also recall that the suspect's father was identified as "Walter *F.* Wilson." Jack Anderson Wilson's birth certificate shows his father as "Alex *F.* Wilson.") "Wilson seemed to prefer the company of low-lifes," Lesnick says, "the moochers, and apparently second-rate female impersonators. He referred to one being connected with a murder in Indianapolis, and he mentions this person working in a bar called the Pair of Jacks, and another joint, Jud Logan's Bar in the same area. He alludes to that room in the 7000 block of West 10th Street, downtown, and all of this having some peculiar skid-row feeling of activity to it, and these talks about rape and murder that are in the transcripts-the methods mentioned by Wilson coming peculiarly close to the actual conditions to do with the bathtub murder of Georgette Bauerdorf. Of course this became of great interest to the unsolved homicide division of the sheriff's department" (Note 27, p. 199-200).

The following is a list of the aliases of Jack Anderson Wilson (Note 27, p. 202):

	Initials
Jack Anderson Wilson	J.A.W.
Jack Olsen	J.O.
Hanns Anderson Von Cannon	H.A.V.C.
Jack A. Taylor	J.A.T.
John D. Ryan	J.D.R
Eugene Deavilen	E.D.
Jack McCurry	J. M.
Jack H. Wilson	J.H.W.
Grover Loving Jr.	G.L.
Grover Loving Wilson	G.L.W.
Jack Anderson McGray	J.A.M.
Jack Smith	J.S.
Arnold Smith	A.S.

It is also interesting to note that Federal agents in St. Louis seized twenty-five-year-old Grover Casey of Troy, Alabama, for making telephone calls to the Degnans saying their child was safe and demanding $500. He was charged with making a threat over interstate communications. On February 15, 1946 Grover Casey was sentenced to five (5) years in a federal penitentiary.

Medford, Oregon Police Department arrest photograph of Jack Anderson Wilson, a/k/a Jack Wilson, November 16, 1960 (photo courtesy of the Museum of Death, Hollywood, California)

Wilson had a five-page rap sheet with a number of aliases and three Social Security numbers. In Tennessee, Wilson was caught having sex with another man in a park. His rap sheet listed Los Angeles as his place of birth and included two separate dates of birth. In Tennessee, Wilson's arrest record listed his birthplace as *Canton, Ohio*, not Los Angeles. Detective Lesnick stated: "It appeared that the mother of either Alex Wilson or Minnie Buchanan came to Canton from the Newland region in North Carolina and lived in that house when Wilson and Minnie relocated to southern California, leaving the boy behind. Apparently he remained in Canton with the relative from Newland. Though it appears he was shuttled back and forth between Canton and North Carolina, most of his early years were spent growing up in Ohio" (Note 27, p. 199). The first

Torso murder in Cleveland occurred in 1935. If Wilson was born in 1920, he would have been 15 years old in 1935. Canton, Ohio is located not far from Youngstown, New Castle and West Pittsburgh, Pennsylvania, and Cleveland, Ohio. The New York Central runs through Minerva, Ohio, twelve miles from Canton.

In her research on the Black Dahlia, the author of *Childhood Shadows*, Mary Pacios tracked down the information on Jack Anderson Wilson. Pacios called author John Gilmore. "Gilmore had relatives in Canton who could obtain Wilson's birth certificate. A few days later a hand-corrected document arrived in the mail. The name on the certificate was Grover Loving, Jr., with a birthdate of August 5, 1920. The name of the father, Grover Loving, was crossed out and the name Alex F. Wilson written in. The mother was listed as Minnie Buchanan. Both mother and father gave North Carolina as their place of birth. An attached affidavit signed by Minnie Buchanan and dated November 10, 1942, listed Jack Anderson Wilson as the correct name of the child with Alex F. Wilson as the correct name of the biological father." Mary Pacios writes:

> Upon my return to San Francisco I visited a library that specializes in genealogy—the Sutro Library. Looking through old census tracts, telephone books, and city directories, I traced the whereabouts of Jack Anderson Wilson and his mother, Minnie Buchanan Wilson. I found a trail of listings that placed Minnie Wilson in the city of Wilmar, a suburb of Los Angeles, between 1939 and 1942. Her name disappeared from the telephone books and city directories in 1943. The 1940 Los Angeles City Directory listed a Jack A. Wilson living on Hill Street in Los Angeles. The 1941 and 1942 city directories had a Jack A. Wilson working at Cogar Brothers Sign Company in Los Angeles with a residence in Wilmar. All the information, with exact dates and addresses, I passed on to John Gilmore.

> John obtained Wilson's military file. Wilson had been in the army from January 12, 1944, to March 15, 1945. I created a chronology combining Wilson's arrest record with the new information, but a major gap appeared—no paper trail existed for Wilson's whereabouts between his entry into the army and his arrest in 1948 for vagrancy and lewd behavior. There was nothing to indicate whether or not Wilson was in the Los Angeles area when Elizabeth Short was murdered (Note 32, p. 166). See information concerning Georgette Bauderdorf's murder on pages 69–71.

It is interesting to note that Jack Anderson Wilson's rap sheet reflects an arrest on 3/22/43, for violation of the Selective Service Act. The related murders in Los Angeles appear to have begun with the death of Georgette Bauerdorf on October 12, 1944. Ross, Brown and Degnan were killed in Chicago during 1945-1946. The Black Dahlia, Jeanne French and other Los Angeles victims were killed from 1947-1949. No arrests appear on Wilson's rap sheet from March 22, 1943-July 26, 1948, after which time he was arrested and incarcerated on a fairly regular basis.

John St. John wanted some tangible evidence that would connect Smith with the Black Dahlia. He wanted to meet with Smith and discuss the details of the Black Dahlia murder.

Eddie introduced true-crime writer John Gilmore to Jack Arnold (Arnold Smith) in the late 60's. They met at "Eddie's" flophouse in Silver Lake where, after a few drinks, Smith would eventually begin to reveal to Gilmore information he knew about the Black Dahlia murder. More than a dozen years later Smith called Gilmore and said, "It's probably time we got together and talked about the murder." "What murder?" Gilmore asked. Smith replied, "Her murder. You know who I mean . . ." (Note 27, p. 228-229). Gilmore met with Arnold Smith at Harold's 555 Club in Los Angeles in early

1980. Smith showed Gilmore a photograph of Elizabeth Short and a handkerchief that he said was in her purse on the day she was killed. Smith related details of the murder to Gilmore that only the killer would have known. Gilmore relayed the information he obtained from Smith to Detective St. John. After meeting with Gilmore, St. John said, "This is the guy that I have got to talk to." He was nearly certain Arnold Smith was the murderer of Elizabeth Short. "He's blaming somebody else for the homicide, but he's got details only the killer could know-or details only the killer could have told him. He either takes us to this other joker or takes the rap for it himself . . . this is the break I've waited for. All I need to make a connection between Smith and Short—linking them together at the same time . . . the perfect piece of evidence is the photograph you saw. With that, we'll bring him in, and I'll close the book on this case. I'll retire after fifty years of working this shit by closing the door on this one." St. John contacted the informant to arrange a meeting with Smith and to find out certain information about the Dahlia murder. "When the informant talked to Smith about getting together at the 555 Club the last of January, he also asked him about a couple of little things that St. John had been interested in—some articles of clothing and a washcloth. Did Smith have any recollection of items like that? Yes, some things were stuffed in a storm drain a couple of miles south of San Pedro. There was blood on the clothes—his clothes, Smith said. He'd wiped all the makeup off her face with a washcloth. He threw that away with the clothes." (Note 27, p. 202).

Unfortunately, just days before his arrest, Jack Anderson Wilson (Smith) died on February 4, 1982, as a result of a fire in the Holland Hotel near downtown Los Angeles. St. John was unable to obtain the corroborative evidence that would establish beyond a reasonable doubt who murdered the Black Dahlia, although Jack Anderson Wilson certainly appeared to be the killer.

As you will see this case has more twists and turns than a bent corkscrew. St. John was close–really close, but according to author John Gilmore, "John St. John's dream of being the cop to 'officially' break the Dahlia case had gone up in smoke with the death of Arnold Smith, a/k/a Jack Anderson Wilson." Contrary to popular belief, this case can be solved even though Arnold Smith has gone up in smoke. When Smith met with John Gilmore in the early 80's Smith made a statement that is of significance. Smith, speaking of the Black Dahlia said, "One time she was giving a blowjob to a sailor in a back booth and nobody was paying fucking attention, well . . . almost nobody. Someone saw it as a betrayal. Going against what someone's got in their thinking. That's why she wasn't living any longer than she did." Smith was also quoted earlier as saying that the killing of the Black Dahlia was "justified." In my estimation Smith may very well been exhibiting jealousy towards the Black Dahlia. If this was in fact the case, then there is a possibility that he stalked her and may have followed her to Chicago in 1945 and 1946. It would be interesting to find out if Illinois State Police records reflect an arrest record on Jack Anderson Wilson during that time. To reinforce the jealousy theory, consider this: Following the murder of the Black Dahlia, Los Angeles policewoman Myrl McBride reported that on the afternoon of January 14, 1947, Elizabeth Short approached her "sobbing in terror." Short told McBride, "Someone wants to kill me." Officer McBride said that Short told her she "lives in terror" of a former serviceman whom she had just met in a bar up the street. McBride added, "She told me the suitor had threatened to kill her if he found her with another man" (Note 28, p. 237). If the former boyfriend was Jack Anderson Wilson, then it would appear that he may have been jealous and if he was a jealous suitor, he may very well have been stalking her. It may then logically follow that Jack Anderson Wilson might have been stalking Elizabeth Short during 1945-1946 when she was in Chicago, at the same time Ross, Brown and Degnan were murdered in that city.

I discovered the corroborating evidence that John St. John needed to connect Arnold Smith with the murder of the Black Dahlia, in the history of a Cleveland Torso Murders that occurred twelve years before the murder of Elizabeth Short. According to the Cleveland Police records in 1937, Cleveland Detective Orley May reported on a tip that was typical of thousands of tips the police department were given regarding the Cleveland Torso murders. Orley is quoted as having said:

> **Detective Musil and I received information from a person who does not want her identity revealed and who stated that while she was in the workhouse, a woman by the name of Helen O'Leary, who was the former wife of a man who was shot and killed several years ago—since got married to Gas House O'Malley, a stage hand, told her that she knew the man that killed Florence Polillo. She asked him who it was and she said "You know, his name is Jack Wilson." We learned from the informer that Jack Wilson was a former butcher and worked for Sam who operated a grocery store and meat market on St. Clair Avenue, and that he was known to carry a large butcher knife. Informant also stated that this Wilson was a sodomist, and that he committed sodomy on a number of persons known by the informant and is committing these decapitated (sic) murders in Kingsbury Run and may be killing them for the purpose of committing Sodomy on the victims, and would be a good suspect in the above murder (Note 26 & Note 20, p. 58).**

Unless there were two sodomists by the name of Jack Wilson during this time period who were butchering people, then it is a reasonable assumption that Jack Anderson Wilson of Los Angeles and Jack Wilson of Cleveland, fingered by the woman from the workhouse as the killer of Flo Polillo and other victims in Kingsbury Run, was one and the same person. That being the case, then Jack Anderson Wilson, a/k/a Arnold Smith, a/k/a Jack Wilson was, more than likely, the Mad Butcher of Kingsbury Run and, as John St. John suspected, but was unable to definitively prove, the murderer of the Black Dahlia.

On July 18, 1990, Dr. Money, a forensic sexologist associated with Johns Hopkins University, commented on the Arnold Smith (Jack Anderson Wilson) interview: "Despite the incoherency of parts of the interview, the overall content is consistent with the possibility that Ms. Short met her death as the victim of a lust murderer. Lust murder is one of the 40 different paraphilias. Its Greek name is erotophonophilia . . . . I think it is very likely that Arnold Smith himself was the murderer of Ms. Short." Keep in mind that in the case of Suzanne Degnan, Dr. Jerry Kearns of the coroner's office indicated that her killer was "motivated by a powerful sex obsession" (Note 24).

There has always been a question surrounding the Cleveland Torso Murders regarding the reason for lack of resistance that was exhibited by the Butcher's victims. It was reported that a few of his victims may have been decapitated while still alive, which is highly unusual. Typically a person is killed by some other means and then the body is dismembered. For example, acting detective Charles O. Nevel theorized that the Tattooed Man had arrived in Cleveland by rail and had fallen asleep in Kingsbury Run. Nevel said, "While he was sleeping the maniac attacked him. First he cut his throat. Then he hacked away at the neck. Then he undressed the victim" (Note 20, p. 65). Torso witness Helen O'Leary thought that Jack Wilson "was committing sodomy on his victims." Keep in mind that there were reports of sexual perversion and promiscuity associated with several of the Torso Murders victims. Now consider what Arnold Smith (Jack Anderson Wilson) stated in his taped recordings when speaking about the Black

Dahlia murder in Los Angeles: "See, she made my dick hard every time I looked at her mouth." Remember also that Jack Anderson Wilson had been arrested on May 9, 1948, for having sex with another man in a park. Wilson hung out with female impersonators and in 1958 while incarcerated in the Oakland City Prison he spoke about a queer's head he had seen at the 1936 Great Lakes Exposition in Cleveland. I suspect that a reasonable explanation for the lack of resistance exhibited by the victims of the Torso Killer may have been the result of immediate decapitation by the killer following a sexual act performed on the executioner by his victims. This may also account for the heads that were never found in several of the Torso Murders.

Jeanne Axford French (The Red Lipstick Murder)

Jeanne Axford French lived an interesting life in Los Angeles, albeit a short one. To her credit she had been an actress, registered nurse who traveled with famous people, and one of America's first female pilots. She became known as "the Flying Nurse." Like the Black Dahlia, Jeanne French became famous not in life but as a result of her untimely death at the hands of a deranged killer. On February 9, 1947, Jeanne French's life went into a tailspin. At 7:30 p.m. Sunday, February 9, she was seen with two men at the Plantation Café 10984 Washington Boulevard in Los Angeles. One of the men had "dark hair and a small mustache." French had been drinking heavily and appeared intoxicated. After she finished her meal at the Plantation she left the restaurant possibly with both men. At 10:00 p. m. that evening witnesses reported seeing French at the Turkey Bowl restaurant 11925 Santa Monica Boulevard. Half an hour later she was seen at a bar at 10421 Venice Boulevard. Fifteen minutes later she was at her estranged husband's home at Sanford and Colorado Boulevards. The two argued and she eventually drove off in her 1928 Ford Roadster. Just after midnight she showed up at the Picadilly drive-in restaurant at 3932 Sepulveda

Boulevard. Again witnesses reported seeing her with "a dark-haired man with a small mustache." Detectives speculated that she latter left the Picidilly and drove off with the dark-haired man. A little after 8:00 a.m. in the morning of February 10, 1947, exactly twenty-seven days after the murder of the Black Dahlia, construction worker Hugh Shelby discovered the nude body of Jeanne French in the 3200 Block of Grandview Avenue. According to Captain Jack Donahoe, she had been beaten with "a heavy weapon, probably a tire iron or a wrench, as she crouched naked on the highway" (Note 28, p. 189-195).

On November 15, 1950, Lt. Frank Jamison gave the following report on the Jeanne French murder:

> The body of Jeanne French was discovered at 8:15 A.M. on February 10, 1947, at a spot in the weeds, lying face up with her feet sixteen feet from Grand View Avenue, at a point 303 feet north of Indianapolis Street in West Los Angeles. Her body was nude and her clothes were piled on top of her body. Her shoes were found some fifty or sixty feet in two different directions, apparently thrown by the murderer into the field. Her pocketbook was lying some ten feet from her body. A piece of lipstick was found just under the body, and written on the body in lipstick was the writing, "Fuck you, B.D." and "Tex." These writings were on the lower abdomen of the body. Her face was completely covered with bruises, blood and mud. The face had been apparently beaten into a pulp. There were no knife cuts on the body. The tissues of the anus were bruised about one-eighth of an inch. There was no death weapon found. There were several wounds in head, apparently administered by a steel blunt instrument, and which could have been, according to Autopsy Surgeon Newbarr, a socket wrench. These blows on the head did not cause death. The cause of death was due to hemorrhage and

> shock from fractured ribs and multiple injuries caused by stomping no doubt with feet, as heel prints were visible on the chest of the victim and a small heel print appeared in the mud right near the victim's face which appears to be smaller in size (six or seven shoe in men's sizes). There were other footprints further away from the body which were prints of larger sizes; however, the Crime Laboratory Chief, Lee Jones, believes they could have been caused by the newspaper reporters coming up later. According to Dr. Newbarr, the victim no doubt took some period of time to die after the administration of the stomping and the crushing of the ribs, which had penetrated her lung and liver causing hemorrhage, and which caused the victim to slowly bleed to death, as she was no doubt knocked unconscious by the blow on the head in the first instance. The physical evidence establishes the victim was murdered at the scene where the body was found, but apparently she had been knocked unconscious, possibly by the suspect's car, and dragged from the car into the field where he administered the stomping. See the enlarged photographs attached and also the crime Lab. Plaster cast of the killer's heel. Dr. Newbarr stated that it was possible that this victim was administered this beating and stomped as early as 2:30 A.M. or 3:00 A.M., February 10, 1947.

This crime became known as "the Lipstick Murder." The Los Angeles detectives thought that the murder of Jeanne French might have been linked to the murder of Elizabeth Short. Short had been killed on January 14, 1947. After the murder of Elizabeth Short a Corporal Joseph Dumais had supposedly signed a bogus confession to the crime. Detectives theorized that the Black Dahlia Avenger may have killed French in order to establish that Dumais was not the killer. There also has been as much speculation that the murder of Jeanne French was a completely separate murder and in no way connected to the murder of Elizabeth Short. There are clues that point towards the same killer that should be considered:

1. There may have been two individuals involved in the murder of Jeanne French, one of which may have worn size 6-7 men's shoe size. Keep in mind that two men may have been involved in the kidnapping/murder/dismemberment of Suzanne Degnan in Chicago on January 7, 1946.
2. The Los Angeles detectives found a man's white handkerchief at the scene of the French murder. A man's "balled-up handkerchief" was associated with the murder of Suzanne Degnan in Chicago and a man's "balled-up handkerchief" was found at the murder scene of Gladys Eugenia Kerns, February 14, 1948, in Los Angeles, exactly one year after the murder of Elizabeth Short. Some Los Angeles detectives thought the Kerns murder may have been related to the murder of The Black Dahlia.
3. The killer of Jeanne French had draped her coat, trimmed with red fox fur-cuffs, and her red dress over the body before leaving the scene. The Mad Butcher of Kingsbury Run wrapped the severed head of the Tattooed Man in his pants and the killer of Josephine Ross and Frances Brown wrapped a dress and pajamas around the heads of his Chicago victims.
4. The killer of Jeanne French wrote in red lipstick on her abdomen, "Fuck you, B.D." The killer of Frances Brown left a message on her wall written in red lipstick. The Mad Butcher of Kingsbury Run wrote the word "NAZI" on the abdomen of one of his victims.
5. The murder of Jeanne French occurred exactly 27 days after the murder of the Black Dahlia. The murder of Suzanne Degnan occurred exactly 27 days after the murder of Frances Brown in Chicago.

6. The body of Jeanne French was deposited in a vacant lot in Los Angeles. The body of Elizabeth Short was deposited in a vacant lot in Los Angeles.
7. On Tuesday, February 11, 1947, Los Angeles cab driver Charles Schneider discovered a note in his cab possibly written by the killer of the Black Dahlia. The note read: "Take it to examiner at once, I've got the number of your cab. $20,000 and I'll give B.D. up. Is it a go? B.D." Following the murder of Suzanne Degnan, her killer left a ransom note in her bedroom demanding $20,000.

In 1946, Captain Donahoe "told the public that in his opinion the Black Dahlia and the Lipstick Murders were likely connected" (Note 28, p. 195).

Is it possible that the same person or persons who killed Ross, Brown and Degnan also killed the Black Dahlia and Jeanne French the following year? Could the killer or killers have traveled from one state to another and committed similar crimes? If it could be established that whoever killed the Black Dahlia and Jeanne French in 1947, also killed Ross, Brown and Degnan in Chicago, then obviously it would be physically impossible for William Heirens to have committed the offences he was charged with because he was in custody in Chicago at the time the Black Dahlia and Jeanne French were killed in Los Angeles in 1947. From a statistical standpoint it is unlikely that a sadistic psychopathic killer would be dismembering a child in Chicago in January, 1946, and a different individual would commit a similar crime in Los Angeles one year later. From a probability standpoint it may be more plausible that the same individual was involved in both series of murders. For Mr. Heirens' benefit both the Los Angeles and the Chicago murders should be reevaluated to see if there is any connection.

Here is an odd coincidence: according to A. L. Brodie's Coroner's Report dated January 8, 1946, Suzanne Degnan was born in Worchester, Massachusetts, in 1940. Before moving to Miami Beach in 1942, Elizabeth Short lived with her mother in Medford, Massachusetts, approximately 35 miles from Worchester. Could there be some connection here that went unnoticed? Was Elizabeth an acquaintance of the Degnan family? According to published reports, she may have been in Chicago in 1946 when Suzanne Degnan was murdered. There is also some speculation that Elizabeth Short had a great deal of interest in the Degnan murder. Jim and Helen Degnan (parents of Suzanne Degnan) had grown up on the East Coast and had moved only recently from Baltimore, Maryland, where they resided while Jim Degnan traveled to Washington, D.C., to his position with the Office of Price Administration, popularly known as the OPA. The OPA had been created during the war in order to issue ration cards and keep prices under control. Degnan had been instrumental in its formation, but already the organization was meeting resistance from areas under control, particularly the meat and dairy industry, where black market meat was continuing to thrive in the oppressed market. Degnan had been transferred to Chicago to assist in the administration of the troubled Midwest contingency. It is interesting to note that according to his rap sheet, one of Jack Anderson Wilson's many social security numbers may have been obtained while in the State of Maryland.

OTHER LOS ANGELES VICTIMS

Ica Mable M'Grew

On Wednesday, February 12, 1947, two days after the murder of Jeanne French, twenty-seven-year-old Ica Mable M'Grew reported that she was kidnapped and forcibly raped in Los Angeles. She reported that two men forced her into their car and drove her to an isolated location on East Road in Los Angeles where they both raped her. One of her attackers warned her, "Don't tell the police, or I'll do to you the same as I did to the Black Dahlia." A news article described the two rapists as "two swarthy men."

Evelyn Winters

On March 12, 1947, the nude body of Evelyn Winters was found on a vacant lot at 830 Ducommun Street, near railroad tracks. She had been severely bludgeoned. The cause of death was due to "blunt force trauma causing a concussion and hemorrhage to the brain" (Note 28, p. 402). The killer had wrapped the victim's dress around her neck. (Recall the case of Josephine Ross in Chicago, June 5, 1945, in which her killer wrapped her head in a dress.) Evelyn Winters was an alcoholic who frequently visited downtown bars on Hill Street in Los Angeles. The police believed her murder was related to the deaths of Elizabeth Short and Jeanne French. The LAPD listed the following similarities in the murders of Elizabeth Short, Jeanne Axford French and Evelyn Winters:

1. All three girls frequented cocktail bars and sometimes picked up men in them.
2. All three were slugged on the head (although Mrs. French was trampled to death and Miss Short tortured and cut in two).
3. All three were killed elsewhere and taken in cars to the spots where the bodies were found.
4. All three were displayed nude or nearly so.
5. In no case was an attempt made to conceal the body. On the contrary bodies were left where they were sure to be found.
6. Each had been dragged a short distance.

7. Each killing was a pathological case, apparently motivated by psychological lust.
8. In each case the killer appears to have taken care not to be seen in company with the victim.
9. All three women had good family backgrounds.
10. Each was identified by her fingerprints, other evidence of identity having been removed.
11. Miss Short and Miss Winters were last seen in the same Hill Street area. For whatever it is worth, I am adding another similarity:
12. Evelyn Winters was an alcoholic. On the night she was abducted and murdered, Jeanne French had a blood alcohol content of .30, twice what was then considered legally drunk. By all accounts Elizabeth Short was well liked and a very good person. There has been, however, some speculation, although unproven, that she may have prostituted herself and was down on her luck. All of the women seemed to fit the type of person this predator looked for.

Laura Elizabeth Trelstad

On May 11, 1947, Laura Elizabeth Trelstad's body was found in the 3400 block of Locust Avenue in Long Beach, California. The cause of death was strangulation with "a piece of flowered cotton cloth, believed torn from a man's pajamas or shorts." She had been raped and the autopsy confirmed the presence of semen. If still available, there may be a possibility of DNA analysis.

Rosenda Josephine Mondragon

On July 8, 1947, the body of Rosenda Josephine Mondragon was located at 129 East Elmyra Street in Los Angeles near railroad tracks.

She was drunk the night of her murder. A silk stocking was found wrapped around her neck. Her right breast had been slashed. (Recall that the right breast of Elizabeth Short had been severed.)

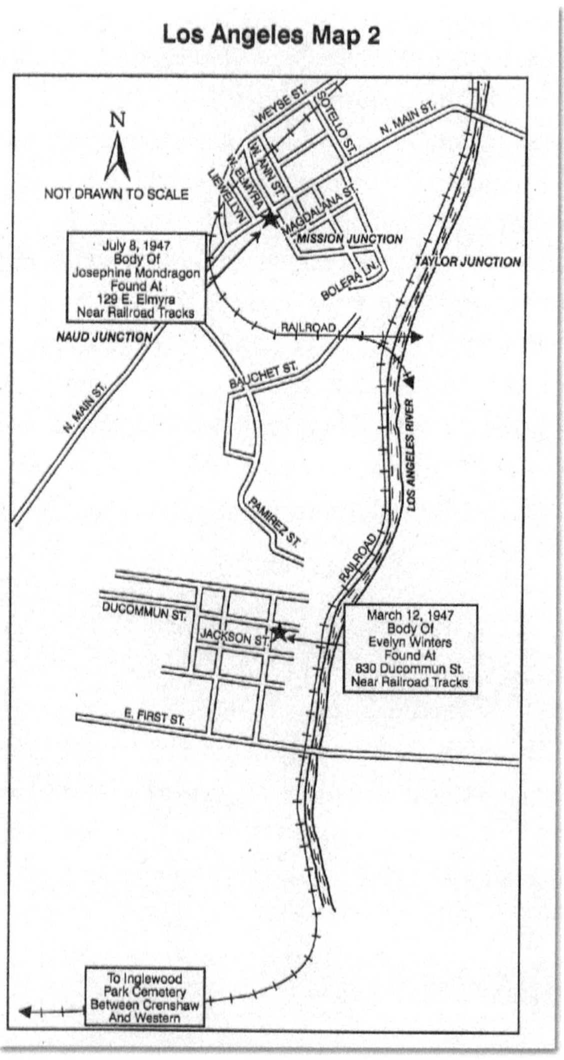

Los Angeles map showing the location of the bodies of Josephine Mondragon and Evelyn Winters. Note the close proximity to railroad tracks

Viola Norton

On February 14, 1948, Viola Norton was savagely attacked near the location where the Black Dahlia had been killed. "Two men both appearing to be approximately 40 years of age approached her in a car and asked her to get in." She was walking home from a cocktail lounge in Alhambra near Los Angeles. She was forced into the car and severely beaten on her face and head with a tire iron. Her assailant left her for dead four blocks from where the Black Dahlia had been found a little more than one year earlier on January 15, 1947.

Louise Margaret Springer

On June 13, 1949, Louise Margaret Springer was kidnapped and murdered in Los Angeles. She was strangled with a thin white clothesline cord. She worked at a beauty parlor in a department store at Santa Barbara and Crenshaw just two blocks from where Elizabeth Short's body had been found two and a half years earlier (Note 30, p. 411). Her assailant inserted a 14-inch length of finger-thick tree branch into her vagina. Witnesses reported the assailant of Louise Margaret Springer as a "white man with curly hair."

Similarities Between Jack Anderson Wilson, the Cleveland Torso Killer and the killer of Josephine Ross, Frances Brown and Suzanne Degnan

If Jack Anderson Wilson did in fact commit the Torso Murders between 1935-1938, in Cleveland and the murder of the Black Dahlia on January 14, 1947, it is a fairly safe bet that he committed other murders somewhere else between those time periods. Josephine Ross, Frances Brown and Suzanne Degnan were all killed during the years 1945-1946. Los Angeles County Detective Joel Lesnick stated: "With his 'rightful name' documented, Wilson now shows up in L.A., working as a sign hanger for Coger Brothers on Bixel Street. He gets picked up by the police for a Selective Service violation, then leaves the sign hanging job and drifts back to Indianapolis. He seems to hang out again with a female impersonator and turns twenty-four in August, 1943. He is bumbling around the city until a young female, a WAC, is murdered in a downtown hotel. And it seems that immediately Wilson leaves Indianapolis and turns up back in Los Angeles." Keep in mind that Josephine Ross was murdered on June 5, 1945, in Chicago. Indianapolis is located approximately 185 miles from Chicago. The New York Central runs from Indianapolis to Chicago.

1. Jack Anderson Wilson spent his early years in Ohio, and he admitted attending the Great Lakes Exposition in Cleveland in 1936.
2. The Cleveland Torso Murders began in 1934, and "officially" ended in 1938.
3. Jack Anderson Wilson "appeared in Los Angeles in the late 1930's."
4. Additional Torso murders took place from 1938-1942, in Pennsylvania.
5. Wilson reappeared in Los Angeles in 1942.
6. Wilson was regarded as a probable suspect in the murders of Georgette Bauerdorf and Elizabeth Short.
7. The killer of Elizabeth Short used a large knife to bisect her.
8. Wilson may have discarded clothing and other evidence down storm drains. The Cleveland Torso Killer and the killer of Suzanne Degnan discarded body parts and other evidence down storm sewers.
9. The New York Central runs from Indianapolis to Chicago and from Indianapolis to Cleveland. Jack Anderson Wilson was in Indianapolis when he turned 24. "He is bumbling

around the city until a young female, a WAC, is murdered in a downtown hotel. And it seems that immediately Wilson leaves Indianapolis and turns up back in Los Angeles" (Note 27, p. 200-201). One of the victims William Heirens pled guilty to killing, Frances Brown, was a WAVE.

10. Cuyahoga County Coroner Samuel Gerber speculated that the Butcher was probably right-handed and dismembered his victims with a large heavy butcher's knife. As Arnold Smith's (Jack Anderson Wilson's) transcript provided, "Then he said there was a larger knife like a long butcher knife that was two inches, the width of the blade near the handle" (Note 27, p. 188).

11. Victim No. 6 was found in Kingsbury Run September 10, 1936. At the scene the police found a twelve-by-sixteen-inch piece of faded green underwear bearing the laundry mark "J.W." on the waistband. Could the initials have stood for "Jack Wilson"?

12. The bloody underwear found with the remains of Victim No. 4 (the "Tattooed Man") had the following laundry marks: "J.D.A." or J.D.X." One of Jack Anderson Wilson's alias's was "Jack Deavilen." Could the initials have possibly stood for "Jack Deavilen Anderson or Jack Deavilen?" The "X" was usually included as a laundry mark if two laundry customers have the same last name.

13. Torso witness Helen O'Leary indicated that the person who killed Flo Polillo in 1935, was "Jack Wilson." She also indicated that Jack Wilson was a former butcher who worked in a Cleveland butcher shop, carried a large butcher knife and was a sodomist.

14. Jack Anderson Wilson was a convicted sodomist.

15. The Cleveland Torso killer was a necrophiliac.

16. The person who killed Elizabeth Short was a suspected necrophiliac.

Similarities Between the Cleveland Torso Murders and the Murder of the Black Dahlia

Cleveland Torso Murders	Black Dahlia
1. Torso victim Edward Andrassy had rope burns on his wrist.	**1.** She had rope burns on her wrists.
2. Torso Victim No. 2 may have been immersed in some sort of fluid before being dumped at the base of Jackass Hill in Cleveland.	**2.** She may have been immersed in water before being dumped in a vacant lot. Detective Finnis Brown stated, "maybe she's been in water" (Note 27, p. 13).
3. The body of Edward Andrassy had been drained of all its blood by his killer before being dumped.	**3.** Her body was drained of all blood before being dumped in the vacant lot.
4. The Torso Killer transported some body parts in burlap sacks and baskets.	**4.** Her lower torso was carried from the killer's vehicle on a cement bag.
5. Authorities thought the Torso Killer had either medical training or was a butcher. If Jack Wilson of Cleveland and Jack Anderson Wilson of Los Angeles were the same person and if he was in fact born in 1920, then Wilson would have been just over 15 years old on January 23, 1936, when Flo Polillo was murdered and dismembered in Cleveland.	**5.** Her killer had the "finesse of a surgeon."

6. When disposing of his victims, the Torso Killer "manifested an odd combination of obsessive neatness and casual sloppiness." The killer of Victim No. 4 (the "Tattooed Man") placed his shoes about twenty feet from the head, their laces tied together and stuffed with a pair of dark striped socks with orange tops. The head of the fourth victim had been carefully rolled up in his pants and deliberately deposited under a willow tree, just as pieces of Flo Polillo's body had been neatly wrapped in newspapers, placed in burlap bags, packed in baskets and deposited behind Hart Manufacturing Plant 2340 East 22nd in Cleveland six months before (Note 20, p. 63).	**6.** Her killer carefully "arranged her shoes on either side of her head an equal distance of approximately ten feet. "The upper torso appears to have been placed asymmetrically approximately twelve inches above the lower portion and offset to the left approximately six inches. Both of the victim's arms are raised above the head, the right arm at a forty-five-degree angle away from the body, then bent at the elbow to form a ninety-degree angle. The left arm extends at a similar angle away from the body, and then bends again to form a second ninety-degree angle that parallels the body. This was no normal 'dumping' of a victim to get rid of a corpse quickly. In fact, the body had been carefully posed, just six inches from the sidewalk at a location where the victim was certain to be discovered, to create a shocking scene" (Note 28, p. 13).
7. Torso Killer inserted a pants pocket into a female victim's rectum.	**7. Her killer cut flesh from her leg and pushed it up her rectum.**

8. The Torso Killer left deep gashes in the thighs of Victim No. 10.	**8**. Her killer cut a chunk of flesh from her thigh.
9. The Torso Killer left his victims' bodies naked.	**9**. Her killer left her body naked.
10. Some of the Torso Killer's victims were killed in one location and transported to another.	**10**. She was killed elsewhere and dumped in a vacant Los Angeles lot.
11. The Torso Killer used a large, sharp knife.	**11**. Her killer used a large, sharp knife.
12. The Torso Killer drenched a victim's body in oil.	**12**. Her personal belongings were drenched in gasoline.
13. The Torso Killer taunted the police with their inability to catch him.	**13**. Her killer taunted the police with their inability to catch him.
14. The Torso Killer was an "organized killer."	**14**. Her killer was an "organized killer."
15. On December 23, 1938, someone sent a letter to the Chief of Police in Cleveland suggesting that he might be the Torso Killer, that he had gone to Los Angeles for the winter, and that he buried a head "without the features" on Century Boulevard between Crenshaw and Western in Los Angeles.	**15**. On or about January 14, 1947, the severed body of the Black Dahlia was found on the corner of 39th and Norton between Crenshaw and South Western in Los Angeles.

16. The Torso Killer may have refrigerated a body of one of his victims.	**16.** Detectives thought her body may have been frozen before being severed.
17. According to the Cleveland police, the Torso Killer was probably a necrophiliac.	**17.** Her body "was lacerated in an area below the naval down to the pubic area. The attacker may have had some usage of this area of the body." In other words he may have been a necrophiliac if sexual activity was after the victim was dead.
18. The Torso Killer bisected the bodies of six of his victims.	**18.** Her body was bisected.
19. One of the Torso Killer's victims' palms was burned. He may have been tortured.	**19.** She was tortured by her killer. She may have been burned on her breasts, possibly with cigarettes, although this was never confirmed, and possibly forced to eat human feces. I reviewed this issue with a highly respected Michigan coroner because similar granular material was found in Suzanne Degnan after she was dismembered. The coroner indicated that force applied to the body could push the person's own feces into the upper areas of the body.

20. The skull of Victim No. 8, tentatively identified as belonging to Rose Wallace, was found under the Loraine-Carnegie Bridge in Cleveland in 1936. "On the afternoon of her disappearance Merylo learned Wallace had been doing her laundry when a friend arrived and informed her that an unidentified man wanted to see her at an East 19th and Scoville bar close to her home. She left her laundry in the tub and headed for the sleazy establishment. According to witnesses, she later left with a dark-skinned white man named **Bob** for a party on the west side. Later still, a woman identified only as Mrs. Carter of Hazen Court reported seeing her in a car with three white men, but after that Rose Wallace simply vanished" (Emphasis added) (Note 20, p. 115).	**20**. On February 3, 1947, the *Los Angeles Herald-Express* ran an article about a forcible rape that occurred "near the Dahlia murder spot. A 30-year-old woman named Sylvia Horan had gone to Los Angeles alone to watch a movie. Afterwards she was standing on the corner of 7th Street and Broadway when a 'suave stranger', driving a black coupe, offered to drive her home. 'I accepted the ride,' she said, 'due to the late hour.' The stranger, who identified himself as '**Bob**,' drove her to a lonely spot on Stocker Boulevard between Crenshaw and LaBrea Avenues, only eight blocks from where the body of Elizabeth Short had been found, and forcibly raped her. Sylvia Horan might have been an important living witness to detectives in the Black Dahlia investigation had they linked the Horan crime to the Short case." (Emphasis added) (Note 28, p. 184).

21. **Flo Polillo, Victim No. 3, was bisected at the second lumbar vertebra★ and a longitudinal incision ran the length of the lower half★ (Dr. Reuben Straus, County Pathologist).**	21. **"The incision was performed through the abdomen above the naval and then through the second and third lumbar vertebrae.★ There is a gaping laceration of four-and-one-half inches which extends longitudinally to the superficial lacerations★** (Dr. Frederic Newbarr, Chief Autopsy Surgeon for the County of Los Angeles). The incision may have been used as an artificial vagina postmortem. To quote Vincent Bugliosi in his book *And The Sea Will Tell*, "Aloha evidence."
22. It was speculated that the Torso Killer was a "large powerful man" (Note 20, p. 39).	22. The killer may have been "abnormally strong."
23. The Mad Butcher of Kingsbury Run "flaunted his crimes and horrified society with his atrocities." "The urge to show off his butchery was evident in the Torso Murder's decision to leave his final pair of Cleveland victims on the busy lakefront in full view of city hall and the Office of Safety Director Ness (Note 31, p. 216).	23. The Black Dahlia Avenger was an egomaniac who planned the murder to show the world he was a superman, someone who could, "outwit and outthink the whole world." The killer had placed the body where it would be quickly found and mutilated it so horribly to attract the greatest attention on the part of the police and public (Note 28, p. 164-165). The killer of Suzanne Degnan fits the same mold.

24. Three murder victims were found at McKees Rocks, Pennsylvania, on May 3, 1940. One of the victims had the word "NAZI" carved in his chest. The pattern of dismemberment strongly resembled that practiced by the Torso murderer. Dr. P. R. Heimfold, a coroner's physician in Pittsburgh indicated that the killer tried to burn the bodies. He also indicated that the bodies had been cut "by an expert who had some knowledge of anatomy **or was a butcher"** (Emphasis added) (Note 22, p. 153).	**24**. The killer of Jeanne French wrote the words, "Fuck You B.D." on the midsection of her body in red lipstick.
25. The body of Victim No. 9, unlike any other, had been dismembered. The entire abdomen had been split open and its contents gutted. The heart had also been removed; the killer had cut through the chest with a single decisive stroke and ripped out the organ with his hand. None of the internal organs were ever located (Note 20, p. 120).	**25**. Detective Herman Willis indicated that, "the killer had cut out parts of some basic female organs." There was an apparent cavity where it appeared that organs had been removed from the body (Note 27, p. 5).

26. Victim No. 11 was found at the East 9th Lake Shore dumpsite in Cleveland. The human torso was wrapped in **heavy brown paper** used by butchers (Note 20, p. 134).	**26**. Following the murder of the Black Dahlia, a mysterious package was located at the Biltmore Hotel. The package was **wrapped in brown paper.**
27. Deputy Coroner Chamberlain reported that Edward Andrassy had a mysterious, small pock-mark like scar on his forehead.	**27**. The killer of the Black Dahlia carved a scar on her forehead.
28. The sex organs were mutilated on No.'s 1,2,3 & 7. Detective Merylo believed the murderer committed crimes "solely for the sexual satisfaction he secured."	**28**. The Black Dahlia's killer performed a postmortem hysterectomy on her.
29. The thighs of Victim No. 11 were held together with rubber bands.	**29**. Arnold Smith brought a See's Candy box held together with rubber bands.
30. Cuyahoga County Coroner Samuel R. Gerber indicated "He may have been a doctor or medical student sometime in the past, a butcher, osteopath, chiropractor, orderly, nurse or hunter in order to accomplish the dissection with such finesse" (Note 22, p. 168).	**30**. The Black Dahlia was bisected by someone "with the finesse of a surgeon."

31. The torso of Victim No. 9 was found in 1937 packed in a burlap bag that was labeled "One Hundred Pounds of Purina Chicken Feed." The bag also contained a "perplexing clue": a cheap woman's silk stocking, in good condition, which contained a lone black and white dog hair and several short blond human hairs (Note 20, p. 118). Victim No. 9 was a forty-year-old man. Was the victim or his killer wearing silk stockings?	**31.** Several subsequent victims associated with the Black Dahlia murder were found strangled with silk or nylon stockings.

---

* Pathological Report on Suzanne Degnan dated January 8, 1946: "The trunk has been divided *at the level of the umbilicus* anteriorly and the *2nd lumbar vertebra* posteriorly," (Emphasis added) What you have here are two bisections at exactly the same location at the second lumbar vertebra, followed by a longitudinal laceration on the lower portion of the torso. This, coupled with the facts that the victim is nude, the blood has been completely drained from the body, and the bisection was done by someone with a great deal of skill, may cause the accusing finger to be pointed in one direction and one direction only. That there were two sadistic psychopathic killers in this same approximate time period, performing nearly identical incisions and mutilations on the bodies of their victims is not very likely. In the 1930's and 1940's the authorities determined that several different torso killers had mysteriously begun to appear in various locations in the United States. The torso killers manifested several of the same behaviors: In New Castle and in Cleveland they buried the head of a victim near the body in such a manner so that the police were sure to find it. They did not bury the body. In Cleveland, New Castle, West Pittsburgh, Haverstraw and Youngstown they all deposited torsos along or near railroad tracks; the bodies were nude, in several of the different locations the head was not with the torso, the blood was drained from the bodies, the dismemberments were completed by someone with a great deal of skill, and so on.

Similarities Between the Murder of the Black Dahlia and the Murder of Suzanne Degnan

The Black Dahlia	Suzanne Degnan
1. The Black Dahlia's body was bisected on or about January 14, 1947.	**1.** Just over a year earlier on January 7, 1946, the dismembered body of Suzanne Degnan was found in Chicago.
2. In the Jeanne French case, which was thought to be related to the Black Dahlia murder, the killer left a ransom note demanding $20,000.	**2.** The killer of Suzanne Degnan left a ransom note at the scene of the crime demanding $20,000.
3. The Black Dahlia Avenger wrote a note following the murder of the Black Dahlia: "Here is the photo of the Werewolf's killer's I saw him kill her." (California newspapers also described the killer of the Black Dahlia as the "werewolf," so the fact that the Chicago newspapers made reference to a werewolf may or may not mean anything.)	**3.** Following the arrest of William Heirens in 1946, a Chicago daily newspaper wrote "The Werewolf was in Chains."
4. *Degnan* Boulevard is located approximately 370 feet from the corner of 39th and Norton in Los Angeles where the Black Dahlia was killed.	**4.** Suzanne *Degnan* was killed in January, 1946.
5. The killer of the Black Dahlia is suspected of using a tub and a knife in his murder.	**5.** The killer of Suzanne Degnan used a tub and knife in his murder.

6. Jack Anderson Wilson indicated that he discarded evidence in storm drains.	**6.** The killer of Suzanne Degnan deposited body parts and other evidence in sewers (storm drains).
7. Jack Anderson Wilson burned evidence after the Black Dahlia was bisected.	**7.** The "confession" of William Heirens in the Suzanne Degnan case indicates that evidence may have been burned following dismemberment.
8. The cut went straight through the narrowest part between the bottom of her ribs and navel.	**8.** Pathological Report on Suzanne Degnan: The trunk has been divided at the level of the umbilicus anteriorily and the 2nd lumbar vertebra posteriorly."
9. Gladys Eugenia Kerns was killed in Los Angeles February 14, 1948. The man had dark curly hair. The murder weapon was an eight-inch jungle knife wrapped in a man's handkerchief. A balled-up handkerchief was found in the kitchen sink near the body. In the Jeanne French homicide a man's white handkerchief was found near her body. Author Steve Hodel wrote on page 317 in *Black Dahlia Avenger:* "In my experience—which included the investigation of more than three hundred homicides—I have never encountered a case in which a suspect left a handkerchief at the scene of his crime. It is as if this was a 'calling card,' like dropping an ace of spades on the body."	**9.** Two men's handkerchiefs were found at the Degnan murder scene. One found close to a loop of wire and the other rolled into a ball that may have been used as a gag (Note 22).

10. Black Dahlia's killer soaked her purse and belongings in gasoline to destroy trace evidence.	**10**. Her killer poured oil on the ransom note to destroy trace evidence.
11. "She was trussed up by ropes or maybe ***wire*** from some of the marks . . ." (Emphasis added) (Captain Jack Donahoe at Central Homicide). Marian Davidson Newton had been strangled in Los Angeles July 16, 1947, with a thin ***wire*** or cord." Arnold Smith talked about using wire on the Black Dahlia: "I don't mean the wire part of the hanger but like you got on the other kind of hanger, that's the hook on the top part of it, going over the clothes pole, but it wasn't like that, it was soft and around the frame part" (Transcript of Arnold Smith a/k/a Jack Anderson Wilson at the Los Angeles County Sheriff's Department).	**11**. A loop of ***wire*** may have been used to strangle her.
12. Henry Silver, a document expert hired by the *Los Angeles Examiner* in 1947, said, "The sender is an egomaniac and **possibly a musician.** The fluctuating base line of the writing reveals the writer to be affected by extreme fluctuations of mood, dropping to melancholy" (Emphasis added) (Note 28, p. 173-174).	**12**. Arthur C. Becker, noted musical scholar, pointed out that resemblances of the ransom note to the letters in musical signs **indicated that the slayer of Suzanne Degnan was a musician** (Emphasis added). "Investigators speculated yesterday on whether the slayer could have been a musician.

	The speculation arose after it was noted that some of the letters were similar to notes and symbols used in writing music. Musical scholars said an accomplished musician might unconsciously form letters to resemble the symbols (Note 25). In the murder investigation of Frances Brown, several of her musician friends were questioned since a few of the letters in the "red lipstick" message resembled musical notes.
13. On January 23, 1947, James Robinson, editor of the *Los Angeles Examiner,* received a telephone call from someone claiming to be the killer of the Black Dahlia. The caller indicated that he had certain items that belonged to the Black Dahlia, including "her address book and her birth certificate and a few other things she had in her handbag."	**13.** "Earlier today it was reported a mysterious man telephoned the Degnan home, demanded the ransom and asserted that he had a lock of Suzanne's blond hair and a piece of her blue pajamas."
14. The Black Dahlia's body was bisected on or about January 14, 1947.	**14.** Just under one year earlier, on January 7, 1946, the dismembered body of Suzanne Degnan was found in Chicago. One year earlier on January 14, 1945, Eunice Rawlings disappeared in Chicago.

15. The Black Dahlia was killed and bisected at one location and discarded in another.	**15**. The killer of Suzanne Degnan dismembered her at one location and discarded her body in another.
16. The Black Dahlia was bisected by someone "with the finesse of a surgeon."	**16**. Suzanne Degnan was dismembered by someone with the "skill of a butcher."
17. Georgette Bauerdorf was murdered in her Los Angeles apartment. The bottom portion of her pajamas was removed and she was found draped over her bathtub. The outside light to her apartment had been tampered with prior to her murder. She had been raped as she lay dying or was already dead.	**17**. Frances Brown was murdered in her Chicago apartment. Her killer had removed the bottom portion of her pajamas. She was found draped over the bathtub. Questioning in the William Heirens "confession" in the Suzanne Degnan murder case indicated that an outside light may have been tampered with by her assailant prior to the abduction. She may have been sexually assaulted.
18. Mimi Broomhower disappeared on August 24, 1949, in Bel Air. An unidentified witness found her white purse at 9331 Wilshire Blvd. in Beverly Hills, with a note written directly onto the purse. The note read, "POLICE DEPT,—WE FOUND THIS AT BEACH THURSDAY NIGHT" (Note 28, p. 322).	**18**. Eighteen-year-old Eunice Rawling's torso was found on a Lake Michigan beach in Chicago on August 12, 1946. She had been missing since January 14, 1945. Her head and arms were missing and at the time the police determined the case to be a suicide. On January 17, 1945, a purse containing the girl's name on

	a slip of paper was found on the lake shore rocks near Addison. Eunice Rawlings lived in an apartment on Roscoe near Josephine Ross and Frances Brown. Does it make any sense that she would end her life by voluntarily jumping into the frigid waters of Lake Michigan in the middle of the winter? This is not a typical method for a young woman to commit suicide. Two days before she disappeared, Eunice was out looking for employment. It sounds a little odd for someone contemplating suicide to be out looking for a job. Could she have been forced to write the suicide note that indicated she could be found in Lake Michigan?
19. On June 13, 1949, Louise Margaret Springer was strangled to death in Los Angeles with a white sash cord. On July 16, 1947, Marion Newton was strangled to death in Los Angeles with a thin wire or cord (Note 28, p. 407).	**19**. Two sash cords, apparently blood-stained were found in the alley near the Suzanne Degnan crime scene. "A loop of wire with a handkerchief was found north of the Degnan home" (Note 29, p. 49).
20. The killer of Jeanne French wrote on her body in **red lipstick**, February 11, 1947, in Los Angeles.	**20**. The killer of Frances Brown wrote on her living room wall in **red lipstick**, December 10, 1945 in Chicago.

21. Los Angeles County Coroner Chief Surgeon, Fredrick Newbarr, noted that Elizabeth Short's stomach "was filled with greenish **brown granular material**, mostly fecal matter and other particles" (Emphasis added).	**21**. The Pathological Report on Suzanne Degnan dated January 8, 1946, indicated that "the mucosa of the posterior pharynx, the aryepiglottic fold epiglottis and larynx were swollen and wrinkled pinkish red in color and covered with a **brownish granular viscid material**" (Emphasis added).
22. Following the murder of the Black Dahlia, the *Los Angeles Herald Express* received the following in pasted letters, "To Los Angeles Herald Express **I will Give up** in Dahlia Killing **If I Get 10 years.** Don't try to find me" (Emphasis added).	**22**. Shortly after the murder of Suzanne Degnan, Chicago Police Chief Walter G. Storm received the following communication: "Why don't you catch me. If you don't ketch me soon, I will cummit suicide. There is a reward out for me. **How much do I get if I give myself up.** When do I get that 20,000 dollars they wanted from the Degnan girl at 5901 Kenmore Avenue. You may find me at the Club Tavern at 738 E. 63rd St. known as Charlie the Greek's or at Conway's Tavern at 6247 Cottage Grove Av. Please hurry now" (Emphasis added). Jack Anderson Wilson was an alcoholic. In each series of murders bars become a meeting place.

Consider this:

Cleveland Torso Murders: Victim # 8, Rose Wallace. On the afternoon of her disappearance, Merylo learned Wallace had been doing her laundry when a friend arrived and informed her that an unidentified man wanted to see her at an East 19th and Scoville bar close to her home.

William Heirens Case: The killer wrote "you may find me at the Club Tavern at 738 East 63rd St. known as Charlie the Greeks or at Conway's Tavern at 6247 Cottage Grove Avenue.

Black Dahlia Murder: Jack Anderson Wilson met John Gilmore at Harold's 555 Club in Los Angeles. "In Indianapolis he (Wilson) mentions this person working in a bar called the Pair of Jacks and another joint Jud Logan's Bar in the same area."

Both individuals wrote a letter shortly after committing a murder. Both wrote the same content in their letters:

1. One wrote: "If I get ten years." The other one wrote: "How much do I get"
2. The other one wrote: "If I give up." The other one wrote: "I will give up."

Keep in mind that both killers murdered and bisected a human shortly before writing the letter (if in fact the letters were written by the killers). Both killers wrote a limited number of short communications, so with this in mind the similarities are striking.

Take notice the sequence of events in the Black Dahlia case that are followed by a message written by her killer:

1. On January 14, 1947, Elizabeth Short is murdered and professionally bisected in one location and then secretly transported to another location where her body is deposited.
2. Soon after her murder the killer writes a note to the *Los Angeles Herald-Express*.
3. The note reads:
   To Los Angeles Herald-Express
   I will give up in
   Dahlia killing if I *Get*
   10 years
   Don't try to find me (Emphasis added)

Now compare this to the sequence of events in the Suzanne Degnan case:

1. On January 7, 1946, Suzanne is taken secretly from one location to another where she is professionally dismembered and then taken to other locations where her body parts are discarded.
2. Soon after her murder her killer writes a note (ransom note) that reads:

   Get $20,000
   Reddy &
   Waite
   For Word
   Do not notify
   FBI or
   Police
   Bills in 5's &
   10's (Emphasis added)

Both messages start out with a statement that includes the word "get" and end with a command that included either the word "don't" or the words "do not."

Here is another interesting comparison:

A fifth note sent by the Black Dahlia Avenger on January 29, 1947, provided;
A certain girl is going to get same as E.S.
got if she squeals on us.
We're going to Mexico City-*catch* us if
You *can* (Emphasis added)

Now compare this to the red lipstick message written on the wall of Frances Brown's apartment following her murder on December 10, 1945:

For heavens
sake *catch* me
before I kill more
I **can**not control myself (Emphasis added)

Note # 4 from the Black Dahlia Avenger to the *Los Angeles Herald-Express* reads as follows:

To Los Angeles Herald Express
I will give up in
Dahlia killing *if I get*
10 years
Don't try to find me (Emphasis added)

Following the murder of Suzanne Degnan, Chicago Police Chief Walter G. Storms received the following communication:

Why *don't* you catch me. *If* you
don't ketch me soon *I will*
cummit suicide. There is a
reward out for me. How much
do *I get if I* give
myself up. When do *I get*
that 20,000 dollars they
wanted from that Degnan girl at
5901 Kenmore Avenue.
You may find me at the Club
Tavern at 738 E. 63rd St
Known as Charlie the Greeks. Or
At Conway's tavern
At 6247 Cottage Grove
Av
Please hurry now.

(It is interesting to note that the Degnan home was located:

5943 Kenmore Avenue.

The place of dismemberment:

5901 Winthrop Avenue.)

23. On January 30, 1947, The Black Dahlia Avenger wrote a pasted note to Captain Donahoe: "Have changed my mind, **you** would not give me a square deal. Dahlia Killing justified" (Emphasis added).	**23**. In the letter to Chief Storm, following the murder of Suzanne Degnan, the killer wrote, "**You** may find me at the club Tavern . . ." (Emphasis added)

24. The nude body of Rosenda Josephine Mondragon (Los Angeles, July 8, 1947) was found with a silk stocking wrapped around her neck. The body of Geneva Hilliker Ellroy was found June 22, 1958, in El Monte, California, with a nylon stocking wrapped around her neck (Note 28, p. 418). Elspeth Long was found January 22, 1959, in La Puente, California strangled to death. The suspect used Long's nylon as a ligature (Note 28, p. 420).	**24.** Josephine Ross had a dress wrapped around her head securely tied with a silk stocking.
25. On January 14, 1947, the Black Dahlia is murdered in Los Angeles. Twenty-seven days later on February 10, French is brutally murdered and her killer writes on her body in red lipstick.	**25.** On December 10, 1946, Frances Brown is brutally murdered in Chicago. Her killer left a message on her living room wall in red lipstick. Twenty-seven days later Suzanne Degnan is murdered and dismembered.
26. At 7:30 p. m. Sunday, February 9, 1947, the day before she was killed, Jeanne French was seen in the company of two men. Waitress Christine Studnicka described one of them as having, "dark hair and a small moustache." Studnicka observed that the two men appeared, "to be arguing over which one was going to accompany the victim.	**26.** On the night Suzanne was murdered, Cecelia Flynn heard the sound of two men arguing on the street below. Several months earlier two men had driven up to the Degnan house and attempted to force Suzanne into the car with them as she was returning home for lunch. Her screams had brought neighbors to the win

On February 14, 1948, Viola Norton was approached near the east-southeast city limits of Los Angeles by two men in a car. The two men, both appearing to be approximately 40 years of age, approached her in a car and asked her to get in. "Viola was kidnapped by the two men, beaten savagely about the face and head. Her skull was fractured with a tire iron, and the two men left her for dead in an isolated area just four blocks from where the body of Elizabeth Short had been found thirteen months earlier."

Twelve hours later, Gladys Eugenia Kern was found at 4217 Cromwell Avenue. She had been stabbed with an eight-inch jungle knife that was found in the kitchen sink wrapped in a man's bloody handkerchief. Two witnesses, Japanese gardeners working across the street from the murder scene at the hillside mansion, were located by the police and told of seeing "two men coming out of the mansion, and down the steps on Saturday afternoon, the day of the murder."

dow and the men had fled, but it seemed more than coincidental.

27. "The broom was where the mop was and the mop and the rags were used and then these things went down and were put in the incinerator and lighted on fire" (Transcript of Jack Anderson Wilson on file at the Los Angeles County Sheriff's Department).	**27.** "Charles Wilson, head of the police crime laboratory, disclosed that bits of cotton fabric saturated with blood found in the laundry room drain of the apartment house at 5901 Winthrop Avenue indicated that the basement room in which police believe the girl's body was dismembered subsequently had been mopped."
28. Following the murder of the Black Dahlia, her killer washed her body in a tub.	**28.** Following the murder of Frances Brown, her killer washed her body in a tub.
29. Jack Anderson Wilson was employed in Los Angeles as a sign hanger for Cogar Brothers on Bixtel Street.	**29.** A length of picture wire drawn into a noose was associated with the murder of Suzanne Degnan.
30. Los Angeles County Sheriff's Detective Joel Lesnick indicated that "Wilson (Jack Anderson Wilson) seemed to prefer the company of lowlifes, the moochers and apparently second-rate female impersonators. He referred to one being connected with a murder in Indianapolis and he mentions this person working in a bar called the Pair of Jacks and another joint, Jud Logan's Bar in the same area."	**30.** In the communication received by Chicago Chief of Police Walter G. Storm the individual stated: "You may find me at the Club Tavern at 738 E. 63rd Street known as Charlie the Greeks or at Conway's Tavern At 6247 Cottage Grove Av. "

31. Cleveland's director of Public Safety, Elliot Ness's assistant, was John R. Flynn.	**31**. Louis and Cecelia Flynn occupied the second floor of the building at 5943 Kenmore in Chicago where the Degnan family lived. Cecelia Flynn was also involved with the OPA.
32. A pasted note, possibly mailed by the killer of the Black Dahlia, was addressed to Los Angeles Captain Donahoe, following her murder.	**32**. Chicago Police Chief Storm received a note in 1946, following the murder of Suzanne Degnan, possibly mailed by her killer.
33. "Of the times the informant met with Smith, he said the man never referred to Elizabeth Short by name. 'He did not call her Elizabeth, or the Short girl, or Beth. He would say **her**, or like he would say **her**, who we're talking about'" (Emphasis added) (Note 27, p. 181).	**33**. Suzanne Degnan's killer wrote on the reverse side of the ransom note, "BuRN This FoR **heR** SAfeTY" (Note 28, photo following p. 200).
34. Wrote large letter before small letter in same word of a note: "To HeralD-EXPess BUiLD-iNG1234 TReNton.St. Zone is LoS ANGele" (Note 20, p. 178)	**34**. Wrote large letter before small letter in the same word in the ransom note (See No. 33 above).
35. Letter "P" in word "EXPRESS" on the Black Dahlia Avenger's envelope to *Los Angeles Herald Express,* postmarked Jan. 28, 1947, is similar to letter "P" in the Suzanne Degnan ransom note. (Note 28, p. 175)	**35**. Letter "P" in the Suzanne Degnan ransom note is similar to letter "P" on the Black Dahlia Avenger's envelope postmarked January 28, 1946 (Note 29, photo following p. 200).

36. While in Indianapolis Jack Anderson Wilson associated with female impersonators. Twenty-one-year-old Dorothy French had befriended Elizabeth in Los Angeles. Elizabeth stayed with her for a while. After the murder, Dorothy recalled an incident that took place shortly after Elizabeth was killed: "A couple of days later some people came to our door and knocked. There was a man and a woman, and another man was waiting in a car parked on the street in front of the house. Beth became very frightened—she seemed to get panicky and didn't want to see the people or answer the door. They finally went back to the car and drove away. Even our neighbors thought all of this was very suspicious" (Note 29, p. 110).	**36.** On the night of her abduction a witness saw a woman carrying a large bundle in both arms in the vicinity of the Degnan home. "She got into what seemed to be a waiting automobile where a balding man sat behind the wheel."
37. The FBI suspected that Jack Anderson Wilson's friend "Eddie," was involved in an earlier kidnapping."	**37.** Suzanne Degnan was kidnapped. At first the detectives suspected that two men might have been involved in the kidnapping.
38. Captain Jack Donahoe was of the opinion that a woman may have been the murderer based on the nature of the injuries and the spite with which they were inficted. (Possibly a female impersonator?)	**38.** In the murder of Frances Brown detectives speculated that a woman was involved because of wording in the lipstick message: "For Heavens Sake." Frances Brown and Josephine Ross were both viciously attacked.

39. On the afternoon of January 14, 1947, Elizabeth Short was identified by Los Angeles police officer Myrl McBride as the woman who ran up to her "sobbing in terror" and told her that "someone wants to kill me." Short said that she had come from a bar up the street and had just run into an ex-boyfriend. Officer McBride said that Short told her she "lives in terror" of a former serviceman whom she had just met in a bar up the street. McBride added, "She told me the suitor had threatened to kill her if he found her with another man." McBride said she walked the victim back into the Main Street Bar, where she recovered her purse. A short time later, McBride again observed the victim "reenter the bar, and then emerge with two men and a woman" (Note 28, p. 236-237).	**39**. On the night of Suzanne's abduction and murder Cecelia Flynn recalled hearing two men talking in the street near the Degnan home.
40. Jeanne French's killer draped her blue coat and her red dress over her body before leaving the scene (Note 28, p. 190). Evelyn Winters was found with her dress wrapped around her neck (Note 28,	**40**. Josephine Ross' head was wrapped in her daughter's red dress (Note 29, p. 35). Frances Brown was found draped over her tub, half covered with a housecoat and her pajamas looped around her neck.

p. 403). Louise Springer's body was found draped and covered with a white cape-type material which belonged to the victim (Note 28, p. 411). Geneva Ellroy's killer placed her dark blue coat over the lower portion of her body (Note 28, p. 418).	
41. The cause of Evelyn Winter's death was listed as "blunt force trauma causing a concussion and hemorrhage to the brain (Note 28, p. 402). Viola Norton's skull was fractured with a tire iron (Note 28, p. 410).	**41.** Josephine Ross was hit repeatedly in the head with a heavy object. Her killer stuck a knife four times in her throat (Note 29, p. 35).
42. Following the murder of the Black Dahlia a witness by the name of John Jiroudek told detectives he saw Elizabeth Short at the corner of Hollywood Boulevard and Highland Avenue. She was a passenger in a 1937 Ford Sedan. A blond female was driving the car (Note 28, p. 236).	**42.** On January 7, 1946, on the morning of the kidnapping, a witness by the name of Robert Reisner saw a man and a woman in a "1940 or 1941 Ford four door sedan, and the first two numbers of the 1945 Illinois license were 11 (Note 29, p. 47-48). The design of a 1937 Ford sedan, and a 1940 Ford sedan, although slightly modified, were very similar. Keep in mind that the witness reports were made over six years after the date of the crimes in 1946, and 1947, respectfully and one of the vehicles was sited after dark at 2:00 a.m.

In Appendix D to the book *Childhood Shadows: The Hidden Story of the Black Dahlia Murder*, author Mary Pacios included a list of major suspects in the Black Dahlia case.

The Cleveland Butcher is listed on page 249 and Jack Anderson Wilson is listed on page 250. Unknown at the time her book was written, these two suspects, identified on back-to-back pages, might have been the same person. Jack Anderson Wilson might have been the Mad Butcher of Kingsbury Run, the killer of the Black Dahlia and more than likely the killer of Jeanne French, Georgette Bauerdorf, Josephine Ross, Frances Brown, Suzanne Degnan and several other individuals during the 1930's and 1940's.

Chapter 4

THE PHANTOM KILLER OF TEXARKANA

This is the true story about one of the most feared and elusive serial killers of all time. It begins on a cold night in February, 1946, in Texarkana one hundred seventy five miles northeast of Dallas, Texas. Texarkana is now located on Interstate 30 between Dallas, Texas, and Conway, Arkansas, directly across the eastern Texas State line. In 1946, together with its twin city, Texarkana, Texas, its population was about forty thousand. On February 22, 1946, 19-year-old Mary Jeanne Larey attended a local Texarkana movie theater with her friend, 24-year-old Jimmy Hollis. After the movie was over the couple drove down and parked off Richmond Road. Mary Jeane's report of what happened next appeared the next day in the *Texarkana Gazette:*

> Jimmy and I parked about 11:45 P.M. just off Richmond Road about a mile north of Beverly. We had been there about ten minutes when a man walked up. He wore a white mask over his head with cutout places for his eyes and mouth. He was pointing a flashlight and pistol at us. He came up on the driver's side of the car, shined his flashlight into our faces and told Jimmy something like this 'I don't want to kill you fellow, so do what I say.' We both got out of the car on Jim-

> my's side and stood by the man. The man then told Jimmy to 'take off your (expletive deleted) britches.' I told Jimmy to please take them off because I thought if he did, we wouldn't be hurt. After Jimmy had taken off his corduroy trousers, the man hit Jimmy twice on the head. The noise was so loud I thought Jimmy had been shot. I learned later that the sound was his skull cracking. I picked up Jimmy's pants and took the billfold out of his pocket. I said 'Look, he doesn't have any money.' The man told me I was lying. He said that I had a purse but that I told him I had not. Then he hit me. I thought with a piece of iron pipe. He knocked me to the ground but I managed to get up.

The man told her to run. She went towards the ditch, but he told her to go down the road. She passed an old car parked along the road. Mary Jeanne recalled: "Just after I got past the car the man overtook me and asked me why I was running. I told him because he told me to run. He called me a liar again and then I knew he was going to kill me." The man struck her again and she fell to the ground (Note 35). He sat on top of her then coughed, then wheezed, then snorted like a bull (Note 34). He did not rape her but she said he "abused her terribly." News reports later indicated that he used the barrel of his gun to sexually assault her. Both Mary Jeanne Larey and Jimmy Hollis survived the attack. Hollis later gave the police a statement. There was one key difference in Mary Jeanne's and Jimmy's account. She thought he was a light-skinned black man. Mary Jeanne "believed he was a Negro because of the way he pronounced the curse words he growled at her" (Note 36, Sunday, June 2, 1946). Jimmy thought he was a dark-tanned white man. Mary Jeanne described her attacker as a six-foot tall male.

A little over one month later on March 24, 1946, local war veteran, 29-year-old Richard Griffin and 17-year-old Polly Ann Moore, an employee of the Red River Arsenal, were found murdered in a car near Highway 67 on South Robinson Road one mile out of the Texarkana city limits. Their car and bodies were found not far from the Highway 67 nightspot called Club Dallas. Did someone stalk them from Club Dallas? Griffin and Moore were both shot in the back of the head. Their bodies were found in the rear seat of Griffin's car on the outskirts of Texarkana (*Washington Times-Herald*, April 15, 1946). According to Arkansas State Trooper Max Tackett, Moore had been killed in front of the car on a blanket and placed in the vehicle after she had been murdered. The couple was last seen around 10:00 P.M. the previous Saturday night in a West Seventh Street café where they ate dinner with Griffin's sister, Eleanor Griffin (*Texarkana Gazette*). Bullets found at the scene of the murders matched those fired from a .32 caliber pistol believed to be a Colt that was used in other of the Phantom killings.

One month later on April 13, 1946, Betty Jo Booker, a pretty 15-year-old brunette, was playing her saxophone with a band in a high school orchestra called the Rhthmaires at a local VFW dance hall at Fourth and Oak Streets in Texarkana. The dance was for "young people" (FBI Report on Phantom Killings). At about 1:30 A.M. 16-year-old James Paul Martin picked up Betty Jo after the dance and drove her to Spring Lake Park in Texarkana. The next day Martin's lifeless body was found on the side of Cork Lane north of Interstate 30. Betty Jo Booker's body was later located in a wooded area about a mile and a half away north of Interstate 30. Both victims had been shot dead with a .32 caliber Colt revolver (*Texarkana Gazette*). Bette Jo's saxophone was missing but was located four months later in a marshy area in the vicinity where her body was discovered. According to Jerry Akins, a member of the Rhythmaires Band, someone knew it was there and told authorities where to look for it. Did some other young person in the 15-16 age bracket, who attended the young people's dance, stalk and kill Booker and Griffin, or was someone waiting to stalk them as they left the dance?

In May, 1946, in Texarkana, Mrs. Aleene Peavy, age 30, was shot dead and Mrs. J. C. Johnson, age 42, was in critical condition from gunshot wounds. Mrs. Peavy had been shot in the head and died instantly. According to Bowie County Sheriff, W.H. Presley, "Mrs. Johnston was shot in the head, the bullet entering on the right side near the ear and leaving through the top of her skull." A revolver "of small caliber" was found beside Mrs. Johnston's body. Officers did not believe the attacks were the work of the Phantom Killer.

The Phantom Murders occurred on weekends. Each murder was approximately one month apart. On May 3, 1946, the Phantom Killer struck again, this time nine and one-tenth miles north of Texarkana on U.S. Highway 67. A 36-year-old farmer by the name of Virgil Starks sat quietly reading his newspaper when someone fired two shots from a .22 caliber semiautomatic from three feet through a closed front porch window of his farm house. Stark was struck in the back of his head and died instantly. His wife, Katy Starks was also shot by the same assailant through her right cheek and jaw but managed to escape and fled to a neighboring farmhouse owned by A. V. Prater. Three twenty-two long rifle Super X cartridge casings were found at the scene, together with a questionable footprint impression made with a left shoe, the size of which was approximately 9 ½ to 10 ½. The Texas Rangers investigated the string of unsolved Phantom Murders. Captain Manuel (Lone Wolf) Gonzaullas was the lead investigator. The Rangers were joined by at least forty-seven police officers, including Bowie County Sheriff W.H. "Bill" Presley, the Federal Bureau of Investigation and Sheriff W.E. Davis of Arkansas' Taylor County.

At the time detectives had very few clues to work with.

The Dallas Morning News reported on February 24, 1946, that "a woman clad in a nightgown, a housecoat and a street coat was found shot to death on the sidewalk in the 3600 block of Wendelkin shortly after midnight Monday." The lady's name was Beatrice Graham Thraser. "A .32 revolver with one shot fired was found lying at her feet." "The woman's crumpled body lay approximately in the middle of the block on the east side of the street. A single bullet hole was behind her right ear."

Texas Rangers had arrested a suspect in the Phantom Murders by the name of Youell Swinney. Swinney had a long arrest record. He was eventually convicted of car theft and was sentenced. Authorities questioned whether Swinney was the Phantom Killer because when he was in jail two murders, similar to the Phantom Murders, took place at Dania Beach in Fort Lauderdale, Florida. Edythe Elaine Eldridge, age 24, from South Chatham, Massachusetts, and Lawrence Overman Hogan, age 23, of Miami, Florida, formerly of Roanoke, Virginia, were found shot to death near Hogan's parked car on a lonely, secluded area on Dania Beach near the ocean. The weapon used was a .32 caliber.

In February, 2006, I received the complete FBI Report on the Phantom Murders under the Freedom of Information Act. Based on the information I have researched regarding the Phantom Murders, it is my understanding that most of the information contained in the FBI Report was never made public and, unless released in federal court at a later date, I doubt that anyone at a later date copied the non-disclosed information. According to the FBI Report on the Phantom Murders, a Mr. Clark Brown of 1417 Locust Street, Texarkana, the stepfather of Betty Jo Booker, received a letter and envelope after the murder of his stepdaughter. The letter was dated December 19, 1946, and was postmarked at Texarkana, Arkansas, on December 12, 1946, at 4:30 PM.

DL #9-616

found on the morning of April 14, 1946, at approximately 6:30 AM near Spring Lake Park north of Texarkana, Texas. The victim's car was found approximately 1½ miles southeast of his body. The body of BETTY JOE BOOKER was discovered at approximately 11:30 AM on the same date in a wooded area southwest of the body of JAMES PAUL MARTIN. BETTY JOE BOOKER had been shot twice; once through the left side of the nose and the other through the left fifth rib. PAUL MARTIN had been shot four times; once through the nose to the left of the nasal arch, another bullet through the left level of the fourth rib, a third bullet wound in the right hand, and the fourth bullet in the right part of his head to the right of the middle line level of the upper portion of the ear. A .32 automatic was again used, and the gun is identical with the gun used in the first double murder. BETTY JOE BOOKER had definitely been assaulted. These cases remain unsolved.

b6

b7C

At approximately 9:15 PM on May 3, 1946, VIRGIL STARKS, a farmer and special deputy sheriff of Miller County, Arkansas, residing approximately 9½ miles north of Texarkana, Arkansas, was killed instantly while sitting in his home. [redacted] The gun used was a .22 caliber similar to a Colt Woodsman pistol. This case is also unsolved.

The stepfather of BETTY JOE BOOKER is CLARK BROWN, an employee of the Gifford-Hill Company, Texarkana, Texas, and who formerly resided in the Sussex Downs Addition of Texarkana, Texas, until approximately October of 1946, at which time he moved to 1417 Locust Street, Texarkana, Arkansas. Since December, 1946, BROWN has received the following letters:

1st Letter - Postmarked: Texarkana, Arkansas-Texas
December 17, 1946
At 4:30 PM

Addressed to: Mr. Clark Brown
1417 Locust St
City

"MR. BROWN:

THIS IS ADDRESSED TO YOU PERSONALLY AND IS ONLY TO HELP YOU AND MRS. BROWN. THE FOLLOWING INFORMATION IS CONFIDENTIAL AND IF YOU DO NOT CARE FOR IT BURN IT UP IMMEDIATELY. CANNOT COME TO EITHER OF YOU PERSONALLY. THIS CAR NUMBER AND PARTIES WAS SEEN BY YOUNG GIRL WHO DOES NOT AND WILL NOT COME TO YOU

- 2 -

DL #9-616

"ON ACCOUNT OF FEAR AND FOR HER SAKE IF NOT USED PLEASE BURN. INFORMATION WAS GIVEN TO BOTH LAWS HERE AND ANOTHER AUTHORITY SO BE CAREFUL AND FOR YOUR BENEFIT AND SUCCESS IN THIS USE HIGHER AUTHORITIES. [redacted] [redacted] [redacted] AND THAT IS WHY PROTECTED. KEEP THIS INFORMATION CLOSE AND SORRY CANNOT SIGN AND SEE YOU PLEASE BURN IF OF NO VALUE BUT IT IS IF YOU ONLY KNEW IT. BE CAREFUL AND IF USED TRY HIGHER AUTHORITIES AND PLEASE DO NOT QUESTION THIS AT ALL. THIS IS ONLY GIVEN FOR YOUR SAKES AND NOTHING WANTED OR ASKED ONLY SUCCESS IF USED. MANY KIND THOUGHTS FOR BOTH OF YOU AND USE CONFIDENTIAL"

* * * *

2nd Letter - Postmarked: Texarkana, Arkansas-Texas
January 3, 1947
At 6:00 PM

b6
b7C

Addressed to: Mr. Clark Brown
1417 Locust Street
City

"AS A FOLLOW UP OF LETTER WRITTEN TO YOU SOME FEW DAYS AGO. THE CAR LICENSE NUMBER GIVEN YOU WAS RIGHT AND THIS CAR HAS RECENTLY BEEN SOLD. ALSO ASK HOW COME FBI TO CHECK BLOCK AT [redacted] SOME TIME AGO AND WHO WITHIN THIS WAS RELATED IN A MANNER TO THESE PEOPLE AT FARM. ALSO HOW WAS GUN TRANSFERRED TO NOT BE IN JUST ONE HAND AND IS STILL KEPT GOING FROM [redacted] [redacted] WITH VIRGIL STARKS JUST ONE OR TWO HOURS BEFORE HIS DEATH. ALSO HIGHER AUTHORITIES THAN THESE HERE WOULD BE THE ONES FOR YOU TO GO FOR HELP. ALSO BOTH LETTERS HAVE BEEN WRITTEN BECAUSE WAS TOLD YOU HAD INFLUENCE WITH RIGHT AUTHORITIES AND PLEASE IF NOT USED WOULD YOU BE KIND ENOUGH TO BURN WHEN READ [redacted]

* * * *

3rd Letter - Postmarked: Texarkana, Arkansas-Texas
March 21, 1947
At 5:30 PM

- 3 -

Typed in upper CASE

DL #9-616

Addressed to: Mr. Clark Brown
1417 Locust Street
Texarkana, Arkansas

"SORRY YOU DID NOT BELIEVE IN LETTERS SENT YOU LAST YEAR AS YOU EITHER DID NOT OR ELSE LONG TIME USING SAME. SEEMS IT WOULD BE SO EASY BY GIVEN GOOD INFORMATION AS GIVEN. THESE SAME PARTIES ARE STILL MOLESTING AND IF YOU HAD OF THOUGHT INFORMATION GIVEN YOU AS BENEFICIAL YOU WOULD HAVE CAUSED OTHER GIRLS LESS SUFFERING. BUT CANNOT BLAME YOU AND ONLY WISHED YOU HAD. OF COURSE IT IS BETTER TO GO FACE TO FACE, BUT IN THIS CASE THAT COULD NOT BE DONE AND SORRY HEARTACHE AS WELL AS YOURS CANNOT BE EASED. RIGHT PARTIES COULD OF RUN THIS DOWN. MONEY WAS NOT AND IS NOT NOW THE INTENTION OF THIS AND REMEMBER [redacted] THIS IS NOT MADE UP. WHY IS THIS WRITTEN? WELL IF YOU ONLY COULD OF HAD RIGHT PARTIES TO LOOKED INTO THIS A BODY OF A YOUNG GRIL WHO IS STILL LIVING BARELY THOUGH WOULD CEASE CRYING AND HURTING. NOT FOR A MINUTE WOULD I APPEAL TO YOUR SYMPATHY ONLY SORRY YOU CANNOT USE THE INFORMATION GIVEN. PLEASE DO IF YOU CAN."

b6
b7C

****

4th Letter - Postmarked: Texarkana, Arkansas-Texas
May 2, 1947
At 5:30 PM

Addressed to: Mr. Clark Brown
1419 Locust St
City Personal

"SOMETIME AGO YOU WERE WRITTEN AND GIVEN VALUABLE INFORMATION AND NOTHING SEEMS TO COME OF IT. THE NAMES GIVEN YOU AND ALL WAS CONFIDENTIAL AND DO NOT MEAN TO SORRY OR REMIND YOU. MUST BE IF YOU TRIED TO FIND OUT THEY PLAYED INNOCENT. JUST A LITTLE WHILE BACK THERE WAS A DEATH OF A GIRL AND YOU NO DOUBT READ ABOUT IT THERE POSSIBLY WILL BE ANOTHER IF YOU HAVE ANY INFLUENCE WOULD BE SO GLAD YOU USE IT. MAYBE YOU

- 4 -

DL #9-616

"DID NOT RECEIVE LETTER WILL REPEAT NAMES GO TO HIGHER OFFICIALS AS THESE PEOPLE ARE HELPED BY THE LAW. [redacted] DO NOT BE MISLEAD ABOUT ANY OF THIS. ALL OF THIS WAS HEARD NEAR STARKS ALSO BLOOD NEAR MARTINDALE FARM THE NIGHT YOUR STEP FATHER KILLED THEY MET THERE LATER. NOT ALL THIS AT MURDERS BUT PLAYED THEIR PARTS AND ACCORDING TO ANY LAW WILL BE GUILTY DO NOT BE MISLEAD. KEEP THIS CONFIDENTIAL. BURN THIS JOT NAMES DOWN. [redacted] PLEASE IF YOU HAVE ANY INFLUENCE CARRY THIS TO HIGHER AUTHORITIES. DO NOT GIVE TO THESE HERE FOR THEY WILL TELL YOU NOTHING TO IT. YOU CAN SEE WHY CAN'T YOU. HURRY. MAYBE YOU DID NOT GET FORMER LETTERS THIS WILL BE LAST WRITTEN. WISH YOU COULD DO SOMETHING AS THAT WILL BE MORE. SYMPATHY WITH YOU AND YOURS BY MANY BE ASSURED OF THAT AND ONLY TOO GLAD TO HELP TO BRING JUSTICE DON'T THINK FOR ANY OTHER PURPOSE. KEEP THIS CONFIDENTIAL AND MANY THANKS IF YOU CAN DO ANYTHING ABOUT THIS."

b6

b7C

All of the above four letters have been typewritten in upper case and all except the letter postmarked March 21, 1947, have been submitted to the FBI Laboratory for examination.

Reference is made to the report of Special Agent [redacted] dated May 12, 1947, at Dallas, Texas, which sets out the details of the two extortion letters received by victim FEAGINS, one postmarked April 29, 1947, at 7:30 PM, and the other postmarked May 5, 1947, at 2:30 PM, both at Texarkana, Arkansas-Texas. These letters were also submitted to the FBI Laboratory for examination.

b6

b7C

By letter dated June 2, 1947, the FBI Laboratory advised that the two letters addressed to victim FEAGINS were prepared on the same machine as the typewriting appearing on the first letter and envelope addressed to Mr. CLARK BROWN. This is the letter postmarked December 17, 1946. The Laboratory also advised that they had concluded that the typewriting appearing on the letters addressed to Mr. BROWN bearing the postmarks of January 3, 1947 and May 2, 1947, were also prepared on the same machine. This typewriting corresponds with the Laboratory standards of Underwood elite type, spaced 12 letters to the inch. Type similar to this may be found on both Underwood

- 5 -

FBI Report in case DL #9-616 in the Phantom Murders; letters to Clark Brown, stepfather of Betty Jo Booker.

It is interesting to note the following with regard to the Clark Brown letter:

1. The letter was written by an unknown sender to the stepfather of a young girl who had been brutally murdered.
2. The letter was mailed to the stepfather almost exactly eight months after Betty Jo Booker was killed.
3. The letter was neatly typewritten.
4. The letter was typed entirely in upper case.
5. The first line of the letter begins with the words: "This is . . .".
6. The content of the letter is written as an offer to assist.
7. Nearly all of the Phantom attacks and murders occurred on weekends.

The FBI determined that an Underwood typewriter was used by the author of the Clark Brown letter in 1947. No latent fingerprints were found on the envelope or the letter.

Elmer Feagins lived close to Clark Brown at 3119 Locust Street, Texarkana, Arkansas. He received a letter mailed April 29, 1947, demanding three thousand dollars in cash to be delivered to Spring Lake Park, Texas. Later additional letters were mailed by the same suspect in the Booker/Martin murders to Elmer Feagins.

The following are excerpts from the FBI Report regarding the Brown and Feagin letters:

FBI Report: Phantom Murders

The three bullets referred to above as specimens Q11, Q12 and Q13 were found to be most similar to caliber .22 long rifle Western lubaloy bullets. These specimens were too mutilated to ascertain definitely the type of weapon from which they were fired. There is some indication, however, that they may have been fired from a weapon with a barrel having six lands and grooves with a left hand twist. This would indicate that they were fired from a caliber .22 Colt automatic pistol or caliber .22 Colt revolver. There are no individual microscopic markings present on these bullet specimens suitable for comparison purposes in the event a suspect weapon is recovered.

The three cartridge cases referred to above as specimens Q14 and Q15 are Western Super-X caliber .22 long or long rifle cartridge cases. These were compared microscopically with each other and it was possible to identify them as having been fired in the same weapon and that they have been loaded into and extracted from an auto loading weapon similar to the caliber .22 Colt Woodsman pistol.

As a result of grouping tests conducted on the human blood appearing on the pieces of linoleum, specimen Q1, it was ascertained that this blood was derived from an individual belonging to International Blood Group "O". The human blood contained in the two vials, specimens Q5 and Q6, was determined to have been derived from an individual belonging to International Blood Group "O". Two small spots of human blood were also found on the brown wrapping paper, specimen Q2; however, the amount of blood on this paper was too limited for a grouping determination. Preliminary chemical tests for blood were obtained on the right kitchen window curtain, specimen Q3, but the amount of stain thereon was too limited to confirm the presence of blood or to determine its origin. No blood was found on specimen Q4.

Traces of soil were found on the pieces of linoleum numbered 1, 2, and 3 and also on specimen Q3. The soil on the number 1 and 3 pieces of linoleum was different in color from K1 but was contaminated with blood which may have affected the color. The amounts were too small to analyze and compare. The soil removed from the number 2 piece of linoleum was different in color and other characteristics from K1 and did not come from the same source. The trace of soil on the curtain, Q3, was too small to compare with K1.

Specimen Q4 contained a trace of cobwebs and insect material and a small sliver of wood, the significance of which is not known. The pieces of linoleum numbered 4 and 5 contained no soil of value. No further material of significance was found on the curtains.

No hair was found in the folded paper, specimen Q7; however, one dark purple wool fiber was found in the cellophane wrapper in which the paper was contained. The source of this fiber is not known.

The questioned footprint impression listed above as Q10 was made with a left shoe, the size of which is approximately 9½ to 10½. From the submitted

PC-17228 Page 2

FBI Report Phantom Murders

DL #9-616

portable and standard typewriters. On special request type similar to this may be found on other makes of typewriters. The letter also advised that the typewriting on the letter to Mr. BROWN postmarked December 17, 1946, and the two letters to Mr. FEAGINS corresponds with the Laboratory standards of Underwood Pica type, spaced 10 letters to the inch. This style of type is usually found on various types of Underwood typewriters. On special request type similar to this may be found on other makes of typewriters.

No latent prints of value were developed on the letters and envelopes addressed to Mr. E. E. FEAGINS. However, the Laboratory advised by letter dated May 28, 1947, in the case entitled "UNKNOWN SUBJECT; BETTY JOE BOOKER; JAMES PAUL MARTIN - VICTIMS; MURDER, April 14, 1946, TEXARKANA, TEXAS; POLICE COOPERATION", that one latent palm print had been developed on the typewritten message beginning "Sometime ago you were written and given valuable..." which was received by Mr. CLARK BROWN with the letter postmarked Texarkana, Arkansas-Texas, May 2, 1947.

All of the envelopes used in the six letters are large size stamped envelopes that can be purchased at the Post Office, with the exception of the letter postmarked December 17, 1946, to Mr. CLARK BROWN. This envelope appears to be a personal envelope. The paper used in writing the messages appears to be regular typewriting paper 8½ inches wide, but in each instance a portion of the paper has been torn and only part of the sheet sent each time. The only exception to this is the letter to FEAGINS postmarked April 29, 1947, which appears to have been written on a scratch pad of some type, and the bottom of the sheet has also been torn as the other sheets. The only paper bearing any watermark is the message contained in the envelope addressed to BROWN postmarked March 21, 1947, and this paper bears the watermark "Atlantic Bond". This letter and this envelope have been secured from the Sheriff's Office, Texarkana, Texas, and are being forwarded to the FBI Laboratory for examination.

It should be noted that none of the individuals mentioned in the letters to Mr. BROWN have previously been considered suspects in the murder cases by the local officers. It should also be noted that Mr. BROWN moved to the Locust Street address in October of 1946 and received his first letter postmarked December 17, 1946. Mr. FEAGINS moved to 3119 Locust Street on April 2, 1947, and received his first letter postmarked April 29, 1947. It should also be pointed out that the first letter to FEAGINS instructed him to [redacted] the proposed "pay-off spot". It should be noted that this location is only approximately 200 yards from where the car being used by victim BOOKER and MARTIN was abandoned near Spring Lake Park, and that it is the opinion of the investigating officers from the evidence secured that the subject of the murder cases first approached victims

b6
b7C

- 6 -

FBI - LITTLE ROCK MAY 2, 1947 5-45P CST HHB

DIRECTOR - URGENT

b6
b7C

UNSUB, E. E. FEAGINS, THREE ONE ONE NINE LOCUST ST., TEXARKANA, ARK. - VICTIM, EXTORTION..... VICTIM RECEIVED LETTER MAILED APRIL TWENTYNINE, SEVEN THIRTY PM, TEXARKANA, ARK-TEX., DEMANDING THREE THOUSAND DOLLARS IN CASH TO BE DELIVERED TO SPRING LAKE PARK, TEXAS, BETWEEN EIGHT AND [redacted] EIGHT FIFTEEN TODAY. LETTER TYPEWRITTEN AND REQUESTED VICTIM BRING MONEY TO PARK [redacted] [redacted] AND AFTER LEAVING MONEY AT DESIGNATED SPOT, TO DRIVE BACK HOME [redacted] LETTER RECEIVED BY VICTIM APRIL THIRTIETH BUT ONLY ADVISED POLICE THREE PM TODAY. VICTIM NOT ABLE TO PAY RANSOM BUT WILLING TO CARRY OUT DIRECTIONS WITH EXCEPTION OF [redacted] [redacted] ONE FLOYD KILCREASE, TEXARKANA, ARK., SUSPECT DUE TO DEALINGS WITH FEAGINS RE PURCHASE OF HOME BY FEAGINS. KILCREASE KNOWN TO BE HEAVY DRINKER AND PRESENTLY HAVING DOMESTIC TROUBLES. PAY-OFF SPOT BEING COVERED BY AGENTS THIS OFFICE AND DALLAS OFFICE WITH ASSISTANCE OF LOCAL POLICE, ARK. AND TEXAS SIDES. BUREAU WILL BE KEPT ADVISED.

MORLEY

RECORDED & INDEXED 62-80844-102

EX-37

A AND H

58 MAY 16 1947 FBI WASH-DC CCW

cc. Mr. Ladd

Mr. Tolson
Mr. E. A. Tamm
Mr. Clegg
Mr. Glavin
Mr. Ladd
Mr. Nichols
Mr. Rosen
Mr. Tracy
Mr. Carson
Mr. Egan
Mr. Gurnea
Mr. Harbo
Mr. Hendon
Mr. Pennington
Mr. Quinn Tamm
Mr. Nease
Miss Gandy

FEDERAL BUREAU OF INVESTIGATION

Form No. 1
THIS CASE ORIGINATED AT LITTLE ROCK, ARKANSAS FILE NO. 9-616 MJH

REPORT MADE AT	DATE WHEN MADE	PERIOD FOR WHICH MADE	REPORT MADE BY
DALLAS, TEXAS	5-12-47	5-2 & 6-47	b6 b7C

TITLE	CHARACTER OF CASE
UNKNOWN SUBJECT; ELMER EDWARD FEAGINS - VICTIM	EXTORTION

SYNOPSIS OF FACTS: Victim, a resident of Texarkana, Arkansas, received note 4-30-47 instructing him to leave $3,000 in Spring Lake Park, Texarkana, Texas, on Friday, 5-2-47, at 8:15__. Surveillance of pay-off negative. Victim then received second note on 5-6-47, advising him that his accusations were wrong. No additional instructions as to pay-off received. Notes forwarded to FBI Laboratory.

\- RUC -

DETAILS:

Mr. ELMER EDWARD FEAGINS, 3119 Locust Street, Texarkana, Arkansas, contacted the writer at the Resident Agency, Texarkana, Texas, at approximately 3:00 PM, on May 2, 1947. He furnished the writer with a stamped envelope addressed to E. E. FEAGINS, 3119 Locust Street, City, bearing the postmark "Texarkana, Ark-Tex, 7:30 PM, April 29, 1947". Mr. FEAGINS advised that he received the envelope and the enclosed note on the morning of April 30, 1947, at his residence in Texarkana, Arkansas. He did not decide to report the matter until May 2, 1947. Enclosed in the envelope was the following typewritten note:

"WHEN YOU HAVE BEEN A RAIL ROADER YOUR SELF YOU NO DOUBT UNDERSTAND RAILROADING. SINCE YOU HAVE DONE THIS THEN YOU UNDERSTAND THE GAME. SINCE THIS IS THE CASE YOU DID IT IN THE PAST WILL ASK FOR RET URN WITH INTEREST. AT THE SPRING LAKE PARK VAULT AFTER ENTERING GATE AT HEAD OF SPRING AT VAULT ON EAST SIDE PUT THIS SPONDULUX. IN AN OILCLOTH OF DARK COLOR AND THEN TIED WITH DARK STRING CAN'T FIND PAINT OILCLOTH THIS AMOUNT OF MONEY IN AS SMALL BUNDLE

G. L. R. -2

APPROVED AND FORWARDED: SPECIAL AGENT IN CHARGE

DO NOT WRITE IN THESE SPACES

62-80864-105

RECORDED & INDEXED 132

COPIES DESTROYED
11 NOV 16 1964

COPIES OF THIS REPORT
3 - Bureau
3 - Little Rock (Enc.)
2 - Dallas

62 MAY 20 1947

COPY IN FILE

F B I
31 MAY 16 1947

EX-27

U. S. GOVERNMENT PRINTING OFFICE 7—2084

DL #9-616

"AS POSSIBLE IN AS LARGE AMOUNT OF MONEY AS POSSIBLE. LARGE BUNDLE SO AS TO NOT MAKE POSSIBLE. PUT THIS ON FRIDAY OF THIS WEEK BETWEEN EIGHT AND EIGHT FIFTEEN [redacted] [redacted] THEN LEAVE GO HOME STAY QUIET. WITHOUT ALLOWING ANYONE TO KNOW ABOUT THIS IN ANY WAY YOU KNOW WHAT I MEAN. THE AMOUNT IS THREE THOUSAND DOLLARS THIS IS ONLY FIRST REQUEST TO GET BACK YOUR REQUEST OR RAILROADING? REMEMBER??? YES YOU DO. DON'T HAVE ANY WATCH DOG OR PROWLERS. KEEP QUIET ABOUT THIS OR ELSE. YOUR RAILROADING OTHER PEOPLE IS OVER. REMEMBER YOUR FAMILY AND KEEP RULES AND MUM OR??????"

b6
b7C

It should be particularly noted in the note that the victim was instructed to put the bundle on Friday of this week (which was May 2, 1947) between 8:00 and 8:15. The note does not state whether A.M. or P.M. However, since the victim did not report the matter until after 8:15 A.M., arrangements were made to surveil the pay-off spot in Spring Lake Park, Texarkana. The victim stated that he did not have $3,000 but agreed to place a package at the point designated in the note. He did not desire to have [redacted] and requested that an officer be left at his residence while he was making the trip from his residence to the park, and that an officer accompany him concealled in his automobile. A surveillance of the pay-off spot was maintained by the writer and Special Agent [redacted] of the Little Rock Division, and Bowie County Deputy Sheriff [redacted] A surveillance was maintained at the entrance of the park by Special Agent [redacted] of the Little Rock Division and Miller County, Arkansas, Deputy Sheriff [redacted] Arkansas State Policeman [redacted] remained at the victim's residence, and Arkansas State Policeman [redacted] accompanied the victim from his residence to Spring Lake Park. The victim placed the package at the appointed place at approximately 8:10 PM. A surveillance was maintained at the various places from approximately 7:15 until 11:00 P.M. Nothing of value was noted at any of the above-mentioned points.

b6
b7C

At the time the victim reported the receipt of the letter, he stated that he suspected only one individual. This individual was FLOYD KILCREASE, a former owner of a welding shop and garage at Dudley and Jackson Streets, Texarkana, Arkansas. The victim had purchased the residence at 3119 Locust Street from KILCREASE approximately one month prior to the receipt of the letter. He furnished the following information which caused him to suspect KILCREASE. KILCREASE was in California at the time he negotiated through [redacted] real estate dealer, with [redacted] for the purchase

- 2 -

DL #9-616

"MANY A SLIP HAS BEEN MADE BETWEEN THE CUP AND THE LIP. YOUR LIP DID IT TOGETHER WITH YOUR FAMILY. YOU ASKED FOR IT. YOUR VERSION WRONG ACCUSATION WRONG LIP TOO BIG. YOU ASKED FOR IT TOGETHER WITH OTHERS LIP. YOU WERE TOLD TO DO SOMETHING. IT IS WHAT YOU HAVE DONE IN PAST NOT OTHERS. YOU AND YOUR LIPPERS WILL FIND THIS OUT IN TIME. YOU ASKED FOR IT."

b6
b7C

Again FEAGINS advised that the only individual he could suspect would be FLOYD KILCREASE. He stated that this note was not handled, and it was immediately placed in a cellophane envelope. He described KILCREASE as being approximately 5' 10½" tall, weight 135 to 140, age approximately 45, slightly gray hair, brown eyes, and slender build. He did not know KILCREASE until he transacted the real estate deal [redacted] [redacted] KILCREASE through the Jennings Real Estate Company.

The extortion notes and envelopes are being forwarded to the FBI Laboratory.

ENCLOSURES TO LITTLE ROCK - Photostatic copies of the two extortion notes.

REFERRED UPON COMPLETION TO THE OFFICE OF ORIGIN

- 4 -

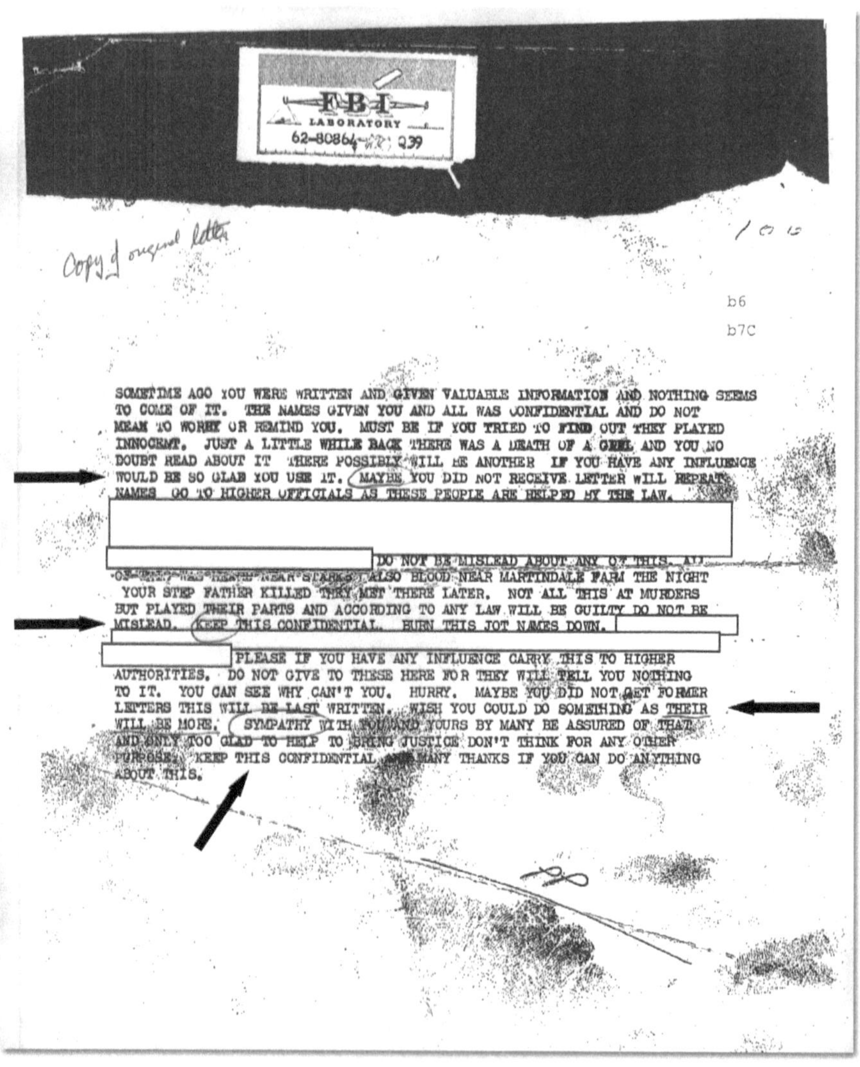
FBI LABORATORY
62-80864

Copy of original letter

b6
b7C

SOMETIME AGO YOU WERE WRITTEN AND GIVEN VALUABLE INFORMATION AND NOTHING SEEMS TO COME OF IT. THE NAMES GIVEN YOU AND ALL WAS CONFIDENTIAL AND DO NOT MEAN TO WORRY OR REMIND YOU. MUST BE IF YOU TRIED TO FIND OUT THEY PLAYED INNOCENT. JUST A LITTLE WHILE BACK THERE WAS A DEATH OF A GIRL AND YOU NO DOUBT READ ABOUT IT THERE POSSIBLY WILL BE ANOTHER IF YOU HAVE ANY INFLUENCE WOULD BE SO GLAD YOU USE IT. MAYBE YOU DID NOT RECEIVE LETTER WILL REPEAT NAMES GO TO HIGHER OFFICIALS AS THESE PEOPLE ARE HELPED BY THE LAW. DO NOT BE MISLEAD ABOUT ANY OF THIS. [illegible] NEAR STARKS ALSO BLOOD NEAR MARTINDALE FARM THE NIGHT YOUR STEP FATHER KILLED THEY MET THERE LATER. NOT ALL THIS AT MURDERS BUT PLAYED THEIR PARTS AND ACCORDING TO ANY LAW WILL BE GUILTY DO NOT BE MISLEAD. KEEP THIS CONFIDENTIAL. BURN THIS JOT NAMES DOWN. PLEASE IF YOU HAVE ANY INFLUENCE CARRY THIS TO HIGHER AUTHORITIES. DO NOT GIVE TO THESE HERE FOR THEY WILL TELL YOU NOTHING TO IT. YOU CAN SEE WHY CAN'T YOU. HURRY. MAYBE YOU DID NOT GET FORMER LETTERS THIS WILL BE LAST WRITTEN. WISH YOU COULD DO SOMETHING AS THEIR WILL BE MORE. SYMPATHY WITH YOU AND YOURS BY MANY BE ASSURED OF THAT AND ONLY TOO GLAD TO HELP TO BRING JUSTICE DON'T THINK FOR ANY OTHER PURPOSE. KEEP THIS CONFIDENTIAL AND MANY THANKS IF YOU CAN DO ANYTHING ABOUT THIS.

b6
b7C

DL #9-616

BOOKER and MARTIN in Spring Lake Park at a point only approximately 200 yards from the spring mentioned in the first extortion letter to FEAGINS. According to Sheriff W. H. PRESLEY, [redacted] description as victims BOOKER and MOORE. Sheriff PRESLEY stated that from his personal observation, he felt that [redacted] for either victim BOOKER or victim MOORE. It should also be noted that the individuals mentioned in the letters to BROWN reside in the same general neighborhood as FEAGINS.

Sheriff PRESLEY has determined that there is an individual by the name of [redacted] It should be noted that the word "spondulux" has been used in the first letter to Mr. FEAGINS, and that the writer of the letter also speaks of the "head of the spring". These expressions are not frequently used.

[redacted] company was the sole wholesale distributor for Atlantic Bond paper in the Texarkana, Texas-Arkansas territory. The paper is manufactured by the Eastern Manufacturing Company of Bangor, Maine. [redacted] examined the paper used in the four letters to Mr. BROWN. He stated that the letter postmarked March 21, 1947, was written on Atlantic Bond paper, while the other letters are written on what he described as a Number 4 bond paper which contains no watermark and is produced by practically all of the paper companies. The first letter to Mr. FEAGINS is written on what he described as a cheap memo pad paper with a gum label at the top. The second letter to Mr. FEAGINS which bore the postmark May 5, 1947, is written also on the Number 4 bond paper and bears no watermark. According to [redacted] the majority of all firms in Texarkana, Texas, would use Atlantic Bond paper and also have available for use a Number 4 bond paper. Both are used for letterheads. This should be particularly noted since a portion of each sheet has been torn off. The memo pad paper used in the first letter to FEAGINS, according to [redacted] is made from pure wood pulp and has no rag content. [redacted] stated that it would nearly be impossible to identify the business firms using the paper in question inasmuch as it is a common grade of paper used by all places of business.

[redacted] the Ragland Office Equipment Company, 218 Main Street, Texarkana, Texas, and

- 7 -

FBI Report in the Phantom Murders covering letters to E.E. Feagins.

It is interesting to note the following:

1. All of the suspect letters were neatly typed in upper case.
2. In the letter marked DL #9-116, the fourth sentence from the bottom begins with the word "Maybe" and the last sentence begins with the word "Keep."
3. The follow-up Feagin letters are fairly lengthy and by the tone of the letters the writer seems to be getting perturbed because of lack of attention.
4. One of the letters mentions "the game."
5. The first Feagin letter was mailed April 29, 1947.
6. One of the Phantom letters mentions the word "sympathy" followed in the same letter with the word "justice" (see page____).
7. One of the Phantom letters indicates that if some action is taken "you would have caused other girls less suffering."
8. One of the letters written to Mr. Feagin identified as Q39 includes the following sentence: "wish you could do something as their will be more."
9. One of the letters to Mr. Feagin included the word "lip."
10. The letters written in the Phantom case contained odd words including: "head of the stream" and "spondulux."

Floyd Kilcrease, operator of a welding and repair shop in Texarkana, Arkansas, received a *hand printed* letter, postmarked 1-29-47, at Texarkana, Arkansas-Texas. (The Zodiac letters were hand printed. See Chapter 5.)

It should be noted that as a result of an examination by the Federal Bureau of Investigation Laboratory, the FBI determined that the anonymous letters to Mr. Brown and the extortion letter to Mr. Feagins were prepared on two typewriters found in the office of W.C. Kuhl, 108 East Third Street, Texarkana, Arkansas. The FBI further identified a forty-year-old woman by the name of Madeline Mary James as the suspect- author of the extortion communications directed to Victim Feagins. James had been employed at the office of W.C. Kuhl and resided at 3112 Locust Street, Texarkana, Arkansas, which address is directly across the street from the home of Mr. Feagins.

The subject James was interviewed by the Little Rock Office of the FBI in 1947, and denied writing the Feagins letters or any other letters involved in these related cases. The August 15, 1947, FBI Report states: "As the subject has continually denied authorship of any of these communications, it is observed that the evidence in connection with the letters addressed to Victim Feagin is only circumstantial inasmuch as Feagin's letters were prepared on the typewriter located in the W.C. Kuhl Realty Office."

The United States Attorney at Fort Smith, Arkansas, authorized the filing of a complaint against James. On August 26, 1947, a Federal Grand Jury returned a two count indictment against James. On September 24, 1947, she entered a "not guilty plea" to each count of the indictment before Judge Harry J. Lemley at Texarkana, Arkansas. A trial date was set for November 10, 1947. On November 11, 1947, when the trial of James opened, defense attorneys Ned Stewart and Ben Shaver "vigorously contested the admissibility of these specimens." Judge Lemley denied the defense motion to suppress and the evidence was deemed admissible. James' trial was postponed from November 10, 1947, to November 11, 1947. On Wednesday, November 12, 1947, a psychiatrist found the defendant, James, "mentally ill and not in possession of sufficient mental competency to understand the nature of the proceedings against her and rationally unable to advise with counsel as to her defense." On Thursday, November 13, 1947, due to the facts in the psychiatrist's report, United States Attorney R.S. Wilson made a motion that the proceedings against James be dismissed. The motion was granted by Judge Lemley and the case against Madeline Mary James was dismissed.

Now let's move the clock ahead twenty years and track the killer to Riverside, California.

Chapter 5

THE ZODIAC KILLER

OCTOBER 30, 1966

CHERI JO BATES

On Sunday, October 30, 1966, Cheri Jo Bates went to church with her father, Joseph Bates, at St. Catherine's Catholic Church in Riverside, California. On Halloween her lifeless mutilated body was found by a college groundskeeper. She was a very pretty, blond-haired, blue-eyed, five-feet-three, 110-pound, eighteen-year-old freshman cheerleader at the Riverside City College. Cheri was studying at the college library on that fateful Halloween night. Unknown to her, at the same time, someone lingered in the darkness near her lime-green Volkswagen Beetle in the college library annex parking lot. Had the same person seen her earlier at St. Catherine's Church? Whoever it was knew the car was driven by Cheri Jo Bates. Detectives determined that her killer had tampered with her vehicle's engine by pulling out the electrical distributor coil and disconnecting a wire to the distributor. Cheri eventually left the library and went to her car. She tried to start her Volkswagen but to no avail. At that moment a man approached Cheri and probably offered assistance or a ride home. The stranger persuaded Cheri to go with him down an unlit gravel path leading out of the parking lot, a walk that would end in tragedy. The stranger assaulted Cheri with a small knife, slamming her to the ground. A neighbor would later recall that he heard two screams between 10:15 and 10:45 P. M. . . . Her assailant kicked her in the head then slashed her face and throat, cutting her jugular vein and voice box, almost severing her head from her body. Her purse was found next to her body, and nothing appeared to have been taken. She was not sexually assaulted. Detectives were puzzled by the motive of this vicious murder. As her lifeless body lay on the cold gravel, the mysterious killer disappeared into the darkness.

The case did eventually take a strange turn. Within thirty days after the death of Cheri Jo Bates, the Riverside Police and the *Riverside Press-Enterprise* received identical typewritten letters entitled: "The Confession"

By ____________________

The author of this letter typed the document all in upper case through approximately twelve carbon papers. The copy mailed was taken from the last copy, rendering a typewriter trace nearly impossible. The killer wrote:

The Confession (FBI Laboratory)   *Typed in upper CASE*   Page 1 of 2

FBI LABORATORY

THE CONFESSION

BY________________

SHE WAS YOUNG AND BEAUTIFUL. BUT NOW SHE IS BATTERED AND DEAD. SHE IS NOT THE FIRST AND SHE WILL NOT BE THE LAST. I LAY AWAKE NIGHTS THINKING ABOUT MY NEXT VICTIM. MAYBE SHE WILL BE THE BEAUTIFUL BLOND THAT BABYSITS NEAR THE LITTLE STORE AND WALKS DOWN THE DARK ALLEY EACH EVENING ABOUT SEVEN. OR MAYBE SHE WILL BE THE SHAPELY BLUE EYED BROWNETT THAT SAID NO WHEN I ASKED HER FOR A DATE IN HIGH SCHOOL. BUT MAYBE IT WILL NOT BE EITHER. BUT I SHALL CUT OFF HER FEMALE PARTS AND DEPOSIT THEM FOR THE WHOLE CITY TO SEE. SO DON'T MAKE IT TO EASY FOR ME. KEEP YOUR SISTERS, DAUGHTERS, AND WIVES OFF THE STREETS AND ALLEYS. MISS BATES WAS STUPID. SHE WENT TO THE SLAUGHTER LIKE A LAMB. SHE DID NOT PUT UP A STRUGGLE. BUT I DID. IT WAS A BALL. I FIRST PULLED THE MIDDLE WIRE FROM THE DISTRIBUTOR. THEN I WAITED FOR HER IN THE LIBRARY AND FOLLOWED HER OUT AFTER ABOUT TWO MINUTS. THE BATTERY MUST HAVE BEEN ABOUT DEAD BY THEN I THEN OFFERED TO HELP. SHE WAS THEN VERY WILLING TO TALK WITH ME. I TOLD HER THAT MY CAR WAS DOWN THE STREET AND THAT I WOULD GIVE HER A LIFT HOME. WHEN WE WERE AWAY FROM THE LIBRARY WALKING, I SAID IT WAS ABOUT TIME. SHE ASKED ME "ABOUT TIME FOR WHAT". I SAID IT WAS ABOUT TIME FOR HER TO DIE. I GRABBED HER AROUND THE NECK WITH MY HAND OVER HER MOUTH AND MY OTHER HAND WITH A SMALL KNIFE AT HER THROAT. SHE WENT VERY WILLINGLY. HER BREAST FELT VERY WARM AND FIRM UNDER MY HANDS, BUT ONLY ONE THING WAS ON MY MIND. MAKING HER PAY FOR THE BRUSH OFFS THAT SHE HAD GIVEN ME DURING THE YEARS PRIOR. SHE DIED HARD. SHE SQUIRMED AND SHOOK AS I CHOAKED HER, AND HER LIPS TWICHED. SHE LET OUT A SCREAM ONCE AND I KICKED HER HEAD TO SHUT HER UP. I PLUNGED THE KNIFE INTO HER AND IT BROKE. I THEN FINISHED THE JOB BY CUTTING HER THROAT. I AM NOT SICK. I AM INSANE. BUT THAT WILL NOT STOP THE GAME. THIS LETTER SHOULD BE PUBLISHED FOR ALL TO READ IT. IT JUST MIGHT SAVE THAT GIRL IN THE ALLEY. BUT THAT'S UP TO YOU. IT WILL BE ON YOUR CONSCIENCE. NOT MINE. YES I DID MAKE THAT CALL TO YOU ALSO. IT WAS JUST A WARNING. BEWARE...I AM STALKING YOUR GIRLS NOW.

CC. CHIEF OF POLICE
ENTERPRISE

http://www.zodiackiller.com/FBIConfession.html   3/3/2006

"The Confession" letter written in the Zodiac case
(courtesy of Tom Voigt, *zodiackiller.com)*

May 1, 1967

On May 1, 1967, the Riverside Police Department and the *Riverside Press-Enterprise* received hand-addressed envelopes, each postmarked locally and mailed with double postage. Inside each envelope was the following message:

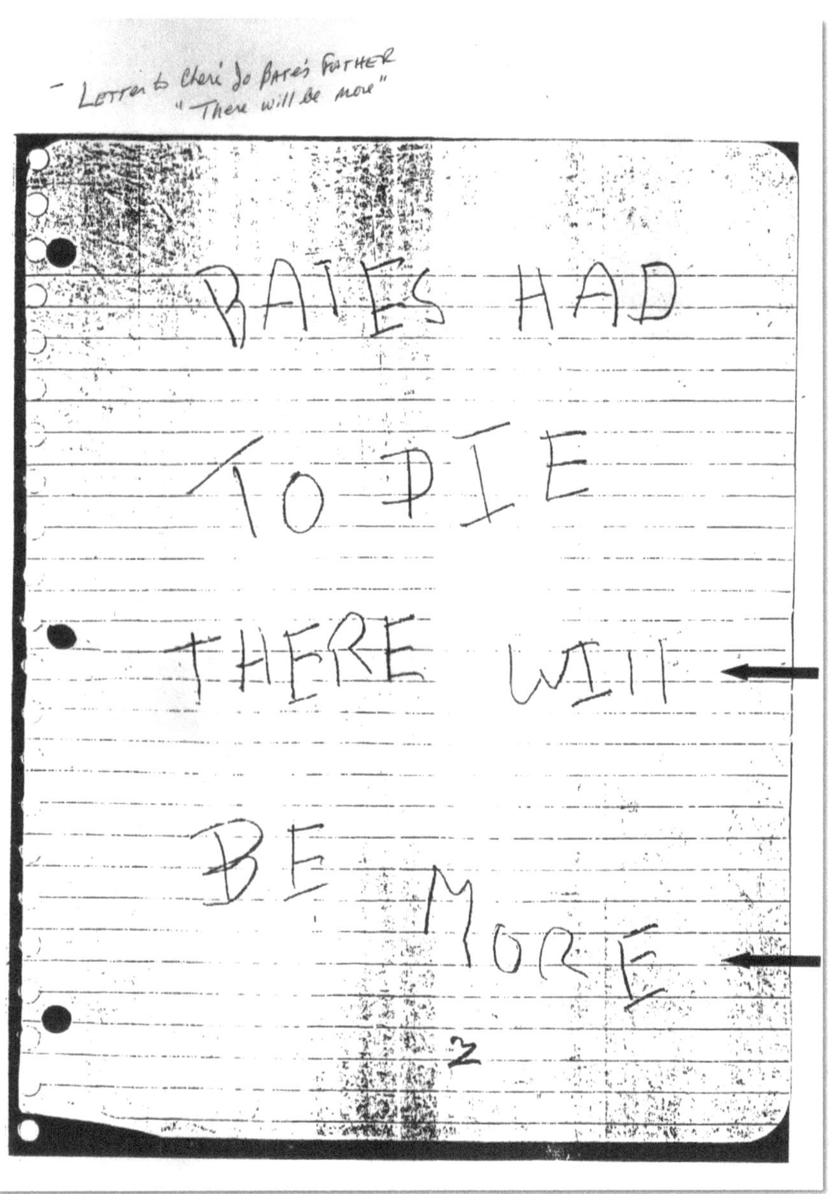

- Letter to Cheri Jo Bates Father
"There will be more"

BATES HAD
TO DIE
THERE WILL
BE MORE
Z

"Bates Had To Die" letter writt en in the Zodiac case
(courtesy of Tom Voigt, *zodiackiller.com)*

This time the notes were signed with either a "2" or a "Z." An identical letter was mailed to Joseph Bates, father of Cheri Jo Bates. This murder case grew cold with no promising leads. Four years later and several hundred miles to the north in San Francisco, detectives there learned that the death of Cheri Jo might be related to a series of random murders and attacks in their jurisdiction.

The following clues and facts can be ascertained from the information associated with the death of Cheri Jo Bates:

1. Her assailant wanted publicity and his name in the newspaper.
2. He wrote the police and a newspaper following a murder he committed.
3. The letter he wrote was lengthy, typewritten in capital letters, and single spaced.
4. Her assailant was interested in poetry and quoted poetry.
5. She was slashed in the face and her head was almost severed from her body.
6. Following the murder, her assailant wrote a letter to Cheri Jo Bates's father. The letter was written in block letters like those a child would write.
7. In his letter to the *Riverside Press-Enterprise* the killer threatened to cut off female parts and deposit them for the whole city to see.

No one was ever arrested and charged with the murder of Cheri Jo Bates. All that now remains is cold file #352-481 at the Riverside Police Department. It is interesting to note that:

1. The "Confession" letter was entirely typed in upper case
2. The "Confession" letter mentions "**the game**."

3. The "Confession" letter includes a sentence that starts with the word "**Maybe**" followed shortly thereafter by a sentence that starts with the word "**Keep**."
4. The "Bates Had To Die" letter was mailed to Joseph Bates, father of Cheri Jo Bates after Cheri Jo had been brutally murdered.
5. The "Bates Had To Die" letter was mailed to Joseph Bates on April 30, 1967, exactly six months after Cheri Jo Bates was murdered.
6. The poet John Keats (1795-1817) wrote in *Hyperion:Book II* "And just as thou wast *not he first* of powers so art thou *not the last*." If the phrase "not the first and not the last" was borrowed from the works of John Keats, then one could deduce that the writer of "The Confession" letter may have a keen interest in the poetry and writings of Keats. It is well known that Keats wrote volumes of material, so it may not be surprising that several of the words used by the Zodiac are also found Keats's work including but not limited to: Zodiac (*Lines On the Mermaid Tavern*), whence, I am here, leave me alone, wandering, spray, blast, paradise, delicious, slaves, dripping, collecting, rile, wipe, cheer, clean, mask, Phantom, sensible, inflict, twitched (*The Eve of St. Agnes*) happy, and so on.
7. Detectives suspected that the Zodiac used a portable Royal Typewriter to type the "Confession" letter.
8. The Zodiac indicated in this letter that if some action is taken "It just might save that girl in the alley."
9. "The Confession" letter written by the Zodiac included the word "lip."
10. The Zodiac's "Bates Had To Die" letter included the following words:" There will be more."

11. The Zodiac wrote odd words in his letters including "unflappable," "Mask the sound," and "positively ventalate."
12. The Zodiac signed his "Count Marco" letter: "The Red Phantom (red with rage)"
13. Zodiac began most of his letters with the words: "This is . . ."
14. The 1977, movie entitled *The Town That Dreaded Sundown* may provide additional clues. Although based on a true story, several of the factual accounts concerning the Phantom Murders depicted in the movie are not completely accurate. For example, the cloth-hood worn by the Phantom Killer in the movie had holes for the eyes but not the mouth (The Phantom Killer and the Zodiac both wore cloth-hoods with cutout holes for the eyes and the mouth). There are a few scenes from the movie that I mention here for whatever value they may be worth:
    a. In the movie, the Phantom Killer is seen opening the hood of the automobile driven by a character depicting Phantom Victim, Jimmy Hollis, and removing several wires before attacking the couple.
       In the case of Cheri Jo Bates, the Zodiac Killer opened the hood of her Volkswagen and "pulled out the distributor coil and the condenser and disconnected the middle wire of the distributor" (Note 37, page 165).
    b. In the movie, the character depicting Betty Jo Booker is tied up and then stabbed with a knife several times in her back by a man with a clothhood over his head.
       Zodiac Victim, Cecelia Shepard, was stabbed with a knife five times each in the front and back by a man with a cloth-hood over his head.
    c. In the movie, the Phantom Killer uses a gun with some sort of silencer attached to it.

Zodiac Victim, Mike Mageau, "got the impression the gun had some sort of silencer on it" (Note 37, page 27).

Confidential

Editor—
Put Marco back in the hell-hole
from whence it came — he has
a serious psychological disorder—
always needs to feel superior. I
suggest you refer him to a shrink.
Meanwhile, cancel the Count Marco
column. Since the Count can
write anonymously, so can I —
the Red Phantom
(red with rage)

"Count Marco" letter written in the Zodiac case
(courtesy of Tom Voigt, www.zodiackiller.com)

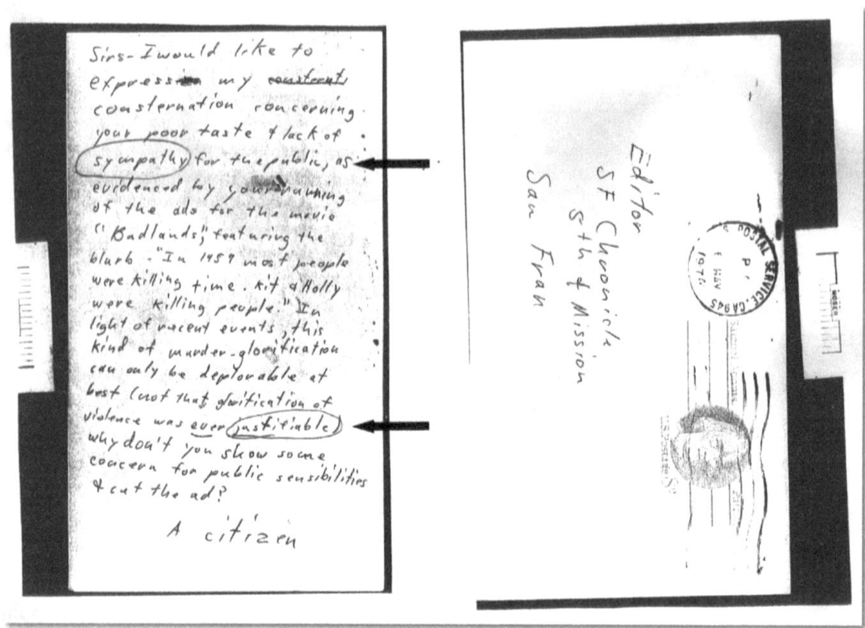

Sirs- I would like to express my consternation concerning your poor taste & lack of sympathy for the public, as evidenced by your running of the ads for the movie "Badlands", featuring the blurb - "In 1959 most people were killing time. Kit & Holly were killing people." In light of recent events, this kind of murder-glorification can only be deplorable at best (not that glorification of violence was ever justifiable) why don't you show some concern for public sensibilities & cut the ad?

A citizen

Editor
SF Chronicle
5th & Mission
San Fran

"Citizen" letter written in the Zodiac case
(courtesy of Tom Voigt, zodiackiller.com)

BETTY LOU JENSEN AND DAVID ARTHUR FARADAY

December 20, 1968

The Zodiac had migrated from the Los Angeles area to San Francisco by late 1968. At that time no one knew he might have been responsible for the savage murder of Cheri Jo Bates two years earlier in Riverside, California. The Zodiac was smart. He didn't continue to commit his deadly crimes in the same location for a very long period of time. This would have increased the chance of being identified and eventually apprehended. One small mistake could lead to the evidence that would end his career as a serial killer. He was too clever to allow the authorities time enough to set a trap that would snare him. Over the course of a couple of years the Zodiac would do exactly what he eventually wrote: "I shall change the way the collecting of slaves. I shall no longer announce to anyone. When I commit my murders, they shall look like routine robberies, killings of anger, and a few fake accidents, etc. The police shall never catch me because I have been too clever for them" (Zodiac's letter to the *San Francisco Chronicle*, November 9, 1969). I believe the Zodiac may have read and studied true crime, detective magazines, the history of Jack the Ripper and other famous serial killers to educate himself so that he would not get caught after committing his murders. He knew that if he continued to kill in the same location for an extended period of time he stood a better chance of being caught, tripped up by some act of indiscretion.

It is also interesting to note that on Sunday, April 19, 1970, "a man in a late-model hardtop at the corner of Bay Street and Embarcadero seemed to have an obsession about the crime rate in San Francisco. He went on in great detail to list all thirty-five of the city's murders so far that year. 'It's not safe to walk alone,' he told Christopher Edwards, a ship's steward, 'with all the muggings, murders, rapes, and crime.' Edwards had stopped to ask directions while walking to Fisherman's Wharf and he was getting 'bad vibrations' from the stranger. The man identified himself as a British engineer who had lived in San Francisco for ten years; he offered the steward a lift. Edwards declined, but listened while the stranger went on with great knowledge about all of the murders in the city, save those that were on the minds of most people-the Zodiac killings.

The stranger's reluctance to talk about Zodiac impressed Edwards, and he could not shake the incident from his mind. As soon as he got to the wharf, he called the police. Later at Central Station, he identified the man from a composite drawing of Zodiac" (Note 37, page 142).

On Friday, December 20, 1968, the Zodiac had set his deadly

web in Vallejo, 25 miles north of San Francisco. Two young people, sixteen-year-old Betty Lou Jensen and seventeen-year-old David Arthur Faraday went on a date. They were typical California teenagers out for a good time, enjoying life. David drove his mother's 1961 Rambler station wagon to Betty Lou Jensen's home in Vallejo. The couple drove to Mr. Ed's, a drive-in, and after drinking a Coke drove to a lover's lane off Lake Herman Road. Not long after they had parked a car pulled up alongside of the Rambler. The authorities later reconstructed the events of that fateful evening: They thought a stranger exited his car and walked up to the side of the Faraday vehicle, where he probably ordered David and Betty Lou out of their car. At first the couple might have ignored his order so he drew a gun and fired two shots, one of which went through the side of the rear window of the Rambler. Both Jensen and Faraday started to flee from the vehicle. Davis was met by the stranger as he attempted to exit the vehicle. He was shot behind the left ear and the bullet lodged in his brain. David Faraday was mortally wounded. The gunman then turned his rage on Betty Lou Jensen who had dashed from the car screaming in terror. The gunman raised his weapon and fired five shots at the fleeing victim striking her five times in the back. Betty Lou Jensen's life ended where she fell.

Mrs. Stella Borges lived on Lake Herman Road a little over two miles from where David Arthur Faraday and Betty Lou Jensen had been murdered. At 11:10 p.m. that evening Mrs. Borges went for a ride with her mother-in-law and daughter to Benicia. They came upon the gruesome scene and summoned the police. When the police arrived they had no clue who had committed these crimes. There were no fingerprints or other physical evidence except the expended shell casings and slugs recovered at the crime scene. The bullets were made by Winchester and appeared to be a .22 caliber that may have been fired from a J.C. Higgins Model 80 or a Hi Standard Model 101. The killer used Winchester Super X copper-coated long rifle bullets. The bullets recovered had a right hand twist with six land groves, a "six and six" (for definition see page 10, *Zodiac*).

On August 1, 1969, the *Vallejo Times-Herald*, the *San Francisco Chronicle,* and the *San Francisco Examiner* all received variations of the following letter from the Zodiac killer:

Dear Editor
This is the murderer of the
2 teenagers last Christmass
at Lake Herman & the girl
on the 4th of July near
the golf course in Vallejo
To prove I killed them I
Shall state some facts which
only I & the police know.
Christmass
1 ~~Brand name~~ of ammo
Super X
2 10 shots were fired
3 the boy was on his back
with his feet to the car
4 the girl was on her right
side feet to the west
4th July
1 girl was wearing paterned
slacks
2 The boy was also shot in
the knee.
3 Brand name of ammo was
Western
Over

Here is part of a cipher the
other 2 parts of this cipher are
being mailed to the editors of
the Vallejo times + SF Exam
iner.

I want you to print this cipher
on the front page of your
paper. In this cipher is my
idenity.

If you do not print this cipher
by the afternoon of Fry. 1st of
Aug 69, I will go on a kill ram-
Page Fry. night. I will cruse
around all weekend killing lone
People in the night then move
on to kill again, untill I end
up with a dozen people over
the weekend.

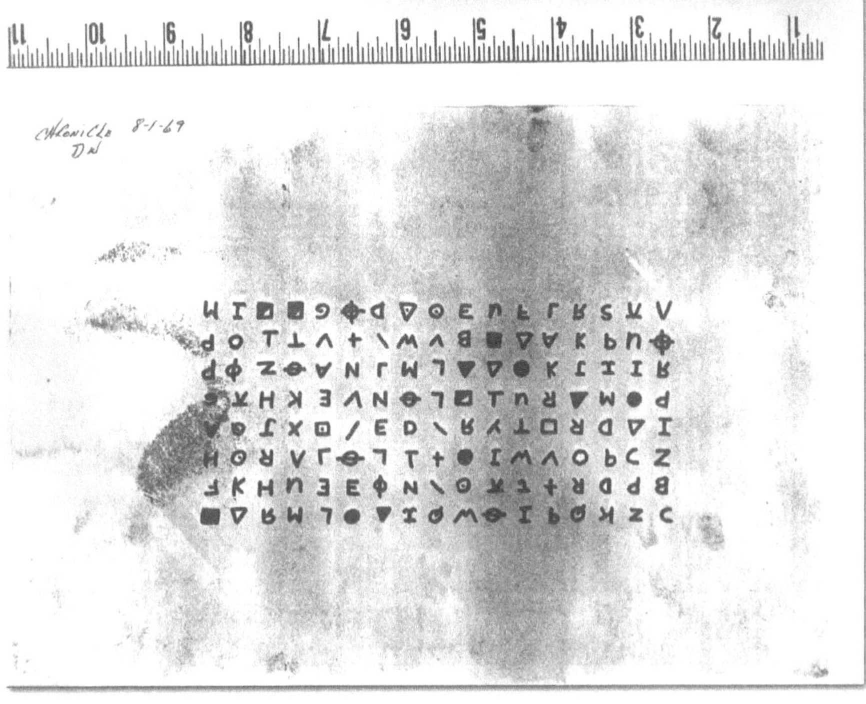
Chronicle 8-1-69
DN

Dear Editor

I am the killer of the 2 teenagers last christmass at Lake Herman & the girl last 4th of July. To prove this I shall state some facts which only I & the police know.

Christmass

1 brandname of ammo - Super X
2 10 shots fired
3 Boy was on his back with feet to car
4 Girl was lyeing on right side feet to west

4th of July

1 girl was wearing patterned pants
2 boy was also shot in knee
3 ammo was made by Western

Here is a cipher or that is part of one. The other 2 parts are being mailed to the Vallejo Times & S.F. Chronicle

I want you to print this cipher on the front page by Fry afternoon Aug 1-69. If you

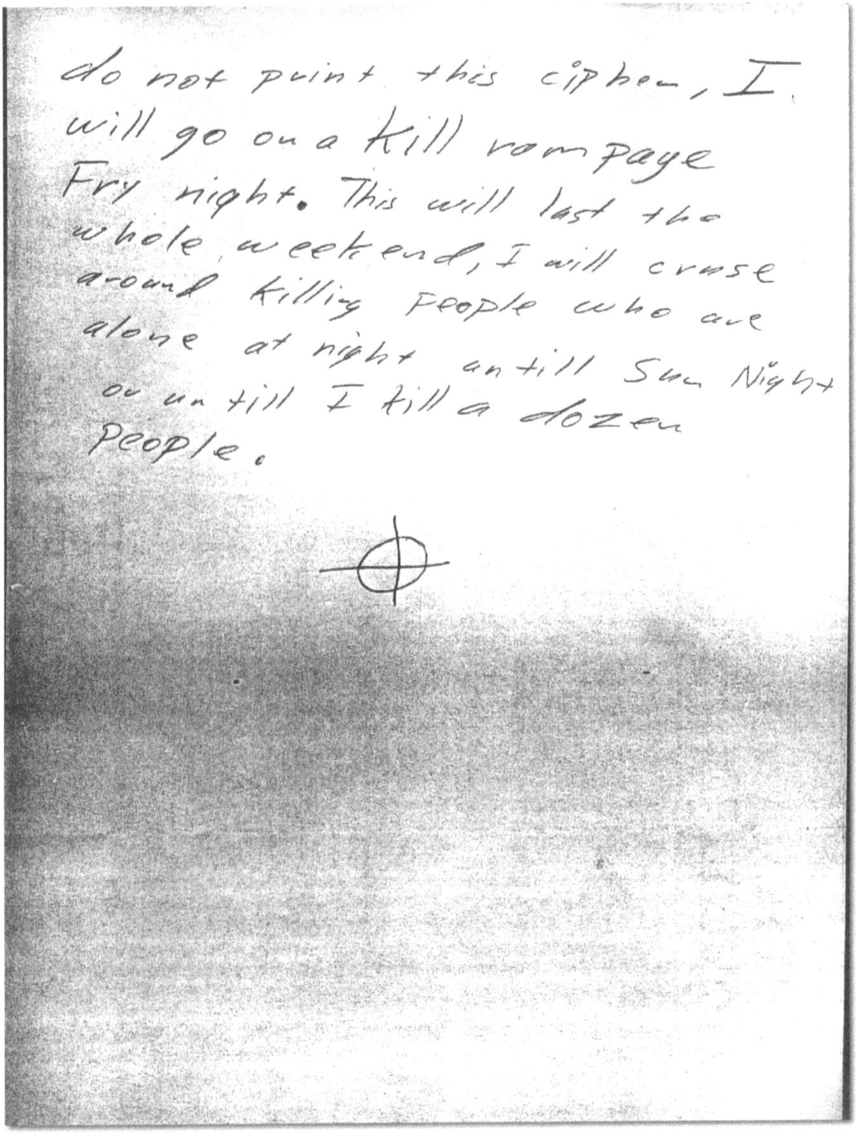

do not print this cipher, I
will go on a kill rampage
Fry night. This will last the
whole weekend, I will cruse
around killing People who are
alone at night untill Sun Night
or un till I kill a dozen
People.

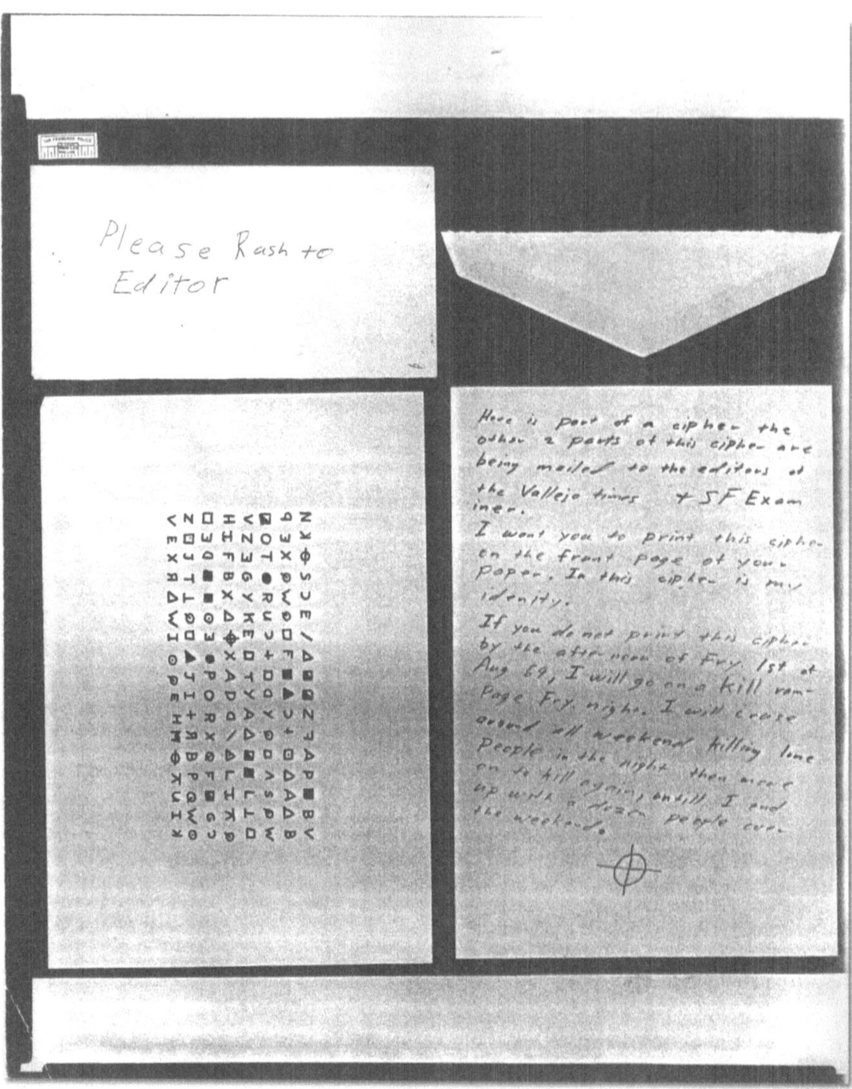

Please Rush to
Editor

Here is part of a cipher the
other 2 parts of this cipher are
being mailed to the editors of
the Vallejo times + SF Exam
iner.
I want you to print this cipher
on the front page of your
paper. In this cipher is my
idenity.
If you do not print this cipher
by the afternoon of Fry. 1st of
Aug 69, I will go on a kill ram-
Page Fry. night. I will crose
around all weekend killing lone
people in the night then move
on to kill again, untill I end
up with a dozen people over
the weekend.

August 1, 1969, letter and ciper sent to the *San Francisco Chronicle* and August 1, 1969, letter sent to the *San Francisco Examiner,* in the Zodiac case. (courtesy of Tom Voigt, www.zodiackiller.com)

The letter was completed by a symbol, a circle with two lines through it.

From July 5, 1969, through August 10, 1969, the front page articles of the *San Francisco Chronicle* and the *San Francisco Examiner* were devoted to the murders committed in Michigan by John Norman Collins and the murders of Sharon Tate, Jay Sebring and Abigail Folger by the Manson Family. The Zodiac had not been receiving the front page press that he craved.

DARLENE FERRIN AND MICHAEL MAGEAU

July 4, 1969

In 1962, sixteen-year-old Darlene Ferrin traveled to Texas with her Mother and sisters, Pam, Linda and Christina. At that time Darlene was a shapely, blue-eyed brunette. She changed her hair color a couple of years later from brunette to blond. They visited relatives in the Dallas/Fort Worth area where they met a couple of men who appeared to be in the Navy and another man who I will refer to as the "stranger." At the time, Darlene's sister, Pam, had very long hair that was quite attractive. In a bowling alley the stranger paid special attention to Pam's long hair and commented on how pretty her eyes were. To Pam's displeasure the stranger would try to run his hand through her hair. The incident caused such concern with Pam that she elected to have her hair cut upon returning to Vallejo. In the bowling alley the stranger tried to "come on to" Darlene but she refused his advances and "told him to get lost" in no uncertain words. Pam could remember that one or more of the individuals they had met in Texas obtained their Vallejo telephone number and address. When Darlene Ferrin and her family returned to Vallejo they received several unwanted telephone calls that might have been placed by the men they had met in Texas. Their mother got so upset with the calls she had her telephone number unlisted.

In January, 1969, a stranger was seen hanging around Darlene Ferrin's home in Vallejo. Darlene was heard to say, "I guess he's checking up on me. He doesn't want anyone to know what I saw him do, I saw him kill someone." Four months later, in May, Darlene and her husband Dean Ferrin had an open house. A stranger arrived, uninvited. No one could remember his name but it was "Bob or Joe or Lee, something like that."

On Friday, July 4, 1969, at 11:45 p.m. Darlene went on a date with her friend Michael Mageau. She picked up Michael at his home and when they started to drive away a stranger started to follow them. Darlene tried to elude the stranger but to no avail. As she pulled into the Blue Rock Golf Course the stranger pulled in behind them. He then sped off in his car but soon reappeared. When the stranger returned he stepped out of his car and shined a flashlight into the Ferrin vehicle. (Had this individual carried a flashlight in one hand and a gun in another during a prior assault? If so, then through trial and error, he would have learned that it would be less encumbering to have a flashlight attached to his weapon, thus freeing the other hand to subdue his victim, if necessary. Keep in mind that the Phantom Killer held a gun in one hand and a flashlight in the other.)

The stranger walked up to the passenger side of the Ferrin vehicle where Michael was seated. There was a sound of metal from the gun barrel hitting his window. Without warning, shots were fired. Michael was shot in his jaw and slug passed through his tongue. Bullets hit Darlene. Darlene was shot nine times, two in the right arm, two in the left arm and five times in her back (note 38, page 12). Had Darlene been killed by someone she met years earlier? Perhaps in Texas? There was speculation by the detectives that Darlene Ferrin's killer may have met her at one time or another. The next day on July 5, 1969, her killer called the Vallejo Police Department from a public pay phone and stated. “I want to report a double murder. If you go one mile east on Columbus Parkway to the public park, you will find kids in a brown car. They were shot with a 9mm Lugar. I also killed those kids last year, goodbye.” By the time the police had traced the call the man had left the phone booth.

On August 7, 1969, the *Chronicle* received the following letter from the Zodiac:

“Last ***Christmass***	**Christmas**	**S**
In that *epasode* the police were	**Episode**	**A**
Wondering as to how I could		
Shoot & hit my victims in the		
Dark. They did not openly state this,		
But implied this by saying it was a		
Well lit night & I could see		
Silowets on the horizon	**Silhouette**	**W,U,T,E & H**
Bullshit that area is *srounded*	**Surrounded**	**U & R**
By high hills and trees. What		
I did was tape a small *pencel*	**Pencil**	**E**
Light to the barrl of my gun. If		
You notice, in the center of the beam		
Of light if you aim it at a wall or		
Ceilling you will see a black or	**Ceiling L**	
Darck	**Dark**	**C**
Circle of light about 3 to 6 in.		
Across		
When taped to a gun barrel, the		
Bullet will strike exactly in the		
Center of the black dot in the light.		
All I had to do was spray them. . .		
No address. (Emphasis added)		

Proposed Solution:

The misspelled words might spell the name: **CHARLES**

(I believe this may be the correct solution because the last letter **S** is the first letter in the first misspelled word and the last letter in the name Charles. The **C** is the last letter in the final incorrect word which is the first letter in the name Charles. However, this is only a guess on my part. There are obviously additional letters that are unaccounted for, namely the letters W, U, T and E.)

CECELIA SHEPARD AND BRYAN HARTNELL

September 27, 1969

Cecelia Ann Shepard and Bryan Hartnell had both attended Pacific Union College in Angwin, California. On September 27, 1969, they decided to go on a date to Lake Berryessa, located north of San Francisco. Bryan drove his 1956 white Karmann Ghia coupe. The couple found a location on a peninsula, laid out a blanket and began to enjoy the day. At around 4:00 o'clock in the afternoon, as they sat on a blanket a man approached them with a gun in hand wearing a square-hooded cloth outfit over his head and shoulders with a white circle and cross-stitched on a tunic that appeared to have been professionally sewed on. It seems to me that the executioner's hood might have been prepared by someone who could have tried this method before. Perhaps in the commission of an earlier assault the assailant had placed a cloth bag over his head and then eventually realized that while committing his crime the bag became more of a nuisance than an effective disguise. That method of concealment was cumbersome, so this time the refined hood might have been constructed so that it fit squarely on his head, allowing for better vision.

The stranger wore a lone knife in a wooden sheath on his side hip and several lengths of white plastic clothesline hung from his belt. The man's stomach hung over his belt. Cecelia said to Bryan, "My God, he's got a gun."

The stranger at first demanded their money and keys. The man said he had escaped from prison in Montana, that he had killed a guard in the process, and needed a car in which to escape to Mexico. Soon after, his true intentions became known to Cecelia and Bryan. This person intended to kill them both. He said to Cecelia, "You tie the boy up." When she failed to properly tie Bryan Hartnell with the rope, the stranger took over. He first tied up Cecelia, then Bryan. Once Bryan was securely tied up, their assailant said, "I'm going to have to stab you people." The Zodiac had struck again. He began stabbing Bryan Hartnell in the back with his foot-long knife. Hartnell was stabbed six times in his back, one blow coming within a fraction of an inch of his heart. The man "gave a ghastly, frenzied sound and, letting out a low exhalation, began stabbing the girl in the back." He continued to thrust his bayonet-type knife into her breasts, groin and once in her abdomen. Her aorta had been cut in two places. The next afternoon, Cecelia Shepard died in the hospital from her wounds. Bryan Hartnell survived the attack after crawling over three hundred yards from where the Zodiac first tied him up.

The police were able to obtain very few pieces of evidence from the crime scene. Bryan was able to describe his attacker's voice: "It was a remarkably calm voice, a voice that was not high or low pitched, a monotone." Bryan further stated, "That voice... it was like a student's. But kind of a drawl; not a Southern drawl though." Detectives found deep footprints that confirm the Zodiac weighed over 200 pounds. Police determined the Zodiac Killer wore size 10 ½ Wing Walker shoes that may have been purchased under military contract for distribution to the Navy and Air Force on the west coast. It appeared that the Zodiac might be somehow connected to the armed forces when he committed the Lake Berryessa crimes.

At 7:00 p.m., one hour and ten minutes after the knifings, the phone rang at the Napa Police Department. The caller on the line said, "I want to report a murder--no, a double murder. They are two miles north of park headquarters. They were in a white Volkswagen Karmann Ghia." The police traced the call to a pay phone located at 1231 Main Street at the Napa Car-wash. Then the police arrived at the phone booth, the caller had disappeared. The caller left the receiver dangling from the phone. The following facts and clues could be ascertained from this crime:

1. The perpetrator wore a cloth hood over his head that may have been a modification of a cloth hood that had obstructed his vision during a prior crime.
2. The man said he needed a car to escape to Mexico.
3. The man forced the female victim to tie up the male victim.
4. The female victim was not sexually assaulted.
5. After the attack the perpetrator called the police from a pay telephone and in a short message reported a double murder, told the emergency dispatcher where the victims could be found, and then left the receiver dangling from the phone.
6. The man may have had sewing skills as exhibited by the cross stitched on his tunic.
7. The man had a drawl, not a southern drawl, and spoke in a monotone voice.
8. While attacking the female victim the perpetrator gave a "ghastly, frenzied sound and let out a long, low exhalation before he began stabbing the girl" (Note 37, page 71).

PAUL LEE STINE

October 11, 1969

The official police report submitted by officers Pelisetti and Peda regarding the murder of taxi driver, Paul Lee Stine, who was killed by the Zodiac on October 11, 1969, is written as follows:

> Upon responding to the above location officers Peda and Pelisetti found Yellow Cab #912 parked at the northeast corner of Washington St. at the corner of Cherry St. The reporters together with two other witnesses __________ , age 14 and __________ , age 13, same address and phone as reported, stated that they saw the below described suspect in the front seat of the Yellow cab, mid to the passenger side, with the victim slumped partially over his lap. The suspect appeared to be searching the victim's pockets. (Witnesses never heard a gun shot). The suspect then appeared to be wiping (fingerprints) on the interior of the cab, leaning over the victim to the driver's compartment. The suspect then exited the cab by the passenger side front door, also wiping with a white rag, possibly a handkerchief. The suspect then walked around the cab to the driver's side and proceeded to wipe the exterior of the left door area. The suspect then fled (walking) north on Cherry St. towards the Presidio of S.F. R/Os immediately checked the interior of the cab and found the victim to be slumped over the front seat with his upper torso in the passenger side, head resting on the floorboard, facing north. Ambulance was summoned, Code Three, and other units were requested for an immediate search of the area. Description was obtained from reporters whose observation point was directly across the street (50ft.) and unobstructed. Description was broadcast and

numerous units responded to institute a search of the area. P.E.H. ambulance #82 responded, Stewart Dousette, victim was examined and pronounced dead at 10:10 pm.

Inspector Krake responded and summoned dog units and fire department "spotlight" vehicle to assist in the search. R/Os called for Crime Lab Coroner, Yellow cab officials, and a tow.

Assistant traffic manager of Yellow Cab, LeRoy Sweet responded and gave reporting officers the victim's identification. Mr. Sweet further stated the last dispatch given the victim was at 9:45 pm to 500 9th Ave. apt #1. Victim allegedly never arrived at the above location as the dispatch was reassigned to another cab at 9:56 pm. R/Os noted that the meter of the cab was running, indicating that the victim possibly picked up another fare (suspect) en route to the original assignment. (The meter read $6.25 at exactly 10:46 pm.) ***A check with Yellow Cab Co. revealed that the victim had arrived at work at approximately 8:45 pm and had only one fare prior, that being from Pier 64 to the Air Terminal.*** (emphasis added). Sgt. Falk responded in G #10, Lt. Kiel also responded. The military police headquarters of the Presidio of S.F. was also notified and an intense search of the Julius Kahn area was made by seven dog units, other Richmond and C.P. units--to no avail. The coroner responded, Deputy Schultz and Kindred, and took charge of the deceased. Coroner's receipt attached to this report. Crime Lab responded and took necessary photographs of the preserved Scens-Dagitz and Kirkindal--all physical evidence was retained by crime lab for I.D. The auto, Yellow cab #912 Calif. Lic. Y17413, was towed to the Hall. Impounded for homicide prints, Tow slip attached this report. Room 100 was notified, given description, and advised to have broadcast continuous throughout the morning as per insp Armstrong's direction. Crime lab's initial investigation showed that the victim was devoid of any U.S. currency, nor did he have possession of a wallet; the ignition key for the cab was also missing.

According to the official police report this is the sequence of events:

1. Paul Lee Stine arrives at work at 8:45 pm.
2. Between 8:45 pm and 9:45 pm, Stine picks up a fare at Pier 64 in San Francisco and delivers the fare to the air terminal.
3. A last dispatch to 500 9th Ave. Apt 31 was radioed to Stine.
4. 9:58 pm, the last dispatch was reassigned to another cab.
5. 10:10 pm, Stine is pronounced dead.

When Paul Stine dropped off the fare at the Air Terminal there was a good chance that he may have picked up a new fare at that time. If my theory is correct, Paul Stine may have picked up a fare at the airport and that person may have been the individual who murdered him in San Francisco. The police report indicated that Stine "possibly picked up another fare (suspect) en route to the original assignment."

Unfortunately the police operator made a mistake and reported the perpetrator as a NMA (Negro male adult) instead of the initial and correct identification of the perpetrator as a WMA (white male adult). Did the assailant appear to the witnesses to be a black man when he was possibly a dark-tanned white man?

As later developments would reveal, the Zodiac had disappeared into the shadows of the night in the direction of the Presidio. After an extensive search the police were unable to locate the suspect. The Zodiac killer had vanished into the night.

October 14, 1969

On Tuesday, October 14, 1969, the *San Francisco Chronicle* received the following message:

Zodiac's October 13, 1969, letter to the *San Francisco Chronicle*, in which he enclosed a bloody scrap of Paul Stine's shirt.

This is the Zodiac speaking. I am the murderer of the taxi driver over by Washington St & Maple St last night, to prove this here is a blood stained piece of his shirt. I am the same man who did in the people in the north bay area.

The S.F. Police could have caught me last night if they had searched the park properly instead of holding road races with their motorcicles seeing who could make the most noise. The car drivers should have just parked their cars & sat there quietly waiting for me to come out of cover.

School children make nice targets, I think I shall wipe out a school bus some morning. Just shoot out the front tire & then pick off the kiddies as they come bouncing out.

October 13, 1969 letter sent to the *San Francisco Chronicle* in the Zodiac case. (courtesy of Tom Voigt, www.zodiackiller.com)

Two police officers did encounter the Zodiac Killer while searching for the murderer of Paul Lee Stine near the Presidio in San Francisco. A police artist was able to create a new composite drawing of the Zodiac. The following description of the Zodiac was provided: 5'11", thirty-five to forty-five, 200 pounds, short brown hair. The second police composite drawing changes the hair line, widens the jaw, shows a drooping eyelid and opens the mouth of the Zodiac.

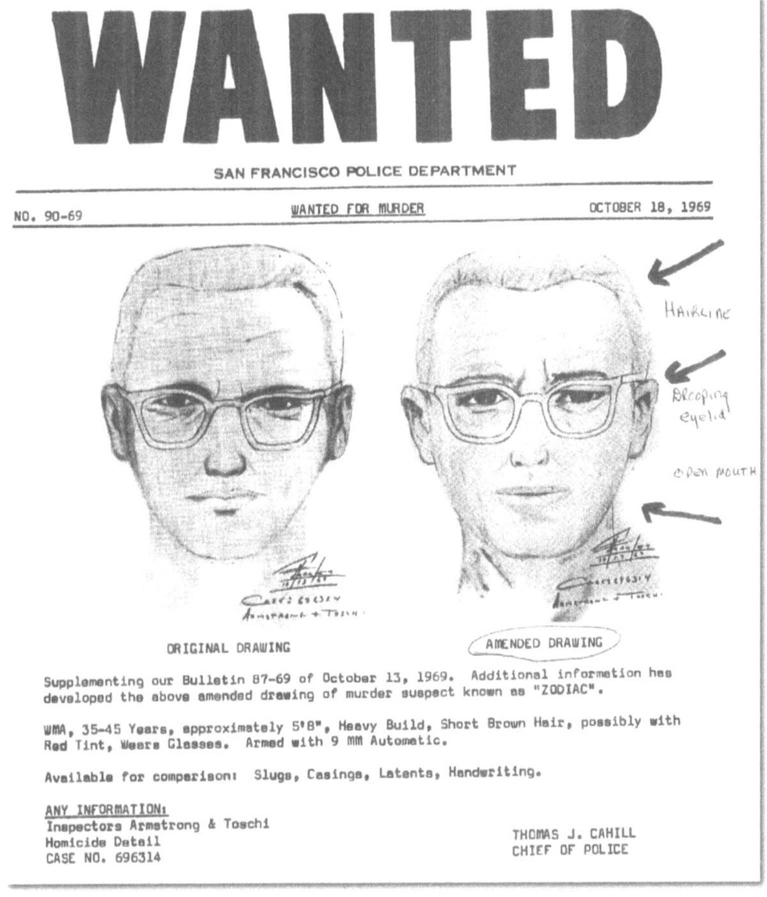

WANTED

SAN FRANCISCO POLICE DEPARTMENT

NO. 90-69 WANTED FOR MURDER OCTOBER 18, 1969

HAIRLINE

Drooping eyelid

open MOUTH

ORIGINAL DRAWING AMENDED DRAWING

Supplementing our Bulletin 87-69 of October 13, 1969. Additional information has developed the above amended drawing of murder suspect known as "ZODIAC".

WMA, 35-45 Years, approximately 5'8", Heavy Build, Short Brown Hair, possibly with Red Tint, Wears Glasses. Armed with 9 MM Automatic.

Available for comparison: Slugs, Casings, Latents, Handwriting.

ANY INFORMATION:
Inspectors Armstrong & Toschi
Homicide Detail
CASE NO. 696314

THOMAS J. CAHILL
CHIEF OF POLICE

October, 1969, composite drawing of the Zodiac Killer (courtesy of Tom Voigt, www.zodiakiller.com)

WHAT DID THE SIGN OF THE ZODIAC REPRESENT?

The Zodiac included a crossed circle at the end of the October 14, 1969, letter to the *San Francisco Chronicle*. No one ever determined exactly what the sign of the Zodiac stood for. I have my own theory.

Look carefully at what the Zodiac wrote in the letter to the *Chronicle* on July 24, 1970:

This is the Zodiac speaking

I am rather unhappy because
you people will not wear some
nice ⊕ buttons. So I now
have a little list, starting with
the woeman + her baby that I
gave a rather intersting ride
for a coupple howers one
evening a few months back that
ended in my burning her
car where I found them.

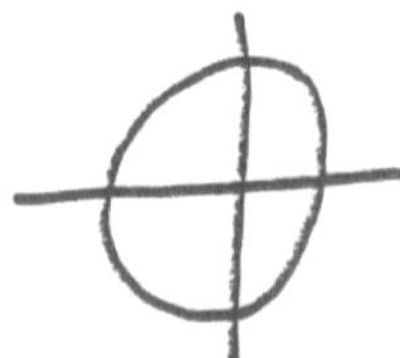

This is the Zodiac speaking

Being that you will not wear
some nice ⊕ buttons, how about
wearing some nasty ⊕ buttons.
Or any type of ⊕ buttons that
you can think up. If you do
not wear any type of ⊕
buttons I shall (on top of every
thing else) torture all 13
of my slaves that I have
wateing for me in Paradice.
Some I shall tie over ant hills
and watch them scream + twich
and sqwirm. Others shall have
pine splinters driven under their
nails + then burned. Others shall
be placed in cages + fed salt
beef untill they are gorged then
I shall listen to their pleass
for water and I shall laugh at
them. Others will hang by
their thumbs + burn in the
sun then I will rub them down
with deep heat to warm

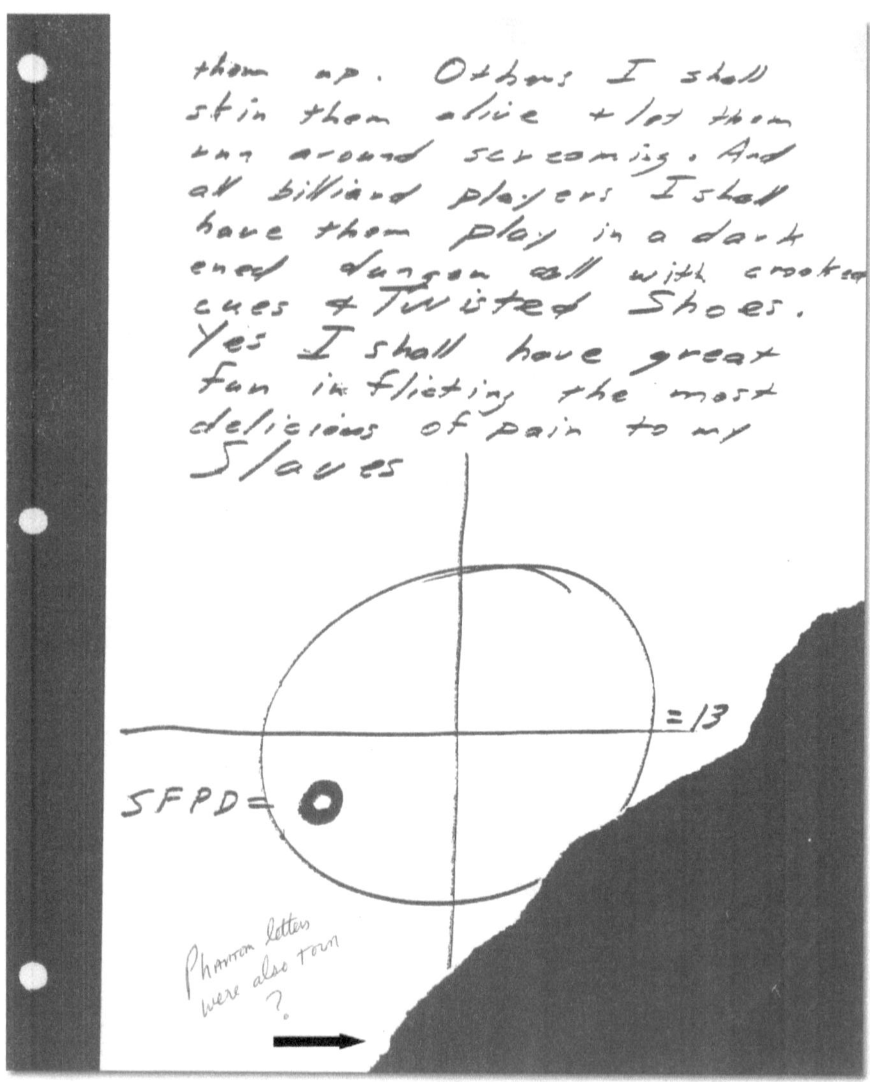

them up. Others I shall
skin them alive + let them
run around screaming. And
all billiard players I shall
have them play in a dark
ened dungen all with crooked
cues + Twisted Shoes.
Yes I shall have great
fun inflicting the most
delicious of pain to my
Slaves

= 13

SFPD = 0

Phantom letters
were also torn
?

Portion of the July 24, 1970, letter sent to the San Francisco Chronicle in the Zodiac case. (courtesy of Tom Voigt, www.zodiackiller.com)

In my opinion the Zodiac was specifically referring to the sign of the Zodiac as a "button." The repeated mentioning of the sign of the Zodiac immediately in front of the word "buttons" suggests, in no uncertain terms, that the sign of the Zodiac was in fact a button. If you take an ordinary sewing button and run thread through the button holes then cut the threads what emerges is the sign of the Zodiac.

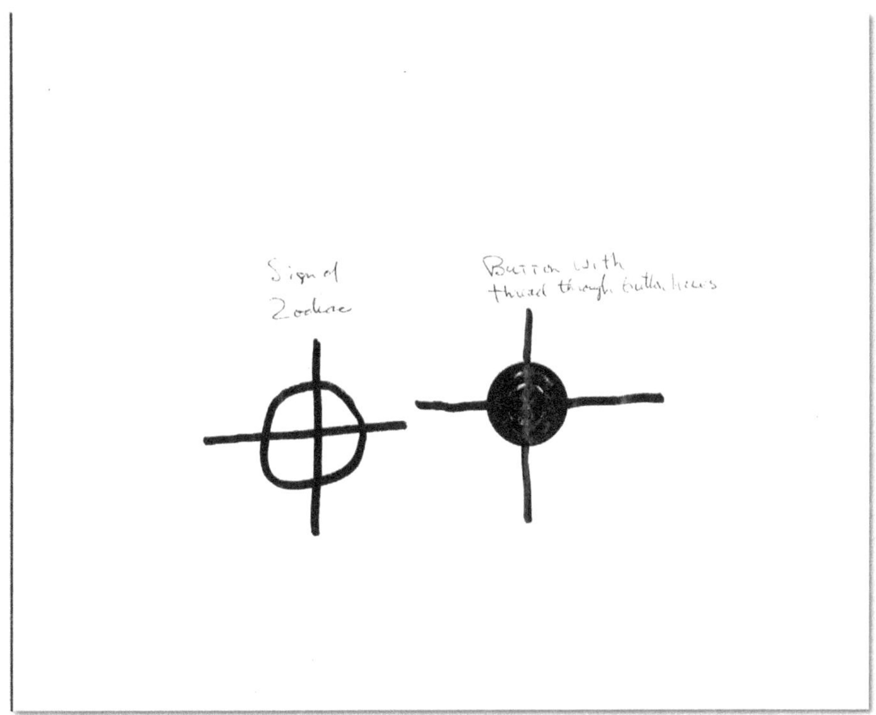

Sign of the Zodiac?

Zodiac Letter mailed to the San Francisco Chronicle 11/9/69

1/6

This is the zodiac speaking up to the end of Oct I have killed 7 people. I have grown rather angry with the police for their telling lies about me. So I shall change the way the collecting of slaves. I shall no longer announce to anyone. when I comitt my murders, they shall look like routine robberies, killings of anger, + a few fake accidents, etc.

The police shall never catch me, because I have been too clever for them.

1 I look like the description passed out only when I do my thing, the rest of the time I look entirle different. I shall not tell you what my descise consists of when I kill

2 As of yet I have left no fingerprints behind me contrary to what the police say

2/6

in my killings I wear trans-
parent finger tip guards. All it
is is 2 coats of airplane cement
coated on my finger tips - quite
unnoticible & very efective.
3 my killing tools have been bought
en through the mail order out-
fits before the ban went into
efect. except one & it was
bought out of the state.
So as you see the police don't
have much to work on. If you
wonder why I was wipeing the
cab down I was leaving fake clows
for the police to run all over town
with, as one might say, I gave
the cops som bussy work to do to
keep them happy. I enjoy needling
the blue pigs. Hey blue pig I
was in the park - you were useing
fire tracks to mask the sound
of your cruzeing prowl cars. The
dogs never come with in 2
blocks of me & they were to
the west & there was only 2

3/6

groups of barking about 10 min
apart then the motor cicles
went by about 150 ft away
going from South to north west.
ps. 2 cops pulled a goof abot 3
min after I left the cab. I was
walking down the hill to the
park when this cop car pulled up
& one of them called me over
& asked if I saw any one
acting supicisous or strange
in the last 5 to 10 min & I said
yes there was this man who
was runnig by waveing a gun
& the cops peeled rubber &
went around the corner as
I directed them & I dissap-
eared into the park abblock &
a half away never to be seen
again.

Must Print in Paper

Hey pig doesnt it rile you up
to have you noze rubed in your
booboos?
If you cops think I'm going to take
on a bus the way I stated I was,
you deserve to have holes in your
heads.

4/6

Take one bag of ammonium nitrate fertlizer + 1gal of stove oil + dump a few bags of gravel on top + then set the shit off + will positivily ventalate any thing that should be in the way of the Blast.
The death machiene is allready made. I would have sent you pictures but you would be nasty enough to trace them back to developer + then to me, so I shall describe my masterpiece to you. The nice part of it is all the parts can be bought on the open market with no quest ions asked.
1 bat. pow clock - will run for aprox 1 year
1 photoelectric switch
2 copper leaf springs
2 6V car bat
1 flash light bulb + reflector
1 mirror
2 18" cardboard tubes black with shoe polish in side + oute

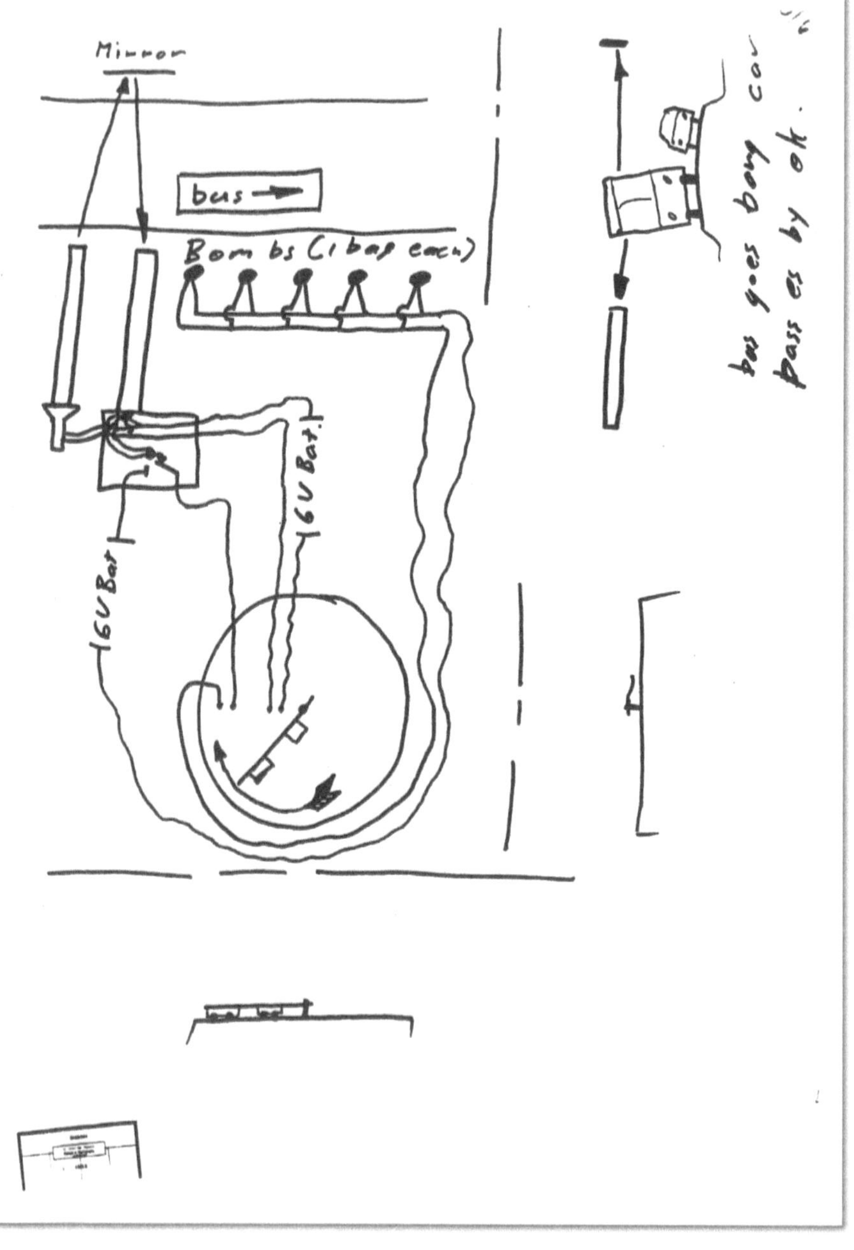
Mirror
bus
Bombs (1 bag each)
6V Bat
6V Bat.
bus goes boom car
passes by ok.

6/6

the system checks out from
one end to the other in my
tests. What you do not know
is whether the death machine
is at the sight or whether
it is being stored in my
basement for future use.
I think you do not have the
man power to stop this one
by continually searching the
road sides looking for this
thing. & it wont do to re roat
& re schedule the busses bec
ause the bomb can be adapted
to new conditions.
Have fun!! By the way
it could be rather messy
if you try to bluff me.

PS. Be shure to
print the part I
marked out on
page 3 or I shall
do my thing

To prove that I am the Zodiac, Ask the Vallejo cop about my electric gun sight which I used to start my collecting of slaves.

November 9, 1969, letter sent to the *San Francisco Chronicle* in the Zodiac case (courtesy of Tom Voigt, www.zodiackiller.com)

By November 9, 1969, the Zodiac had already killed at least six individuals, usually in secluded areas. These killings and his taunting, enigmatic letters to police and newspapers generated a great deal of fear in the general public. As though this weren't enough to satisfy his need for publicity and power, he added a new level of terror to his madness. Seldom do serial killers change their pattern or method of killing, including the type of victims. However, on November 9, 1969, the Zodiac threatened to do just that by sending a letter to the *San Francisco Chronicle* together with a drawing of a "bus bomb." The Zodiac indicated that the "bomb" was intended to be used to blow up a school bus full of children. At this point it is important to remember that the Zodiac had his own sense of humor that he wove into his deceptive writings. The Zodiac had written several phrases throughout his various letters that indicated he was having a "good time." For example, on August 7, 1969, he wrote, "By the way, are the police having a good time . . ." On November 8, 1969, the Zodiac wrote in his letter to the *San Francisco Chronicle*,

"I thought you would need a good laugh before you hear the bad news." On November 10, 1969, he wrote in another letter to the *Chronicle*, "Have fun." On April 19, 1970, he wrote on a greeting card, "I hope you enjoy yourselves when I have my Blast." The Zodiac seemed to get a great deal of enjoyment, not only writing and taunting the police, but also from fooling them. I believe that for some sort of personal satisfaction, he wrote his "bus bomb" letter intending to instill fear in the public and gain the attention he craved. I also believe he received personal gratification knowing full well that his "bus bomb" was no bomb at all; in my opinion, it may have been a drawing of his sewing machine. To the Zodiac, this was great fun. I am confident that I can establish that the Zodiac's "bus bomb" was in fact a drawing of a sewing machine. Keep in mind that the Zodiac wrote in his November 10, 1969, letter to the *Chronicle*, "If you cops think I am going to take on a school bus the way I stated I was, you deserve to have holes in your head." He may have been referring to his method referred to in his October 14, 1969 letter in which he wrote, "School children make nice targets, I think I shall wipe out a school bus some morning. Just shoot out the front tire & then pick off the kiddies as they come bouncing out." Or, on the other hand, he may have been referring to his "bus bomb" described in his letter of November 9, 1969. In any event let's take a closer look at the Zodiac's "bus bomb" drawing that he included with his November 9, 1969, letter to the *Chronicle:*

Upon close examination, you can see the spool, thread, stitches, pressure plate, needle, shuttle (bus), mirror and side lever that are all parts that are associated with a sewing machine.

Zodiac Map 1

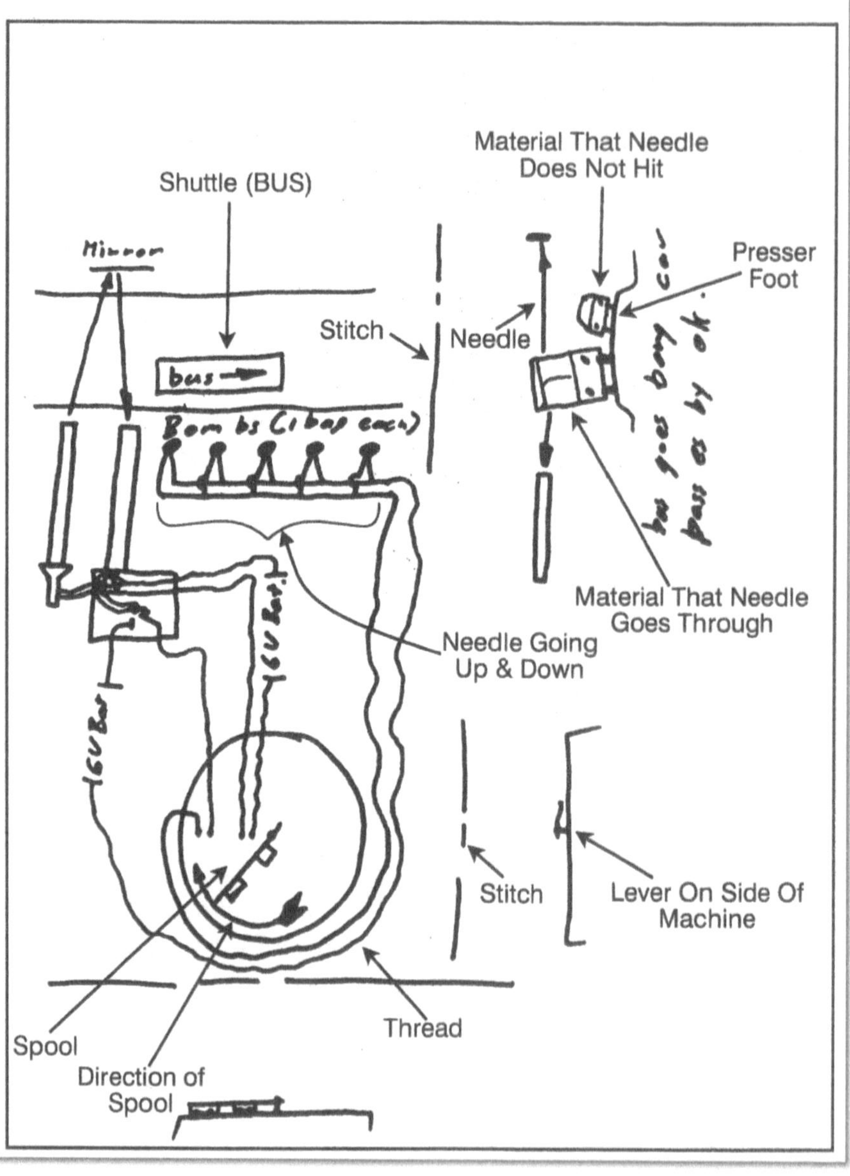

Zodiac's "Bus Bomb" appears to have been a drawing of a sewing machine

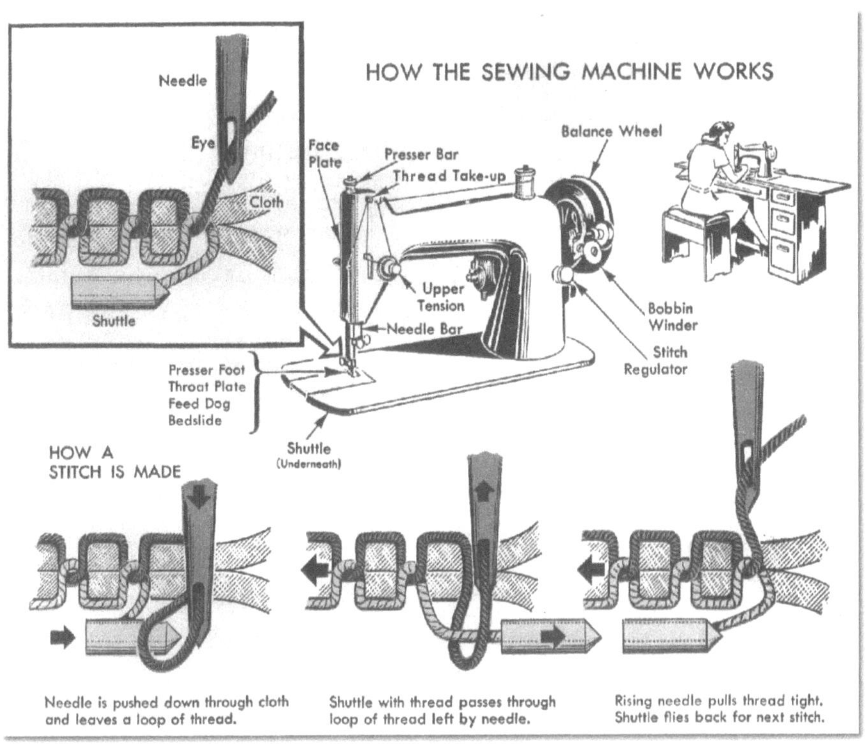

Illustration of a sewing machine from *The World Book Encyclopedia*, copyright World Book, Inc. By permission of the publisher, www.worldbook.com

The Zodiac was proficient at sewing (Note 37, page 320).

In his November 9, 1969, letter, the Zodiac referred to his "bus bomb" as a "**death machine**." He wrote "The system checks out from one end to the other in my tests. What you do not know is whether the **death machine** is at the sight or whether it is being stored in my basement for future use" (emphasis added). If you switch the word "sewing" for the word "death" and then figure the Zodiac used his imagination, while looking at his sewing machine, to concoct his grand story about the construction of a bus bomb it starts to make sense. He then mailed his letter to the *Chronicle* and received the attention he was looking for and personal satisfaction derived by fooling the detectives.

Unless, of course, you believe the Zodiac's version, on its face, that the drawing was in fact a bomb that included "mirrors on the side on the highway that reflects light to photoelectric cells that work only in daylight and cause several separate 'bombs' to go off that will strike a moving school bus (not a truck or other tall vehicle) and that will not strike a moving car. If you believe that, then I have a bridge for sale that you might be interested in purchasing.

CHANNEL SEVEN TALK SHOW

At 2:00 A.M., October 22, 1969, the Oakland California Police Department received a telephone call that may have come from the Zodiac killer. The caller requested a meeting with either attorney F. Lee Bailey or Melvin Belli. The caller wanted one otr the other to appear on a T.V. program known as the Channel Seven Talk Show. The meeting was scheduled; Melvin Belli appeared and received several telephone calls. The first of these calls may have come from the Zodiac Killer. Mr. Belli asked the caller if he could refer to him by a name other than Zodiac. The caller responded "Sam." Belli asked the caller where they could meet and the response was, "At the top of the Fairmont Hotel," a statement that may prove to be important in connection with later developments. It was reported that subsequent telephone calls to Mr. Belli were traced to a mental patient at the Napa State Hospital.

"DEAR MELVIN LETTER"

December 20, 1969

San Francisco attorney Melvin Belli received the following Christmas letter from the Zodiac on December 20, 1969:

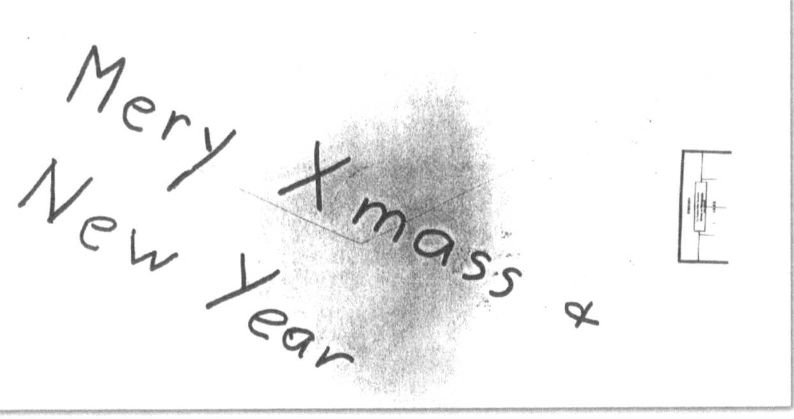

Dear Melvin

This is the Zodiac speaking I wish you a happy Christmass. The one thing I ask of you is this, please help me. I cannot reach out for help because of this thing in me wont let me. I am finding it extreamly dif-icult to hold it in check I am afraid I will loose control again and take my nineth & posibly tenth victom. Please help me I am drownding. At the moment the children are safe from the bomb because it is so massive to dig in & the triger mech requires much work to get it adjusted just right. But if I hold back too long from no nine I will loose ~~complet~~ all controol of my self & set the bomb up. Please help me I can not remain in control for much longer.

⊕

December 20, 1969, letter to Melvin Belli in the Zodiac case. (courtesy of Tom Voigt, www.zodiackiller.com)

PROPOSED SOLUTION:

In the letter you will notice the following:

"I am **fi**nding	I am	**F**	
"I am **a**fraid"	I am	**A**	
The letter contains five words with Extra letters:			
Christmass		**S**	
Extre**a**mly		**A**	
Nin**e**th	**E**		
Drownding			**D**
Contro**o**l		**O**	
There are three words with missing letters:			
Dificult	**F**		
Posibly	**S**		
Triger		**G**	
And the word:			
Vic**to**m	**TO**		
The word "complet" is crossed out and not finished. All the Zodiac had to do to finish this word was to add the letter "e," instead, he drew a single line through the unfinished word and continued with the letters:	**ALL**	**ALL**	

In my opinion, the word puzzle
might go like this: I AM F A GO TO S E DALLAS

KATHLEEN JOHNS

March 17, 1970

On March 22, 1970, Kathleen Johns was traveling with her ten-month-old baby on Interstate 5 near Bakersfield, California, on her way to Travis Air Force Base. At about midnight, when she turned onto Highway 132, she noticed headlights in her rear view mirror from a car that seemed to be following her. She slowed her vehicle down to let the other car pass. The car didn't pass her. Instead, she noticed blinking lights from the other vehicle. A stranger signaled her that one of her wheels was malfunctioning and to pull over and stop along the road. Kathleen was pregnant and apprehensive. She eventually pulled over and stopped her vehicle on the side of Highway 132. She allowed the stranger to attend to her wheel as she waited in her car. When she again started to drive, the wheel came completely off. The stranger stopped his vehicle and again approached her and offered assistance. "Oh no," he said. "The trouble's worse than I thought. I'll give you a ride to the service station." The stranger offered to drive her to a service station so she could summons help for her disabled vehicle. Kathleen could see the lights of an ARCO station about a quarter mile up the road. Kathleen was reluctant at first to accept a ride with him but then eventually accepted his offer. The stranger drove past the ARCO station and then past two exits. Kathleen's apprehension turned to fear not only for herself but also for her baby. She turned to the unknown driver, "Do you always go around helping people on the road like this?" He responded, "When I get through with them, they don't need any help." Kathleen Johns became totally afraid at this point. She knew she was in trouble. After driving down a lonely dirt road, the man said, "You know I'm going to kill you. I'm going to throw the baby out." Kathleen, although frightened, kept her head. She made a mental note of everything she could about her abductor and the contents of his vehicle. Her heart was pounding when she decided to make a run for it. When the stranger slowed down at a stop sign, Kathleen grabbed her baby and jumped from the moving car. She ran into tall grass and hid until the stranger was run off by a semi-truck driver (Robert Graysmith's interview with Kathleen Johns).

Later, at a local police station, Kathleen identified her abductor as the same person in the composite drawing of the Zodiac. Kathleen and her baby had apparently been riding with the Zodiac killer.

ALTERED PHILLIPS 66 MAP

June 26, 1970

The Zodiac sent a letter to the *San Francisco Chronicle* on June 26, 1970, stating:

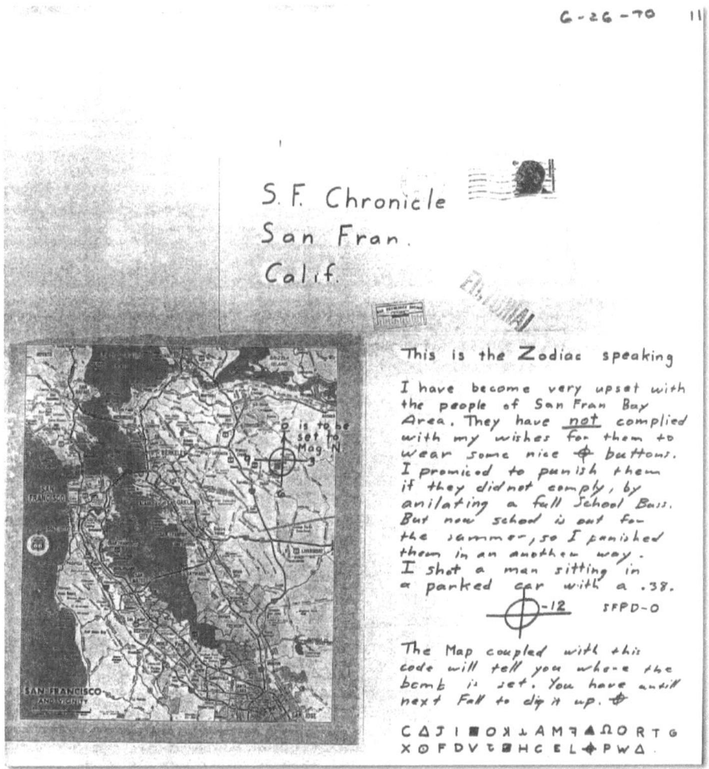

6-26-70

S.F. Chronicle
San Fran.
Calif.

This is the Zodiac speaking

I have become very upset with the people of San Fran Bay Area. They have not complied with my wishes for them to wear some nice buttons. I promiced to punish them if they did not comply, by anilating a full School Buss. But now school is out for the summer, so I punished them in an another way. I shot a man sitting in a parked car with a .38.

-12 SFPD-0

The Map coupled with this code will tell you where the bomb is set. You have untill next Fall to dig it up.

June 26, 1970 Phillips 66 Map in the Zodiac case.
(courtesy of Tom Voigt, www.zodiackiller.com)

A radian is a unit of measurement used by engineers and mathematicians of 57 degrees, 17 minutes, 44 seconds. It is an angle over an arc whose length is equal to the radius of a circle, of which the arc is a part.

The corporate headquarters for Phillips 66 is in the state of Oklahoma. The Phillips 66 sign on the Zodiac's map is located in the Pacific Ocean approximately eighty miles from the center of the sign of the Zodiac on the map. Dallas, Texas, is located approximately eighty miles south of the state of Oklahoma. Could the Phillips 66 decal on the map have anything to do with the solution to the Zodiac's puzzle?

GILBERT AND SULLIVAN'S: THE MIKADO

July 24, 1970

On July 24, 1970 the Zodiac sent his twelfth letter to the *San Francisco Chronicle*. In the letter he paraphrased a portion of Gilbert and Sullivan's *Mikado* from memory.

Here is a copy of the Zodiac's twelfth letter:

As some day it may hapen that a victom must be found. I've got a little list. I've got a little list, of society offenders who might well be underground who would never be missed who would never be missed. There is the pestulentual nucences who whrite for autographs, all people who have flabby hands and irritating laughs. All children who are up in dates and implore you with implatt. ~~All people~~ who are shakeing hands shake hands like that. And all third persons who with unspoiling take thoes who insist. They'd none of them be missed. They'd none of them be missed. There's the banjo seranader and the others of his race and the piano orginast I got him on the list. All people who eat pepermint and phomphit

in your face, they would
never be missed They would
never be missed And the
Idiout who phraises with in-
thusastic tone of centuries
but this and every country but
his own. And the lady from
the provences who dress like
a guy who doesn't cry and
the singurly abnomily the
girl who never kissed. I don't
think she would be missed
Im shure she wouldn't be
missed. And that nice impriest
that is rather rife the judic-
ial hummerest I've got him on
the list All funny fellows, com-
mic men and clowns of private
life. They'd none of them be
missed. They'd none of them be
missed. And uncompromiseing
kind such as wachamacallit,
thingmebob, and likewise, well-
-nevermind, and tut tut tut tut,
and whatshisname, and you know

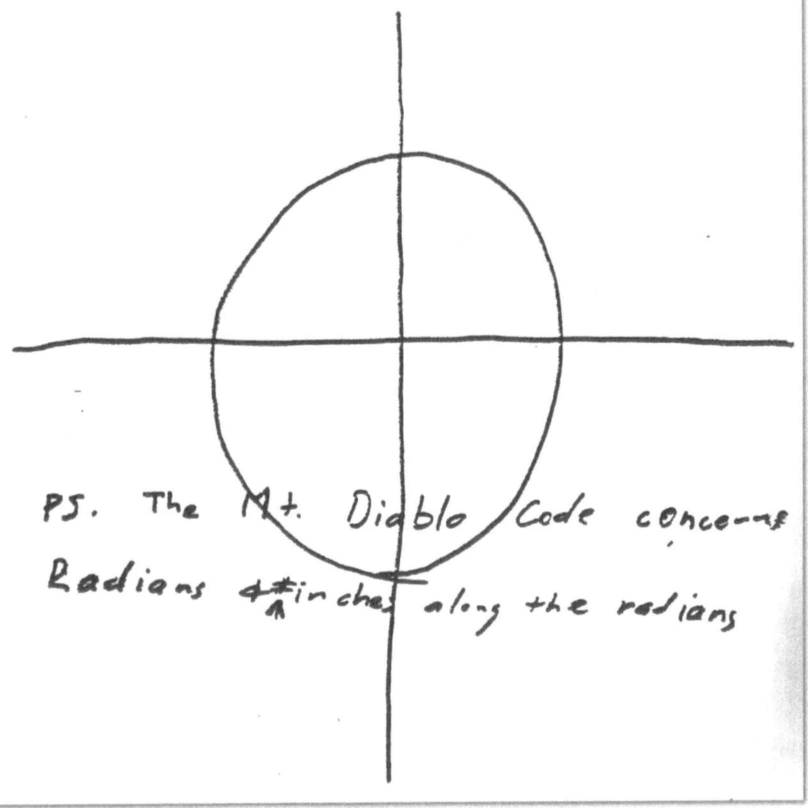

who, but the task of filling
up the blanks I rather leave
up to you. But it really does-
n't matter whom you place
upon the list, for none of
them be missed, none of
them be missed.

PS. The Mt. Diablo Code concerns
Radians & # inches along the radians

June 24, 1970, "Mikado" letter in the Zodiac case (courtesy of Tom Voigt, www.zodiackiller.com)

One line of the Zodiac's version reads as follows:

"All children who are up in dates and *implore* you with implatt"

The correct verse from the *Mikado* is written as follows:

"All children who are up in dates and *floor you* with em flat. . ."

The Zodiac misquoted the original *Mikado* by using the word "Implore" instead of "floor you." The word "implore" is a word that is not commonly used. John Keats, included the word "implore" in his poem "The Eve of St. Agnes."

"Buttress'd from moonlight, stands he and implores."

If the Zodiac was in fact an admirer of the works of John Keats, it could be possible that he misquoted the *Mikado* by substituting a word from the Keats' poem that was buried in his memory.

ZODIAC'S HALLOWEEN CARD

October 28, 1970

On Wednesday, October 28, 1970, *San Francisco Chronicle* crime reporter Paul Avery received a Halloween card from the Zodiac. The Zodiac enjoyed sending greeting cards and may have been particularly fond of holidays. This could account for the number of murders that took place on holidays that coincide with traditional greeting cards, i.e. St. Patrick's Day, Valentines Day, Labor Day, Christmas and so on. Avery's Halloween card stated in two places "sorry no cipher." This card was not a cipher. In my opinion it was a different kind of puzzle. This time a seek-a-word puzzle. The trick might be to discover his name written in the puzzle.

Here is a picture of the Paul Avery Halloween card:

Zodiac Halloween card. (courtesy of Tom Voigt, www.zodiackiller.com)

The name "FRED" can be found in what might be a word puzzle.

AIRMAIL LETTER

Here are some interesting facts that relate to the Zodiac killings:

a. Practically every one of the Zodiac murders occurred on weekends or on holidays.

b. On February 26, 1969, Darlene Ferrin mentioned to her babysitter, "I heard he was back from out of state." when referring to a stranger who had been parked outside her home at 560 Wallace in Vallejo, California.
c. On September 27, 1969, Bryan Hartnell and Cecelia Shephard were attacked by the Zodiac at Berryessa Lake. Bryan Hartnell told the police: "That voice. . . It was like. . . a student. But kind of a drawl not a Southern drawl though."
d. March 22, 1970, another victim, Kathleen Johns, described the Zodiac as follows: "I remember thinking he may be a serviceman."
e. The police had speculated that the Zodiac may have been a Navy man who committed his crimes while docked in San Francisco Harbor. Several eyewitness accounts identified the Zodiac as having a military-style crew cut, that he wore a Navy-type windbreaker, that his pants were pleated and his shoes spit shined.
f. On March 15, 1971, the *Los Angeles Times* received a letter from the Zodiac. The letter contained this phrase: "The longer they fiddle and fart around the more slaves I will collect for my afterlife" (emphasis added). Author Robert Graysmith argued in his book *Zodiac*, that the term "fiddle and fart around is a phrase used by older people around the state of Texas, most commonly in Lubbock County, Texas."
g. The word "AIRMAIL" took up one third of the envelope used by the Zodiac to mail the March 15, 1971, letter to the *Los Angeles Times*.

Zodiac's "Airmail letter." (courtesy of Tom Voigt, www.zodiackiller.com)

What this indicates to me is that the Zodiac may very well have been from a state other than California. When he writes the word "AIRMAIL," he is almost shouting out that he air-mailed the letter himself. Several coincidences seem to point to the state of Texas as being the home of the Zodiac. The letters may have been personally air-mailed when the Zodiac was transported to California by military aircraft. The known California murders committed by the Zodiac killer took place between the years 1966-1969, at the same time the Vietnam War was being waged in Southeast Asia. Soldiers and sailors were being transported by the thousands in the United States at that time from one military installation to another. Few restrictions that I know of were imposed to gain access to military flights. There were few, if any, background checks, no metal detectors to go through, just a review of the person's identification, and a thumb print. It was possible for someone to forge the required identification needed to fly "seat waiting" on military aircraft. If the person appeared as an officer, very few questions would be asked. If someone was military personnel, dependent of military personnel, or if that person had forged documents with the necessary picture identification and dressed as an Air Force or Navy man. He could have easily flown from Texas to California on a Friday afternoon and returned to Texas on Sunday night without detection. This person would probably have known that military manifests would be routinely destroyed approximately two years after each flight, thereby eliminating the evidence linking him to his method of transportation from one state to another. California has several Air Force and Naval air stations near the locations of each Zodiac murder.

Kathleen Johns was abducted by a person thought to be the Zodiac while on her way to her mother's house in Petaluma.

March Air Force Base is located near Riverside, California, where Cheri Jo Bates was murdered. The Grand Prairie Naval Air Station (Dallas NAS) was located near Dallas, during this time period. The Carlswell Air Station was located in Fort Worth near Dallas during the Vietnam War. The Grand Prairie Naval Air Station and Carlswell Air Force Base have since either been closed or incorporated into the Fort Worth Naval Air Station in Fort Worth.

DONNA LASS

September 6, 1970

Samuel Clemens once said about Lake Tahoe, "The lake burst upon us, a noble sheet of blue water lifted six thousand three hundred feet above the level of the sea, and walled in between a rim of snow-clad mountain peaks . . . thought it must surely be the fairest picture the whole earth affords."

My brother owned a cottage near the famous Donner Pass just west of Truckee off Highway 89. We vacationed in this area and skied the mountains at Heavenly and Squaw Valley. We also tried our luck at the Boomtown Casino playing black jack, so I became somewhat familiar with this area. This is a beautiful and fascinating part of America, rugged and unforgiving, full of history of the American West, including the story of a group of unfortunate emigrants who, in late fall 1846, found themselves at the foothills of the Sierra Nevada Mountains. They were ill equipped and totally unprepared for the onslaught of one of the worst snowfalls in decades that descended upon them. George Donner, Jacob Donner, James Reed, Charles Graves, Franklin Graves, Lewis Keseberg, their families and several other weary travelers became trapped in what would become, for several in their party, a wintry tomb. Up to twenty feet of snow fell during the first week of their captivity. It wasn't long before food supplies became depleted. Starvation soon followed. The historical account of the plight of the emigrants reflects cannibalism among some of the survivors. After the ordeal was finally over and the survivors rescued in the spring of 1847, Keseberg was tried for the murders of George and Tamzene Donner, Lavinah Murphy, George Foster, Samuel Donner and Mr. Wolfinger. He was acquitted because of lack of evidence.

On Labor Day, September 6, 1970, a twenty-five year old nurse by the name of Donna Lass mysteriously disappeared from a South Lake Tahoe Hotel. The authorities never found her or her remains. There are several remote locations in this vast expanse that have not been explored by humans for years. A body could easily be hidden off a dirt road and never be found. The remains of more than one murder victim have been found in remote areas north of Lake Tahoe over the years. The police were at a standstill, no clues, no body, just a pretty young nurse missing and a family desperate to find her.

On Monday, March 22, 1971, Paul Avery of the *San Francisco Chronicle* received a postcard written in the Zodiac's hand.

On the reverse side of the card the Zodiac had glued an advertisement that had run in the *Chronicle* two days before. It was an artist's drawing of the Forest Pines Condominiums Village located near Lake Tahoe. The Avery postcard contains the words, "Pass Lake Tahoe Areas." The first letters of each word in this phrase are **PLTA**. These letters, when switched around, spell "**PLAT**." A plat is a map. Was the Zodiac sending a clue that may include the directions to the body of Donna Lass?

The South Lake Tahoe Police considered the possibility of a connection between the disappearance of Donna Lass and the Zodiac killer. For years the search for Donna Lass went on without any success. On January 30, 1974, nearly three years after her disappearance, the *San Francisco Chronicle* received the following note in the Zodiac's handwriting:

I saw + think "The Exorcist"
was the best saterical com-
idy that I have ever seen.

Signed, yours truley :

He plunged him self into
the billowy wave
and an echo arose from
the sucides grave
titwillo tit willo
titwillo

Ps. if I do not see this
note in your paper, I
will do something nasty,
which you know I'm capable of
doing

Me - 37
SFPD - 0

Zodiac's "Exorcist" letter.
(courtesy of Tom Voigt, www.zodiackiller.com)

The "Exorcist" was not a satirical comedy; it was a horror movie. The words satirical and truly are misspelled, as are other words.

SAT	eri	*CAL*
Tru	*LEY*	

These misspelled words may spell **SATLEY, CAL**. Sattley, California, is a small town located on State Highway 89 in Sierra County, north of Lake Tahoe. The symbols that follow the Zodiac's "Exorcist" letter may represent roads leading to Sattley, from Lake Tahoe, California.

The mark on the left side of the map may represent the location of the remains of Donna Lass.

Additional comparisons between the Phantom Killer letters and the Zodiac letters are shown below.

(1947, FBI Report on Phantom Killer of Texarkana)

b6
b7C

DL #9-616

letter which bears postmark of "June 24, 1946, 3 PM, Texarkana, Ark. Tex. This letter is typewritten in the lower case. The third letter was also postmarked during 1946 but the remaining part of the postmark has been torn off. This letter was received by [redacted] and is a handwritten letter. The last two letters were mailed in a three cent stamped envelope of the long type that can be purchased at the Post Office. The first letter is in a small envelope and the stamp has been placed on the envelope. These letters are being set forth:

I. "Soon as read no time to lose for lives are in danger [redacted]

The writer would like to meet you personally, but every movement is being watched, on account thinking writer overheard conversation or least portion of it. Wish you would never give me away ever if you knew as my life would not be worth any more to these parties than was of those lately murdered.

"Please believe this, gun of German make, using .45 or 38 caliber, was borrowed recently for more trouble, so watch this week end for something or later. They said that had gotten by with so much [redacted] is carrier of gun, gotten from [redacted] [redacted] [redacted] they said had 40 or 50 to cover up for alibis if ever questioned. [redacted] said like first girl murdered, well enought no one else not to have her did not mention last couple. [redacted] is clever and cunning gotten by with stealing and rapping and has plenty to help him, as his dad is law on Ark side.

"Said [redacted] was carrying gun for own protection and would have good alibi of March 24. This is true and hope you will see into this as are getting braver please burn this, even tho true, writer would be killed if ever known, this is valuable to you. Shake him down. But please burn. Writer will not signname as want to live."

II. [redacted]

"Some time ago you were written a letter, concerning three different parties, addressed to you at Texas Police Station, and whether you got it or not, is not known.

- 2 -

FBI misspelling? weekend written as two words WR

See letter to Vallejo Times Herald 8/1/69 pages 108-109 Zodiac by Robert Graysmith

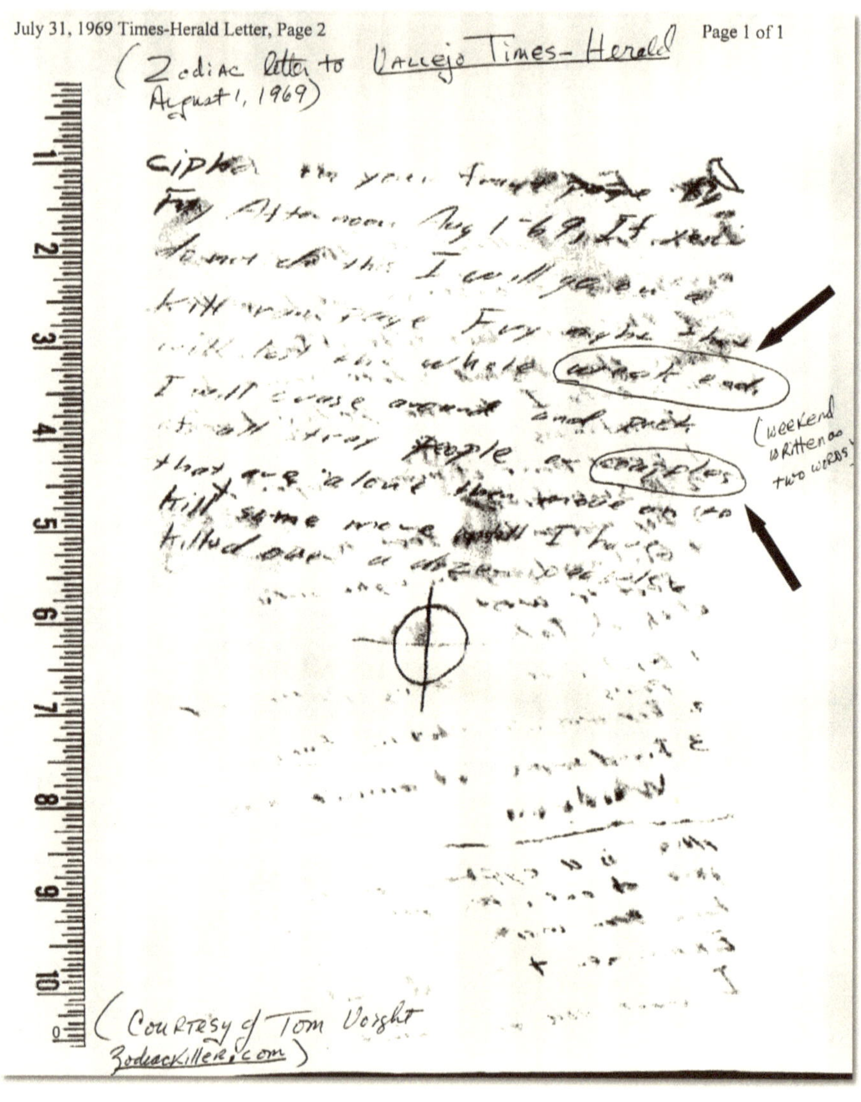

July 31, 1969 Times-Herald Letter, Page 2 Page 1 of 1

(Zodiac letter to Vallejo Times-Herald August 1, 1969)

cipher [illegible] your [illegible]
[illegible] Afternoon Aug 1-69, It [illegible]
[illegible] I will [illegible]
kill rampage Fry [illegible]
[illegible] whole week end.
I will [illegible] around and pick
[illegible] people or couples
that are alone [illegible]
kill some more until I have
killed over a dozen [illegible]

(weekend written as two words)

(Courtesy of Tom Voigt Zodiackiller.com)

Zodiac Letter mailed to the San Francisco Chronicle 11/9/69

6 (Zodiac Killer Letter Written 11/9/69) 1/6

This is the zodiac speaking
up to the end of Oct I have
killed 7 people. I have grown
rather angry with the police
for their telling lies about me.
So I shall change the way the
collecting of slaves. I shall
no longer announce to anyone.
when I comitt my murders,
they shall look like routine
robberies, killings of anger, +
a few fake accidents, etc.

The police shall never catch me,
because I have been too clever
for them.
1 I look like the description
passed out only when I do
my thing, the rest of the time
I look entirle different. I
shall not tell you what my
descise consists of when I kill
2 As of yet I have left no
fingerprints behind me contrary
to what the police say

(Courtesy of Tom Voight
ZodiacKiller.com)

(1947, FBI Report on Phantom Killer of Texarkana)

DL #9-616

(letter cont'd)

"Sometimes letters written like this seem to be maybe to you people not too much importance, but to others possibly would mean their life. This letter referred to was written in time before the Starks' murder and you were given three names and this is another note or letter written in behalf of lives of people who care to live, but cannot come to you. Trusting you are not favoring no certain Ark. Law man or his friend, which is not written in any way, shape or manner, as an accusation of any kind with reference to our laws or you. If you will do some questiong think you will have something, as as what we need in this town is co-operation and no pay off. Talk getting mighty big and brave and time getting ripe, so get busy and watch these people.

"Trust you will keep this confidential as you said you would in the newspaper, is not written with spirit of ralling things up, but with all good intention to help protect the lives of not only one person, but possibly many.

"If you will check Blue two door Sedan, without top, you, of it had been the findings, no doubt would of been an advantage to you. This Sedan belongs to boy not over 24, North of Texarkana, Arkansas. Has been washed and rewashed, and had two friends to help him, and gun was returned to one of them. Keep that confidential, confidential as it measn the lives of more than one."

III [redacted]

"As some people have hobbies I have one looking at different license number, especially State licenses and have tried to find you in or on the phone and am told you were out and wish you would keep this confidential. While travelling out highway toward Little Rock noticedcar parked near railroad track and it backed out, since then learned car the night Mr. Stark's was murdered was parked close to railroad track, road where told [redacted] went across to sisters house and this car number [redacted] and saw it since on trips to Texarkana, but just recently learned the

b6

b7C

- 3 -

(Zodiac letter written 11/9/69) 2/6

in my killings I wear trans-
parent finger tip guards. All it
is is 2 coats of airplane cement
coated on my finger tips—quite
unnoticible & very efective.
3 my killing tools have been bought
en through the mail order out-
fits before the ban went into
efect. except one & it was
bought out of the state.
So as you see the police don't
have much to work on. If you
wonder why I was wipeing the
cab down I was leaving fake clows
for the police to run all over town
with, as one might say, I gave
the cops som (bussy) work to do to
keep them happy. I enjoy needling
the blue pigs. Hey blue pig I
was in the park—you were useing
fire trucks to mask the sound
of your cruzeing prowl cars. The
dogs never come with in 2
blocks of me & they were to
the west & there was only 2

39

(Courtesy of Tom Voigt, zodiackiller.com)

(Zodiac letter written 11/9/69) 3/6

groups of parking about 10 min
apart then the motor cicles
went by about 150 ft away
going from South to north west.
ps. 2 cops pulled a goof abot 3
min after I left the cab. I was
walking down the hill to the
park when this cop car pulled up
& one of them called me over
& asked if I saw any one
acting supicisous or strange
in the last 5 to 10 min & I said
yes there was this man who
was runnig by waveing a gun
& the cops peeled rubber &
went around the corner as
I directed them & I dissap-
eared into the park a block &
a half away never to be seen
again.
Hey pig doesnt it rile you up
to have you noze rubed in your
booboos?
If you cops think I'm going to take
on a bus the way I stated I was,
you deserve to have holes in your
heads.

Most Print in Paper

(Courtesy of Tom Voight, ZodiacKiller.com)

(Zodiac Killer letter. July 24, 1970) 7

As some day it may hapen
that a victom must be found.
I've got a little list. I've
got a little list, of society
offenders who might well be
underground who would never
be missed who would never be
missed. There is the pestulentual nucences who whrite
for autographs, all people who
have flabby hands and irritating laughs. All children who
are up in dates and implore
you with im platt. All people
who are shakeing hands shake
hands like that. And all third
persons who with unspoiling
take thoes who insist. They'd
none of them be missed. They'd
none of them be missed. There's
the banjo seranader and
the others of his race and
the piano orginast I got him
on the list. All people who
eat pepermint and phomphit

(Courtesy of Tom Voigt
ZodiacKiller.com)

7

(1947, FBI Report on Phantom Killer of Texarkana)

DL #9-616

"AS POSSIBLE IN AS LARGE AMOUNT OF MONEY AS POSSIBLE.
LARGE BUNDLE SO AS TO NOT MAKE POSSIBLE. PUT THIS ON
FRIDAY OF THIS WEEK BETWEEN EIGHT AND EIGHT FIFTEEN [redacted]
[redacted] THEN LEAVE GO HOME STAY
QUIET. WITHOUT ALLOWING ANYONE TO KNOW ABOUT THIS IN ANY
WAY YOU KNOW WHAT I MEAN. THE AMOUNT IS THREE THOUSAND
DOLLARS THIS IS ONLY FIRST REQUEST TO GET BACK YOUR REQUEST
OR RAILROADING? REMEMBER??? YES YOU DO. DON'T HAVE ANY
WATCH DOG OR PROWLERS. KEEP QUIET ABOUT THIS OR ELSE.
YOUR RAILROADING OTHER PEOPLE IS OVER. REMEMBER YOUR FAMILY
AND KEEP RULES AND MUM OR??????"

b6
b7C

6 question MARKS

It should be particularly noted in the note that the victim was instructed to put the bundle on Friday of this week (which was May 2, 1947) between 8:00 and 8:15. The note does not state whether A.M. or P.M. However, since the victim did not report the matter until after 8:15 A.M., arrangements were made to surveil the pay-off spot in Spring Lake Park, Texarkana. The victim stated that he did not have $3,000 but agreed to place a package at the point designated in the note. He did not desire to have [redacted] and requested that an officer be left at his residence while he was making the trip from his residence to the park, and that an officer accompany him concealled in his automobile. A surveillance of the pay-off spot was maintained by the writer and Special Agent [redacted] of the Little Rock Division, and Bowie County Deputy Sheriffs [redacted]. A surveillance was maintained at the entrance of the park by Special Agent [redacted] of the Little Rock Division and Miller County, Arkansas, Deputy Sheriff [redacted] Arkansas State Policeman [redacted] remained at the victim's residence, and Arkansas State Policeman [redacted] accompanied the victim from his residence to Spring Lake Park. The victim placed the package at the appointed place at approximately 8:10 PM. A surveillance was maintained at the various places from approximately 7:15 until 11:00 P.M. Nothing of value was noted at any of the above-mentioned points.

b6
b7C

At the time the victim reported the receipt of the letter, he stated that he suspected only one individual. This individual was FLOYD KILCREASE, a former owner of a welding shop and garage at Dudley and Jackson Streets, Texarkana, Arkansas. The victim had purchased the residence at 3119 Locust Street from KILCREASE approximately one month prior to the receipt of the letter. He furnished the following information which caused him to suspect KILCREASE. KILCREASE was in California at the time he negotiated through [redacted] real estate dealer, with [redacted] for the purchase

- 2 -

7

(Zodiac's "dripping pen" greeting card, Nov 8, 1969)

This is the Zodiac speaking
I though you would need a
good laugh before you
hear the bad news
You won't get the
news for a while yet
PS could you print
this new cipher
in your frunt page?
I get awfully lonely
when I am ignored,
So lonely I could
do my Thing!!!!!!

and i can't do a thing with it!

(6 exclamation marks)

(6 lines under word "Thing")

Des July Aug
Sept Oct = 7

(Courtesy of Tom Voight
ZodiacKiller.com)

Chapter 6

COMPARISONS BETWEEN THE ZODIAC KILLER AND THE EYEBALL KILLER

"When the moon is in the seventh house
And Jupiter aligns with Mars
Then peace will guide the planets
And love will steer the stars."
—The 5th Dimension,
Aquarius/Let the Sunshine In, 1969

Several years ago I was researching a series of unsolved murders. During my investigation a seasoned homicide detective in Dallas, Texas, informed me that "all serial killers are alike." To me this sounded like stereotyping and too sweeping, too simplistic, given the many differences in serial killer's motivations and methods. Other murders that I had studied, that had been committed by different individuals, were, in some ways, similar and in other ways different. Age of the victims, time and methods of perpetrating the crimes, weapons used, signatures, crime scene evidence and so on were all different in some respect. Humans are victims of habit and although they may try to hide their identity they are still subject to certain personality traits and interests that may eventually reveal their identity. Someone may have an interest in electronics, sports, women, fast cars, fine wines, tattoos, opera, sex, and a myriad of other interests. It therefore seems hard to believe that all serial killers are alike beyond the most general level (i.e., that they all commit more than one murder and tend to have signature methods). But it seems crucial to consider the degree to which serial killers might have very specific traits in common, other than just the obvious comparisons the detective may have had in mind with his remark. If at a more detailed level serial killers tend to be unique, what would it mean if we found very unusual, seemingly unique details in common between a pair of serial killers? What if the Texas detective's idea could be revised as "Serial killers may often share a few very broad traits but are usually quite distinct in their methods, their manner of expression, and their interests or hobbies other than in their criminal acts. So if we discover similarities between any two killers in these special, unusual characteristics, we should pay close attention." That is the purpose of this chapter, then, to look for the possibility of such specific similarities between two well known serial killers: convicted serial killer Charles F. Albright in Texas and the yet-to-be-identified Zodiac Killer associated mostly with California.

On August 10, 1933, Charles F. Albright was born in Amarillo, Texas. He was adopted by Fred Albright and Delle Albright, husband and wife, and lived in Oak Cliff, Texas, about 180 miles from Texarkana where the Phantom Murders took place in 1946. He learned taxidermy at age nine and received his first gun shortly thereafter. Stuffed dead birds were exhibited in the Albright home. By age thirteen he had been convicted of aggravated assault. Years later, during an interview with a reporter, Albright recalled how he ". . . vividly remembers a quarter pound of hamburger meat that stayed in the side door of the refrigerator. Over the weeks it was there, the refrigerator door opened and closed so many times that the meat would thaw a little bit and refreeze. By the time Delle got around to cooking it, the meat was pretty rank, but she mixed it up with all sorts of filler and served a big plate of meatballs. Charlie snuck bites onto a little ledge under the table and fed them to the dog" (Note 39, p. 138). Such a bizarre incident regarding tainted meat would seem to be unique to Albright's childhood, but consider a statement by the Zodiac Killer: On July 24, 1970, Zodiac wrote in a letter to the *San Francisco Chronicle*: "Others shall be placed in cages and fed salt beef until they are gorged then I shall listen to their pleass for water and I shall laugh at them" (Note 40, p. 152-153). Albright also indicated in an interview given in 1991, that his mother "put him in a dark room as punishment for chewing on her tape measure." "When he wouldn't take a nap she would tie him to his bed" (Note 41, p. 341-342). With a similar set of particulars, Zodiac continued in his July 24th letter: "Some I shall tie over ant hills and watch them scream & twitch and squirm," "all billiard players I shall have them play in a darkened dungen all with crooked cues and Twisted shoes" (Note 40, p. 152-153). As a child, Albright was surrounded by stuffed animals and birds, but they differed from the usual taxidermied practice in how the eyes were created. Instead of putting glass eyes in the taxidermied birds, Albright's mother, who was a seamstress, took buttons out of her sewing bag and sewed them into the bird's eye sockets. Albright recalled this information over thirty-five years after the date his mother used buttons instead of taxidermist's eyes. An early interest in eyes and buttons as substitutions for them obviously played into Albright's serial killings, but a fixation with buttons isn't confined to what we know of the Texas killer, Zodiac wrote about "buttons" in several of his letters. For example, on April 29, 1970, he wrote in a letter to the *San Francisco Chronicle*: "I would like to see some nice Zodiac butons wandering about town. Everyone else has these buttons like (peace symbol), black power, Melvin eats blubber, etc. Well it would cheer me up considerably if I saw a lot of people wearing my buton." In his eleventh letter to the *Chronicle* mailed on June 26, 1970, Zodiac wrote in part "They have not complied with my wishes for them to wear some nice (Zodiac sign) buttons."

Hobbies and acquired skills would seem to be among the traits likely to differ from serial killer to serial killer, yet here, too, a comparison can be made. Taxidermy involves sewing. In his twelfth letter to the *Chronicle* Zodiac wrote "I am rather unhappy because you people will not wear some nice (Zodiac sign) buttons." Because Albright's adoptive mother was a seamstress and because he was into taxidermy at age nine, I suspect he learned how to sew at an early age. "Zodiac knew how to sew well" (Note 40, p. 320).

Albright's mother made him wear glasses because he had headaches (Note 41, p. 349-350). Zodiac wore glasses and may have claimed to have headaches (Note 40, p.115).

At age 18, Albright cut the eyes out of a friend's ex-girlfriend's photographs and pasted them on the dorm walls of dorm room at the Arkansas State Teacher's College. It was later determined that Albright had some psychological attraction to eyes. Albright's victims in Texas had their eyes surgically removed at the time they were murdered. On October 27, 1970, Zodiac mailed a Halloween greeting card addressed to Paul Avery to the *Chronicle.* Inside the card, "Zodiac had pasted a totally different skeleton, a portion of another card, and had drawn exaggerated pictures of peering eyes . . ." "The card had come originally with only one peering 'evil eye'. Zodiac had added twelve more, and had given the printed skeleton eyes as well" (Note 40, p. 159-160). Compare the skeleton in a photo of a Halloween party found by the author in Albright's file at the Dallas District Attorney's Office in 2001, with the skeleton drawn by the Zodiac in his Halloween greeting card addressed to Paul Avery on October 28, 1970. The teeth in the skeletons, the eyes and marking on the skulls show a close resemblance. The skull of the skeleton in the Albright photo may just be a mask and, if so, of no significance.

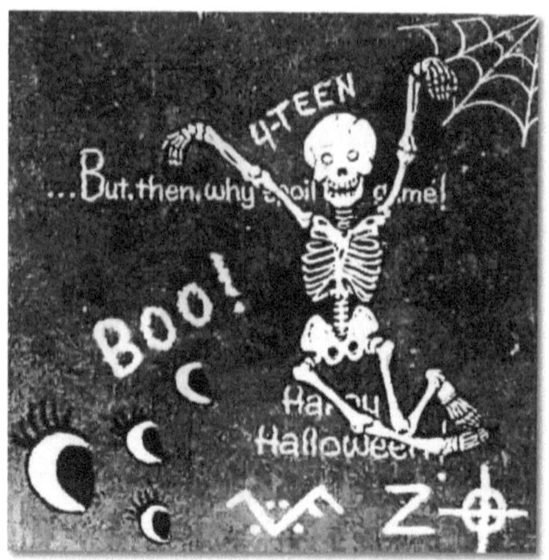

Zodiac's drawing of skeleton on Paul Avery greeting card to San Francisco Chronicle October 27, 1970.
(photo courtesy of Dallas County District Attorney's office)

Photo of skeleton at Albright's Halloween Party.
(photo courtesy of Dallas County District Attorney's office)

Besides these very unusual and seemingly unique comparisons, there are similarities between Albright and the Zodiac in physical appearance, educational or career backgrounds, and methods used in their crimes. Albright rarely kept the same job for more than three months. During his prosecution, it was made clear that Albright killed his victims at close range. Zodiac is a serial killer who profilers thought would not be able to hold a job and who killed at close range. In physical appearance Albright is 5'11" and in 1969, wore his short, brown curly-hair military style. From witness reports, we know that Zodiac was 5'11" and wore his short, brown, curly-hair military style in 1969.

Composite drawing of Zodiac supplementing the San Francisco Police Department Bulletin 87-69, October 13, 1969. (note partially open mouth)

Photo of Charles F. Albright taken in 1969, at Crandall High School where Albright was employed as a school teacher and school bus driver.

Albright

FORM 137-Rev. 77

SHERIFF'S DEPARTMENT
CASE REPORT

Disposition		Filed	
Date		Date	April 3, 1991 Time
Court		With	Geyer
Docket		By	Oliver #651
Method		Court	CDC
Disposition		Docket	
		Location of Defendant	In Jail (other charges)

5' 11"

SS [redacted]
TX D.L. [redacted]

Defendant: ALBRIGHT, Charles Frederick (Last) (First) (Middle) Race: W Sex: M D.O.B. 8/10/33

Height: 71" Weight: 186 Hair: gray Eyes: brown Scars/Tattoo: none

Alias: none

Residence Address: 1035 Eldorado, Dallas TX Identification No. (LAI): 115120

Place of Arrest: Date of Arrest:

Magistrate's Hearing: Date Time Magistrate

Offense: Date February 10, 1991 Time 8:00 am Service No. 91-02517 Offense No. 91-02517

Complainant: PETERSON, Susan Beth (Last) (First) (Middle) Race: W Sex: F D.O.B. 9/25/63

Where Committed: Roadway, 10000 Beckleyview, Dallas County, Texas

How Committed: He intentionally commits murder pursuant to the same scheme or course of conduct

Charge: Capital Murder, Sec. 19.03 TPC, a Capital Felony

Property Taken and Value: none

Evidence and Seizures: blue blanket and quilt with blood, hair, and fibers that match hair and fibers found on the body of the complainant.

Voluntary Statement: none

Accomplices: none

Summary of Case: On February 10, 1991 at 8:00a.m., Oscar Martinez found the nude body of Complainant Peterson lying just off the roadway in the 10000 block of Beckleyview in Dallas County, Texas. Mr. Martinez notified the Sheriff's Department by use of a neighbor's phone in this residential area. The nude body appeared to have been dumped at that location after death. At the autopsy

Witnesses and additional information placed on reverse side

Dallas County Sheriff's Department report dated April 3, 1991, indicating that Albright is 5' 11" and weighs 186 pounds.

Albright taught at Crandall High School near Dallas, Texas, in 1969. He also drove school bus at that time. The 1970 Crandall High School High School Yearbook included artwork depicting the zodiac wheel that "appeared to have been drawn by someone with a draughtsman's background." A former football player associated with Crandall High School in 1969, confirmed that Albright may have had input in the Yearbook artwork because he worked fairly close with the yearbook advisor. In college Albright had been "business manager of the yearbook" before becoming a teacher at Crandall High School (Note 39, p. 150). Having a zodiac theme in the 1970 yearbook seemed odd to a current member of the Crandall High School staff because "Crandall is such a small, extremely Christian town, and people here still get upset if we run a horoscope in the newspaper."

Published with permission of Crandall High School.

Cover of the 1970 Crandall High School Yearbook showing signs of the Zodiac. (Yearbook photos courtesy of Crandall High School, Crandall, TX)

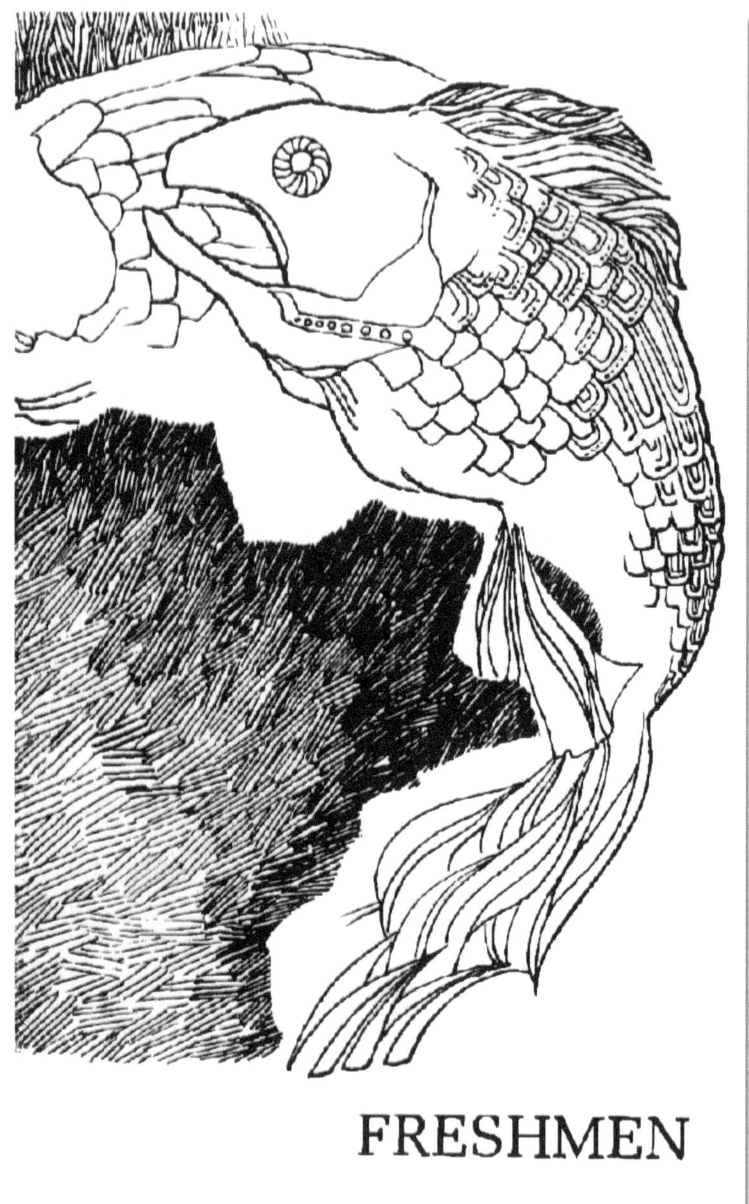

Published with permission of Crandall High School.

Sign of the Zodiac drawing in 1970 Crandall High School Yearbook.

... to Crandall, we were, to say the least, very happy," said former Crandall School Trustee, Lovel Griffith. "He had made high marks in school and was an honor student at East Texas State."

The principal had been searching all summer for a teacher and Albright came along just in time with a master's degree in biology and starting on his Ph.D. So he was put to work as a health teacher, biology teacher, bus driver, and the junior high coach.

"Everything was going perfect," said Griffith, "all the young guys seemed to get along with him and all the young girls loved him."

... faked, too," said Griffith. "He had been kicked out of college well before he ever graduated."

Albright was wearing out his welcome quickly. Griffith and a fellow board member, Edward Key, were advocates of removing him as soon as possible.

"It came down to who would take over his bus route," said Griffith, who was becoming more and more frustrated, "so I volunteered to drive the afternoon route and Edward Keys took the morning route."

Both Crandall ISD and ETSU decided to keep a lid on things,

... face when she got to his mug shot.

After being told that if she identified her attacker the police w... put him in jail where he could no lo... hurt her, she looked up and quickly tu... Albright's picture over, and signed ... name.

At approximately two a.m. o... morning of March 22, 1991 a team of ... tical officers prepared to invade Albri... 1035 Eldorado house.

"It was a cool, eerie morni... recalled former Dallas S.W.A.T. t... member of almost 14 years, Sergeant ... die Fuller, the father of Pirate Press ... writer Amanda Fuller. "We parked ... vans a couple of blocks away and ther...

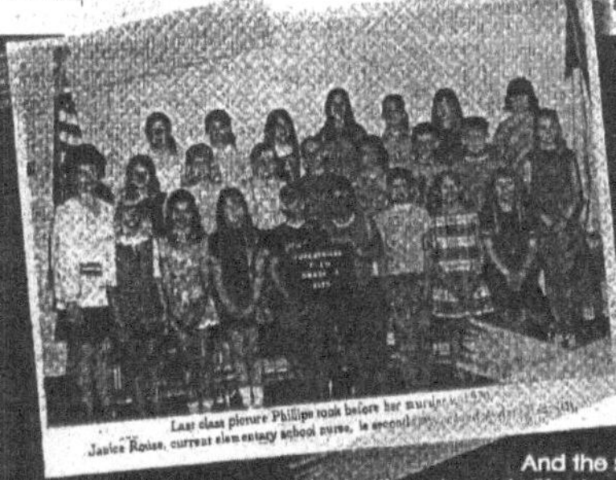

Last class picture Phillips took before her murder ... Janice Rouse, current elementary school nurse, is second ...

It was the murder that shocked Kaufman Cou... daughter of Kaufman ISD Superintendent James ... death on the night of Sunday, August 9, 1970. He... of Kaufman, right off an old dusty road that lead... A teacher at Forest Ridge Elementary School in ... and was friends with a lot of area schoolteache...

On that night she was killed, she had attend... talking with a fellow teacher from nearby Cran... Dallas Police Lieutenant Regina Smith said th... years until notorious serial killer Henry Lee Luc... were quickly closed on the Phillips murder, and ... quite happy to place her investigation in the "...

But Lucas confessed to a rash of killin... have killed over 3,000 people. Investigators qu... fessions were little more than a hoax to keep h... ter all, they couldn't kill him if he was the key w...

And the state of Texas didn't kill him. In 1998, then-Gove... sole death sentence to life. Lucas died in prison of cancer in 2001.

Smith said that when she was investigating Albright, she went to the Kaufman County Sheriff's Office to ... there. It had been misplaced after the case was closed with Lucas' confession.

In an odd twist of fate Crandall Elementary nurse, Janice Rouse, was one of Phillips fourth grade student...

"Linda was the sweetest, most fun, and highly respected teacher," recalled Rouse.

When Phillips died, Richardson neighborhoods gathered in mourning.

"I remember that most people didn't know where Kaufman was," said Rouse, "but my mom's friend di... al."

Lt. Smith said she doesn't know if Albright had anything to do with Phillips murder or not, but she said ... weren't his only victims.

"You cannot convince me that a 57 year old man just up and decided to start killing," said Smith, "I...

14

Published with permission from the Crandall High School Pirate Press

Page from Crandall High School Pirate Press indicating that Albright drove school bus in 1969.

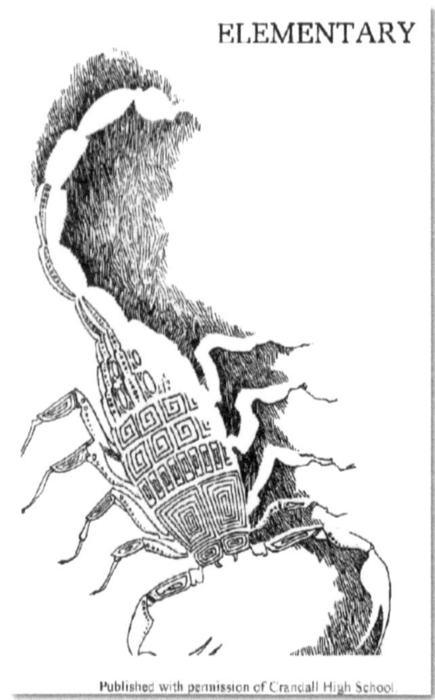

Drawing of sign of Zodiac in the 1970 Crandall High School Yearbook.

Drawing of sign of the Zodiac in the 1970 Crandall High School Yearbook.

Detectives speculated that Zodiac may have been a school teacher based on information presented in the Zodiac letters. Zodiac wrote in a letter received by the *Chronicle* on Tuesday, October 14, 1969, "School children make nice targets, I think I shall wipe out a school bus some morning & then pick off the kiddies as they come bouncing out" (Note 40, p.102). A school bus driver could certainly become upset with unruly children he transported.

Albright was into astrology. "He can name all of the constellations in the sky" (Note 41, p. 341). "A friend of Albright had marked her calendar the day one of Albright's victims, Mary White, had died and had begun plotting the phases of the moon. She spent many hours listening to his theories, and was sure that he had killed

This is the Zodiac speaking

I have become very upset with the people of San Fran Bay Area. They have not complied with my wishes for them to wear some nice ⊕ buttons. I promiced to punish them if they did not comply, by anilating a full School Buss. But now school is out for the summer, so I punished them in an another way. I shot a man sitting in a parked car with a .38.

⊕-12 SFPD-0

The Map coupled with this code will tell you where the bomb is set. You have untill next Fall to dig it up. ⊕

Zodiac's letter to the *San Francisco Chronicle* June 26, 1970, threatening to annihilate a school bus.

the women at times that corresponded with phases of the moon" (Note 39, p. 302). Zodiac killed according to phases of the moon (Note 40, p. 321).

Albright Dixie Austin Deposition

Dixie Austin: From a Altoona High School, in Pennsylvania.

Paul Shannon: Were you a good student?

Dixie Austin: Average.

Paul Shannon: What was Charlie's educational background? What did he (inaudible)?

Dixie Austin: From what I, uh, he of course graduated from high school when he was 15 years old. And, uh,

Paul Shannon: Kind of young isn't it?

Dixie Austin: Very.

Paul Shannon: What did he say about that?

Dixie Austin: Uh, not a whole lot, just that he was, he was a lot smaller than everybody when he graduated. And, uh, that's, that's about all he said about,

Paul Shannon: How did he graduate when he was 15, was he accelerated or something?

Dixie Austin: I can't, I really don't know. I don't know that.

Paul Shannon: Was he smarter than the other kids?

Dixie Austin: He's extremely smart.

Paul Shannon: Give us some examples.

Dixie Austin: Uh, uh, he knows uh, like astronomy. He just he knows every, you know, everything about, in Science. He's smart in, you know, scientific things. He's, uh, a marvelous carpenter, finish carpenter. And he is, uh, he sings like Pavarotti. He, uh, plays the piano and, uh, he just seems to remember, you know, a lot of things.

Paul Shannon: What did he do after high school?

Dixie Austin: I think we went to North Texas State. I'm not sure about that.

Paul Shannon: How long did he go there?

Albright

16

Page from Dixie Austin's deposition indicating that Albright knows astrology.
(photo courtesy of Dallas County District Attorney's office)

Albright has a high IQ of 140 and is abnormally strong. He can do 600 sit-ups non-stop. Zodiac is highly intelligent and strong (Note 40, p. 322). Albright speaks in a low, soft voice that was almost a monotone (Note 39, p.104). "He pronounces the words 'eyes' with the accent of deep Texas so that the vowel is drawled out, hard and flat" (Note 39, p.146). Zodiac victim Bryan Hartnell described the Zodiac's voice as follows: "It was a remarkably calm voice that came from beneath the hood, a voice that was not high-or low-pitched, a monotone . . ." "That voice . . . it was like a student's. But kind of a drawl, not a Southern drawl, though" (Note 40, p. 67). "The words were even spoken," Hartnell added. Switchboard operator Nancy Slover indicated that Zodiac's voice "was even and consistent, soft but forceful" (Note 40, p. 33).

Albright was an expert at forgery. He had no problem forging papers to deceive the U.S. Army. "Once, when a neighborhood boy wanted to join the Army but wasn't old enough to get in he complained to Charlie that his parents wouldn't sign for him. Charlie forged a set of papers he needed and the boy was gone before his parents knew what happened" (Note 39, p. 158). Zodiac "had a pretty thorough knowledge of identification techniques" (Note 40, p. 167). "He devised a method that would frustrate the best experts. It went something like this: First he set his typewriter to all caps. Then he made a book of typewriter paper and carbon, about thirteen pages of paper, twelve of carbon. By sending one of the last copies of the letter he insured that these would be so blurred that identification of the make of the typewriter would be tough" (Note 40, p.168).

Albright "was a masterful painter" (Note 41, p. 339). "He had been a professional photographer in a downtown motel" (Note 39, p. 116). Zodiac knew photography. "The procedure was probably this: Zodiac photographed onto a strip of 35-mm film individual letters of the alphabet collected from a variety of sources, such as friends or people that he worked with. The film strip was placed into a photographic enlarger, and each individual character was projected from above by the enlarger one at a time onto the paper and traced with a blue tip pen." "The fact is inescapable that not even a professional artist could lay out 340 cipher symbols so neatly in block form, each character identical in size and slant, without some sort of grid" (Note 40, p. 218-219).

Albright "had been a draftsman, a designer for a company that built airplanes, and an illustrator" (Note 39, p. 116). Zodiac "had lettered on the back in white ink such as artists and draughtsmen use" (Note 40, p. 159). Zodiac "knows drafting" (Note 40, p. 320).

Albright can recite difficult poetry from memory. He can recite 42 verses of *The Eve of St. Agnes* by John Keats (Note 39, p. 366). Zodiac could recite verses from Gilbert and Sullivan's *The Mikado* from memory. "Because of the variations from Gilbert's original lyrics detectives Armstrong and Toshi knew their man wrote the lyrics from memory rather than copying them directly from the libretto" (Note 40, p. 131 and 156)

John Keats' poem *The Eve of St. Agnes* includes the seldom-used word "implores" in the IX stanza. Zodiac misquoted a line from *The Mikado* when he wrote in one of his letters: "All children who are up in dates and implore you with im platt" (Note 40, p. 154). The correct verse from *The Mikado* was written as follows: "All children who are up in dates, and floor you with em flat . . ."

Albright drove a Corvette in 1970. According to a police report given by possible Zodiac witness Sandra Sue Betts on June 7, 1970, Zodiac may have driven a Corvette in 1970. Betts also thought this person was approximately 38-years-old in 1970. Albright was born on 8/10/33 and was 37, two months and three days short of his 38th birthday in 1970.

Blue Rock Springs Report, Page 70 Page 1 of 2

VALLEJO POLICE DEPARTMENT

CRIME REPORT SUPPLEMENT

243 146

CRIME	DATE	CLASSIFICATION

VICTIM'S NAME - LAST, FIRST, MIDDLE	ADDRESS ☐ Residence ☐ Business	PHONE

shown a composite drawing from the San Francisco Police Department and immediately identified the subject Paul as baring an extremely striking resemblance to the "Zodiac"composite. in fact, BETTS stated "that's him." BETTS and ████ left at approx. 1am and this subject left at the same time. He was observed to be driving a small black car possibly a Corvette, however subject BETTS was the only one that observed the vehicle and does not know types of cars very well. BETTS drew a picture of subject Paul after leaving the Coronado Inn on the back of a photograph. Picture attached to this supplement. Subject BETTS advises that she frequents the Coronado Inn and if she should observe this subject again will call VPD.

Zodiac

REPORTING OFFICERS	RECORDING OFFICER	TYPED BY	DATE AND TIME	ROUTED BY
	Sgt. Dewart	ns	6/7/70–9pm	ns

COPIES TO: DATE DATE

DETECTIVE ☐ CII

☐ INVEST. COMM. ☐

☐ DIST. ATTNY. ☐

REVIEWED BY DATE

1 | 2 | 3 | 4 | 5 | 6 | 7 | 8 | 9 | 10 | 11 | 12 | 13 | 14 | 15 | 16 | 17 | 18 | 19 | 20 | 21 | 22 |
23 | 24 | 25 | 26 | 27 | 28 | 29 | 30 | 31 | 32 | 33 | 34 | 35 | 36 | 37 | 38 | 39 | 40 | 41 | 42 | 43 | 44 |
45 | 46 | 47 | 48 | 49 | 50 | 51 | 52 | 53 | 54 | 55 | 56 | 57 | 58 | 59 | 60 | 61 | 62 | 63 | 64 | 65 | 66 |
67 | 68 | 69 | 70 | 71 | 72 | 73 | 74 | 75

Back to Darlene Ferrin and Mike Mageau

vw.zodiackiller.com/DFR70.html 1.

Vallejo Police Departments Crime Report Supplement #243 146, dated 6/7/70, indicating that Zodiac may have driven a Corvette.

INVESTIGATIVE NOTES

SUBMITTING OFFICER: McNear DATE: 4-4-91 TIME:

INFO OBTAINED BY PHONE [ ] DATE AND TIME OF CALL:

INFO OBTAINED THRU INTERVIEW [—] DATE AND TIME OF INTERVIEW:

(list all persons present in narrative) LOCATION OF INTERVIEW:

INFO OBTAINED THRU OTHER METHODS [ ]

NARRATIVE: I contacted Shirley Baucom, 286-0256, who advised that in 1970 she was a 10th grade Biology student of Charles Albright's at Crandal High School. She said one day Albright asked her if she wanted to go to Arkansas with "them" to hunt for salamanders. She told him to ask her mother. Her mother told him no, she couldn't go. Shirley started checking to see who "them" were. She found out that no one else was scheduled to go except she and Albright. She started receiving low grades on her report cards, when she was actually making good grades. When her mother confronted Albright about it, he told her that Shirley was friendly and had a bad attitude. Albright drove a green Corvette all the time and wore pointed alligator shoes.

Dallas County Police Department Notes dated 4/4/91, indicating that Albright drove a Corvette.

According to investigative notes Albright may have cut off female parts of his victims. Zodiac wrote in his "The Confession" letter: "But I shall cut off her female parts and deposit them for the whole city to see" (Note 40, p. 168-169).

Albright was dressed very neatly and was "positively distinguished" (Note 41, p 339). When he was arrested in 1991, his car was very messy. A copy of Anne Rice's book T*he Mummy* was found in his vehicle along with items on the dashboard. In 1991, Albright was asked by a reporter "Well, what kind of person would be able to cut out the eyeballs of some hooker?" Albright responded "Someone who is sadistic? Just one mean son of a gun? I don't know the purpose behind it unless that person thought the women wouldn't be able to see without their eyes in the next world-which is sort of ignorant" (Note 39, p. 351). When he was arrested in 1991, detectives photographed two plastic scouring pads at Albright's house in Oak Cliff, Texas. A surviving victim of the Zodiac, Kathleen Johns reported seeing two plastic scouring pads on the dashboard of Zodiac's vehicle (Note 40, p. 138).

Albright

INVESTIGATIVE NOTES

SUBMITTING OFFICER: Hamilton DATE: 3-27-91 TIME:

INFO OBTAINED BY PHONE [ ] DATE AND TIME OF CALL:

INFO OBTAINED THRU INTERVIEW [ ] DATE AND TIME OF INTERVIEW:

(list all persons present in narrative) LOCATION OF INTERVIEW:

INFO OBTAINED THRU OTHER METHODS [ ]

NARRATIVE: I interviewed [redacted] at Decker and took an affidavit. She is very cooperative and told me of another prostitute named "Susie" that also had an encounter with "him" where he cut off the nipple of her right breast. She will try to locate Susie and get her to call me for an affidavit.

Each time he cut part of her clothing he would take the razor from it's handle and throw it in a nearby drainage creek. I was thinking we might get her to show us the exact spot and we might find some razor blades.

Detective's investigative notes dated 3/27/91 on Charles F. Albright.

Detective's Investigative Notes dated 3/27/91 on Charles F. Albright.
(courtesy of Dallas County District Attorney's office)

THE CONFESSION

BY________________

SHE WAS YOUNG AND BEAUTIFUL. BUT NOW SHE IS BATTERED AND DEAD. SHE IS NOT THE FIRST AND SHE WILL NOT BE THE LAST. I LAY AWAKE NIGHTS THINKING ABOUT MY NEXT VICTIM. MAYBE SHE WILL BE THE BEAUTIFUL BLOND THAT BABYSITS NEAR THE LITTLE STORE AND WALKS DOWN THE DARK ALLEY EACH EVENING ABOUT SEVEN. OR MAYBE SHE WILL BE THE SHAPELY BLUE EYED BROWNETT THAT SAID NO WHEN I ASKED HER FOR A DATE IN HIGH SCHOOL. BUT MAYBE IT WILL NOT BE EITHER. BUT I SHALL CUT OFF HER FEMALE PARTS AND DEPOSIT THEM FOR THE WHOLE CITY TO SEE. SO DON'T MAKE IT TO EASY FOR ME. KEEP YOUR SISTERS, DAUGHTERS, AND WIVES OFF THE STREETS AND ALLEYS. MISS BATES WAS STUPID. SHE WENT TO THE SLAUGHTER LIKE A LAMB. SHE DID NOT PUT UP A STRUGGLE. BUT I DID. IT WAS A BALL. I FIRST PULLED THE MIDDLE WIRE FROM THE DISTRIBUTOR. THEN I WAITED FOR HER IN THE LIBRARY AND FOLLOWED HER OUT AFTER ABOUT TWO MINUTS. THE BATTERY MUST HAVE BEEN ABOUT DEAD BY THEN. I THEN OFFERED TO HELP. SHE WAS THEN VERY WILLING TO TALK WITH ME. I TOLD HER THAT MY CAR WAS DOWN THE STREET AND THAT I WOULD GIVE HER A LIFT HOME. WHEN WE WERE AWAY FROM THE LIBRARY WALKING, I SAID IT WAS ABOUT TIME. SHE ASKED ME "ABOUT TIME FOR WHAT". I SAID IT WAS ABOUT TIME FOR HER TO DIE. I GRABBED HER AROUND THE NECK WITH MY HAND OVER HER MOUTH AND MY OTHER HAND WITH A SMALL KNIFE AT HER THROAT. SHE WENT VERY WILLINGLY. HER BREAST FELT VERY WARM AND FIRM UNDER MY HANDS, BUT ONLY ONE THING WAS ON MY MIND. MAKING HER PAY FOR THE BRUSH OFFS THAT SHE HAD GIVEN ME DURING THE YEARS PRIOR. SHE DIED HARD. SHE SQUIRMED AND SHOOK AS I CHOAKED HER, AND HER LIPS TWICHED. SHE LET OUT A SCREAM ONCE AND I KICKED HER HEAD TO SHUT HER UP. I PLUNGED THE KNIFE INTO HER AND IT BROKE. I THEN FINISHED THE JOB BY CUTTING HER THROAT. I AM NOT SICK. I AM INSANE. BUT THAT WILL NOT STOP THE GAME. THIS LETTER SHOULD BE PUBLISHED FOR ALL TO READ IT. IT JUST MIGHT SAVE THAT GIRL IN THE ALLEY. BUT THAT'S UP TO YOU. IT WILL BE ON YOUR CONSCIENCE. NOT MINE. YES I DID MAKE THAT CALL TO YOU ALSO. IT WAS JUST A WARNING. BEWARE...I AM STALKING YOUR GIRLS NOW.

CC. CHIEF OF POLICE
ENTERPRISE

Zodiac's "The Confession" letter written in 1969, wherein he threatened to "CUT OFF FEMALE PARTS AND DEPOSIT THEM FOR HE WHOLE CITY TO SEE."

1991 photo of interior of Albright's automobile.
(courtesy of Dallas County District Attorney's office)

1991 photo of interior of Albright's automobile. (note items on dashboard)

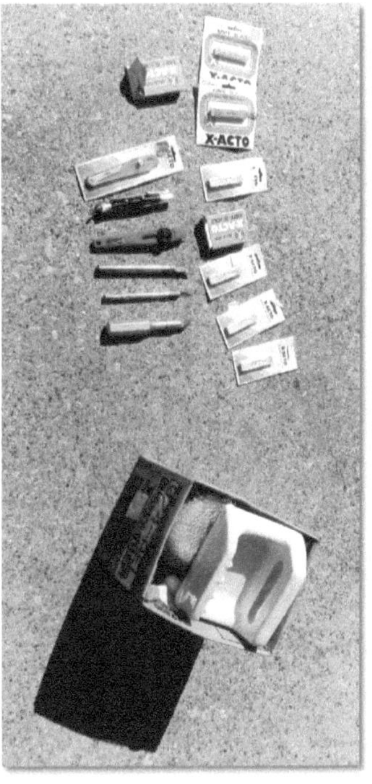

Two colored plastic scouring pads photographed by detectives at Albright's home when he was arrested in 1991. (courtesy of Dallas County District Attorney's office)

Zodiac "dressed neatly but the interior of his car was messy." Johns also stated that "the car's interior was messy, with papers, books and clothes strewn about the front and back seats even on the dashboard. The clothing was mostly a man's but mixed in were some small T-shirts with patterns such as a child age eight to twelve might wear" (Note 40, p. 138). Johns stated that this person dressed in a dark blue-black nylon windbreaker type jacket over black bell-bottom pants" (Note 40, p. 317). Zodiac wrote in several letters about collecting slaves for the afterlife, a striking similarity to Albright's reference to "the next world."

Albright's mug shot taken after his arrest in 1991, shows acne scarring on the left side of his chin. Kathleen Johns indicated that Zodiac's chin was traced with scars of some past acne infection" (Note 40, p.138). Note in the mug shot below Albright has his mouth partially open. The amended drawing of the Zodiac rendered by the police artist shows Zodiac with his mouth partly open.

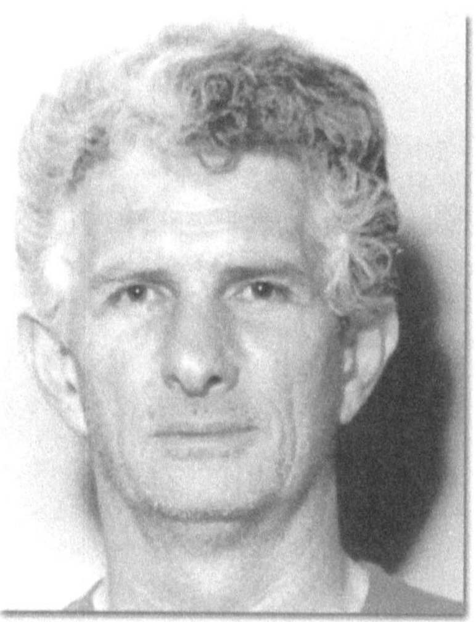

Mug shot of Charles F. Albright taken in 1991.
(note partially open mouth and curly hair)

The similarities between these two killers range across still other particulars, ones that seem too odd or particular to be coincidental. Albright sings opera. Zodiac had knowledge of Gilbert and Sullivan's *The Mikado* which is light opera.

Albright - sings Opera

INVESTIGATIVE NOTES

SUBMITTING OFFICER: Westphalen DATE: 3/25/91 TIME: 1:10 PM

INFO OBTAINED BY PHONE [ ] DATE AND TIME OF CALL:

INFO OBTAINED THRU INTERVIEW [ ] DATE AND TIME OF INTERVIEW:

(list all persons present in narrative) LOCATION OF INTERVIEW:

INFO OBTAINED THRU OTHER METHODS [ ]

NARRATIVE: Jeanette Henderson, WF 12-4-56, H# 258-0843 and 331-1783 called with the following information on Charles Albright. She met him about five years ago and said he was real strange. She advised Albright has rent houses on Cotton Valley. Jeanette said that a few times when they had sex, Albright would paint his face like a clown. When they had sex, he wouldn't ejaculate. She didn't date except for a month. She also said he sang opera and played the piano.

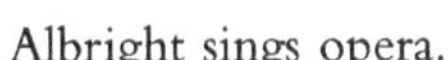

Albright sings opera.

Albright "loved giving greeting cards and gifts" (Note 39, p. 117). He is a prolific letter writer. Zodiac "mailed humorless greeting cards" (Note 40, page 147) *Zodiac* and mailed at least 25 letters to the *San Francisco Chronicle* and other newspapers. Zodiac may have left gifts at Darlene Ferrin's home in 1969.

Published with permission
from the Dallas District
Attorney's Office
Re: Charles F. Albright

BILL HILL
CRIMINAL DISTRICT ATTORNEY
Frank Crowley Courts Building
133 N. Industrial Boulevard, L.B. 19
Dallas, Texas 75207-4399
Office: 214.653.3600

FACSIMILE COVER SHEET

DATE: 10/3/02 Total Pages, Including Cover:

To: Bill Rasmussen	Dept./Agency:
Fax #: 281/946-0882	Phone #:

From: Lamisa T. Ro... Reply to Fax #:
Dept./Agency:

Comments: Found greeting cards,

Please find attached copies
of Albright's written notations
I don't know how much will clearly transmit
Will send hard copies via mail

CONFIDENTIALITY NOTICE

The information contained in this facsimile message is privileged and confidential and is intended only for the exclusive use of the addressee. The term "privileged and confidential" includes, without limitation, attorney-client privileged communications, attorney work product, and any other proprietary information. Nothing in this facsimile is intended by the attorney to constitute a waiver of the confidentiality of this message. If the reader of this message is not the intended recipient, or employee/agent of the intended recipient, you are hereby notified that any use, disclosure, dissemination, duplication, distribution or the taking of any action because of this communication is unauthorized and strictly prohibited. If you have received this facsimile transmission in error, please notify us by telephone immediately so that we can arrange for the return of the original documents.

Greeting cards found in Albright's evidence file at the Dallas County District Attorney's office.

Albright may have used the phrase "fiddle and fart around." Albright's girlfriend Dixie Austin spoke the words "fiddle around" in her deposition in 1991. The phrase "fiddle and fart around" may have been used in the Albright household.

Albright

Deposition of Dixie Austin

Dixie Austin: Uh, I usually would take a twenty minute nap when I got home and uh then I'd fix dinner or Charlie'd fix dinner and, uh, uh, we'd watch TV, I didn't watch a lot of TV. I would fiddle around the house and do things but, uh, uh, and we we didn't go out very often at night, sometimes we'd go dancing but not, you know, not too often. And a lot of his, uh, time was taken up playing ball at night. They played ball mostly at night.

John Westphalen: Did you go to most of his,

Dixie Austin: Most all of them.

John Westphalen: What time, I know mens softball couldn't start at 6 or,

Dixie Austin: Well,

John Westphalen: You know, go, go late, what time was most of his games, or what time did he usually get in from them?

Dixie Austin: Most the games, most of the games there were very few that were early, uh, they would be 7 and 9 o'clock games. Sometimes, I think, now I'm not sure about that.

John Westphalen: That's all right.

Dixie Austin: But we'd get in about, uh, we were always home by 11:00.

John Westphalen: Okay. Uh, what about your social life? Did you, did, uh, you and Charlie go out a lot at night, other than softball or,

Dixie Austin: Uh, we would go to some friend's house for dinner and, um, we, uh, then once in awhile we'd go out with some friends to, uh, uh, you know, to like Spaghetti Warehouse or someplace like that and eat.

John Westphalen: Sure. Who who were these friends that you'd go out with, if you remember their names?

Dixie Austin: Uh, Lafraudas, now they've moved to Lynchberg,

Albright

9

Page from Dixie Austin's deposition.
(courtesy of Dallas County District Attorney's office)

Zodiac wrote on March 15, 1971: "Because the longer they fiddle and fart around. . ." Author Robert Graysmith wrote: "The phrase fiddle and fart around is an antiquated one and led investigators to suspect Zodiac was a much older man than they had thought. I learned that the phrase 'fiddle and fart around" is used in areas of Texas, principally around Lubbock County" (Note 40, p.176). On August 8, 2002, Pam Huckaby sister of Darlene Ferrin told the author that a man her family met at a Fort Worth, Texas, motel and bowling alley in 1963, kept using the phrase fiddle and fart around. Fort Worth is next to Dallas and Oak Cliff where Albright lived in 1963.

Albright wore glasses (Note 39, p. 142) and made baseball bats with a wood lathe (Note 41, p. 358). On March 22, 1970, Zodiac victim Kathleen Johns said that Zodiac wore "black-rimmed glasses held in place by an elastic band like a machinist might wear (Note 40, p. 317).

Albright wore a softball cap with a "twisted coat hanger inside so the cap would fit perfectly on his head" (Note 41, p. 373). Zodiac wore a cloth hood at Berryessa Lake on September 27, 1969. The hood stood upright on his head and may have been held in position by use of wires (see drawing of Zodiac, Note 40, p.108-109).

Albright went to beauty school, received his beautician's license and then persuaded the salon to hire him with no experience at all as a stylist. Albright took to calling himself "Mr. Charles" (Note 41, p. 358). "Albright was a very effeminate man," remembered Mark, a Crandall senior of 1973, "and I went out of my way to make fun of him." Albright taught Mark's science class, where he noticed how bizarre Albright's habits were" (See No Evil, 11/15/06 by Chelsea Flores www.piratepressonline.com).

Recently a former Crandall High School student, that Albright coached football in 1969–1970, indicated that Albright "talked about going to California all the time." According to possible Zodiac witness Sandra Betts, the Zodiac "Had somewhat effeminate actions and walked with a swayback manner (Vallejo Police Department Crime Supplement, see report above). On July 10, 1974, Zodiac mailed a letter to the *Chronicle* with this demand: "Put Marco back in the hell-hole from whence it came . . ." Count Marco Spinelli was a former hairdresser that wrote a column for the *Chronicle.*

In 1991, Albright told a reporter in a jail house interview that he "regularly went to the Venetian Room at the Fairmont Hotel to get autographs from the stars performing there" (Note 41, p.358). The Fairmont Dallas opened in 1969, and its "Venetian Room was styled after the Venetian Room of its sister hotel, The Fairmont San Francisco." A person, thought by some to be the Zodiac, wanted to meet Melvin Belli, a famous attorney, at the Fairmont Hotel in San Francisco in 1969.

Albright was calm in a crisis situation. "After being literally blown out of bed and wrestled to the ground, he was perfectly calm and quiet. Eerily quiet, as though he were at peace" (Note 39, p. 101). Zodiac was "calm in a crisis" (Note 40, p. 321).

Blue Rock Springs Report, Page 69 — Page 1 of 2

VALLEJO POLICE DEPARTMENT

CRIME REPORT SUPPLEMENT

243 146

CODE SECTION	71. CRIME	DATE	72. CLASSIFICATION

73. VICTIM'S NAME - LAST, FIRST, MIDDLE (FIRM IF BUS.)	74. Address [ ] Residence [ ] Business	75. PHONE

6/7/70-7pm

Writer contacted at station a Sandra Karen BETTS, WF, 31 yrs., DOB 8/14/38, presently living at 2157 Navarro St., Napa, no phone, and her girlfriend a Margo Blaine ██████ WF, 22 yrs., DOB 10/13/47, of 150 ██████, Vallejo, she has a phone which has recently been installed and she does not know the number. Both subjects stated that on 6/6/70 at approx. 10-10:30pm they were at the Coronado Inn on Highway 37 where subject ██████ first observed a WM who was acting strangely. This subject strongly resembled the pictures they had seen of the composite drawing of the "Zodiac." ██████ and BETTS observed this subject for some period of time describing him as a WM, approx 38 yrs., brown hair which receded approx. to the middle of the head and a bald spot on the back of the head, approx. 5-11, 180 lbs, hazel eyes, wearing glasses with dark brown frames, he had on a nylon sweater shirt with short sleeves, dark pants, black shoes which appeared to be military type and were extremely shiny. He had somewhat effeminate actions and walked in a swaybacked manner, held his glass with his fingers extended in a feminine way. Subject BETTS danced with this person and determined his name was Paul and that he was stationed in Vallejo. Subject Paul was evasive in his answers to BETTS, however, was determined that his favorite song is "Proud Mary" that he knew the name of the band that had played at the Coronado Inn previously approx. 2 months ago. BETTS and ██████ were both

REPORTING OFFICERS	RECORDING OFFICER	TYPED BY	DATE AND TIME	ROUTED BY
STATS	Sgt. Hawart	ns	6/7/70-9pm	ns

COPIES TO: DATE — DATE
DETECTIVE [ ] CII
[ ] INVEST. COMM. [ ]
[ ] DIST. ATTNY [ ]
REVIEWED BY — DATE

1 | 2 | 3 | 4 | 5 | 6 | 7 | 8 | 9 | 10 | 11 | 12 | 13 | 14 | 15 | 16 | 17 | 18 | 19 | 20 | 21 | 22 |
23 | 24 | 25 | 26 | 27 | 28 | 29 | 30 | 31 | 32 | 33 | 34 | 35 | 36 | 37 | 38 | 39 | 40 | 41 | 42 | 43 | 44 |
45 | 46 | 47 | 48 | 49 | 50 | 51 | 52 | 53 | 54 | 55 | 56 | 57 | 58 | 59 | 60 | 61 | 62 | 63 | 64 | 65 | 66 |
67 | 68 | 69 | 70 | 71 | 72 | 73 | 74 | 75

Back to Darlene Ferrin and Mike Mageau

http://www.zodiackiller.com/DFR69.html — 1/1/2003

Vallejo Police Department Crime Report Supplement dated June 7, 1970 indicating that Zodiac may have had effeminate actions and walked in a swaybacked manner.

Zodiac wrote in his November 9, 1969, letter to the *Chronicle* "I have grown rather angry with police for telling lies about me." Albright wrote in one of his letters that people were telling lies about him.

1/6

This is the zodiac speaking
up to the end of Oct I have
killed 7 people. I have grown
rather angry with the police
for their telling lies about me.
So I shall change the way the
collecting of slaves. I shall
no longer announce to anyone.
when I comitt my murders,
they shall look like routine
robberies, killings of anger, +
a few fake accidents, etc.

The police shall never catch me,
because I have been too clever
for them.
1 I look like the description
passed out only when I do
my thing, the rest of the time
I look entirle different. I
shall not tell you what my
descise consists of when I kill
2 As of yet I have left no
fingerprints behind me contrary

Zodiac wrote in his November 9, 1969, letter to the *Chronicle* that the police were telling lies about him.

The perverted D.A.'s still weren't happy. They decided to have me smeared some more. Their next "Dido" was to have me tied to some Old Murders in the State of Arkansas. No Problem! They picked some woman prosecutor and gave her a chance to "Shine". She, of course, called the "Puppet Newspaper". It reported that Albright was to be charged with a Fifth, Sixth, and Seventh Murder. This "Lady" D.A. was quoted as saying, "It looks really good on this" - (tying me to these SUPPOSED cases in Arkansas). It turns out that there NEVER was the slightest chance of tying me to these cases, IF Indeed they ever existed. When I asked my lawyer about this, months later, he said, "Well, the fingerprints didn't match, and the description of the Pick-up Truck didn't match". Guess what? It doesn't take some Ignorant, "Lady" Prosecutor, or any of her "Crooked Cronies", OR some un-ethical, "Puppet Newspaper" to figure-out that they could have learned Over The Phone, or Fax Machine, that I was NOT to be considered a Suspect in a Fifth, Sixth, and Seventh Murder. NO, of course the "Friendly" Newspaper didn't do anything to correct the damage done. IF they printed something True about someone their "Buddies" were trying to smear, or IF they admitted that they printed Lies, (at the request of the County Prosecutors), It Might hurt their Image. So true to form, they did Nothing.

Dallas is Infamous for its "Miscarriages of Justice" One famous, and fairly recent one, is the case of Randall Dale Adams. This case was the subject of a Television Documentary Film, entitled "The Thin Blue Line". Anyone, who is interested in Justice, should read his book, "Adams vs. Texas" - even though he "takes it easy on" Ignorant Jury Members, "Crooked" Cops, and "Sleazy" Prosecutors. There was a "Crooked" Prosecutor in Adams' case, way back in 1976. He KNOWINGLY sent an innocent man, Randall Adams, to "Death Row". (Nothing changes in this Perverted "Justice System", it just gets Worse. This Un-Ethical, D.A. is Now an Un-Ethical Lawyer in Dallas.

At the time of the Randall Dale Adams case, this "Perjurious" District Attorney had one assistant who was so "Talented", that he's Now a Judge. In fact, He was the Judge who resided over MY trial. The unethical EX-D.A. came to see me to offer me his services, and I decided to use a Court Appointed Attorney instead. The point is, that Dallas learns nothing from its Illegal Acts. The "PLOTS" change, But the "Characters" are Still there, and Still Dishonest, and they're simply playing different roles. This is the Pedigree of the Dallas Courts.

The Court Of Appeals, in Dallas, is a complete FARCE. In My case, Three of its "Judges" Conspired with the D.A.'s, (Operating outside the Law), to deprive me of an Honest appeal, as is Guaranteed under the Federal Constitution. These three "CHIPS off the Dallas Block", were So Anxious to do the D.A.'s Bidding, that they went Solely by the D.A.'s Statement, about My case. In doing so, they added Perjury to their "List of Achievements".

This "Court's" Statement, or Ruling, was forwarded to the next "Court" in Austin. This Statement, contained More than a dozen, just Plain Lies. These were FACTS which were NEVER in Evidence; (They Never Once consulted The Record from the "Trial" Proceedings). The purpose of these Perjured Statements was to prevent the Higher Court from ruling on the True Facts. These men in the Court Of Appeals, are disgusting excuses for Judges. They hide behind their Supposed Immunity, and Black Robes, and are Nothing More than Frauds. They accept their "Salaries of Office", and do very little to earn it.

8

CHARLES F. ALBRIGHT LETTER

Albright wrote in a letter that newspapers printed lies about him.

THE CONFESSION

BY________________

SHE WAS YOUNG AND BEAUTIFUL. BUT NOW SHE IS BATTERED AND DEAD. SHE IS NOT THE FIRST AND SHE WILL NOT BE THE LAST. I LAY AWAKE NIGHTS THINKING ABOUT MY NEXT VICTIM. MAYBE SHE WILL BE THE BEAUTIFUL BLOND THAT BABYSITS NEAR THE LITTLE STORE AND WALKS DOWN THE DARK ALLEY EACH EVENING ABOUT SEVEN. OR MAYBE SHE WILL BE THE SHAPELY BLUE EYED BROWNETT THAT SAID NO WHEN I ASKED HER FOR A DATE IN HIGH SCHOOL. BUT MAYBE IT WILL NOT BE EITHER. BUT I SHALL CUT OFF HER FEMALE PARTS AND DEPOSIT THEM FOR THE WHOLE CITY TO SEE. SO DON'T MA[KE] IT TO EASY FOR ME. KEEP YOUR SISTERS, DAUGHTERS, AND WIVES OFF THE STREETS AND ALLEYS. MISS BATES WAS STUPID. SHE WENT TO THE SLAUGHTER LIKE A LAMB. SH[E] DID NOT PUT UP A STRUGGLE. BUT I DID. IT WAS A BALL. I FIRST PULLED THE MIDD[LE] WIRE FROM THE DISTRIBUTOR. THEN I WAITED FOR HER IN THE LIBRARY AND FOLLOWED HER OUT AFTER ABOUT TWO MINUTS. THE BATTERY MUST HAVE BEEN ABOUT DEAD BY THEN I THEN OFFERED TO HELP. SHE WAS THEN VERY WILLING TO TALK WITH ME. I TOLD HER THAT MY CAR WAS DOWN THE STREET AND THAT I WOULD GIVE HER A LIFT HOME. WHEN W[E] WERE AWAY FROM THE LIBRARY WALKING, I SAID IT WAS ABOUT TIME. SHE ASKED ME "ABOUT TIME FOR WHAT". I SAID IT WAS ABOUT TIME FOR HER TO DIE. I GRABBED HER AROUND THE NECK WITH MY HAND OVER HER MOUTH AND MY OTHER HAND WITH A SMALL KNIFE AT HER THROAT. SHE WENT VERY WILLINGLY. HER BREAST FELT VERY WARM AND FIRM UNDER MY HANDS, BUT ONLY ONE THING WAS ON MY MIND. MAKING HER PAY FOR TH[E] BRUSH OFFS THAT SHE HAD GIVEN ME DURING THE YEARS PRIOR. SHE DIED HARD. SHE SQUIRMED AND SHOOK AS I CHOAKED HER, AND HER LIPS TWICHED. SHE LET OUT A SCRE[AM] ONCE AND I KICKED HER HEAD TO SHUT HER UP. I PLUNGED THE KNIFE INTO HER AND I[T] BROKE. I THEN FINISHED THE JOB BY CUTTING HER THROAT. I AM NOT SICK. I AM INSANE. BUT THAT WILL NOT STOP THE GAME. THIS LETTER SHOULD BE PUBLISHED FOR ALL TO READ IT. IT JUST MIGHT SAVE THAT GIRL IN THE ALLEY. BUT THAT'S UP TO YOU. IT WILL BE ON YOUR CONSCIENCE. NOT MINE. YES I DID MAKE THAT CALL TO YOU ALSO. IT WAS JUST A WARNING. BEWARE...I AM STALKING YOUR GIRLS NOW.

CC. CHIEF OF POLICE
ENTERPRISE

Zodiac typed in upper case in his "The Confession" letter that "MISS BATES WAS STUPID. . ."

Albright

As soon as I know if that's the author of your book, I'll start in. There are two statements on the cover of the book, that I can show you in a hurry are nothing but lies. The Cops, sat down & filled-out Police Reports on 3 crimes (which were never committed) by any one, of these are what I was originally arrested for. He was so stupid that he charged me with two crimes, 15 miles away from each other, at the same time. A physical impossibility. He anticipated a book, I think, & he started lying from the very moment I was put into his squad car, at about 2:30 a.m.

THAT I WISH TO MAKE SOMEONE DELERIOUSLY
HAPPY, IN EVERY WAY, MIGHT NEVER COME TRUE
ARE WE MEN ALL ALIKE? (STUPID)? EVERYTHING

Albright wrote in a letter "He was so stupid . . ."

Zodiac letters included the following "I was not happy," "to keep them happy," "I am rather unhappy," "I shall be very happy to . . .," and "Happy Christmas" (written on a Christmas message to Melvin Belli December 20, 1969. Albright wrote in letters "I'm not very happy about that," "The perverted D.A.'s still weren't happy," and "I HOPE YOU ARE WELL AND HAPPY." (written on a Holiday Card 1/8/07)

Semester, I managed to make a "G" in Algebra, and I wasn't concerned about it, at all. (I guess that was about a 40 to 50 grade average.) I knew that I could not have done any better; for one thing, I needed a good teacher. Years later, after several College tries, I found that teacher. I just barely missed an "A" in his class, and I felt as if he had changed my whole outlook on Life. He was an old retired Farmer, who taught for the sheer joy of teaching. Later, when I taught problem Children, (School Dropouts, etc.), MATH and Algebra, I had just what was necessary to teach them that those courses could be helpful, and FUN.

By the time I got here, making that 4.00 Grade Point Average, was important to me. Somewhere in life, excelling in Courses became important to me. I have taken 152 College Hours, since I have been here, I think. I'm sending you a copy of an early transcript. Copy it and then return it to me, that is IF it holds any interest for you. Not shown is an "Automotive" Vocational Course, in which I made the highest grade - 24 hrs. of "A". Of six Data Processing courses, listed on the left side of the page, 4 of them were "A's", and two of them were "B's". I think my GPA is now, 3.87, and I'm not too happy about that. My vocations and avocations, over the years, somehow developed in me, a desire to achieve perfection, in all that I do. Everyone who knows me, is aware of this.

Not that it may mean anything to you, but it seems to me, that the real killer in my case/s, showed no intelligence, or any attention to detail, so to speak, and the Police just happened to find me, the morning after the 3rd murder? Yet they did NOt arrest me for any murders? Get serious, Samantha; There is something rotten, in Denmark - about this, as the saying goes.

I have drifted away from answering some of the questions that you asked me. I did teach Biology, and coach football. I did help name 7 different Turtles, in two Summers, and I was working on a Thesis for a Masters Degree, the name of which would have been, "The Salamanders of Arkansas". I played lots of Fast Pitch Softball and I was very good at it. I designed and made my own Bat. Everyone attributed my good hitting to the special bat. I got orders for lots of custom-made bats, and I had them in 22 states, at one time. I took good action photographs, at the games and tournaments that I played in, and this hobby helped me become known for my bats, too. I'll stop with this page. and this means I will have to write another letter, just to finish answering all of the questions you asked, that I didn't get answered. I will have to spend time, in making comments on that "Gulino Paper, too. Be Patient, and I know you will. I wish you the best, until next time, Charles Albright

Albright letter "I'm not very happy about that."

The perverted D.A.'s still weren't happy. They decided to have me smeared some more. Their next "Dido" was to have me tied to some Old Murders in the State of Arkansas. No Problem! They picked some woman prosecutor and gave her a chance to "Shine". She, of course, called the "Puppet Newspaper". It reported that Albright was to be charged with a Fifth, Sixth, and Seventh Murder. This "Lady" D.A. was quoted as saying, "It looks really good on this" - (tying me to these SUPPOSED cases in Arkansas). It turns out that there NEVER was the slightest chance of tying me to these cases, IF Indeed they ever existed. When I asked my lawyer about this, months later, he said, "Well, the fingerprints didn't match, and the description of the Pick-up Truck didn't match". Guess what? It doesn't take some Ignorant, "Lady" Prosecutor, or any of her "Crooked Cronies", OR some un-ethical, "Puppet Newspaper" to figure-out

Albright letter "The perverted D.A.'s still weren't happy."

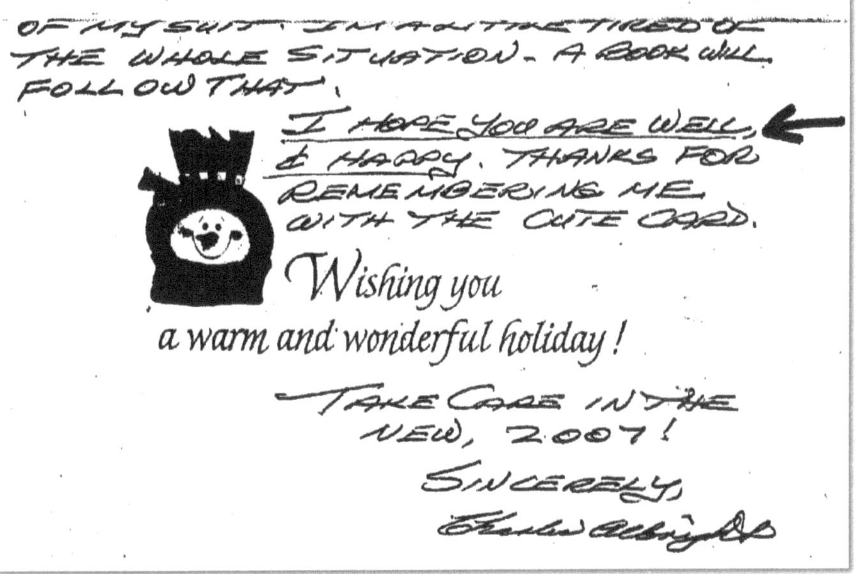
OF MY SUIT. I'M A LITTLE TIRED OF
THE WHOLE SITUATION - A BOOK WILL
FOLLOW THAT.

I HOPE YOU ARE WELL,
& HAPPY. THANKS FOR
REMEMBERING ME
WITH THE CUTE CARD.

Wishing you
a warm and wonderful holiday!

TAKE CARE IN THE
NEW, 2007!
SINCERELY,

Albright holiday card 1/8/07: "I HOPE YOU ARE WELL, & HAPPY."

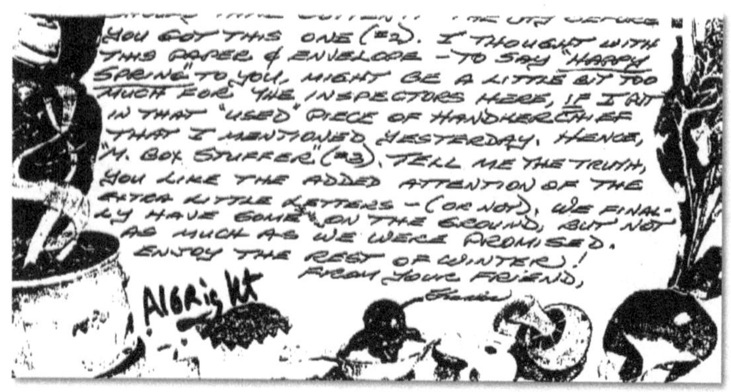
YOU GOT THIS ONE (#2). I THOUGHT WITH
THIS PAPER & ENVELOPE - TO SAY "HAPPY
SPRING" TO YOU, MIGHT BE A LITTLE BIT TOO
MUCH FOR THE INSPECTORS HERE, IF I AT
IN THAT "USED" PIECE OF HANDKERCHIEF
THAT I MENTIONED YESTERDAY. HENCE,
"M. BOX STUFFER" (#3). TELL ME THE TRUTH,
YOU LIKE THE ADDED ATTENTION OF THE
EXTRA LITTLE LETTERS - (OR NOT). WE FINAL-
LY HAVE SOME ON THE GROUND, BUT NOT
AS MUCH AS WE WERE PROMISED.
ENJOY THE REST OF WINTER!
FROM YOUR FRIEND,

Albright wrote in a letter "Happy Spring."

Zodiac wrote in his November 90, 1969, letter to the *Chronicle* "As of yet I have left no fingerprints behind me **contrary to what** the police say" Albright wrote in a letter "AND **CONTRARY TO WHAT** YOU THINK . . ."

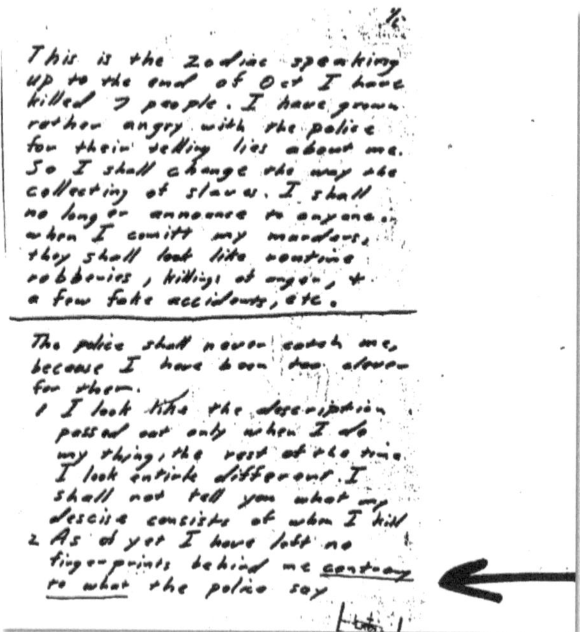
This is the zodiac speaking
up to the end of Oct I have
killed 7 people. I have grown
rather angry with the police
for their telling lies about me.
So I shall change the way the
collecting of slaves. I shall
no longer announce to anyone.
when I comitt my murders,
they shall look like routine
robberies, killings of anger, &
a few fake accidents, etc.

The police shall never catch me,
because I have been too clever
for them.
1 I look like the description
passed out only when I do
my thing, the rest of the time
I look entirle different. I
shall not tell you what my
descise consists of when I kill
2 As of yet I have left no
finger-prints behind me contrary
to what the police say

Zodiac's letter dated November 9, 1969, in which he wrote "contrary to what."

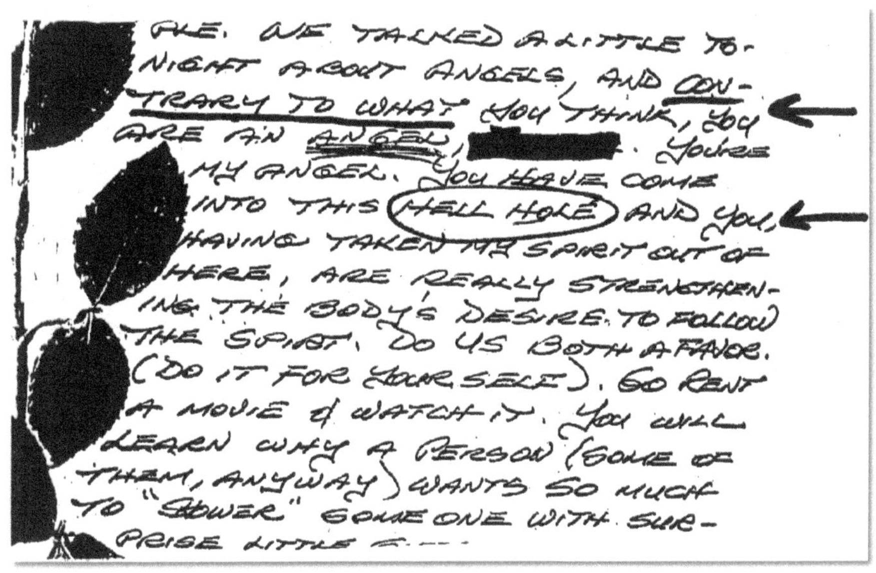

ME. WE TALKED A LITTLE TO-
NIGHT ABOUT ANGELS, AND CON-
TRARY TO WHAT YOU THINK, YOU
ARE AN ANGEL, [redacted]. YOU'RE
MY ANGEL. YOU HAVE COME
INTO THIS HELL HOLE AND YOU,
HAVING TAKEN MY SPIRIT OUT OF
HERE, ARE REALLY STRENGTHEN-
ING THE BODY'S DESIRE TO FOLLOW
THE SPIRIT. DO US BOTH A FAVOR.
(DO IT FOR YOURSELF). GO RENT
A MOVIE & WATCH IT. YOU WILL
LEARN WHY A PERSON (SOME OF
THEM, ANYWAY) WANTS SO MUCH
TO "SHOWER" SOME ONE WITH SUR-
PRISE LITTLE ---

Albright wrote "CONTRARY TO WHAT" in a letter. There are several other similarities in the writings of the Zodiac, Albright and the letters that followed the Phantom Murders in Texarkana.

Addressed to: Mr. Clark Brown
1417 Locust Street
Texarkana, Arkansas

"SORRY YOU DID NOT BELIEVE IN LETTERS SENT YOU LAST YEAR AS YOU EITHER DID NOT OR ELSE LONG TIME USING SAME. SEEMS IT WOULD BE SO EASY BY GIVEN GOOD INFORMATION AS GIVEN. THESE SAME PARTIES ARE STILL MOLESTING AND IF YOU HAD OF THOUGHT INFORMATION GIVEN YOU AS BENEFICIAL YOU WOULD HAVE CAUSED OTHER GIRLS LESS SUFFERING. BUT CANNOT BLAME YOU AND ONLY WISHED YOU HAD. OF COURSE IT IS BETTER TO GO FACE TO FACE, BUT IN THIS CASE THAT COULD NOT BE DONE AND SORRY HEARTACHE AS WELL AS YOURS CANNOT BE EASED. RIGHT PARTIES COULD OF RUN THIS DOWN. MONEY WAS NOT AND IS NOT NOW THE INTENTION OF THIS AND REMEMBER THIS IS NOT MADE UP. WHY IS THIS WRITTEN? WELL IF YOU ONLY COULD OF HAD RIGHT PARTIES TO LOOKED INTO THIS A BODY OF A YOUNG GRIL WHO IS STILL LIVING BARELY THOUGH WOULD CEASE CRYING AND HURTING. NOT FOR A MINUTE WOULD I APPEAL TO YOUR SYMPATHY ONLY SORRY YOU CANNOT USE THE INFORMATION GIVEN. PLEASE DO IF YOU CAN."

* * * *

4th Letter - Postmarked: Texarkana, Arkansas-Texas
May 2, 1947
At 5:30 PM

Addressed to: Mr. Clark Brown
1419 Locust St
City Personal

"SOMETIME AGO YOU WERE WRITTEN AND GIVEN VALUABLE INFORMATION AND NOTHING SEEMS TO COME OF IT. THE NAMES GIVEN YOU AND ALL WAS CONFIDENTIAL AND DO NOT MEAN TO SORRY OR REMIND YOU. MUST BE IF YOU TRIED TO FIND OUT THEY PLAYED INNOCENT. JUST A LITTLE WHILE BACK THERE WAS A DEATH OF A GIRL AND YOU NO DOUBT READ ABOUT IT THERE POSSIBLY WILL BE ANOTHER IF YOU HAVE ANY INFLUENCE WOULD BE SO GLAD YOU USE IT. MAYBE YOU

Letter typed in upper case to Mr. Clark Brown in 1947, following the murder of his stepdaughter during the Phantom Murders in Texarkana (note the words "CANNOT BLAME YOU AND ONLY WISH YOU HAD." followed by the words "FACE TO FACE, BUT."

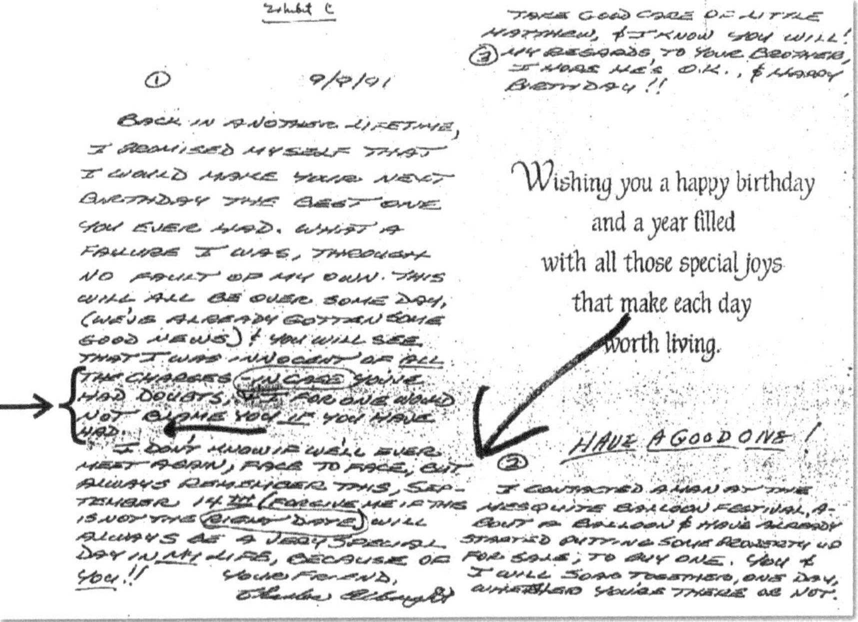

Exhibit C

① 9/9/91

BACK IN ANOTHER LIFETIME,
I PROMISED MYSELF THAT
I WOULD MAKE YOUR NEXT
BIRTHDAY THE BEST ONE
YOU EVER HAD. WHAT A
FAILURE I WAS, THROUGH
NO FAULT OF MY OWN. THIS
WILL ALL BE OVER SOME DAY,
(WE'VE ALREADY GOTTEN SOME
GOOD NEWS) & YOU WILL SEE
THAT I WAS INNOCENT OF ALL
THE CHARGES - IN CASE YOU'VE
HAD DOUBTS, I FOR ONE WOULD
NOT BLAME YOU IF YOU HAVE
HAD.

I DON'T KNOW IF WE'LL EVER
MEET AGAIN, FACE TO FACE, BUT
ALWAYS REMEMBER THIS, SEP-
TEMBER 14TH (FORGIVE ME IF THIS
IS NOT THE RIGHT DATE) WILL
ALWAYS BE A VERY SPECIAL
DAY IN MY LIFE, BECAUSE OF
YOU!!

YOUR FRIEND,
Charles Albright

TAKE GOOD CARE OF LITTLE
MATTHEW, & I KNOW YOU WILL!
③ MY REGARDS TO YOUR BROTHER,
I HOPE HE'S O.K., & HAPPY
BIRTHDAY!!

Wishing you a happy birthday
and a year filled
with all those special joys
that make each day
worth living.

HAVE A GOOD ONE!

② I CONTACTED A MAN AT THE
MESQUITE BALLOON FESTIVAL, A-
BOUT A BALLOON & HAVE ALREADY
STARTED PUTTING SOME PROPERTY UP
FOR SALE, TO BUY ONE. YOU &
I WILL SOAR TOGETHER, ONE DAY,
WHETHER YOU'RE THERE OR NOT.

Letter written in upper case by Charles F. Albright on 9/9/91,
(note the words "WOULD NOT BLAME YOU IF YOU HAVE HAD."
Followed by the words "FACE TO FACE, BUT."

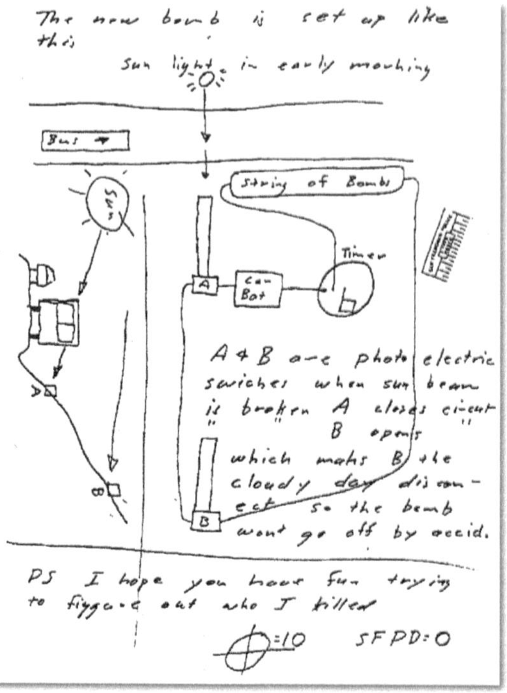

Zodiac's drawing of "bus bomb."

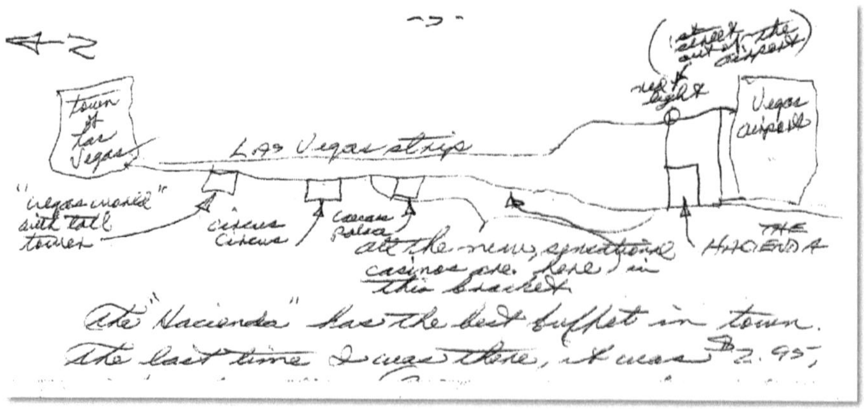

Albright's drawing of Las Vegas Strip (compare the arrows to the arrows drawn by Zodiac in his "bus bomb" drawing).

2/6

in my killings I wear trans-
parent finger tip guards. All it
is is 2 coats of airplane cement
coated on my finger tips - quite

From Zodiac's letter to Chronicle dated November 9, 1969

cases, and if I were still there, they could say, SEE, he lives in the midst of
it all, and that's just what they did, in my cases. (In the middle column, and
under the map, about where "Until recently" is, is where two girls were dropped

Line from Charles F. Albright's letter.

Zodiac and Albright's letters using the double verb "is is."

enough to track ... ...
developer & then to me, so I
shall describe my masterpiece

From Zodiac's letter to Chronicle dated November 9, 1969.

TO DETRACT FROM YOU. HIS LEFT HAND COULD
LIE BY HIS HEAD ON HER TUMMY, & THERE
COULD BE A COLORFUL SHAWL ? PARTLY COVER-
ING HER RIGHT BREAST NOW THIS WOULD BE A
MASTERPIECE AND MAYBE ONLY TWO FEET TALL,
TWO SMALLER COMPANION PIECES WOULD MAKE

Line from Charles F. Albright's letter.

Zodiac and Albright letters using the word "masterpiece."

Editor—
Put Marco back in the (Hell-hole)
from whence it came—he has
a serious psychological disorder—
always needs to feel superior. I
suggest you refer him to a shrink.
Meanwhile, cancel the Count Marco
column. Since the Count can
write anonymously, so can I——
the Red Phantom
(red with rage)

Zodiac wrote the words "Hell Hole" in his Count Marco letter.

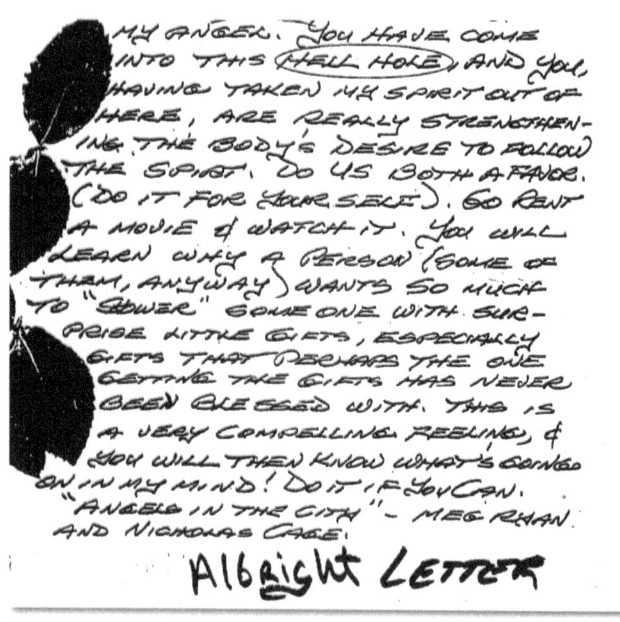

MY ANGEL. YOU HAVE COME
INTO THIS (HELL HOLE), AND YOU,
HAVING TAKEN MY SPIRIT OUT OF
HERE, ARE REALLY STRENGTHEN-
ING THE BODY'S DESIRE TO FOLLOW
THE SPIRIT. DO US BOTH A FAVOR.
(DO IT FOR YOURSELF). GO RENT
A MOVIE & WATCH IT. YOU WILL
LEARN WHY A PERSON (SOME OF
THEM, ANYWAY) WANTS SO MUCH
TO "SHOWER" SOME ONE WITH SUR-
PRISE LITTLE GIFTS, ESPECIALLY
GIFTS THAT PERHAPS THE ONE
GETTING THE GIFTS HAS NEVER
BEEN BLESSED WITH. THIS IS
A VERY COMPELLING FEELING, &
YOU WILL THEN KNOW WHAT'S GOING
ON IN MY MIND! DO IT IF YOU CAN.
"ANGELS IN THE CITY" - MEG RYAN
AND NICHOLAS CAGE.

Albright LETTER

Letter written by Albright using the words "Hell Hole."

DL #9-616

"DID NOT RECEIVE LETTER WILL REPEAT NAMES GO TO HIGHER OFFICIALS AS THESE PEOPLE ARE HELPED BY THE LAW. [redacted] DO NOT BE MISLEAD ABOUT ANY OF THIS. ALL OF THIS WAS HEARD NEAR STARKS ALSO BLOOD NEAR MARTINDALE FARM THE NIGHT YOUR STEP FATHER KILLED THEY MET THERE LATER. NOT ALL THIS AT MURDERS BUT PLAYED THEIR PARTS AND ACCORDING TO ANY LAW WILL BE GUILTY DO NOT BE MISLEAD. KEEP THIS CONFIDENTIAL. BURN THIS JOT NAMES DOWN. [redacted] PLEASE IF YOU HAVE ANY INFLUENCE CARRY THIS TO HIGHER AUTHORITIES. DO NOT GIVE TO THESE HERE FOR THEY WILL TELL YOU NOTHING TO IT. YOU CAN SEE WHY CAN'T YOU. HURRY. MAYBE YOU DID NOT GET FORMER LETTERS THIS WILL BE LAST WRITTEN. WISH YOU COUID DO SOMETHING AS THAT WILL BE MORE. SYMPATHY WITH YOU AND YOURS BY MANY BE ASSURED OF THAT AND ONLY TOO GLAD TO HELP TO BRING JUSTICE DON'T THINK FOR ANY OTHER PURPOSE. KEEP THIS CONFIDENTIAL AND MANY THANKS IF YOU CAN DO ANYTHING ABOUT THIS." b6 b7C

All of the above four letters have been typewritten in upper case and all except the letter postmarked March 21, 1947, have been submitted to the FBI Laboratory for examination.

Reference is made to the report of Special Agent [redacted] dated May 12, 1947, at Dallas, Texas, which sets out the details of the two extortion letters received by victim FEAGINS, one postmarked April 29, 1947, at 7:30 PM, and the other postmarked May 5, 1947, at 2:30 PM, both at Texarkana, Arkansas-Texas. These letters were also submitted to the FBI Laboratory for examination.

By letter dated June 2, 1947, the FBI Laboratory advised that the two letters addressed to victim FEAGINS were prepared on the same machine as the typewriting appearing on the first letter and envelope addressed to Mr. CLARK BROWN. This is the letter postmarked December 17, 1946. The Laboratory also advised that they had concluded that the typewriting appearing on the letters addressed to Mr. BROWN bearing the postmarks of January 3, 1947 and May 2, 1947, were also prepared on the same machine. This typewriting corresponds with the Laboratory standards of Underwood elite type, spaced 12 letters to the inch. Type similar to this may be found on both Underwood b6 b7C

- 5 -

FBI Report in case DL #9-616 in the Phantom Murders; letters to Clark Brown, stepfather of Betty Jo Booker.

FBI Report in Phantom Murders DL #9-616
(note writer ended paragraph with the words typed in upper case "IF YOU CAN DO ANYTHING ABOUT THIS").

Addressed to: Mr. Clark Brown
1417 Locust Street
Texarkana, Arkansas

"SORRY YOU DID NOT BELIEVE IN LETTERS SENT YOU LAST YEAR AS YOU EITHER DID NOT OR ELSE LONG TIME USING SAME. SEEMS IT WOULD BE SO EASY BY GIVEN GOOD INFORMATION AS GIVEN. THESE SAME PARTIES ARE STILL MOLESTING AND IF YOU HAD OF THOUGHT INFORMATION GIVEN YOU AS BENEFICIAL YOU WOULD HAVE CAUSED OTHER GIRLS LESS SUFFERING. BUT CANNOT BLAME YOU AND ONLY WISHED YOU HAD. OF COURSE IT IS BETTER TO GO FACE TO FACE, BUT IN THIS CASE THAT COULD NOT BE DONE AND SORRY HEARTACHE AS WELL AS YOURS CANNOT BE EASED. RIGHT PARTIES COULD OF RUN THIS DOWN. MONEY WAS NOT AND IS NOT NOW THE INTENTION OF THIS AND REMEMBER

THIS IS NOT MADE UP. WHY IS THIS WRITTEN? WELL IF YOU ONLY COULD OF HAD RIGHT PARTIES TO LOOKED INTO THIS A BODY OF A YOUNG GRIL WHO IS STILL LIVING BARELY THOUGH WOULD CEASE CRYING AND HURTING. NOT FOR A MINUTE WOULD I APPEAL TO YOUR SYMPATHY ONLY SORRY YOU CANNOT USE THE INFORMATION GIVEN. PLEASE DO IF YOU CAN."

* * * *

4th Letter - Postmarked: Texarkana, Arkansas-Texas
May 2, 1947
At 5:30 PM

Addressed to: Mr. Clark Brown
1419 Locust St
City Personal

"SOMETIME AGO YOU WERE WRITTEN AND GIVEN VALUABLE INFORMATION AND NOTHING SEEMS TO COME OF IT. THE NAMES GIVEN YOU AND ALL WAS CONFIDENTIAL AND DO NOT MEAN TO SORRY OR REMIND YOU. MUST BE IF YOU TRIED TO FIND OUT THEY PLAYED INNOCENT. JUST A LITTLE WHILE BACK THERE WAS A DEATH OF A GIRL AND YOU NO DOUBT READ ABOUT IT THERE POSSIBLY WILL BE ANOTHER IF YOU HAVE ANY INFLUENCE WOULD BE SO GLAD YOU USE IT. MAYBE YOU

A Letter written to Mr. Clark Brown in 1947, following the Phantom Murders ended with the following words type in upper case "PLEASE DO IF YOU CAN."

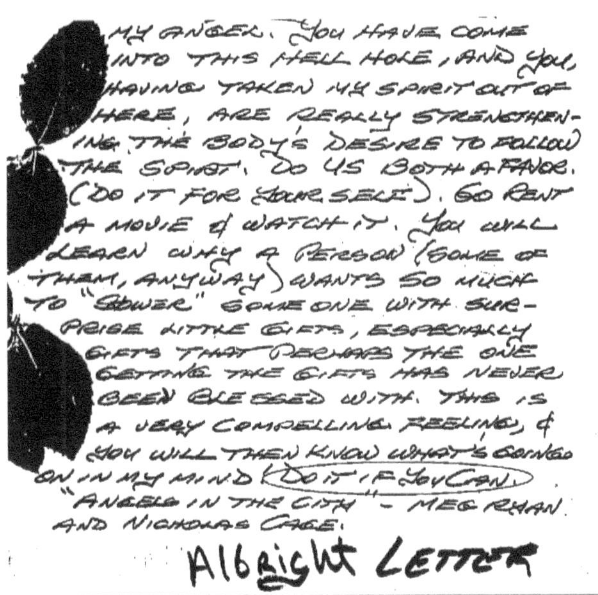

MY ANGEL. YOU HAVE COME INTO THIS HELL HOLE, AND YOU, HAVING TAKEN MY SPIRIT OUT OF HERE, ARE REALLY STRENGTHEN-ING THE BODY'S DESIRE TO FOLLOW THE SPIRIT. DO US BOTH A FAVOR. (DO IT FOR YOURSELF). GO RENT A MOVIE & WATCH IT. YOU WILL LEARN WHY A PERSON (SOME OF THEM, ANYWAY) WANTS SO MUCH TO "SHOWER" SOME ONE WITH SUR-PRISE LITTLE GIFTS, ESPECIALLY GIFTS THAT PERHAPS THE ONE GETTING THE GIFTS HAS NEVER BEEN BLESSED WITH. THIS IS A VERY COMPELLING FEELING, & YOU WILL THEN KNOW WHAT'S GOING ON IN MY MIND (DO IT IF YOU CAN). "ANGELS IN THE CITY" - MEG RYAN AND NICHOLAS CAGE.

Albright LETTER

Albright wrote at the end of a letter in upper case "DO IT IF YOU CAN."

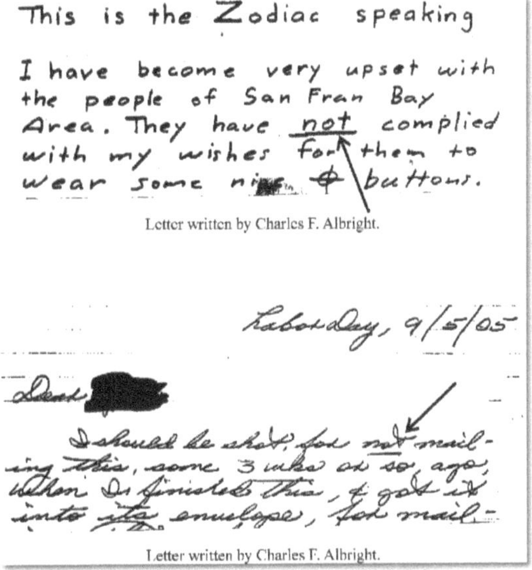

This is the Zodiac speaking

I have become very upset with the people of San Fran Bay Area. They have not complied with my wishes for them to wear some nice ⊕ buttons.

Letter written by Charles F. Albright.

Labor Day, 9/5/05

Dear

I should be shot, for not mail-ing this, some 3 wks or so, ago, when I finished this, & got it into its envelope, for mail-

Letter written by Charles F. Albright.

Zodiac and Albright both underlined the word "not" in letters.

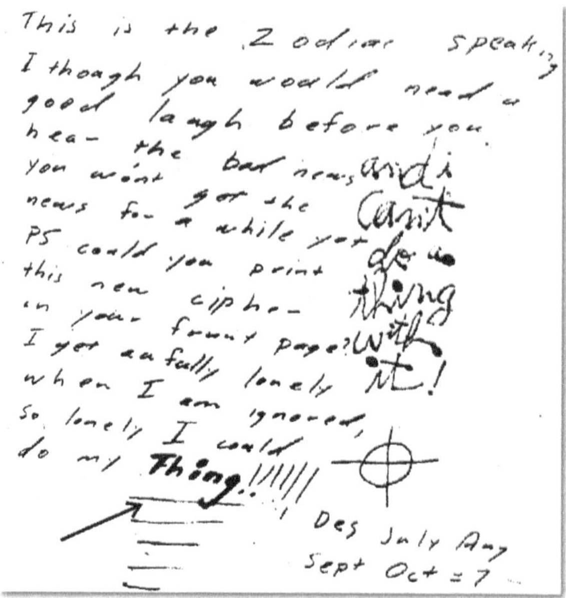
This is the Zodiac speaking
I though you would need a
good laugh before you
hear the bad news
You won't get the
news for a while yet
PS could you print
this new cipher
in your front page?
I get awfully lonely
when I am ignored,
So lonely I could
do my Thing!!!!!!

Des July Aug
Sept Oct = 7

and i can't do a thing with it!

Zodiac underlined the word "thing" in a letter.

LOVE DOES
NOT TAKE
INTO ACCOUNT
A WRONG, SUFFERED.
LOVE DOES NOT REJOICE
IN UNRIGHT- EOUSNESS, BUT
REJOICES WITH THE TRUTH. AND
LOVE BEARS ALL THINGS.
LOVE BELIEVES ALL THINGS,
LOVE * ENDURES ALL THINGS,
LOVE NEVER FAILS.
I WILL NEVER FAIL YOU,

SIGNED [signature].

Albright

Albright underlined the words "ALL THINGS" in a letter.

Sirs- I would like to
express my ~~constant~~
consternation concerning
your poor taste & lack of
sympathy for the public, as
evidenced by your running
of the ads for the movie
"Badlands," featuring the
blurb - "In 1957 most people
were killing time. Kit & Holly
were killing people." In
light of recent events, this
kind of murder-glorification
can only be deplorable at
best (not that glorification of
violence was <u>ever</u> justifiable)
why don't you show some
concern for public [illegible]

Zodiac underlined the word "<u>ever</u>" in a letter.

YOU WANT, WHEN YOU FEEL READY TO, & DON'T FEEL
THAT I'M PUTTING ANY PRESSURE ON YOU. I
WOULD NEVER, <u>EVER</u> MAKE YOU DO ANYTHING YOU
DIDN'T WANT TO DO, [redacted], (I'LL SETTLE FOR A BLUE,
OR PINK, DRESS, ☺).
ABOUT THE 50 ROSES, I HAVE ONLY DONE ABOUT
HALF OF THEM. I MAY NOT DO ANY MORE OF THEM.
REMEMBER, THEY TOOK ALL OF MY COLORS, ON THE
5TH OF THIS MONTH, EXCEPT FOR MY COLORED PENCILS.
I HAVE 5 OR 6 WHICH ONLY NEED SOME FINAL TOUCHES
WITH COLORED PENCILS, INCLUDING YOUR NO. 3, AND I HAVE

Albright

Albright underlined the word "<u>ever</u>" in a letter.

This is the Zodiac speaking
By the way have you cracked
the last cipher I sent you ?.
My name is —

A E N ⊕ ⊗ K ⊗ M ⊗ ⫫ N A M 

I am mildly cerous as to how
much money you have on my
head now. I hope you do not
think that I was the one
who wiped out that blue
meannie with a bomb at the
cop station. Even though I talked
about killing school children with
one. It just wouldnt doo to
move in on someone elses teritory.
But there is more glory in killing
a cop than a cid because a cop
can shoot back. I have killed
ten people to date. It would
have been a lot more except
that my bus bomb was a dud.
I was swamped out by the
rain we had a while back.

Zodiac wrote the words "glory," "cop," and "cop" in a letter.

OPENING STATEMENT,
CONTINUED

ions, and twelve years of his life. The Plaintiff's Possessions were viciously stolen at will, by the Dallas Detectives; viciously removed from their Storage Areas – so they could be stolen by "Passerbys" - in deference to the Police's own policy to secure personal Property; and viciously destroyed certain items – maybe accidentally, but laughing about it at the time. The Dallas Police took many items of Personal Property, supposedly for their Investigation, and most of them were taken illegally, without Warrants, and none of them were ever returned. An Honest Police Department – and its Officers, aren't supposed to do anything Viciously, and outside the Law, to the Correct Suspect. Dallas will do anything illegal and unethical, to anyone. This action must be investigated, and stopped.

The Dallas County District Attorneys Office has been Corrupt for Decades. A complete upheaval should be implemented, to once again make this an honest Department, with honest Attorneys working in it. The Case now before this Court will show that a Malicious Prosecution is nothing unusual in the Dallas County D.A.'s Office. No Illegal and unethical Act is beneath this Office.

An Investigation of the Dallas "Crimes Against Persons" Department should be implemented. They were guilty of: the "Planting" of Evidence; the Coercion of Witnesses; the Threatening of Witnesses; the Tampering of Evidence; giving Perjured Testimony at Trial, and Conspiring with Corrupt Members of the F.B.I., to defraud the Plaintiff of "Justice". This little corrupt Dept. is the Modern Day, Dallas "Homicide Squad", that worked with the F.B.I. at the time of the Kennedy Assassination, to distort the Truth. A disgusting, symbiotic relationship. Several of the **Dallas Conspirators** lied in this Case, for Personal Glory. The Cop who lied the the most, **Conspirator COP Matthews**, got credit for solving this Case/s, along with his Police-Woman partner, **Regina Smith**. He lied , time and time again, to the Media, and also in Court at the Plaintiff's Trial. Not only were his Perjuries for his own Personal Aggrandizement, but he lied, to **help** his fellow Conspirators. (This is Not to mention that he was writing a Book about the Case – at the time, and he needed to invent many "things", and situations, in order to make his manuscript more saleable). **Matthews**, showing his good Dallas, "lack of Training to be

Albright wrote the words "glory," "cop," and "cop" in his Opening Statement.

Dear Melvin

This is the Zodiac speaking I wish you a happy Christmass. The one thing I ask of you is this, please help me. I cannot reach out for help because of this thing in me wont let me.

Zodiac's letter to Melvin Bell.

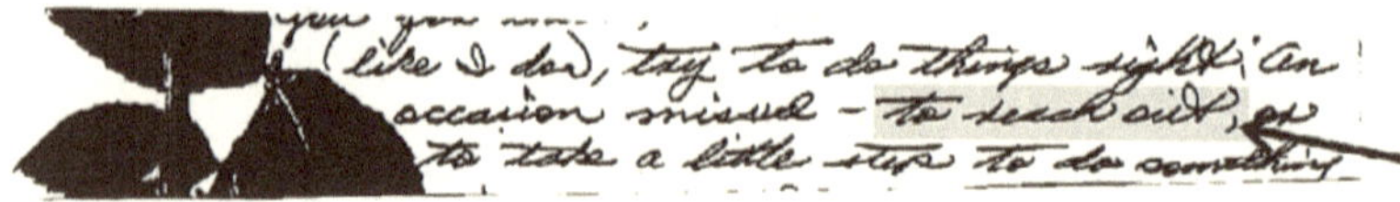
(like I do), try to do things right; An occasion missed – to reach out, or to take a little step to do something

From Charles F. Albright's letter.

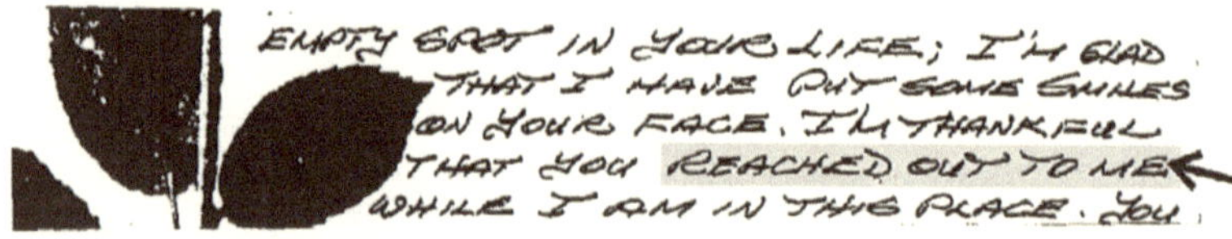
EMPTY SPOT IN YOUR LIFE; I'M GLAD THAT I HAVE PUT SOME SMILES ON YOUR FACE. I'M THANKFUL THAT YOU REACHED OUT TO ME WHILE I AM IN THIS PLACE. YOU

From Charles F. Albright's letter.

Zodiac wrote in his Dear Melvin letter the words "reach out" and Albright wrote the words "reach out" in at least two letters.

groops of barking about 10 min
apart then the motor cicles
went by about 150 ft away
going from South to north west.
ps. 2 cops pulled a goof abot 3
min after I left the cab. I was
walking down the hill to the
park when this cop car pulled up

From Zodiac letter to the Chronicles dated November 9, 1969.

"Phantom Hair". They've faked evidence, TWICE, in this case, Thanks to the F.B.I.! Guess what! A "Crooked" F.B.I. Man is as big a FOOL as any other "Crook". They gambled again on this case, and Goofed again. This Dog is the only Dog we ever owned. It wasn't even born in October, 1988. It wasn't born until December, of 1989 - over a year later. We bought the Dog from a Man and Woman, both of whom worked for the Dallas County Sheriff's Department. There was absolutely NO doubt about it.

From Charles F. Albright's letter.

Zodiac wrote in a letter "cops pulled a goof" and Albright wrote in a letter that an FBI man "goofed again."

DL #9-616

"MANY A SLIP HAS BEEN MADE BETWEEN THE CUP AND THE LIP. YOUR LIP DID IT TOGETHER WITH YOUR FAMILY. YOU ASKED FOR IT. YOUR VERSION WRONG ACCUSATION WRONG LIP TOO BIG YOU ASKED FOR IT TOGETHER WITH OTHERS LIP. YOU WERE TOLD TO DO SOMETHING. IT IS WHAT YOU HAVE DONE IN PAST NOT OTHERS. YOU AND YOUR LIPPERS WILL FIND THIS OUT IN TIME. YOU ASKED FOR IT."

Again FEAGINS advised that the only individual he could suspect would be FLOYD KILCREASE. He stated that this note was not handled, and it was immediately placed in a cellophane envelope. He described KILCREASE as being approximately 5' 10½" tall, weight 135 to 140, age approximately 45, slightly gray hair, brown eyes, and slender build. He did not know KILCREASE until he transacted the real estate deal [redacted] [redacted] KILCREASE through the Jennings Real Estate Company.

The extortion notes and envelopes are being forwarded to the FBI Laboratory.

ENCLOSURES TO LITTLE ROCK - Photostatic copies of the two extortion notes.

Letter following Phantom Murders in Texarkana.

SOMETHING BY FRIDAY, APR. 28TH. I WOULD THINK.
MY MIND IS FILLED WITH NICE THOUGHTS OF YOU.
(YOU ASKED FOR THIS [redacted]) AND YOU WILL BE MY ONLY ROSE,
FOR AS LONG AS YOU LIKE (YOU ASKED FOR THIS TOO.)
I LOVE PLEASING YOU, [redacted]. DON'T FORGET
TO WRITE!

YOUR
CHARLIE

Albright

From Charles F. Albright's letter.

A letter following the Phantom Murders in Texarkana included the words typed three times in upper case "YOU ASKED FOR IT." Albright wrote two times in a letter in upper case the words "YOU ASKED FOR THIS."

Zodiac spent a great deal of time devising his ciphers

ture of the face. I have several times spent 80 to 100 hours, just painting a woman's clothes. I'm all about being "perfect", whether it is as an Artist, a Photographer, an amateur Softball player, or as a person who tries to sup-

From a letter that Charles F. Albright wrote.

Zodiac and Albright were very meticulous.

Zodiac mailed ciphers to newspapers, one of which was decoded.

Now [redacted], look at the "Message" I got today, as I decoded this simple puzzle. I don't need it! My mind is already made up. I am sending it on

Charles F. Albright wrote in a letter that he had "decoded this simple puzzle" not that he had "solved" this simple puzzle.

Zodiac mailed ciphers to newspapers. Albright wrote in a letter "I decoded this simple puzzle."

One of my readers wrote that "Rasmussen probably will say that the Zodiac was the second gunman on the grassy knoll when President John F. Kennedy was assassinated in 1963." I have never said that, nor have I ever implied it. However, I do suggest that Mr. Albright may have known Lee Harvey Oswald in 1963, when Oswald rented a room at Gladys Johnson's rooming house located at 1026 North Beckley, Oak Cliff, Texas. Albright lived at 1035 Eldorado, Oak Cliff, approximately five hundred feet from where Lee Harvey Oswald was living in 1963, at the time Kennedy was murdered. This area was sparsely populated in 1963, and there is a good possibility that Albright may have met Oswald at a bar, a strip joint, at Mrs. Johnson's rooming house or somewhere in the Oak Cliff neighborhood during the six weeks Oswald stayed at Mrs. Johnson's rooming house. (See map search on Google or Yahoo to see locations of these two properties).

Michael Granberry of the *Dallas Morning News* reported in an article dated March 9, 2006, that "Patricia Puckett Hall, granddaughter of Gladys Johnson remembers no fewer than 16 tenants standing by the piano singing hymns as Grandma 'Mimi' played her heart out, on Thanksgiving, Christmas and Easter. . . She remembers the dapper gentleman who brought his daughter to the house on weekends, giving Ms. Hall a treasured playmate." Charles F. Albright lived close by the Johnson rooming house in 1963. He "looked positively distinguished" (Note 41, p. 339), played the piano, sang and had a daughter. Was Albright the dapper gentleman that Patricia Puckett Hall was referring to? The fact that a person, who years later was convicted of murder, lived so close to Oswald's rooming house in 1963, is information that was unknown in 1963, and was not included in the Warren Commission Report or considered by the House Select Committee on Assassinations. Albright was convicted of murder in 1991. The reason I mention this is that eleven days after the Kennedy assassination a letter was mailed from Lancaster, California, addressed to Jack Rubenstein a/k/a Jack Ruby. Ruby operated the Carousel Club, a topless stripper-joint located at 1312 ½ Commerce Street in Dallas. "The Carousel was the after hours place in Dallas in 1963. Students, attorneys and police officers all mingled here." North Beckley ends at Commerce Street not far from where Oswald and Albright lived in 1963. The Lancaster letter was in some ways similar to the "Bates Had to Die" letter mailed by the Zodiac after Cheri Jo Bates was murdered in Riverside, California, on October 30, 1966. Whoever wrote the letter addressed to Rubenstein was obviously upset that Ruby had killed Oswald. The writer called Ruby a "dirty low stinking Jew" which may indicate that the writer of the Rubenstein letter could have been an acquaintance of Oswald and someone who obviously disliked Jack Ruby. Albright may not have liked Jews. When he was arrested in 1991, detectives found "Nazi memorabilia, including a portrait of Adolf Hitler painted by Albright" in his Texas home (Note 39, p. 173). Lancaster, California, is located close to Edwards Air Force Base.

A serial killer is an individual, either a man or woman, who kills two or more people at different times for some psychological reason. Several, if not all, of the serial killers that terrorized California between 1960–1990, including but not limited to Richard Ramirez, Randy Kraft, William Bonin, Douglas Clark and Ted Bundy, Angelo Buono Jr., Kenneth Bianchi, Juan Corona and Charles Manson were not expert photographers, draftsman, experts at astrology and forgery. They did not kill according to phases of the moon. They did not love to send greeting cards and they were not prolific letter writers. They didn't speak in low, soft monotone voices and have a drawl. They were not known to be someone who could write difficult poetry from memory or be neatly dressed and drive a messy car. They weren't known to be calm in a crisis situation. They weren't known to be interested in opera. Even though no one has ever determined the true identity of the Zodiac Killer, one thing has to be said about the detective's remark that "all serial killers are the same," and that is that at least two known serial killers are remarkably similar.

Maybe there is something to astrology. I mentioned above that Charles F. Albright was born on August 10th, so was I.

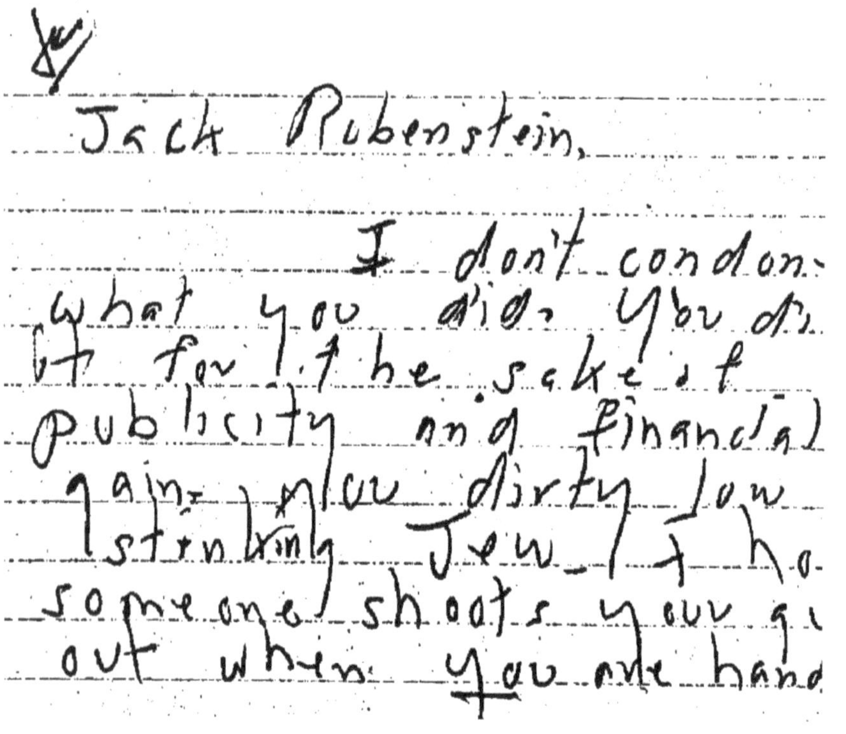

Jack Rubenstein,

I don't condon what you did. You did it for the sake of publicity and financial gain. You dirty low stinking Jew. I ho someone shoots your gu out when you are hand

In1963, Lee Harvey Oswald kept a room at Gladys Johnson's home located at 1026 North Beckley, Oak Cliff, Texas. Charles F. Albright lived at 1035 Eldorado, Oak Cliff, Texas (do Google map search). The area was sparsely populated in 1963. Did Albright know Oswald who registered as "O.H. Lee?" The writer of the Jack Rubenstein letter was clearly upset that Ruby had killed Oswald. Also check Google map search for 214 West Neely, Oak Cliff, Texas.

Letter to Jack Rubenstein mailed from Lancaster, California, eleven days after the assassination of President John Kennedy. Charles F. Albright died on August 22, 2020, while incarcerated at the West Texas Regional Medical Facility in Lubbock, Texas.

Chapter 7

THE MYSTERIOUS MURDER OF VALERIE PERCY KENILWORTH, ILLINOIS, SEPTEMBER 18, 1966

September 18, 1964, *Time Magazine* Article on Charles Harting Percy

The cover of the September 18, 1964, issue of *Time Magazine,* Volume 84, No. 12, features a painting of Charles Harting Percy, Republican candidate for Governor of the State of Illinois. Percy was well liked, home spun, religious and a family man. Some even thought he could be a future candidate for President of the United States. He had made his fortune moving up very fast in the ranks at Bell and Howell, a leading supplier of media equipment for schools and offices. At age 23 he was named to its board of directors and soon after became president of Bell and Howell. He was well on his way to becoming a young millionaire. In 1962, he became the chairman of Bell and Howell's executive board. Percy's run for Governor was not successful, and he lost the 1964 governor's race to Democrat Otto Kerner.

The September 18, 1964, issue of *Time Magazine* featured the well known politician, his family and a postcard-size photo of the Percy's sprawling 17-room Tudor mansion, called Windward, located at 40 Devonshire in upscale Kenilworth, Illinois, north of Chicago between Winnetka and Wilmette. Kenilworth consists of about 850 homes and had a population of less than 3000 in 1966. A Percy family photo on page 35 of the magazine included Roger, 17; Gail, 11; Mrs. Lorraine Percy, 37; Charles H. Percy; Mark, 9; and Sharon, 19. A footnote to the family photo indicated that "Sharon's twin sister Valerie is away at school in France." Valerie was studying in Paris at the time.

Time Magazine has national circulation and was readily available to anyone in 1964. The Percy mansion fronts on and faces Lake Michigan. A public street ending near Mahoney Park at the Kenilworth-Wilmette border at Lake Michigan allows access to the Percy's beach front and north yard of the Percy estate.

In 1966, Charles Percy's daughter Valerie had just graduated from Cornell University in Ithaca, New York. Valerie was an attractive, 21-year-old, blue-eyed blonde who was very well liked and had no known enemies. Charles Percy had decided to run for the United States Senate, so in 1966, Valerie was back in Kenilworth to work on her father's campaign.

September 18, 1966, the Murder of Valerie Percy

On Sunday, September 18, 1966,[1] exactly two years after the subject *Time Magazine* article was published, featuring the Percy family, someone with the intent to murder hid in the darkened bushes off the cold waters of Lake Michigan near the north yard of the Percy estate.[2] Had a serial killer been attracted to the painting of Charles Harting Percy on the cover of the September 18, 1964, *Time Magazine* and did he pursue and murder Valerie Percy on September 18, 1966? Did the painting of Charles Percy and the anniversary date have some connection to the murder of Valerie Percy?

The killer may have gained access to the Percy property from the public access located south of the estate. The mansion had huge windows facing Lake Michigan. It would have been easy to see someone on the inside of the building at night from the Lake Michigan side of the Percy property. From the north portion of the Percy estate, concealed in the bushes, a prowler watched a dinner party in the Percy home that included Valerie, guests James Mann, Tully Friedman-both workers in Charles Percy's campaign for U.S. Senate-Valerie's twin sister Sharon, their half sister Gail and half brother Mark. At approximately 10:00 pm Valerie excused herself from the dinner party and ascended the spiral staircase to her second floor bedroom located in the northeast corner of the mansion. The dinner guests also dispersed at this time. When she arrived at her bedroom, which was located adjacent to her sister Sharon's room, Valerie turned on her bedroom light, got ready for bed, watched television until 11:30 pm and then eventually turned off the light in her room. It should be noted that no family members actually saw Valerie in her bedroom from 10:00 pm-11:30 pm until her sister Sharon stopped by the bedroom and returned a raincoat that she had borrowed from Valerie. Sharon told detectives: "Val was in her nightclothes, sitting up in bed watching television." Anyone watching from outside the mansion would have seen her leave the dinner party, go up the stairs and see her bedroom light go on and off. They would have known exactly where her bedroom was located. On that night Charles Percy and Mrs. Percy were at the Germania Club on the north side of Chicago where Charles was giving a speech. They returned home at 12:30 am and retired to their bedroom about one hour later. Around 4:45 am the home was dark and all of its occupants were asleep when the unknown assailant, under the cover of darkness, entered the mansion from the north yard by cutting a four-inch square section from the copper-screen door and then cutting a panel of glass from a French door with a glass cutter. The intruder either pulled out or knocked the remaining glass from the door frame. Fingerprints were found on the piece of glass located between the door and drapery. He then entered the music room on the northeast side of the house. With the aid of his flashlight he moved through the large living room and the vestibule and crept silently up the 18-step spiral stairway past Sharon's bedroom directly to Valerie's bedroom, where she lay sleeping. In addition to the flashlight, the intruder carried with him a glass cutter, a blunt object shaped like a ball peen hammer with one end sharpened and possibly a double-edged army bayonet with 10-inch blade as he slithered through the occupied mansion. Detectives later pondered as to how he accomplished this feat, traveling through the mansion without detection.[3]

Valerie was asleep in her third floor bedroom when he entered her room. Without warning, he viciously struck her four times in the left side of her head with a heavy object similar to a ball peen hammer or fireplace poker with a conical or triangular head, fracturing her skull. She was then stabbed six times around her nose and left eye, once in the neck, one time in each breast and twice in the abdomen.[4] It appears that someone entered the Percy mansion with the sole purpose of brutally killing Valerie Percy. Robbery was ruled out as a motive. Valerie had defensive wounds that indicated she had tried to fight off her attacker. Director Dan Dragel of the Chicago Police Crime Lab thought that from the amount of blood in Valerie's room, the killer's clothing must have been badly stained.

At approximately 5:00 am Lorraine Percy, Valerie's stepmother, asleep in the master bedroom, was awakened by the sound of a breaking glass and moans from down the hallway in the vicinity of either Sharon's of Valerie's bedrooms. Mrs. Percy thought someone had knocked a water glass off a night stand and went to investigate. When she approached Valerie's bedroom and peered in the intruder startled her. She was temporarily blinded by his flashlight as he left the room and fled down the stairway, through the music room, out the French doors and into the north yard, where he made his escape.[5] Mrs. Percy, overcome with fear, ran screaming to her husband in the master bedroom. She immediately pushed a button that triggered an alarm located on the roof of the mansion. The alarm pierced the early morning silence and then shut off. Mr. Percy switched it on again and the siren shut off for the second time. By this time the intruder had vanished. When later questioned by detectives, Lorraine Percy said she saw the bludgeoned body of Valerie lying on her blood-soaked bed with her nightgown pulled up over her shoulders. Mrs. Percy also advised detectives that she pulled the nightgown down to Valerie's knees and wiped some blood off Valerie's face. Although not documented for public disclosure, it would appear that the killer pulled the nightgown up to expose her nude or semi-nude body. Authorities began to question whether this may have been a sex killing, although the post mortem determined that Valerie had not been raped.[6] Following the murder, police checked several other sex murders in which victims had been stabbed to death. None were ever connected to the murder of Valerie Percy.

The Clues

Valerie Percy died in the house from her wounds and her killer has never been identified. Police and twenty-five members of the Wilmette Explorer Scout Post 2 scoured the grounds and Lake Michigan beach for clues to the murder. The U.S. Coast Guard was called in with heavy magnets to search the water off shore to try to find any weapon the killer may have thrown into Lake Michigan after he exited the building. Eight hundred feet south of the Percy mansion and forty feet off shore scuba divers found an **army bayonet with a 10-inch-long, double-edged blade** and 4-inch plastic handle that may have been used to inflict the stab wounds. Searchers also found on top of a bush in a gully 30 feet from the Percy mansion a black wool glove with a leather palm, the kind used by "someone who may have driven a sports car." Fibers found on the cut screen were analyzed and found to match the black fibers found on Valerie's bed and the fibers from the black glove. Police were certain the black wool glove they found was worn by Valerie's killer. They were never able to conclusively determine that the bayonet had been used in the murder.[7] Hundreds of footprints were found in the sand on the beach. Police interviewed the Percy's neighbors to find out if they had seen anything unusual on the night of the murder. One neighbor reported to Chief of Police Daley seeing a man in a gray suit, about 32, driving a green station wagon near the Percy home after the murder. If this was a possible suspect in Valerie's murder the driver would have been born sometime between 1933-1934.

Boy Scouts searching for evidence at the Percy property

Investigators searching for evidence at the Percy property

Police were baffled over a possible motive of the killing. The position of her body did not indicate that she had caught someone in the act of stealing from her or ransacking her bedroom. Detectives searched her dresser drawers and found a large amount of money that could have easily been found by a cat burglar. Nothing else in the home was reported missing. She was bludgeoned about her head as she lay sleeping, and she was probably targeted by the intruder. Dr. Andrew J. Toman, Cook County Coroner, stated that "The attacker obviously came to the house to murder someone." Killing the daughter of Charles H. Percy in a mansion occupied by several other family members would certainly gain national attention. Newspapers all over the United States would carry the story. The killer must have expected this result before the murder was committed. You could then speculate that a possible motive for the murder might have been to succeed in gaining national attention, for whatever twisted reason the killer might have, through reports printed in the newspapers and broadcast in the radio and television news.[8]

In May, 1966, Charles H. Percy had received a three-page double-spaced, typewritten letter threatening him with a "one way ride." The letter was addressed to Percy and was signed "The Boys from Out of Town," The letter warned: "We hope we don't have to take you on a one-way ride. Be careful of what you are saying . . . first watch what you say from now until June." Also mentioned in the letter were:

1. Senator W. Russell Arrington, Republican, Evanston
2. Former Vice president Richard M. Nixon
3. Senator Everett Dirksen, Republican, Illinois
4. Rep. Gerald R. Ford, Republican, Michigan
5. Senator Barry Goldwater of Arizona [9]

The letter went on to say; "We've been ordered to watch such men when they come to town." (Referring to Goldwater, Nixon and Dirksen)[10] Curiously, Goldwater, Nixon and Dirksen are all mentioned in the *Time Magazine* article on Charles Percy dated September 18, 1964. (Vol. 84, No. 12) On page 36 of the *Time* article there is also a photograph of Senator Dirksen with Charles Percy.

Summary

The murder of Valerie Percy appears to have been committed by someone who was well prepared and not an amateur. He probably came to the Percy mansion, wearing gloves so that he wouldn't leave any fingerprints, equipped with a flashlight, glass cutter, possibly a ball peen hammer or fireplace poker and possibly an army bayonet. He had devised some way to transport all of these items; the most logical solution would be by way of a carpenter's belt. Police theorized that the killer might have been familiar with the floor plan of the Percy home but this was never positively determined. If he waited in the darkened yard and bushes from before 10:00 pm during the dinner party, and the time Valerie went upstairs to her bedroom until approximately 4:45 am-5:00 am to enter the mansion after everyone was asleep, one could surmise that the perpetrator had a great deal of patience. One might also draw the conclusion that the killer had experience. After killing Valerie and then being approached by Lorraine Percy, the killer exhibited composure by shining his flashlight in Mrs. Percy's eyes and then descending the staircase taking all the tools he brought with him, then exiting the property without being detected, and escaping the area by what may have been a preplanned escape route.

Possible Solution

As indicated, following the murder of Valerie Percy, the police checked, to no avail, several other sex murders where the female victims were stabbed to death. It is my suggestion that a more comprehensive search using "specific indicators" that were present at the Percy murder might uncover the identity of the killer. Such "indicators" would be: Valerie was not only stabbed to death, during the commission of the attack, she was also stabbed one time in each breast with no sexual assault. I think this is significant. All attacks on females during this time period should be checked wherein the victim was stabbed one time in each breast and not raped. The fact that this offence occurred in the state of Illinois does not necessarily mean that the same individual could not have committed a similar attacks in different states. Valerie was struck in the head with an object shaped like a ball peen hammer. All crimes against females during this time period involving blows to the head with a hammer should be reviewed for similarities. Valerie was stabbed multiple times including several stab wounds near her left eye. An army bayonet may have been used by her killer as a murder weapon. All crimes against women during this time period wherein a bayonet was used as a weapon and where a woman was stabbed around her eyes should be reviewed and cross checked. The killer temporarily blinded Mrs. Lorraine Percy with the bright light of a flashlight. Crimes involving the murder of young women (or other victims with at least some similarities) should be re-examined to see if they involve some of these details.

It is also my recommendation that the authorities conduct DNA testing on all letters and stamps associated with this case that may have been licked by the sender and were received before and after the murder of Valerie Percy.

Whoever entered the Percy mansion on September 18, 1966,

and murdered Valerie was, in my opinion, a person who came well prepared and was not an amateur killer. It appears the killer entered the mansion with the intention of killing Valerie Percy and no one else. The person must have known that killing a daughter of a famous person in an occupied home in upscale Kenilworth, Illinois, would surely create national news. The killer may have reveled in the attention his crime created, not by the newspapers mentioning his real name but just knowing that he created the national attention. Was this the underlying motive for the crime?[11] With this in mind, detectives should take a close look at the facts and circumstances surrounding the Zodiac Murders that took place before and after the murder of Valerie Percy and compare them to the murder of Valerie Percy.

Footnotes:

All page numbers below refer to the page in the publication referred to in the note.

1. The Zodiac Killer had a habit of writing letters on the anniversary of his attacks and murders. (Note 42, page 157) There may have been something in his mind that involved astrology, signs of the Zodiac, etc. that resulted in revisiting events on anniversary dates.
2. Zodiac killed near water. (Note 42, page 321)
3. On September 27, 1969, the Zodiac Killer wore a bayonet-type knife, "**at least a foot long**," in a sheath attached to his belt. **The blade was sharpened on both sides.** On his right side was a black holster and several lengths of hollow-core plastic clothesline. Zodiac was also known to carry a flashlight. (Note 42, pages 66-69)

4. On Sunday, October 30, 1966, Zodiac Victim Cheri Jo Bates was stabbed one time in each breast. Her autopsy report indicated that she had a 1.4 cm vertical gapping sharp edge laceration in the upper medial quadrant of the left breast and a 1.9 cm gapping sharp edge laceration of the lower medial quadrant of the right breast. On September 27, 1969, Zodiac Victim Cecelia Shepard was stabbed 24 times including once in the abdomen and once in each breast. (Note 42, page 71) Bates was killed 42 days after Valerie Percy was murdered. The Zodiac was active during this time period. Were Valerie Percy and Cecelia Shepard each stabbed in a "V" shaped pattern? (See Chapter 9, pages 327–328)
5. On July 4, 1969, the Zodiac Killer temporarily blinded Mike Mageau by shining a powerful flashlight directly in his eyes. (Note 42, page 27)
6. Zodiac did not rape his victims.
7. Zodiac wore black gloves when he attacked Bryan Hartnell and Cecelia Shepard on September 27, 1969, at Lake Berryessa north of San Francisco. (Note 42, page 68)
8. Zodiac had a very large ego and demanded front page press. (Note 42)
9. On May 2, 1978, a letter was mailed to KHJ-TV in Los Angeles. The police thought the letter was sent by the Zodiac Killer. The writer wrote in the letter that he had plans to kill five people in the next three weeks:

    1. Chief piggy Darrel Gates
    2. Ex chief piggy Ed Davis
    3. Pat Boone
    4. Eldridge Cleaver
    5. Sharon Atkins, a member of the Charles Manson Family

10. In the Phantom Murders of Texarkana murder victim Betty Jo Booker's step father, Clark Brown, received a letter dated May 2, 1947, that may have been mailed by her killer. In the Zodiac Murders, Joseph Bates, father of murder victim, Cheri Jo Bates, received a letter on April 30, 1967, two days before May 2, from the Zodiac.

11. Zodiac wrote in a letter to the *Los Angeles Times* on or about March 15, 1971: "The reason I am writing the *Times* is because they don't bury me on the back pages." Zodiac was not the real person's name. I would say it was his stage name. On May 2, 1978, Zodiac wrote in part to KHJ-TV in Los Angeles: "whoever plays me has his work cut out for him." A possible Zodiac letter mailed on April 25, 1978, to the *San Francisco Chronicle* included the following: "I am waiting for a good movie about me, who will play me." (Note 42, page 207) The point is, Zodiac was an egomaniac and wanted his accomplishments headlined in major newspapers.

Chapter 8

THE MURDERS OF RICHARD ROBISON AND HIS FAMILY, GOOD HART, MICHIGAN, JUNE 25, 1968

In the spring of 1968, Richard Robison appeared to be a successful publisher of the arts and entertainment magazine *Impresario.* Robison's company, R. C. Robison and Associates had several major advertisers including Delta Faucet, National Bank of Detroit and Chrysler. He lived near Detroit in upscale Lathrup Village at 18790 Dolores with his wife Shirley and their four children, Susan, Randall, Gary and Ritchie. The Robisons were upper middle class, living a life that most people would envy. Richard was an active supporter of the civic opera[1] and a man "who could do oil paintings of professional quality." It was later discovered that his picture-perfect business had its shortcomings. The company was financially distressed. Between January and June, 1968, only $3,500.00 in advertisements had been sold, and money was missing from the business. Later, Robison's business associate, Joseph "Joe" Raymond Scolaro III, became a suspect in its disappearance.

Odd, unexplained things began to happen with Richard Robison in early June, 1968. He made two visits to hotels in San Francisco and spent three nights and two days in a hotel 20 miles from his Lathrup Village home. Apparently, he had a multi-million dollar business deal in the works to build "computerized warehouse operations and support cultural centers." The New Hudson Airport in Oakland County north of Detroit was going to be the site of Robison's dream development, a development that could reach the lofty sum of one hundred million dollars to complete. A mysterious investor in the development by the name of "Mr. Robert" or "Mr. Roebert" was later mentioned by associates of Robison. One of the associates thought the name sounded French and stated that Mr. Roeberts had a monotone voice, with frequent pauses in his speech, "an unusual robotic quality."[2] Robison had made plans to travel on June 16, 1968, with his family to their secluded cottage located 100 feet from the edge of Lake Michigan[3] beneath a bluff in a resort known as Blisswood, 1.9 miles north of Good Hart, a small village between Harbor Springs and Cross Village in Emmet County, Michigan. Mr. Roebert was supposed to fly into the Pellston Airport and then meet Richard Robison at his cottage on June 25, 1968, the day Robison and his entire family were murdered.

Richard Robison Family

The Murders

On July 22, 1968, all six members of the Robison family were found murdered in their secluded lake-front cottage in Good Hart. This was no ordinary crime scene. Approximately thirty days after the Robisons were last seen, a horrible stench emanated from the vicinity of the Robison cottage. Local resident Monnie Bliss and an Odawa Indian named Steve Shananaquet investigated the source of the terrible odor. Smoke was coming out of the cottage windows. They thought maybe a raccoon had died under the cottage. Subsequently realizing that there was something dead inside the building, they forced the door open. What they discovered was astounding, an absolutely horrific crime scene. At the time, the two men saw what appeared to be the body of a woman lying on the wooden floor partially covered with a red plaid blanket. The ladies bottom portion of her legs remained uncovered. They immediately left the

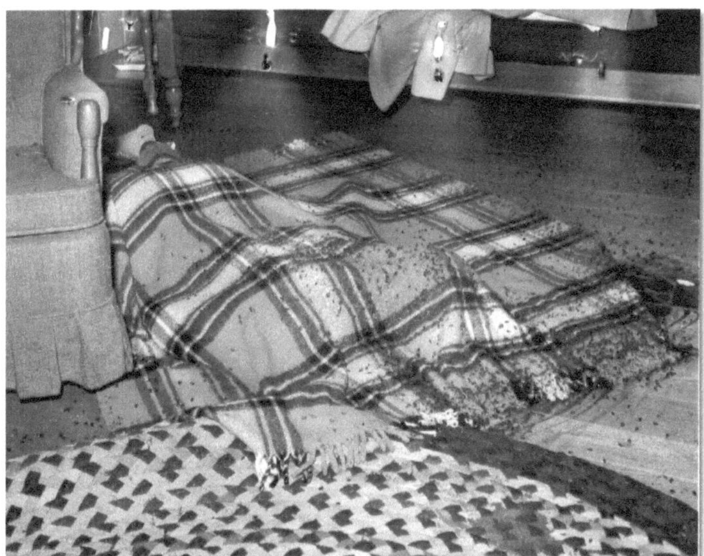

Red plaid blanket covering Shirley Robison's body at the Robison cottage.

building and summoned the Emmet County Sheriff's Department, which in turn called the Michigan State Police for assistance. What would ultimately be revealed in this grisly setting were all six decaying bodies of the Robison family, covered with maggots and thousands of flies. Detectives arrived and, after donning gas masks, began their investigation. Michigan State Police Trooper Edward Hancock wrote, "The smoke was caused by the furnace, a floor-hung type that was under some of the bodies in the hallway. Particles of flesh and such were falling on the furnace and causing it to smoke."[9]

On July 22, 1968, C.C. Cole, deputy sheriff of the Emmet County Sheriff's Department, described the mass murders as follows:

> The undersigned was summond to the sheriff's office by Chief Deputy John Theisen and instructed to go to Blisswood as it was believed there was a body of a person or animal found in one of the cottages. This cottage was owned by Richard Robison. I immediately left for the assignment and was on the Harbor Springs road when the office called and told me to pick up the undersheriff (Clifford Fosmore) at the Ted Gokee residence. The undersheriff was there because his radio sending unit was out and he had been unable to answer the office when it called him. Undersheriff Fosmore and myself then proceeded to the Blisswood site. When we went down to the lower road at Blisswood, we saw Chauncy Bliss and some others, working on a new building. Mr. Bliss and Steve Shananaquet came out to the road to meet us and Mr. Bliss then informed us that he had opened the door of the Robison cottage and found what he believed was a human body with a rug thrown over it, on the living room floor. He stated that he then closed the door and immediately called the sheriff's department. He stated that he had disturbed nothing. Mr. Shanaquet had nothing to say at that

time and left the talking up to Mr. Bliss. Mr. Bliss did say that Mr. Shanaquet was with him at the time he (Bliss) went to the cottage. Fosmore and myself then proceeded up the road to the Robison cottage. I was driving the car and I pulled directly up in front of the cottage. There was a very strong odor coming from the cottage and was recognized as putrified flesh. Fosmore got out of the car and went to the front door and opened it while I backed the car out of the flow of air. Mr. Fosmore did not enter the building at that time, but returned to the car and called the coronor and prosecuting attorney. I then went to the building and entered by the door on the east side (toward the road) and saw a body of what appeared to be a woman (this determined by the shoes) lying on the floor and covered down to the calves of the legs by a floor rug. I then went out and back to the car to get a Polaroid camera. I then re-entered the building and took a picture of the body. I then went back out and the undersheriff and myself decided that we should open the door on the lake side to allow air through the building to dissipate some of the odor. I entered the building and the undersheriff went around the south end of the building to the back door. This door was secured with a knife type latch with a draw string said string being on the inside of the door. I tried to open the door by this string but was unsuccessful. (I was in a hurry) so I hit the knife latch with the palm of my hand and pulled the door open. It was then I saw a trail of blood (dried) leading from the doorway, around the back of a couch which was in the middle of the room. A small throw rug was in front of the door and had been over the blood trail until I moved it by opening the door. I then unhooked the screen door and Fosmore pulled it open and I went out for air. It was while I was passing through the living room to open the lakeside door that I saw what appeared to be several bodies in the hallway leading from the living room. I informed Mr. Fosmore of this and we decided to wait for the medical examiner and prosecuting attorney to arrive before proceeding with the investigation. Upon arrival of the afore mentioned officials, we re-entered the building with the aid of gas masks, and I took a picture of the bodies in the hallway. There were three bodies in a pile miday down the hall and the lower part of another body was protruding from the bedroom on the west (Lake) side of the building. The bodies in the hallway were of two males and a female, while the one in the bedroom was a male. We then went back out and got permission from the prosecuting attorney to break a window on the north end of the building to check on the body in the bedroom. Undersheriff Fosmore broke a pane of glass and opened the window on the northwest bedroom and looked in and said there was another body lying next to the bed. I then reached inside the window and took two shots of the body. (The first one was too fuzzy) Fosmore then went to the window on the northeast corner and opened it and entered the building through this window. When he emerged he had a billfold that he stated had been picked up from the floor in the hallway next to the pile of bodies. He put the billfold on the ground and I used the erasure end of a pencil to turn the partitions of the billfold. This article was identified as belonging to a Richard Robison and contained several pieces of identification and family pictures. By this time there were quite a number of people on the scene, some of whom were, Jim Jensen of the Petoskey Police Department, Vic Thompson of the Petoskey Fire Dept. Fred Lovelace of the Petoskey News Review and several others including the prosecutor and Medical examiner. After a few minutes, I was

> back by my car when Mr. Fosmore came out with a hammer. He was carrying it with a handkerchief, and told me to take a picture of it, which I did. I then re-entered the building with Mr. Fosmore and he replaced the hammer on the couch in approximately the same place it had been removed from, and I took a picture of it again. It was shortly after this that Mr. Fosmore informed all present that he was calling for the Michigan State Police crime lab for assistance on the case and that the area was to be sealed off. Mr. Fosmore directed Deputies Wilton and Mikulski that they were to protect the area and allow no one to enter. Mr. Fosmore and myself then left the area and I returned Fosmore to his car in Harbor Springs. I personally had no further contact with the murder scene until the following Saturday when Deputies Wilton, Mikulski and myself used magnets to drag the cove area in front of the cottage, looking for a possible weapon.

The police determined that someone must have approached the Robison cottage either during the late afternoon or at night from the yard facing Lake Michigan on the north side of the property. Mr. Robison was in his leather lounge chair in the southeast corner of the cottage reading, and the children were all occupied in various locations throughout the cottage. Mrs. Robison sat in an armchair nearby. The killer, with expert precision, fired four rounds in a tight pattern with a 22 semi-automatic[4] through a glass window pane near the front door. The first shots struck Mr. Robison twice in the chest. His son, Gary, was struck in the back. The killer then turned his vengeance on Mrs. Robison. He fired his weapon again and struck his mark. Mrs. Robison fell to the floor and died. A bullet grazed 7-year-old Susan across the top of her head. She also fell to the ground and lay unconscious. Then the assassin entered the cottage, left a bloody size-10 ½ shoe print,[5] stalked and killed each of the three sons. Had the act of terror ended here it would appear, based on the money trail that was subsequently uncovered, that Joseph Scolaro or a professional hit man hired by Scolaro was responsible for the murders. Unless the killer was attempting to leave a false trail, the extenuating circumstances that followed seem to suggest the work of a completely different perpetrator. After murdering the sons the killer went back to the living room, took a carpenter's hammer and smashed little Susan Robison's skull ending her life.[6] Had he located Robison's 25 caliber Beretta revolver and elected to fire two rounds through son Gary's head and one shot through the heads of most of the other victims? He then dragged Richard's dead body down the hallway and placed him on his stomach on a hot air register. Next he dragged the youngest son, Randall, down the hallway and lifted him face down on top of his father.[7] He then partially covered the father and son with a lavender rug that was taken from in front of the fireplace. Susan was then hauled from the living room and positioned face up next to Randall and Richard's bodies. The killer then proceeded back to the living room where Mrs. Robison lay mortally wounded on her stomach. He pulled her dress up to her waist and yanked her undergarments down to her ankles. On August 19, 1968, under sheriff Clifford Fosmore reported that "Mrs. Robison was wearing a sanitary belt, and this belt, along with other under garments were down around her ankles. They found that the sanitary belt had been stabbed seven different places in the upper left side with a sharp instrument." (Emmet County Sheriff's Department Supplementary Report dated August 19, 1968, by Clifford L. Fosmore, under sheriff.)[8] Then he covered her dead body, except for her legs below the calves, in a plaid blanket. The killer then closed all of the windows and taped a note written on a paper towel on one of the windows near the front door. The note read, "WILL BE BACK 7-10 ROBISON." Handwriting experts determined the note had been written by Richard Robison. The killer then closed the window shades, turned up the heat on the furnace thermostat,[9] left the building, padlocked the rear door and then vanished into the night. Whoever committed these crimes intended to have the bodies discovered long after he had disappeared.

Outside window of the Robison cottage with bullet holes and attached note.

Emmet County undersheriff Clifford Fosmore holding
a hammer outside the Robison cottage.

Authorities gather outside the Robison cottage.

Police with gas masks searching for clues at the Robison cottage.

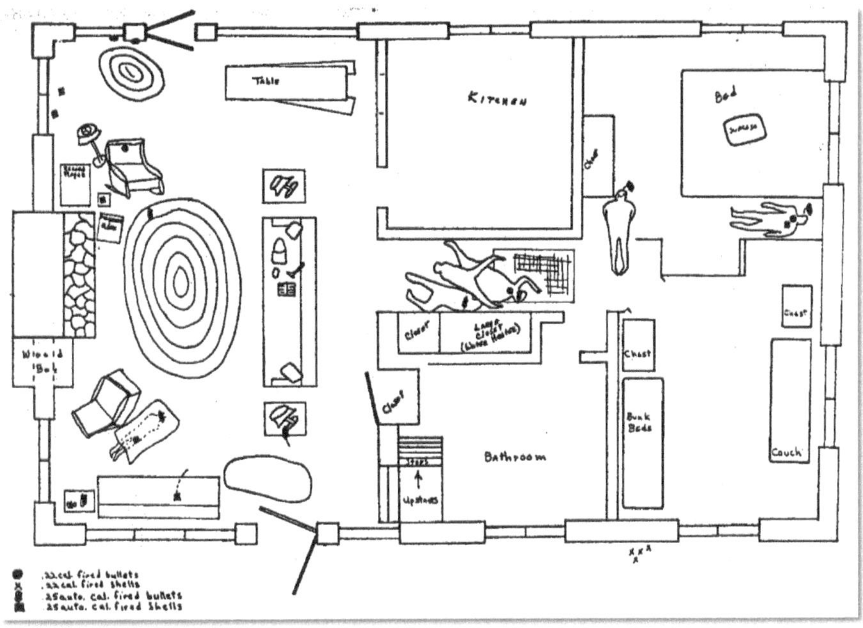

Michigan State Police diagram of murder scene of the interior of the Robison cottage after the bodies were found.

Once the crime scene evidence had been gathered and analyzed, lab technicians from the Michigan State Crime Lab determined that the weapon used for the initial shooting was probably an AR-7, 22 semi-automatic rifle. Coincidentally, this was the same type of rifle featured in the James Bond movie *From Russia with Love* when Q issues one in Bond's attaché case. Bond uses the AR-7 to assassinate a soviet agent with a suppressor and infrared telescopic sight on the weapon. Bond also used an AR-7 to kill a crewmember of a helicopter. This same type of weapon was used by Tilly Masterson in the James Bond movie, *Goldfinger* (1964) when she attempted to kill Auric Goldfinger. The AR-7 was a weapon that was well known by the movie going public. The AR-7 was manufactured by Armalite from 1959-1973, and could be readily purchased by the public. The AR-7 is chambered for the .22 long rifle cartridge. I located a curious note in Michigan State Police Complaint No. 78-785-68 in the Robison Murders dated 10/4/68. The note reads as follows: "weapon **rifled with six lands and grooves with a right twist**. The rifling specifications are similar to weapons manufactured by the Stevens-Savage Corporation, but these weapons may bear brand names of department or chain stores such as Sears (**J. C. Higgins**), Ward (Western Field) or Gambles (Pioneer). However, no suspected weapon should be overlooked." The note is signed by Detective Sergeant Kenard Christensen and Trooper Hugh Fish of the Crime Laboratory. It's possible that the killer had an original AR-7 or any of the close variations retailed under other names by major chain stores. In any case, the markings on the shell casings have similarities to other crime scene findings.[10]

Four (4) .22 caliber Remington Peters brand expended shell casings were found on the outside of the Robison cottage. The shell casings were located between 12 and 16 feet to the north of the window which had the bullet holes through it. There is no mention in the Michigan State Police Additional Complaint Report whether investigators determined the distance shell casings would eject from an Armalite AR 7 as compared to the distance shell casings would eject from a J. C. Higgins .22 semi-automatic.

Because a narrow roadway leads from M-119 to the Robison property, it is unlikely the killer drove his vehicle to the cottage. He probably left his car near a public access located within walking distance and traveled by foot along the Lake Michigan beach where he could approach the north side of the cottage under the cover of darkness. He would have had a full view of the living room and some of the occupants of the cottage.[11] If the killer had driven directly to the cottage police could have boxed him in had a neighbor reported a disturbance at the time the crimes were committed. The killer appears to be too organized to let that happen.

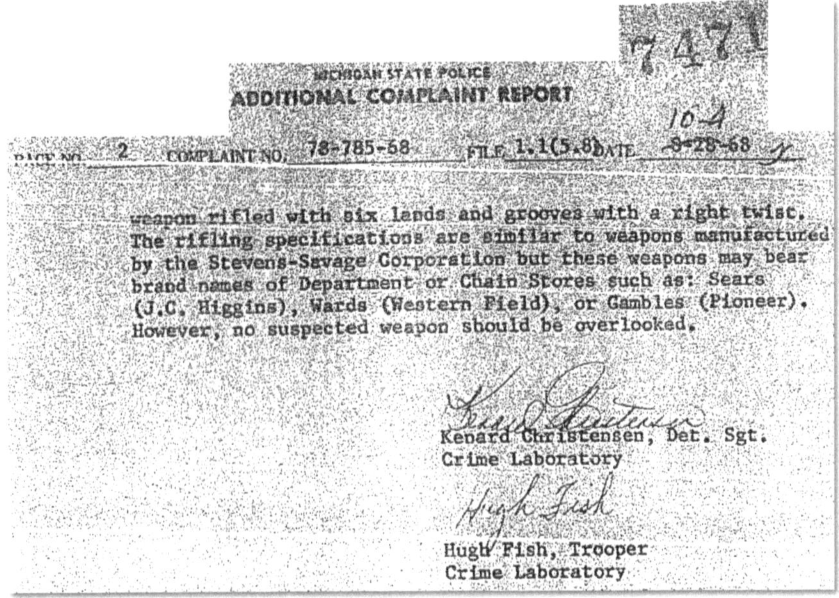
7471

MICHIGAN STATE POLICE
ADDITIONAL COMPLAINT REPORT

104

PAGE NO. 2 COMPLAINT NO. 78-785-68 FILE 1.1(5.8) DATE 8-28-68

weapon rifled with six lands and grooves with a right twist. The rifling specifications are similar to weapons manufactured by the Stevens-Savage Corporation but these weapons may bear brand names of Department or Chain Stores such as: Sears (J.C. Higgins), Wards (Western Field), or Gambles (Pioneer). However, no suspected weapon should be overlooked.

Kenard Christensen, Det. Sgt.
Crime Laboratory

Hugh Fish, Trooper
Crime Laboratory

Page from the Michigan State Police Additional Complaint Report in the Robison Murders that closely matches the investigative report in the Jensen/Faraday Murders committed by the Zodiac.

Trail to the Robison cottage near Good Hart, Michigan.

If Robison's business associate Joseph Scolaro wanted Richard Robison dead, why would he have killed the entire family? He knew that all of the Robisons would be at Summerset during their annual summer vacation. If Scolaro hired a hit man to kill Richard Robison, why would all of the Robisons be targeted? A hit man would have been told that the Robison family was at Summerset and it would have been obvious that the cottage was occupied by more than Richard Robison. Would a professional hit man have used an AR 7? Unless the hit man and/or Scolaro was a sexual predator, completely deranged, why would they commit the methodical acts that followed the murders-pulling down Mrs. Robison's dress, removing her undergarments after she was dead, and then stabbing her with a sharp instrument seven times in the upper left side of her sanitary belt, smashing seven-year-old Susan Robison and Richard Robison in the head with a carpenter's hammer, dragging Richard and Randall down the hallway and placing them on top of each other on a hot air register, dragging little Susan next to her dead father and brother, then turning up the heat to the furnace, slowly cooking his victims, close all of the curtains, leave a piece of cardboard over the bullet holes in the window, leave a handwritten note written on the door on the north side of the building, and padlock the back door when he left the cottage? None of the acts that followed the murders indicate the killer was in a hurry to vacate the property and the facts do not seem to point directly at Scolaro or a hit man. In almost every instance, with few exceptions, where a hit man is hired, he is paid a portion in advance, targets his victim, pulls the trigger, collects the balance of his blood money and that ends the story. Scolaro had no known history either before or after the murders of any violent and deviant sexual behavior. It appears to me that these acts of violence may have been committed by a previously unidentified individual, someone with experience, patience and a desire to commit murders that were intended to shock and disturb those that investigated and eventually the public, based on the amount of press the crimes would generate. The murders did have that end result. The *New York Times*, *Detroit News* and several other major and local newspapers carried the story. Several books have been written on the Robison murders. Even *True Detective* did a feature article on the Robison murders using fictitious names. If national attention is what the killer was seeking, he accomplished his goal. Could this have been a motive for the killings?

The Chief Suspect

Joseph Scolaro became and remains the leading suspect in the Robison murders. Most, if not all law enforcement assigned to this case, believe that Scolaro was responsible in some way for the murders. The forensics findings, Scolaro's own web of lies and the mounting circumstantial evidence certainly create a great deal of circumstantial evidentiary weight against him. Police determined the motive may have been embezzlement. Scolaro gave the police an alibi for his whereabouts on June 25, 1968, but, upon investigation, not everything in his alibi was corroborated. Detectives Lloyd G. Stearns and John Flis of the Michigan State Police provided the following summary of the investigation of Joseph Scolaro:

> The suspect was left in charge of the business for about three months prior to the murder and was left with signed blank checks. During this period his salary increased from $600.00 take home semi-monthly to $2000 take home semi-monthly. He was also receiving expense checks ranging from $300.00 to $1000 as often as twice a week. The investigation indicates that the victim was not aware of this until 6-25-68. This can be verified by the accountant and the records. It is believed that he did learn of it on 6-25-68 and confronted the suspect with it by phone 4 times.

On 2-4-68 the suspect purchased two .25 caliber Beretta model 950-B pistols, serial numbers 47910 and 47836 along with 100 rounds of .25 caliber SAKO brand ammo. The suspect still has serial number 47910 which has been checked out. Serial number 47836 is missing and the suspect states he gave the gun along with the 100 rounds of SAKO to the victim on the day after he purchased them. However, officers' investigation has failed to turn up anything that would substantiate this. (NOTE: The suspect's wife told the officers that the suspect had both of the guns at the house from the time he purchased them until about June, 1968 when he took one of them to work one day. About a week later he told her that he had given the gun to the victim.) The SAKO brand ammo is so rare that neither the laboratory officers or the field officers could locate any of it in Michigan for comparison. Some was eventually obtained from Military Intelligence.

On 9-30-66 the suspect purchased an Armalite, model AR-7, 22 caliber rifle, serial #68314. On 11-28-66 he purchased another like rifle with serial #75878. Shortly after he purchased #68314 he gave it to a friend in Chicago. Officers have checked this out and it was not the weapon used in the murder. Sometime in the warm weather, believed to have been in the spring or summer of 1967, the suspect and his brother-in-law fired #75878 on some private property near Union Lake. Officers recently checked that location and located numerous empty casings. The crime lab has checked these as having come from the same gun that was used in the murder. The suspect advised officers that he had given this gun to his brother-in-law sometime prior to the murders but this has been found to be false. This gun is also still missing. NOTE: This gun is so rare and unusual that even most sport and gun shops have never handled or even seen them.

On 6-25-68 the suspect left the office in Lathrup Village about 11:00 am and didn't arrive home until after 11:00 pm this is by his own statement and was confirmed by his wife. He gave officers an alibi as to his activities and whereabouts on that day but officers have checked this out and found it to be false.

Joseph Scolaro (left), chief suspect in the Robison Murders.

The police report indicated that one of Scolaro's polygraph tests was inconclusive and that he failed two additional polygraph tests, could not accurately account for his whereabouts on June 25, 1968, was embezzling from Robison's company, knew the remote and secluded location of the Robison cottage, owned the same types of weapons that were used in the murders and, according to the Michigan State Police Crime Lab, four shell casings found at the crime scene were fired by the very same weapon that fired five shell casings at a private gun range frequented by Scolaro in Oakland County. Was Scolaro a sociopath who had turned into a socio-psychopathic killer? It should be noted that an unscrupulous individual could collect discarded brass casings fired from a weapon and "salt" a gun range thereby leaving false evidence and increasing the workload for investigators. (see Firearm Micro Stamping, *Wikipedia*) Did Mr. Roebert obtain information from Richard Robison concerning the type of weapons Scolaro owned and where he target practiced? Probably not, but it is something to consider.

Joseph Scolaro suggested that shortly before the death of Richard Robison, he (Robison) may have had a mistress. Scolaro told Ed Goss, a polygraph examiner for the Michigan State Police, "I felt that at that point he was getting a mistress. A secretary mistress. He was being supplied like anybody in the advertising business could supply a girl in a strange town or something like that." Scolaro was in the advertising business. My question is: Did Scolaro have a mistress and could this have accounted for the inaccuracies in his whereabouts on June 25, 1968?

Even with all of the circumstantial evidence that tied Scolaro to the Robison murders, Emmet County Prosecuting Attorney Donald Noggle felt there was not enough evidence to issue a warrant for his arrest. Michigan Attorney General Frank Kelly came to the same conclusion. The police report did not put Scolaro at the Robison cottage at the time of the murders. In order to have a warrant authorized against him, Scolaro would either have to admit the crimes in a confession or be placed at the scene of the murders. Neither of these ever happened. It should also be noted that following one of the most grisly murders in Michigan, Scolaro voluntarily agreed to take three polygraph examinations, waived his right to an attorney, did not flee the state following the murders, purchased the R. C. Robison business from the Robison Estate, continued to run the business until it went bankrupt, had no known history of violence and continually denied having any involvement in the murders, even in his eventual suicide note.

It should also be noted that if the murders were committed at approximately 8:30 pm on June 25, 1968, and if Scolaro returned to his home by automobile in Birmingham, Michigan, at approximately 11:15 pm on June 25th*, he would have had to drive the 280 miles in the rain at an average speed of 101 miles per hour, without getting a speeding ticket, to accomplish that goal. If the witness is correct and unless Scolaro flew an aircraft to and from the Detroit area on the day of the murders (the police files do not address this issue) and then somehow located a vehicle to drive the 16 miles to and from the Robison cottage, the facts seem to indicate that it was nearly impossible for Scolaro to have committed the Robison murders. Records at the Department of Transportation, Federal Aviation Administration do not indicate that Joseph Scolaro was ever a licensed pilot. (*Scolaro's wife Lora Lee Scolaro verified that her husband returned to their home in Birmingham, Michigan at approximately 11:15 pm on June 25 "during the 11 o'clock news or shortly thereafter." The police investigative reports on the Robison murders do not indicate that detectives doubted Mrs. Scolaro's recollections of the time Joseph Scolaro returned to his home on the evening in question.) The number of steps taken by the killer following the murders i.e. dragging the bodies down the hall way, stacking the bodies, stabbing Mrs. Robison in her sanitary napkin, shutting the drapes, turning up the heat in the cottage, leaving a note near the door, taping a piece of cardboard over the bullet holes in the window and padlocking the rear door, do not sound like a person who was in any hurry to flee the scene of the crime. In fact, the steps taken following the murders, suggest the work of a methodical, calm and well organized killer.

If Scolaro was upset with Richard, why would he have to kill the entire Robison family? If words were exchanged between Scolaro and Robison on June 25, 1968, that enraged Scolaro, wouldn't a five-hour drive from Lathrup Village to Good Hart be a sufficient time to cool off and reconsider the use of violence?

Detectives theorized that the motive for the murders arose from Scolaro's fear of being discovered for embezzling from Robison's company. If fear of being caught was Scolaro's motive, then wouldn't Scolaro have to cover up the embezzlement by also killing the managing editor of *Impresserio*, Ernest Gilbert, Ted Stegmeyer Jr., the executive editor, probably their families, Calvin Maurice Mackey the CPA and bookkeeper for R.C. Robison and Associates and Richard's secretary Glenda Sutherland?

If Robison had a multi-million dollar deal in the works, why would Scolaro kill or plot with someone else to have the goose that was about to lay a golden egg killed?

Scolaro, deep in debt, subject to criminal prosecution for forgery and the murder of the Robison family and constantly hounded by police detectives, decided to end his misery. On March 8, 1973, he committed suicide at 29350 Southfield Road, Suite 112, in Southfield, Michigan. Scolaro left a suicide note on his desk addressed to his mother. In the note Scolaro wrote: "P.S. I had nothing to do with the Robisons-. I'm a cheat but not a murderer (s) Joe"

U.S. Department of Transportation
Federal Aviation Administration

Flight Standards Service
Airmen Certification Branch, AFS-760

P.O. Box 25082
Oklahoma City, Oklahoma 73125-008
WEB Address: http://registry.faa.

March 19, 2010

WILLIAM T RASMUSSEN
ATTORNEY AT LAW
PO BOX 993
TRAVERSE CITY MI 49685

Dear Mr. Rasmussen:

RE: FOIA #2010-003527F7

Thank you for your request of March 12, 2010, made under the provisions of the Freedom of Information Act (FOIA), wanting to know if Joseph Raymond Scolaro, a/k/a Joe Scolaro, a/k/a Joseph R. Scolaro III, a/k/a Joseph Raymond Scolaro III, was ever licensed to fly airplanes.

We have checked our files and are unable to locate any airman records for Joseph Raymond Scolaro, a/k/a Joe Scolaro, a/k/a Joseph R. Scolaro III, a/k/a Joseph Raymond Scolaro III, based on the information provided.

If you require further assistance, please contact the Airmen Certification Branch at (405) 954-3261 or toll free 1-866-878-2498.

Sincerely,

Tona K. Gates

Tona K Gates
Manager, Airmen Certification Branch

Federal Aviation letter dated March 19, 2010, indicating that Joseph Scolaro was not a licensed pilot.

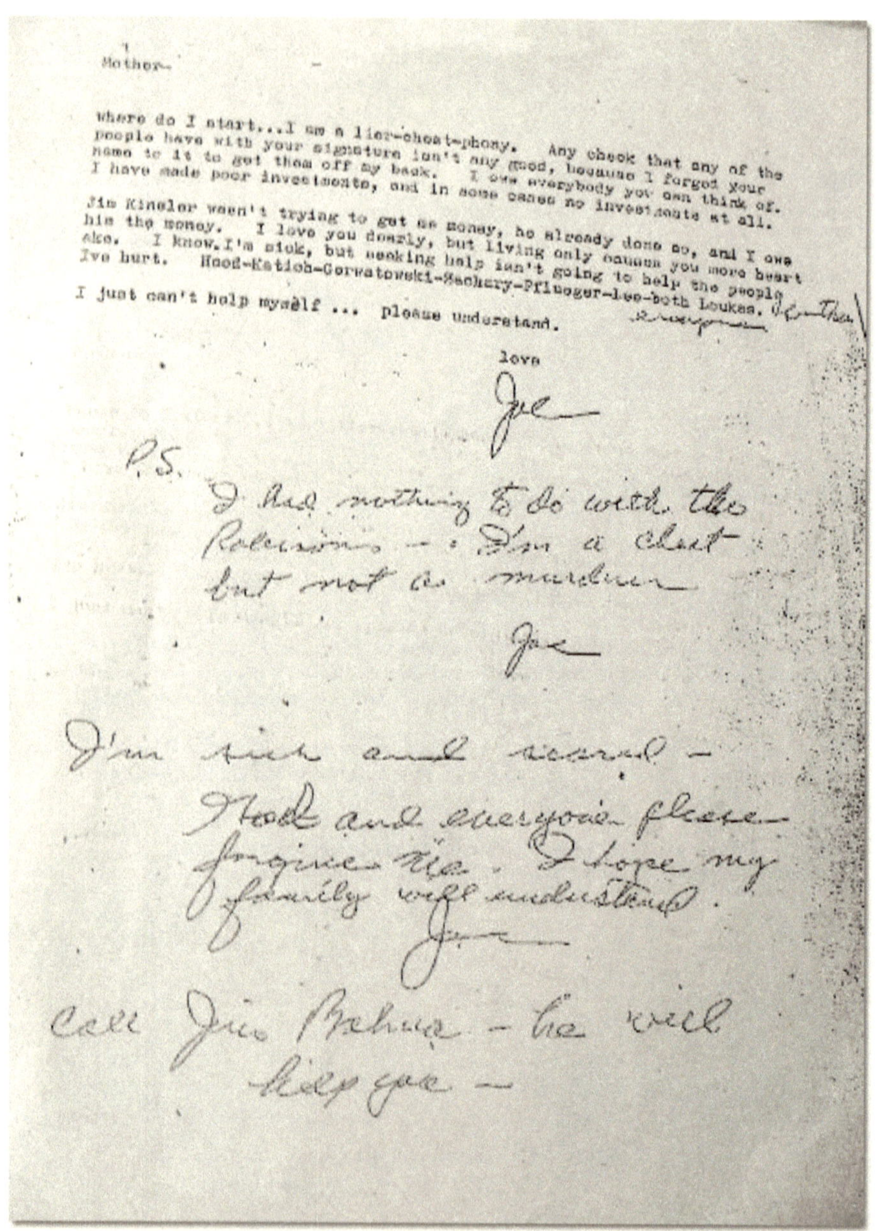
Mother-

where do I start...I am a lier-cheat-phony. Any check that any of the people have with your signature isn't any good, because I forged your name to it to get them off my back. I owe everybody you can think of. I have made poor investments, and in some cases no investments at all.

Jim Kinsler wasn't trying to get me money, he already done so, and I owe him the money. I love you dearly, but living only causes you more heart ake. I know. I'm sick, but seeking help isn't going to help the people Ive hurt. Hood-Katich-Gorzatowski-Zachary-Pflueger-Lee-both Loukas. & everyone

I just can't help myself ... please understand.

love

Joe

P.S.

I had nothing to do with the Robinsons — I'm a cheat but not a murderer

Joe

I'm sick and scared —

Hood and everyone please forgive me. I hope my family will understand.

Joe

Call Jim [illegible] — he will help you —

Suicide note partially typewritten and partially written in longhand by Joseph Scolaro shortly before he killed himself on May 8, 1973.

Did Scolaro write his suicide note to appease his elderly mother and did he go to see his maker without admitting his guilt and asking forgiveness, or was he telling the truth about not having anything to do with the Robison Murders?

Was Richard Robison Anti-gun?

Joseph Scolaro purchased two nine-shot semiautomatic .25 caliber Beretta handguns and one hundred rounds of Sako ammunition in the spring of 1968. After the Robison murders Scolaro was interviewed by detectives. He said that Richard wanted one of the Berettas. Scolaro said that he gave one of the weapons to him along with several rounds of the Sako ammunition. The police reports that were drafted following the murders question whether Robison would have accepted a Beretta from Scolaro because he was "anti-gun." One of the reports from an Oakland County assistant prosecutor provided: "Friends and family of the deceased Richard Robison state, inter alia, that he was anti-gun and that the prospect of him accepting a pistol and ammunition as alleged by the perpetrator is inconsistent with his stated belief." Dr. Roger Felding Smith a close friend of Robisons, told detectives that, "he was shocked to hear Richard had purchased a gun as he appeared to be "anti-gun." Dr. Smith stated that he purchased a gun for himself in February, 1968 to carry while he was going to and from the hospital. He told Richard about this and Dr. Smith believes that if Richard had a gun or was planning to buy one, he would have mentioned it to him at that time." (Michigan State Police Report Complaint No. 78-785-68 dated 7/23/68 - 7/28/68)

Many people in the State of Michigan were purchasing weapons for their protection following the riots in Detroit in 1967. The Michigan State Police Complaint Report on the Robison Murders also provides the following: Item # 12, Fourteen .22 caliber

Western Super X expended shell casings, which were found in the Robison cottage. Significance: None. These shells were identified as having been fired by a Mossberg Model 342K bolt action rifle that was found in the cottage, which belonged to the Robisons. If the Robisons possessed a Mossberg 22 rifle at their cottage, it appears that they were not anti-gun. With this in mind, Robison may have accepted a .25 caliber Beretta hand gun and Sako ammunition from Scolaro. This weapon may have been kept at the cottage, found and used by the perpetrator in the commission of the crimes. The weapon may have been discarded by the killer, possibly in Lake Michigan, after he fled the scene.[12]

Mr. Roebert

What about the mysterious "Mr. Roebert"? Was he a real person or someone Scolaro created to establish an elaborate alibi for the premeditated murders of the members of the Robison family? If Mr. Roebert was a real person, the question is, did he know that Richard Robison would be at his Good Hart Cottage on June 25, 1968, and did he have directions to the secluded cottage? My research suggests that Mr. Roebert was a real person, although the name is probably fictitious. On June 12, 1968, Robison told Arnold Park and William McKinley, managers of the New Hudson Airport, to expect a telephone call from Mr. Roebert. Roebert wanted to set up an appointment with them to work out the specific details of the new airport-cultural enterprise development. At 5:00 p.m. on June 12, 1968, a man who identified himself as Mr. Roebert called the new Hudson Airport. A discussion ensued and Roebert said he would call back later. Richard Robison called Arnold Park to see if Mr. Roebert had called and Park said he had. On June 12, 1968, Robison told Arnold Park that he was leaving for his cottage at Good Hart. On June 21, someone again identifying himself as

Mr. Roebert called Arnold Park at the New Hudson Airport. It is known the Mr. Roebert was supposed to fly to the Pellston Airport located in Pellston, Michigan, in his Lear jet on the day Richard Robison and his family were murdered. Was Mr. Roebert an imaginary investor created by Richard Robison to present the appearance that a great deal of money was forthcoming for the pending development? Based on the facts of this case, it appears that neither Scolaro nor Robison created Mr. Roebert. According to the police report, Richard Robison did not suspect Scolaro of misuse of company funds until a few days before he was murdered. Robison put a hold on the company's funds just before he was murdered. If embezzlement or a severe lecture by Robison caused Scolaro to become enraged enough to drive from Lathrup Village for over five hours to kill Richard Robison and his family, this would appear to be a compulsive act and not something that had been planned for a considerable period of time. You will recall that the person who identified himself as "Mr. Roebert," called the New Hudson Airport on June 12, 1968, and Robison may have received correspondence from Mr. Roebert before that date. Robison and Scolaro did not have a falling out until on or about June 24, 1968. If Richard Robison created "Mr. Roebert" then why did the coroner find a round gold St. Christopher medal on a thin chain around Robison's neck during his autopsy. The medal included the following inscription: "Richard to my chosen son and heir-God Bless you. Roebert." No one alive had ever seen Robison wearing the medal and it was covered by his shirt and jacket. This would be extremely odd item to be wearing if Robison had in fact created Mr. Roebert as a fake investor. Under the word "Richard" on the medal are two small triangular marks. There are dots under the middle letters of "Roebert." (*Detroit News*)

A five-page letter dated May 17, 1968, written by Richard and addressed to "Dear Roebert (My Father)" was found in Richard's office by Scolaro after the murders. Another memo entitled "Superior Table" was also located. Copies of both of these papers can be found in the exhibits in this book. Detectives were unable to determine who authored the "Superior Table" memo. If you look under the word "Roebert" in the "Superior Table" memo you will see three asterisk marks under the letters "ebe." Three dots can also be found under the letters "ebe" in the name "Roebert" in Richard's letter dated May 17, 1968. This may suggest that Richard authored the "Superior Table" memo, possibly at the direction of the person calling himself "Mr. Roebert."

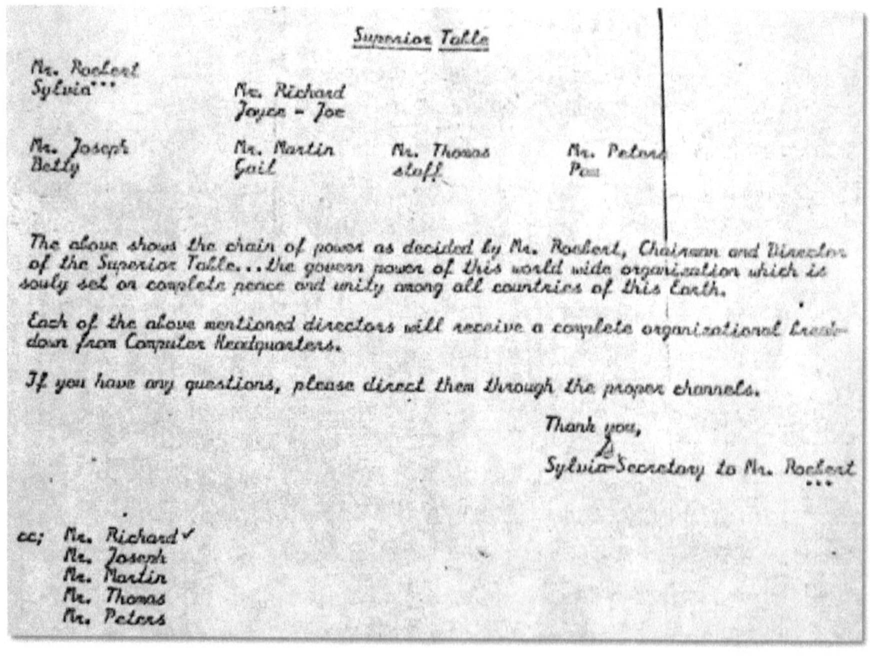

Superior Table

Mr. Roebert
Sylvia***

Mr. Richard
Joyce - Joe

Mr. Joseph
Betty

Mr. Martin
Gail

Mr. Thomas
staff

Mr. Peters
Pam

The above shows the chain of power as decided by Mr. Roebert, Chairman and Director of the Superior Table...the govern power of this world wide organization which is souly set on complete peace and unity among all countries of this Earth.

Each of the above mentioned directors will receive a complete organizational breakdown from Computer Headquarters.

If you have any questions, please direct them through the proper channels.

Thank you,

Sylvia-Secretary to Mr. Roebert
***

cc; Mr. Richard✓
Mr. Joseph
Mr. Martin
Mr. Thomas
Mr. Peters

Superior Table letter in the Robison Murders.

IMPRESARIO
Magazine of the Arts

. . . richard c. robison
editor-publisher

Dear Roebert (My Father) . . . 5/17/68
1:20 P.M.

I'm most honored and pleased with the message given me by "Steamboat Joe" this morning. I have it where we decided and have instructed Joe not to allow me to "drop my wallet". Also - if something (how?) should happen to me to take the entire wallet and pass it "up" to where the proper people would know what to do with it.

Please forgive me for writing so many words to you. I should not take

printers of IMPRESARIO
SWENK-TUTTLE PRESS, INC.
320 SPRINGBROOK, ADRIAN, MICHIGAN 49221
Area 313 – 263-4615 • 265-2862

539

Letter addressed from Richard Robison to "Dear Roebert."

IMPRESARIO
Magazine of the Arts

2.

. . . richard c. robison
editor-publisher

your precious time over anything but important matters. In the future, when Joyce arrives I'll be sending far better, more-easily-read messages.

Ted Seemeyer, Jr. (Exec. Editor) and Ernest Gilbert (The educated idiot) (and Managing Editor) drive cars. Ted - The Mustang and Ernie - The Thunderbird.

Ernie - with his increase, was told his car allowance was included - so he could make his choice as to lease at his own expense... or buy. In one day he bought a '65 THUNDERBIRD. Ted, when told, also, that his new wage included his auto

printers of IMPRESARIO
SWENK-TUTTLE PRESS, INC.
320 SPRINGBROOK, ADRIAN, MICHIGAN 49221
Area 313 – 263-4615 • 265-2862

540

Letter addressed from Richard Robison to "Dear Roebert." (continued)

IMPRESARIO
Magazine of the Arts

. . . richard c. robison
editor-publisher

3.

quickly stated his "Mustang" was still very good... and he was happy.

Now... a favorite story of mine was the one where a fellow arrived at work excited about the "Tremendous" collision that must have taken place on the company's corner earlier. No one was aware of it... but he insisted a Mustang and Thunderbird had to have hit, head on 'cause there were feathers and horse (manure) all over the place.

Now... It should prove, in the future, most interesting to see whether we have

printers of IMPRESARIO
SWENK-TUTTLE PRESS, INC.
320 SPRINGBROOK, ADRIAN, MICHIGAN 49221
Area 313 – 263-4615 • 263-2862

541

Letter addressed from Richard Robison to "Dear Roebert." (continued)

IMPRESARIO
Magazine of the Arts

. . . richard e. robison
editor-publisher

4.

a simular mess strewn about the halls of 'ole Impresario' via Ted, the Mustang and Ernie, the Thunderbird. It will be interesting to see if wonderful "Steamboat" has a keen sense of smell.

Now, I promise, I'll stop writing selfishly and stick to more and clearer facts in the future. Anyway, by the sound of your voice, you health is to the point where you no longer require "trivial humor."

I thank God for you, father,

Your son, always,

Richard

printers of IMPRESARIO
SWENK-TUTTLE PRESS, INC.
320 SPRINGBROOK, ADRIAN, MICHIGAN 49221
Area 313 – 263-4615 • 265-7862

542

Letter addressed from Richard Robison to "Dear Roebert." (continued)

IMPRESARIO
Magazine of the Arts

. . . richard c. robison
editor-publisher

P.S.

Incidentally – 'Ole Joe' really had a "full head o steam" this time. He was MOST controlled!

(Incidentally – I did not try the knee-slapping trick today since I fully intend my #1 son to have a "hard Top and NOT some "do-it-yourself convertable".)

I'm looking forward with great anticipation and love to the day when we finally meet – soon, I hope.

Always – your son
Richard

AGAIN:
Thank You, Father!

printers of IMPRESARIO
SWENK-TUTTLE PRESS, INC.
320 SPRINGBROOK, ADRIAN, MICHIGAN 49221
Area 313 – 263-4615 • 265-2862

(OVER)

543

Letter addressed from Richard Robison to "Dear Roebert." (continued)

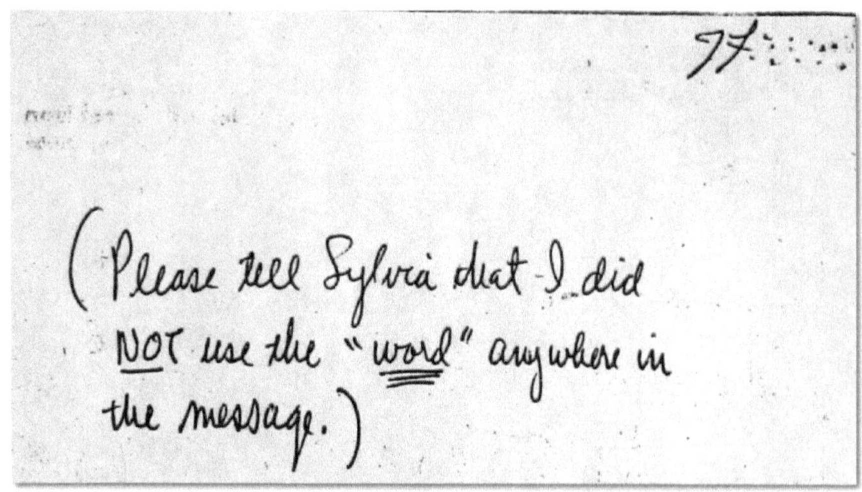

Letter addressed from Richard Robison to "Dear Roebert."

Time Line

Here is a time line that might help establish the existence of a third party calling himself "Mr. Roebert":

3/65	Scolaro starts to work for R.C. Robison and Associates
1966	Scolaro purchases 2 AR-7's
07/67	Detroit Riots
2/4/68	Scolaro purchases 2 .25 cal. Berettas.
4/4/68	Robisons on vacation in Hawaii, Scolaro in charge of R.C. Robison Associates.
Beginning of May, '68	Scolaro gets a substantial raise in wage at R.C. Robison and Associates.
4/5/68	Scolaro obtains two permits for his Berettas.
5/17/68	According to a 5-page letter found in Robison's office by that had been written by Richard Robison to Mr. Roeberts,

	Richard addresses the letter to "Dear Roebert (My Father)." There is no address on the letter. The letter includes the words "if something (how?) should happen to me." Robison writes in the letter, "I'm looking forward with great anticipation and love to the day we finally meet soon I hope. Always-your son Richard." It appears that Robison had contact with Mr. Roebert prior to 5/17/68. It does not appear that Richard had ever mailed the letter.
Sometime in May '68	Richard and Scolaro are at the Lansing Airport. Scolaro investigators wrote in their report that Scolaro claimed that Richard mentioned the name "Roebert" at various times.
6/4/68	Richard is at the San Francisco Hilton in San Francisco, meeting with investors. A total of 18 telephone calls were placed during this time between the San Francisco Hilton and Scolaro in Michigan.
Mid April-June, 1968	Richard and Scolaro are seen almost daily driving around the new Hudson Airport; on occasion Richard is seen with another male subject.
6/12/68	Richard is at the New Hudson Airport. He tells Park and McKinley to expect a call from Mt. Roebert. (If Mr. Roebert is a real person Richard must have talked to him, been with him or received word that Roebert would be calling the airport.)

June 12, 13 & 14, '68	Richard is staying at the Detroit Metro Airport Hotel.
4:45 pm 6/12/68	A person calling himself "Mr. Roebert" calls the New Hudson Airport and talks to Arnold Park. Parks later described the caller as an elderly man with a low, monotone voice and that he had frequent pauses in his speech. Parks stated that it was a "very unusual voice and he got the feeling that he was talking to some robot."
4:54 pm 6/12/68	Nine minutes later Richard calls the New Hudson Airport and talked to Arnold Park. He wants to know if Mr. Roebert called.
6/8/68-6/15/68	Mrs. Roger Smith talks on the telephone with Mrs.Robison.
6/13 or 6/14/68	Mrs. Robison tells Mrs. Smith that Richard Robison called and said a man is coming to visit them at the cottage and spend a few days. **She said Richard handed the phone to the expected visitor and this person talked to Shirley Robison. Mrs. Robison told Mrs. Smith that the man told her not to make any fuss at the cottage as they were going there to relax. He asked her to make some of the pasties that Richard told him about.** At this point Shirley told Mrs. Smith that she and the children were driving to the cottage on 6/16/68 and that Richard was coming up later with the visitor (Michigan State Police Complaint Report No. 78-785-68 dated 7/23/68). Shirley

makes no mention to Mrs. Smith about the St. Christopher medal that may have been hanging on a chain around Richard's neck. (page 5 Michigan State Police Additional Complaint Report Complaint No. 78-785-68, dated 7/23/68-7/28/68)

6/13/68 Robison's banker, Frank Joity, receives a telephone call from Robison. At this time Richard says he is calling long distance and leaves the impression that he is on the West Coast.

6/15/68 Richard Robison arrives at the Lathup Village home. Shirley is surprised that he has returned earlier than expected. Richard indicates that they will drive to the cottage and that the visitor would be arriving later.

6/15/68 Richard Robison is at his home in Lathrup Village, so is his father, Ross C. Robison. Richard and Ross sit down and talked for a time. **Richard says a Mr. Roebert is coming up to the cottage in a few days to spend a few days at the cottage with them.** He states Mr. Roebert is flying a two-engine jet plane and would be landing at the Pelston Airport. After he spent a few days there, the whole family was going with Mr. Roebert in the jet to Lexington, Kentucky, and Naples, Florida. At Lexington, Richard was planning to buy a horse farm as his daughter liked horses. At Naples he was either going to build or buy a villa. He also mentioned something about Spain, but Ross could not remember what it was. Richard told his father that now there was no reason why his father couldn't go to Florida this winter. Richard then told Shirley that she wouldn't have to do any work at the new places as they would be fully staffed. Richard stated that he was winding up a big deal, but was keeping it a secret as he didn't want his competitors to learn of it until it was all over. He remarked that when the deal was over with he would be a tycoon. He told Shirley to pack extra suits for the trip. Richard said they would be on this trip for about three weeks. Richard also told his father he was having a pool and two guest houses constructed at the cottage and that they should be completed by the time he returned from the trip. Richard remarked: "When I get back from the trip, I will have something big to tell you." He also told his father to contact Joe if he needed anything while they were gone. (Michigan State Police Additional Complaint Report, Complaint 78-765-68, dated July 23-28, 1968)

6/16/68 The Robison family left for Good Hart in two vehicles.

6/21/68 Arnold Park says a man calling himself Mr. Roebert called the New Hudson Airport again. The caller promised to call back in a week to schedule appointments. This is the last time Mr. Roebert was heard from by anyone except possibly Richard on June 25.

6/23/68 Richard meets Frederick Adolph Meyn in his car near the Robison cottage. He asks how long Fred and his family would be up at their cottage. He also asks him to stop over at the cottage that evening (6/23/68). Richard stated they were leaving the following morning on a trip but did not say where they were going or how long they would be gone. Richard states that they had just been out to eat and they were all dressed up at the time. They did not say where they had eaten but did eat sometimes at **Kenilworth** Restaurant in Mackinaw City.

6/23/68 Shirley Robison talks to her mother, Aileen Fulton, on the telephone and tells her the family is having a good time. There was no mention of a trip and apparently no mention of the St. Christopher medal that Richard may have worn around his neck on a chain. It would seem that Shirley would have noticed the St. Christopher medal on Richard either in bed or in the bathroom when he had his shirt off. Because Robisons were Lutheran and not Catholic, it also seems that the medal could have been of concern to Shirley and she would have mentioned it to either Mrs. Smith or her mother. Was the medal placed on Richard's neck after he was murdered?

6/24/68 Richard tells the Bliss family that they are leaving the next day (June 25) for Kentucky

	and Florida and that they would be gone for 2-3 weeks.
6/24/68 (8:22 pm)	A telephone call is made from Scolaro's home in Birmingham, Michigan, to the Robisons' cottage near Good Hart. The call lasted 9 minutes.
6/24/68 (8:42 pm)	A second telephone call is made from Scolaro's home to Robison's cottage. This one lasted less than one minute.
9:00 am 6/25/68	Richard Robison tells Russell Figg (tree trimmer at the cottage) that they were waiting for an airplane and would leave the following day (June 26, 1968). He also informs Figg that he was waiting for a long distance call that would tell him when the airplane was in. Richard tells Figg not to disconnect the telephone line until he received the anticipated telephone call.
Before 9:45 am 6/25/68	Scolaro says he called Richard from the Robison home in Lathrup Village. Richard wants to know if Scolaro had received the endorsed business checks he had mailed. Scolaro says he had not received them yet.
9:45 am 6/25/68	Glenda Sutherland, receptionist for R. C. Robison and Associates, receives a call from Richard Robison. Robison wants to know if the endorsed checks had arrived at the office. Glenda tells him she does not have the checks. Robison is very angry or upset and talks extra loud. Robison instructs her to call his banker Mr. Joity about the STOP PAYMENT order. Scolaro is handed the

phone and tells Glenda he will take of it, so Glenda did not make the call to Mr. Joity. Richard appears to have been upset because the endorsed checks he had mailed had not arrived at the R. C. Robison and Associates office, not because he had become aware of any alleged embezzlement from the company funds by Scolaro.

10:00 am 6/25/68 Robison calls his banker, Frank Joity, requesting to know if a $200,000.00 deposit had been made to his account. Mr. Joity checked and advised him that it had not. Richard indicated that it should have been there and also stated there was $2,000.000.00 more coming. He stated that it was coming from Bank of America, but gave no further details. He also told Mr. Joity to stop payment on all checks from his business. (Scolaro contacted Robison and advised him that he had located the signed checks that Robison had mailed to the company address at R. C. Robison Associates, Inc., 28081 Southfield, Lathrup Village.

Between 10:15-10:30 Richard calls Mr. Joity and tells him to lift the STOP Payment order on the business checks.

10:30 am 6/25/68 Richard calls his secretary Glenda Sutherland and advises her to disregard contacting Mr. Joity as he has taken care of it.

10:33 am 6/25/68 Scolaro calls from R. C. Robinson Associates in Lathrup Village and talks on the telephone with Robison at the cottage

	in Good Hart. Scolaro says that Richard told him they were leaving for Kentucky and Florida on June 25.
Around 10:30 am	Scolaro leaves the R. C. Robison and Associates office and is not seen again until approximately 11:15 pm by his wife at their Birmingham home.
12:00 noon 6/25/68	In a police interview Scolaro tells officers that he called Richard at the cottage from the R. C. Robison and Associates office at 12:00 noon 6/25/68.
12:00-1:00 pm 6/25/68	Were the Robisons having their lunch at this time?
1:30 pm 6/25/68	Richard tells Russell Figg that he received his telephone call (about when the airplane would be arriving to take the Robisons to Kentucky and Florida?). He advised Figg to go ahead and disconnect the telephone line to complete the tree trimming.
4:30 pm 6/25/68	Robison pays tree trimmer Russell Figg $170.00 cash for trimming trees at his cottage near Good Hart.
8:30-9:00 pm 6/25/68	Robison's neighbors, Mr. and Mrs. William R. Freeman, hear gun shots. "These shots came from the south and she set the time about 9:00 pm as it was light enough** that she thought on the first shot that someone was shooting gulls. She heard the first shot

** According to the Astronomical Application Department US Naval Observatory, Washington, D.C. the sun set in Michigan on June 25, 1968, at 8:32 pm. (See usno.navy. mil/usno/astronomical-applications/data-services-one-year)

	and about two or three seconds she heard four or five more in rapid succession and then she thought that it must have been target practice. After the shootings she heard the voice of a woman and that of a man and they were excited and this too made her think of target practice. Her sister, who lives just north from her, heard the same shots, but she thought there were eight shots. Officers contacted her but she has nothing further to offer." Michigan State Police Report Complaint No. 78-785-68 dated 8/1/68.
11:15-11:30 pm 6/25/68	Joseph Scolaro returns to his home at 659 Wallace Street, Birmingham. Lori Lee Scolaro, wife of Joseph Scolaro, tells detectives that her husband returned home that night "during the 11 o'clock news or shortly thereafter."
6/25/68	It rains throughout the day in Michigan.
9:30 am 6/26/68	Russell Figg returns to the Robison cottage.
2:30 pm 6/26/68	Scolaro and his family drive to Indianapolis on a pleasure trip.
7/22/68	The Robison family is found murdered at their cottage near Good Hart.

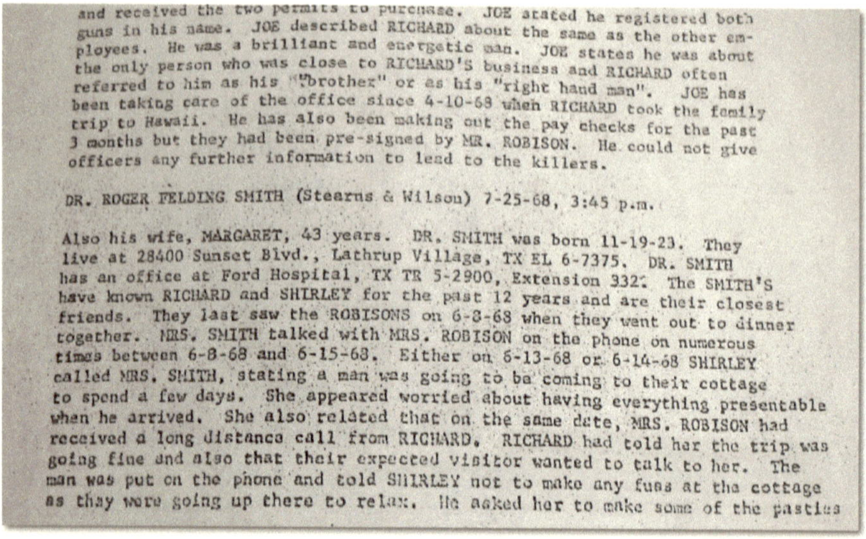

and received the two permits to purchase. JOE stated he registered both guns in his name. JOE described RICHARD about the same as the other employees. He was a brilliant and energetic man. JOE states he was about the only person who was close to RICHARD'S business and RICHARD often referred to him as his "brother" or as his "right hand man". JOE has been taking care of the office since 4-10-68 when RICHARD took the family trip to Hawaii. He has also been making out the pay checks for the past 3 months but they had been pre-signed by MR. ROBISON. He could not give officers any further information to lead to the killers.

DR. ROGER FELDING SMITH (Stearns & Wilson) 7-25-68, 3:45 p.m.

Also his wife, MARGARET, 43 years. DR. SMITH was born 11-19-23. They live at 28400 Sunset Blvd., Lathrup Village, TX EL 6-7375. DR. SMITH has an office at Ford Hospital, TX TR 5-2900, Extension 332. The SMITH'S have known RICHARD and SHIRLEY for the past 12 years and are their closest friends. They last saw the ROBISONS on 6-8-68 when they went out to dinner together. MRS. SMITH talked with MRS. ROBISON on the phone on numerous times between 6-8-68 and 6-15-68. Either on 6-13-68 or 6-14-68 SHIRLEY called MRS. SMITH, stating a man was going to be coming to their cottage to spend a few days. She appeared worried about having everything presentable when he arrived. She also related that on the same date, MRS. ROBISON had received a long distance call from RICHARD. RICHARD had told her the trip was going fine and also that their expected visitor wanted to talk to her. The man was put on the phone and told SHIRLEY not to make any fuss at the cottage as they were going up there to relax. He asked her to make some of the pasties

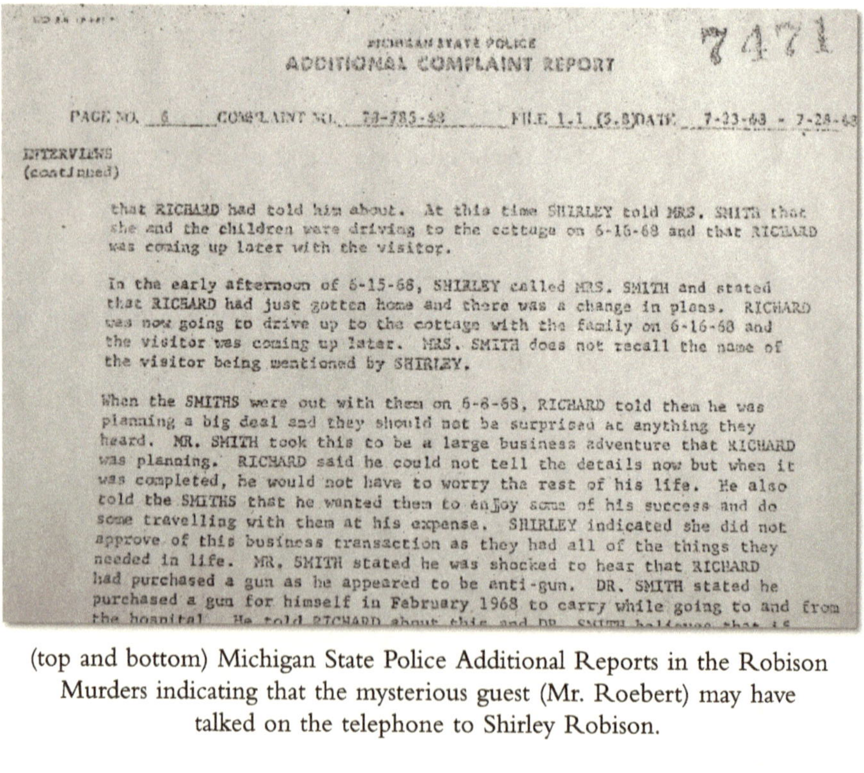

MICHIGAN STATE POLICE
ADDITIONAL COMPLAINT REPORT

7471

PAGE NO. 6 COMPLAINT NO. 73-785-68 FILE 1.1 (5.8) DATE 7-23-68 - 7-28-68

INTERVIEWS
(continued)

that RICHARD had told him about. At this time SHIRLEY told MRS. SMITH that she and the children were driving to the cottage on 6-16-68 and that RICHARD was coming up later with the visitor.

In the early afternoon of 6-15-68, SHIRLEY called MRS. SMITH and stated that RICHARD had just gotten home and there was a change in plans. RICHARD was now going to drive up to the cottage with the family on 6-16-68 and the visitor was coming up later. MRS. SMITH does not recall the name of the visitor being mentioned by SHIRLEY.

When the SMITHS were out with them on 6-8-68, RICHARD told them he was planning a big deal and they should not be surprised at anything they heard. MR. SMITH took this to be a large business adventure that RICHARD was planning. RICHARD said he could not tell the details now but when it was completed, he would not have to worry the rest of his life. He also told the SMITHS that he wanted them to enjoy some of his success and do some travelling with them at his expense. SHIRLEY indicated she did not approve of this business transaction as they had all of the things they needed in life. MR. SMITH stated he was shocked to hear that RICHARD had purchased a gun as he appeared to be anti-gun. DR. SMITH stated he purchased a gun for himself in February 1968 to carry while going to and from the hospital. He told RICHARD about this and DR. SMITH believes that it

(top and bottom) Michigan State Police Additional Reports in the Robison Murders indicating that the mysterious guest (Mr. Roebert) may have talked on the telephone to Shirley Robison.

The Changing Itinerary

On either June 13 or June 14, 1968, Shirley Robison spoke on the telephone to her good friend, Mrs. Roger Smith. She indicated that a man was going to be coming to their cottage to spend a few days. At that time Shirley told Mrs. Smith that she and the children were driving to the cottage on 6/16/68, and that Richard was coming later with the visitor. In the early afternoon of 6/15/68, Shirley called Mrs. Smith and stated that Richard had just gotten home and there had been change in plans. Richard was now going to drive up to the cottage with the family on 6/16/68, and the visitor was coming up later.

Ross C. Robison, father of Richard Robison, was at the Robison's Lathrup Village home about noon, June 15, 1968. When he got there, Shirley told him that Richard was away on a trip and that she and the three children were going to drive to the cottage on June 16, 1968, with both cars. She stated that he was expected home from the trip on Wednesday, June 19, 1968, and would fly to the cottage with a friend. About an hour later, Joe (Scolaro) brought Richard to the Robison home in Lathrup and everyone was surprised to see him. The plans were then made for Richard to go to the cottage with the family by car. Richard said a Mr. Roebert was coming up to the cottage in a few days to spend a few days at the cottage with them. He stated that Mr. Roebert was flying a two-engine jet plane and would be landing at the Pellston Airport. After he spent a few days there, the whole family was going with Mr. Roebert in the jet to Lexington, Kentucky, and Naples, Florida. At Lexington, Richard was planning to buy a horse farm as the daughter liked horses. At Naples he was either going to build or buy a villa. "He also mentioned something about Spain." (Michigan State Police Complaint No. 78-7856-68, dated July 23-July 28, 1968) At 9:00 am on June 25 Richard told tree trimmer Russell Figg that they were waiting for a plane and would leave the following day (June 26). Again the itinerary changed. Why was the visitor no longer going to "spend a few days?"

At 1:30 pm on June 25, Richard told Russell Figg that he had received the awaited telephone call and that Figg could disconnect the telephone line and complete the tree trimming project. The itinerary must have changed again. Here is why: If the Robison family was going to be traveling to Kentucky and Florida on June 26 for two weeks, they would have had their suitcases packed with clothing, swimming suits, suntan lotion, toiletries, beach towels, etc. The only suitcase identified in the police reports was one located in the back bedroom of the cottage. Now remember the conversation between Shirley Robison and Mrs. Smith on either June 13 or 14 in which Shirley told her that Richard handed the phone to the visitor. The visitor told Shirley "not to make a fuss at the cottage as they were going there to relax." On June 15 Richard told his father, Ross Robison, that "a Mr. Roebert was coming up to the cottage in a few days to spend a few days at the cottage with them."

If the call Richard received before advising Russell Figg to disconnect the telephone line was from Mr. Roebert, then this would account for the Robisons not having their suitcases packed and located either by the door or in their vehicle. The person who made the telephone call to Richard may have been the one who said he would be staying "to relax for a few days at the cottage." If the call was made by the same person who identified himself as Mr. Roebert, then it would seem that Richard would have recognized his distinct monotone-voice. Or was the call made by Scolaro? In an interview with the police, Scolaro told them the last call he made to Richard at the cottage was at 12:00 noon on the 25th.

From the Michigan State Police Interview with Joseph Scolaro

Scolaro: I did not kill the Robisons', but I feel the people from this business deal, this Mr. Roberts and those people quite possibly could have.

Officer: All right, now, we are getting down to business.

Scolaro: Yes sir.

Officer: Now tell me about this business deal, about this Roberts and bear in mind one thing . . .

Scolaro: Yes sir.

Officer: But if they're involved in the killing, I want to find out who killed the Robisons'.

Scolaro: Yes sir.

Officer: Whether you stand to gain a half million dollars or your best finances in life, good deal Joe, but I want to know who killed these people.

Scolaro: Yes sir.

Officer: And that's why I say, if this financial dealing is involved there and you were just sitting here telling me not two minutes ago how close you were with Dick, you've got to know.

Scolaro: That's right.

Officer: All right, let's have it.

Scolaro: Dick was going down to Kentucky and Florida and he was suppose to meet this Mr. Roberts, who by the way I have not met and only know by name.

Officer: All right.

Scolaro: He was supposed to meet Mr. Roberts and they were going together.

Officer: Where did he meet Mr. Roberts?

Scolaro: The way he originally told me, it was supposed to be up there. But then the way he talked when I talked to him on the phone, I gathered that he was possibly going to be meeting him someplace else.

Officer: What day on the phone did you talk to him?

Scolaro: The 25th.

Officer: All right.

Scolaro: And they were going, positively going?

Officer: On the 25th, he told you that he was going to meet Roberts where?

Scolaro: He told me that they were, on the 25th, he told me that they were going. And I said, "Are you flying?" And he said, "That hasn't been established yet, we may drive." And I said, "Are you going with anyone?" And he said, "That hasn't been completely established yet." But he said, "If I go with somebody," he said, "you don't know who they are." That's the way he put it which was very true. I did not know who Mr. Roberts was.

Officer: Um-hum.

Scolaro: Now, he had told me that he had, you know, cinched this whole deal for everything.

Officer: Everything for what?

Scolaro: For the magazine, the purchasing deal, his, you know, news service, the television deal, he was going into travel business and all the money to support the travel business, he was going to open up offices in other countries because they wanted it that way that if he, they had offices in foreign countries, they could, you know, get information in and out, people could go in and out if they wished under the guide of the magazine, writers and artists and so forth. Excuse me. And he did say that when he was in California that he had met three other people.

Officer: Who?

Scolaro: And he told me he had met Thomas, Peter, and Joseph. Those were the names he gave me, period.

Officer: First names or are those the last names?

Scolaro: I don't know, those are the names, Thomas, Peters, and Joseph.

Officer: Um hum.

Scolaro: And Thomas was supposed to be the financial man of this group. It was like a treasurer or something like that and Peters was suppose to be the personnel manage. He didn't say anything about Joseph.

Officer: Um hum.

Scolaro: And when he came back, we talked a lot of times when he was in California, when he came back, he told me that he was, you know, about going out to Metropolitan Airport.

Officer: Yah, why did he go out to the airport and tell his family he was going the other way?

Scolaro: He told me that he was going to be picked up at the airport. When we got there, he said that this was going to be the base of operation. He would be operating, you know, in and out of here. And I said, "Well, then why, will, do you want a car?" And he said, "No, no, no, I'll just be operating in and out of here, this will be my base of operation, period." And I said, "Will I be picking you up?" And he said, "No." His original plans were that he was going to be flown because the group had their own airplane. He was going to be flown up north and meet, you know, Shirley and the kids up north. And then he called me after that. Either he called me or it was when I was calling him because he gave me times to call him. And he said that the plans were changed, that he wanted to be picked up Saturday morning that he was going to drive up with Shirley and the kids. And I said, you know, "Are you going to be spending the entire summer up north?" And he said, "Oh no, I'm still going to go to Kentucky and Florida." And he was supposed to be getting a farm, he was also, this group was suppose to be buying him a twin engine, Sessna airplane. That was one of the things he was suppose to get from them. And, Mr. Roberts, from what I gathered was the key.

Officer: Who was Mr. Roberts?

Scolaro: I don't know. But Mr. Roberts was the key.

Officer: How much money was involved here, Joe?

Scolaro: I had thought in the beginning when Dick was talking about the purchasing thing, maybe five, ten million dollars, but then when Walt Mulenhagen spoke, I'm going by what Walter said, they were talking fifty to one-hundred million dollars on one deal and they were talking, maybe, again I don't know building and everything, but the airport thing, the detectives tell me that could have gone up to twenty-five to fifty million dollars.

Officer: They could have hired you to handle something like that.

Scolaro: I should think so, or a group of people that had money. Now, Dick had explained that these people had money.

Officer: Thomas, Peters and Joseph.

Scolaro: And Roberts.

Officer: And Roberts. Who did he meet out in San Francisco?

Scolaro: He was suppose to meet them all.

Officer: Where?

Scolaro: He didn't say where. He was staying at the San Francisco Hilton. I know that much.

Officer: How many men met him at the airport out there? You talked to him at the airport constantly.

Scolaro: I did and he didn't say any, all he said was that he was in a series of meetings.

Officer: Where were these meetings being held?

Scolaro: I asked him if they were in his room or where he was and he said, "I've been in a series of meetings" and he said, "I'm in and out of here quite a lot." That's what he told me.

Officer: Um hum.

Scolaro: And I said, "Well, does Shirley know where to reach you?" And he said, "Oh Christ, no, I told her I went out of state." I said, "Okay, fine." He told me not to tell her where he was.

Officer: How much of this haven't you told Stearns and Flis?

Scolaro: The part about knowing about completely about Roberts and so forth and who he was.

Officer: Who is Roberts?

Scolaro: He is head of the whole thing.

Officer: Is that his true name or it sounds like he made, there's a Roberts, Thomas, Joseph and Peters, sounds like a bunch of a . . .

Scolaro: These are names that Dick gave. And Dick when he said that his name was, as far as they were concerned his name was Mr. Richards.

Officer: Now, it seems to me that these men were telling me about some letter they have with the names on it, now are you, you told them about that, that you mentioned that or that you knew about that?

Scolaro: I found the letter when we were going through things with your Latent Print people.

Officer: Where was this letter?

Scolaro: It was in Dick's desk.

Officer: Did you type the letter? Is that the one you typed?

Scolaro: I didn't type any letter. This was a handwritten letter, I'm talking about.

Officer: How about a typed letter with all of those names on it. Now we are getting back up here on June the 25, how, did he tell you, how was he going to go down to Kentucky and to Florida?

Scolaro: He was either going to leave by plane or by car. But that wasn't established when I talked to him, he said, "We haven't finalized on that," but he said, "The car is ready to go." And I said, "Well, I hope that if you're taking the whole family, you will go by car." That's all I told him.

Officer: Um hum.

Scolaro: And he said, "Well," he said, "If we go by plane, it will be" you know, "plenty big enough, and don't worry about it pal," he said.

Officer: Okay, then two months ago, you mentioned he was to meet this Roberts. Had he told you?

Scolaro: Prior to this, he had told me he was going to meet Roberts.

Officer: Where?

Scolaro: Roberts was suppose to come up there.

Officer: Up to the cottage?

Scolaro: Um hum.

Officer: Didn't you just tell me that he was going to meet Roberts in Kentucky or Florida?

Scolaro: No, no, no, I told you that he was going to meet Roberts and he was going to Kentucky and Florida.

Officer: With Roberts.

Scolaro: With Roberts and then they were suppose to meet some other people, part of a group.

Officer: Had there been any negotiations made to buy this, you mentioned, farm or the horses or . . .

Scolaro: I don't know that. I don't know that. He was supposed to . . . His words were that he was going to acquire.

Officer: You know Joe, this could very well be true, but based upon what I have seen, what I have seen right here on these charts.

Scolaro: Um hum.

Officer: And talking to the other officers and what you've told me here and how you were so intimately associated with Dick and his business dealings.

Scolaro: And Shirley.

Officer: And Shirley, that I just cannot see how you did not know more, know about this than what you have told me.

Scolaro: Well Bob . . .

Officer: To me, Roberts, Thomas, Joseph and Peters are obviously phony names. Somebody is hiding behind something. Whether it be the Mafia or some big industrialist, I don't know. But I, I, as far as I'm concerned, the key is sitting right here in front of me.

Scolaro: Bob, I have never met a Mr. Roberts, I have never met any of those gentlemen. Dick met with those gentlemen alone and arranged this thing alone. I did not have an active role in any part of this. My active role was to be with the magazine, to be with the advertising agency. As these things were completely developed to where I could be taught about them.

Officer: Seems strange to me Joe. As I, I, what little you've told me that you haven't told these officers, just Thomas, Joseph and Peters caused all this.

Scolaro: I told them those names.

Officer: But you didn't tell them about Dick and the bit in San Francisco, is that right?

Scolaro: No.

Officer: And all your phone calls to this man when he was at Metro, do you have any reason to believe that he was not there all the time or that he was gone, maybe . . .

Scolaro: He told me that he would be gone and to call him at a certain time.

Officer: You talked to him enough, I mean could have he had time to go to Los Angeles and back? Or to go to Florida and back?

Richard Robison's conversation with his father, Ross Robison

Scolaro's statements and those of Ross Robison, made to him by Richard Robison, are similar. Both seem to confirm that Richard Robison had come in contact and had made plans with an individual called "Mr. Roebert." In addition, both Scolaro and Ross Robison suggest that the itinerary for the trip to the Robison cottage and itinerary for the following trip to Kentucky and Florida had either changed or had not been finalized. Are they pieces to the puzzle in the Robison murders? Was Mr. Roeberts going to fly to the Pellston airport and transport the Robisons on his jet to Kentucky and Florida, or was this all a ruse? If Roberts was flying to the Pellston airport, how was he going to be transported from the airport to the Robison's cottage? Did the itineraries continue to evolve because Mr. Roberts realized he would need transportation from the Pellston Airport to the cottage and that didn't fit into his scheme to murder the Robison family? Did Mr. Roberts determine from Richard Robison where the secluded cottage was located, when the Robisons would be at their cottage and then drive an automobile to Good Hart and the Lake Michigan public access, walk the beach to Robison's cottage, murder the Robison family, and then leave the area undetected on June 25, 1968, in his automobile?

On July 22, 1968, detectives at the scene noted that there was an open suitcase on the bed in one of the back bedrooms and, "three dressy coats-a man's, a woman's and a little girl's spread neatly over the back of the couch." On June 25, 1968, were the Robison's getting ready to take a trip? A trip they planned to take with Mr. Roberts, the expected visitor?

New Clues?

Following the Robison murders the Michigan State Police were so incensed by the horror and macabre crime scene they contacted the *Detroit News* and requested a publication of the account of the Robison murders in its "Secret Witness Reward" Program. Although the *Detroit News* "Secret Witness Reward Program" was originally intended to be limited to crimes committed in and around Wayne, Oakland and Macomb counties, an exception was made and the newspaper's editorial staff agreed to run an article on the Robison murders on August 11, 1968. Several responses were received, one in particular I found of interest. A reader wrote that he had information, ". . . but in order to get it law enforcement officials had to place the following ad in the *News* personal column:[13]

> **"Dr.Guidini: Your prescription good. However, need additional. Zodius."**

"There is additional information," he wrote, "and you may contact this writer through the *Detroit News* personal column."

The ad was placed in the *Detroit News* once in September, 1968, and again in January, 1969, under the headline, 'Is key to Robison's killer in classified ad?' There was no response, and, as far as anyone knows, the informant was never heard from again. The identity of 'Dr. Guidini' and 'Zodius' have never been determined. I also found it very interesting that the word "Zodius"[14] was written in a letter following the murder of six individuals and that the writer indicated that a newspaper must print the letter in order to receive more information. No one had ever heard of the Zodiac Killer when the "Dr. Guidini" letter was received by the *Detroit News* because Zodiac did not identify himself as the "Zodiac" until nearly a year later on August 7, 1969, in a letter to the *San Francisco Chronicle*. If the Zodiac Killer did in fact write the letter to the *Detroit News*, I thought that he might have included a clue in the classified advertisement. What I noticed is that by combining the words "**Dr**" and "**Guidini**" you can spell: **DRGU ID IN I** or "**ID IN DRUG**." The letter's author's name appears to be: "Zodius."[15] Was the clue to the identity of the Robison's killer "Zodius"? When he wrote:

Is key to Robisons' killer in classified ad?

MANUFACTURERS CLEARANCE!

LOOK! SAVE 3.07 on every sq. yard

IMPORTANT NOTICE! Since this is a limited time only sale of a highly desirable broadloom, you'd better phone today, if you cannot come in Monday! PHONE 881-0100 NOW . . . our operators are on duty round the clock Sunday to take your Call! We'll bring samples to you!

Headline of the *Detroit News* on page 27A, Sunday, January 5, 1969: "Is key to Robisons' killer in classified ad." (Published with permission of the *Detroit News*

"Your prescription good. Need additional" did he mean that killing individuals was the prescription and that he needed additional victims? On October 22, 1969, famed attorney, Melvin Belli, may have had a telephone conversation with the Zodiac Killer, however; this has been disputed for years. In the conversation the caller mentioned that he had headaches. The caller stated, "I have headaches. If I kill I don't get them." Belli asked, "How long have you been having these headaches?" The caller responded, "Since I killed a kid". (Note 43, page 15) Was Zodiac's prescription for headaches killing people? Did the Zodiac kill the Robison family?

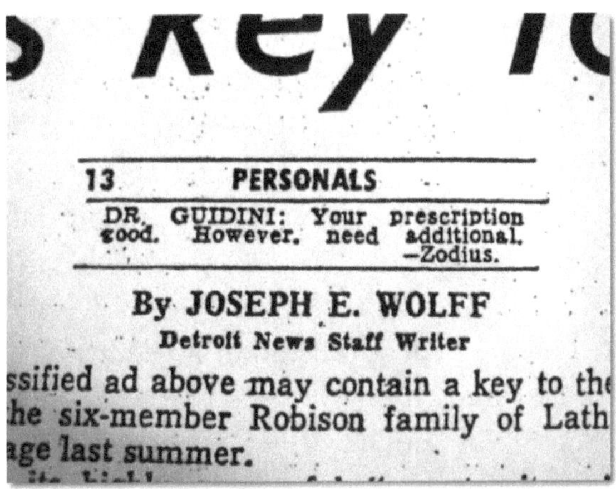

13 PERSONALS

DR. GUIDINI: Your prescription good. However, need additional. —Zodius.

By JOSEPH E. WOLFF
Detroit News Staff Writer

ssified ad above may contain a key to th
he six-member Robison family of Lath
ge last summer.

"Zodius" tip in the Robison Murders mailed to the *Detroit News* about four months before Betty Lou Jensen and David Faraday were murdered by the Zodiac in California. (Published with permission of the *Detroit News*)

On August 1, 1969, Zodiac mailed a code message to the *San Francisco Examiner*. The code was deciphered by Donald Harden and his wife. The remaining letters at the end of the enciphered message, "EBEORIETEMETHHPITI" were deciphered to possibly read: "ROBERT EMMET THE HIPPIE." (Note 43, pages 57-58) "Mr. Robert" or "Mr. Roebert" was the name of the mysterious investor in the Richard Robinson case and Emmet is the exact spelling of Emmet County where the Robison family was murdered. Did Richard Robison unknowingly come in contact with a very clever serial killer? Did this person obtain inside information from Robison that he used to his advantage. For example did he find out from Robison what types of weapons Scolaro owned, where the Good Hart cottage was located and exactly when the Robisons would be vacationing in Good Hart?

Possible Solution

The murder of the Richard Robison family has never been solved. Joseph Scolaro remains the main suspect. If the individual who mailed the "Dr. Guidini" letter to the *Detroit News* in 1968, had anything to do with the Robison murders then, if it hasn't already been done, it might be worth attempting to obtain DNA from the envelope the letter was mailed in and the stamp, then enter the results in the Combined DNA Index System (CODIS), a DNA database funded by the Federal Bureau of Investigation. It also might be a good idea to compare the DNA from the envelope and stamp to known DNA of the Zodiac Killer at the San Francisco Police Department Crime Lab.

Theory

Unless Mr. Roberts was a figment of Richard Robison's imagination it appears that, based on the testimony of Mrs. Roger Smith, Ross Robison, Arnold Park, and Joseph Scolaro, Richard was dealing with a real person. Richard may have had a meeting or meetings with Mr. Roebert in San Francisco between June 4-7, 1968. Robison may have again met Mr. Roebert in Detroit on either June 13 or June 14, as evidenced by remarks made by Mrs. Roger Smith when she stated that Shirley Robison called her and said Richard had called and indicated a visitor would be coming to the cottage and that Richard handed the phone to the alleged visitor who spoke to Shirley. Between 9:45 a.m. and 10:30 a.m. on June 25, 1968, Richard called his banker and wanted to know if $200,000.00 had been deposited in his account. This could have been enough money to purchase a horse farm in Kentucky or a Villa in Naples. Did Richard contact Mr. Roebert between 9:45 and 10:30 a.m. on that day regarding the $200,000.00 deposit that was supposed to be coming from Bank of America? Did Mr. Roebert tell Richard that he decided to hand deliver the money instead of depositing it in Robison's bank account? He was going to Good Hart that day anyway. If Richard and Joe Scolaro were seen at the New Hudson Airport nearly everyday from mid April-mid June, 1968, and if Richard Robison was working on a multi-million dollar deal that was going to make him a tycoon, why would he leave his Lathrup Village business and go on a vacation from June 16 through at least July 10, 1968, and leave the development, the airports, the negotiations etc., unless he thought he would be meeting with the investor(s) and consummating a portion of the money transaction associated with the development?

Detectives in the Robison Murders should redirect their attention on "Mr. Roebert" and for the time being let Joseph Scolaro rest in peace.

Footnotes:

All page numbers below refer to the page in the publication referred to in the note.

1. Zodiac was into light opera. He recited a portion of the light opera The Mikado from memory. (Note 43, pages 153-155)

2. "Zodiac spoke in a monotone voice," "man was reading or had a rehearsed speech," "He spoke very precisely," "The caller sounded mature," "The most monotone voice I had ever heard." (Note 43, page 314) "There was no trace of accent in the voice and it seemed to Nancy that the man was reading what he was saying or had rehearsed it." (Note 43. page 33)
3. Zodiac killed near water. (Note 43, page 321)
4. Phantom Victim, Virgil Starks was shot in the head with a 22 semi-automatic. Shots were fired in a tight pattern through a window of his farm house. He was shot while sitting in his easy chair reading the paper.
5. Zodiac's shoeprint is size 10 ½. (Note 43, page 317)
6. Valerie Percy was struck in the head with a blunt instrument that may have been a ball-peen hammer. She was killed in the Percy home off of Lake Michigan near a public access. In the Robison case detectives searched the cove in front of the cottage with magnets looking for the murder weapon. Should they have also searched the water in Lake Michigan along the shore from the cottage to the public access located near the Robison cottage?
7. Zodiac Victims Linda Edwards and Robert Domingos were murdered on a beach Santa Barbara in 1963. They were then dragged into a shack where Edwards was placed on top of Domingos. The top of Edward's bathing suit was cut, exposing her breasts. In 1972, Santa Barbara County Sheriff John Carpenter issued the following Press Release:

   In June of 1963, a young teenage couple was found shot to death near an isolated stretch of beach, north of Santa Barbara. The victims, both of Lompoc High School seniors, had been shot several times and their bodies placed in a small lean-to shack a short distance from the beach. An extensive investigation by Sheriff's Detectives failed to reach a successful solution to the killings. Although the case was never closed, no substantial leads could be developed. Over a year ago, Sheriff's Detectives began a thorough study of the case, examining and re-evaluating all aspects of the crime. A recent development has provided information that appears somewhat promising. Considerable evidence points to the murders of Linda Edwards and Robert Domingos as being the work of the infamous ZODIAC. Although the anticipated response to this statement would be one of skepticism, let me say that we do not make this assertion frivolously. Many hundreds of hours, over the past several months, have been spent compiling information concerning the possibility that this man could have been responsible for the killings in 1963. Sheriff's Detectives have met with investigators from those areas where ZODIAC has, admittedly, been responsible for several murders. These agencies have conducted intensive investigations for the past several years in an effort to identify ZODIAC. After conferring with the officers in those other jurisdictions, we have found that it appears to be a high degree of probability that this subject is responsible for the double murder in our County. Several significant similarities between our case and the others, as well as other evidence which I am not at liberty to disclose at this time, all tend to connect ZODIAC to this crime. In addition, we have information, to be investigated further, which may place him in the Santa Barbara area in 1963. All possibilities will be investigated thoroughly to confirm, or disprove, their validity. I would like to emphasize that we are not using the notoriety of ZODIAC to dispose of a difficult case, nor are we closing our minds to the possibility that he may not be responsible. Very simply, this office feels that sufficient evidence exists to warrant further investigation into the feasibility of this assumption. It is hoped that a more factual determination can be gained by combining our efforts with those of other law enforcement agencies already working along these lines.

8. Phantom Victim, Mary Jeane Larey was sexually assaulted with a gun barrel. (Note 44, page 3)
9. Phantom Victim, Virgil Stark's heating pad was smoking when police arrived. Zodiac attempted to set fire to the shack where Edwards and Domingos were placed. Zodiac set fire to Kathleen John's vehicle.
10. Zodiac killed Betty Lou Jensen and David Faraday near Vallejo, California on December 20, 1968, six months after the Robisons had been murdered. On August 7, 1969, Zodiac wrote in a letter: "What I did was tape a small pencil flash light to the barrel of my gun. If you notice in the center of the beam of light if you aim it at a wall or ceiling you will see a black or darck spot in the center of the circle of light about 3 to 6 in. across when taped to a gun barrel, the bullet will strike exactly in the center of the black dot of light. All I had to do was spray them." Coincidentally this was the same letter that contained the enciphered message that was deciphered to read "ROBERT **EMMET** THE HIPPIE." (emphasis added)

Did Zodiac use an AR-7 with infrared telescopic sight? Was Zodiac telling the truth in his letter? Could a "pencil flash light attached to a rifle actually work like Zodiac said it would? The weapon he used to kill David Faraday and Betty Lou Jensen on December 20, 1969, was a .22 caliber. "The murder weapon proved likely to be a .22 caliber **J.C. Higgins Model 80** or Hi Standard model 101. The bullets were Super X copper-coated long rifle ammo made by Winchester since October, 1967, which made them pretty new." Each recovered bullet had a "**right hand (clockwise) twist with six lands and grooves a six by six.**" (Note 43, pages

9 -10) (emphasis added) Criminal Identification and Investigation in Sacramento provided the following: "In addition to subjecting to further tests any **J. C. Higgins**, Model 80 automatic pistol recovered, further tests should be made on any weapons having the following characteristics:

Cartridge cases: Semicircular firing pin impressions at 12 o'clock position, small extractor markings at 3 o'clock position. Very faint ejector markings at 8 o'clock position (latter may not always be detectable)

Weapon barrel or tests bullets: Six right-hand grooves, land and groove ratio 1:1 +. Bullet groove width approximately .056 inch. Bullet land width approximately .060 inch. Due to lack of sufficient unique structure it appears that considerable difficulty will be encountered in positively identifying the responsible weapon if it should be recovered . . . from our examination it appears that a conclusive identification of the responsible weapon will be extremely difficult, if not impossible, even though it should be recovered." (Note 43, page 11.)

11. The murder of Valerie Percy took place just off of Lake Michigan. Access to the Percy mansion may have been gained from a public access and then along the beach.

12. A bayonet that may have been used in the murder of Valerie Percy was found approximately 800 feet down the beach from the Percy mansion about 40 feet off shore.

13. Zodiac insisted that his "The Confession" letter be printed in the *San Francisco Chronicle*. In a letter mailed on November 9, 1969, by Zodiac, he insisted that a portion of the letter be published in the *Chronicle*.

14. Type a sentence on your computer using the word Zodius and then do spell check.

15. The spelling of Zodiac and Zodius are very similar.

Chapter 9

FROM WEST COAST TO EAST COAST-POSSIBLE CONNECTIONS BETWEEN UNSOLVED MURDERS

A series of unsolved serial murders separated by over two thousand miles may have been committed by the same perpetrator. Then again they may also not be connected, but the fact of the matter is none of these murders has ever been solved, so I am going to present information in this chapter that may connect the Zodiac Killer to the Santa Rosa Hitchhiker Murders and several murders that took place on the eastern side of the United States between 1971 and 1989. It seems highly unlikely that one person was responsible for so much human suffering without being caught. It is more likely that separate individuals are responsible for the carnage. The purpose of this chapter is to present information that may assist investigators in determining the identity of the killer or killers.

It is known that the Zodiac Killer was alive from October 5, 1970, to April 24, 1978, based on the dates of the letters he mailed to the *San Francisco Chronicle,* Paul Avery and the *Los Angeles Times.* It is fairly safe to figure that he was probably killing someone, somewhere during that time period. Unless the Zodiac was dead, incarcerated or in a mental institution from 1978–1989, he was also probably killing someone somewhere during this time period as well. The questions that should be addressed are: Where was he killing and who did he kill after the abduction of Kathleen Johns on March 22, 1970? Zodiac wrote in his letter to the *Chronicle* on November 9, 1969: "So I shall change the way the collecting of slaves. I shall no longer announce to anyone. when I comitt my murders, they shall look like routine robberies, killings of anger, & a few fake accidents, etc. The police shall **never catch me**, because I have been too clever for them." By his own admission Zodiac was going to continue killing after 1969, in at least three different ways without "announcing to anyone" when he committed his murders. If Zodiac continued to be capable of killing, it is just plain folly to assume that he stopped killing after March 22, 1970. He may have just relocated from the West Coast to the East Coast of the United States and again changed his methods of killing to obstruct police investigations. With that in mind here are several interesting series of unsolved murders that followed the known Zodiac murders:

The Freeway Phantom

Six African-American girls between the ages of 10 and 18 were abducted, raped and strangled near Washington, D.C. between April, 1971, and September, 1972. The killer became known as the Freeway Phantom. On March 13, 1971, Zodiac mailed a letter to the *Los Angeles Times*. In this letter he wrote in part:" If the Blue Meanies are **ever going to catch me**, they had best get off their fat asses & do something."

The Victims:

> Forty-three days after the Zodiac letter was mailed on **April 25, 1971**, 13-year-old Carol Spinks was abducted near Washington, D.C. Her lifeless body was found next to the northbound lanes of I-295.

On July 8, 1971, Darlenia Johnson, 16, disappeared. Her body was located within feet of where Carol Spinks body was found. A witness reported seeing Darlena after she had been abducted in an old black automobile driven by a Black man.

On July 27, 1971, 10-year-old Brenda Crockett vanished. Her body was found along Route 50, near I-295 in Prince George's County, Maryland. Brenda had been raped and strangled, and a scarf was knotted around her neck.

On October 1, 1971, 12-year-old Nenomoshia Yates was kidnapped, raped and strangled. Her body was found near Pennsylvania Avenue in Prince George's County. A Washington D.C. newspaper named the killer the "Freeway Phantom."

On November 15, 1971, Brenda Woodward, 18, was last seen boarding a city bus in Washington, D.C. Her body was found a short time later near an access ramp to Route 202 from the Baltimore/ Washington Parkway. She had been stabbed and strangled to death. Her killer placed a coat over her chest. In one of the coat pockets investigators found a note with impressive words from her killer.[1]

> "This is tantamount to my insensitivity to people especially women. I will admit the others **when you catch me** if you can.[2]
>
> s/ Free-way Phantom"[3]

On September 5, 1972, Diane Williams, 17, was last seen boarding a bus. Her body was found along I-295 immediately south of the District line.

Evidence:

Green synthetic carpet fibers were found on the bodies of all but one of the victims. (Automobiles, including station wagons during that time period, that were originally painted green, probably had green carpet with synthetic carpet fibers.)[4]

The Santa Rosa Hitchhiker Murders

Between February 4, 1972, and December 22, 1973, someone killed eight young girls near Santa Rosa, California. These murders became known as the Santa Rosa Hitchhiker Murders and remain unsolved. The Zodiac Killer is considered one of the possible suspects. The Victims:

Yvonne Weber and Maureen Sterling were last seen on February 4, 1972, getting into someone's vehicle near the Redwood Empire Ice Arena in Santa Rosa. Their skeletal remains were found ten months later. The cause of death was listed as "unknown."

Kim Allen had left her place of employment in Larkspur in Marin County and was headed towards her home in Santa Rosa. She never made it, and her nude body was found on Sunday, March 5, 1972, in a ravine south of Santa Rosa. She had been strangled to death.

Jeannette Kamahele, a Santa Rosa Junior College student, vanished on Tuesday, **April 25, 1972**, hitchhiking north on Highway 101 to Santa Rosa Junior College. Her remains have never been found and the cause of death remains "unknown." She was last seen exactly one year after Carol Spinks disappeared in Washington D.C. on April 25, 1971.

Lori Lee Kursa's nude body was found on December 14, 1972. She had been missing near Santa Rosa since Saturday, November 11th of that year. Her neck had been broken. Kurska was a known hitchhiker.

Carolyn Davis was hitchhiking on Highway 101 near Garberville when she disappeared. Her body was later located where Yvonne Weber's and Maureen Sterling's bodies were located. She had been poisoned.

Therese Walsh disappeared Sunday, December 22, 1973. She was last seen hitchhiking on Highway 101. Her nude body was found in Mark West Creek near Santa Rosa. Zodiac wrote a letter to the *San*

Francisco Chronicle on January 29, 1974 (thirty-eight days after the last murder in Santa Rosa).

On July 2, 1979, the remains of a Jane Doe were located buried in a laundry sack near the area where Lori Lee Kurska's body had been found several years earlier. The coroner determined that her remains had been there between five and seven years. (Both the location of Jane Doe's remains and the use of a sack bring to mind an earlier murder: a drifter by the name of Robert Brent Bowman who has been directly tied to the murder of 13-year-old Eileen Adams near Ypsilanti, Michigan, in December, 1969. The killer placed Adams' body in a sack. Bowman was arrested on October 2, 2008, in Riverside, California. Jane Doe was murdered in California sometime between 1972 and 1974.)

The Connecticut River Valley Killer

Between October 24, 1978, and August 6, 1988, seven women were murdered near Claremont, New Hampshire, and an eighth victim was stabbed several times and managed to survive. The serial killer became known as the Connecticut River Valley Killer. On May 2, 1978, after four years of silence, the Zodiac Killer wrote a letter to KHJ-TV in Los Angeles, California. In the letter he wrote in part: "I have decided to begin killing again. . ."

The Connecticut River Valley Murders remain unsolved.

The Victims:

> On October 24, 1978, Cathy Millican, 26, was murdered after **photographing birds at the Chandler Brook Wetland Preserve** in New London, New Hampshire. She was stabbed over twenty nine-times in the upper body and abdomen in a "V" shape. There was no sign of sexual assault.

On July 25, 1981, Mary Elizabeth Critchley disappeared while hitchhiking near the Massachusetts/Vermont border. Her body was located on August 9, 1981, in Unity, New Hampshire.

On May 20, 1984, Heidi Martin, 16, went for a run. The next day her dead body was found in a swampy area behind Hartland Elementary School in Hartland, Vermont.[5]

On May 30, 1984, Bernice Courtemanche, a nurse's aide, vanished after hitchhiking along Route 12 in Claremont.

On July 20, 1984, Ellen Fried, 27, a supervising nurse at Valley Regional Hospital, disappeared. She had stopped to use a payphone outside Leo's Market in Claremont. Her remains were found on September 19, 1985, near the bank of the Sugar River in Kelleyville, New Hampshire.

On July 10, 1985, Eva Morse, 28, was hitchhiking near the border of Claremont and Charlestown, New Hampshire, when she was last seen.

On April 15, 1986, Lynda Moore, 36, was found dead in Saxton's River, Vermont.

Witnesses reported seeing a "slightly stocky, dark haired male with a blue knapsack" near the crime scene on the day of the murder. "The man was cleanshaven with a somewhat round face wearing dark-rimmed glasses." They thought this person was between 20 and 25 years old. (Except for the age, this description closely matches that of the Zodiac Killer.)

On September 19, 1986, an abandoned car belonging to Sarah Hunter, 36, was discovered at a gas station near Route 7A in Manchester Center, Vermont. She was a golf pro in Manchester Center. Two months later her remains were located at the edge of a cornfield in Pawlet, Vermont. Hunter had been strangled to death.[6]

The remains of Bernice Courtemanche were found about 1000 yards from where Ellen Fried's remains were located. A mere 500 feet from where Mary Critchley had been discovered searchers came across the remains of Eva Morse. Both victims had knife wounds to their necks. Fried had an injury to her head.

On January 10, 1987, a nurse by the name of Barbara Agnew, 38, was murdered after a ski outing in Stratton, Vermont. Here green BMW was found at a rest stop on northbound I-91 in Hartford, Vermont. Agnew had been stabbed to death in a "V" shaped pattern. A large snowstorm engulfed the area on the night she disappeared.[7]

On August 6, 1988, Jane Boroski, 22, was attacked near a closed convenience store in West Swanzey, New Hampshire. She was stabbed 29 times before her attacker drove away. [8] Boroski survived the attack and was the last known victim of the Connecticut River Valley Killer. Boroski was seven months pregnant when she was attacked.[9]

The Colonial Parkway Murders

During the years 1986-1989, six individuals were murdered (two young women and two couples) and another couple was presumed dead after having been missing since April 9, 1988, along the Colonial Parkway in the state of Virginia. Detectives suspect the murders were committed by a serial killer.

The Victims:

On October 12, 1986, the bodies of a lesbian couple, Cathleen Marian Thomas, 27, and Rebecca Ann Dowski, 21, were found near the Colonial Parkway between Ringfield Plantation overlook and the York River in York County, Virginia. They had been strangled with a rope and had their throats cut. Their purses and money were still in their white 1980 Honda Civic. The car had been pushed down an embankment and both bodies were found inside the vehicle. Cathleen's wounds were so severe that she was nearly decapitated. Neither had been sexually assaulted. Rope burns were found on their necks and wrists. There was no sign of sexual assault.

On Saturday, September 19, 1987, 20-year-old David Lee Knobling and 14-year-old Robin M. Edwards were shot in the back of the heads. Their killer dumped the bodies in the James River **in the Ragged Island Wildlife Refuge** in Isle of Wright County, Virginia.

Saturday, April 9, 1988, 20-year-old Richard Keith Call and 18-year-old Cassandra Lee Hailey were last seen leaving together in Richard's car. Richard's abandoned car was located the next morning by his father at the York River Overlook off the Colonial Parkway near Yorktown, Virginia. The male victim's glasses, wallet and watch were found in the vehicle along with Cassandra's purse, bra and shoes. Neither body has ever been recovered and they are presumed dead.

Labor Day weekend, 1989, 21-year-old Daniel Lauer and Anna Marie Phelps, 18, disappeared. Daniel's car was found in a rest area in New Kent County, Virginia, on the westbound side of I-64 between Williamsburg and Richmond, Virginia. The next month their skeletal remains were found less than a mile from where his vehicle was earlier located. Anna Marie's body had been wrapped in a blanket. Each had been stabbed to death. Daniel's keys were in the ignition and articles belonging to Daniel and Anna Marie together with her untouched purse were found in the vehicle.

The Bedford Highway Killer

Between July, 1988 and June, 1989, nine women were murdered near New Bedford, Massachusetts. Two additional women disappeared and are presumed dead. All of the victims were either prostitutes or known substance abusers. Any convicted serial killer who killed prostitutes and/or known female drug abusers from before and after the last known Bedford Highway Murder should be considered a possible suspect.

The Victims:

In April, 1988, Robin Rhodes, 28, was last seen near New Bedford. Her dead body was located on March 28, 1989, off southbound Mass. Rte 140 across the highway where another victim by the name of Debra Meadows would soon be found.

May 27, 1988, Debra Maseiros, 30, was last seen near a New Bedford exit ramp off Mass. Rte 140.

July 11, 1988, Nancy Pavia, 36, and Deborah DeMello, 34, disappeared. On July 30, 1988, the remains of Pavia were located on an I-195 exit ramp. On November 8, 1988, the remains of DeMello were located close to where the body of Pavia had been discarded earlier.

November 4, 1988, Dawn Mendes, 25, disappeared. Her remains were located seven days later on November 11 along I-195.

December 1, 1988, the remains of Deborah McConnell, 25, were located off Rte 140 near New Bedford.

December 10, 1988, the remains of Rochelle Clifford Dopierla, 28, were found near the location where DeMello and Paiva were discarded.

July 16, 1988, the remains of Mary Rose Santos, 26, were located off Route 88.

April, 1988, Robin Rhodes was last seen alive.

April 24, 1989, the remains of Sandy Botelho, 24, were found along I-195.

In May and June, 1988, two other women, Christine Monteiro, 19, and Marilyn Roberts, 34, disappeared. Investigators considered that both of these women were possible victims of the Bedford Highway Killer.

Clues that may connect the Zodiac Killer to the Santa Rosa Hitchhiker Murders

As of December 1, 2010, the Santa Rosa Hitchhiker killer and the Colonial Parkway killer had not been identified. Several suspects have been investigated and subsequently eliminated as the perpetrator of these crimes. The murders may or may not have been committed by the same individual; however, certain similarities between these and other previously highlighted murders reviewed in this book are worth mentioning.

1. **Direction of the Zodiac Murders**
   You will notice that the Santa Rosa Hitchhiker murders took place from 1972-1974, near Santa Rosa, California. The progression of the Zodiac Killer in the earlier cases may have begun with Edwards and Domingos near Santa Barbara, California, in 1963, and then moved north to Riverside, California in 1966 when Cheri Jo Bates was murdered. Following her murder Zodiac again moved north towards San Francisco and Vallejo. On September 27, 1969, he attacked Bryan Hartnell and killed Cecelia Shepard north of Vallejo near Lake Berryessa.
2. **Killed on weekends**
   Most of the Santa Rosa murders occurred on weekends as did most of the Phantom Murders and the Zodiac Murders.
3. **White clothesline**
   Santa Rosa victim Jeannette Kamahale had been "tied with her hands and ankles bound to her neck." White cloth line was wrapped around her neck four times by her killer. Zodiac used "two-and-one-half to three-foot lengths of hollow clothesline" to bind Bryan Hartnell and Cecelia Shephard. (Note 45, pages 69-70)

4. **Hogtied**
   Santa Rosa victims Therese Walsh and Carolyn Davis may have been hogtied by their killer. Zodiac victims Bryan Hartnell and Cecelia were hogtied by the Zodiac. (Note 45, page 70)
5. **Mt. Diablo/Devil's Kitchen**
   On December 28, 1972, the remains of Yvonne Weber and Maureen Sterling were found and on July 31, 1973, and the remains of Carolyn Davis were located near Devil's Kitchen in Franz Valley. A witchcraft symbol made of sticks was located nearby. "The sign: two crude rectangles joined by a stick, is an old English witchcraft symbol that was used in connection with death rituals meant to hurry the spirits on to the afterlife." Zodiac wrote in his letters about collecting slaves for the afterlife. A possible Zodiac letter mailed on Valentine's Day, 1974, to the *San Francisco Chronicle* made reference to "an old Norse word meaning to kill." Devil's Kitchen is a summit in Sonoma County, California. It has an elevation of 277 meters, or 909 feet. A Zodiac letter received by the *Chronicle* in June, 1970, made reference to "Mt. Diablo." "Diablo" is Spanish for "Devil." Mt. Diablo has an elevation of 3864 feet.

Clues that may connect the Zodiac Killer to the Colonial Parkway Murders and other Murders:

1. **Nearly decapitated, "V" shaped stabbing pattern**
   Colonial Parkway victim Cathleen Marian Thomas had "injuries so extreme that she was nearly decapitated." Zodiac victim Cheri Jo Bates's "jugular was severed as was her voice box and she was almost decapitated." (Note 45, page 155) Cecelia Shepard was stabbed in a "V" shaped pattern.

2. **Killed on weekends**
Murders may have occurred on Saturday, September 19, 1987; Saturday, April 9, 1988; and Labor Day Weekend, 1989.
3. **Attacks on couples at night in secluded areas near a body of water**
The Colonial Parkway Killer attacked couples in secluded areas near a body of water at night. Several of the Phantom murders in Texarkana and the Zodiac murders exhibited the same characteristics.
4. **No sexual molestation**
The victims in the Colonial Parkway Murders were not sexually assaulted. The Phantom and Zodiac victims were not sexually assaulted (except Phantom victim Mary Jeanne Larey who was violated with a pistol).
5. **Detectives theorized that a policeman or someone acting like a police officer may have been involved in the Colonial Parkway murders**
When Daniel Lauer's vehicle was located police noted that the driver's window was cracked open, the keys were in the ignition and his wallet was on the dashboard. All of these facts indicated that a person posing as a police officer may have approached his vehicle. On Friday, July 4, 1969, Zodiac victim Michael Mageau thought a policeman was approaching his vehicle. Mageau recalled that he said to Darlene Ferrin, "Here come the cops, you better get your identification out." The driver's window to Mageau's car was down. (Note 45, pages 24-27)
6. **Lone killer with a pistol**
In the Colonial Parkway murders detectives wondered how a lone assailant could overpower two individuals. Some detectives thought two assailants may have been involved in the

attacks. In both the Phantom Killer of Texarkana and the Zodiac cases a single individual appears to have been responsible. He overpowered his victims using a gun as a means of persuasion.

7. **Hogtied**
   Colonial Parkway victims Rebecca Ann Dowski and Cathleen Marian Thomas were found with rope burns to their necks and wrists. They may have been hogtied.
8. **Set vehicles on fire, left wooden matches at scene of fire**
   Colonial Parkway victims Cathleen Thomas and Rebecca Dowski's vehicle had been doused with diesel fuel. Wooden matches were found outside their car. Someone attempted to set their vehicle on fire. Zodiac victims Linda Edwards and Robert Domingos were killed and dragged inside a shack in Santa Barbara in 1963. Their killer attempted to set the shack on fire. Wooden matches were found at the scene of the attempted fire. Zodiac victim Kathleen John's vehicle was torched by the Zodiac. (Note 45, page 140)
9. **Purses in the vehicle untouched**
   Colonial Parkway victims Rebecca Ann Dowski's and Cathleen Marian Thomas's purses were found untouched in their vehicle. In the Phantom murder case of Polly Ann Moore her untouched purse was lying beside her body in her vehicle. It rained the night Polly Ann Moore was murdered.
10. **Tiger Salamander (*Ambystoma Tigrinum*)**
    There may be another interesting connection between York County, Virginia, where the Colonial Parkway Murders took place and Santa Rosa, California, where the Santa Rosa Hitch-hiker Murders took place. The Tiger Salamander is an endangered species in the State of Virginia and is found in only four of its counties. One of the Virginia counties

where the Tiger Salamander is found is in York County. The Tiger Salamander is also known to inhabit the Santa Barbara region, Mt. Diablo and Sonoma County in California, especially the Laguna de Santa Rosa where the Santa Rosa Hitch-hiker murders took place. The Tiger Salamander is active at night in the spring and fall, usually when it rains. A flashlight or some other form of artificial light source is usually necessary to locate them.

11. **Opposite sides of the United States**
    The Colonial Parkway Murders and the Santa Rosa Hitch-hiker Murders took place at almost opposite sides of the United States. This may indicate the killer chose strategic locations separated by great distance hoping that the exchange of information between law enforcement agencies would be limited. If the same individual committed both sets of murders and if this was in fact his strategy, detection was avoided and the outcome was successful.
12. **Eight victims**
    There were eight known victims in the Santa Rosa Hitch-hiker Murders, eight in the Connecticut River Valley Murders and eight victims in the Colonial Parkway Murders. Zodiac attacked eight individuals from Riverside to Lake Berryessa in California: Bates, Jensen, Faraday, Mageau, Ferrin, Hartnell, Shepard and Stine. Kathleen Johns was abducted with her child but was not injured. Was it part of his overall plan to attack eight individuals in one general area and then move on to a new jurisdiction in order to avoid detection?
13. **Shot, strangled and stabbed**
    The method of killing varied in the Zodiac Murders and the Valley River Murders. Some victims were shot others strangled and stabbed.

14. **Military installations**
    There are many military installations in Virginia like there are in California.
15. **Blanket over victims**
    In the Colonial Parkway Murders of Phelps and Lauer their killer placed a blanket over their bodies. In the 1963 Santa Barbara beach murders of Robert Domingos and Linda Edwards their killer may have covered their bodies with a blanket. In the Good Hart Murders Mrs. Robison's body was covered with a blanket by her killer.
16. **Failed attempt to burn bodies**
    In the Domingos and Edwards case their killer attempted to burn their bodies. In the Colonial Parkway Murders of Dowski and Thomas their killer attempted to burn their automobile and bodies.
17. **Killed on anniversary dates**
    Zodiac Victim Paul Stine was killed on October 11, 1969. The Dowski-Thomas murders took place on October 12, 1986. Possible Zodiac Victim Donna Lass was killed on Labor Day Weekend, 1970. Colonial Parkway Victims Daniel Lauer and Anna Marie Phelps disappeared on Labor Day Weekend, 1989.
18. **Exposed breasts**
    Santa Barbara beach victim Linda Edwards had here bikini cut and her breasts exposed by her killer. Colonial Parkway victim Robin Edwards had her bra lifted off and around her neck exposing her breasts.

Footnotes:

1. Zodiac used words in his letters intended to impress the reader including "consternation," "sensibilities," "glorification," "deplorable," "psychological," & "anonymously."

A letter that followed the Phantom Murders in Texarkana included the word "spondulux."

2. It may not be of much significance but you will notice that Zodiac wrote the word "people" in several of his letters:

August 1, 1969:	"killing lone people," "I have killed over a dozen people"
August 4, 1969:	"I like killing people"
November 9, 1969:	"I have killed 7 people"
April 28, 1970:	"If I saw a lot of people wearing my buton"
July 24, 1970:	"You people will not wear some. . ."

3. Zodiac signed his July 10, 1974 letter "Red Phantom."
4. In the Michigan Co-Ed Murders when Jane Mixer was killed "some youngsters had noticed a late-model **green station wagon** cruising slowly around the perimeter of the cemetery at dusk the previous evening." (Note 45, page 49) On the night Valerie Percy was murdered a taxi driver told police: "he saw a **green station wagon** pull out of the Percy driveway between 4:30 am and 5:30 am." (Page 8, Section 1, *Chicago Tribune*, Monday, September 19, 1966)
5. Possible Zodiac victim Nancy Gidley's nude body was dumped in the parking lot of George Washington High School on July 15, 1973. The body of possible Zodiac victim Angela Thomas was found in the playground at Ben Franklin Junior High School on July 2, 1973.
6. Zodiac victims Mike Mageau and Darlene Ferrin were attacked on July 4, 1969, near the Blue Rock Springs Golf Course.

7. On September 6, 1970, a Lake Tahoe nurse and possible Zodiac victim by the name of Donna Lass, 25, disappeared after leaving work at the Sahara Hotel in Stateline, Nevada. On March 22, 1971, Zodiac sent a postcard to Paul Avery. The postcard included the words: "around in the snow."
8. Zodiac victim Cecelia Shepard was stabbed 24 times.
9. On March 22, 1970, Kathleen Johns and her ten-month-old daughter were abducted at night, possibly by the Zodiac Killer. She survived after escaping from Zodiac's vehicle. Johns was the last known victim of the Zodiac. She was seven months pregnant at the time of her abduction.

AFTERWORD

(Author's note: William Heirens died on March 5, 2012. The Afterword was written and originally published before his death)

It is my intention to revisit these cold cases and hopefully rekindle some interest and possibly lead to a resolution of these matters once and for all. If only a portion of my ideas and theories are accurate, then the contents of this book might lead to some evidence that may be used to determine the identity of the killers. The individuals involved in the Cleveland Torso Murders, the murders of Georgette Bauerdorf, Jeanne Axford French, Suzanne Degnan and other murder victims mentioned are probably all dead by now. William Heirens is still alive as of this writing and remains incarcerated by the State of Illinois in Dixon, Illinois. I believe there is a high probability that the Zodiac Killer is still alive and is more than likely incarcerated in a penal institution for some other similar crime. Based on all of the research I have completed, I would suspect that if he is alive the Zodiac is probably incarcerated in the State of Texas. Dr. Donald Schrag wrote in 1979, "All multiple or mass murderers either become incarcerated for life as a common criminal, are declared psychopathic and are placed in a criminal institution or realize the hopelessness of their condition and seek intensive psychiatric assistance (*Wichita Eagle-Beacon*, August 5, 1979). If the DNA of all criminals between the ages of fifty-seven to seventy-five years old currently incarcerated for serial murder could be tested and their DNA compared to the known DNA of the Zodiac, the odds might favor ferreting out the culprit. I selected the representative age group based on possible eyewitness accounts in the Zodiac case. A possible witness in the Cheri Jo Bates murder on October 10, 1966, reported the possible age of her assailant at thirty-five. If this was an accurate report, then the Zodiac would have been born in 1931, and would be seventy-six in 2006. In the Darlene Ferrin case a possible witness indicated the "man at Terry's: thirty-five to thirty-eight in 1969. If this witness report was accurate, the Zodiac's birth date would have been 1931-1934, and he would be seventy-two to seventy-five in 2006. Zodiac witness Michael Mageau (who was not considered to be reliable because of his condition at the time) thought his attacker was between twenty-six to thirty years of age in 1969. If Mageau was correct in his assessment, the Zodiac would be between the ages of sixty-three to sixty-seven in 2006, and would have been born between 1939-1943. A possible witness on October 11, 1969, described the Zodiac as being thirty-five to forty-five years old. If accurate, the Zodiac's date of birth would have fallen between the years 1924-1934, and he would be seventy-two to eighty-two years old in 2006. Possible Zodiac witness, Sandra Betts, described the man as being thirty-eight years old in 1969. If accurate and if see did run into the Zodiac, he would have been born in 1934 and would be 73 years old in 2006.

It is quite possible that the Zodiac is imprisoned for some other offense other than serial murder. With that in mind a prisoner profile could be conducted using certain parameters as guidelines. The study could be narrowed by eliminating all black men and all women because there has never been any indication (other than Mary Jeanne Larey) that the Zodiac was a woman or a black man. The search should concentrate on strong, highly intelligent white male between 5'8" and 6'4" tall, weighing between 180-220 pounds when originally incarcerated, who enjoy poetry and opera. The inmate might have a background in the teaching profession and enjoy sewing. He may be involved in softball or baseball in the prison system. Eliminate from the search any prisoner with an arm or leg missing unless the limb was severed after 1977. Focus on an inmate who was convicted for killing a stranger, not a spouse or relative. Concentrate on inmates who killed women or couples. Look for an inmate who killed at close range either with a knife or gun. Look for an inmate who killed more than one person, who has a large ego and who enjoys mailing greeting cards and postcards. For years the emphasis has been trying to solve the clues sent by the Zodiac. Finding the Zodiac in prison might be the easiest and best route to take.

If the authorities wait too long the same thing might happen to the Zodiac's DNA that happened to author Patricia Cornwell's suspect in the Jack the Ripper case, namely, Walter Sickert. All known DNA of Walter Sickert was destroyed when his body was cremated in 1942 (unless of course DNA from the remains of Sickert's natural mother could be analyzed). Worse yet, if the Zodiac is currently incarcerated, he may someday be freed as a "harmless old man," by an uninformed, sympathetic parole board. At the very least DNA samples of all convicted murderers who fit the Zodiac's profile should be preserved in the event of their deaths as a method of trying to resolve these old cold cases.

Any legal restraints or constitutional issues concerning this method of inmate profiling and DNA testing should be overcome. If the profiling created a reasonable belief that a particular inmate might be responsible for any of the murders mentioned in this text, then in that event DNA testing and comparisons would be appropriate. In a 2-1 decision in 2003, the Ninth Circuit Court of Appeals in San Francisco ruled that a law requiring parolees to give blood for a DNA databank used to investigate crimes violates the Fourth Amendment ban on unreasonable searches and seizures. The reason given was that blood would be extracted from parolees who are not suspected of committing new crimes. The Court, in its decision, did mention that other inmates, like parolees, retain certain rights of privacy. "Even parolees maintain a reasonable expectation of privacy in their own bodies," said Judge Stephen Reinhart in the majority decision. Inmates who are incarcerated for murder and other serious crimes who fit the test of "probable cause" based on a reasonable belief that they may have committed additional felonies should be subject to DNA testing. This is not a difficult or terribly expensive task and should be conducted for the benefit of the victims.

Based on the following clues I would suggest that the prisoner profiling and DNA comparisons begin with inmates in the 61-80-year-old category in the State of Texas:

1. The Phantom Killer wore a cloth-hood over his head and attacked couples on secluded lover's lanes at night.
2. The Phantom Killer attacked and murdered his victims at close range approximately 175 miles from Dallas, Texas.
3. Two of the Phantom Killer's victims were murdered in Texarkana, Arkansas, not far from a night club called Club Dallas.
4. In 1946, the Phantom Killer appeared to be inexperienced at his trade based on the fact that he wore a loosely fitting cloth-hood over his head that probably interfered with his eyesight. The hood had slits for the eyes and mouth but not the nose. He carried a gun in one hand and a flashlight in his other hand. In addition Betty Jo Booker and Jimmy Hollis were playing in a band at a "young people's dance" that might have also been attended by their stalker who also may have been a young person.
5. In different attacks in California in 1969, the Zodiac wore a hood over his head that did not interfere with his vision and he used a rifle with a flashlight attached to the barrel, thus freeing the other hand. The hood had slits for the eyes and mouth but not for the nose.
6. In 1969, the Zodiac wrote in one of his letters "Because the longer they fiddle and fart around, the more slaves I will

collect." The author Robert Graysmith has suggested that this form of slang is used predominately by older people, most commonly around Lubbock, Texas.

7. On August 7, 1969, the Zodiac wrote in a letter, "Bullshit that area is surrounded by high hills and trees." The word "bullshit" is used throughout the United States but quite frequently in the Lone Star State, famous for its Long Horn Steers.
8. Darlene Ferrin and her family visited the Dallas/Fort Worth area in 1962, and gave a stranger their Vallejo, California, address and phone number. When in Texas, Darlene told a man who was with them in a bowling alley to "push off" and in effect snubbed his advances.
9. The Zodiac's "Dear Melvin" letter may provide a clue that indicates that he was from Dallas, Texas.
10. The Zodiac may have, and in my estimation probably did, originate from a state other than the State of California. He killed several individuals in California on weekends and holidays but for some reason not during the week. The murders occurred at a time when the United States was engaged in war in Vietnam and Cambodia. A serviceman, or someone pretending to be a serviceman, dressed like a serviceman and with the proper, forged documents, could easily travel freely throughout the United States on either domestic or military flights.
11. During the Vietnam War there was a military naval air station in Dallas, Texas and a military air station in Fort Worth, Texas. The State of California has several military and naval air stations some of which are located close to the sites where the Zodiac committed his murders.
12. In 1969, Paul Stine was killed by the Zodiac in San Francisco in his taxi. Two hours earlier Stine had been at the airport.

13. One of the envelopes sent by the Zodiac included the words "AIRMAIL" written in large letters. However the letter not sent by the US Postage Service by airmail.
14. On March 22, 1970, Kathleen Johns was traveling to the Travis Air Force Base when she was abducted by a person that fit the description of the Zodiac Killer.
15. In the Phantom Murders and in the Zodiac murders several of the letters were typed in upper case. Letters were mailed to the stepfather and father of a victim who had been brutally murdered.
16. Nearly all of the Zodiac murders and attacks occurred on weekends and holidays.
17. The Phantom's shoe size was estimated at 9 ½-10 ½. The Zodiac's shoe size was estimated at 10 ½.

Solving the Zodiac murders in California becomes more and more difficult as time passes. Witnesses die; original detectives assigned to the cases retire or pass away; police agencies become burdened with several hundred if not thousands of murders, rapes, burglaries and other crimes that call for more immediate attention. After the murders, people grow older, a new generation emerges, and the general public, although somewhat interested, becomes apathetic towards these cold cases. Those who survive and were directly affected by the acts of terror and brutality never forget. Their lives were forever changed. They became burdened with the great loss and agony suffered as a result of a seemingly senseless crime that touched their lives somewhere in the distant past. Establishing the identity of a killer after years have passed since the crimes took place is a discouraging task, but not an impossible one. With some additional detective work, a little luck and forensics, one or more of these killers may be eventually identified.

SYNOPSIS OF VICTIMS: TORSO MURDERS AND RELATED CASES

DATE	VICTIM
September 5, 1934	A torso of a woman identified as "the Lady of the Lakes" is located near 156th Street in Cleveland.
September 23, 1935	An individual described as Victim No.1 is found at the foot of Jackass Hill in Cleveland. Victim No. 2, later identified as Edward Andrassy, is found near the body of Victim No.1. Both had been decapitated and emasculated.
January 26, 1936	The torso of Victim No. 3, Flo Polillo, is discoved behind Hart Manufacturing Plant in Cleveland.
June 5, 1936	Victim No. 4, known as the "Tattooed Man," is found in Cleveland's Kingsbury Run.
July 22, 1936	Victim No. 5 is found decapitated on Cleveland's west side.
September 10, 1936	Victim No. 6 is found dismembered in Cleveland.
May 5, 1937	Victim No. 7's upper torso is found in Lake Erie off of East 30th Street in Cleveland.
June 6, 1937	The skull of Victim No. 8 is found in Cleveland under the Lorain-Carnegie Bridge.

July 6, 1937	Searchers in Cleveland scour the banks of the Cuyahoga River for the remains of victim No. 9.
July 9, 1937	The lower half of Victim No. 10 is discovered in Cleveland floating down the Cuyahoga.
August 16, 1938	The dismembered torsos of Victim No. 11 and Victim No.12 are discovered at the East 9th-Lake Shore dump site in Cleveland.
1939-1942	At least five more torso victims are found in Pennsylvania.
October 12, 1944	Georgette Bauerdorf is found murdered in her Los Angeles apartment.
June 5, 1945	Josephine Ross is murdered in Chicago.
December 10, 1945	Frances Brown is murdered in Chicago. Her killer leaves a note on her bedroom wall in red lipstick.
January 7, 1946	Twenty-seven days later, 6-year-old Suzanne Degnan is murdered and dismembered in Chicago by someone with the skill of a butcher.
September 4, 1946	Seventeen-year-old William Heirens pleads guilty to the murders of Ross, Brown and Degnan.
September 5, 1946	William Heirens is handed three consecutive life sentences for the murders and one year to life for burglaries and assaults.
January 14, 1947	Almost exactly one year after the murder and dismemberment of little Suzanne Degnan, Elizabeth Short (the Black Dahlia) is mutilated, killed and cut in half, by someone "with the skill of a surgeon" in Los Angeles. The killer calls himself the Black Dahlia Avenger.

February 10, 1947	Exactly 27 days later Jeanne French is murdered in Los Angeles. A note in red lipstick is written on her body.
February 12, 1947	Ica Mable M'Grew is kidnapped and raped in Los Angeles. The Black Dahlia Avenger is a possible suspect.
March 12, 1947	The nude body of Evelyn Winters is found near railroad tracks in Los Angeles. The Black Dahlia Avenger is a possible suspect.
May 11, 1947	Laura Elizabeth Trelstad is found strangled in Long Beach, California. The Black Dahlia Avenger is a possible suspect.
July 8, 1947	Rosenda Josephine Mondragon's body is found near railroad tracks in Los Angeles. The Black Dahlia Avenger is a possible suspect.
February 14, 1948	Viola Norton is savagely beaten by two men near the location where the Black Dahlia's bisected body was found one year earlier. The Black Dahlia Avenger is a possible suspect.
June 13, 1949	Louise Margaret Springer is kidnapped and murdered in Los Angeles. Her assailant violated her with a 14-inch finger-thick tree branch. She worked two blocks from where the body of the Black Dahlia was discovered January 15, 1947. The Black Dahlia Avenger is a possible suspect.
June 12, 1950	Cuyahoga County Coroner Dr. Gerber estimates that forty-four-year-old Robert Robertson was killed on June 12, 1950, the same day he disappeared. Robertson's torso and other body parts were found near

Norris Brothers Company Movers at 2138 Davenport Avenue in Cleveland on July 22, 1950. If Dr. Gerber's estimated date of death was correct, then this murder could not have been committed by Jack Anderson Wilson because on June 12, 1950, according to his five-page rap sheet, Wilson was arrested and charged in Los Angeles with suspicion of burglary. Robertson was a suspected homosexual (page 191, *Torso*).

CHRONOLOGY OF THE TORSO MURDERS AND OTHER RELATED MURDERS

August 5, 1920	Birthdate of Arnold Smith, a/k/a Jack Anderson Wilson, whose birthdate is also reported as 8/5/24. Wilson is born in Canton, Ohio, and spends his early years in that state.
September 5, 1934	First torso murder victim found in Cleveland is known as the "Lady of the Lakes."
1935	Elliot Ness becomes Cleveland's Director of Public Safety.
September 23, 1935	Edward Andrassy, Victim No. 1, and Victim No. 2 are found at the foot of Jackass Hill 1in Cleveland. The killer may have tried to burn one of the victims.
January 26, 1936	Body parts of Flo Polillo (Victim No. 3) are discovered behind Hart Manufacturing Plant in Cleveland.
June, 1936	The headless torso of a white male is found in an abandoned box car near New Castle by railroad detectives. The individual may have been killed in Cleveland and later located in a box car that moved by rail to New Castle.

June 5, 1936	The "Tattooed Man" (Victim No. 4) is discovered in Cleveland's Kingsbury Run. His head is wrapped in his pants.
June 27-October 4, 1936	The Great Lakes Exposition takes place in Cleveland. Jack Anderson Wilson attends.
July 22, 1936	The decapitated torso of Victim No. 5 is located on Cleveland's west side.
September, 1936	Detectives Orley May and Emil Musil were told that a woman who had been in the workhouse said that, "Another inmate named Helen O'Leary had identified Jack Wilson, a former butcher who had worked at a meat market on St. Clair, as the murderer of Flo Polillo. Wilson, according to the nameless informant, was a known "Sodomist" who carried a large butcher knife. May and Musil spoke to Detective Cooney, who knew of the deviant former butcher and promised to haul him in for questioning. Whether Jack Wilson was ever questioned is not known, but police were apparently unable to implicate him in Flo Polillo's murder" (Note 46, p. 58).
September 10, 1936	Victim No. 6 is found in Cleveland's Kingsbury Run near East 37th Street.
October, 1936	The decapitated torso of a white male is found along railroad tracks near Haverstraw, New York. The New York Central passes near Haverstraw. The killer used a saw to behead this victim.

March, 1937	The upper half of Victim No. 7 is discovered in Cleveland.
June, 6, 1937	The head of Victim No. 8 is found under the Lorain-Carnegie Bridge in Cleveland.
July 6, 1937	Body parts of Victim No. 8 are recovered from the Cuyahoga River in Cleveland.
July 10, 1937	The lower half of Victim No. 10 is discovered floating down the Cuyahoga River.
April 8, 1938	Body parts of Victim No. 10 are found about three feet from a storm sewer outlet along the Cuyahoga River.
August 16, 1938	The severed bodies of Victims No. 11 and No. 12 are found at the East 9th-Lake Shore dumpsite in Cleveland.
December 29, 1938	Cleveland postal workers find a letter dated December 23, 1938, postmarked from Los Angeles. The author of the letter claims he buried a head of one of his victims between Western and Crenshaw in Los Angeles. A copy of the correspondence is dispatched to Los Angeles police to search for the author of the letter.
-Late 1930's	Glover Loving, Jr., a/k/a Jack Anderson Wilson a/k/a Jack Wilson, surfaces in Los Angeles.
1939-1942	Six additional torso murders occur in Pennsylvania similar to the Cleveland Torso murders. In a torso murder that

occurred in New Castle sometime between September and October, 1939, the killer used a saw to separate the victim's head from his torso. Detective Peter Merylo is convinced that the Mad Butcher of Kingsbury Run is back at work by late 1939. The victim's palms had been burned either before or after the killing. Some lawmen theorized that if the burning occurred before the murder, then the killer, by 1939, was torturing his victims. By 1939, was the Mad Butcher of Kingsbury Run changing his method and manner of killing?

1942 — Jack Anderson Wilson reappears in Los Angeles.

Mid 1942 — Los Angeles detectives tentatively identify the author of the December 23, 1938, letter to Cleveland Chief of Police Matowitz. Detective Merylo dismisses the identified letter as that of a "raving crank."

1943?-April, 1946 — Elizabeth Short is not in California (Note 50, p. 95).

March 22, 1943 — Jack Anderson Wilson is arrested in Los Angeles for suspected violation of the Selective Service.

August 5, 1943 — Jack Anderson Wilson turns 24 years old while in Indianapolis, Indiana. "He is bumbling around the city until a young female, a WAC, is murdered in a

	downtown hotel. He then immediately leaves Indianapolis and ends up in Los Angeles" (Note 47, p. 200). Indianapolis is located approximately 185 miles from Chicago. Wilson is known to have been in Indianapolis on August 5, 1943.
1944	Jack Anderson Wilson is in the Army for a short time (Jan. 12, 1944-March 15, 1945).
	Pilot Joseph Gordan Fickling meets Elizabeth Short in Southern California.
October 12, 1944	Georgette Bauerdorf is found murdered lying face down in her bathtub in her apartment on Fountain Avenue in West Hollywood. She had been raped as she lay dying. A tall man with a limp dressed like a soldier was seen near her abandoned car shortly after the murder.
November 12, 1944	Elizabeth Short is in Tucson, Arizona.
1945-1946	Elizabeth Short travels by train from Los Angeles to Chicago. She may have taken an interest in the Chicago murder of Suzanne Degnan.
At times during 1945-1946	Elizabeth Short is in Chicago. She meets Pilot Joseph Gordan Fickling, and she meets with a doctor in Hammond, Indiana.
During 1945	Elizabeth Short visits relatives in Medford, Massachusetts. While in Medford, Elizabeth "made collect calls from a pay phone attempting to secure employment—modeling in

	Miami through Duffy (Duffy Sawyer) or perhaps in Chicago—maybe in Indianapolis" (Note 47, p. 53).
January-June, 1945	Several other women are reported murdered in Chicago, the former home of Elliot Ness. The women are pathologically cleaned by their killer, postmortem.
January 14, 1945	Eunice Rawlings disappears from her Roscoe Street apartment in Chicago. (Rawlings' apartment is located near the Ross and Brown apartments.)
January 17, 1945	A purse containing Eunice Rawlings' name is found on a Lake Michigan beach in Chicago.
June 5, 1945	Josephine Ross is murdered in Chicago. Her killer wraps her head in her dress. A passenger train known as the Red Line runs within one block of her apartment. She is murdered exactly ten years after the "Tattooed Man" was found murdered in Cleveland.
September 2, 1945	Elizabeth Short is in Medford, Mass.
December 10, 1945	Frances Brown is murdered in Chicago. Her killer wraps her head in her pajamas. A large knife is found lodged in her neck by detectives.
January 7, 1946	Six-year-old Suzanne Degnan is murdered and dismembered in Chicago not far from railroad tracks and near Lake Michigan. Her body parts are discarded by her killer in the Chicago

	sewers. (Several body parts of the victims of the Mad Butcher of Kingsbury Run were discarded in Cleveland's sewer system near Lake Erie.) Her killer leaves a ransom note demanding $20,000, soaked in oil.
February-April, 1946	Elizabeth Short is in Medford, Massachusetts.
May-June, 1946	Elizabeth Short is in Hammond, IN.
June 24-July 12, 1946	Elizabeth Short is in Chicago (Los Angeles D.A.'s files).
June 26, 1946	Seventeen-year-old William Heirens is arrested in Chicago and later charged with the murders of Josephine Ross, Frances Brown and Suzanne Degnan.
July, 1946	A Chicago newspaper reports that Heirens confessed to the murders of Ross, Brown and Degnan.
August 12, 1946	The headless, armless torso of Eunice Rawlings washes up on a Chicago beach. Her death is ruled a suicide.
September 5, 1946	William Heirens is handed three consecutive life sentences for the Chicago murders.
December, 1946	At Elvera French's apartment in San Diego, Elizabeth Short wrote a letter to Gordan Fickling: "I think I'm going to be coming back to Chicago to do some work (modeling job with "Jack") . . . I am sorry that you feel as you do, and I hope that you can find a nice young lady to kiss every New Year's Eve. I

believe it would have been wonderful if we belonged to each other now. I do want you to know that I'll never forget coming West to see you. Even though it has not worked out that you did take me in your arms and keep me there. Honey, it was nice as long as it lasted . . ." (Note 47, p. 109). (Compare to Appleton letter on pages 47-48)

January 14, 1947 Almost exactly one year after the murder/dismemberment of Suzanne Degnan, E1izabeth Short is tortured, killed and severed in Los Angeles. Her killer drains the blood from her body. X's are carved into her upper pubic region. Part of the female organs have been cut out of her body and her mouth has been cut into a grotesque smile.

January 25, 1947 The Black Dahlia Avenger sends a package containing belongings of Elizabeth Short. The package is drenched in gasoline.

January 27, 1947 "Had my fun with police" postcard is mailed by the Black Dahlia Avenger to the *Los Angeles Examiner* by the Black Dahlia Avenger.

January 27, 1947 Letter received by the Los Angeles District Attorney's Office, "Sorry Greenwich Village, not Cotton Club."

January 29, 1947 Three additional notes from the Black Dahlia Avenger are received by Los Angeles police and newspapers:

"Dahlia's killer cracking," "I will give up,'" and "We're going to Mexico."

He also wrote on a postcard: "If he confesses you won't need me." (Was he referring to William Heirens or to Daniel Vorhees, who may have confessed to the murder of the Black Dahlia?)

January 30, 1947 The Black Dahlia Avenger sends a note addressed to Captain Jack Donahoe: "Dahlia killing justified."

January 31, 1947 Six additional messages, possibly mailed by the Black Dahlia Avenger, are published by the *Los Angeles Herald-Express*: "Here is the photo of the werewolf" killer's I saw him kill her a friend." (Note the possessive-pasted word "killer's" possibly indicating that the photo of the werewolf killer was intended to be a reference to the writer's). Was the Black Dahlia Avenger alluding to William Heirens who had been called a "werewolf" in the Chicago newspaper six months earlier?

February 3, 1947 Sylvia Horan is raped on Stocker Street between La Brea and Crenshaw Avenue in Los Angeles eight blocks from where Elizabeth Short was murdered January 14, 1947.

February 10, 1947 Jeanne French (Red Lipstick Murder) is killed in Los Angeles.

February 10, 1947	Following the murder of Jeanne French the *Los Angeles Herald-Express* publishes a special edition headline: "WEREWOLF STRIKES AGAIN KILLS L.A. WOMAN WRITES 'B.D.' ON HER BODY."
February 12, 1947	Ica Mabel M'Grew is kidnapped and raped in Los Angeles. Possibly connected to the Black Dahlia murder.
1947 after the murder of Black Dahlia	In Los Angeles, following the murder of the Black Dahlia, there are six additional murders that detectives feel might be related. Gordan Fickling told Charlotte, North Carolina, detectives he had received a final letter from Elizabeth Short dated January 8, 1947, in which she told him not to write anymore at her address in San Diego because her plan was to relocate to Chicago (Note 48 p. 140).
March 11, 1947	Evelyn Winters is murdered in Los Angeles and her body is dumped near railroad tracks. Before the killer left the scene he wrapped the victim's dress around her neck (Note 48, p. 403). The victim's shoes and undergarments were found at commercial and Center Streets, one block from where the body was located. The Black Dahlia Avenger is a suspect.
May 12, 1947	Laura Elizabeth Trelstad is strangled in Los Angeles with a piece of flowered

	cloth believed to be torn from a man's pair of pajamas or shorts. The Black Dahlia Avenger is a suspect.
July 8, 1947	Rosenda Josephine Mondragon is strangled to death in Los Angeles. Her right breast is slashed. The Black Dahlia Avenger is a suspect.
July 16, 1947	Marian Davidson Newton is strangled to death in San Diego with a thin wire or cord. Two men's handkerchiefs are found near her body. The Black Dahlia Avenger is a suspect.
February 14, 1948	Viola Norton is abducted by two men in Los Angeles and beaten on the head and face with a tire iron. The Black Dahlia Avenger is a suspect.
May 9, 1948	Jack Anderson Wilson is arrested in Los Angeles for vagrancy, lewd behavior.
July 26, 1948	Jack Anderson Wilson is arrested in Los Angeles and charged with battery.
June 13, 1949	Louise Margaret Springer worked two blocks from where the Black Dahlia's body was found on January 15, 1947. Her killer strikes her in the head and strangles her to death with a white sash cord. He then inserts a 14-inch finger-thick length of tree branch into her vagina. The Black Dahlia Avenger is a suspect.
May 23, 1950	Jack Anderson Wilson is arrested in Los Angeles for being drunk.
June 3, 1950	Jack Anderson Wilson is arrested in Los Angeles for being drunk.

June 12, 1950	Jack Anderson Wilson is arrested in Los Angeles and charged with burglary and suspicion of burglary.
June 12, 1950	Robert Robertson disappears from the Wayfarer's Lodge in Cleveland.
July 22, 1950	Robertson's dismembered torso is found behind a factory on East Twenty-Second Street in Cleveland. Police discovered with the body pages 457 and 458 of the Cleveland phone directory which contained listings for the letter "k" (Note 49, p. 191). Cuyahoga County Coroner Dr. Gerber estimates that June 12, 1950, was the date of death. Detective Merylo was convinced that this was the work of the Mad Butcher of Kingsbury Run. In 1947, the Black Dahlia Avenger signed one of his notes "2 k's." If he was in Los Angeles on June 12, 1950, then Jack Anderson Wilson is probably not Robert Robertson's killer.
August 21, 1950	Jack Anderson Wilson is charged with suspicion of armed robbery in Los Angeles.
February 21, 1951	Jack Anderson Wilson is charged with grand theft in Los Angeles.
May 2, 1951	Jack Anderson Wilson is charged with Susp. 487.3 PC (grand theft) in Los Angeles.
July 4, 1957	Jack Anderson Wilson is charged with intoxication in Los Angeles.

1958	Jack Anderson Wilson, while incarcerated in Oakland City Prison, tells an inmate a story about a "queer's head" he'd seen in a glass box in Cleveland. The head was that of the "Tattooed Man." A casting of his head was displayed at the Great Lakes Exposition in Cleveland in 1936.
November 27, 1963	Karyn Kupcinet, daughter of *Chicago Sun Times* columnist Irv Kupcinet, is murdered in Hollywood. Inspectors at the sheriff's department think her murder might be connected to the deaths of the Black Dahlia and Georgette Bauerdorf (Note 50, p. 172).
February 4, 1982	Jack Anderson Wilson dies in a fire at the Holland Hotel in Los Angeles before Detective John St. John has the opportunity to question him.
1991-1992	Cleveland Police Chief Edward Kovacic receives an official request from the Los Angeles authorities to look into a possible connection between the Cleveland Torso Murders and the murder-dismemberment of the Black Dahlia in 1947. Kovacic hands the assignment to Sergeant John Fransen, who quickly disposes of the notion that the same individual could be responsible for the murders in both cities . . ." (Note 46, p. 215).

COMPARISON OF QUOTES FROM EXPERTS

Cleveland Torso Killer

Cuyahoga County Coroner Dr. Samuel R. Gerber suggested that the Mad Butcher of Kingsbury Run could be, among other things, a "prosector butcher" (page 79, *Butcher's Dozen*). Gerber added, "He may have been a doctor or medical student sometime in the past, a butcher, osteopath, chiropractor, orderly, nurse or hunter in order to accomplish the dissection with such perfect finesse." "He is a pervert who sometimes drugs his victims and may lead a normal life when not absorbed with his sadistic passion" (page 168, *In the Wake of the Butcher*).

Detective Merylo was convinced the Butcher was a sexual pervert (page 74, *Butcher's Dozen*).

Cuyahoga County Coroner Arthur J. Pearce: "The killer would have to possess the skill and anatomical knowledge of a surgeon to sever the head from the body so cleanly" (page 71, *In the Wake of the Butcher*).

Cleveland Director of Public Safety Elliot Ness: "The Torso Murderer was a big man with the strength of an ox."

Pathologist Straus: "The killer is apparently a sex maniac of the sadistic type. This is indicated by the condition of his victims. He is probably a muscular man. The slayer definitely has expert knowledge of human anatomy. The incisions of his knife are clean and were made without guesswork. He may have gathered his knowledge as a medical student. Or it is possible that he is a butcher" (page 79, *In the Wake of the Butcher*).

Sergeant James Hogan: "The Butcher had cut the skin around the arms and legs and wrenched them from the socket" (pages 57-58, *In the Wake of the Butcher*).

On July 6, 1937, Dr. Hurbert S. Reichle, head of pathology at City Hospital: After carefully examining the grisly pieces, Reichle declared that, "his department never dissected a body in such a manner but whoever had made the incision in the lower trunk clearly knew something about anatomy" (page 119, *In the Wake of the Butcher*).

In December, 1938, Dr. P. R. Heimbold, a coroner's physician in Pittsburgh: The bodies had been cut "by an expert who has some knowledge of anatomy or was a butcher" (page 153, *In the Wake of the Butcher*).

Suzanne Degnan Murder

Dr. Jerome J. Kearns, the coroner's physician: "The killer had to be an expert in cutting meats because the body was separated at the joints. Not even the average doctor could be so skillful. It had to be a meat cutter" (page 49, *William Heirens: His Day In Court*); "a person with a knowledge of anatomy," "motivated by a powerful sex drive" (January 12, 1946, *Chicago Sun*).

Dr. William D. McNally, toxicologist: reported to Coroner Brodie that a sharp knife had been used to dissect Suzanne and that the expertise could only have come from a butcher or a hunter accustomed to the dissection of animals" (page 49, *William Heirens: His Day In Court*).

Chicago Chief of Police Walter G. Storms: "The girl's murderer was either a physician, a medical student, a very good butcher, an embalmer or perhaps a livestock handler" (page 49,*William Heirens: His Day In Court)*.

Coroner Brodie: "It was a very clean job with absolutely no signs of hacking as would be evident if a dull tool was used. The bones were intact, carefully wrenched from their sockets (page 49, *William Heirens: His Day In Court*).

The seventy-four pound child may have been carried down a ladder. Police theorized that it may have been the work of two men. Could it have been the work of one very strong, tall man?

Black Dahlia Murder

Detective John St. Johns: "The perpetrator may have had some knowledge of anatomy but he wasn't necessarily in the medical profession" (page 133, *Severed*).

Lieutenant Jess Haskins: "They [the detectives] speculated that the killer was someone who had medical knowledge or who was familiar with anatomy, possibly a mortician" (page 71, *Childhood Shadows*).

Los Angeles Detective Finnis Brown: "Of course it's a sex crime and we're looking for a pervert" (page 121, *Severed*).

If Jack Anderson Wilson was in fact the person who killed the Black Dahlia and also was the Cleveland Torso Killer, then the remarks made by the experts could be combined and compared to the experts' reports in the Suzanne Degnan case. Comparing the reports would then provide the following conclusions concerning the killer:

- **a.** He was very strong.
- **b.** He was a sexual pervert.
- **c.** He was possibly a butcher or meat cutter.
- **d.** He had knowledge of anatomy.

e. He used a large sharp knife.
f. He wrenched the bones from the sockets.

Now compare these clues to additional similar facts identified between the Cleveland Torso murders, Black Dahlia murder and the murder of Suzanne Degnan. In each set of cases the killer:

1. Dismembered a human body during a time period when the known killer was still active at his trade. Suzanne Degnan was dismembered January 7, 1946, and the Black Dahlia was severed on January 14, 1947.
2. Removed the victim from one location, dismembered at a separate location and then discarded the body parts at a third location undetected.
3. Discarded body parts and other evidence in city storm sewers.
4. Killed in cold winter nights in the month of January.
5. Killed on June 5.
6. Used a tub and water in the dismembering process.
7. Dismembered the body in an area that had coal in it.
8. Mopped the floor after the dismemberment.
9. Wrapped a torso in a sugar sack or may have left a sugar sack at the scene of the crime.
10. May have used a balled-up handkerchief to gag his victim.
11. Left a striped pillow cloth or striped pillowcase at the scene of a murder.
12. Left a ransom note following a murder demanding $20,000.
13. Wrote a note in large letters followed by small letters.
14. Wrote a note in red lipstick.
15. Burned evidence following a murder.
16. Soaked evidence in either gasoline or oil.

17. May have turned out or broken a yard light before entering the dwelling to commit the crime.
18. May have had some musical background.
19. Killed near railroad tracks in a large city.
20. Killed near Lake Michigan or Lake Erie where sewers from the city flow towards the big lake.
21. Wrote letters to newspapers or telephoned someone associated with the crime following a murder.
22. May have sexually assaulted the victim, possibly postmortem.
23. Wrapped an article of clothing around the victim's neck.
24. Wrapped a silk stocking around the victim's neck.
25. May have used a thin wire as a ligature.

The clues and evidence seem to indicate that Jack Wilson might have been at Suzanne Degnan's bedside in the early morning of January 7, 1946 and not 17-year-old William Heirens as the press, police and public hastily concluded in their rush to judgment.

WILLIAM HEIRENS' MURDER CONFESSION: SUZANNE DEGNAN

Mr. Crowley

Q: What is your name?
A: William George Heirens.
Q: Where do you live?
A: 4175 Tuohy Avenue.
Q: How old are you?
A: Seventeen.
Q: With whom do you live?
A: I live with my mother and father and brother.
Q: Where do you go to school?
A: University of Chicago.
Q: Now calling your attention to Jan. 7, 1946, early Monday morning, did you on that date kidnap and murder Suzanne Degnan?
A: Yes, sir.
Q: What did you do with the body?
A: The body was—part of that is not clear to my memory, but as things stand I have the knowledge it was deposited in different sewers in the neighborhood.
Q: Did you cut it up before you put it in the different sewers?
A: To my knowledge, yes, it was cut up when it was put in the sewers.
Q: What kind of an instrument did you use to cut it with?

A: A knife was used.
Q: What did you do with the knife?
A: It was deposited on an elevated station—not an elevated station, but the elevated tracks.
Q: Where?
A: North of Glenlake.
Q: North of Glenlake?
A: Yes.
Q: How far away from Thorndale is Glenlake?
A: A block.
Q: And is it the block north?
A: Yes, sir.
Q: Did you deposit it in a particular place or just throw it?
A: I threw it.
Q: Where were you when you threw the knife away?
A: Down on the bottom of the siding of the "L."
Q: Where were you going?
A: I was going north.
Q: Walking?
A: Yes, sir.
Q: Where did you finally arrive at walking north after throwing the knife away?
A: At the Granville "L" Station.
Q: Then where did you go?
A: Back to school.
Q: How?
A: Back on the Jackson Park Express.
Q: Did you board the train at Granville?
A: Granville "L" Station.
Q: What time did you get back at school?
A: Six o'clock.
Q: In the morning?

A: Yes.
Q: Where did you go when you got back there?
A: I went back to my room.
Q: At that time did you have a roommate?
A: No, sir.
Q: You were living alone at that time?
A: Yes, sir.
Q: What particular location at the university did you live in January of 1946?
A: Snell Hall, it is practically on the corner of 57th and Ellis.
Q: What was your room number?
A: 51.
Q: Did you go to bed?
A: No, I stayed up and studied.
Q: On your ride from the north side to the university did you meet anyone that you knew?
A: No.
Q: Were there other passengers on the elevated train at the time?
A: Very few.
Q: You didn't recognize any of them as persons you knew?
A: No.
Q: How long after you disposed of the last part of the body was it before you threw the knife away?
A: Oh, I would say an hour and a half.
Q: What did you do for an hour and a half after you disposed of the last part of the body?
A: Well, to my knowledge—well, what I know myself from what I remember myself, the last part of the body was disposed of—I don't know, I think they were the arms, they were disposed of near Broadway, on the other side, on the west side of the "L" Station?

Q: After the cover fell on your finger, when you disposed of the arms, did you then go immediately to the Glenlake "L" Station?
A: No.
Q: What "L" Station?
A: Then I went—I am not sure of this, but I am quite sure I went directly back to the basement, because to my recollection I was in the basement.
Q: What basement did you go back to?
A: To the one where the cutting up was supposed to have taken place.
Q: And do you know where that is located?
A: No.
Q: It is a basement in an apartment building on Winthrop Avenue, is it?
A: Yes.
Q: And would it be in the 5900 block?
A: It is south of the Degnan home.
Q: Just south of the Degnan home?
A: Yes.
Q: But on the block west of the Degnan home?
A: It would be in the 5800 block.
Q: When you got back to the basement, what did you do?
A: When I got back to the basement I seen there was blood in the tub there. I had some inkling of what happened, I realized—I didn't know the exact facts what happened until later I read about it, and it was made known to me that way, but I knew of it, then I realized something terrible happened. I washed up what was there and cleaned it up, and then it dawned on me something must of happened to the child. The last thing I remember I was with the child, and after a while—after I disposed of the bag—I was holding it I

remember like that, and while I was there the thing was on the edge and it dropped down, and it caught my finger and it woke me up to the fact.

Q: That is when you were putting the arms in the sewer?

A: Yes.

Q: You knew you were putting the arms in the sewer?

A: No, I didn't know what they were.

Q: Were the arms in the bag?

A: Whatever it was was in the bag.

Q: You had made other trips to other sewers before that and put parts of the body in other sewers?

A: That is what I don't know, whether I did or not, but from what I put together, that is what happened. To my knowledge I do not know anything previous to where I dropped that thing on my finger.

Q: You remember writing the ransom note?

A: That was after.

Q: When did you write that note?

A: In the basement.

Q: Was that after you disposed of the body?

A: Yes.

Q: Which basement did you write the ransom note in?

A: The basement where the blood was.

Q: Where the body was cut up?

A: Yes, sir.

Q: Well, now, tell us how you happened to write that ransom note?

A: It came into my head that I had done something as I told you before, and I realized it must have been the child, and I didn't address the note because I didn't know the name of the people, so to relieve the parents in all ways possible I could would be to give them some hope the child was alive and that was the manner in which I wrote it.

Q: In what particular part of the basement were you when you wrote the ransom note?

A: I was in the rear part.

Q: When you wrote it were you standing or sitting?

A: Standing.

Q: Did you have the paper placed against anything?

A: Yes, sir.

Q: Against what?

A: A broken locker door.

Q: Did you have more than one sheet of paper?

A: No.

Q: Was that a full sheet of paper you had at the time you wrote the ransom note?

A: Yes.

Q: Did you tear it at any time?

A: No, I had torn it before I wrote the ransom note.

Q: Where were you when you tore it?

A: Down there.

Q: What did you do with the part of the paper you tore off?

A: I think I either left it there or put it back in my pocket, but it was in my pocket for such a long time that the torn part of it got dirty and I used the clean part, and I tore the dirty part off.

Q: Had you been carrying that sheet of paper around in your pocket?

A: Yes.

Q: Was it folded before you did any writing on it?

A: Yes.

Q: Did you write with a pencil?

A: Yes.

Q: Did you hold the paper up to the wall and write—
A: Yes.
Q: —or standing up? This locker you referred to as a broken locker, do you know whose locker that was?
A: No.
Q: Do you know, of course, how it happened to be broken, don't you?
A: No.
Q: Didn't you break into that locker?
A: No, not to my knowledge, I did not, no.
Q: Not to your knowledge?
A: No.
Q: Didn't you take some rags and some bags out of that locker?
A: No.
Q: Didn't you take some bags out of the locker and place parts of Suzanne's body in the bags?
A: No. Mr. Crowley, I would like you to understand something. I am not repeating or I mean repeating some of the things I had knowledge of from the papers. I shall not repeat anything, just from my own, what I know myself to be actual facts. It will not be anything I read in the papers. The actual thing, I do not know if I broke the lock myself or took a bag out.
Q: Let us go back then. How did you happen to pick out this particular house in which Suzanne Degnan lived as a place to commit a crime?
A: Because of the low windows.
Q: How did you happen to observe those low windows?
A: From passing by.
Q: When was it that you passed by there that you first noticed the low windows?
A: About 2:45 that morning, January 7.

Q: 2:45 A.M.?
A: About that time, yes.
Q: Had you ever noticed that place prior to that?
A: No.
Q: Had you ever been in that vicinity before?
A: Yes.
Q: When was the time prior to January 7, that you had been in that same vicinity?
A: Well, to my knowledge I believed it was, I do not know the name or the time or the person, to my knowledge I believe it was an apartment, or a big apartment building nearby.
Q: You were in an apartment of a man named Gold?
A: Yes.
Q: That apartment building is just north of the Degnan home?
A: Yes.
Q: Did you observe the Degnan home at that time?
A: No.
Q: At 2:45 a.m. January 7, when you observed the low window, what were you doing?
A: Well, I had, shall I start at the beginning? Do you want it in chronological order from the time I left?
Q: Tell it in your own words.
A: I left school. We were drinking. I had about six shots. I had gone to my room. I had taken off my coat, prepared for bed. Then it just came on me to go out, and I went out. I had no intention of doing, I intended to go to the "L" station and get on the "L." I got there all right and I fell asleep until Lawrence Avenue, where I woke up, and after getting my bearings I got off at Thorndale. I walked east until Glenlake. I turned east again. From there I went to the alley, Kenmore and Sheridan alley on Glenlake, and I turned south, and on the right-hand side.

Q: You turned south into an alley?

A: Yes. In the right-hand side, in the back yard, rather, behind a building, I think it was. I do not know how many feet, I say it was about fifty feet off the street in, and there was a ladder lying in the back yard, which I could see over the fence, so I took it. Then I went further down into that big apartment building.

Q: Carrying the ladder with you?

A: Yes.

Q: Where were you going then?

A: I intended to burglarize at the time.

Q: Do you know where particularly you were going?

A: No, there was a large apartment building there, and I entered there and I went, it was on the north side of the large apartment building. I entered there and I tried one of the windows on the first floor, near the front of the building. I could not reach it with a ladder because of my condition at the time, so I gave up that.

Q: Where was that apartment building?

A: It is a big one. I believe it is the Gold Apartment, yes, it would be the Gold Apartment.

Q: In the same building where the Gold Apartment is?

A: Yes.

Q: Go ahead?

A: I took the ladder back, because I could not get in that way. Then I walked for a lower window, when I see the Degnan home. I went to the window that was least lighted. There was a light in the back near the door.

Q: Did you do anything to that light?

A: No, then I went east, north, I went west then, and after I turned that corner going in sort of "Z" corner, I went in and looked for the window that was least lighted, I found it and I entered.

Q: Did you use the ladder?
A: Yes.
Q: Before you entered that room did you do anything to the electric light that was lighted outside?
A: No.
Q: Did you hit the bulb with your hand in order to break it?
A: No.
Q: You went into the room with the electric light on?
A: Yes.
Q: Was it pretty well lit up back there?
A: Yes.
Q: When you entered the window of the Degnan home for what purpose did you enter?
A: Burglary.
Q: By that you mean to steal what you could?
A: Just burglary, that is, went in to steal what I could, just burglary.
Q: When you got in there you intended to take something that did not belong to you?
A: Yes, I guess that would be it, but notice I did not intend to take anything special.
Q: When you got inside the window what next happened?
A: I noticed somebody sleeping on the right-hand side in the bed. Then I went toward the door and as dizzy as I was, I may have awakened whoever it was by brushing against the bed, or something of that sort, but anyway, whoever was there, before I had reached the door to open it, got up in bed, sat up. It started talking. That is where I got her, I took the person, I did not know it was a child at this time, and did not know until I read it in the paper it was a child. Then I knew it must have been a female because of the long hair, which I seen by the flashlight.

Q: Did you have a flashlight with you?
A: Yes, I had a flashlight with me all the time.
Q: Did you put the flashlight on the person in the bed?
A: Well, yes, I put it on, not directly, but I must have shone it in that direction.
Q: Then you could have seen it was a girl, couldn't you?
A: A female, yes, the long hair. My vision was not too good.
Q: Then what did you do?
A: Then I strangled her.
Q: When you say you strangled her, how did you strangle her?
A: With my fingers.
Q: Around her neck?
A: Yes.
Q: Had the child said something to you before you did that?
A: No. She made some utterances. I do not know what they were, too inarticulate to make out.
Q: How long did you keep your hands on her neck, would you say?
A: About two minutes.
Q: You squeezed as hard as you could?
A: Until everything went limp.
Q: As soon as the body of the child went limp you released your grip on her throat, is that right?
A: Yes.
Q: Then what did you do?
A: Then I got back, so I picked up the body and carried it down. Going down the ladder I believe I stepped my right leg over the first onto the lower rung and I carried her down to the lower. From that position I would be carrying the child in my arms in front.
Q: At the time you got to the ground what did you do with the child?

A: Proceeded to the alley and turned north, and from there on I do not know what happened. I got to the apartment building.

Mr. Tuohy

Q: What alley did you proceed to?
A: The alley that I came down when I came down with the ladder.
Q: Between Sheridan and Kenmore?
A: Yes.
Q: And you proceeded north?
A: Yes, after I got past the apartment building I do not know what took place after that. I do not know how, what grounds from or just how everything happened.

Mr. Crowley

Q: You finally took the child into a basement of an apartment building on Winthrop Avenue, didn't you?
A: Not to my knowledge, no. I don't know.
Q: The basement where you wrote the ransom note and cleaned up the blood in the sink, you know where that basement is located?
A: I do not know the number, but I know it is south of the Degnan home.
Q: You remember being there that night?
A: Yes, I was there that night?
Q: Now –
A: That morning, rather.
Q: Yes, that morning, don't you remember cutting up the body?
A: No.

Q: Where did you get that knife?

A: Well, from any number of various places, any burglary that may have been committed by me. I do not know what place it is taken from.

Q: You mean that you had taken that knife in a burglary?

A: Yes.

Q: Do you remember where?

A: No.

Q: Did you take it with you when you left the University of Chicago that night?

A: Yes, it was, it would be in my regular coat pocket.

Q: Why did you carry the knife that night?

A: Well, a matter of prying windows open or anything of the sort.

Q: Then you had the knife with you when you entered the Degnan home?

A: Yes, sir.

Q: And you had it with you when you carried the girl out of the Degnan home?

A: I must have.

Q: And you had it with you when you were in the basement after you disposed of the arms and the body?

A: Yes, sir.

Q: Did you wash the knife off then?

A: It was laying across a basin there and as I washed the tubs I must have washed the knife also.

Q: At that time you knew you had used that knife in cutting up the body, did you?

A: I didn't know what I had cut up.

Q: You knew that you had cut something up, didn't you?

A: I didn't know I was doing cutting up as far as that is concerned, but there was blood in the wash tub and at that time

my mind was quite clear—not too clear, but clear enough to realize it must have been used for some purpose of that sort.
Q: So you washed it off?
A: Yes.
Q: And you threw it away?
A: Yes.
Q: Why did you throw it away?
A: On previous times when I realized what happened, like a burglary, I had the habit of throwing things away. Quite a few times I had thrown weapons away when I knew what I was doing.
Q: Well, do you know how many times you were in and out of that basement that night?
A: No, I don't.
Q: Do you know if you were in and out of there more than once?
A: No.
Q: Don't you know how you got into that basement?
A: No, I don't.
Q: Was the door open?
A: When I came back from what I remember, the door was open.
Q: Was the light lit?
A: No, there was no light.
Q: Didn't you have a light at any time in that basement?
A: I had a flashlight.
Q: Do you remember at the time you wrote the ransom note whether the light was lit?
A: Yes, I had the flashlight.
Q: You mean you wrote by using a flashlight for your light at the time?
A: Yes, sir

Q: Well, do you know whether or not when you first entered that basement with the girl's body, whether or not the door was open?
A: No, I don't know.
Q: Do you know whether or not you had to go through any window first and open the door?
A: No, I don't.
Q: Was the girl dead at the time you entered the basement with her body?
A: Presumably, yes. I strangled her in her room.
Q: Well, at the time you carried her out of the room did you believe she was dead then?
A: Yes, I believed it.
Q: Why did you take her out of the room if you believed she was dead at the time?
A: I don't know. In fact, I didn't have the realization of it until going down the stairs. And after that I had the realization. When I got to the alley was the first time I had the realization of it.
Q: Did you use an automobile any time that night?
A: No, not that I know of.
Q: Did you use a wire at any time that night around her neck?
A: I might have because of the fact I carry wire in my pocket of the type they found.
Q: Don't you remember that you did?
A: No.
Q: After you got the girl out of the house and started to go north in the alley between Kenmore and Sheridan Road, don't you remember stopping at any time on the journey with that body?
A: No.
Q: Did you just carry the girl in your two arms?

A: Yes. I carried her until I got to this big apartment building, and I don't know how I carried her after that.
Q: Do you know where the big apartment building is located?
A: Yes.
Q: What is the address?
A: I don't know that.
Q: What Street is it on?
A: It is on Kenmore.
Q: How far from the Degnan home?
A: 150 feet about.
Q: Do you remember stopping at any apartment building on the block west of the Degnan home?
A: No.
Q: And about a block north of the Degnan home?
A: No.
Q: Do you know how you happened to reverse your direction and come back south to the place where the body was cut up?
A: No, I don't know.
Q: Do you remember cutting the girl's head off?
A: No.
Q: Do you remember cutting her torso, the body?
A: No.
Q: Do you remember cutting the arms?
A: No.
Q: Or the legs?
A: No.
Q: Don't you know you did that?
A: No, I didn't know.
Q: Do you know where the head was found?
A: I believe I have knowledge of the fact through what I have read, but personally I don't know where it was found.

Q: Doesn't that refresh your recollection as to where you put the head?
A: No.
Q: Don't you know you put the head in a sewer?
A: No.
Q: Do you know where the left leg was found?
A: No.
Q: Haven't you any idea where you put the left leg?
A: No.
Q: Do you know where the torso was found?
A: No.
Q: That is the part of the body above the waist and below the neck?
A: No.
Q: You don't remember where the buttocks and the right leg were found?
A: No.
Q: Do mean to tell us you can't recollect putting those parts of the body in the various sewers they were found in?
A: No. I don't know what sewers I put them in or anything of that sort.
Q: Do you know how long you were in the basement from the time that you first went there until you were through washing off the knife and washing up the tubs?
A: I think I was in the basement about half an hour washing up the tubs.
Q: That is when you were washing the tub it took you a half hour?
A: Yes.
Q: How long were you in there before you did that?
A: I don't know.
Q: Haven't you any idea?

A: I can't figure it out. I would say an hour.
Q: You would say an hour?
A: Yes.
Q: How do you figure that out?
A: I got back to school at six o'clock and it takes an hour for the trip, and it would put me there at five o'clock and—no, it would be less than an hour and a half because I went to a restaurant to get something to eat, and that took about a half hour. Then a half hour there.
Q: When did you go to the restaurant?
A: After five-thirty, before I boarded the "L" I went to Granville Avenue.
Q: Did you have the knife with you at that time?
A: No.
Q: Had you thrown the knife away before you went to the restaurant?
A: Yes.
Q: Where was that restaurant located?
A: On Granville Avenue.
Q: Do you know the name of it?
A: No.
Q: Were there people in the restaurant at the time you were there?
A: There was a policeman in there and a waitress.
Q: Was the policeman in uniform?
A: Yes.
Q: Did you know him?
A: No.
Q: Did you know this waitress?
A: No.
Q: Was she an elderly lady or a younger lady?
A: Middle-aged.

Q: Had you ever eaten there before?
A: Yes, sir.
Q: How long were you there this particular morning?
A: About half an hour.
Q: What did you eat?
A: Doughnuts and coffee.
Q: Did it take you half an hour to eat doughnuts and coffee?
A: Well, probably yes. It is just a fair judgment of mine how long it was.
Q: And when you left the restaurant where did you go?
A: I went to the Granville "L" Station.
Q: Do you remember how you lifted the sewer cover in which you put the arms?
A: No. But when the thing was up and I was holding it up like that, my fingers were under like that, they had those things in it that went around, and my fingers were through the end.
Q: Then do you remember you lifted it with your hands?
A: No, I got it up, and I was holding it up like that. That is how it fell down and caught my finger.
Q: What hand did you have on the sewer cover?
A: My right.
Q: And what hand got hurt when the sewer cover fell down?
A: My right.
Q: You mean to say your fingers were pinched between the sewer cover and the rim into which it fit?
A: No, it didn't get into the rim, it fell on the ground.
Q: You had taken the sewer cover completely off the hole?
A: Yes.
Q: After it fell down and hurt you fingers, did you put it back on the hole again?
A: Yes, sir.
Q: How were you dressed at the time?

A: I had a tan coat, it was a weather coat, sort of like a raincoat.
Q: Do you still have those clothes?
A: No. As I was coming down the alley, I burned the coat.
Q: In what alley?
A: Down the alley next to the "L" station.
Q: What "L" station?
A: That didn't take long at all, five minutes for that. I burned it. When the alley comes to Granville, it turns and goes up and comes down, it makes a Z-shape turn there, and right in the corner that is where I burned the coat.
Q: How far from where you threw the knife?
A: About a block, I believe, or a block and a half or two blocks.
Q: Is the coat the only thing you burned?
A: Whatever was in the pockets.
Q: Why did you burn the coat?
A: There was some blood on one of the wrists.
Q: Is that the only part that had blood on it?
A: Yes, sir.
Q: Is that the reason you burned it?
A: Yes, sir.
Q: Did you have a gun with you that night?
A: I believe so, yes.
Q: What gun did you have?
A: I think it was—I am quite sure it was the one I threw away on the Loyola tennis courts. I threw it away, I think sometime later.
Q: Sometime after that?
A: Yes.
Q: You didn't throw it away that night?
A: No, it was not in my coat, and it was not so big.
Q: Where did you carry it?
A: In my pocket.

Q: After you threw away your topcoat, did you have a suit coat on?
A: A sweater.
Q: And did you carry the gun in your pants pocket?
A: Yes, sir.
Q: In your back hip pocket? Or the side pocket?
A: Side pocket.
Q: Was it a large gun?
A: It was fairly large, yes.
Q: Do you know what caliber?
A: No, I would say about a .32.
Q: A .32 caliber?
A: Yes.
Q: Where had you gotten that?
A: I don't know where I got that.
Q: This wire that you referred to that you carried with you, did you always carry wire with you?
A: Yes, I had the wire already in my coat pocket.
Q: Do you know where you got that?
A: No, some burglary.
Q: What kind of wire was it?
A: It was picture wire.
Q: Picture wire, used to hang pictures, ordinary light silver-colored wire?
A: Yes, sir.
Q: Did you have any handkerchiefs with you that particular night?
A: No.
Q: None at all?
A: No, I had one big one.
Q: What kind of a handkerchief, white?

A: No, I think it was more on the order of a babushka because after I left the note there and took the ladder away, there was a man coming down the alley and I put the thing over my head, and tied it all the way down here, so it must have been a big handkerchief.
Q: Did you have your hat with you then?
A: No.
Q: Had you already burned your hat?
A: I never wear one.
Q: You didn't wear one that night?
A: I never wore a hat.
Q: Well, after you washed the tubs and washed the knife and wrote the ransom note, where did you go then when you left the basement?
A: Then I went directly to the home and put the note in and left.
Q: And did you carry the knife with you on that trip?
A: Yes, the knife was with me.
Q: What did you do with the ransom note?
A: Then I pushed it in the window.
Q: Did you climb the ladder to do that?
A: About one rung.
Q: Was the ladder still in the same position it was when you took the girl out of the window?
A: Yes.
Q: Did you do anything with the ladder after you put the ransom note in the room?
A: I took it out to the alleyway.
Q: You took it out to the alleyway?
A: Yes.
Q: You mean the alley just east of the house?
A: Yes.

Q: That is the alley between Kenmore and Sheridan Road?
A: Yes, sir.
Q: Where did you place it?
A: I seen this man coming out of the alley, directly forward—I heard him first and he didn't come into view in the alley, and I dropped the ladder and I put the thing over my head, and I proceeded towards the south cutting across the lawn, but I would say I kept about 150 feet in front of him all the time.
Q: You went south?
A: South, cutting across the lawn of the Degnan home, and went to Kenmore and went north on Kenmore until I got to Glenlake, and he was still behind me, and he turned in a building on the end corner there, and I proceeded to the alley—beside the elevated and disposed of the knife and sheath and went to the alleyway and disposed of my coat and turned the corner and got something to eat.

Mr. Crowley

Q: Where was the man when you first noticed him?
A: When I noticed him he was approaching the street lamp.
Q: From what direction?
A: He was coming north.
Q: Coming north in the alley?
A: Yes, sir.

Mr. Tuohy

Q: Coming north or coming from the north?

The Witness

A: He was coming north-he was coming north-he was coming from the south side of Thorndale in the alley, the same alley that runs straight through.

Mr. Crowley

Q: And then you say he followed you west on Thorndale?
A: West on Thorndale until Kenmore and then I turned north keeping on the west hand side of the street, and he stayed on the east side until he got to the corner of Glenlake on the east side, and he went in there and I proceeded west.
Q: Was he a short or tall man?
A: I would say between tall and medium.
Q: Did you just continue walking?
A: I waited for a while.
Q: Where did you wait?
A: To see where he was going.
Q: Where were you when you waited?
A: I went into a doorway there. I started to go west.
Q: Started to go west on what street?
A: Glenlake.
Q: Did you have your gun with?
A: Yes.
Q: Did you take it out?
A: No, I didn't take it out, I had it in my pocket, and there was no need to take it out.
Q: Did you believe the man was following you?
A: Well, the way he—yes, I believed he was following me.
Q: And did you have any idea what you were going to do if he caught up with you?

A: I had no reason to know why he would catch up with me at first. I thought he was a robber.
Q: You thought he was a robber?
A: Yes, he followed me that distance.
Q: Now, in this restaurant did you have any conversation with the waitress?
A: I just asked for my order, that is all.
Q: She didn't ask you where you had been or what you were doing in the neighborhood or anything like that?
A: No.
Q: You didn't talk about anything else to her?
A: No. At the time she was having a conversation with the policeman.
Q: Well, when you got back to the University of Chicago, did you still have the wire?
A: No, that was in my coat. I burned it with the coat or I don't know what happened to it. Whatever was in my pockets was burned.
Q: So that if you didn't use the wire in putting it around the girl's neck, it could have been left in you coat pocket?
A: Yes.
Q: But you could also have used it in putting it around the girl's neck?
A: Yes, sir.
Q: And you could have thrown it away?
A: Yes.
Q: As a matter of fact, didn't you do that?
A: No, not that I know of.
Q: Well, on this journey that you say you don't remember, after taking the child, don't you recollect that you tried to get into a basement at the corner of Glenlake and Kenmore? Do you remember that?

A: No.

Mr. Tuohy

Q: Or the east side of Winthrop?

The Witness

A: No.
Q: The corner of Winthrop and Glenlake?
A: No, I have no recollection of that.

Mr. Cowley

Q: When you were in the Degnan home just before you choked this girl, do you know whether the door from her room leading into the apartment was open or closed?
A: Closed, because I went to open it up.
Q: You say it was closed?
A: Yes.
Q: You didn't close it yourself?
A: No.
Q: Did you know who lived in the apartment at that time?
A: No.
Q: Why were you carrying this particular piece of blank paper in your pocket that night?
A: It is a habit of mine going to school, to carry paper in my pocket, to take notes on short notice.
Q: You don't carry dirty white paper in your pocket for that purpose?
A: It gets dirty in my pocket.
Q: How long had you been carrying it?

A: About a week.
Q: Had you planned on using it as a kidnap ransom note at that time?
A: No.
Q: How did it get oil on it?
A: After I had gone and wrote the ransom note in the basement, then I noticed a can of oil on the floor, and I wanted to disguise anything that had been on it, and I squirted the oil on it.
Q: What kind of oil was that, do you know?
A: It was round can on the basement floor of the locker room where I was writing the note.
Q: How big a can?
A: About so high.
Q: Did you put that can on top of the paper?
A: I may have.
Q: Was that can full of oil?
A: No, just a little bit.
Q: Did you turn the oil can over on the paper and force the oil on the paper?
A: I turned it there and pushed it so the oil would squirt out.
Q: Did it have a long funnel on it?
A: No.
Q: Was it an open can at the top?
A: No, it had a regular oil feeding thing.
Q: What?
A: An oil feed, things that are on 3-in-1 Oil cans, but it was not a 3-in-1 Oil can.
Q: You mean it had a spout out of which the oil comes when you force it?
A: Yes.

Q: Did you put that can on the paper at any time and press it to wipe off some of the dirt and oil off the can onto the paper?
A: No, I was holding the thing up, and I noticed that after I had written the note already and I then squirted it on and I threw it away or burned it with my coat.
Q: The can?
A: Yes.
Q: How big was it?
A: A small one.
Q: A small one about an inch in diameter?
A: Yes.
Q: Was it round?
A: Yes.
Q: It was not a large can?
A: No.
Q: Why did you put the oil on?
A: To disguise anything that was on the paper.
Q: What did you expect to be on the paper?
A: My fingerprints for one thing.
Q: And what reason did you say you wrote that ransom note?
A: To get the parents away from the idea their child may have been killed.
Q: What good was that going to do?
A: Lessen the burden for them.
Q: The child was not going to return, you knew that?
A: Yes.
Q: How could you lessen their burden by writing a ransom note?
A: At the time they would get the idea that the child would be kidnapped, and anything might happen and prepare themselves for anything that would happen.

Q: Don't you remember putting a gag in the mouth of the girl?
A: No.
Q: When you were carrying the knife, how did you carry it, in a sheath?
A: Yes.
Q: You would recognize the knife again if you saw it, would you?
A: No.
Q: Does that appear to be the size and kind of knife you had and threw away (Mr. Crowley showing the witness a knife)?
A: It would be about the size, yes.
Q: And about that kind and type?
A: It does not look exactly like that. My memory was not so clear that night anyhow. It is about the size, yes.

Mr. Tuohy

Q: Is that the knife?

The Witness

A: I don't know for sure, Mr. Tuohy.

Mr. Crowley

Q: But in appearance this could be the knife?
A: Yes.
Q: It looks like the knife to you?
A: Yes, sir.
Q: I asked you a little while ago how you were dressed and you told us about your topcoat. What kind of trousers did you wear?

A: I think they were—I don't know what color, I suppose they were my brown trousers.
Q: What kind of a sweater did you have on?
A: Brown.
Q: Do you remember the color of your shoes?
A: I wear brown shoes.
Q: Was it a pull-over sweater?
A: Yes.
Q: A V-neck?
A: You have the sweater. I didn't get it cleaned before that.
Q: The police have the sweater you wore that might?
A: Yes.
Q: And it is a brown sweater?
A: Yes.
Q: Do you remember whether or not at any time you touched the private parts of Suzanne Degnan?
A: No.
Q: Did you attempt to get any sexual satisfaction from taking Suzanne Degnan out of that apartment?
A: No.
Q: Why did you disguise your handwriting or attempt to disguise your handwriting in the ransom note?
A: It was not an attempt to disguise it as much as the thing I was writing on. It was a rough board.
Q: Well, you tried to write some of the letters different, didn't you?
A: Yes.
Q: In other words, you didn't want to be caught, is that right?
A: That is right. I didn't want to be caught.
Q: Then you knew you did something wrong?
A: Naturally I knew I did something wrong.

Q: And you knew you had destroyed this girl's body, didn't you?
A: Well, I didn't know what happened to the girl's body, but the blood was there and it was evident to me what happened.
Q: When you wrote the ransom note so the people would get the idea the child was kidnapped and you would relieve their mind that was the reason you wrote the ransom note, certainly you knew the body was destroyed at the time, is that right?
A: That was evident, yes.
Q: And when you wrote the ransom note you didn't want to leave your normal handwriting there so you would be caught, did you?
A: It was my normal handwriting as far as most of the characteristics, but from what I was writing on, I think there was twice I tried to disguise it, and at the time the handwriting I didn't just—my head was not clear at the time, it was getting clearer, and I began to realize.
Q: How did you conceive of asking for $20,000?
A: It is a most logical amount. It could have been two or any amount for that matter.
Q: Why did you pick twenty?
A: It didn't matter to me, it could have a hundred for that matter.
Q: Why did you say, do not notify the F.B.I. or police?
A: That is usually done in ransom notes.
Q: How did you know that?
A: It is reasonable.
Q: Why did you ask that the money be delivered in five and tens?
A: Well, if it was a ransom note, asking for ransom, they don't want big bills, they want small bills. So, I put medium, five and tens.

Q: If the note was intended to simply placate the parents and help the parents in their grief, at the loss over their child, why were you so particular in writing the ransom note in that fashion?
A: Because I had to make it seem convincing.
Q: Your mind was very clear on how to draft a ransom note and make it convincing, was it?
A: At the time it was clear, yes.
Q: Your mind was very clear then, wasn't it?
A: No, it wasn't very clear then. I was hazy when I left my room.
Q: Did you remove any of the clothes off this girl while you were in the basement there?
A: I don't know.
Q: Did you take any of her clothes home with you?
A: No. I did not have anything of that sort.
Q: Sir?
A: I did not have anything of that sort. It may have been, it might have been in a pocket of my coat or something like that and burned.
Q: Did you attempt at any time that night to rent a room in the Fleetwood Hotel?
A: No.
Q: Are you sure of that?
A: Quite sure, yes.
Q: Are you sure you did not go to a hotel and attempt to register at the hotel and ask a lady there whether or not she had a room that she would rent?
A: No.
Q: This paper on which you wrote the ransom note, did you get that out of your room at the university?
A: No.

Q: Where did you get that from?
A: I got it from Harper's Library.
Q: From where?
A: From Harper's Library.
Q: Where is that located?
A: That is at, off 59th and Ellis, Ellis and University and 59th.
Q: Do you remember when you obtained that particular sheet?
A: It was about quite some time before the incident had happened and it was upstairs in the reference library with a lot of desks, and all long tables rather. It was a plain sheet there and it was near by me, and it was probably left there by some student who had taken notes previously.
Q: Did you just take one sheet?
A: Yes, that is all that was there.
Q: You carried it around with you how long?
A: About a week.
Q: Why did you take this odd piece of paper from a strange location and use that particular piece of paper in the ransom note?
A: That is a habit of mine, to take paper of that sort, when it is, well, when it is convenient, for me, that is all.
Q: At the time you took that piece of paper didn't you have in mind then writing a ransom note on it?
A: No.
Q: You are sure of that?
A: I am sure.
Q: In writing this ransom note, Mr. Tuohy will show it to you. The character "and." Mr. Tuohy: That is a picture of it.

Mr. Crowley

Q: It is made on that note, do you notice that?

A: Yes.
Q: Do you remember discussing with Mr. Tuohy the fact that you did not know how to make the character "&"?
A: That is right.
Q: You do know how to make that character, don't you?
A: Made an "S" but I did not know how to make that. I never made that character before in my life.
Q: Before you made that character on that ransom note?
A: Yes.
Q: That is a photostat. No, that is a photograph of the ransom note that was written, that is exactly how you wrote it, isn't it?
A: Yes.
Q: Can you see that?
A: Yes.
Q: That is how you made it, isn't it?
A: Yes.
Q: Where did you write these words on that are on the back?
A: While I wrote the other note.
Q: You mean you wrote that all at the same time?
A: Yes.
Q: With the same pencil?
A: No.
Q: You say no?
A: No.
Q: Did you use a different pencil?
A: Yes. This one here I wrote with a pencil, was on the floor in that locker room where the oil can was too, that one here.
Q: Why did you change pencils?
A: Disguise.
Q: What?
A: For disguise.

Q: How many pencils did you have with you that night?
A: One.
Q: When you wrote the face of the note did you immediately then write the other words on the back of the note?
A: No.
Q: How much time between the time you wrote the face of the note and the time you wrote the back of the note?
A: I read it over once and then I figured it was, that was all right. I wanted to add something and there was no room so I turned it over on the other side.
Q: Why didn't you use the same pencil?
A: I had already put it in my pocket.
Q: Why didn't you take it out of your pocket?
A: Because the other was more convenient. It was lying on the floor.
Q: It was more convenient to pick up a strange pencil off the floor than to take the one you had used out of your pocket?
A: It was more convenient and it was also that I wanted to disguise, too.
Q: How was that going to disguise it?
A: I do not know, two different leads I suppose.
Q: What?
A: Two different types of lead.
Q: Did you have that in mind at the time you wrote it?
A: I thought that would help.
Q: That was an extra precaution you took, is that right?
A: It was not extra. It was, say convenient precaution.
Q: You felt that would make it more confusing if they found it was written by two pencils?
A: I had the pencil in my back pocket and I had the coat over it and I could not get it out so well, and I could not get it out.

Q: Are you sure you wrote the ransom note in the basement?
A: Yes.
Q: Are you sure you are telling us the truth about the ransom note being written that way?
A: Yes.
Q: You did not add those words on that ransom note after you got into the room, did you?
A: No. It was a rough board that I wrote it. It would have left a mark on. Later I left a few marks, the line and the five, it was a rough board.
Q: You know you misspelled the word wait on the note, don't you?
A: Yes.
Q: That is the way you continued to misspell that word, isn't it?
A: No, not all the time.
Q: What?
A: Not all the time.
Q: Nearly all the time, isn't it?
A: Most of the time, yes.
Q: You know that when you gave us samples of your handwriting you misspelled it that way, isn't that right? You know you insisted you found it in the dictionary?
A: Yes.
Q: You spelled it "waite", didn't you?
A: I insisted on it, yes.
Q: The word "safety," you misspelled "safety" the way it is spelled on the ransom note?
A: Not all the time. About the only time I spell words wrong is when I am nervous. This word here.
Q: You were nervous when you wrote the ransom note, were you?
A: Yes.

Q: It accounts for your misspelling those words?
A: Yes.
Q: Were you nervous when you gave us samples of your handwriting in the Bridewell Hospital?
A: Yes.
Q: That accounts for the fact that you misspelled it again?
A: The same way, yes, like the comma. I never make the comma like that, never at all, never on anything else.
Q: You did on the samples you gave to us, too?
A: I do not know why I did it. In all my writings at school and all my figures and all, I do not write a comma like that.
Q: Did you have any particular reason for tearing that part of the paper?
A: The other part was dirtier.
Q: Is that the only reason?
A: Yes.
Q: When you were in the room with the little girl did you hear any of the other persons in the house moving around?
A: No.
Q: Did you hear any noise in the house at all?
A: No.
Q: Did you hear any dogs growling upstairs or barking?
A: I did not hear nothing.
Q: Did you know there were dogs in the apartment upstairs?
A: No.
Q: Did you know how many families lived in that building?
A: No.
Q: Did you get any satisfaction out committing this particular crime?
A: No, the only thing I get satisfaction out of is the burglaries.
Q: What kind of satisfaction?
A: Is that necessary?

Q: Yes.
A: Sexual satisfaction.
Q: Will you describe that to us?
A: Well, the time, it all depends on the burglary. If I have an erection, and ejection at the place, then I go out without taking anything. That is the satisfaction I get out of it.
Q: When you say ejection, you mean an emission?
A: Yes.
Q: You mean you go in, and after you get into a place you have an erection?
A: Yes, before I get in.
Q: Even before you get in?
A: Yes.
Q: After you get in you have an emission?
A: Yes, not all the time, though.
Q: Sometimes?
A: Yes, sometimes.
Q: If you have an emission you go right out?
A: Yes.
Q: If you don't, you do something else?
A: Yes, until, but it is only when I, after the emission I realize what is going on and I leave.
Q: Did you have an erection on this particular night?
A: Going in, I did.
Q: Where did that erection take place?
A: It started when I tried to get into the other building.
Q: Did it remain with you all the time?
A: Yes. That is another.
Q: Did you have an emission after you got into the place?
A: No, not that I know of.
Q: How long did the erection continue then?

A: I do not know. I know I dropped this thing on my finger, I did not have it any more.
Q: Did you take the girl for the purpose of having sexual intercourse with her?
A: No.
Q: When you left the university to go back north you did not have any erection then, did you?
A: No. I just had the feeling of it, that's all.
Q: Just the feeling of it?
A: No, no, at the time I did not. From the drink and all I don't know whether I did or not.
Q: Let us get back to that Sunday night, that Sunday afternoon prior to the time you went to the Degnan home, were you at your mother and father's home on Touhy Avenue?
A: Yes.
Q: Had you spent the weekend there?
A: Yes.
Q: What time did you leave your mother and father's home to return to school?
A: On the 7:07 bus.
Q: What is the answer?
A: On the 7:07 bus leaving from Touhy and Keeler, on the corner.
Q: The bus leaves seven minutes after seven?
A: Yes.
Q: Where does it take you?
A: Howard Street.

Mr. Tuohy

Q: Howard and what?

The Witness

A: Howard.
Q: Howard and Paulina?
A: And Paulina, yes, the "L."

Mr. Crowley

Q: Then where did you go?
A: Then I went up and took the Jackson Park Express back to school.
Q: To where?
A: Back to either University or Cottage, University Avenue.
Q: To where?
A: Back to either University or Cottage, University Avenue.
Q: How long did it take you to get from your mother's home to school?
A: A good hour. At that time of the day it would be more than an hour.
Q: So it was sometime around 8:15 p. m., or later, that you arrived at school?
A: About 8:30, because it took the bus a while to arrive. The bus usually arrives at Howard twenty minutes after the hour.
Q: What did you do at 8:30 when you got there?
A: I went up to my room.
Q: How long did you remain in your room?
A: I studied for a while and then I went to the washroom to get a drink of water, and I met Gene in there washing his clothes out.
Q: What time would that be, approximately?
A: About nine o'clock.
Q: Then what did you do?

A: Gene invited me into his room to have some drinks with Joe Costello.
Q: Are you sure that is who you drank with, Gene and Joe Costello?
A: Positive.
Q: Could you be mistaken about that?
A: No, I was sick that night.
Q: How is that?
A: I was sick that night, drank too much.
Q: Don't you know Joe Costello was sick in his room that night?
A: No, because I came out before he came out, I went to my room before he went.
Q: How long did you remain in Gene's room?
A: For about, until 12:30. It was after twelve o'clock.
Q: After twelve o'clock midnight?
A: Yes.
Q: Then where did you go?
A: Then I went to my own room.
Q: Then what did you do?
A: I started undressing. I got undressed and I then laid down for a while, but then I got up and went out.
Q: Did you get up right away?
A: No, not right away.
Q: What?
A: Two minutes or so, until I just lay down, I did not even take the covers off the bed. I just laid down and got up again.
Q: Did you go right out and take the "L" train?
A: Yes, I went right to the "L" train.
Q: What time did you get the "L" train?
A: About one o'clock.
Q: About 1:00?

A: 1:30, rather, because it took me sometime to get dressed, too.
Q: Couldn't it have been earlier than that?
A: No.
Q: How do you fix the time at 1:30?
A: Because I got out of Gene's room. I undressed, and it takes you fifteen minutes or more to walk to the "L" station. I had to get dressed over again. I did not have the same clothes on that I wore that day, when I came home.
Q: How do you fix the time you left Gene's room?
A: It was after twelve o'clock.
Q: How do you know that?
A: I looked at my watch, it was after twelve o'clock, as I said myself.
Q: The drinks had not affected you so that you could tell the time of day?
A: No, it had not affected me at all, not much. I usually know when I get enough.
Q: You were not drunk, were you?
A: No, I would not say I was drunk because I got to my room all right.
Q: You say you became ill?
A: No, I did not become ill.
Q: You were not nauseous?
A: No, not unless I get too much, I fall asleep.
Q: I am talking about this night?
A: No.
Q: Did you look at your watch again at the time you left your room?
A: No, I did not take my watch with me. I took it off that night.
Q: You did not have it with you then?

A: No.
Q: So you had no way of telling the time when you were en route going north?
A: No.
Q: You were just giving us an estimate of your time then?
A: An estimate.
Q: If you did not sleep very long and got right up and dressed, you would have got up north a little earlier than 2:30, is that right?
A: Yes.
Q: You could have been up there much earlier than 2:30, couldn't you?
A: No. No, not much earlier, approximately between 2:00 and 2:30.
Q: Did you see anybody else at the university outside of Gene and Joe that particular evening, Sunday, Jan. 6, 1946?
A: No, not that I remember. There may have been, but I was in my room all the time, and I recall to mind that far back Joe and Gene and me being together.
Q: When you were at your mother's house over the weekend did you have the knife and the gun with you?
A: No.
Q: And the piece of paper?
A: No, the paper may have been with me. I think it was in my other pants pocket.
Q: Well, was it with you or wasn't it?
A: I don't know.
Q: Why did you take the knife and a gun and the wire and a piece of paper with you when you went out that night?
A: Well, in burglaries you take a gun.
Q: Burglaries you take a gun?

A: I always had that wire in my packet because on previous burglaries where I wired the front door.
Q: What was the knife for?
A: The knife was to pry open windows and all. I usually carried a knife. Almost always it was something heavy on the order of a knife that could open something.
Q: Why did you bother with a piece of paper?
A: That was in my pocket. I had no reason for that.
Q: Did you take a pencil with you?
A: Yes. I always carried a pencil.
Q: What kind of pencil?
A: It was an ordinary.
Q: Just an ordinary lead pencil?
A: Yes.
Q: Why did you take it with you?
A: That was in my pocket, too.
Q: The paper and pencil would not help you in any burglary, would they?
A: No.
Q: When you started north, didn't you know that you were going to go to the Degnan home?
A: No, I did not. I remember disputing with myself whether I should get off at Granville or Thorndale, but Granville is too far out. I could have been over there.
Q: Do you know why you picked Thorndale to get off?
A: No, it was just a matter of choice.
Q: You disputed with yourself, what do you mean, disputed between Thorndale and Granville?
A: If I wanted to get off at Thorndale I would have to get up in a hurry before the door closes, before it left the station. I wanted to sit until Granville, so I got up and went out.
Q: Where did you get off at?

A: At Thorndale.
Q: At Thorndale?
A: Yes.
Q: That is the place where you had to hurry to get out?
A: Yes.
Q: Now, to get back to this piece of paper, you say you picked it up about a week before, will you tell us again just where you were when you picked that up?
A: In Harper Library.
Q: What were you doing?
A: I was doing some research work, encyclopedias.
Q: Did you have a notebook with you?
A: Yes.
Q: Where was this piece of paper at?
A: It was laying right near me. I had the whole table to myself.
Q: Was it attached to a pad?
A: No.
Q: Was it lying loose as a single sheet?
A: Yes.
Q: How did you fold that paper?
A: End over end. Just fold it in half and fold it quarter. Then fold it a long quarter and a half.
Q: Will you fold this piece of paper in the manner you say you folded it? (folds paper)
Q: What did you do with that after you folded it that way?
A: Put it in my pocket.
Q: Did you have any idea what you were going to use it for at that time?
A: No.
Q: Yet you had lots of paper in your room at the university?
A: Not too much, enough, though.
Q: One sheet of paper is not very valuable to you?

A: No.
Q: Why would you take all the pains to pick up a single sheet of paper in Harper's Library and fold it so carefully as you folded that piece of paper?
A: Well, because by my taking notes in lectures and any time to take notes.
Q: Couldn't you take a sheet of paper from your own pocket?
A: In fact I did not have it with me. I would not have the paper with me all the time.
Q: You always have it with you if you put it in your pocket?
A: Just like people make it a business to carry a pencil.
Q: If you made it your business to carry a pencil and paper with you, why didn't you have paper with you and not find it necessary to take particular sheet?
A: I had no notebook with me.
Q: You are sure that piece of paper was not attached to any pad?
A: Yes.
Q: It was lying there loose?
A: Yes.
Q: You just stuck it in your pocket for note paper?
A: Yes.

Mr. Tuohy

Q: Was the pad close by?

Mr. Crowley

Q: Do you know who had been using this particular piece of paper before you?
A: No.

Q: When you got off of the elevated at Thorndale Avenue Station where did you go?
A: Then I went east.
Q: East on Thorndale Avenue?
A: Yes, sir.
Q: How far east did you go?
A: To Winthrop, I went down Winthrop.
Q: Then did you turn Winthrop?
A: Yes, then north.
Q: How far north on Winthrop did you go?
A: Glenlake.
Q: Then where did you go?
A: Then I turned east and went to the alley between Kenmore and Sheridan, and turned south in that alley until I came to the back yard, about fifty feet off the main road, Glenlake. Then I seen the ladder and I take the ladder. I proceeded north and I tried to get into one of the windows. From there I proceeded after failure, back to the alley and started south again, and I came to the Degnan home.
Q: Did you at any time cut across Kenmore Avenue in a southeasterly direction from the corner of Glenlake and Kenmore to the east side of Kenmore Avenue?
A: Glenlake? What are the streets again? Glenlake.
Q: And Kenmore. You crossed Kenmore Avenue on Glenlake, you said?
A: Yes.
Q: At any time did you walk from the corner of Kenmore to Glenlake in a southerly direction to the east side of Kenmore Avenue?
A: No.
Q: Did you pass in front of an automobile with the light going on Kenmore Avenue just south of Glenlake?

A: No.
Q: After you took Suzanne Degnan's body out of her room you walked east to the alley between Kenmore and Sheridan?
A: Yes.
Q: Where did you go from there?
A: I went north.
Q: How far north?
A: To my knowledge I went up to the apartment building, the big apartment building where I tried to get into.
Q: Where was that apartment building which you tried to get into?
A: It is going north, it is east, on my east side, I mean my left side.
Q: How far from the Degnan home is that?
A: About two houses.
Q: Did you stop there?
A: No.
Q: Where did you go from there?
A: I don't know. I must have continued north. I do not know where I went from then on, but I was going that direction.
Q: Where did you find yourself when you next recollect your whereabouts?
A: I was near Broadway, on the west side of the "L," on the west side of the "L" tracks. I do not know what street it was. Some place south.
Q: It would be Hollywood?
A: I guess so—no, it was some place south.
Q: The alley west of the elevated?
A: Yes.
Q: Between Ardmore and Hollywood?
A: I don't know the street. It could be up in here (pointing at the plan on the table).

Q: Have you been back in that neighborhood since January 7?
A: I do not think so.
Q: When did you throw the gun on the tennis courts at Loyola?
A: It may have been before, it may have been after, but I know there was snow on the ground.
Q: Those tennis courts are located at the head of Winthrop and Sheridan Road, where Sheridan Road runs east and west, isn't that so?
A: Yes the gun was dismantled I believe. I think I took the barrel off, the thing that goes around it and threw it in there and I threw the other part in too.
Q: What time did you get back to the university in the morning of January 7?
A: About six o'clock.
Q: Where did you go?
A: I went to my room.
Q: How long did you stay in your room?
A: I studied until, I listened to the radio about, I would say at least a quarter to nine. No, it was about eight o'clock because I know I went to get something to eat that morning.
Q: Where did you go get something to eat?
A: The cafeteria, Hutchinson College.
Q: How long were you there?
A: I was there about half an hour.
Q: Then where did you go?
A: Then I came back to my room, got my books and went to class.
Q: What time was the first class you attended that morning?
A: Ten o'clock.
Q: What did you do between the time you had breakfast and the time you went to class?
A: Continued to study.

Q: Did you make a telephone call to the Degnan home?
A: No.
Q: During that period. Did you ever make a telephone call to the Degnan home?
A: No, never.
Q: How long did that class last?
A: An hour. Fifty minutes. They give you ten minutes.
Q: It was about ten minutes of eleven?
A: Yes.
Q: What did you do then?
A: At ten minutes to eleven I went to the next class.
Q: What time was that out?
A: That was ten minutes to twelve.
Q: Then where did you go?
A: To my next class.
Q: Where did you go the afternoon of January 7?
A: Went to class.
Q: Till how long?
A: Around five o'clock.
Q: Then what did you do?
A: I went back to my room and studied, as usual.
Q: Were you back in the neighborhood of the Degnan home at any time after five o'clock on January 7?
A: No.
Q: Were you present at any time in the Degnan neighborhood when parts of Suzanne's body were recovered?
A: My classes ended between five and six, and I had not eaten all day, so I must have taken breakfast, too, that was about seven o'clock.
Q: What did you do at seven o'clock?
A: After that I was studying.
Q: Where did you study?

A: In my room.
Q: With whom?
A: With myself, nobody.
Q: Was anybody else there?
A: No.
Q: Did anybody see you that day?
A: Everybody was in class.
Q: Outside of the class hour?
A: I think me and Joe Costello ate the next day. I mean for suppertime, because I know wrestling class ends about five-thirty or so and my afternoon class and lecture at three o'clock ends at four.
Q: Did you learn at any time during the day—
A: No, it was a full day.
Q: —that there had been a kidnapping from the Degnan home?
A: No.
Q: Did you read in the newspapers?
A: No.
Q: Or listen to the radio and hear reports of this kidnapping?
A: No. I did not listen to the radio until, I think it was January 8, because January 7 in the morning I listened to the radio until I went to class, after that I listened to—
Q: When you listened to the radio, did you hear any radio report that Suzanne Degnan had been kidnapped?
A: No.
Q: Did you hear anybody discussing the kidnapping of Suzanne Degnan on the morning of January 7?
A: No.
Q: Did you discuss that kidnapping with any of your friends or associates on the day of January 7?
A: No, I did not.

Q: When did you first learn that parts of the body of Suzanne Degnan had been recovered?
A: It was a couple of days after it happened. I believe January 8 I found out.
Q: How did you find out?
A: From radio reports.
Q: Was there any discussion with any of your friends on January 8 about it?
A: No.
Q: Never?
A: No.
Q: Did you ever discuss it?
A: It may have been mentioned, but I never discussed it.
Q: Did you ever discuss it at home?
A: No.
Q: Did your mother ever ask you if you were the boy that did that?
A: No.
Q: Did you ever know anybody by the name of George Murman?
A: I know the name George, I didn't know the name George Murman.
Q: You didn't know anybody by the name of George Murman?
A: That has all been attached to myself. It was practically the truth all what I told you that evening, except like I always have the habit of doing—it just seems a fight with him and me.
Q: George Murman is in reality a name you concocted for yourself, when you do something that you, Bill Heirens, don't want to admit to?
A: You can say that, yes, but the name was concocted right around the time I was at Gibault, that was about five years

ago. No, that is about three years ago, and from then on I just seemed to be in a fight, that is all. To tell me he is real. But when you get down to other people, he is not real.

Q: What do you mean by that?

A: He is as real as anybody else to me.

Q: Does he exist? Does he live in flesh and blood outside of your head?

A: No, he doesn't. I realize he is a concoction of my imagination.

Q: Was it a name you concocted to use as an alias?

A: No.

Q: How did you happen to give him the name Murman?

A: There was no reason for that, just anything that popped in my head when you asked me. George was already in my mind.

Q: That is your middle name?

A: Yes, sir.

Q: And it is your father's name?

A: Yes.

Q: And that is how you happened to use the name George?

A: No, it was not the reason at all. I don't know what brought the name about in my head.

Q: When you talk of George Murman, you mean the same individual as Bill Heirens, don't you?

A: As to you, yes. You can accept George as being me.

Q: Do you think that George Murman and Bill Heirens are two separate individuals within the same body?

A: I don't know.

Q: But he does not exist as a living person that you could bring in and introduce to me, and that you know where he lives?

A: When you questioned me as to where he lived, I could not tell because I didn't know.

Q: But he had no existence outside of your imagination, is that right?

A: Well he seems very real to me. He exists. When I say he brings things for me to use, I actually mean it. He brought things in for me to use and I took it as that. Just like the note I wrote, I thought I had sent him away, he was going to Mexico.

I thought he would go like that and I wrote the note to myself.

Q: Did you send the note to him?

A: I kept the note. I wrote a lot of notes.

Q: But you knew in reality you were writing those notes to yourself?

A: Not at the time I wrote them, but after a while they seemed to be different.

Q: Did you ever mail a note to George Murman?

A: No.

Q: Did you ever see him?

A: No.

Q: Did you ever talk to him?

A: A couple of times I had talks.

Q: But he was not physically present?

A: No.

Q: So in reality you were just talking to yourself?

A: Yes.

Q: So there is no person George Murman that you know of, other than Bill Heirens?

A: No, there is no other person.

Mr. Tuohy : Let the Sheriff take Bill Heirens over to Mr. Crowley's office for a moment. His counsel can go with him.

(William Heirens left the room at 1 p. m. and returned to Mr. Tuohy's office at 1:05 p. m.)

Mr. Tuohy

Q: Bill, have you any recollection of washing off the parts of Suzanne's body after you cut it up in the basement?
A: No, I have not.
Q: Would you have any objection to going out with us and identifying for us the particular window in which you climbed into the Degnan home?
A: No.
Q: Will you go out with us and identify it if we ask you to?
A: Yes.

Mr. Tuohy

Q: Does counsel have any objection to that?

Mr. John Coghlan

A: No.

Mr. Tuohy

Q: Would you have any objection to going to the basement of the apartment building where the body of Suzanne Degnan was dismembered and identifying that for us?

The Witness

A: No.

Mr. Tuohy

Q: Does the counsel have any objection to that?

Mr. Mal Coghlan

A: No.

Mr. John Coghlan

A: No objection.

Mr. Rowland Towle

A: No.

Mr. Tuohy: I think that is all on this statement.

ANALYSIS OF CLEVELAND TORSO MURDERS, SUZANNE DEGNAN MURDER AND THE BLACK DAHLIA MURDER

In addition to the possible—or as I believe, probable—connections between the central cases and Jack Anderson Wilson already examined in preceding chapters, there are further sources of corroboration and evidence supporting the theory that two or more perpretrators were working together to commit these crimes. One source would be to employ DNA technology and the other appears in various news articles and books that I have found only after completing the main body of the text. These are analyzed and included here.

JACK ANDERSON WILSON'S DNA

The charred body of Jack Anderson Wilson was cremated following his death in 1982. If Wilson's mother, Minnie Buchanan Wilson, was not cremated following her death, then her remains could be exhumed and a mitochondrial DNA analysis could be conducted. Wilson's biological mother would have the same DNA as her son, Jack Anderson Wilson. This DNA could then be compared with the known DNA samples in the Cleveland Torso Murders, the murder of the Black Dahlia and the murder of Suzanne Degnan, if available.

JACK ANDERSON WILSON CLUE

As recently as 1990, the Los Angeles Police Department thought the murder of the Black Dahlia might have been connected to the Cleveland Torso Murders. Cleveland Detective Peter Merylo believed that the Mad Butcher of Kingsbury Run "was responsible for the more recent Black Dahlia murder case in Los Angeles" (page 75, *Greatest Crimes of the Century*, 1954, by A.W. Pezet and Bradford Chambers). Los Angeles Detective John St. John suspected that Jack Anderson Wilson killed the Black Dahlia but did not feel Wilson was involved in the Cleveland killings. St. John's assessment that the murder of the Black Dahlia and the Cleveland Torso Murders exhibited separate and distinct "signatures" was based on incomplete information supplied by the Cleveland authorities. Had St. John received all of the facts concerning the Cleveland Torso Murders, including the fact that more than one of the Cleveland Torso Victims was tortured before being killed, then his assessment of the murders could very well have been consistent with that of Detective Merylo.

I recently found some other information that may be worth mentioning and that may shed some light on this mystery. Note, however, that as of the date of this writing I have not found verification of the following information. I read a book written by Max Allen Collins entitled *Angel In Black*, published by Signet in 2002. Mr. Collins' book is, in his words, "based on history although it is a work of fiction." Before writing his book Mr. Collins and his research associate, George Hagenauer, did extensive research on the Cleveland Torso Murders in Cleveland. Collins' book included three entries that caught my attention:

1. Page 202: "We even had a suspect, a young homosexual who worked in the butcher shop of a St. Clair Avenue grocery . . . but this never panned out."

2. Page 269: "You had a suspect . . . some fag butcher . . ." "A young homosexual, yes, who worked on St. Clair Avenue. Like Watterson, he liked to prowl the skid row sections of town, preying on society's dregs. And his name, as you've guessed, was Arnold Wilson." "Yes, but the description of the St. Clair butcher shop boy was not common: he was a very pockmarked kid, very thin, very tall, Merylo said . . . perhaps as much as six four."
3. Page 317: (Here Collins makes reference to his factual account in *Angel In Black*: "Although my pairing of Wilson and the Mad Butcher of Kingsbury Run may seem fanciful, one of Wilson's aliases is in fact the name of a suspected accomplice of the Kingsbury Run Butcher." This clue and the source of Collin's information are of importance because more than one person may be involved. See: "Two Men and a Female Impersonator Clue" below.

I spoke with Mr. Collins and his recollection was that the information contained in numbers 1, 2 & 3 above was based directly on his and his assistant's research of the Cleveland Torso Murders. I have not personally located the source of this information, but it makes sense that the Cleveland detectives would have followed up on the tip received by Detective Orley May from the woman in the Workhouse. They could have located a young 6'4" sodomist-former butcher who worked for "Sam" on St. Clair Avenue in Cleveland during the time of the Cleveland Torso Murders. There may very well be a police report or an article in *The Plain Dealer* that expressly identified the sodomist-former butcher fingered by the lady in the Workhouse in 1937. If so, then it appears that the Cleveland detectives were investigating a 6'4" sodomist by the name of Jack Wilson as a suspect in the Cleveland Torso Murders but couldn't pin the murders on him, just as the Los Angeles detectives, years later, identified a 6'4" sodomist by the name of Jack Anderson Wilson (a/k/a Jack Wilson) as a suspect in the murder of the Black Dahlia, but couldn't find the corroborating evidence necessary to make an arrest.

According to his Ohio birth certificate Jack Anderson Wilson was born on August 5, 1920. He would have been fourteen-years-old going on fifteen in 1935, when Flo Polillo was killed and dismembered in Cleveland, and twenty-six-years-old in 1947, when Elizabeth Short was killed and severed in Los Angeles.

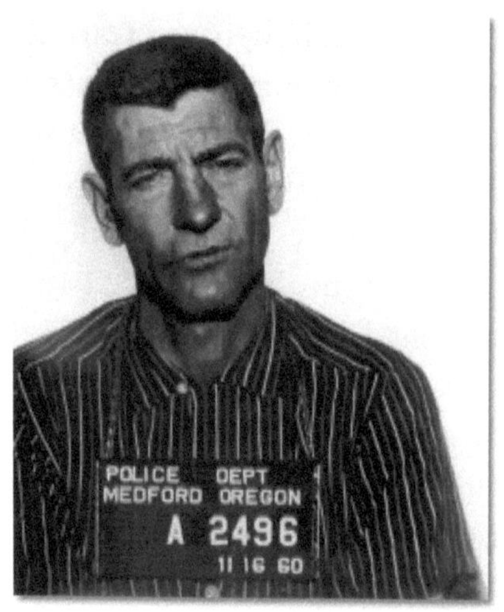

Jack Anderson Wilson

If Wilson had been born in 1920, he would have been 40-years-old in 1960, when his mug shot was taken in Oregon. I have asked several people to look at his photo and guess his age. Everyone indicated that he looks at least 50 or older. His appearance in 1960 could be the result of hard drinking and smoking, or possibly his birth certificate is not accurate. His father's name was altered. Was his date of birth? Note that his birth certificate is on a form that reads 19120. His birth certificates filed in Canton, Ohio, and in Columbus, Ohio, are identical.

PLACE OF BIRTH
County of Stark
Township of
or
Village of
or
City of Canton
Francis Ave S.W.
Ward.

STATE OF OHIO
BUREAU OF VITAL STATISTICS
CERTIFICATE OF BIRTH 80166

AFFIDAVIT ATTACHED

Registration District No. 5306 File No.
Primary Registration District No. 8482 Registered No. 1260

FULL NAME OF CHILD Grover Loving, Jr. (If child is not yet named, make supplemental report, as directed)

Sex of Child Male | Twin, triplet, or other? - | Number in order of birth 1 | Legitimate? no | Date of birth Aug 5th, 1920 (Month) (Day) (Year)
(To be answered only in event of plural births)

FATHER		MOTHER	
FULL NAME	~~Alex F Wilson~~ Grover Loving	FULL MAIDEN NAME	Minnie Buchanan (Wilson)
RESIDENCE	Francis Ave S.W. Canton	RESIDENCE	Francis Ave S.W.
COLOR OR RACE	White; AGE AT LAST BIRTHDAY 26 (Years)	COLOR OR RACE	White; AGE AT LAST BIRTHDAY 23 (Years)
BIRTHPLACE	North Carolina	BIRTHPLACE	North Carolina
OCCUPATION AND INDUSTRY	Machinist	OCCUPATION AND INDUSTRY	House W. Jr.
NUMBER OF CHILDREN BORN AND LIVING: Number of children born alive to this mother, including this child (if born alive)	1	Number of children of this mother living, including this child (if born alive)	1

CERTIFICATE OF ATTENDING PHYSICIAN OR MIDWIFE*

I hereby certify that I attended the birth of this child born to Mrs Alex F. Wilson (Mother's Name) and that the child was Born alive (Born alive or Stillborn) at 8 A. M., on the date above stated.

(Signature) A. R. Olmstead (Physician or Midwife)
Address 1717 Navarre Rd Canton Ohio

*When there was no attending physician or midwife, then the father, householder, etc., should make this return. A stillborn child is one that neither breathes nor shows other evidence of life after birth.

Given name added from a supplemental report ....191....
REGISTRAR

Filed Aug 12, 1920 Margarette McAbee REGISTRAR

THIS IS A CERTIFIED COPY OF THE RECORD ON FILE IN THE CANTON CITY HEALTH DEPARTMENT

7/6/05 DATE
Robert e Pattison LOCAL REGISTRAR

Birth Certificate of Jack Anderson Wilson a/k/a Grover Loving, Jr.

On November 10, 1942, shortly after the murders in McKee's Rocks ended, an affidavit was filed at the Canton, Ohio, Department of Vital Statistics. This affidavit appears to have been signed by his mother, Minnie Buchanan Wilson, in the state of North Carolina and lists the name of Wilson's father as Alex F. Wilson.

STATE OF [illegible] } ss. COLUMBUS
COUNTY OF Avery } AFFIDAVIT

I, Mrs. Minnie Buchanan, Wilson being first duly sworn, say that I am the Mother of Jack Anderson Wilson and that (h is) original birth certificate on file with the Ohio Department of Health is incorrect.

The following is a true and correct statement:

NAME Jack Anderson Wilson FILE NO. 80166

DATE OF BIRTH August 5, 1920 PLACE OF BIRTH Canton, Ohio.

NAME OF FATHER Alex F. Wilson

MAIDEN NAME OF MOTHER Minnie Buchanan.

REMARKS

(SIGNATURE OF FATHER OR MOTHER) Minnie Buchanan Wilson

Sworn to before me and subscribed in my presence, this 10th day of November nineteen hundred and 42.

My Commission Expires June 24, 1943.
(SEAL)

Stella Hampton Lowe
Notary Public
OFFICIAL TITLE

V.S.28 (This affidavit must be typewritten)

THIS IS A CERTIFIED COPY OF THE RECORD ON FILE IN THE CANTON CITY HEALTH DEPARTMENT

2/16/05 Robert E. Pattison
DATE LOCAL REGISTRAR

affidavit signed by Minnie Buchanan Wilson dated November 10, 1942

Wilson could have killed Flo Polillo in 1935, in concert with others, when he was fourteen-years-old. Consider the following:

1. In 1935, the United States was in the middle of the Great Depression. The Great Depression began on Black Friday in October, 1929, and didn't end until 1942, after the United States had entered World War II.
2. Little, if any, attention was paid to Child Labor Laws in 1935. It would certainly have been possible for a fourteen-year-old to work in a Cleveland grocery-butcher shop at that time. Keep in mind that this is the era of John Steinbach's *Grapes of Wrath*.
3. Due to the state of the economy in 1935, Wilson was probably forced to work and become a man at an early age. He probably enjoyed a very short childhood.
4. The Cleveland Workhouse included a juvenile section in 1935. (See tip received by Detective Orley May in 1937, from the lady in the Workhouse on page 96 of this text.)
5. If Wilson had been a lust killer he would have had these tendencies at an early age. This is not something that is learned in school or acquired through experience. At age fourteen Wilson would not have been the first young person to commit a murder. Consider the 1874 case of Boston's Jesse Pomeroy. At age eleven he sexually tortured seven young boys and not long after killed and mutilated a ten-year-old girl. A month later he slashed four-year-old Horace Mullen so savagely with a knife that he nearly decapitated him. All of his crimes were committed when he was under the age of fourteen. And what about fifteen-year-old Edmond Kemper who shot and killed both of his grandparents in 1964, in California? Or how about fifteen-year-old Willie Bosket who shot a man in the eye, piercing his brain and then shot

the man again in his right temple killing him in a New York subway in 1978? The list of child killers goes on and on. It is not beyond the realm of possibility for Jack Anderson Wilson to have begun killing in Cleveland at age fourteen and to have acquired the ability to "expertly dismember" a human body by practicing his trade carving up dead animals in a local grocery-butcher shop.

According to the woman in the Cleveland Workhouse, who was interviewed by Detective Orley May in 1937, Jack Wilson was a sodomist and "a former butcher who worked for 'Sam'" on St. Clair Avenue. At the Case Western Reserve Historical Library in Cleveland I located in the *1935 Cleveland City Directory* the following grocery stores located on St. Clair Avenue that were owned by a person with the first name "Sam":

> Sam Kaas Grocery, 4034 St. Clair Avenue
> Sam Gold Grocery, 9115 St. Clair Avenue
> Sam Rocco Grocery, 10819 St. Clair Avenue
> Sam Pistollo (Sam Pistitello) Meats, 15808 St. Clair Avenue

Perhaps someone acquainted with one of these businesses can remember a young 6'4" pock-marked employee during 1935-1937, who may have walked with a limp and carried a large butcher knife.

6. At age fourteen Wilson could have already engaged in acts of sodomy. We know that he was charged with sodomy in California in 1948 (See Max Allan Collins' reference to a young homosexual who worked for a butcher shop of a St. Clair Avenue grocery in Cleveland in the "Jack Anderson Wilson Clue" above).

MURDER OF CORPORAL MAOMA RIDINGS

On August 31, 1943, *The Indianapolis Star* reported that a 32-year-old WAC corporal by the name of Maoma L. Ridings was found murdered in the Claypool Hotel in downtown Indianapolis. She was nude from the waist down. Large gashes, "unusually deep" the paper noted, were found in the left side of her neck. "The coroner said also that the autopsy showed the wrists of the victim were slashed some time after she was cut brutally in her throat and face. This indicated that the assailant tried to show Corporal Ridings attempted suicide, the coroner added." "She had been a frequent week-end visitor at the hotel during the last two months, sometimes coming alone and sometimes being accompanied by another member of the WAC from Camp Atterbury." At this same time period Elizabeth Short was living at Camp Cooke in California with a WAC sergeant. There is some question regarding the date Elizabeth Short left her employment at Camp Cooke. Author Mary Pacios wrote in her chronology that "Bette ends her employment at Camp Cooke on August 25, 1943." (She may have ended her employment at a later date.) It is known that Elizabeth Short traveled through Indianapolis on different occasions (See page 173, *Severed*). Now here is what I found to be very interesting: *The Indianapolis Star* also reported on August 31, 1943, that on the day Maoma Ridings was killed "a black-haired woman in black was seen in the room with Corporal Ridings early Saturday night by two bellboys." Following the murder of Maoma Ridings the woman in black disappeared. One of the theories the police developed was that the "woman with black hair, dressed in black" was not a woman but instead a female impersonator. Jack Anderson Wilson was either a female impersonator or he hung out with someone who was a female impersonator. Wilson was in Indianapolis on August 23, 1943, when Corporal Maoma Ridings was murdered. He left town immediately thereafter (Page 200, *Severed*).

MURDER OF SUZANNE DEGNAN

It is known that Elizabeth Short traveled through Indianapolis and Chicago during the mid-1940's. Duffy Sawyer had modeling jobs for her in both of these cities and that is where she met co-pilot Gordan Fickling. Suzanne Degnan was killed and expertly dismembered on January 7, 1946, in Chicago. Elizabeth Short was in Chicago sometime between June-August, 1946. On January 30, 1947, sixteen days after Elizabeth Short was murdered in Los Angeles, the *Los Angeles Examiner* ran the following article:

> In Chicago, Freddie Woods, 23, who described himself as a "friend" of the Slain girl, revealed that she was "fascinated" with the brutal slaying of six-year-old Suzanne Degnan, which took place in Chicago a year ago. Woods said he met Miss Short last August when she was in Chicago for 10 days. She told him she was a Massachusetts reporter covering the trial of William Heirens who was convicted of the Degnan kidnapping and slaying. "Elizabeth was one of the prettiest girls I ever met," Woods said. "But she was terribly preoccupied with the details of the Degnan murder."

It seems too coincidental to me that Elizabeth Short was murdered and expertly severed on January 14, 1947, less than six months after she had been in Chicago "terribly preoccupied with the details of the Degnan Murder" and pretending to be a reporter from Massachusetts "covering the trial of William Heirens." Did the person responsible for the murder of Suzanne Degnan stalk and eventually kill and expertly sever Elizabeth Short because she was "talking" too much about the Degnan murder? Is that the reason she was so frightened from January 1 through January 8, 1947, the day she was last seen walking towards Sixth Street after

Los Angeles Examiner Jan. 30, 1947

Give Generously of Dimes in War Against Polio! (See Editorial Page)

Los Angeles Examiner

CHARACTER QUALITY · AMERICA FIRST! · ENTERPRISE ACCURACY

AN AMERICAN PAPER FOR THE AMERICAN PEOPLE · THE GREAT NEWSPAPER OF THE GREAT SOUTHWEST

Reg. U. S. Pat. Off. Examiner Telephone Richmond 1212 · Examiner Building, 1111 S. Broadway

LIV—NO. 50 · LOS ANGELES, THURSDAY, JANUARY 30, 1947

Self-Admitted Dahlia Slayer Changes Mind

give me a square deal. 'Dahlia' killing justified."

Police Chemist Ray Pinker was given the letter for analysis.

Donahoe and his aides, Detective Sergeants Harry Hansen, F. A. Brown and Harry Fremont, yesterday discredited the "I did kill Betty Short" confession made by a suspect who did surrender himself.

DON'T JIBE——

This man, Daniel S. Voorhees, 33, formerly of Phoenix but now living with a brother in Van Nuys, was questioned in the county jail hospital where he was committed after telephoning police to arrest him on a downtown corner.

Alternating between insistence that his confession was authentic and denial that he killed "The Black Dahlia," Voorhees claimed he had "dates" in Los Angeles with the girl in 1941.

(Miss Short's mother, Mrs. Phoebe Mae Short, told the Examiner her daughter did not come to Los Angeles until early 1943. This was corroborated by the girl's father, Cleo, in his story to police.)

Voorhees also described Miss Short as having "brown hair," whereas her hair actually was jet black, the basis for her nickname of "The Black Dahlia."

During the day, too, an ex-WAC, Mrs. Emily E. Williams, of Tampa, Fla., surrendered to San Diego police with a confession that:

"Elizabeth Short stole my man, so I killed her and cut her up."

But she also told a story that varied from the known facts and finally admitted she "made the whole story up."

QUIZ WOMAN——

In Chicago, Freddie Woods, 23, who described himself as a "friend" of the slain girl, revealed that she was "fascinated" with the brutal slaying of six-year-old Suzanne Degnan, which took place in Chicago a year ago.

Woods said he met Miss Short last August when she was in Chicago for 10 days. She told him she was a Massachusetts reporter covering the trial of William Heirens, who was convicted of the Degnan kidnaping and slaying.

"Elizabeth Short was one of the prettiest girls I ever met," Woods said. "But she was terribly preoccupied with the details of the Degnan murder."

Last night homicide detectives questioned Phyllis Jean Cyr, 20, of 2705 Tilden avenue, West Los Angeles, about her association with Miss Short.

Miss Cyr told Long Beach officers that she had been mistaken for Miss Short on numerous occasions but that she had not seen the slain girl for many months.

Late yesterday investigators began questioning Mrs. Christenia Salisbury, ex-Follies girl, who told the Examiner she met Miss Short and two women in front of the Tabu Club on the Sunset Strip, the night of January 10.

Mrs. Salisbury knew the Short girl in Florida. She said the girl told her in the January 10 meeting she was living with her two companions in a motel in San Fernando Valley. One of the women was a brunette, the other blonde.

January 10 is the last day she has thus far been reported as having been seen alive.

SUSPECT DISCREDITED—Daniel S. Voorhees, who was eliminated as killer of Elizabeth Short. Voorhees, living in Van Nuys, was arrested after he phoned police and told them he was the slayer. He told of having dates with the "Black Dahlia" in 1941. The girl, however, did not come to Los Angeles until 1943. —Los Angeles Examiner photo.

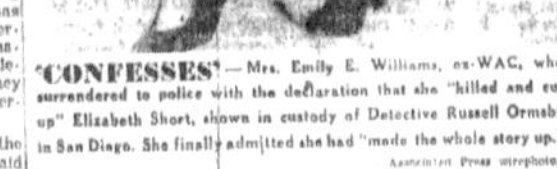

'CONFESSES'—Mrs. Emily E. Williams, ex-WAC, who surrendered to police with the declaration that she "killed and cut up" Elizabeth Short, shown in custody of Detective Russell Ormsby in San Diego. She finally admitted she had "made the whole story up." Associated Press wirephoto.

Lynn Martin Questioned by D. A.; Accuses 10

Lynn Martin, 16-year-old friend of slain Betty Short, has accused 10 men of taking liberties with her during her runaway's life on Hollywood boulevard, Deputy District Attorney Herbert Grossman said yesterday.

Grossman spent much of the day questioning the girl. He said complaints may be issued against

Ex-Councilman Foils Holdup

Franklin P. Buyer, former city councilman, was severely beaten yesterday in foiling a holdup of the American Express Agency office at 10810 South Broadway. He is manager there.

Two men demanded that Buyer put his hands up, announcing:

"This is a stick up."

"Sure," Buyer, who served his last term as councilman in 1939, answered, "sure, I'll put my hands up."

Then he unleashed a left hook at the face of the nearest bandit, flooring him.

The second man hit Buyer on the head with the butt of a revolver, he told police.

Both bandits then fled without taking any money.

Hedge-Hopping Flyer Fined $50

For flying an airplane too low over a congested part of the city, Richard Blake Webster, university student, was fined $50 yesterday by Municipal Judge Ellsworth Meyer.

Witnesses said the plane was flying from 700 feet to 100 feet from the ground over the vicinity of La Cienega boulevard and

Man Hangs Self

LONG BEACH, Jan. 29.—After tying a sheet to the top of an upright folding bed in his room at 140 American avenue today, Joseph Hugershoff, 33, hanged himself, police said.

FEBRUARY SALE FEATURE AT MARILYN FUR CO. GORGEOUS SILVER FOX SCARFS ONLY $86.80 PR. PAY $11.30 AND TAKE YOUR FURS HOME WITH YOU. MARILYN FUR CO., 810 WEST

L. A. TRACKLESS TROLLEYS O[N]

State Also Approves Oth[er] Changes of Transit Lin[es]

Trackless trolleys in downto[wn] Los Angeles and other chang[es] in Los Angeles Transit Lin[es] service were approved yesterd[ay] by the State Public Utilities Co[m]mission, effective February 17.

The company has 60 days fr[om] this date to establish the serv[ice] authorized by the commissi[on]. The city Board of Public Utilit[ies] has already approved the p[ro]gram.

ROUTES——

The new trackless trolleys [will] operate on a line running [on] West Sixth street and Cent[ral] avenue.

Under the plan approved [by] the commission one-way tra[ffic] will be inaugurated east [on] Sixth street and west on F[ifth] street, as approved by city tra[ns]portation officials.

A new motor coach line [will] serve Melrose avenue and T[hird] street on the west and M[ain] avenue and Main street on [the] south. Motor coach lines ["...] and "49" will be extended.

Rail lines "U," "D," "3," and "O" are to be aband[oned] and lines "F," "R" and "S" [re]routed under the plan.

EXTENSION——

Company officials say the program will reduce tur[n] movements by transit veh[icles] by 9000 daily and speed up [and] improve all service.

All abandoned lines will be [re]placed by substitutes.

The commission also appr[oved] extension of the Pacific Ele[ctric] Railway Company's motor [coach] route No. 26 into the San [Fer]nando Valley. The new se[rvice] will be:

From Lankershim and Ven[tura] boulevards via Lankershim [bou]levard, Victory boulevard, W[...]sett avenue, Vanowen st[reet], Lankershim boulevard and S[...]coy street to Tujunga ave[nue]; also along Lankershim boule[vard] between Victory boulevard [and] Vanowen street.

The P. E.'s request to es[tab]lish a new Los Angeles-N[orth] Hollywood-Van Nuys mo[tor] coach line by way of River[side] drive was denied.

SLAVICK'[S]

427 W. 7th • LOS AN[GELES]

TR 9725

9:30 A. M. to 5:45 P. M.

January 30, 1947, *The Los Angeles Examiner*

she left the Biltmore Hotel in Los Angeles? Did Elizabeth Short's killer cut her mouth, not to present a "grotesque smile" as was commonly thought by the detectives, but rather to send a message to the world that she had a "big mouth" because she was talking too much about the Degnan murder? Author Mary Pacios interviewed retired *Los Angeles Dailey News* reporter Gerry Ramlow concerning the murder of the Black Dahlia. She asked Ramlow about the gashes on Bette's face: "Did he know of other murders in which the victim was cut from ear to ear? 'Usually a low level crook, someone who talked too much,' he said, and looked at me as if he had just realized something" (page 74, *Childhood Shadows: The Hidden Story of the Black Dahlia Murder*).

Why was Elizabeth Short preoccupied with the details of a murder in Chicago where a young girl was killed and expertly dismembered? Did Short know who really killed Suzanne Degnan? In order to answer this question it must first be determined that Elizabeth Short knew Jack Anderson Wilson. Following the murder of Georgette Bauerdorf, an eyewitness reported seeing someone fitting the description of Jack Anderson Wilson near her abandoned automobile. Elizabeth Short and Georgette Bauerdorf worked at the same establishment and Bauerdorf mentioned Elizabeth Short by name in her diary (page 201, *Severed*). Georgette dated a very tall soldier. She saw him several times, but for some reason stopped dating him. She was frightened of him. Detectives at the Los Angeles Sheriff's Department suspected that Jack Anderson Wilson had killed Georgette Bauerdorf, but were unable to prove it. According to John Gilmore's taped interview of Jack Anderson Wilson, Elizabeth Short appeared to have known Wilson because she "got into his car and sat with him for a while" (See page 82 of this text or page 185 of *Severed*).

Now, with this in mind, it seems logical to me that Elizabeth Short may have either known who killed Suzanne Degnan and was reasonably sure that Jack Anderson Wilson was involved with the Degnan murder. Being "preoccupied with the details of the Degnan murder" and "reporting on the trial of William Heirens" may very well have led to Short's murder by Jack Anderson Wilson, the same person who may have been involved in the murder/dismemberment of Suzanne Degnan.

WAS JACK ANDERSON WILSON IN CHICAGO WHEN SUZANNE DEGNAN WAS KILLED?

An article in the January 17, 1982, *Los Angeles Herald Examiner* written by Suzan Nightingale, *Herald Examiner* staff writer, included a statement by author John Gilmore concerning "Mr. Jones," who I believe Gilmore later identified as "Al Morrison." Detective John St. John thought Al Morrison was in fact Jack Anderson Wilson. The article reads in part, "Jones was a shy figure, according to Gilmore, **connected with two deaths** *in Chicago* **before he came to Los Angeles** and 'did jobs' for people" (emphasis added). This information fits into my theory that the same person who killed and expertly severed the Black Dahlia was also responsible for the murder and expert dismemberment of Suzanne Degnan in Chicago. I suspect that one of the two murders Jones claimed responsibility for in Chicago before he went to Los Angeles was the murder of Suzanne Degnan.

The most logical reasons nothing shows up on Jack Anderson Wilson's California rap sheet from 3/22/43-5/9/48 are these:

1. He wasn't committing crimes at that time, or was committing crimes and wasn't being caught.
2. He was out of the state of California during most of this time period. In 1944, Wilson was in the military service.

r
y clouds
artly cloudy
on. Chance of
ow. High
68, tomorrow
low 60s.
11

Los ANGELES
HERALD EXAMINER

Sunday
January 17, 1982

Final
edition

50 cents

Southern California's Award-Winning Newspaper (213) 744-8000

id Abscam chief witness lie?

Cowan
Times News Service

WASHINGTON — Justice Department officials have passed along to the trial judge allegations that the government's chief witness in the Abscam case, Melvin Weinberg, lied in some portions of his testimony.

The allegations were said to have been made by Weinberg's wife, Marie, in interviews with a reporter. They have been referred by the Justice Department to Judge George C. Pratt, who presided over five of the Abscam trials in federal court in Brooklyn.

"It's a pending matter before the court," said John Russell, a spokesman for the department. "We're not at liberty to discuss it," he said.

In the Abscam trials, seven members of Congress and other public officials were convicted of accepting money for corrupt purposes from undercover FBI agents. Weinberg played an important role in the investigation and as a witness.

The government's most important evidence against the defendants was a videotape that showed them talking with the undercover agents and taking money. The agents posed as wealthy Arabs.

It appeared that defense lawyers might try to use Mrs. Weinberg's accusations to support their contentions that their clients were denied due process during the trials. Officials said the Justice Department was having difficulty ... tions because she had refused to be interviewed. Her reported assertions about her husband's testimony were made in interviews with Indy Badhwar, a reporter for columnist Jack Anderson.

"He's been interviewing her over three months," Anderson said yesterday. He said Badhwar spoke to Mrs. Weinberg twice at her Florida home and had also spoken with her by telephone. He said columns ... berg said had been distributed for publication next week.

Anderson said that "we made transcripts of some conversations" and that "I submitted them to the Justice Department" through Richard Ben-Veniste, a Washington lawyer representing Howard L. Criden. Criden, a Philadelphia, was c... three other defenda... Abscam trial in Au... ate Mrs. Weinberg'... an aid to defense ... turn the prosecutio... said her stateme... would be "regardec... rial." He added, "...

Abscam/A-6, Col. 3

LACK DAHLIA

thor claims to have found 1947 murderer

m Elizabeth Short and sketches of suspected killer as he may have looked in 1947, left, and 1978.

Suzan Nightingale
ld Examiner staff writer

The fine, light powder she smoothed over her body may have been the only light thing in Elizabeth Short's life.

She moved in dark shadows, frequented k bars, always wore black clothes, and ulti- ately died amid blacker secrets.

They called her the "Black Dahlia."

She died 35 years ago Friday, and she remains as gmatic as on that Jan. 15, 1947, morning when vspaper headlines screamed about "THE MAN- CAL WEREWOLF KILLER" who tortured and n bisected the 22-year-old brunette, abandoning hacked torso in a grassy lot on Norton Avenue ween 39th Street and Coliseum Avenue.

Fanned by the flaming journalistic excesses of day, it was a murder that has horrified and cinated Los Angeles ever since. No motive, no apon and no killer have ever been found.

But John Gilmore — the 13-year-old son of a Los geles cop at the time of the murder — believes has solved the crime that has stumped police for ree decades. After 13 years of research, the thor of books about Charles Manson ("The arbage People") and Charles Schmidt ("The cson Murders") is convinced the killer is alive and nning a bar in Nevada.

Although he is willing to release composite awings of his prime suspect, Gilmore won't reveal e man's name, calling him instead, "Mr. Jones." ilmore's key source is "Mr. Smith," who knew both ones and Elizabeth Short.

"According to Smith, Jones told him he'd done ," Gilmore says. "My source said he sat in the hotel oom and drank an entire bottle of whiskey and told him in great detail what he'd done."

"My source said he sat in the hotel room and drank an entire bottle of whiskey and told him in great detail what he'd done."

Author John Gilmore

Jones was a shady figure, according to Gilmore, connected with two deaths in Chicago before he came to Los Angeles and "did jobs" for people. After holding her against her will in a rented house on 33rd Street, he murdered Elizabeth Short in a fit of frustrated jealousy.

It is the latest theory in a case that has offered as many smoke screens as suspects. The Black Dahlia is, after all, a murder 40 people have confessed to.

"There are people today who confess to the murder even though they weren't born at the time."

But Gilmore, who has talked to "a couple hundred" people in his 13-year quest, is convinced he has finally pieced the story together, building on the collection of shady characters who found their way to Hollywood after World War II.

So certain is Gilmore of his findings, that he took his evidence to the Los Angeles Police Department several weeks ago.

Black Dahlia/A-8, Col. 2

New blast of polar cold in Midwest

Death toll now 253 as much of U.S. shivers

Associated Press

A surge of polar cold nicknamed the Siberian Express blew into the frozen Midwest with paralyzing blizzards yesterday, and the mercury sank to painful lows deep into the Sun Belt.

The frigid winds sent the chill factor to 80 degrees below zero in places and the death toll reached 253 in a wintry assault that began writing weather history last weekend.

"It is one of the most severe outbreaks of cold weather mid-America has seen since the 1800s," said meteorologist Nolan Duke of the National Weather Service in Kansas City.

While temperatures yesterday stopped shy of last weekend's records, such as the all-time low of 26 below in Chicago, readings were close to 30 degrees below zero across parts of Montana, North Dakota and Minnesota, with wind chills below zero as far south as San Antonio, Texas.

More than 120,000 people remained without power in Alabama, Georgia and North Carolina. Freezing rain closed many highways again in north Georgia and snow fell in the Texas Panhandle.

Snow was common from the

Weather/A-6, Col. 4

Fog prompts CHP travel advisories and LAX confusion

By Lennie La Guire
Herald Examiner staff writer

Thick, blinding fog enveloped Los Angeles last night, forcing virtual closure of Los Angeles International Airport and blotting out visibility almost completely in some areas, the National Weather Service announced.

The newest return of Billy Jack

Tom Laughlin, the maverick of the movie back to play his real-life role as a crusader this time is rescuing Filmex and running h

Style/E-1

Bruins and Trojans triumph at home

UCLA's Bruins snagged their first confere against Arizona, and guard Dwight Anders points helped the Trojans defeat Arizona

Sports/B-1

Courting trouble for Brown

Conservatives are looking at rulings by s Court nominee Judge Cruz Reynoso for e use against him — and Gov. Brown.

News/A-3

EDITOR'S REPORT

William Randolph Hearst Jr.
Editor in Chief
The Hearst Newspapers

The same old story from Russia — and U.S. automakers

Comment/F-3

INDEX

Section B
Section C
Section D
Section E
Section F

Examiner sta

January 17, 1982 *Los Angeles Herald Examiner*

There is reason to believe that he was in Indianapolis in 1943, when Corporal Maoma Ridings was murdered in that city and that he was in Calfornia in 1944 when Georgette Bauerdorf was murdered. According to his taped interview with John Gilmore, Wilson, or at least "Al Morrison," was in California in January, 1947, when Elizabeth Short was murdered. If Wilson or "Al Morrison" was in Chicago during 1945-1946, there may be something like an arrest record, social security or wage payment, telephone number, accident report, photograph, etc., that could establish his presence in that city.

HUMAN EAR CLUE:

Following the murder of Suzanne Degnan in 1946, a human ear was mailed to Helen Degnan, along with a threatening note (page 51, *William Heirens: His Day In Court*). Following the murder of the Black Dahlia in 1947, it was discovered that one of her ear lobes had been sliced off (page 74, *Reporters: Memoirs of a Young Newspaperman*, by Will Fowler). If the person who killed Suzanne Degnan did in fact mail the ear lobe to Mrs. Degnan, this would indicate a signature similar to the ear lobe detail in the Black Dahlia case.

SIMILAR NOTES CLUES:

After Suzanne Degnan was murdered, Chicago's Mayor Kelly received a hastily written note that read:

> "This is to tell you how sorry I am I couldn't get ole Degnan instead of his girl. Roosevelt and OPA made their own laws. Why shouldn't I and a lot more? (See page 50: *William Heirens: His Day In Court)*

Published with permission by DOLORES KENNEDY
50 THE MURDERS
William Heirens: His Day in Court

> pretty big sums, as their salaries went, and that Jim indulged in some fancy borrowing to meet creditor claims when pressed.
>
> Could Jim be in debt to anyone of unbalanced mind? Could Jim have turned to less acceptable means of amplifying an income which, though increasing, failed to keep pace with the growth of his tastes? (Incidentally, he is given to gambling for what I'd consider pretty high stakes at cards.) Sinister things can happen to a man who fails to live within his income.

The author offered the names of additional people who knew Jim well upon request.

Questioned by the police about the possibility that Suzanne's death might be an act of vengeance by an unknown enemy, Degnan stated:

> I suppose I have, like anybody else, skeletons in the closet that would be incidents in your life that you would not be too keen to draw out and review, but from the bottom of my heart I can tell you I know of no incident in my life that would not bare full review in a thing like this.
>
> I have made mistakes that presumably would cause prejudices. I have thought of all the places I have been and all the people I know, and the one thing that has been a tremendous degree of satisfaction to me is that no place I have ever been I can't go back and have a lot of friends. I suppose I have people that don't like me, but nobody that I know of that feuded.

An anonymous note reported:

> Mrs. Degnan is responsible for her child's death. The Degnan child was killed by accident in her room that night.

And yet another note from a "former friend" offered:

> You surely cannot believe the father of the Degnan child is innocent. If you only knew the temper he has. He would do anything when he is in a bad mood.... We who know him are not surprised at what happened.

Mayor Kelly received a hastily written note that read:

> This is to tell you how sorry I am I couldn't get ole Degnan instead of his girl. Roosevelt and OPA made their own laws. Why shouldn't I and a lot more?

And Katherine Baker, maid to Marian Murphy of Lake Shore Drive, told police that, according to Mrs. Murphy:

Copy of page 50, *William Heirens: HIS DAY IN COURT*
Published with permission by Dolores Kennedy

Now compare the note mailed to Mayor Kelly with the December 21, 1938, letter mailed to Cleveland Chief of Police Matowitz from Los Angeles:

> "*I felt bad* operating on those people. . . *What did their lives mean in comparison* . . . In both the note to Mayor Kelly and the letter to Chief Matowitz the writer wrote that he was either "sorry" or "felt bad" followed by a question. Again the pattern is very similar.

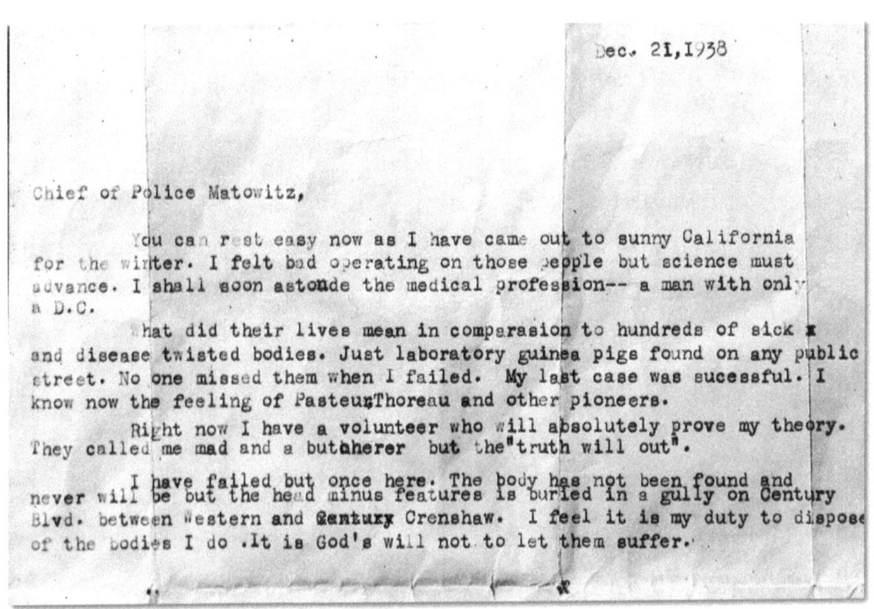

Dec. 21,1938

Chief of Police Matowitz,

You can rest easy now as I have came out to sunny California for the winter. I felt bad operating on those people but science must advance. I shall soon astonde the medical profession-- a man with only a D.C.

What did their lives mean in comparasion to hundreds of sick x and disease twisted bodies. Just laboratory guinea pigs found on any public street. No one missed them when I failed. My last case was sucessful. I know now the feeling of PasteurThoreau and other pioneers.

Right now I have a volunteer who will absolutely prove my theory. They called me mad and a butaherer but the"truth will out".

I have failed but once here. The body has not been found and never will be but the head minus features is buried in a gully on Century Blvd. between Western and Century Crenshaw. I feel it is my duty to dispose of the bodies I do .It is God's will not to let them suffer.

Copy of the 1938 letter to Chief Matowitz
(photograph courtesy of Marjorie Merylo Detnz)

CLUE: SIMILAR LETTERS MAILED FOLLOWING A MURDER:

Here is another interesting clue that may help prove that the same person or persons that killed the Black Dahlia may also have killed

Suzanne Degnan. Following the murder of Suzanne Degnan on January 7, 1946, Chicago Police Chief Walter Storm received the following enticing communication:

> "Why don't you catch me. **If** you don't ketch me soon, **I will** cummit suicide. There is a reward out for me. How much do **I get if I give** myself **up**. When do I get that **20,000** dollars they wanted from the Degnan girl at 5901 Kenmore Avenue

You may **find me** at the Club Tavern at 738 E. 63rd St. known as Charlie the Greeks. Or at Conway's Tavern at 6247 Cottage Grove Av.

Please hurry now" (emphasis added)

(Remember that Jack Anderson Wilson was an alcoholic, spent a great deal of time in bars, met with author John Gilmore in seedy bars over a period of three years, and in both cases the killer demanded the exact amount of money, $20.000.)

Published with permission by Dolores Kennedy

> It was the work of gangsters and they probably wanted to get revenge on the Flynns because I happen to know that the Flynns run a handbook.

Walter Storms received the following enticing communication:

> Why don't you catch me. If you don't ketch me soon, I will cummit suicide. There is a reward out for me. How much do I get if I give myself up. When do I get that 20,000 dollars they wanted from that Degnan girl at 5901 Kenmore Avenue.
>
> You may find me at the Club Tavern at 738 E. 63rd St. known as Charlie the Greeks. Or at Conway's Tavern at 6247 Cottage Grove Av.
>
> Please hurry now.

During the succeeding months, cranks surfaced regularly. Notes of confession were found in hallways of apartment buildings. A human ear was mailed to Helen Degnan, along with a threatening note. On May 31, a twenty-eight-year-old Michigan man appeared at the police station in Houston, Texas, announcing that he knew something about the Degnan case. He stated that "I could tell a story that would knock the Chicago cops off their feet," and promptly leaped to his death from an open window in the building.

The police department filtered the information coming in from various parts of the country—trying not to waste their time on worthless leads, while wary of neglecting anything of value.

The investigation became a dragnet of the city of Chicago. So professional was the dismemberment of Suzanne that the police wiretapped the telephone lines of neighboring butcher shops and tree surgeons, hoping to overhear incriminating conversations. Thousands of persons were questioned, especially those with any hint of sexual misbehavior in their past. A variety of busboys, bartenders, postal clerks, cab drivers, doctors, dentists, businessmen, and ex-convicts paraded before the police. Women turned in their husbands, mothers implicated their sons, and a young woman was apprehended because someone had written on the snow which clung to the trunk of her car: "ketch me before I kill."

The most promising suspects were arrested and, upon those arrests, State's Attorney William J. Tuohy and Chief of Detectives Walter G. Storms would tell the press that this time they were certain they had found the killer. Inevitably, the suspect passed the lie detector test, or came up with an alibi, or the police were forced to admit that the fingerprints did not match.

Chief Storms declared publicly that: "In the heat of public anger over this atrocious killing, there is a tendency to condemn the first person seized."

Page 51 from *William Heirens: HIS DAY IN COURT*
Published with permission by Dolores Kennedy

Now compare the letter to Chief Storm to the letter received by the *Los Angeles Herald Express*, in January, 1947, following the murder of Elizabeth Short:

"To Los Angeles Herald Express
I will give up
In Dahlia Killing **if I get**
10 years
Don't try to **find me**" (emphasis added)

In each letter not only were the exactly the same words used by the writer but also note that the order of the words in each communication was very similar:

First: **"I will"**
Second: **"If I get"** and **"I get if"**
Third: "**find me"**
Fourth: "**give myself up**" and "**give up**"
Fifth: a number, either **20,000** or **10**

I am certainly not an expert in forensic linguistics. I did submit the notes to Alan M. Perlman, PhD, an expert in forensic linguistics analysis. He indicated that "The occurrence of similar words in the two texts means nothing in itself. The longer text has some interesting properties, but the other is too short for meaningful comparisons. I find no evidence of similar or different authorship."

I had another expert (John Pahl, a professor of English and technical writing at Northwestern Michigan College) give his opinion on these two letters. He wrote, "I don't think the wording similarities are all that surprising, at least not the very brief phrases that, in normal English, are almost necessarily the words that one would use to express these thoughts. So I'd look more to the attitudes or

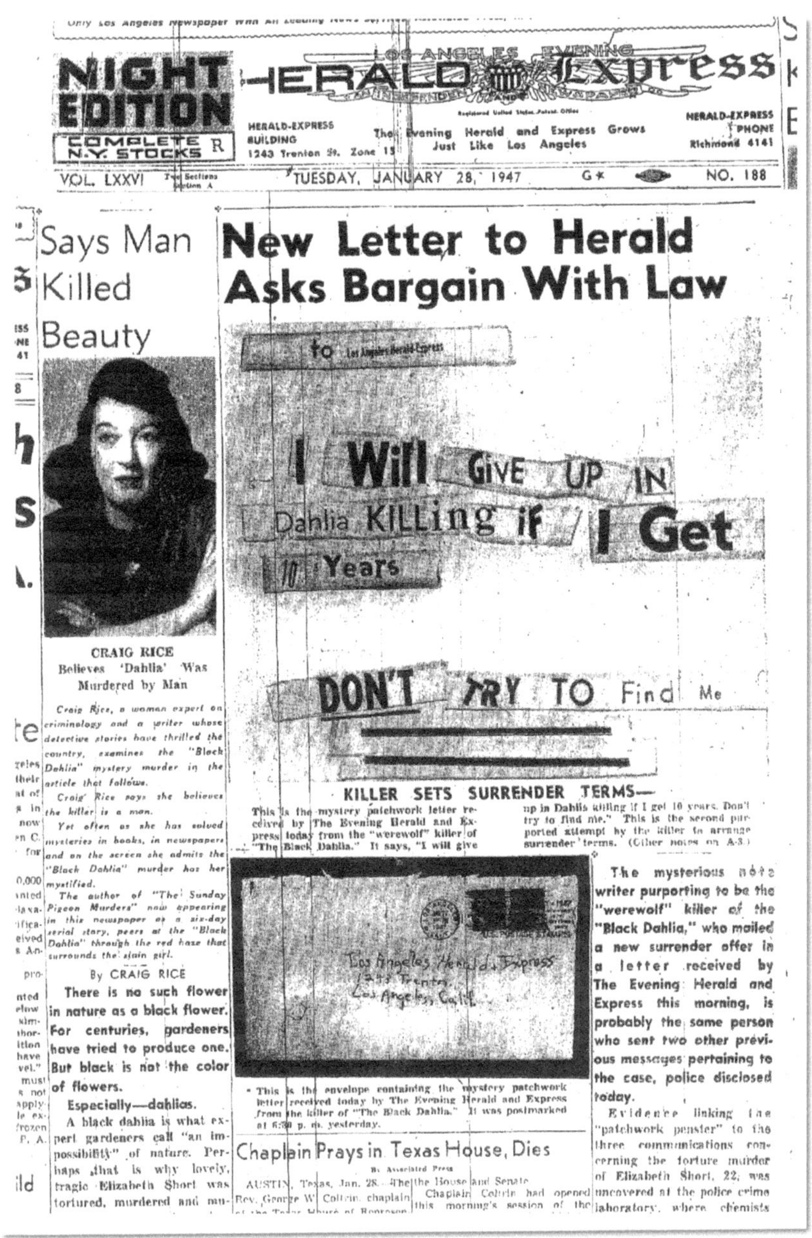

NIGHT EDITION
COMPLETE N.Y. STOCKS R

LOS ANGELES EVENING HERALD AND EXPRESS

HERALD-EXPRESS BUILDING
1243 Trenton St. Zone 15

The Evening Herald and Express Grows Just Like Los Angeles

HERALD-EXPRESS PHONE Richmond 4141

VOL. LXXVI — TUESDAY, JANUARY 28, 1947 — NO. 188

New Letter to Herald Asks Bargain With Law

to Los Angeles Herald-Express

I Will GiVE UP IN Dahlia KILLing if I Get 10 Years

DON'T TRY TO Find Me

KILLER SETS SURRENDER TERMS—

This is the mystery patchwork letter received by The Evening Herald and Express today from the "werewolf" killer of "The Black Dahlia." It says, "I will give up in Dahlia killing if I get 10 years. Don't try to find me." This is the second purported attempt by the killer to arrange surrender terms. (Other notes on A-3.)

Los Angeles Herald-Express
1243 Trenton
Los Angeles, Calif.

• This is the envelope containing the mystery patchwork letter received today by The Evening Herald and Express from the killer of "The Black Dahlia." It was postmarked at 6:30 p. m. yesterday.

The mysterious note writer purporting to be the "werewolf" killer of the "Black Dahlia," who mailed a new surrender offer in a letter received by The Evening Herald and Express this morning, is probably the same person who sent two other previous messages pertaining to the case, police disclosed today.

Evidence linking the "patchwork penster" to the three communications concerning the torture murder of Elizabeth Short, 22, was uncovered at the police crime laboratory, where chemists

Says Man Killed Beauty

CRAIG RICE
Believes 'Dahlia' Was Murdered by Man

Craig Rice, a woman expert on criminology and a writer whose detective stories have thrilled the country, examines the "Black Dahlia" mystery murder in the article that follows.

Craig Rice says she believes the killer is a man.

Yet often as she has solved mysteries in books, in newspapers and on the screen she admits the "Black Dahlia" murder has her mystified.

The author of "The Sunday Pigeon Murders" now appearing in this newspaper as a six-day serial story, peers at the "Black Dahlia" through the red haze that surrounds the slain girl.

By CRAIG RICE

There is no such flower in nature as a black flower. For centuries, gardeners have tried to produce one. But black is not the color of flowers.

Especially—dahlias.

A black dahlia is what expert gardeners call "an impossibility" of nature. Perhaps that is why lovely, tragic Elizabeth Short was tortured, murdered and mu-

Chaplain Prays in Texas House, Dies

By Associated Press

AUSTIN, Texas, Jan. 28.—The Rev. George W. Coltrin, chaplain of the Texas House of Represen- the House and Senate.

Chaplain Coltrin had opened this morning's session of the

copy of January 28, 1947 *Herald-Express* article

psychological tone expressed by the letters, that and their intended effect. There are some similarities here: Both indicate a dare—i.e., Why can't you catch me? (a challenge, a dare) and Don't (you dare) try to find me. Both raise the possibility of giving himself up, if certain conditions are met. Both are looking for some pay-off, in a lighter sentence or in cash. Having said that, I see real differences, too: The first letter provides two places to look for the writer, as though anxious to be caught or at least to be seen among a group of people. The other doesn't want to be caught, but is willing to turn himself in if the punishment is on his terms. Perhaps the most obvious contrast is that the first letter seems to represent a very incoherent train of thought, while the second, though its request for a lighter sentence is totally unrealistic, is logical and straight forward. So there are some striking similarities in what might be called the needs on the part of the writer, but some significant differences, as well, in style and logic. There's no reason they couldn't be the same writer. Even the differences could be a result of the writer behaving or feeling differently after quite different slayings in terms of the two victims or the locations, that and his increasingly urgent state of mind. It's hard to say."

Keep in mind that there were very few communications received by the authorities following the Degnan and Short murders. Each communication was very brief. The chances of two individuals writing the same words, in the same order, would seem to me to be extremely unlikely. If nothing else, one thing is for sure: William Heirens could not have written the above mentioned letter to the *Los Angeles Herald Express* in 1947, because he had been incarcerated in Chicago since July, 1946. Was Elizabeth Short silenced because she knew the real killer of Georgette Bauerdorf and Suzanne Degnan? There were reports that she was extremely afraid of someone shortly before she was murdered. Was her killer concerned that she would talk too much and tip off the authorities? Consider this, on

Wednesday, January 29, 1947, fourteen days after the Black Dahlia was murdered, Federal Inspectors at the Terminal Annex Post Office in Los Angeles received the following note:

> "A certain girl is going to get same as E.S. got if she squeals on us. We're going to Mexico City—**catch** us if you can.
> 2k's" (emphasis added)

The person who wrote this note appears to have been concerned about someone squealing on him. Did the same person(s) kill Elizabeth Short because they were concerned that she was going to "squeal" on them? The writer also used the word "catch" in the communication, the same word that was written in the "red lipstick message" by the person who killed Francis Brown, December 10, 1945, in Chicago:

> "For heavens
> Sake **catch** me
> BeFore I kill more
> I cannot control myself" (emphasis added)

And in the enticing communication to Chicago Police Chief Walter Storm following the murder of Suzanne Degnan:

> "Why don't you **catch** me. If you don't **ketch** me soon. . ."
> (emphasis added)
> (See page 51, *William Heirens: His Day In Court*)

CLUE: ENVELOPE PUNCTUATION

The 1938 letter to Cleveland Chief of Police Matowitz mailed from Los Angeles contains the same odd punctuation marks that were included in the January, 1947 letter that may have been mailed by the Black Dahlia Avenger to the Los Angeles District Attorney. Here is a copy of the 1938 envelope that was mailed from Los Angeles:

Copy of the 1938 Envelope. *Photo courtesy of Marjorie Merylo Dentz*

The 1947 envelope containing the note that may have been mailed by the Black Dahlia Avenger is addressed as follows:

District Attorney,
Hollywood, California.
(See page 170, *Black Dahlia Avenger*)

On both envelopes the first line is followed by a comma, and the last line, after the name of the state is completely spelled out, is followed with a period. Most writers would not put a comma after the first line on an envelope and most writers would not put a period after a non-abbreviated name of a state on the envelope's last line. Yet on an envelope associated with the Cleveland Torso Murders and an envelope associated with the murder of the Black Dahlia someone

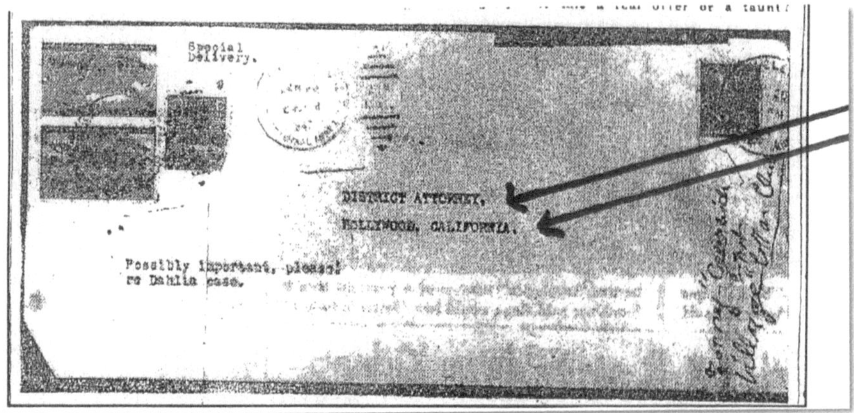

Copy of January 28, 1947 envelope mailed to the *Los Angeles Examiner*

did exactly that. This may simply be a coincidence, but then again when considered with all the other coincidences, it might not be. The envelopes may have been addressed by the same person.

CLUE: MURDER OF THE BLACK DAHLIA

On January 18, 1947, six days after Elizabeth Short had been murdered, the *Los Angeles Examiner* ran the following article:

> **MISS SHORT SOUGHT HELP IN EARLIER PLIGHT**, says Taxi Stand Manager
>
> —Monterey Park, Jan. 17.
>
> "Elizabeth Short came to my hack stand last December 29. Her clothes were torn. She told me a man she worked with had tried to attack her." These statements were made by Cab Stand Manager Glen Chandler this morning at his office, 115 North Garfield Avenue. "It was about 7 p.m. when some people dropped her off at my stand," Chandler said. "She looked wild-eyed and hysterical. Blood came from her knees.

I didn't know whether she was cut or bruised. Her clothes were torn and she didn't have any shoes on.

She told me the well-dressed man who worked with her wanted to take her to Long Beach and cash her weekly pay check for her.

"Instead, he parked his car on a lonely road just south of Garvey Boulevard near Garfield Avenue. There, she told me, was where he tried to attack her. "She fled from the car and got a ride to my stand. I put her in a cab and drove her to a hotel at 512 South Wall Street.

"I waited outside for her to come down to pay my fare. When she came down she was all dolled up. She said she didn't have the money and I figured then that I wouldn't get it.

"I don't know where she worked," Chandler said, "but she said she was a waitress.

"I'm positive that she was Elizabeth Short," he concluded.

Notice that Chandler said in this report that the man "who worked with her" tried to attack her. This would have been seventeen days before she was murdered.

If she had been attacked, as indicated by Chandler (and not otherwise discounted by the Los Angeles detectives) then it seems to me, in all likelihood, that the same person who attacked her two weeks before she was murdered was probably the same person who killed her less than seventeen days later. Assuming the taxi stand manager was correct and he did see Elizabeth Short on December 29, 1946, then ask yourself this question: How often is a girl beaten up by one person and two weeks later tortured and killed by a totally unrelated person? Elizabeth Short's friend and landlady Elvira French recalled that on or about January 2, 1947, "Some people came to our door and knocked. There was a man, a woman, and another

belonged to Miss Short's slayer.

MONEY SENT—

Discovery that the murdered girl's trunk was in Los Angeles was the result of independent investigations by the Examiner. Miss Short apparently left it behind her when she went to San Diego.

"While she was with us, she apparently needed a great deal of money for something," said Miss French. "Just before Christmas she sent a telegram to Mr. Fickling, who was then in North Carolina.

"Two days later, Betty received a Western Union money order from him for $100."

Fickling, whom Miss Short called Gordon—his middle name—had been stationed during part of the war at the Long Beach Army Air Base, now closed.

At the request of Los Angeles investigators, police at Charlotte, N. C., located Fickling.

GOT LETTER—

They telegraphed that Fickling has been back in his home community since last November 9.

He is now a co-pilot for a Chicago-to-Charlotte air line.

He told the Charlotte police he received a letter from Miss Short postmarked January 8 in San Diego. She wrote:

"Do not write to me here, I am planning to go to Chicago to work for Jack."

Jack, Fickling explained, operates an agency for models in Chicago. At one time Miss Short was a model for a hat manufacturer.

"Betty and I met in 1944 before I went overseas," Fickling was quoted. "We met again when I got back last year. We carried on a long correspondence, but there never was any talk of our marrying."

Though Miss French was the one who informed investigators of the wire from "Red," she was able to supply few other details concerning him or her guest's departure.

"Betty left alone, with her [illegible]

FOUND—Joseph G. Fickling, former Army lieutenant who was a friend of Elizabeth Short, was located today at Charlotte, N. C. He is a co-pilot for an air line and has been in North Carolina since November 9.

[illegible] been married. Betty had crossed out the 'not'. She told me the newspaper had made a mistake."

The slain girl's father was found at the South King [illegible] address by two chief [illegible] of the slaying, Detective Sergeants Harry Hansen and F. A. Brown.

"I want nothing to do with this," Short was quoted. "I broke off with the mother and the family several years ago. My wife wanted it that way.

"When I left the family, I provided a trust fund for their support.

"Five years ago, though, Elizabeth wrote to me. So I sent her some money. She came out here and we set up housekeeping in Vallejo. But she wouldn't stay home.

"In 1943, I told her to go her way, I'd go mine.

"After that she was in Santa Barbara, where she was arrested for juvenile delinquency, and later worked in Camp Cooke."

Miss Short's mother was en route by plane to Los Angeles last night.

Mrs. Short learned of her daughter's death from the Los Angeles Examiner, after it had [illegible]

[illegible] hotel, now called the [illegible] at 53 Linden avenue," said Arnold Landers Sr., the pharmacy owner.

"She'd come into our drug store frequently. She'd usually wear a two-piece beach costume which left her midriff [illegible]

Death Victim Looked Worried, Says Landlady

"I felt sorry for her even when she got brutal on the rent. She looked tired and worried."

[illegible]

NOVEMBER 13—

"She came here for a room last November 13. That's a bad day, isn't it?" Mrs. Ringo said.

"She wasn't sociable like the other girls who lived in apartment 501 with her—more the sophisticated type.

"When I went up for the rent last December 3 she didn't have it. I don't think she had a job. That night she got the money somewhere and left the next morning."

BOY FRIEND—

Linda [illegible], who works in the rouge room at Max Factor's, also remembered her "odd" roommate. Eight girls live in the apartment.

"She was out nearly every night. She had a lot of telephone calls, mostly from her *'favorite boy friend,'* Maurice.

"The morning she left she was very anxious," Linda continued.

"She said, *'I've got to hurry—he's waiting for me.'* We never found out who he was. She was supposed to go to live with her sister in Berkeley."

Miss Short Sought Help in Earlier Plight, Says Taxi Stand Manager

MONTEREY PARK, Jan. 17.—"Elizabeth Short came to my hack stand last December 23. Her clothes were torn. She told me a man she worked with had tried to attack her."

These statements were made by Cab Stand Manager Glen Chansler this morning at his office, 115 North Garfield avenue.

"It was about 7 p. m. when some people dropped her off at my stand," Chansler said. "She looked wild-eyed and hysterical. Blood came from her knees. I didn't know whether she was cut or bruised. Her clothes were torn and she didn't have any shoes on.

"She told me the well-dressed man who worked with her wanted to take her to Long Beach and cash her weekly pay check for her.

"Instead, he parked his car on a lonely road just south of Garvey boulevard near Garfield avenue. There, she told me, was where he tried to attack her.

"She fled from the car and got a ride to my stand. I put her in a cab and drove her to a hotel at 512 South Wall street.

"I waited outside for her to come down to pay the fare. When she came down she was all dolled up. She said she didn't have the money and I figured then that I wouldn't get it.

"I don't know where she worked," Chansler said, "but she said she was a waitress.

"I'm positive that she was Elizabeth Short," he concluded.

FROM MAGNIN'S YOUNG THIRD FLOOR

Los Angeles Examiner

CHARACTER QUALITY · AMERICA FIRST! · ENTERPRISE ACCURACY

AN AMERICAN PAPER FOR THE AMERICAN PEOPLE · THE GREAT NEWSPAPER OF THE GREAT SOUTHWEST

Los Angeles Examiner Jan. 18, 1947

January 18, 1947, *The Los Angeles Examiner*

man was waiting in a car parked on the street in front of the house. Beth became very frightened—she seemed to get panicky, and didn't want to see the people or answer the door. They finally went back to the car and drove away. Even our neighbors thought all of this was very suspicious."

CLUE: "WAITRESS"

Jack Anderson Wilson mentioned in his taped message to John Gilmore, "This is what he had in mind for the **waitress**" (See page 89 of the text).

Cab stand manager Glen Chandler is quoted in the January 18, 1947, *Los Angeles Examiner* as follows:

> "I don't know where she worked," Chandler said, "but she said she was a **waitress**."

Was Elizabeth Short working as a waitress? If so, where and who was she working with during the last weeks in 1946, and the first week in 1947? Was Jack Anderson Wilson working in the same establishment?

CLUES FROM AUTOPSY REPORT

Dr. Victor CeFalu assisted Chief Surgeon Dr. Newbarr in the autopsy of Elizabeth Short. The autopsy report contained in part the following information:

> There were multiple lacerations to the midforehead, in the right forehead, and at the top of the head in the midline. There are multiple tiny abrasions and lacerations. The trunk is completely severed by an incision, which is almost straight through the abdomen. There are multiple crisscross lacerations in the suprapublic area, which extend through the skin and soft tissues. There are lacerations of the intestine and kidneys. The uterus is small and no pregnancy is apparent. The tubes, ovaries, and cul-de-sac are intact. Within the vagina and higher up there is lying loose a small piece of skin with

> fat and subcutaneous tissue attached. On this piece of loose skin there are several crisscrossing lacerations. Smears for spermatozoa have been taken. The anal opening is markedly dilated and the opening measures 1" in diameter. There are multiple abrasions. Smears for spermatozoa have been taken. The stomach is filled with greenish brown granular matter, mostly feces and other particles, which could not be identified. All smears for spermatozoa were negative. It appeared as though many of the lacerations, including the dilation of the anal opening were done after the woman's death.

One of the photos of Elizabeth Short taken at the Los Angeles County Morgue shortly after her murder shows possible bruising near her left knee. If the autopsy report makes mention of the bruising and/or lacerations to her knees, this would tend to verify the report given by taxi stand manager Glen Chandler.

See also, for comparison, the photo of victim No.5 on page 3 of this text. His anal opening is markedly dilated. The anal sphincter muscle that closes the anus no longer functions in a dead body. It appears that victim No.5 was either penetrated sexually or with a foreign object after he was killed.

CLUE: "DESPERATELY NEEDED MONEY"

I am going to mention a few other known facts concerning the last days of Elizabeth Short's life that may shed a light on her killer's identity. Keep in mind that in the Cleveland Torso Murders some of the victims were drugged before being murdered. ("An addict named Al may have supplied Torso victim Flo Polillo with drugs.") Let me preface this information by stating that I believe Elizabeth Short was a beautiful young lady whose life and aspirations spiraled down a dark path out of her control into the web of a vicious predator.

A review of known facts concerning the Black Dahlia covering the time period of December 29, 1946, through January 9, 1947, reveals the following:

1. She was broke and virtually penniless. She could not afford cab fare.
2. She could not afford to rent an apartment and was allowed to live at Elvira French's home for $1.00 per day. According to Los Angeles Detective Joel Lesnick, "Elizabeth was on a hard road, couldn't seem to land a job and having to mooch off friends. . . She wasn't following through with long-range plans, I believe, and bounced from situation to situation; hence the number of apartments and rented rooms she was in. Was she a true friend to the drunks and downtrodden, or was it part of an act?"
3. Her teeth were decaying and she could not afford to go to a dentist. (At some point in time did someone offer her some form of addictive pain medication for her tooth aches?)
4. She "desperately needed money." On January 8, 1947, her friend, Gordan Fickling, wired $100.00 to her from North Carolina. (Keep in mind that $100.00 in 1947, would have been the equivalent of approximately $1,000.00 in today's dollars.)
5. She owed Elvira French rent money in San Diego but did not pay her out of the money wired from Fickling.
6. According to Dorothy French, daughter of Elvira French, Elizabeth Short was "down and out."
7. She needed new shoes but instead had Red Manley get her old shoes repaired.
8. She was having mood swings and was "flighty and nervous," according to Elvera French.

9. Elvera French said Beth became very "frightened" she seemed to get "panicky."
10. She was down to her last pair of stockings but didn't purchase new ones out of the $100.00 wired from Fickling.
11. Mrs. French said "she was in constant fear of someone" and "frightened when anyone came to the door."
12. "She had chills all night January 8, 1947, at the motel with Red Manley."
13. "She had scratch marks on her arms," Manley said and that "one of them seemed to be bleeding." Short explained that the scratch marks were from a "jealous boyfriend." The marks on her arms were "on the outside, above the elbows."
14. On January 9, 1947, she got all "dolled up," according to Manley, who dropped her off at the Biltmore Hotel in Los Angeles. Manley had asked her where she wanted to be dropped off. He said, "At the Biltmore?" and her response was, "Yes, at the Biltmore." In her financial condition it seems very unlikely that her intended stay was the Biltmore Hotel. She made telephone calls to someone from the Biltmore.
15. On the evening of January 9, 1947, a doorman at the Biltmore last saw her walking towards Sixth Street and into history.
16. Elizabeth Short's remains are buried at the Mountain View Cemetery in Oakland, California.

CLUE: TWO MEN AND A FEMALE IMPERSONATOR

In all three cases, the Cleveland Torso Murders, the murder of Suzanne Degnan and the murder of the Black Dahlia similar reports appear concerning three individuals. The most likely suspects to me are the individual named "Eddie" who is mentioned in the murder of Cleveland Torso Victim, Edward Andrassy and in association with

Los Angeles Examiner January 27, 1947

Teaches Us Today
(See Editorial Page)

Examiner Telephone Richmond 1212

AN AMERICAN PAPER FOR THE AMERICAN PEOPLE — THE GREAT NEWSPAPER OF THE GREAT SOUTHWEST

Examiner Building, 1111 S. Broadway

VOL. XLIV—NO. 47 — LOS ANGELES, MONDAY, JANUARY 27, 1947

Two Women Tell Dahlia's Fear of Mysterious Trio

...enefactors Reveal Fright Over Visit

Deep-rooted fear of some... e or something claimed po... e attention yesterday in the ...se of Elizabeth Short, the ...ain "Black Dahlia," as new ...tails came to light.

From Mrs. Elvera French and ...r daughter, Dorothy, officials ...arned of a mysterious trio who ...ightened Miss Short shortly ...fore her death.

The slain girl lived in the ...rench home at Pacific Beach ...r a month prior to January 8, ...hen she left for Los Angeles ...d her date with death.

...IRL'S STORY——

Dorothy French said:

"I heard of the two men and woman from a neighbor, since I was sleeping when they came to our home. It was on January 7, the day the telegram came for Betty (Miss Short) from 'Red.'

"The neighbor said the three people went to our door and knocked. They waited, then backed away quickly and ran to their parked car. The door had not opened before they drove off.

"When I heard of the visitors, I asked Betty about them. She admitted hearing them knock and said she peeped at them through the window.

"She was terribly frightened, though, and refused to talk about them. She was evasive when I asked other questions, so I gave up.

"She also told me that a woman chased her and a friend of hers on Hollywood boulevard just before I met her early in December."

BETTY IN FEAR——

Mrs. French added:

"Betty seemed constantly in fear of something. Whenever anyone came to the door she would act frightened."

Detectives Harry Hansen and Jess Haskins immediately asked San Diego police to check on the trio.

Robert "Red" Manley, exonerated friend of Miss Short, conferred with the officers, Mrs. French and her daughter. He reiterated that the "Dahlia" had expressed fear of an "insanely jealous man."

(Picture and additional news on Dahlia killing on Page 2.)

Egypt, British Talks Fail

Pact Meet Collapses; Students Riot

By W. P. Saphir

CAIRO, Jan. 26.—Egypt's Premier Mahmoud Nokrashy Pasha announced tonight that negotiations for revision of the Anglo-Egyptian treaty have been broken off.

Egypt will submit to the United Nations the dispute over sovereignty of the Sudan.

Sixty-four students were arrested in riots that broke out at various universities in Alexandria in demonstrations against latest treaty developments.

Five students and four policemen were injured in clashes in which the police fired buckshot and charged the students with batons.

SEDAN ISSUE——

The Premier said he would air the entire matter before Parliament tomorrow.

Nokrashy Pasha said the treaty negotiations were halted when his cabinet rejected the latest British proposals on the Sudan. The country is now governed jointly by Great Britain and Egypt.

These reportedly suggested establishment of a tripartite commission of Britons, Egyptians and Sudanese to prepare a program for self government by the Sudan.

The British embassy in Cairo said that the British government in London sees no legal grounds for any recourse to the U. N.

The British said that the Egyptian government has insisted that it be allowed to annex Sudan outright, while British representatives are holding out for eventual Sudanese independence, or self-determination.

'Teaching Control' Newest Jap Strike

NAGOYA, Japan, Jan. 26.—(AP)—Sixteen hundred students of Chukyo Commercial School and Girls' School have started a new kind of strike which they call "teaching control."

Demanding "democratization" of the school system, the students barred their teachers from the classrooms but went on with their studies, conducted by upper-grade students.

Allis CIO Wins Bargaining Vote

MILWAUKEE, Jan. 26.—(AP)—Despite failure to receive the majority required by law, striking UAW-CIO local 248 today remained as collective bargaining agent at Allis-Chalmers by defeating the challenging independent workers of Allis-Chalmers in a close election.

The Wisconsin employment relations board, which ordered and supervised the election, announced the CIO local had polled

Texas Quad Girls to Mark Birthday

GALVESTON, Jan. 26.—(INS)—Joan, Jeraldine, Jeanette and Joyce Badgett, the country's youngest all-girl quadruplets, looked forward today to a birth-

KENNEY WARNS OF NORTH POLE ATTACK ON U.S.

25 Million Casualties in First Day, Air General Predicts

WASHINGTON, Jan. 26.—(INS)—General George C. Kenney predicted today that if there is a third world war, the United States will be attacked from the north polar basin.

He said 25,000,000 persons might be on the casualty list in the first 24 hours.

Kenney, commanding general of the Strategic Air Command, declared that this country will be No. 1 on the priority list of objectives which the "next Hitler will hand his boss gunmen."

The general addressed the closing session of the Women's Patriotic Conference, to which 29 organizations sent delegates.

TRAINING URGED——

Secretary of War Patterson told the gathering that universal military training is a "must." Shortly after hearing Patterson the 1200 delegates approved a resolution indorsing "wholeheartedly" a program of universal military training.

The conference adopted resolutions recommending that the atomic bomb be retained as an exclusive secret of the United States and that immigration laws be strengthened rather than weakened.

It urged that all necessary funds be given the House committee on un-American activities.

General Kenney told the conference that he was "not preaching war."

However, he said failure to prepare against the possibility of another war would constitute "criminal negligence" and, he said, "those 300,000 white crosses of World War II will agree with me."

SUPER WEAPONS——

He said that if the United States can be knocked out in the next war, world domination is assured the victor.

Kenney, in picturing the start of another war, declared:

"The attack will come over the shortest air routes from the European-Asiatic land mass, across the north polar basin.

"It will be directed against our centers of industry and population.

"It will be made by both piloted and pilotless aircraft, by radio-controlled missiles, by rockets—all loaded with atomic bombs, super explosives, super incendiaries, bacterial weapons.

"If you need a yardstick to show you that I'm not exaggerating this nightmare, remember that four atomic bombs of the old Hiroshima-Nagasaki type, properly placed, would knock New York City out of commission."

U.S. Ship Aground Off French Coast

NEW YORK, Jan. 26.—(AP)—The 15,199-ton American Victory

GANG KIDNAPS BRITISH BANKER IN JERUSALEM

Victim Taken to Ancient Moslem Cemetery After Being Beaten

JERUSALEM, Jan. 26.—(AP)—Four men and a woman, described by police as members of the Jewish underground, cholorformed and kidnaped a British businessman tonight and then disappeared with him into an ancient Moslem cemetery containing a maze of catacombs.

The dramatic abduction unloosed rumors that other kidnapings had occurred throughout Palestine, all of which were denied by police.

One report, which police said after investigation they were "unable now to confirm," told of the seizing of a British army officer.

FORMER MAJOR——

The businessman who was abducted was identified as H. I. Collins, 48, a former British army major and now director of the Jewish owned British bank in Palestine.

Police said that a girl present at the abduction told them that Collins "was struck with a long wooden handle on the right temple and then on the right wrist as he raised his arms to protect himself."

A search for him was promptly organized.

HEART OF CITY——

Six hundred British troops, carrying machine guns and lighting their way with parachute flares and tracer bullets swiftly surrounded a half-mile-square area of the cemetery, situated in the very heart of Jerusalem. A British officer said, however, that "about all we can hope to find is a dead body."

British officials attributed the kidnaping to Irgun Zvai Leumi, and said it was in "retaliation" for the sentence pronounced on Dova Bela Groner, alleged Irgun member who is under sentence to die Tuesday for an attack on a Palestine police station.

Stromberg Junior Weds in Raleigh

Hunt Stromberg Jr., 23, son of the film producer, was married last night in Raleigh, N. C. His bride is Marilyn Elwell, 20, alumna of the University of Georgia.

After the ceremony the couple flew to New York, where young Stromberg is a theatrical producer.

Chairman Named by YMCA Board

NEW YORK, Jan. 26.—(AP)—James C. Donnell II, of Findlay, Ohio, today was elected chairman of the national board of the YMCA.

22 Stolen Autos in 216 Crimes

In the past 24 hours

Grace Moore, Prince, 20 Ot... in Fiery Air...

PRINCE DEAD—Heir to the Swedish throne, Prince Gustaf Adolf, was among 22 killed in Dutch airliner crash.
Associated Press wirephoto.

SINGER MEETS DE... and film star, who was killed yester... hagen. The singer was en route to ...

Man Plunges 86 Stories

Empire Building Leaper Falls on Woman

(Photo on Page Two)

NEW YORK, Jan. 26.—(AP)—A man identified as David H. Gordon Jr. leaped 1000 feet to his death today from the 86th floor observation tower of the Empire State Building.

He evaded efforts of guards and another spectator to prevent him from jumping.

The body crashed onto Mrs. Frances Coover, 51, of Ames, Iowa, who was walking along 34th street. Mrs. Coover was taken to St. Vincent's Hospital, where she was reported to be suffering from multiple fractures.

The man, who was identified from papers in his pockets, took an elevator to the tower of the building, tallest in the world.

Chief Petty Officer James Lambert, who was looking out over the city, said the man removed his hat, coat and gloves and then put one foot on the parapet.

CALLS FOR HELP——

"What are you going to do?" Lambert asked.

"I'm going to jump," the man replied.

Lambert said he tried to dissuade the man and shouted for help.

Max Furman, an Assistant State Attorney General, identified Gordon as his nephew and said the victim was 28 years old.

The hospital reported Mrs. Coover had suffered a possible fractured left arm, possible fractured neck and the skin was ripped from her left foot below

Housing Sho... Price Drop

WASHINGTON, Jan. 26.-... housing shortage will be "sub... altogether in 1947 came today f... tatives.

A third predicted a buyers' market in real estate.

"If the Government lets us build, the housing shortage will be over by the end of 1947 and home prices will soften simultaneously," said Herbert U. Nelson, executive vice president of the National Association of Real Estate Boards.

The "buyers' market" prediction came from W. Wadsworth Wood, president of the Home Builders' Institute and publisher of the small homes annual, in another interview.

"The peak in prices of old houses has been reached and passed," Wood said. "The classified columns are twice as long as they were six months ago, and for-rent listings are beginning to appear in most cities."

The National Association of Home Builders, announcing that private builders hope to erect 1,000,000 houses this year, declared that "good news is in

Byrd to Lead

copy of *Los Angeles Examiner* article dated Jan. 27, 1947

Jack Anderson Wilson (see *Severed*, page 180); a person by the name of Al Morrison, who is named as the killer of the Black Dahlia in Jack Anderson Wilson's taped message to John Gilmore; more than likely the same person by the name of "Al" who is mentioned in the Cleveland Torso Murders as having supplied Cleveland Torso Victim Flo Polillo with drugs; and of course Jack Anderson Wilson. Remember that Wilson refers to a female impersonator in his taped message and the Indianapolis police suspected a female impersonator may have been connected with the murder of Corporal Maoma Ridings.

Now, with that in mind, look at the facts that arose from each case:

Cleveland Torso Murders

First: In the Cleveland Torso Murders Detective Peter Merylo suspected more than one person was involved in the murders. He surmised that it would have been too difficult for one man to carry the heavy bodies undetected into Kingsbury Run and deposit them. On July 23, 1936, *The Cleveland Press* ran the following article:

POLICE SEEKING THRILL SLAYERS

"A GROUP OF THRILL-SEEKERS IS RESPONSIBLE FOR Cleveland's grisly series of decapitation murders, detectives believed today as they puzzled over the fifth headless body found in the last 11 months."

07/26/2005 18:52 2166879328 CDBM

in open new land developments.

This was the testimony today of Arthur L. Sackett, the company's assistant treasurer, before William B. Woods, special master in bankruptcy.

There was one exception to continuance of pre-depression policies, Mr. Sackett explained. The "assurance contract" given land purchasers would not be resumed. This was a contract under which the Van Sweringen Co. agreed, under certain condition and after death of the original purchaser, to buy back the contracted land.

"Assurances" Released

Mr. Sacket testified under questioning by attorneys representing holders of these "assurance contracts" that the company had in recent years obtained releases from the contracts by paying $1 to holders. He said this had been done in 30 cases of the 104 such contracts held.

He was asked if the company were not insolvent at the time of these $1 releases, but an objection prevented his answer.

Mr. Sackett, outlining the original plan to divide large plots into small estates, to build a Chagrin Falls boulevard to match the present Gates Mills boulevard, and to make a super-highway out of Shaker boulevard, revealed the Van Sweringen tendency to retain ultimate control over the area.

Policy Detailed

This was brought out in testimony that the company retains title and mortgage claims to property originally designed to carry streets.

The Van Sweringen attitude was developed in an exchange between Robert C. Lee, the Van Sweringen expert on reorganization, and Attorneys J. C. Logue and Sidney N. Weitz, representing bondholders.

The Van Sweringen attitude—as expressed by the witness and Attorney Joseph C. Little—was exemplified in a series of exchanges between those two and Attorneys J. C. Logue and Sidney N. Weitz, representing bondholders and opposing some aspects of the plan.

Mr. Logue: Are you unalterably opposed to bondholders being represented on the conversion (liquidation) committee?

Mr. Lee: Not at all; I am of the opinion that they are well represented by the present setup of the qualifications committee.

PRIEST NAMED AS 3D ARBITER

Msgr. Smith Chairman of Board Settling Street Railway Union Dispute

The Rt. Rev. Msgr. Joseph F. Smith, vicar general of the Catholic Diocese, today was named impartial chairman of the arbitration board to settle the dispute between the Cleveland Railway Co. and the Street Car Men's Union.

He was agreed to at a conference today between William H. Boyd, attorney, arbiter for the company,

remark raises an interesting question:

Can a man still be a gentleman and a master in chancery?

POLICE SEEKING THRILL SLAYERS

Fifth Headless Victim Found Indicates Homeless Pursued by Murderers

A group of thrill-killers is responsible for Cleveland's grisly series of decapitation murders, detectives believed today as they puzzled over the fifth headless body found in the last 11 months.

Coroner A. J. Pearse, after exhaustive tests, today established that blood was on the nearby clothing of the middle-aged man, dead at least two months, whose nude body was found yesterday in a gully near the Baltimore & Ohio tracks a half-mile south of the Industrial Rayon Corp.

Dr. Pearse, although he still had not been able to determine how the victim's head was removed from the body, discovered that the right sleeve of the dead man's coat had been slashed as by a knife.

There were no identifying marks on the clothing or papers of any kind in the pockets.

What puzzled Dr. Pearse was how the head could have been removed. It was separated from the spine at the juncture of two vertebrae and gave no signs of having been cut. The skill and anatomical knowledge of a surgeon would have been required to perform a job so neat without leaving evidence of cutting, Dr. Pearse said.

Indications increased that the slayers pick on homeless men not likely to be identified. The latest victim, a man of about 40, had extremely long hair, indicating he probably was a transient.

Likewise the last body—that of a youth of 21—never was identified, despite the presence of numerous tattoo marks all over his body which would have been recognized by friends if he had been a Clevelander.

The youth's body, lying 100 feet from the Kingsbury Run gulch, where his head lay wrapped in his trousers, was found June 6.

Six months before, in January, various portions of the decimated body of Mrs. Florence Sawdey Polillo, 47, began to turn up in lower East Side spots, although her head was never found. In September of last year the headless bodies of Edward Andrassy, 47, and an older man never identified were found in Kingsbury Run not far from where the June victim was found.

police precincts to act on complaints of gambling and vice conditions forwarded directly from the safety director's office, probably will result in further suspensions, it was indicated today by Mr. Ness.

As preparations were being made for the hearing on Saturday of Capt. Lenahan, suspended on charges of intoxication while on duty, the safety director indicated drastic action against negligent police officers.

Inspector Costello was called upon by the director yesterday to explain why the place flourished uninterruptedly, and further why his three sons worked for McGinty at the Bainbridge Race Track at $4 a day.

The inspector admitted his sons worked for McGinty, but insisted they obtained the jobs themselves during vacation to help pay for their education.

No further comment was forthcoming from Capt. Lenahan today. His wife told reporters that the "captain is in bed sick." She added that it was "doctor's orders" that he see no one.

CLEVELANDERS PASS OHIO PHARMACY TEST

Cincinnati Man Tops List With 92 Per Cent Grade

Press State Service

CEDAR POINT, O., July 23—Sixteen Clevelanders today were granted certificates for registration as pharmacists by the Ohio State Board of Pharmacy in session here.

The successful Clevelanders were: Louis E. Golenberg, Charles W. Nevel, Marjorie Loesch, Robert J. Remenyi, Gene W. Johnston, Gustav C. Kostell, Joseph E. Dudas, Maurice Fishman, Meyer H. Kassoff, Benjamin Goldman, Harry Grushcow, Joseph E. Huber, Samuel J. Cantor, V. C. Sidorovich, Alex Saferin, Ann J. Donnelly and Jerry R. Bassichus.

Passing grades were won by 72 of 88 applicants who took the state examinations in Columbus June 16 and 17. S. S. Micall of Cincinnati was high with 92 per cent.

COLONIAL HOTEL OPENS CLUB BAR

Fixtures, Ornaments From Original Rooms Used in New One

Completion of a new "club bar" executed after the traditions of years ago was announced today by the Colonial Hotel, 523 Prospect avenue.

In contrast with the trend toward modernism displayed in similar spots, the new bar is decorated with old bronze pieces and paintings from the estate of the original Colonial Hotel valued at $30,000 by the management.

Two of the old bartenders in Cleveland, Harry Cushing and Bill Carey, will preside. The "club bar" has a capacity of 45 persons, and both food and drinks will be served.

Cleveland Press July 23, 1936 P. 14

Cleveland Press July 23, 1936 P. 14

July 23, 1936 *The Cleveland Press* article

In the case of Cleveland Torso Victim No. 8, Rose Wallace, "A woman identified only as Mrs. Carter of Hazen Court reported seeing her in a car with three white man, but after that, Rose Wallace simply vanished" (page 115, *In the Wake of the Butcher*).

John Bartlow Martin wrote in *Butcher's Dozen* on pages 60-61:

> Captain J.C. Van Buren of the Nickel Plate police believes he carried them along the lee of an embankment a quarter of a mile from East 37th Street; others argue he would have deposited them in a safer jungle of bushes closer to 37th Street and, moreover, that they were too heavy to be carried so far. Van Buren replies that perhaps there were two murderers.

Murder of Suzanne Degnan

Cecelia Flynn remembered hearing two men arguing in the street below at or about the time Suzanne Degnan was kidnapped from her parents' home in Chicago (page 47, *William Heirens: His Day In Court*).

Witness Robert Reisner told police of a dark-gray car parked on Thorndale with a bareheaded, heavy-set man behind the wheel (page 47, *William Heirens: His Day In Court*). Several taxi drivers reported that they saw a man and a woman driving up and down Thorndale Avenue the night Suzanne was murdered.

William Heirens' "confession" mentioned that he wore a babushka over his head. Was the "confession" concocted in such a way that it in effect presents William Heirens as a female impersonator? Again the reports from witnesses, when taken together, may indicate the presence of three individuals, one of which may have been a female impersonator.

Look again at the Heirens "confession" and compare it to the facts of the Suzanne Degnan murder.

Bill Heirens' "confession" includes the following dialog:

Q. Do you remember how you lifted the sewer cover in which you put the arms?
A. No, I got it up, and I was holding it up like that. That is how it fell down and caught my finger.
Q. What hand did you have on the sewer cover?
A. My right.
Q. And what hand got hurt when the sewer cover fell down?
A. My right.
Q. You mean that your fingers were pinched between the sewer cover and the rim which it fit?
A. No, it didn't get into the rim, it fell on the ground.
Q. You had taken the sewer cover completely off the hole?
A. Yes.
Q. After it fell down and hurt your fingers, did you put it back on the hole again?
A. Yes, sir.

It was also suggested that Heirens used the .32 caliber revolver to pry open the storm sewer covers. Again, I don't believe this is possible. The sewer covers are approximately two inches thick and are constructed of heavy gauge solid-iron. If you have a .32 caliber, make sure it is unloaded and give it a try. You won't be able to open the subject storm sewer covers with one. Here is a photo of a .32 caliber:

Photo of .32 caliber

I believe that it is nearly physically impossible for the crime to have been committed by one person as explained in the "confession" of William Heirens. In 1946, as they are today, Thorndale Avenue, Winthrop Avenue, Kenmore and Admore Avenues in Chicago were densely populated areas. Separate body parts were located in storm sewers and catch basins off alleys between Winthrop Avenue and Kenmore Avenue, in an alley between Kenmore Avenue and Sheridan Avenue, in a sewer on Admore Avenue, and in an alley near Hollywood Avenue. I personally retraced the route that was taken by the killers and located each separate storm sewer where Suzanne Degnan's body parts were discarded. Each storm sewer and catch basin is covered by an extremely heavy iron cover that is virtually impossible to remove with your bare hands. They are noisy if moved without assistance. Yet a total of five separate storm sewers, catch basins and sewers were used by the killer(s) to dispose of the body parts. In my estimation no one person could have or would have embarked on such a task. It would have been nearly impossible. It makes no sense. A lone killer would have either left the gory, blood-soaked body parts where he dismembered her, in the laundry room, or in a waste receptacle, or in the first storm sewer he managed to open, and then fled the highly populated area before being detected.

If the sewer cover fell on his fingers as indicated in the Heiren's "Confession" (see page 155 of this text), they would have been crushed, not hurt. As I recall, the storm sewer in the alley where the arms were deposited is a hard surface, so a falling iron storm sewer cover could cause serious injury to a person's fingers. I suspect that William Heirens hurt his fingers when he was hit on the head with a flower pot following an attempted burglary.

A more logical explanation of the way Suzanne Degnan's body parts were discarded would go like this:

The killers knew where the storm sewers were located in advance of the crime. They must have because the crime took place late at night and the alleys and streets were dimly lit in 1946. The January evening was cold and wet, as were the heavy iron sewer covers.

Without gloves they would have been uncomfortable to handle. The killers had to have a tool similar to a pick to pry open the heavy sewer covers. One of them acted as a lookout while the covers were removed and the body parts transported. Timing was all important so that the crime would go undetected. The murder, dismemberment and discarding of a child's body parts in seperate storm sewers were committed with the intended purpose of shocking and horrifying the community just like in the Cleveland Torso Murders and the murder of the Black Dahlia. In the Suzanne Degnan murder her body was "expertly" dismembered, a ransom note in the amount of $20,000 was left by the killers, clothing was burned, oil applied to the ransom note, body parts were deposited in storm sewers, the floor of the crime scene was mopped. This murder-dismemberment shocked the nation. In the murder of the Black Dahlia, her body was "expertly" severed, a ransom note demanding $20,000 was found in a murder case associated with the murder of the Black Dahlia (according to Jack Anderson Wilson's taped message to John Gilmore), clothing was burned following the murder, her purse was found soaked in gas. And, again according to Wilson's taped message to Gilmore, evidence was put into storm sewers and the crime scene floor was mopped. Her murder, too, shocked the entire nation.

In order to prove that I am correct, the Chicago Police Department should attempt to recreate the way Suzanne Degnan's murder took place—this time using a dead animal of similar size and weight and following these steps:

1. Have a seventeen-year-old strong, able-bodied boy carry a seventy-four pound dead animal from 5943 Kenmore Avenue to the laundry room at 5901 Winthrop Avenue.
2. Have the boy dismember the animal in the unlit laundry room with the assistance of a flashlight and a "knife" he carries in his pocket.

3. Have the boy move the head, legs and torso of the animal from the laundry room at 5901 Winthrop Avenue at 1:00 a.m. (Make sure the street lights are dimmed to reflect the lighting present in 1946).
4. Have the boy carry the individual animal parts to the storm sewer in the alley at 5907 Kenmore, to the storm sewer at Admore & Kenmore, to the storm sewer in the alley at 5900 Kenmore, and to the storm sewer in the alley at 5838 Kenmore Avenue.
5. Have the boy lift and remove the heavy, cold storm sewer covers with his bare hands and/or the butt of a .32 caliber revolver (At least one of the storm sewer covers is screwed shut so be sure to remove the screws).
6. Have the boy deposit individual animal parts in the storm sewers, returning each time to 5901 Winthrop Avenue to retrieve the other animal body parts.
7. Drop the last storm sewer cover located at 5701 Broadway Avenue on the boy's right hand fingers.
8. Have the boy then return to the laundry room at 5901 Winthrop Avenue, mop the floor and write a ransom note with an injured hand.
9. Have the boy deliver the ransom note to 5901 Kenmore Avenue—all without being detected. (The Degnan home is no longer at that address.)

I can assure you that the seventeen-year-old boy will not be able to complete the process. Neither could William Heirens or anyone else for that matter, because the fact is—it is next to impossible for one person, acting alone, to complete all of the steps that were followed in the Suzanne Degnan murder. If you don't believe me, give it a try. I guarantee it can't be done the way it is described in the Heirens "confession."

Black Dahlia Murder

After January 1, 1947, a little more than one week before she disappeared, Elizabeth Short was seen in the company of three individuals, two men and a woman. Dorothy French recalled "a couple of days later some people came to our door and knocked. There was a man and a woman and another man was waiting in a car parked on the street in front of the house." (The woman may have been a female impersonator.)

CLUE: $20,000 RANSOM NOTE

On January 7, 1946, the killer of Suzanne Degnan left a ransom note on the window ledge of her bedroom demanding $20,000. On February 11, 1947, in Los Angeles following the murder of Jeanne Axford French, a ransom note was found in the glove compartment of Los Angeles taxi driver Charles Schneider's taxicab demanding $20,000. Detectives thought that the person who killed French also killed the Black Dahlia.

"ITALIAN" CLUE

John Barlow Martin wrote in *Butcher's Dozen* in 1945, on page 65, the following excerpt concerning the murder of Cleveland Torso Victim, Flo Polillo:

> About six weeks before she was murdered, Flo Polillo had returned to the hotel, this time with "an unknown Italian described as twenty-seven-years-old, five feet eight or nine, 135 pounds, dark complexioned wearing a dark cap, a description that nearly matched the description of Andrassy's friend "Eddie." And there was an Italian named "Al" who

was a drug addict and also furnished Florence Martin with drugs.

In the case of Cleveland Torso Victim, Edward Andrassy:

Andrassy told his sister that he had stabbed an Italian in a fight at East 9th Street and Bolivar "and that the gang was after him." He stayed close to home. There was no police report on such a fight. An informer said he had concealed Andrassy for three days, until an Italian drove up in a Dodge touring car, invited the informer to go for a ride (he declined), and took Andrassy away.

On page 60 Martin wrote:

Andrassy left home for the last time at 8:00 P.M. on September 19th, 1935, not saying where he was going. Nobody ever admitted having seen him thereafter. This was a Thursday. The coroner thought he probably was killed Friday. On Monday his body was found below Jackass Hill, a spot he was never known to have frequented. On Friday morning a neighbor had seen two young shabbily dressed Italians park an old Ford coupe at the top of Jackass Hill and walk down towards the spot where the bodies were later found.

In 1991, Will Fowler wrote in his book *Reporters: Memoirs of a Young Newspaperman,* on page 84, the following concerning the Black Dahlia:

Manley said Elizabeth had an Italian boyfriend with black hair "who was intensely jealous of her."

Gladys, a neighbor of Elizabeth on the fifth floor of her apartment building, said:

> "her boyfriend was jealous and he was chasing her."

GANG CLUE

A "gang" is mentioned in the Black Dahlia case that included an Italian by the name of Bobby Savarino. One of the last persons seen with Cleveland Torso Victim, Rose Wallace, was a dark-skinned white man named "Bob." A "gang" was mentioned in the case of Cleveland Torso Victim Edward Andrassy.

CLUE: SIMILAR KIDNAPPING OF YOUNG GIRL IN LOS ANGELES

On January 23, 1947, nine days after the Black Dahlia was murdered, *The Los Angeles Herald Express* ran the following in an article entitled "Werewolves Leave Trail of Women Murders in L.A."

> On Feb. 15, 1946, Rochelle Gluskoter, a smiling child not yet six with long chestnut curls was seen talking to a man who had stopped his black coupe near her home at 1125 East Eighty-Seventh Street. The little girl nodded and smiled as if in answer to his questions. Then she climbed into his car which drove away. A prolonged manhunt ended with the official announcement that little Rochelle must be dead, the victim of the unknown in the black coupe.

Interestingly, Suzanne Degnan was six-years-old when she was kidnapped from her parents' home in Chicago on January 7, 1946, thirty-nine days before Rochelle was kidnapped in Los Angeles. I have absolutely no other information regarding the kidnapping of

May Indicted in Arms Fraud Case

SE-TO-HOUSE SEARCH DAHLIA MURDER CLUE

HERALD EXPRESS

The Evening Herald and Express Grows Just Like Los Angeles

SDAY, JANUARY 23, 1947 — NO. 184

Drop Portal Suit

it of Love and iss at the Train

CLAIRE BORIN AND CHILD, BONNIE JOY

Ex-Rep. May of Ky. Indicted

PRESTONSBURG, Ky., Jan. 23.—Former Rep. Andrew J. May jr., accused by the Federal Grand Jury of corruptly receiving at least $16,000 for his aid to the Garsson munitions combine, today said, "I am not guilty."

WASHINGTON, Jan. 23.—Attorney General Clark announced today the indictment of former Representative Andrew J. May, Democrat of Kentucky, and three officials of a wartime munitions combine on charges of conspiring to defraud the government.

Clark said those named with May in the indictment, returned by a grand jury here, are:

Henry M. Garsson, Murray Garsson and Joseph F. Freeman, all former officers and employes of the Erie Basin Metal Products, Inc., Elgin, Ill., and of Batavia Metal Products, Inc., Batavia, Ill.

Will 'Dahlia' Slaying Join Album of Unsolved Murders?

ELIZABETH SHORT — MRS. ORA MURRAY — GEORGETTE BAUERDORF — GERTRUDE LANDON

Hirohito Emperor Sees the Dawn, Pens a Poem

TOKIO, Jan. 23. A poem by Emperor Hirohito, based on his inspection of reconstruction activities at B-29-blasted Mito City, highlighted the Annual New Year's Day poetry party at the Imperial Palace today.

"As dawn comes to Mito streets
"It is encouraging to hear
"The resounding noise of hammers."

Fog Slows Up L. A. Traffic

Werewolves Leave Trail of Women Murders in L. A.

House Bank Reopens, Ready to Pay 75 Cents on Dollar

David B. Head In Hospital

Comb Death Area

An intensive house-to-house hunt in the neighborhood bounding the ill-fated "Black Dahlia" murder scene was launched by two score uniformed police today in an all-out attempt to unearth a clue leading to the torture chamber where she was hacked to death by a "werewolf" killer.

While the officers were ringing doorbells in the several miles square area, other investigators pressed a search for a mystery witness, the woman who first discovered the brutally-slashed body of Elizabeth Short, 22, and notified police by telephone.

Aug 04 05 09:01a Mike Escalante 323 550-8044 p.2

Copy of *Los Angeles Herald Express* dated January 23, 1947

Rochelle, other than the above-mentioned article, and add this clue, for what its worth. By april 8, 1946, a suspect by the name of William E. Railey was in custody of the Los Angeles County sheriff's office. He was apprehended just as he collected the ransom money in the Rochelle Glusketer kidnapping case.

ADDITIONAL SIMILARITIES BETWEEN THE MURDERS

In the Cleveland Torso Murders, the murder of the Black Dahlia and the murder of Suzanne Degnan certain undisputed facts emerge:

A. The victims in each case were moved from point "A" (safe haven) to point "B," where they were killed, to point "C" (where their body parts were discarded).

B. The victims were all "expertly" severed and/or dismembered by someone with "knowledge of anatomy." *The Cleveland Press* reported on July 23, 1936, that "The skill and anatomical knowledge of a surgeon would have been required to perform a job so neat without leaving evidence of cutting." In the Black Dahlia case it was reported that she was severed by someone with the "finesse of a surgeon."

C. Following each murder the killer(s) "taunted" the police.

D. In the Cleveland Torso Murders and the murder of the Black Dahlia, blood was drained from the bodies by the killer(s) before the bodies were moved.

In the annals of crime there is no question that several people have been killed and dismembered over the years. However, in order for someone to commit a crime similar to the Cleveland Torso Murders, the murder of the Black Dahlia, and the murder of Suzanne Degnan, the person or persons would have to meet all of the following requirements:

1. They would have to want to kill and dismember someone.
2. They would have to possess the fortitude to stomach the gross dismemberment/bisection of a human being.
3. They would require similar expertise to professionally sever and/or dismember a human body.
4. They would require the ability, patience and sleuth to transport a person from one location; move, kill, dismember and/or sever a body; and dispose of the body parts by posing the corpse in a third location, usually in a large, populated city, without being detected.
5. They would have to know how to contact and have the mindset to taunt the police after committing the horrifically gory crime without being apprehended.

If someone other than the Cleveland Torso Killer murdered the Black Dahlia and Suzanne Degnan, and if someone other than the person who killed the Black Dahlia murdered Suzanne Degnan, then one would have to conclude that three separate individuals met the requirements mentioned in the list above within a time span of twelve years (unless, of course the same person(s) were responsible for the murders in two incidents but not the third; then there would have to be at least two separate individuals who met all of the requirements presented above). It is extremely rare to hear about a person who commits a murder/dismemberment and all of the requirements of numbers 1-5 above are met. The likelihood of this occurrence is again significantly reduced when the relatively short time frame (1935-1947) is brought into the equation. The odds that the above-mentioned requirements were met by two or three separate killers or groups of killers is a long shot by any stretch of the imagination.

I have not personally found any statistics regarding the above-mentioned events, but it seems highly unlikely to have two individuals or sets of individuals in addition to the Cleveland Torso Killer, during this relatively short time span, who had similar professional skill and could accomplish what the Cleveland Torso Killer accomplished. Therefore, it would seem logical that, based on the known facts, the Cleveland Torso Killer may have also been responsible for the murders of the Black Dahlia and the murder of Suzanne Degnan.

How many times since the date of the Black Dahlia's murder on January 14, 1947, has a killer fulfilled the requirements listed in items 1-5? If the answer is never, then one would suspect that during the 1935-1947 time frame there might have been one set , and only one set, of killers capable of and responsible for the Cleveland Torso Murders, the murder of Suzanne Degnan and the murder of the Black Dahlia.

Is it reasonable to dismiss Cleveland's sodomist "Jack Wilson" as a different person than Los Angeles' convicted sodomist "Jack Anderson Wilson, who was originally from Canton, Ohio?" The possibility of two separate individuals having the same expertise to sever a human body during this relatively short time span, who was also a sodomist is so far beyond the realm of possibility that the notion becomes an absurdity. The "Jack Wilson" mentioned in conjunction with the Cleveland Torso Murders was more than likely the same "Jack Wilson" who murdered and severed the Black Dahlia. And it is also very likely that he didn't act alone.

SUMMARY

Discovering the killer of the Black Dahlia and the Cleveland Torso Killer may be purely academic at this time but uncovering the true identity of the killer of Suzanne Degnan, Josephine Ross and Frances Brown is more than an exercise in historical study. Suzanne Degnan was surgically dismembered by someone with a great deal of expertise and knowledge of human anatomy. She was kidnapped, strangled, possibly sexually molested, and dismembered in a laundry room with running water and functioning sink. Coal dust was found embedded in her pajamas. Her body parts were discarded in separate storm sewers and catch basins. She was murdered close to a train tract near Lake Michigan on January 7, 1946. The *modus operandi* of the killer(s) and the evidence in the Degnan case parallels the *modus operandi* and evidence in the Cleveland Torso Killings. The method of murder in the Josephine Ross and Frances Brown cases closely parallels the 1943 method of murder in the of Corporal Maoma Ridings case.

Jack Anderson Wilson a/k/a Jack Wilson appears to have been a participant in the Cleveland Torso Murders, the murder of Suzanne Degnan, the murder of the Black Dahlia and several other murders including Corporal Maoma Ridings, Georgette Bauerdorf, Jeanne Axford French, Josephine Ross and Frances Brown. It is highly unlikely that whoever was responsible for the Cleveland Torso Murders stopped killing and dismembering victims after the carnage ended in Cleveland. Similar murders and expert-dismemberments that followed in McKee's Rocks, Youngstown, West Pittsburgh, New Castle, Chicago and Los Angeles all point towards the same perpetrators. There is absolutely no reported indication that Bill Heirens had any experience dismembering animals or human bodies. There is nothing that indicated that Bill Heirens was capable of expertly dismembering Suzanne Degnan. Heirens has been a model prisoner since his incarceration in 1946, and has not exhibited any traits expected of a person who would kidnap, strangle, expertly dismember a six-year-old girl, deposit her body parts in separate storm drains and then taunt the police. On the other hand these are the exact same propensities exhibited by the Cleveland Torso Killer(s) and the person(s) that killed the Black Dahlia.

The Black Dahlia was murdered and expertly severed less than six months after Bill Heirens was incarcerated in Chicago. For some reason Elizabeth Short was "terribly preoccupied with the details of the Degnan murder." She was pretending to be a reporter from Massachusetts covering the trial of William Heirens sometime between June-August 1946, when she was in Chicago. Less than five months later she was murdered and expertly severed in Los Angeles by means that closely matched the Cleveland Torso Murders. Elizabeth Short was expertly severed in Los Angeles, the same city that the suspicious letter was mailed from on December 22, 1938, to Cleveland Chief of Police Matowitz concerning the Cleveland Torso Murders.

Law enforcement should pursue this line of investigation to secure the release of William Heirens. I agree with crime writer Craig Rice, who, in 1946, said of William Heirens: "I said that I believe him innocent—and I think I am right." I will go one step further and say that William Heirens did not kill Suzanne Degnan and that the murder of Suzanne Degnan is directly connected to the murder of the Black Dahlia and the Cleveland Torso Murders. And now, with the additional evidence presented in this revised epilogue, the strong connections between all three cases also suggests two or more perpetrators, one of whom seem most certainly to have been Jack Anderson Wilson.

—William T. Rasmussen

FURTHER ANALYSIS OF CLEVELAND TORSO MURDERS, SUZANNE DEGNAN MURDER AND THE BLACK DAHLIA MURDER

Since the first revision of what I called the original epilogue in *Corroborating Evidence* I have uncovered additional clues and evidence that tend to establish connections between the Cleveland Torso Murders, the murders of Suzanne Degnan, the Black Dahlia and others. These are analyzed and included herein. I have also added two chapters, one on the Phantom Killer of Texarkana and the other on the Zodiac Killer.

WERE JACK ANDERSON WILSON, AL MORRISON AND MAURICE CLEMENT IN CLEVELAND DURING THE CLEVELAND TORSO MURDERS (1935-1938)?

According to Jack Anderson Wilson's taped message to author John Gilmore, a person by the name of Al Morrison was involved in the murder of Elizabeth Short. I, along with Cleveland's detective Peter Merylo, am of the opinion that whoever was responsible for the Cleveland Torso Murders also killed Elizabeth Short. (I have not found in any of the Cleveland Torso police reports any mention of the Suzanne Degnan case.) With this in mind I contacted the Western Reserve Historical Society in Cleveland, Ohio, and requested a search of the names "Jack Anderson Wilson a/k/a Jack Wilson a/k/a Grover Loving, Jr."; "Alex Morrison, a/k/a Al Morrison"; and "Maurice Clement, a/k/a Eddie Clement." Western Reserve returned a search that included the US Federal Census (1920/1930), the Ancestry-Library Edition Index, Cleveland City Directories (1928-1952) and Cleveland telephone Directories (1926-1952), Cleveland Necrology File, and Cuyahoga Marriage Records. The results of the search revealed that a person by the name of "J.A. Wilson" and another person by the name of "Alex Morrison" lived in the same Cleveland neighborhood in 1936. As of the date of this writing it has not been determined if they were the same individuals associated with the Black Dahlia Murder in Los Angeles. The information has been sent to the respective police agencies for their review.

HEAVY SET MAN WITH GRAY HAIR

Cleveland Torso Murders:

> In 1950, "a **heavy**, fiftyish-looking man with **thinning gray hair** came to Norris Brothers Company Movers at 22138 Davenport Avenue every day for six weeks and sunbathed for about twenty minutes on a year-and-a-half-old pile of steel girders at the west end of the company's property. Then one day he stopped coming." Shortly after workmen found the dismembered torso of a white male (Note 51, page 161).

Suzanne Degnan Murder:

> In 1946, in Chicago, a witness by the name of Robert Reisner "told police of a dark gray car parked on Thorndale with a bareheaded, **heavy-set** man behind the wheel." Chicago Chief of Police Walter G. Storms advised the public that "A man was observed in the driver's seat of this car. He was bareheaded and has **gray hair**" (Note 52, pages 47-48).

UNDERGROUND AND OUT OF SIGHT

In the Cleveland Torso Murders Edward Andrassy's headless body was found at the foot of Jackass Hill on September 23, 1935. He was killed and the blood drained from his body at a different location. Detectives questioned as to how he was transported and deposited without anyone noticing anything. Unexplained items were located near Andrassy's body, including pieces of rope, a railroad torch and a two gallon water bucket containing car engine oil (Note 51, page 32).

On a bitterly cold winter-night on January 26, 1936, the dismembered body parts of Victim No. 3, Flo Polillo were discovered in baskets behind Hart Manufacturing Company. No one saw the person or persons who delivered the gruesome packages. The headless body of Victim No. 4, the Tattooed Man, was found in Kingsbury Run on June 5, 1936. The next day, according to Railroad detective Dudley A. McDowell, items of clothing, including worn oxfords, striped socks and a dirty, oily cap were found in the same location. None of these items had been there the day before (Note 51, page 62).

In the case of Torso Victim No. 6 police found "at a point where the water emerged from a large tunnel into a twenty-foot-deep pool, some small bits of human flesh adhering to a ledge, apparently where the killer had thrown the pieces over the edge into a creek" (Note 51, page 76). Lieutenant Harvey Weitzel stated,, "It is my opinion that the missing parts were not thrown into the creek when the torso was thrown in."

Torso Victim No. 7 was found near the foot of East 156th Street in Lake Erie. Two storm sewers emptied into the lake nearby. Detectives Merylo and Zalewski, a Cleveland City Sewer Department employee and a newspaperman, explored a ten-mile stretch of storm drains (Note 51, page 104). During the cold winters in Cleveland during the 1930's, storm drains would not only provide protection from the weather but also an underground passageway where someone could traverse undetected, unseen from street level and patrolling detectives. Someone who knew the streets of Cleveland might also know how to maneuver in the labyrinth of subterranean tunnels that snake under the city. Were Andrassy and Victim No. 2 pulled on a cart through the storm drains? This might explain the rope burns on Edward Andrassy's wrists, the ropes and railroad lantern found near Andrassy's headless body. The railroad torch could have been used to light the way through the storm drains. Use of a railroad torch would have been seen if the body had been transported above ground. The storm drains with their running water could have been used as the killer's abattoir. There, out of sight, the Butcher could have taken time to perform the grisly dismemberments. See pages 7–8 for photos of Cleveland Storm Sewer.

You will recall that I questioned why and how someone would lift a total of five extremely heavy storm sewer and catch basin covers as described in the William Heiren's "Confession." The City of Chicago, Department of Water Management provided me with information that indicates "there has been little or no change to the subject catch basins and storm drains in the area requested from 1946, to present." Here is a copy of a drawing of the 120 lb. manhole and catch basins provided by the city of Chicago, Department of Water Management:

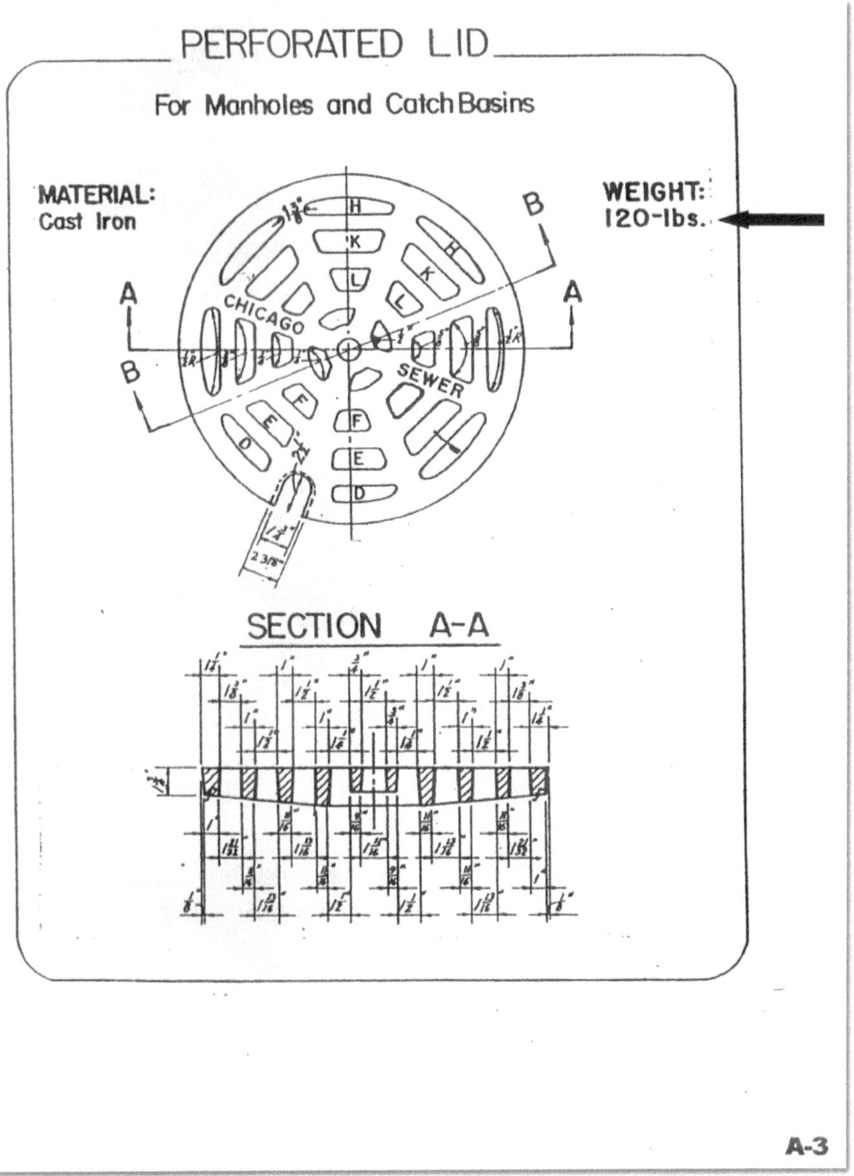

(Courtesy of the City of Chicago Department of Water Management)

5907 Kenmore

Ardmore and Kenmore

5900 Kenmore

5838 Kenmore

Four locations where body parts of Suzanne Degnan were found
(courtesy of Dolores Kennedy)

THE LEFT LEG

According to author John Gilmore, Jack Anderson Wilson walked with a limp and had "one leg shorter than the other (Note 53 page 212). On page 196 of *Severed*, Wilson is referred to as a person "with a crippled leg."

Crime writer Aggie Underwood got a tip that the person seen

walking away from 25th and San Pedro where Georgette Bauerdorf's car was found proceeded with a "halting gait" (Note 53, page 156). My question is, Was Jack Anderson Wilson's left leg either crippled or shorter than his right leg? If so, then consider the following:

a. In the case of Edward Andrassy it looks as though a *severed* penis is positioned close to his left knee (See headless photo of EdwardAndrassy on page 31, *In the Wake of the Butcher*).
b. In the Cleveland Torso Murders the left foot of Victim No. 11 appears to have been sliced from the body

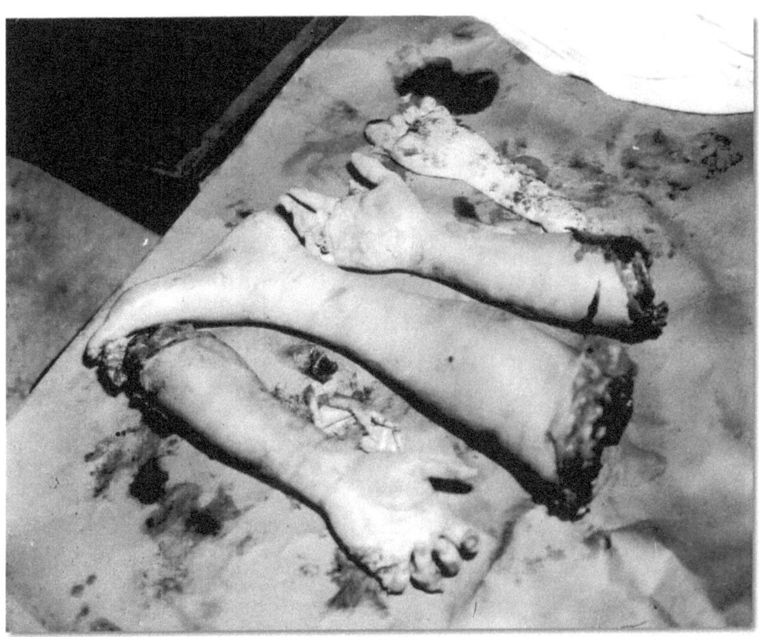

Body parts of Cleveland Torso Victims
(possibly parts of Victim No. 11) including a left leg and a left foot.
(photo courtesy of Marjorie Merylo Dentz).

c. In the Black Dahlia murder her killer cut a chunk of flesh out of her left leg.

NARCOTICS

On August 18, 1952, a letter was written by C.H. Ebbert, Chief of Investigation to Walter R. Creighton, Chief Bureau of Narcotic Enforcement. Here is a copy of the subject letter that I located at the Los Angeles District Attorney's file on the Black Dahlia:

> The letter requested an investigation for narcotic prescriptions (not just any type of prescription) that may have been written by a doctor for Elizabeth Short during 9/1/45-1/31/46 and 6/1/46-1/15/47. the letter appears to have been written for one of two possible reasons: Either the detectives were trying to associate a doctor who may have prescribed a narcotic prescription to the person with "surgical knowledge," or because at the time of her death the autopsy may have revealed Elizabeth Short had narcotics in her tissue, fluids or organs, and they were trying to find the doctor who may have prescribed the drug who in turn may have committed the murder. If the autopsy of Elizabeth Short did in fact reveal the presence of narcotics, this would be similar to the findings in more than one of the autopsy reports in the Cleveland Torso Murders. It was determined that the Cleveland Torso Killer drugged at least one of his victims before the dismemberment. (Note 51, page 131). I also call your attention to the 1938 letter mailed from Los Angeles to Cleveland Chief of Police Matowitz. In that letter the writer wrote in part: "It is God's will not to let them suffer" (See page 33 of this text): "as much as possible, you understand, well . . . there was a purpose to this in such a way though a person undergoes so much it's possible that this person has to be, what you call—anesthesia. It's a word in a crossword puzzle." In both cases the reference may have been to the administration of narcotics prior to the murder/dismemberment.

August 18, 1952

IN REPLY PLEASE GIVE
OUR REFERENCE NUMBER 3.31

Walter R. Creighton, Chief
Bureau of Narcotic Enforcement
156 State Building
San Francisco, California

Dear Sir:

Refering to your conversation on August 18, 1952, at U.C.L.A. with our investigator Walter Morgan. Please check your master narcotic prescription file for a possible prescription written between September 1, 1945 and January 31, 1946, and particularly June 1, 1946 and January 15, 1947, for the following person:

Elizabeth Short, aka Beth Short, E. Short and B. Short

Investigation of the murder of the above named person leads the authorities to conclude that a doctor, or a person with surgical knowledge, may have committed said crime.

The victim suffered female disorders and asthma. A narcotic prescription may have been filled by the deceased during her stay in California between said dates. A copy of such a prescription found in your files would reveal the name and address of the doctor who wrote same.

Your cooperation and assistance in this matter is greatly appreciated.

Yours very truly,

C. H. EBBETS, Chief
Bureau of Investigation

WM:ALS

Case No. 30-1268

August 18, 1952, letter from C.H. Ebbets to Walter R. Creighton in Los Angeles District Attorney's file on Black Dahlia.

OHIO LICENSE

A memorandum in the Black Dahlia case that I found at the Los Angeles District Attorney's office dated January 26, 1950, provides the following information in # 14:

> Identified picture of soldier sitting on_______of chev. Coupe Ohio license # E-640V-4
>
> "name unknown" a new character. As man with Short at Hansen's house in Nov. 46."

MEMORANDUM — JAN. 26 1950

Subject: CONNIE STARR -- and Francis Starr (Mother)
427 So. Mariposa St.
Apt. 310
DU 9-2535

1. Connie is Ann Toth's girl friend.

2. Connie stated that she was invited to dinner at Mark Hansen's by Ann Toth on Saturday January 11, 1947;

3. that the three of them had dinner together and shortly after dinner about 9:00 PM, Beth Short and her boy friend, a young kid with brown hair, arrived;

4. that it was a very cold night and Beth Short did not have a coat and was dressed in a cotton or gingham dress with a pink top bodice and did not have a coat; did not have stockings on;

5. that Beth Short complained of being cold and frozen;

6. that Mark Hansen seated Beth Short on the davenport near the fire-place, put a blanket around xx her shoulders, placed a pair of his socks on her feet, put his slippers on her feet

7. that Mark Hansen asked her XX where she had been, that Beth Short stated that they had been to a movie, that Mark asked if they had been to his theatar, that she answered no, that she had seen the picture at his theater and that they caught an early movie elsewhere;

8. CONNIE stated that she was home when she read of Beth Short's murder and immediately remarked to her Mother that is was just the other day that she just met Beth Short at Mark Hansen's home when she was there for dinner:

9. Connie and her mother should be questioned separately xxxxxxxxxxxxxx xxxxxxx for purposes of corroboration.

10. Connie is an extra-player who obtain's most of her employmant by request calls and a small portion through Central Casting.

11. Connie's moral xxxxxxxx reputation is not too good, XXXXXXXXXXX

12. Connie also stated that she understood that Beth Short had spent the prievious night, Friday, January 10, 1947, at Mark Hansen's home, and was planning to spend Saturday night there also.

13. Places date as just before Ann went to Modesto after they worked together on "[illegible]"

14. [illegible] Picture of Soldier sitting on [illegible] of Chev. coupe Ohio Lic. # E-640V-4. "name unknown" - a new character. as man with Short at Hansen's in Nov. '4[illegible]

January 26, 1950, Los Angeles police memorandum in the Los Angeles District Attorney's file on the Black Dahlia that identifies an Ohio license number.

WRITING ON CHEST OF VICTIM

In the Cleveland Torso Murders on May 3, 1940, three bodies were found at McKee's Rocks in Pennsylvania. Detective Merylo thought the murders were connected to the Cleveland Torso Murders. A size-twelve footprint was located at the scene and a mark made either by a peg leg or a woman's high heel and near it the butt of a cigarette that detective Merylo said had been rolled with marijuana. A single strand of blond hair was found near one of the victims. The word "NAZI" had been carved vertically into the victim's chest from breast to stomach. The letters were crude capitals, the "Z" reversed (Note 51, page 92).

In the Black Dahlia case, Jeanne Axford French was "stomped to death by a fiend who crudely printed an obscene phrase (Fuck You) on her chest." The letters "BD" were written in red lipstick in capital letters vertically from her breasts to her stomach. (For photo see page 195, *Black Dahlia Avenger* by Steve Hodel.)

THE LETTER "K"

Cleveland Torso Murders

At the Norris Brothers crime scene in Cleveland detectives found the dismembered corpse, missing head, no sign of blood at the scene, sports pages from a May, 1949, issue of the *Cleveland News* under the body, and abandoned bits of clothing nearby--though it was not clear if any of it belonged to the dead man. This time, however, there was something new: two pages from the phone book covering the letter **K**" (Note 51, page 161)

Black Dahlia Murder

On Wednesday January 29, 1947, Federal inspectors at the Terminal Annex Post Office in downtown Los Angeles received a fifth note that might have been mailed by the Black Dahlia Avenger. The note read:

> A certain girl is going to get same as E.S. got if she squeals on us We're going to Mexico City-catch us if you can.
>
> **2K's**

(Note 41, page 173)

Maurice Clement

A Maurice Clement was a suspect in the murder of Elizabeth Short.

Here is a copy of the suspects in the Black Dahlia Murder found at the Los Angeles District Attorney's Office:

In 1946, in Los Angeles, Maurice Clement was described as follows:

1. Short, dark complexioned in his late 30's
2. 5' 6" tall, medium build, little fellow about 35-40 (Note 54, page 119)
3. Slight, dapper, olive-skinned man (Note 54, page 130)
4. A procurer for the syndicate call girl ring run by notorious Hollywood madam, Brenda Allen
5. Worked for the talent department at Columbia Studios
6. Elizabeth Short "knew Maurice and was one of the girls he chauffeured" (Note 54, page 120).
7. Based on witness reports, Maurice Clement would have been between 24-29-years-old in 1935. That being the case, he would have been born between 1906-1911.

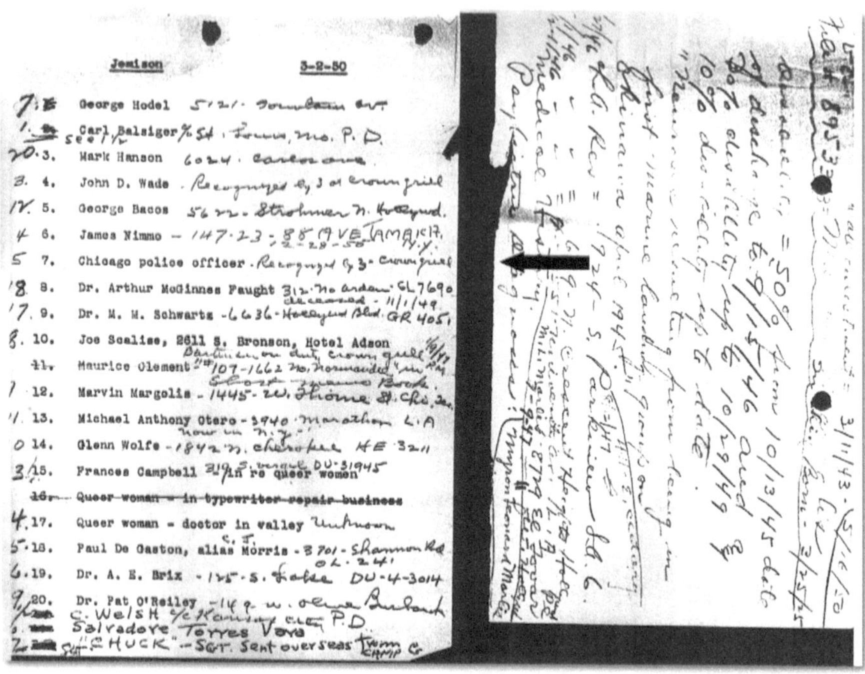

Jemison 3-2-50

1. George Hodel
2. Carl Balsiger
3. Mark Hanson
4. John D. Wade
5. George Bacos
6. James Nimmo
7. Chicago police officer
8. Dr. Arthur McGinnes Faught
9. Dr. M. M. Schwartz
10. Joe Scalise, 2611 S. Bronson, Hotel Adson
11. Maurice Clement
12. Marvin Margolis
13. Michael Anthony Otero
14. Glenn Wolfe
15. Frances Campbell in re queer women
16. ~~Queer woman – in typewriter repair business~~
17. Queer woman – doctor in valley
18. Paul De Gaston, alias Morris
19. Dr. A. E. Brix
20. Dr. Pat O'Reiley

C. Welsh
Salvadore Torres Vera
"Chuck" – Sgt. Sent overseas

March 12, 1950, list of possible suspects in the Black Dahlia Case found in the Los Angeles District Attorney's file on the Black Dahlia Murder.

In the Cleveland Torso Murders a person by the name of "Eddie" was associated with more than one of the Torso Murders. "Eddie" was described by witnesses as follows:

1. 28-30-years-old in 1935
2. Good looking, good set of teeth
3. 5' 6" tall
4. 15 lbs.
5. Was a chauffeur for a wealthy woman in suburban Lakewood (Note 43, page 60)
6. Based on witness reports, if alive, Maurice Clement would have been between 39-41-years-old in 1946. That being the case, he would have been born between 1905-1907

If Maurice Clement mentioned in conjunction with the Black Dahlia had a letter "E" for a middle initial, could his middle name have been "Edward" or"Eddie," and if so, then was the chauffeur driver by the name of "Eddie" mentioned in the Cleveland Torso Murders, the same chauffeur driver by the name of Maurice Clement who was associated with the murder of the Black Dahlia?

On January 7, 1946, at about 2 A.M., the morning of the kidnapping of Suzanne Degnan in Chicago, a woman was seen on Thorndale Avenue between Sheridan Road and Kenmore Avenue carrying a bundle in both arms. She was seen to get into a car parked on Thorndale Avenue. This woman was described as about 130 pounds, 5' 6" tall, wearing a gray coat with a dark fur collar and a small hat" (broadcast to the public by Chicago Chief of Police, Walter G. Storms, January 9, 1946, Note 52, page 48). The description of this "woman" closely matched the description of Maurice Clement in the Black Dahlia case and "Eddie" in the Cleveland Torso Murders. Jack Anderson Wilson was affiliated with a female impersonator.

CLOSE PROXIMITY OF LOS ANGELES CRIMES

I suspect that the same person or persons who killed 6-year-old Suzanne Degnan in Chicago on January 7, 1946, may have also been responsible for the kidnapping of 6-year-old Rochelle Gluskoter on February 15, 1946, in Los Angeles.

Four locations are in the same general area in the city of Los Angeles:

1. The location between 39th and Coliseum on Norton Avenue where the severed body of Elizabeth Short was posed by her killer(s) on January 14, 1947
2. The location, according to the 1938 letter addressed from Los Angeles to Cleveland Police Chief Matowitz, where a

head was buried between Crenshaw and Western on Century Boulevard

3. 1113 East 85th Street where 6-year-old Rochelle Gluskoter was kidnapped on February 15, 1946
4. The residence of Jack Anderson Wilson in the early 1940s

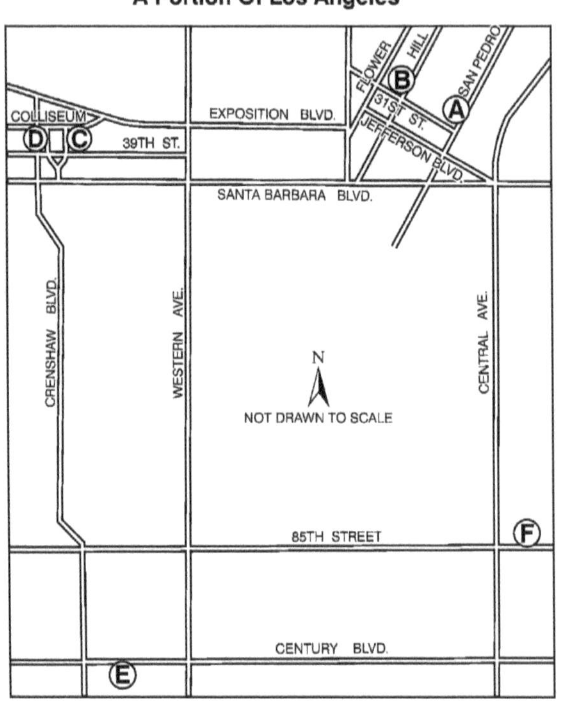

A. "Chinaman's" house in the 200 block no East 31st Street (See page 83 of text).

B. Jack A. Wilson may have lived on Hill Street.

C. Degnan Boulevard

D. Location of Elizabeth Short's severed body on Norton Avenue.

E. A head may have been buried between Crenshaw Boulevard & Western Avenue on Century Boulevard.

F. 1113 East 85th Street — where 6 year old Rochelle Gluskoter was kidnapped on February 15, 1946.

A portion of Los Angeles showing possible crime scene locations.

PERSON DISPLAYING A CHICAGO POLICE OFFICER'S BADGE

Within a few days before Elizabeth Short disappeared a man displayed a Chicago police officer's badge to allow Short to enter the Columbia Broadcasting Studio. Here is a copy of the letter from H. L. Stanley Chief Bureau of Investigators Los Angeles to Mr. John C. Prendergast, Commissioner of Police, Chicago, dated January 31, 1950:

cc: Police Depa[redacted]ent
30-1268

In reply please
refer to 2.6

January 31, 1950

Mr. John C. Prendergast
Commissioner of Police
Chicago, Illinois

Dear Sir:

We have been informed that a man, possibly a Chicago police officer, who definitely displayed a police badge to gain admittance to the Columbia Broadcasting Studios, may have information relative to a Los Angeles murder.

This man showed his badge and it was carefully examined by Jack Egger, who was at that time chief usher at this studio and who now is an employee of this office.

We will appreciate it if you will check your personnel records and determine whether or not any of your officers visited in Los Angeles in connection with an extradition or for a vacation in December, 1946 or in January, 1947.

Will you please also check your files to determine whether or not Marvin Margolis or his father of 1148 Roosevelt Road, Chicago, ever received an honorary Chicago police badge.

Thanks again for your cooperation.

Very truly yours,

H. L. Stanley

H. L. STANLEY, Chief
Bureau of Investigation

FBJ:mrc

Reply:- 2/7/50 attached

January 31, 1950, Los Angeles District Attorney's file letter from H.L. Stanley to Mr. John C. Pendergast commissioner of the Chicago Police Department regarding a suspect in the Black Dahlia Case.

Detective Division  COPY  February 6, 1950

From: Chief of Detectives

To: Commissioner of Police

Subject: Attached communication from H. L. Stanley, Chief, Bureau of Investigation, District Attorney's Office, Los Angeles, Calif.

Report of: Sgt. John T. Martin, Chief Clerk

1. With reference to the attached communication the records of the Detective Bureau and States Attorney's Office do not disclose any police officers of the City of Chicago being in the City of Los Angeles, California during the months of December of 1946 and January 1947, on extradition matters. In response to teletype message #5287 sent through the department received one reply from Sgt. William Barron 14th District stating that while on a disability furlough, he visited some retired Chicago Police Officers in suburban Los Angeles, California, in the latter part of January 1947, but at no time during his visit did they attend a Broadcasting Studio.

2. Upon inquiry of the Chicago Police Pension Board, informed by Miss Kersten, that there are 69 retired Chicago Police Officers residing in California, 20 of whom reside in Los Angeles.

3. Records at the office of the Secretary of Police were checked, and same do not show anyone by the name of Margolis as ever applying for or receiving any Chicago Special Police Badge. The Chicago Police Department does not issue "Honorary" badges.

4. As you will note in the attached communication, same refers to a badge, supposedly a Chicago Police Badge. No further description of this badge is given, as to whether it was the shape of a star, or otherwise. Police Officers of the City of Chicago, as well as numerous other departments of this city and county, are issued stars of various sizes, with the name of their particular department inscribed thereon. Also, previous to Feb. 1st, 1947 retired police officers were issued a replica of their service star, with the word "Retired" inscribed thereon.

5. This department through the Secretary of Police and with the approval of the Commissioner of Police issues "Special Police" badges. These badges are issued only to corporations such as Banks and Utilities, who employ guards, messengers, etc. These employees are carefully checked through the various units of the Chicago Police Department before such badges are issued. This badge is described as an oblong shield, chrome-plated, with a spread-eagle across the top, and a boxband underneath reading "Chicago Special Police Patrolman" - a seal, the Letter Y in center and raised copper numerals underneath.

6. This department is now corresponding with Mr. H. L. Stanley, Chief, Bureau of Investigation, District Attorney's Office, Los Angeles, California, re: Marvin Margolis, Detective Bureau File #50-0304.

/s/ John T. Martin

APPROVED:

/s/ Andrew Aitken
Andrew W. Aitken
Chief of Detectives

February 6, 1950, Los Angeles District Attorney's file letter in the Black Dahlia case from John T. Martin to Commissioner of Police.

Keep in mind that Elizabeth Short was in Chicago in July, 1946, "pretending to be a reporter from Medford, Massachusetts," and "terribly preoccupied with the details of the Degnan murder." The week before she was killed she was scheduled to return to Chicago.

The following individuals knew and came in contact with Elizabeth Short while she was in Chicago in July, 1946:

- **a.** Shg Diamond, a newspaperman whose residence was Park Row Hotel. He claims to have seen Short over a ten-day period and has stated that he had intercourse with her and said that she was always talking about murder cases.
- **b.** Lou Paris, feature writer for the *Chicago Daily Times*, who knew Short and talked with her, at which time she was keenly interested in the famous Heirens Chicago murder case.
- **c.** John Giampa, 3421 West Lexington, who was a mailer for the *Chicago Herald American*. He knew her and said Short knew a Chicago detective who worked on the Heirens' case.
- **d.** Jan Jensen a reporter on the *Chicago Daily News*, who stated he knew the victim in Chicago.

Elizabeth Short was definitely talking in Chicago in July, 1946, about the William Heirens case and about the murder/dismemberment of Suzanne Degnan. Suzanne Degnan was expertly dismembered. Her body parts were placed in separate storm drains and catch basins. Less than six months after being in Chicago, Elizabeth Short was killed and expertly severed in Los Angeles. Her blood was drained from her body. More than one of the Cleveland Torso Victims had their blood drained from their bodies and the body parts of at least one of the Cleveland Torso victims was placed at separate times in Cleveland sewers. Elizabeth Short's face was cut to make it appear that she had a big mouth and was talking too much.

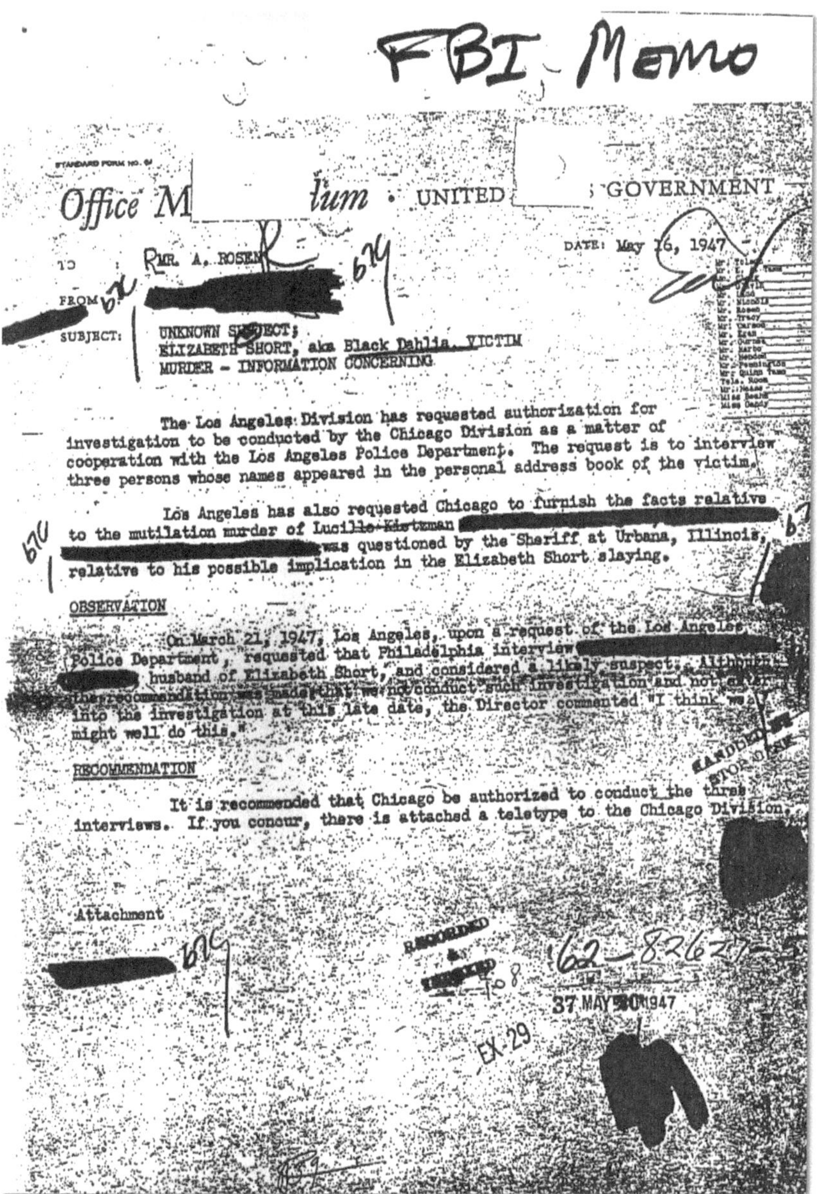
FBI Memo

STANDARD FORM NO. 64

Office M[redacted]dum • UNITED [redacted] GOVERNMENT

TO : MR. A. ROSEN

DATE: May 16, 1947

FROM : [redacted]

SUBJECT: UNKNOWN SUBJECT;
ELIZABETH SHORT, aka Black Dahlia, VICTIM
MURDER - INFORMATION CONCERNING

The Los Angeles Division has requested authorization for investigation to be conducted by the Chicago Division as a matter of cooperation with the Los Angeles Police Department. The request is to interview three persons whose names appeared in the personal address book of the victim.

Los Angeles has also requested Chicago to furnish the facts relative to the mutilation murder of Lucille Kirtzman [redacted] was questioned by the Sheriff at Urbana, Illinois, relative to his possible implication in the Elizabeth Short slaying.

OBSERVATION

On March 21, 1947, Los Angeles, upon a request of the Los Angeles Police Department, requested that Philadelphia interview [redacted] husband of Elizabeth Short, and considered a likely suspect. Although the recommendation was made that we not conduct such investigation and not enter into the investigation at this late date, the Director commented "I think we might well do this."

RECOMMENDATION

It is recommended that Chicago be authorized to conduct the three interviews. If you concur, there is attached a teletype to the Chicago Division.

Attachment

RECORDED & INDEXED

62-82627-

37 MAY 30 1947

EX-29

Federal Bureau of Investigation memorandum dated May 16, 1947, concerning three persons included in Elizabeth Short's personal address book with ties to Chicago.

CARVED LETTER "D"

Some people believe that the "D" cut in the shaved pubic region of Elizabeth Short is the same type of lettering as found on the body of the French woman. Facts reveal that the pubic region of Elizabeth Short's body was not shaved. Experts in handwriting have stated that it would be impossible to determine any type of handwriting from the so-called "D" cut into the pubic region of Elizabeth Short's body. Did the letter "D" cut into the pubic region stand for the "D" in Degnan?

2nd and 3rd LUMBAR VERTEBRAE

In the Black Dahlia Grand Jury investigation LAPD detective Harry Hansen stated: "I think a medical man was involved—a very fine surgeon. I base that conclusion on the way the body was bisected . . . It was unusual in this sense, that the point at which the body was bisected is, according to eminent medical men, the easiest point in the spinal column to severe (between the second and third lumbar vertebrae) and he hit the spot exactly. Dr. Newbarr told Hansen, that the surgery was meticulous and 'couldn't have been done in fifteen minutes, half hour or even an hour.'" The report goes on to state "the murderer had some training in the dissecting of bodies" (Note 54, pages 135-136). "The cut was straight through the narrowest part between the bottom of her ribs and navel" (Note 53, page 4). The FBI Report stated, "It is felt that the murder was committed indoors, where water, drainage facilities and perhaps medical equipment was available" (FBI Report Re: Elizabeth Short, February 15, 1947).

Whoever killed the Black Dahlia and Suzanne Degnan did have plenty of experience in dismembering human bodies. One thing is for certain: William Heirens was in prison in Illinois on January 14, 1947, when the Black Dahlia was killed and expertly severed in Los Angeles.

HANDWRITING COMPARISONS

I don't claim to be a handwriting expert. Usually the best source for making handwriting comparisons with pressure points and spacings are the originals writings. I don't have access to original documents and even if I did I would leave the analysis to the experts. Hopefully all of the known writings in these various cases will be reviewed by handwriting experts. In order to encourage this endeavor, I would like to point out certain similarities for whatever value they may have.

Here is a copy of the ransom note in the William Heirens case concerning the murder of Suzanne Degnan.

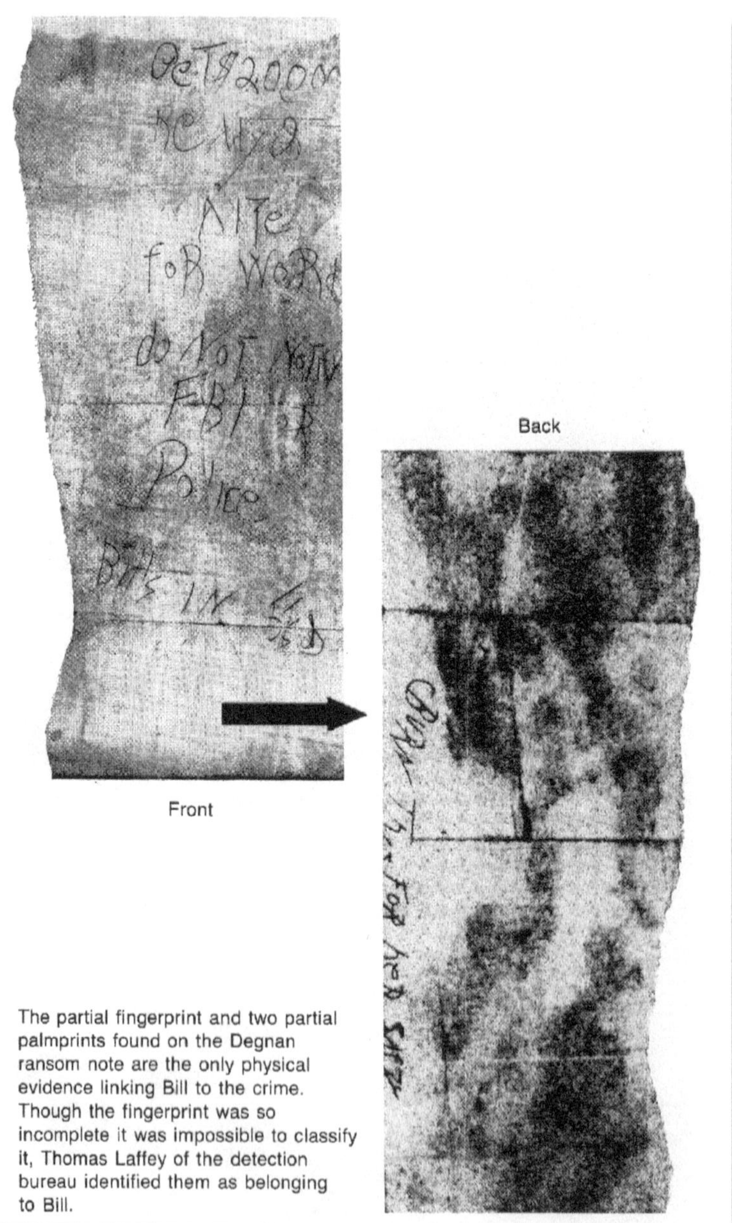

The partial fingerprint and two partial palmprints found on the Degnan ransom note are the only physical evidence linking Bill to the crime. Though the fingerprint was so incomplete it was impossible to classify it, Thomas Laffey of the detection bureau identified them as belonging to Bill.

Ransom note in the Suzanne Degnan Murder
(photo courtesy of Dolores Kennedy).

Now compare the following letters:

The Letter "U"

1. Suzanne Degnan Ransom Note in the word: B*u*rn
2. Black Dahlia Case in Exhibit 28
   (*Black Dahlia Avenger*, by Steve Hodel)
   in the words; cl*u*e, n*u*t and b*u*ilding
3. Mimi Boomhower case:
   In the words: fo*u*nd and Th*u*rsday
4. In the words: f*u*ck and yo*u*
   written in red lipstick on the chest of Jeanne French
   (Note 55, page 195)

Name Used to Aid 5%-ers

5c THE MIRROR

Note Hints Foul Play

PURSE CLOUDS WIDOW'S FATE

Headlines in *The Mirror*, August 26, 1949, including photo of Mimi Boomhower's purse (Copyright, 1949, *Los Angeles Times*. Reprinted with permission).

The Letter "P"

1. In the ransom note in the Suzanne Degnan case in the word: *P*olice
2. In the Black Dahlia case on Exhibit 23 on page 175 of the *Black Dahlia Avenger* in the word: Ex*p*ress

The Letter "R"

1. In the Suzanne Degnan Ransom Note in the word: *R*eddy
2. On Mimi Boomhower's purse in the word: Thu*r*sday

You should also note that the writing on the Boomhower purse reads as follows:

POLICE.
DEPT.-
WE FOUND **THIS**
AT BEACH
THURSDAY NIGHT(emphasis added)

The reverse side of the Suzanne Degnan note reads as follows:

BURN **This** FoR heR SAfTY (emphasis added)

In the Black Dahlia case Federal inspectors at the Terminal Annex Post Office in downtown Los Angeles received the following note:

> A certain girl is going to get same as E.S. got if she squeals on **us** **We're** going to Mexico-catch **us** if you can. **2 k's**
> (emphasis added)
>
> (Note 41, page 173)

The written note on Mimi Boomhower's purse reads in part:

> **WE** FOUND THIS AT BEACH . . . (emphasis added)

THE CASE OF MIMI BOOMHOWER REVISITED (See page 115 of text.)

On August 24, 1949, plump, 48-year-old socialite, Mimi Boomhower of 701 Nimes Road, Los Angeles, disappeared. She had lived alone in a 10-room Spanish style mansion following the death of her millionaire, inventor husband N.E. Boomhower, in 1943. On August 25, 1949, Walter E. Chaney of 3939 Longridge Avenue, Van Nuys, California found her purse in a phone booth. The next day the *Los Angeles Mirror* reported that Boomhower had pawned a diamond-studded wrist watch for $100.00 in Beverly Hills on July 8, 1949. When she pawned her watch Mrs. Boomhower was wearing a 7 ½ karat solitaire ring valued at over $5,000.00.

The *Mirror* further reported on August 26 that several anonymous phone callers reported tips regarding the disappearance of Mimi Boomhower. One anonymous caller "described himself as an ex-policeman and said he saw Evans with Mrs. Boomhower in the bar of the Hollywood Roosevelt Hotel last week."

The *Mirror* further reported:

> Sgt Ferges said today, "It could be that the purse was found on the beach or it could be a hoax. We don't know. But we do know that the purse belongs to Mrs. Boomhower."

Mirror Aug 26, 1949

Socialite Pawned Watch for 'Expenses'

High-spending, fast-living Mimi Boomhower, who vanished from her sumptuous 18-room Bel-Air home a week ago, pawned a diamond-studded wrist watch for $100 in Beverly Hills July 8.

At the time, the missing 48 year old widow told Julius Zimmelman, owner of the Beverly Hills Loan Co.:

"I just want a few dollars to tide me over. I'll be back in about two weeks to get the watch."

Zimmelman said the watch was worth about $800.

He added Mrs. Boomhower was wearing a 7½ karat solitaire ring he would have given $5000 for without a quibble.

Heighten Mystery

These facts about the movements of the woman who lived alone in a rambling mansion heightened her already super-mysterious disappearance.

They came as 20 detectives stubbed their toes for the third day in trying to unravel the riddle of the blackhaired plump widow.

Zimmelman said the woman, who signed herself on the pawn ticket as "Mrs. N. E. Boomhower," using her late husband's initials, did not appear upset.

"She was very charming," the loan company owner said.

Zimmelman, at his Beverly Hills location for seven years, said it was the first time Mrs. Boomhower had come to pawn anything.

Suspects Cleared

Police admitted they were at a dead end in the case as they hurriedly cleared suspect No. 1.

A 250 pound Frenchman, an alleged confidence man and promoter, fingered by one of the scores of anonymous phone callers, was freed today after three hours' questioning by Det. Sgt. Jack Ferges.

Ferges said the North Hollywood promoter was described by the caller as a con man who was bilking the missing Bel-Air socialite in a shady Mexican importing deal.

The woman tipster told police the Frenchman told her he had intended to fleece a wealthy widow of a big game hunter.

The phone caller further described the promoter as a pal of a bookie who was a fugitive from justice. The Frenchman, she said, had been arrested in Florida for impersonating an FBI man.

Officers checked out the leads and released the promoter without even booking him.

Thomas E. Evans, ex-host on Tony Cornero's gambling ship and former dope peddler, is to be questioned in West Los Angeles today.

'Seen in Bar'

Like the promoter, Evans was implicated yesterday by an anonymous phone caller. The caller described himself as an ex-policeman and said he saw Evans with Mrs. Boomhower in the bar of the Hollywood Roosevelt hotel last week.

Said Evans, "Sure I was in the bar at the hotel last week. I'm there every day.

"I never heard of Mrs. Boomhower's name until I saw it in the papers. I'm o.k. with the police and I don't mind seeing them."

Officers said they were quite

BERNARD BETTINGER

The girl in the life of navy chief quartermaster Bernard Bettinger wasn't dockside to meet him today at San Diego.

She was in an airplane at Denver having a son for him.

Mrs. Bettinger gave birth prematurely to a boy as her United Air Lines plane taxied to a stop at Denver.

Child and mother were taken to a Denver hospital.

NEW X-RAY

Doctors See Into Tot's Lung

Six-year-old Carole Brown left Children's hospital today minus a small metal eyelet which she had accidentally inhaled into her lung.

Blonde, brown eyed Carole is the daughter of Mr. and Mrs. Vernon Brown, of 236 Avalon Dr., Sharp Park, a suburb of San Francisco.

Three weeks ago, Aug 4, Carole attended a party at which children were given toy favors. Carole's was a little cardboard doll, with movable joints articulated with one-quarter inch long metal eyelets.

When she was tired of the doll, Carole tried to take it apart by pulling out the eyelets with her teeth. She was lying on her back on the floor.

When the eyelet came loose, it plopped into her mouth and then straight into her windpipe.

Doctors in San Francisco knew that Children's hospital here recently had been presented with a stereoscopic fluoroscope which gives a three dimensional picture of

—AP PHOTO

'OGETHER

. V. E. Bonham, Pomona, recall their wedding day O. They moved to Calid she is 91. They have grandchildren, 13 greatgreat-grandson.

zenship by U.S.

P)—The U.S. circuit court of n of citizenship to three Japd it during wartime.

World War II Legionnaires Pep Up Campaign

PHILADELPHIA, Aug. 26 (AP) elegates to the 31st national merican Legion convention bean streaming into Philadelphia day with many apparently innt on naming a World War II teran as their new commander. As the city gradually took on holiday atmosphere, two vetans of the last war plunged to the business of meeting delgates and lining up support. hey are George N. Craig, Brazil, d., attorney, and Earl Cocke, rmer and railroad man of Dawn, Ga.

August 26, 1949, article in *The Mirror* in the Mimi Boomhower case (Copyright, 1949, *Los Angeles Times.* Reprinted with permission).

Missing persons bureau at Los Angeles said it had received an anonymous call from a man who said he saw the widow and a gambler known to the police "last Thursday or Friday morning." Police said Mrs. Boomhower's companion, if the call stands up, is a known **narcotics** addict and gambler. They are checking out the call.

Now compare these clues to the murder of the Black Dahlia:

a. Shortly before she was murdered the Black Dahlia desperately needed $100.00

b. One of the suspects in the Black Dahlia murder, listed in the Los Angeles District Attorney's file, was a person who flashed a Chicago police officer's badge.

c. In his taped interview with author John Gilmore, Jack Anderson Wilson mentions the Hollywood Roosevelt Hotel:

> They drove further south, to another hotel near 29th Street, also called the Roosevelt Hotel, but not connected to Hollywood's Roosevelt Hotel. (See page 185, *Severed* and page 87 of this text.)

The Hollywood Roosevelt Hotel is a very famous landmark in Hollywood that has been around since 1927. It is known as the birthplace of the academy awards. In his taped message Wilson had already given street directions that placed the Roosevelt Hotel in Los Angeles several miles from the Hollywood Roosevelt Hotel in Hollywood. Was the Hollywood Roosevelt Hotel on Wilson's mind for some other reason other than to make such an insignificant comparison to not being connected with the Roosevelt Hotel near 29th Street?

REVISIT THE CHICAGO CASE OF EUNICE RAWLINGS (See pages 73 and 119 of text).

Rawlings disappeared January 14, 1945, in Chicago. Her headless, armless body washed ashore on a Lake Michigan beach August 12, 1946. On Monday, August 12, 1946, *The Chicago Times* reported that a purse containing "the girl's name on a slip of paper was found on the lake shore rocks near Addison." Her death was ruled a suicide. A suicide note was found a dresser in her apartment. Was she forced to write the suicide note? She disappeared on January 14, 1945, exactly two years before Elizabeth Short was murdered in Los Angeles. When her body washed ashore her head and arms were missing. Was she dismembered before she entered Lake Michigan? Her apartment was located close to the apartments of Frances Brown and Josephine Ross, two of the victims in the William Heirens case. I find it very difficult to believe that a 17-year-old girl who, immediately prior to her demise was actively seeking employment, would choose to end her life by jumping into the frigid waters of Lake Michigan in January. According to an expert I spoke with regarding the Rawlings case, the cold waters of Lake Michigan would act as a refrigerator and preserve the body. Wave action and a myriad of other lake effects could cause an eventual dismemberment, so who knows? Eunice Rawlings' "suicide" and surrounding circumstances just seems peculiar to me.

THE MURDER OF JONBENET RAMSEY

JonBenet Ramsey was born on August 6, 1990, in Atlanta, Georgia. She died at age six sometime in the night of December 25-26, 1996, at her family home in Boulder, Colorado. Her parents were John and Patsy Ramsey. Her brother Burke was three years older. She also had a stepbrother, John Andrew Ramsey, and a stepsister, Melinda Ramsey. John Ramsey was a successful businessman and president and chief executive officer of Access Graphics, a computer service company. Patsy Ramsey was born on December 29, 1956, in Gilbert, West Virginia. In 1977, she won the Miss West Virginia Beauty Pageant. Patsy married John Ramsey on November 5, 1980. On July 4, 1993, while at the Northside Emergency Room in Atlanta, Patsy was diagnosed with ovarian cancer. She died at age 49 in 2006. The Ramseys maintained a summer home in Charlevoix, Michigan, and moved to Boulder in 1991. Access Graphic's headquarters was in Boulder. Patsy entered JonBenet in several child beauty pageants. JonBenet had won several titles including Little Miss Charlevoix, Colorado State All-Star Kids Cover Girl, National Tiny Miss Beauty, America's Royal Miss Colorado, Little Miss Merry Christmas and Little Miss Sunburst.

On December 25, 1996, the Ramseys attended a Christmas party at Fleet and Priscilla White's house in Boulder. Later that evening the Ramseys left the Fleet party and drove back to their Boulder home. On the way Burke and JonBenet fell asleep in the car. Before arriving at their house, John and Patsy delivered gifts at Stewart and Roxy Walker's and Glenn and Susan Stine's houses. After the Ramseys arrived at their Boulder home, John put JonBenet to bed. John then played a game with Burke and then Burke went to bed. John then went to bed. According to the Boulder Police Department report, Patsy told officers Veitch and French that Patsy last saw JonBenet alive at ten that evening. Then Patsy went to bed. Sometime after JonBenet went to bed, estimated at around 1:00 am that night, someone bludgeoned her skull, causing severe injury. She was then carried from her bedroom to an area outside the basement wine cellar and, while still alive, was strangled with a nylon rope attached to a garrote. She was then placed in the wine cellar and her body was covered with a white blanket. The next morning Patsy Ramsey found a ransom note on the stairway as she left her bedroom. It appeared from the ransom note that JonBenet had been kidnapped. JonBenet was not in her bedroom or in other areas of the house that her parents searched. Patsy immediately contacted the Boulder Police Department and reported that their daughter may have been kidnapped. The first police officer arrived at the Ramsey house just before 6:00 am on December 26th. Police treated the case as a kidnapping before realizing that JonBenet had been murdered inside the home. John Ramsey found his daughter's body in the basement wine cellar sometime after 1:00 pm on December 26th. The cause of death was listed by the coroner as "asphyxiation due to strangulation associated with craniocerebral trauma." Jon Benet's official autopsy report by pathologist John E. Meyer indicated that there was a "red-purple area of abrasion" near the hymen and a small amount of dried blood on the outside of the vaginal opening. "On the right side labia majora is a very faint area of violet discoloration measuring approximately one inch by three-eights of an inch." In 1999 a grand jury found that there was evidence to believe JonBenet had been sexually assaulted.

Post Office Box 471 • Boulder, Colorado 80306

Office of the Boulder County Coroner

1777 6th Street • Boulder County Justice Center • Boulder, Colorado 80302 • (303) 441-3535

AUTOPSY REPORT

NAME:	RAMSEY, JONBENET	AUTOPSY NO:	96A-155
DOB:	08/06/90	DEATH D/T:	12/26/96 @ 1323
AGE:	6Y	AUTOPSY D/T:	12/27/96 @ 0815
SEX:	F	ID NO:	137712
PATH MD:	MEYER	COR/MEDREC#:	1714-96-A
TYPE:	COR		

FINAL DIAGNOSIS:

I. Ligature strangulation
   A. Circumferential ligature with associated ligature furrow of neck
   B. Abrasions and petechial hemorrhages, neck
   C. Petechial hemorrhages, conjunctival surfaces of eyes and skin of face

II. Craniocerebral injuries
   A. Scalp contusion
   B. Linear, comminuted fracture of right side of skull
   C. Linear pattern of contusions of right cerebral hemisphere
   D. Subarachnoid and subdural hemorrhage
   E. Small contusions, tips of temporal lobes

III. Abrasion of right cheek

IV. Abrasion/contusion, posterior right shoulder

V. Abrasions of left lower back and posterior left lower leg

VI. Abrasion and vascular congestion of vaginal mucosa

VII. Ligature of right wrist

Toxicologic Studies

blood ethanol - none detected
blood drug screen - no drugs detected

CLINICOPATHOLOGIC CORRELATION: Cause of death of this six year old female is asphyxia by strangulation associated with craniocerebral trauma.

John E. Meyer, M.D.
John E. Meyer, M.D.
Pathologist

jn/12/27/96

John E. Meyer, M.D.
Coroner/Medical Examiner

Thomas J Faure
Chief Medical Investigator

Page 1 of Coroner's Report

NAME: RAMSEY, JONBENET AUTOPSY NO: 96A-155 Page 4

present on the skin below the ligature furrow on the left lateral aspect of the neck. Located on the right side of the chin is a three-sixteenths by one-eighth of an inch area of superficial abrasion. On the posterior aspect of the right shoulder is a poorly demarcated, very superficial focus of abrasion/contusion which is pale purple in color and measures up to three-quarters by one-half inch in maximum dimension. Several linear aggregates of petechial hemorrhages are present in the anterior left shoulder just above deltopectoral groove. These measure up to one inch in length by one-sixteenth to one-eighth of an inch in width. On the left lateral aspect of the lower back, approximately sixteen and one-quarter inches and seventeen and one-half inches below the level of the top of the head are two dried rust colored to slightly purple abrasions. The more superior of the two measures one-eighth by one-sixteenth of an inch and the more inferior measures three-sixteenths by one-eighth of an inch. There is no surrounding contusion identified. On the posterior aspect of the left lower leg, almost in the midline, approximately 4 inches above the level of the heel are two small scratch-like abrasions which are dried and rust colored. They measure one-sixteenth by less than one-sixteenth of an inch and one-eighth by less than one-sixteenth of an inch respectively.

On the anterior aspect of the perineum, along the edges of closure of the labia majora, is a small amount of dried blood. A similar small amount of dried and semifluid blood is present on the skin of the fourchette and in the vestibule. Inside the vestibule of the vagina and along the distal vaginal wall is reddish hyperemia. This hyperemia is circumferential and perhaps more noticeable on the right side and posteriorly. The hyperemia also appears to extend just inside the vaginal orifice. A 1 cm red-purple area of abrasion is located on the right posterolateral area of the 1 x 1 cm hymenal orifice. The hymen itself is represented by a rim of mucosal tissue extending clockwise between the 2 and 10:00 positions. The area of abrasion is present at approximately the 7:00 position and appears to involve the hymen and distal right lateral vaginal wall and possibly the area anterior to the hymen. On the right labia majora is a very faint area of violet discoloration measuring approximately one inch by three-eighths of an inch. Incision into the underlying subcutaneous tissue discloses no hemorrhage. A minimal amount of semiliquid thin watery red fluid is present in the vaginal vault. No recent or remote anal or other perineal trauma is identified.

REMAINDER OF EXTERNAL EXAMINATION: The unembalmed, well developed and well nourished caucasian female body measures 47 inches in length and weighs an estimated 45 pounds. The scalp is covered by long blonde hair which is fixed in two ponytails, one on top of the head secured by a cloth hair tie and blue elastic band, and one in the lower back of the head secured by a blue elastic band. No scalp trauma is identified. The external auditory canals are patent and free of blood. The eyes are green and the pupils

Page 4 of Coroner's Report

Photo of Garrote

No one has ever been brought to trial and convicted of her murder. Boulder police suggested several theories and motives for the murder, among them were the Linda Hoffman-Pugh "housekeeper theory," the Mervin Pugh "handyman theory," the Brian Scott "landscaper theory," the "sexual predator theory," and the "family insider theory." Former Colorado Springs detective Lou Smit focused on the "intruder theory." Despite the variety of theories, Boulder police strapped on blinders and became fixated on the parents, John and Patsy Ramsey. None of these suggested theories has produced a suspect that has ever been convicted of JonBenet's murder. The case has grown cold. In this chapter I have focused on two theories regarding the murder of JonBenet that should be revisited. The first theory explores the possibility that she may have been murdered to eliminate her from dance, talent or pageant competition. The murder may have been committed by an intruder to prevent her from competing. This would not be the first time someone has been injured or nearly murdered for the sake of eliminating competition. This possibility implies an outsider, rather than an employee of the

Ramseys or one of the Ramseys themselves, was responsible for the murder of JonBenet. Detective Lou Smit may have been on the right track by suggesting an intruder, but in this case a very specific sort of intruder, someone connected to the competitive world of dance, talent and beauty pageants featuring young girls. John Ramsey was interviewed on June 23, 1998. Present were detective Lou Smit, Deputy District Attorney for Boulder County Mike Kane, John Ramsey's Boulder attorney Bryan Morgan and private investigator for Bryan Morgan, David Williams.

Included in the transcript of the interview on pages 443-446 is the following dialog:

> **Michael Kane:** I want to back into what happened that day. I think it was John Andrew when he was interviewed he said that-he was talking about the beauty pageants and the possibility of this being a work of a, you know, a jealous parent or whatever. And of course there have been instances where I think there was one that was really well publicized about a cheerleading, problem of a cheerleader mom or something like that. What do you think about that?
>
> **John Ramsey:** I think its plausible. Neither Patsy nor JonBenet or I took those very seriously. It was just a fun thing for her generally to do. She looked at it as it's a way to build her confidence and presence, you know, in front of people and those kinds of things. But it was just fun. There wasn't any—whether she won or lost wasn't really a big deal. It was just fun being there. There were parents there that were just intent on winning.
>
> **Mike Kane:** So what do you think about that in terms of a theory of who—

John Ramsey: Well, I mean I thought it was very odd and very unhealthy that they felt that way. That to us wasn't why we were doing that, you know. But in terms of who, you know, we hardly knew those people. Usually it was a very small group. The girls and their parents, grandparents. Some siblings maybe, that was about it. (Emphasis added, see first sentence in ransom note.)

Mike Kane: Were you aware that there were people that really took this pageant stuff seriously, can you give me some examples?

John Ramsey: Well, just when they would announce the winners. Everybody won 472 something, nobody went home without a big trophy and there were always ones that were favorite trophies, and these parents were just like their team just won the Super Bowl. I mean they just [won] within one point, and it was just really tense emotion that they won, I always thought that was not very healthy.

Mike Kane: Did you witness that any of the time you were there.

John Ramsey: Yeah.

Mike Kane: Yeah? Okay. What happened, what kind of atmosphere, what kind of atmosphere would that create?

John Ramsey: It was really nothing other than just, you know, they would say yes, and they would hug each other and you know. That was about it.

Mike Kane: Did you ever in looking back on it, do you think that any—anybody—was so wrapped up in this that I think you said its plausible. Is it possible?

John Ramsey: I don't think so. Because well, I don't know. I mean I just don't think that way, but I mean there were girls that had been to forty, fifty pageants, and just every weekend. I mean it was just, that was JonBenet went once in a while. Just kind of when they felt like it and they had time. So she wasn't-she didn't win that often. She would win the talent thing usually, she was very good, but she rarely won—she was young I mean, know, relative to some of the girls that were there we just didn't take it that serious, and just kind of a fun thing for her to do. And I think had they been one of these everyone you know competing, it might have, you know, potentially could have been some hostilities, there because there were some pretty intense emotions going on the part of the parents.

The case Mike Kane was referring to in the first portion of his interview with John Ramsey, included above was the 1991 case in Texas in which Wanda Holloway attempted to hire a hit man to kill Verna Heath, mother of a cheerleader, and her cheerleader daughter, Amber. Wanda Holloway wanted to be sure that a spot on the Johnson Junior High School cheerleading squad would be available for her daughter Shanna. The driving force behind this unbelievable crime was jealousy. Tape recorded conversations presented to the jury showed that Wanda Holloway attempted to entice her brother-in-law, Terry Harper, to hire a hit man to kill Verna Heath and possibly Heath's daughter, Amber. Holloway wanted to eliminate the competition. People do crazy things. I have learned that, when it comes to murder, nothing is beyond the realm of possibility. Was

JonBenet killed in order to remove her from the competition? Pageants are expensive and demanding but can lead to scholarships and financial gain. Prizes for winning a Little Miss Beauty pageant can exceed $2,000.00 in value, cash prizes, modeling contracts, crowns, trophies, prestige, etc. Some parents of young beauty contestants have confessed to spending over $30,000.00 annually on their child's beauty pageants. There can be a great deal of animosity and jealousy associated with these events. JonBenet was not a one-time wonder in child beauty contests. Over a couple of years she had competed against and defeated several other young girls. Someone associated with the beauty contests may have grown resentful and jealous enough to take an extreme step to make sure someone other than JonBenet had a chance of winning first place. Mrs. Holloway admitted in trial testimony that the driving force behind her action was "irrational jealousy" of Mrs. Heath and her star cheerleading daughter. Jealousy can become a powerful influence on a weakened disposition. The results can be deadly.

Also, consider the case of Olympic ice skater Nancy Kerrigan. In the 1991 World Figure Skating Championships, she won the bronze medal. Her teammates Kristi Yamaguchi won the gold medal and Tonya Harding won the silver medal in that event. In 1992, Kerrigan received a bronze medal in the 1992 Winter Olympics. She continued to skate and compete in major competitions, with a few setbacks. On January 6, 1994, Jeff Gillooly, ex-husband of Tonya Harding, conspired with Shawn Eckardt to have Shane Stant club Kerrigan in the right knee with a police baton. The intended purpose was to eliminate Kerrigan from the competition in the US Figure Skating Championship taking place at Cobo Arena in Detroit.

At age five JonBenet became Little Miss Colorado and again at age six in Denver. The last pageant JonBenet entered was held at the Southwest Plaza Mall in Denver on December 22, 1996, four days before she was murdered. On December 13, 1996, the Ramseys sponsored a dinner at their Boulder, Colorado, home. Sixty guests were in attendance. Sixty guests may have had access to the layout of the Ramsey's house and may have had access to the notepad used in the ransom note that was found on the stairway following the murder of JonBenet.

Now look closely at the ransom note in the JonBenet murder case:

Mr. Ramsey,

Listen carefully! We are a
group of individuals that represent
a small foreign faction. We
respect your bussiness but not the
country that it serves. At this
time we have your daughter in our
posession. She is safe and unharmed
and if you want her to see 1997,
you must follow our instructions to
the letter.

You will withdraw $118,000.00
from your account. $100,000 will be
in $100 bills and the remaining
$18,000 in $20 bills. Make sure
that you bring an adequate size
attache to the bank. When you
get home you will put the money
in a brown paper bag. I will
call you between 8 and 10 am
tomorrow to instruct you on delivery.
The delivery will be exhausting so
I advise you to be rested. If
we monitor you getting the money
early, we might call you early to
arrange an earlier delivery of the

Page 1 of Ransom Note

money and hence a earlier ~~delivery~~ pick-up of your daughter.
Any deviation of my instructions will result in the immediate execution of your daughter. You will also be denied her remains for proper burial. The two gentlemen watching over your daughter do not particularly like you so I advise you not to provoke them. Speaking to anyone about your situation, such as Police, F.B.I., etc., will result in your daughter being beheaded. If we catch you talking to a stray dog, she dies. If you alert bank authorities, she dies. If the money is in any way marked or tampered with, she dies. You will be scanned for electronic devices and if any are found, she dies. You can try to deceive us but be warned that we are familiar with Law enforcement countermeasures and tactics. You stand a 99% chance of killing your daughter if you try to out smart us. Follow our instructions

Page 2 of Ransom Note

and you stand a 100% chance
of getting her back. You and
your family are under constant
scrutiny as well as the authorities.
Don't try to grow a brain
John. You are not the only
fat cat around so don't think
that killing will be difficult.
Don't underestimate us John.
Use that good southern common
sense of yours. It is up to
you now John!

Victory!

S.B.T.C

Page 3 of Ransom Note

The ransom note starts out: "Listen Carefully! We are a group of individuals that represent a small foreign faction." The writer of the ransom note indicated that he/she represented a "group of individuals." What group was the ransom note author referring to? Was it the other pageant, talent and dance contestants that competed against JonBenet? The ransom note may have been written before the abduction and murder of JonBenet. It would have been extremely difficult for any normal person to keep their thoughts together following the gruesome murder of a small child in a home occupied by the murdered child's parents. I believe that whoever wrote the ransom note wanted JonBenet dead. The ransom note seems to me to have a feminine feel to it. Retired FBI agent and leading forensic linguistics expert James Fitzgerald suggested that the language in the ransom note was "maternalistic." It was clearly printed, mostly in lower case. The ransom note when read in its entirety suggests that JonBenet would die. The writer included the following words in the ransom note: "immediate execution," "daughter being beheaded," "she dies," "she dies," "she dies," "she dies," "killing your daughter" and "don't think killing will be difficult." If the ransom note was in fact written prior to the murder of JonBenet, then the note itself would suggest that the writer intended that JonBenet die. The injuries sustained do not appear to be inflicted in a fit of anger or rage but rather calculated to insure that the victim died. If this is the case, the murderer was not interested in ransom money, but could have been interested in eliminating the competition. Then this was no kidnapping case that went too far in capturing and silencing the victim.

The ransom note ends with the word "Victory." In other words they won, the competition is gone. Could the letters "SBTC" that followed the word "Victory" stand for **S**ilenced **Be**net **T**he **C**ompetition? The only person who really knows what the initials stand for is the person who wrote the ransom note.

If this theory has merit, then the best thing going in the investigation is the passage of time. If someone associated with the past competition list of characters is responsible for JonBenet's murder, there may be someone out there who heard something or knows something, but who has not been investigated or interviewed. People change over time, feelings change, romantic connections change. Time has a way of changing people. Someone may have grown a conscience or is consumed with guilt. They might have been in a relationship and now they are not. (Note 1, p. 312) Did anyone in a past pageant or dance circuit ever refer to JonBenet as a "brat," a "bitch" or in some other derogatory way? For example, several comments were made by a "very bitter woman in Boulder" about a costume JonBenet wore to her school Halloween party. (Note 2) Did any parent ever keep their child out of a competition merely because JonBenet was a participant? Someone connected with the past competitions might know something that connects the dots and might be a missing piece to this unsolved mystery. Cold case detectives should go back and interview everyone involved in JonBenet's past dance classes, talent and pageant competitions. If the authorities haven't already done so, they should examine the families and associates of other pageant, talent and dance contestants who competed in those contests the Ramsey girl had competed in, including families and associates of girls who were planning to compete in contests scheduled for dates following her death. The list should include those associated with contestants likely to compete, even if not registered to do so, based on previous participation in contests JonBenet had competed in. Whoever murdered JonBenet may now want to tell the truth. They may have told someone something—something revealing or even incriminating, shared with a best friend, a relative, a partner, or family member of other pageant contestants. Leaving no stone unturned is often the only way to find the truth.

Evidence of foreign DNA was found on JonBenet's underwear at the time of her death in 1996. Boulder District Attorney Mary T. Lacy indicated that on the date of the murder a "match of male DNA" was found on two separate items of JonBenet's clothing. A debate has continued over the years with the experts concerning "transfer DNA" arguments. The DNA was used by the District Attorney's office to exonerate John and Patsy Ramsey. Gordon Coombes, who worked as an investigator in the Boulder District Attorney Office, questioned the results of "touch DNA." Here is my point regarding the suspect DNA as it pertains to the Ramsey murder: There is questionable DNA from an unknown male that was lifted from JonBenet's long johns and there was questionable DNA identified from blood found on her underwear. No male suspect has ever been connected to the DNA in question. There has been no DNA match in the Combined DNA Index System (CODIS) or the

National DNA Index System (NDIS). It might be advantageous to compare the known DNA samples with any potential suspects ferreted out of the competition pool of individuals. Of course, if someone involved with the pageant or dance competitions committed the murder, or is responsible in some way for the murder, it is quite possible that the person never committed any other crime, before or after the JonBenet murder, that resulted in the person's DNA being entered into CODIS or NDIS—but it would still be worth checking for a DNA match among those involved with the competitions, at least those who might appear to be suspects after interviews and other investigations.

On December 27, 1996, pathologist John E. Meyer, MD conducted the autopsy on JonBenet. Detective Linda Arndt and Detective Tom Trejillo were in attendance when the autopsy was conducted. Dr. Meyer reported that "pieces of yellow to light green-tan apparent vegetable or fruit material which may represent fragments of pineapple" were found in JonBenet's small intestine. Some have suggested that she had eaten pineapple shortly before her death because the fruit hadn't had time to digest before she was killed. That would suggest that the parents may have fed JonBenet when they returned home on the night of December 25th. Both John Ramsey and Patsy Ramsey denied giving JonBenet pineapple when they returned home that night. They insisted that JonBenet was sound asleep in the car and was carried by John Ramsey directly from the car to her bedroom. This raised a question as to who was telling the truth. The autopsy report on page seven provides the following:

NAME: RAMSEY, JONBENET AUTOPSY NO: 96A-155 Page 7

stomach contains a small amount (8-10 cc) of viscous to green to tan colored thick mucous material without particulate matter identified. The gastric mucosa is autolyzed but contains no areas of hemorrhage or ulceration. The proximal portion of the small intestine contains fragmented pieces of yellow to light green-tan apparent vegetable or fruit material which may represent fragments of pineapple. No hemorrhage is identified. The remainder of the small intestine is unremarkable. The large intestine contains soft green fecal material. The appendix is present.

Lymphatic System: Unremarkable.

Musculoskeletal System: Unremarkable.

Skull and Brain: Upon reflection of the scalp there is found to be an extensive area of scalp hemorrhage along the right temporoparietal area extending from the orbital ridge, posteriorly all the way to the occipital area. This encompasses an area measuring approximately 7 x 4 inches. This grossly appears to be fresh hemorrhage with no evidence of organization. the superior extension of this area of hemorrhage is a linear to comminuted skull fracture which extends from the right occipital to posteroparietal area forward to the right frontal area across the parietal portion of the skull. In the posteroparietal area of this fracture is a roughly rectangular shaped displaced fragment of skull measuring one and three-quarters by one-half inch. The hemorrhage and the fracture extend posteriorly just past the midline of the occipital area of the skull. This fracture measures approximately 8.5 inches in length. On removal of the skull cap there is found to be a thin film of subdural hemorrhage measuring approximately 7-8 cc over the surface of the right cerebral hemisphere and extending to the base of the cerebral hemisphere. The 1450 gm brain has a normal overall architecture. Mild narrowing of the sulci and flattening of the gyri are seen. No inflammation is identified. There is a thin film of subarachnoid hemorrhage overlying the entire right cerebral hemisphere. On the right cerebral hemisphere underlying the previously mentioned linear skull fracture is an extensive linear area of purple contusion extending from the right frontal area, posteriorly along the lateral aspect of the parietal region and into the occipital area. This area of contusion measures 8 inches in length with a width of up to 1.75 inches. At the tip of the right temporal lobe is a one-quarter by one-quarter inch similar appearing purple contusion. Only very minimal contusion is present at the tip of the left temporal lobe. This area of contusion measures only one-half inch in maximum dimension. The cerebral vasculature contains no evidence of atherosclerosis. Multiple coronal sections of the cerebral hemispheres, brain stem and cerebellum disclose no additional abnormalities The areas of previously described contusion are characterized by purple linear streak-like discolorations of the gray matter perpendicular to the surface of the cerebral cortex. These extend approximately 5 mm into the

Page 7 of Coroner's Report

Dr. Meyer's autopsy report did not indicate that JonBenet's small intestine contained material that was pineapple. What he indicated was, "the small intestine contains fragmented pieces of yellow to light green-tan apparent vegetable or fruit material which may represent fragments of pineapple" (emphasis added). My question is: Were the fragmented pieces of "pineapple" ever tested in a lab to determine, with certainty, that they were in fact fragments of partially digested pineapple? If the fragments were not partially digested pineapple that would indicate that the Ramseys were in fact telling the truth.

As I mentioned earlier in this chapter, former detective Lou Smit suggested that an intruder entered the Ramsey home through a broken basement window. Boulder police video footage shot on the night of the murder shows an undisturbed spider web on the subject basement window sill. This would suggest that an intruder could not have entered or exited through the broken basement window. John Ramsey told Boulder investigators that he had broken the window once when he locked himself out of the house. That does not eliminate the possibility of an intruder in the Ramsey house on the night JonBenet was murdered. How difficult is it to enter a house during the day when the doors are unlocked? Many people do not lock their house entrance doors when they are home during the day. Someone may have entered an unlocked door before Ramseys left the property on December 25th or somehow obtained a house key entered the house through the front door, waited in the house until the Ramseys went to bed, entered JonBenet's bedroom, bludgeoned her head with a blunt object, transferred the body to the entrance of the basement wine cellar and then strangled her with a garrote. It is also possible that an intruder may have entered the garage to Ramsey's house when the family returned home and opened the garage door on the night of December 25th.

ABC News' Tom Berman and Gail Deutsch in late 2016, contributed to a report that provided the following information: Former Boulder County District Attorney Mary Lacy recently told ABC News "20/20" that "during a walk-through of the Ramsey home in the days after the murder, an indention in the carpet was spotted just around the corner from JonBenet's room on the second floor. "It was a butt print. We all saw it. The entire area was undisturbed except for that place in the rug," said Lacy, who was then the chief deputy district attorney heading up the Sexual Assault Unit under then-Boulder County District Attorney Alex Hunter. "Whoever did this sat outside of her room and waited until everyone was asleep to kill her."

Joe Barnhill, a neighbor of the Ramseys in Boulder, indicated that "many people may have had keys to the house including caterers, a house cleaner, gardeners and landscapers." What that indicates is that keys to the Ramsey home were readily available. The Ramseys hosted three separate Christmas parties in December, 1996. A house guest, at some point in time, could have lifted an entrance key to the Ramsey's home and later gained entrance in a clandestine manner. The were reports of several other recent residential burglaries in the area where JonBenet was murdered.

This is not the first time a child has been taken from her bed while her parents were asleep in the same building one floor above. See Chapter 2 involving the kidnapping and murder of six-year-old Suzanne Degnan. (Note 3, p. 50) One of the many questions that has been analyzed in the present case is "could an intruder have gained access to the Ramsey house on the night JonBenet was murdered?" Ramseys admitted that the house was not secure during the night of December 25, 1996, and that the house alarm was not on. This is not in dispute. Lack of footprints in the snow near the Ramsey house on the night of the murder has been put forth to weaken the intruder theory. What is not in dispute is that snow did not cover the sidewalks and walkways to the Ramsey house on the morning of December 26th. If someone walked up the sidewalk and walkway and entered the front door, either when it was not locked or gained access with a stolen key, then this would account for the absence of footprints in the snow.

There is also a question that has been debated as to whether or not the butler's door to the house was unlocked and open on December 26th. John Ramsey acknowledged that the house alarm was not set on the night JonBenet was murdered. In fact, the alarm had not been used for approximately three years before the murder. If an intruder had already gained access to the house, either during the Ramseys absence or when they returned home, he or she could have committed the crime, written the long ransom note and easily vacated the house undetected. The exit point could have been through the butler's door, which was a short distance from the spiral staircase where the ransom note was found and within view of the pad of paper on which the ransom note was written.

It may still be possible to solve the mystery that surrounds the murder of JonBenet if the authorities focus on the motives of jealousy, greed and envy as they relate to those associated with JonBenet's beauty pageants, talent and dance competitions. This may or may not result in a resolution of this complex case. However, it is another path, another direction, that should be thoroughly investigated.

If, as seems quite evident, an outsider could have entered the home and killed JonBenet, what sort of person might have done so? If it was not someone from the world of competitive beauty and talent pageants, what other sort of person might have done so?

The second theory that should be revisited involves the possibility that JonBenet may have been assaulted and murdered by a sexual predator. Lou Smit identified a registered sex offender by the name of Gary Oliva as a possible suspect in JonBenet's murder. It is my understanding that Mr. Oliva has since been discarded as a suspect. In 2005 "48 Hours" reported: "Within a two—mile radius of where the Ramseys once lived 38 of their neighbors are registered sex offenders." It is certainly possible that a sex predator could have been responsible for JonBenet's death. Here is an example of a similar abduction, assault and murder of a young girl that took place seven and a half years after the murder of JonBenet: Late in the evening on June 6, 2004, as three-year-old Riley Fox slept soundly on a couch in her family's home in Wilmington, Illinois, someone entered the occupied home through an unlocked door, put his hand over Riley's mouth, picked her up and kidnapped her. This all happened while her father, Kevin Fox, slept in his bedroom with a fan running next to his bed. Riley's mouth and hands were bound with duct tape. She was placed in the kidnapper's car and driven to a restroom at the Forsythe Woods Country Forest Preserve, where she was sexually assaulted on the floor of a restroom. Riley was then taken to the edge of a tributary of the Kankakee River called Fork Creek in the Preserve and forcefully drowned by her assailant. Searchers found her body later that day in Fork Creek. The medical examiner noted light bruising on Riley's head. On the same night of Riley's abduction, another house in the same block was burglarized. Will County Sheriffs detectives strapped on blinders and became fixated on Riley's father, Kevin Fox. Here is how some of the investigation proceeded: Kevin's wife, Melissa Fox, indicated that detective Scott Swearengen laid out the "accident" scenario for the death of Riley. Swearengen thought Kevin hurt Riley's head, possibly when he opened the bathroom door, and then panicked when it looked like she was dead. Swearengen then thought Kevin applied duct tape and then sexually assaulted Riley to make it look like a kidnapping. Melissa thought the detective's theory was crazy. Melissa told detectives that even if Kevin had hurt Riley's head he would have tried to resuscitate her. Kevin was certified in CPR. As for the sexual abuse claim made by detectives, Melissa said, "I'm not a stupid person. If someone was abusing my child, I would have known about it. There would have been some sign. I knew it wasn't true." (Note 4) Kevin was eventually arrested and after fourteen and a half hours of grueling interrogation by detectives, signed a false confession and agreed to plead guilty to the assault and murder. Prosecutors sought the death penalty against Kevin. He served over eight months in prison before DNA tests determined that he was not the real killer.

The real killer may have left his DNA in the form of saliva in Riley's vagina (although tests came back "inconclusive"), as well as leaving a pair of muddy boots near Fork Creek. The killer's name was written on the tongue of the boots. However, this fact was not properly communicated between police agencies and overlooked by investigators, including the Will County Sheriffs Office, FBI and the state's attorney office. DNA eventually connected a sexual predator by the name of Scott Wayne Eby to the abduction and murder. On November 10, 2010, thirty-eight-year-old Eby pled guilty to the 2004, murder and sexual assault. He received a life sentence without the possibility of parole. Eby is currently incarcerated at the Menard Correctional Center in the town of Chester in Randolph County, Illinois, 50 miles southeast of St. Louis.

The case histories of Riley Fox and JonBenet Ramsey have uncanny similarities:

1. The assailant gains entrance to an occupied house late at night.
2. Parent is asleep while a young, sleeping girl is abducted.
3. Duct tape, probably brought to the residence by the killer, is used to cover the girl's mouth.
4. Possibility of oral assault.
5. Her hands are bound.
6. Both had injury to the head.
7. Both may have been sexually assaulted in a small room (a restroom and a wine cellar).
8. In both cases the killer made sure the victim died, one by drowning, the other by strangulation, as the victim struggled.
9. There were recent residential burglaries of other homes nearby the scene of the crimes.
10. The letters "SBTC" are found in the name "Scott Eby."

There are obvious differences in the two crimes:

1. Leaving the victim in the home vs taking the victim to a remote location away from the home.
2. Strangulation vs drowning.

Mr. Eby was also convicted of forgery in 1992, burglary in 1992, 1993, and 2000, in the State of Illinois. In his conviction for Residential Burglary in 1993, he received a four-year sentence, beginning September 23, 1993, in the Illinois Department of Corrections. He was paroled on March 23, 1995, and discharged from parole on March 23, 1997. On July 12, 1996, Eby married Robin Condiff at the Joliet, Illinois Courthouse. She filed for divorce from Eby in October, 2001. During the marriage they lived in Illinois, Florida, Pennsylvania and California. Condiff told a reporter "Trouble with the law prompted most moves." Scott Eby worked for a moving company. (Note 5) On October 15, 1996, Eby was living in Ronks, Pennsylvania, where he was caught stealing $360.00 worth of clothing from a store in East Lampeter Township but fled before the case went to trial. I have not been able to locate any records in Lancaster County, Pennsylvania, or through the Illinois Department of Corrections, that indicate Eby was incarcerated on December 25, 1996, or monitored on parole. Pennsylvania officials, especially in Lancaster County, should provide information concerning whether Eby was incarcerated in December, 1996. If he was then Mr. Eby will no longer be a person of interest in the JonBenet Ramsey murder. He is a convicted residential burglar and if he can be placed in Boulder, Colorado, in December, 1996, he may have yielded to his sexual perversion when learning that a young beauty-pageant winner lived in an affluent Boulder, Colorado, neighborhood. JonBenet performed live at the Southwest Plaza Mall Pageant in Denver on December 22, 1996. She could have been seen by a sexual predator at that time. This is all circumstantial evidence, and if Mr. Eby's DNA was found in the Ramsey's home, and if the DNA samples lifted from JonBenet's clothing were from the individual who attacked her, and if the samples were sufficient, there should have eventually been a match through CODIS because Eby's DNA profile would have been entered in CODIS as a result of his conviction in the Riley Fox murder. Regardless, Eby may fit the profile of an individual who should be considered a possible perpetrator, a new suspect, despite the geographic distance involved in the JonBenet Ramsey murder, as well as any other sexual predators with similar *modus operandi* before and after the murder of JonBenet. The search should be a on a national level and not limited to registered sex offenders who lived in close proximity to the Ramsey's former Boulder, Colorado, home.

NOTES

1. Fletcher, Connie. *Crime Scene: Inside the World of the Real CSI'S.* New York: St. Martin's Paperbacks, 2007
2. Paugh, Pam. Q&A www.webslueths.com, November 11, 1999.
3. Rasmussen, William T. *Corroborating Evidence IV*. Santa Fe: *Sunstone Press*, 2012
4. Smith, Bryan. "The Nightmare: A Look at the Riley Fox Case," *Chicago Magazine*, July 3, 2006
5. Schorsch, Kristen. *Chicago Tribune*, June 20, 2010

NOTES

CHAPTER 1: The Torso Murders

(1) Badel, James Jessen. *In the Wake of the Butcher: Cleveland's Torso Murders*

CHAPTER 2: The Case against William Heirens

(2) Badel, James Jessen. *In the Wake of the Butcher: Cleveland Torso Murders*
(3) *Chicago Daily Times*. August 7, 1946
(4) *Chicago Daily Times*. August 12, 1946
(5) *Chicago Daily Tribune*. January 8, 1946
(6) *Chicago Daily Tribune*. January 12, 1946
(7) *Chicago Daily Tribune*. January 12, 1946
(8) *Chicago Daily Tribune*. January 15, 1946
(9) *Chicago Daily Tribune*. January 17, 1946
(10) *Chicago Daily Tribune*. January 18, 1946
(11) *Chicago Tribune Press*. January 7, 1946
(12) *Chicago Sun*. January 12, 1946)
(13) *Chicago Sun*. January 8, 1946
(14) *Crimelibrary.com*
(15) Gilmore, John. *Severed: The True Story of the Black Dahlia Murder*
(16) Hodel, Steven. *Black Dahlia Avenger*
(17) Kennedy, Dolores. *William Heirens: His Day in Court*

(18) Martin, John Bartlow. *Butcher's Dozen and Other Murders*
(19) Nickel, Steven. *Torso: The Story of Elliot Ness and the Search for the Psychopathic Killer*

CHAPTER 3: Georgette Bauerdorf, Elizabeth Short (The Black Dahlia), Jeanne Axford French (The Red Lipstick Murder) and Other Los Angeles Victims

(20) Badal, James Jessen. *In the Wake of the Butcher: Cleveland's Torso Murders*
(21) *Chicago Daily Tribune*. January 15, 1946
(22) *Chicago Daily Tribune*. January 18, 1946
(23) *Chicago Sun*. January 10, 1946
(24) *Chicago Sun*. January 12, 1946
(25) *Chicago Times*. August 12, 1946
(26) *Crimelibrary.com: The Cleveland Torso Murders, Elliot Ness Serial Killer Case*
(27) Gilmore, John. *Severed: The True Story of the Black Dahlia Murder*
(28) Hodel, Steven. *Black Dahlia Avenger*
(29) Kennedy, Dolores. *William Heirens: His Day In Court*
(30) Martin, John Bartlow. *Butcher's Dozen and Other Murders*
(31) Nickel, Steven. *Torso: The Story of Elliot Ness and the Search for the Psychopathic Killer*
(32) Pacios, Mary. *Childhood Shadows: The Hidden Story of the Black Dahlia Murder*
(33) *Cleveland Plain Dealer*

CHAPTER 4: The Phantom Killer of Texarkana

(34) *Crime Library*
(35) *Texarkana Gazette, The Phantom at 50. 1996*

(36) *The Kansas City Star. Sunday, June 2, 1946*

CHAPTER 5: The Zodiac Killer

(37) Graysmith, Robert. *Zodiac*
(38) *True Crime-Time Life Books. 1993*

CHAPTER 6: Comparisons between the Zodiac Killer and the Eyeball Killer

(39) Matthews, John and Wicker, Christine. *The Eyeball Killer*
(40) Graysmith, Robert. *Zodiac*
(41) Hollandsworth, Skip. *See No Evil-Texas Crime Chronicles*

CHAPTER 7: The Mysterious Murder of Valerie Percy

(42) Graysmith, Robert. *Zodiac*

CHAPTER 8: The Murders of Richard Robison and his Family

(43) Graysmith, Robert. *Zodiac*
(44) *Texarkana Gazette, The Phantom at 50. 1966*

CHAPTER 9: From West Coast to East Coast-Possible Connections Between Unsolved Murders

(45) Graysmith, Robert. *Zodiac*

CHRONOLOGY

(46) Badal, James Jessen. *In the Wake of the Butcher*
(47) Gilmore, John. *Severed: The True story of the Black Dahlia*

(48) Hodel, Steven. *Black Dahlia Avenger*
(49) Nickel, Steven. *Torso: The Story of Elliot Ness and the Search for the Pathological Killer*
(50) Pacios, Mary. *Childhood Shadows: The Hidden Story of the Black Dahlia Murder*

FURTHER ANALYSIS OF CLEVELAND TORSO MURDERS, SUZANNE DEGNAN MURDER AND THE BLACK DAHLIA MURDER

(51) Badel, James Jessen. *In the Wake of the Butcher*
(52) Kennedy, Dolores. *William Heirens: His Day in Court*
(53) Gilmore, John. *Severed: The True Story of the Black Dahlia*
(54) Wolfe, Donald H. *The Black Dahlia Files*
(55) Hodel, Steve. *Black Dahlia Avenger*

BIBLIOGRAPHY

Books

Badel, James Jessen. *In the Wake of the Butcher: Cleveland's Torso Murders*. Kent State University Press, 2001.

Celebrity Murders. Edited by Art Crockett. Pinnacle Books, Windsor Publishing Corporation, 1990.

Chambers, Bradford and Pezet, A. W. *Greatest Crimes of the Century*, 1954.

Collins, Max Allen. *Angel In Black*. Signet, 2002.

Douglas, John and Mark Olshaker. *The Cases that Haunt Us*. New York, Lisa Drew Books/Scribner, 2000.

Ellroy, James. *The Black Dahlia*. Warner Books, Inc., 1987.

Fisher, Jim. *Hopewell: Setting the Record Straight in the Lindbergh Case*. Southern Illinois University Press, 1999.

Fowler, Will. *Reporters: Memoirs of a Young Newspaperman*. Roundtable Publishing, Inc., 1991.

Gilmore, John. *Severed: The True Story of the Black Dahlia Murder*. San Francisco: Zanja Press, Amok Books, 1994.

Graysmith, Robert. *Zodiac*. Berkley Publishing Group, 1976.

Hodel, Steve. *Black Dahlia Avenger*. New York: Arcade Publishing, Inc., 2003.

Hollandsworth, Skip. *See No Evil-Tdexas Crime Chronicles.*

Kennedy, Dolores. *William Heirens: His Day in Court/Did an Innocent Man Confess to Three Grisly Murders?*.Chicago: Bonus Book, Inc., 1991.

Link, Mardi. *When Evil Came To Good Hart*, University of Michigan Press, 2008.

Matthews, John and Wicker, Christine. *The Eyeball Killer.*

Martin, John Bartlow. *Butcher's Dozen and other Murders*. New York: Harper & Brothers, 1950.

Nickel, Steven. *Torso: The Story of Elliot Ness and the Search for the Psychopathic Killer.* Winston-Salem, N.C.: John F. Blair Publisher, 1989.

Pacios, Mary. *Childhood Shadows: The Hidden Story of the Black Dahlia Murder.* 1st Books, revised 5/23/00.

Pecora, James J. *Dead End.* Trafford Publishing, 2007.

Rice, Anne. *The Mummy,* Millennium Publications, 1990.

True Crime.Time Life-Books, 1993.

Wolfe, Donald H., *The Black Dahlia Files.* Regan Books, 2005. *World Book Encyclopedia.*

Internet References

Crimelibrary.com. Court TV. Serial Killers, Sexual Predators/William Heirens/Lipstick Killer.

piratepressonline.com

zodiackiller.com. Tom Voigt

Newspapers

Chicago Daily News

Chicago Daily Times

Chicago Daily Tribune

Chicago Defender

Chicago Herald American

Chicago Sun

Chicago Tribune Press

Dallas Morning News
Detroit News
Impresario
Kansas City Star
Los Angeles Herald Examiner
Los Angeles Mirror (*The* Mirror)
Los Angeles Times
Riverside Press-Enterprise
San Francisco Chronicle
San Francisco Examiner
Texarkana Gazette
The Chicago Times
The Cleveland News
The Cleveland Plain Dealer
The Cleveland Press
The Indianapolis Star
Washington Times-Herald
Wichita Eagle-Beacon
Vallejo Times-Herald

Magazines

Martin, John Bartlow. "Butcher's Dozen: The Cleveland Torso Murders." *Harper's Magazine*, November 1948:55-69.
Time Magazine, Volume 84, No. 12, Sept. 18, 1964
Time Magazine, Volume 88, No. 14, Sept. 30, 1966

INDEX

www.ingramcontent.com/pod-product-compliance
Lightning Source LLC
Chambersburg PA
CBHW050031110726
47973CB00032B/284/J
* 9 7 9 8 9 9 0 4 8 0 4 0 7 *